Barbara Mortimer

March 1993

Edinburgh.

BRITISH DIRECTORIES

BRITISH DIRECTORIES:

A Bibliography and Guide to Directories published in England and Wales (1850-1950) and Scotland (1773-1950)

Gareth Shaw and Allison Tipper

University of Exeter

LEICESTER UNIVERSITY PRESS 1988
(a division of Pinter Publishers)
London and New York

First published in 1989 by Leicester University Press
(a division of Pinter Publishers)

Editorial offices
Fielding Johnson Building, University of Leicester, University Road,
Leicester, LE1 7RH

Trade and other enquiries
25 Floral Street, London, WC2E 9DS

British Library Cataloguing in Publication Data

Shaw, Gareth
British directories: a bibliography and guide to directories published in
England and Wales (1850-1950) and Scotland (1773-1950)
1. Great Britain. Geographical features,
Historical sources. Directories.
Bibliographies.
I. Title   II. Tipper, Allison
016.911'41

ISBN 0-7185-1292-8

Designed by Douglas Martin
Filmset in Linotron Ehrhardt
by Communitype Ltd, Leicester
Printed and bound in Great Britain
by Biddles Ltd, Guildford and King's Lynn

Contents

Contents

PART THREE LIBRARY HOLDINGS AND INDEX

List of figures

List of tables

Acknowledgments

The authors are indebted to the British Academy and the Marc Fitch Foundation for funding this research. We also extend our thanks to the many librarians without whose co-operation and interest this research would have been virtually impossible. Special thanks must go to those who were able to allow us access to bookstacks which are normally closed to the public, thus saving a great deal of time in our checking process. Although we would like to credit individually all those who helped, space only permits us to mention the following in particular: Mr Harry Horton of Manchester Central Library, whose help matched his considerable professional and personal interest in the research; Mr L.W. Lawson-Edwards, who kindly allowed us to consult the impressive collection at the Society of Genealogists in London without charge; Mrs Pauline Staite, who allowed us into Falmouth Library at a time when it was otherwise closed; and finally thanks to Miss Margaret Deas of the National Library of Scotland, Dr John Chandler of Trowbridge, and Miss Diana Winterbotham of the Lancashire Libraries Headquarters, all of whom were especially helpful and interested.

At the University of Exeter, the practical advice of George Foot and Ray Burnley of the Computer Unit was invaluable in helping to shape the bibliography for publication, as were the typing skills of Judy Gorton and Jane Skinner.

Part One

Introduction and Guide

Chapter 1
INTRODUCTION

Not only to Persons in Town who reside, but
likewise to Thousands who from it live wide;
A useful Directory all will agree,
A much wanted, pleasing Companion would be.
(Chapman's Birmingham Directory, 1800)

1.1   Previous works and guides

Directories are one of the most frequently used sources within historical studies
and are consulted by a wide range of research workers. Such interest in
directories dates back at least to the early 1930s, with the publication by Goss of a
guide to *The London Directories, 1677-1855*, and of Walker's detailed account of
Birmingham directories, which traced their evolution during the eighteenth
century.[1] Goss in his work suitably highlighted the importance of these
publications when he described the street directory as 'a perfect epitome of local
history', which 'opens up a vast field of quite interesting research'.[2] Even today
few would argue with these sentiments, whilst more recent publications have only
served to emphasize the importance of directories within historical studies.[3]

The early recognition of directories as useful sources of historical information
has had two important consequences. The first is that the demand and use of
directories by local historians has helped to preserve a relatively good stock of
these publications in most county libraries. The build-up of such provincial
collections can be illustrated by the case of Manchester Reference Library: in
1899 the Library held some 261 directories covering both Britain and overseas,
but by 1939 their collection had grown to about 800 directories.[4] The second
consequence of this interest is that a few libraries and local history societies have
been prompted to publish bibliographies of their holdings of county and local
directories. Perhaps the most comprehensive of these local guides are those for
Lancashire and Staffordshire. In the case of Lancashire an initial start was made
by Smyth in 1966 for the holdings of trade directories in the Manchester Library,
although the main guide for the county was compiled by Tupling.[5] An equally
ambitious project was the compilation of a union listing of Staffordshire
directories, which covered the collections held in 12 local libraries.[6] Both
publications present lists of directories in slightly different fashions, with the
Lancashire ones organized by date and those for Staffordshire by type of
directory and then by date. Such variations are typical of local guides, especially
in the case of smaller publications: for example, the guide to the directories of
Bath simply lists in chronological order local directories published between 1753
and 1972.[7] In other cases smaller publications have modelled themselves on the
structure used in earlier, larger works.[8]

Many provincial libraries have no specific bibliographies of their directory
holdings, but rather general guides on local sources, including directories, which

are often aimed at research within the field of family history.[9] Similar general guides have also been published by local societies, although these often only give a brief introduction to historical sources.[10] In a number of libraries the best that can be offered is an unpublished list of their directories, but in many cases even these are not available.[11] Where a local guide does not exist then the researcher may be faced with additional problems and delays, as in many cases provincial libraries do not classify directories under title, but rather by town or area.

In addition to the local bibliographies only one national guide exists, and this only covers the English and Welsh provincial directories published before 1856.[12] Norton, in compiling this work, selected the date to complement the earlier guide by Goss for London directories, and furthermore did not have the resources to undertake a similar survey of Scotland. Consequently, no comprehensive guide to Scottish directories exists, nor to those published in England and Wales after 1855. The search for directories not covered by Norton must therefore be undertaken at a local level, assuming the availability of provincial listings.

There are also some other alternatives, although none can really claim to provide any comprehensive, national coverage. Thus, a fairly general picture of titles, but not temporal coverage, can be built up from the catalogue of the British Library, although this fails to provide a complete cover, as may be illustrated by the fact that the holdings of the British Library and London Guildhall Library together only accounted for around 55 per cent of the titles contained in this survey. Indeed, the research conducted for the compilation of this bibliography revealed that many local publishers often produced long runs of local directories relating to smaller settlements, and that many of these never found their way into the copyright libraries.

Other national coverage is provided by Anderson's bibliography of British topography, which includes those directories containing topographical information.[13] Obviously as a guide it is limited to directories containing local topographies; and the inclusion of such information tended to be associated with particular types of directories published during the second part of the nineteenth century. It therefore not only omits many general town directories, but also those concerned with specific trades. Indeed, the latter receive no mention in Norton's work and only figure in a few of the local bibliographies such as the one for Staffordshire.[14]

Mention should also be made of the bibliography produced by the Society of Genealogists which provides a national, though not comprehensive, coverage of the British directories held in their library.[15] This lists directories by county and chronologically and it includes those that cover four or more counties in a national section. Its coverage spans the period from the late eighteenth century to the present, but it again suffers from the same problem as the British Library Catalogue, in that it relates to just one specific collection.

1.2   Aims of the guide

Given the severe limitations of previous bibliographies, then, clearly considerable scope exists for the publication of a comprehensive guide and bibliography of British directories which will extend and complement Norton's work. With this in mind the aims of this publication are threefold. First, to extend the work of Goss and Norton to provide a listing of directories published after 1856 and up to 1950 for England and Wales (including London). Second, to provide comprehensive coverage of all Scottish directories published prior to 1950; and third, to produce a bibliography of miscellaneous directories of specific trades, which have not been included in previous bibliographies.

In one sense, therefore, this work builds on the previous guides of Goss and Norton, although there are significant differences in the organization of the bibliography. Moreover, given the different areas and time periods covered in this publication it is hardly surprising that it contains a far greater number of directories than any previous guide. For example, Norton identified 875 individual directories in her work, compared with over 2,200 titles listed in this bibliography, representing some 17,943 volumes – which gives some idea of the scale of this survey and its comprehensive coverage. These directories represent the holdings of 120 library collections which have been visited as part of this work.

The book is organized in three major parts. Part One provides an introductory guide to British directories, which explains their evolution as well as discussing the different types of directories and their contents. Part Two concentrates on the bibliography, which is organized in chapters covering England, Wales and Scotland, and within each of these countries, by region and county. There is also a chapter on specialized directories arranged by date and title. Finally, Part Three gives a guide to the different libraries covered by the survey and the organization of these individual collections.

Given its aims, the guide and bibliography will fulfil a dual role, first by giving detailed information about library holdings for each title, and secondly in providing a guide to the type and range of directories available for given areas and subjects.

Notes

1. C.W.F. Goss, *The London Directories, 1677-1855* (1932); B. Walker, 'Birmingham directories', *Trans. and Proc. Birmingham Archaeological Soc., 58* (1934), 1-36.
2. Goss, *op. cit.*
3. G. Shaw, *British Directories as Sources in Historical Geography* (1982).
4. A.L. Smyth, 'Trades, professional and official directories as historical source material', *Manchester Rev.* (1966), 39-58.
5. Smyth, *op. cit.*; G. Tupling, *Lancashire Directories, 1684-1957* (1968).
6. N. Emery and D.R. Beard, *Staffordshire Directories: A Union List of Directories Relating to the Geographical County of Stafford* (1966).
7. Bath Municipal Libraries, *Bath Guides, Directories and Newspapers* (1973). A similar approach is taken by P. Drinkall and K. Maggs, *A Guide to the Croydon Street Directories* (1984).
8. For example J.H. Farrant, *Sussex Directories, 1784-1940* (1980), models the approach on J.E. Norton, *Guide to the National and Provincial Directories of England and Wales, excluding London, published before 1856* (1950).
9. A.V. Steward, *A Suffolk Bibliography* (1979); Warwickshire County Library, *Family History and Local Studies* (1985).
10. See for example, J. Jamieson (ed.),

Family History: A Guide to Ayrshire Sources (1984).

11. Examples of such unpublished lists are: J. Chandler, 'Directories and lists of inhabitants in Wiltshire' (n.d.); V. Wright, 'Berkshire directories' (n.d.); Southampton University, 'Hampshire directories' (n.d.).

12. Norton, *op. cit.*, ref. 8.

13. J.P. Anderson, *The Book of British Topography* (1881).

14. Emery and Beard, *op. cit.*, ref. 6.

15. L.W.L. Edwards, *Catalogue of Directories and Poll Books in the Possession of the Society of Genealogists* (1984); the first edition was compiled by J.M. Sims and published in 1964.

Chapter 2
EVOLUTIONARY TRENDS IN DIRECTORY PUBLICATION, FORM AND CONTENT

2.1 The evolution of British directories

In Britain the first recognizable directories made their appearance towards the end of the seventeenth century and were chiefly concerned with enumerating the numbers of traders and merchants. These early directories appear to have originated from two main sources and followed different evolutionary routes. One group of directories originated over a relatively long period of time, from the lists of traders kept by the earliest registry offices. In contrast, other directories made their appearance in a more spontaneous fashion to meet the needs of increased trade among the London merchants. Behind both these developments, however, there lay a common motivation, the driving force of commerce. From the seventeenth century onwards the increased number of traders, the trend towards the separation of industrial skills, and the geographical spread of business linkages, were all factors that created a new demand for informative literature on aspects of commerce and industry – a fact noted by Sketchley in an advertisement to sell his directory in the *London Chronicle* of 1763, which stated, 'This Day was Published, Price 1s. Very necessary for all Merchants and Tradesmen who have any Dealings in the Town of Birmingham; Stretchley's [sic] Birmingham Director'.[1] Indeed, it was such commercial perspectives that distinguished the earliest directories from other printed lists, which had usually been designed with some specific administrative purpose in mind. It is extremely difficult to identify the precise moment when commercial interests were sufficient to necessitate the publication of a directory, or indeed when a publisher appeared with enough foresight and speculative instinct to produce one. The earliest known list is entitled *The Companyes of all Crafts and Mysteries in London*, which was published in 1538, and listed 2,600 householders who were Freemen of the City Livery Companies.[2] Much earlier versions of this type of list date back to such organizations as the Guild Merchants who attended the Preston Guild, whose records started around 1328.[3] It was, however, only in 1677 that a recognizable directory appeared, with the publication by Samuel Lee of a list of London merchants.[4] Contemporary evidence, sparse though it is, seems to suggest that this work was Lee's original idea and that he had no previous examples to draw upon.[5] Certainly the fact that it took him at least two years to complete the work may be some indication of its innovatory nature. Despite the apparent success of this publication it seems that no successor appeared until 1734, when a directory of London merchants was compiled by James Brown and finally published by Henry Kent. This directory was revised annually by Kent up to 1771, and afterwards by a variety of other people, until being finally discontinued in 1826.[6]

The earliest links between published directories and the work of registry offices is to be found in France, where a Bureau d'Addresse et de Rencontre was opened by Renaudot in 1629.[7] From these offices of information lists of advertisements were periodically published containing names and addresses of traders and it was just such material that formed the basis of the first Paris directory in 1691. It ran to a second edition in 1692, which included new classified sections on such topics as medical wares, antique shops and amusements.[8] In Britain, although permission was granted to Sir Arthur Gorges and Sir Walter Cope to establish a registry office as early as 1611,[9] it would seem that such developments did not stimulate the immediate publication of directories. This is possibly because of the chequered history and slow growth of registry offices in this country in the mid and late seventeenth century, and certainly before the Restoration. However, these early registry offices, which attempted to provide information on all aspects of trade, had started to publish lists of the goods and services they offered and brought into life the first advertisements.[10] After 1695, when the press became free, the advertising sheets of these registry offices declined, as newspapers became more common and devoted more of their space to advertisements. From this period onwards the activities of many registry offices became more restricted. Some became small employment agencies, often acquiring dubious reputations. In addition, by the eighteenth century, these agencies had spread outside London into most provincial towns, stimulated largely by the success of Fielding's Universal Register Office, which was opened in 1751.[11]

It is during the eighteenth century that the link between registry offices and directories appears strongest in Britain, as many owners of employment agencies also published directories. This relationship is clearly illustrated in the case of Birmingham where the first registry office was opened in 1752 by Thomas Juxon, who the same year also compiled a catalogue of the names and addresses of the principal inhabitants and tradesmen of the city.[12] Unfortunately, no copy of this work has ever been found so it may well have never been published on a commercial basis. By 1760 a second registry office had been opened in Birmingham by James Sketchley and he also decided to produce a directory, which was published in 1763 and which contained an alphabetical list of the names and addresses of merchants and tradesmen.[13] In both instances the information and expertise gained from operating registry offices seemed to lead quite naturally on to directory publication. This is not surprising since both Juxon's 'Office of Intelligence' and Sketchley's 'Birmingham Universal Registry Office' were involved in almost every conceivable line of commerce from the buying and selling of property to the employment of apprentices and the hiring of journeymen.[14]

Similar circumstances seem to have operated in Manchester, where the first directory was published by Elizabeth Raffald in 1772.[15] She also ran a registry office, though on a much smaller scale than those in Birmingham. The date of foundation of this office is unknown, although it certainly seems to have been in operation some time before 1774 as the following notice suggests: 'As several of Mrs Raffalds friends in the country have mistook the terms of design of her Register Office, she begs leave to inform them that she supplies Families with

Servants, for any place at One shilling for each.'[16] It would also appear from this advertisement that Mrs Raffald's 'Registry for Domestic Servants' was nothing more than a simple employment exchange.

The early pioneers of directories were drawn from a wide variety of backgrounds, not all of which provided the necessary skills to succeed with such publications. Those drawn from registry offices represented a small but significant number of the many people tempted to turn their hand towards the compilation and publication of directories. A great number of the authors of early directories also came from the fields of printing and publishing, which did give them some insight into the problems and potentialities of directories. Probably the best known of these was Edward Baines, who started his career as an apprentice printer and then founded his own printing business before becoming involved in directory publishing.[17] However, he quickly withdrew from directory publishing and devoted his attention to the printing of other people's volumes. Other common occupations among directory compilers were land and house agents, auctioneers, post office officials and policemen, all lines of work which allowed these people to come into contact with information concerning names and addresses. A few of the early directory compilers were also attracted to the trade because of business failures elsewhere; for example, Charles Pye of Birmingham pursued at least three different occupations (watchmaker, wine merchant and collector of the window and hearth tax) before he turned to directory publishing.[18]

The work of these early directory publishers also gives an insight into the methods employed to gain information and the time taken to publication. For example, Pye, working in Birmingham, had obtained information through personal canvass in order to collect names, which were inserted in the directory free of charge. However, by 1800 he had decided to make no more personal applications, but to ask people to send in their names, together with a payment of sixpence, if they wanted to appear in his directory. This approach was not a success, as Pye only received sufficient names to fill twelve pages in 1800, compared with the 81 pages that comprised his 1797 directory.

The net effect of such a variety of experiences was twofold: first, it casts some doubt on the reliability of some of the more locally produced directories and, second, it led to a very high mortality rate among firms publishing directories. Some indication of the rate of business failure is given by the number of firms that only published one directory; these accounted for nearly 30 per cent of all the directory publishers operating between 1760 and 1800 in England, Wales and Scotland. This trend was to intensify during the mid and late nineteenth century, as the evidence from Lancashire suggests: of the 81 people publishing directories in that county between 1790 and 1900, almost 52 per cent produced only one directory.

2.2 The work of principal directory publishers

Reference has already been made to the small and ephemeral nature of many of the directory publishing firms that existed in the eighteenth century. However, at the other end of the size spectrum some fairly large organizations were beginning to develop that attempted to cover not only individual towns and their immediate areas, but also substantial parts of the country. The first person to publish a directory covering a large geographical area was William Bailey, who in 1781 issued his *Northern Directory*, which he claimed contained 'every principal town from the River Trent to Berwick upon Tweed; with London and Westminster, Edinburgh and Glasgow'.[19] Publication of this directory continued up to 1787, with gaps in 1782 and 1786. In terms of coverage, Bailey's most comprehensive directory was that published in 1784 under the title of *Bailey's British Directory*, the four volumes of which covered all the main towns of England.

After the relatively quick decline of Bailey's directories no national directory was issued until 1790, when the *Universal British Directory* was published. This was compiled largely by John Wilkes and issued in five main volumes and 69 parts at irregular intervals between 1790 and 1799. Wilkes was partnered and supported in the whole venture by Peter Barfoot, a relatively wealthy gentleman from Hampshire. This partnership clearly illustrated the need to draw on a fairly large capital sum to get the directory compiled and marketed. In the compilation of these large-scale directories substantial numbers of local agents needed to be recruited throughout the country. This not only took time and organization, but was also a costly exercise. There is strong evidence, however, to suggest that the publishers of the *Universal British Directory* cut corners by pirating previously published directories. Thus, Pye in Birmingham complains of his directory of 1791 being pirated by Barfoot and Wilkes and issued as part of their 1792 directory.[20] A similar practice has been exposed in other towns, such as Hull, where there is strong evidence to suggest that Wilkes copied *Battle's Hull Directory* of 1791 and re-issued it as part of the *Universal British Directory* in 1794.[21]

To a great extent the success of a directory depended on its price, and therefore the costing exercise prior to publication was extremely important. This was the hard lesson that William Holden learned when his series of provincial directories ran into financial difficulties around 1814. Holden had begun a series of directories in 1805, but each edition became more ambitious and costly. Thus, his first *Triennial Directory*[22] for 1805 cost £1 19s 6d per volume, but this had risen to £2 12s 6d per volume just six years later.[23] Due to such increased prices, sales fell and Holden finally went out of business in 1814. These first national and regional directories are obviously important, although it should be stressed that their coverage was extremely variable, especially in the case of the *Universal British Directory*.

One person to make a success of producing provincial and national directories was James Pigot, who started his career as an engraver in Manchester. His first provincial directory was issued in 1814 [24] (and incidentally sold for less than half the price of Holden's works). By 1820 Pigot had embarked upon the first of a series of national directories that continued until 1853. These publications may be divided into five general surveys that covered the whole of Britain.[25] The first survey between 1820 and 1826 started in Scotland and the North of England and then moved to cover the southern counties. In 1839, Pigot formed a partnership with Isaac Slater, who was a one-time manufacturer of straw hats, and more importantly, an engraver living in Manchester. By 1840, however, which marked the end of the third general survey, Pigot and Slater had withdrawn from publishing London directories in the face of competition from Kelly.[26] The scale and success of these directories was due entirely to Pigot's organizational abilities, as illustrated by the fact that he even employed an agent in Paris to market his directories on the Continent. Most of Pigot and Slater's directories were in the form of a classified list of trades, with the information being collected by personal canvass. The training given by the firm was obviously rigorous, since some of its agents, like J. Bentley and W. Parson, went on to produce their own directories. Pigot issued new directories in a series of regional surveys every six or seven years. The first was between 1820 and 1826, the second from 1826 to 1830, the third between 1831 and 1840 and the final one, 1848 to 1853. The firm was finally taken over by Kelly's, although Pigot's name was retained until 1882.

The development of the large-scale directory firms was, it seems, conditioned by two main factors. First, there needed to be a fairly substantial demand for such publications, a condition that was met by increasing economic and urban development. Second, many of the compilers of provincial and national directories required fairly sizeable amounts of capital, which was often provided from outside resources and sponsors. One notable exception to the latter trend was the business built up by Kelly in London. In his case the capital necessary to produce provincial directories on a large scale, from 1845 onwards, was undoubtedly accumulated from his earlier favourable link with the Post Office, on which his success was built.

The publication by Kelly of his London directory with the aid of Post Office employees put a considerable strain on the relationship with the Post Office. The link had been established in London as early as 1800 with the publication of the London Post Office Directory, initially entitled the *New Annual Directory*, which had been compiled by two inspectors of inland letter carriers, Ferguson and Sparke.[27] The first edition gave the names and addresses of almost 12,000 inhabitants along with their occupations and general postal information for London. It was published annually, changing its name in 1801 to the *Post Office Annual Directory*, and in 1803 acquired a third compiler, another Post Office inspector by the name of Critchett. By 1806 Critchett had taken over sole authorship of the directory, which he retained until 1835 when he sold the copyright to Frederick Kelly, who was then chief inspector of the inland letter carriers.

In the 1840s a number of allegations were raised against Kelly and his use of Post Office resources to compile the directory, by Jonathan Duncan of Kennington, who was proprietor of a newspaper called *The Sentinel*. The main complaint against Kelly was the misuse of public money through using both Post Office materials and employees to carry out the production of his directory. The campaign culminated in a number of questions being put to the House of Commons over the conduct of Kelly and a move for a select committee to inquire into the affairs of the Post Office.[28] Kelly's activities were described to the House of Commons as 'a gross job, converting a great public establishment into a sort of lucrative printing office, to the injury and disadvantage of all engaged in the establishment'.[29]

The reports to questions asked in the House give some interesting insights into the publication of the directory. For example, it appears that the information contained in the directory was collected by letter carriers, who circulated forms on their respective postal rounds. According to Duncan these were 'compulsorily employed throughout the year' and 'in many instances the Post Office servants have been occupied during official hours at the printing office of these Directories'.[30] The forms on which the information was collected were headed 'Post Office Directory', and were thereby given some official status (though it should also be added that some of this information was required by the Post Office irrespective of the directory).[31] The letter carriers also delivered the completed directory and gained a commission on the number of volumes they sold.

It was also claimed by Kelly's opponents that the directory was overpriced and had an unfair advantage over other directories. For instance, in 1843 Robson's London directories were finally discontinued because of competition from Kelly. Such difficulties had, 'driven [Robson] to the workhouse, and ultimately to insanity, by the unfair advantages which had been given by the Post Office authorities to another publication'.[32] This lack of competition led also, it was claimed, to an inaccurate directory which 'contained no less than 16,000 blunders'.[33] These wranglings dragged on for a number of years with the issue being raised in the House of Commons, until finally Kelly was forced to curtail his use of Post Office employees.[34] He did, however, retain the title of Post Office Directory for all his publications and there is little doubt that the title itself was a considerable boost, inspiring as it did public confidence in works that bore an official title. By the 1850s Kelly had become the dominant provincial directory publisher within the south of England. The dominance of the firm at a national level was complete when Kelly took over the business of Isaac Slater during the second half of the nineteenth century.

By the first quarter of the nineteenth century the scale and pace of urban change was such that it prohibited the production of national directories. Thus, in the late eighteenth century Bailey had been able to publish a directory covering all the main settlements in one four-volume issue; by the 1820s such a task could only be achieved over a two- or three-year period. In addition, by the mid-nineteenth century, the large-scale directory publishers had switched from producing directories for selected major towns within a region and had started to move towards county/provincial directories that attempted a coverage of all settlements. This system was especially favoured by Kelly (see Chapter 4) and goes some small way towards explaining his success as a directory publisher.

Kelly's was by far the largest, but not the only, sizeable publisher to operate during the second half of the nineteenth century and in the years up to 1950. As table 1 shows, there were many other firms that issued substantial numbers of directories, either throughout the whole of the country or within a particular region. An example of the latter was the firm of Robinson & Pike, which published 18 different titles and some 429 volumes during the period 1872 to 1940. Based in Brighton, they focused mainly on the towns of south-east England. Similarly, Wright's directories were concentrated in the East Midlands. The firm's first directory was published in 1854 by Christopher Wright, who started his career as a printer in Birmingham. By the mid-1870s he had moved to Leicester where he began a successful directory publishing business. This was eventually taken over by Kelly's in 1900, although the original name was retained. In contrast, other publishers attempted to cover a national market by producing town directories throughout the country. Some, like J.S.C. Morris, were organizations of long standing that had started during the 1860s. Others, despite the competition of Kelly's, had begun publishing in the later years of the nineteenth century. The most famous of these was the Edinburgh-based firm of Town & County Directories Ltd, which published its first directory in 1898; by 1950 the company had issued 53 different titles. Unfortunately, little else is known about this firm since very few details are given in the preface of their directories. It would appear, however, that the success of Town & County Directories was based on cheap, basic publications that were issued quickly.

Many of the medium sized publishers met with less success and were only active over relatively small periods of time. Excessive competition was at the root of most closures, particularly when these organizations came up against Kelly's. In London, for example, by the end of the nineteenth century Kelly's had eliminated all their main rivals, with the demise of Green & Co. in the mid-1870s, and Hutchings & Crowsley's directories in 1886.

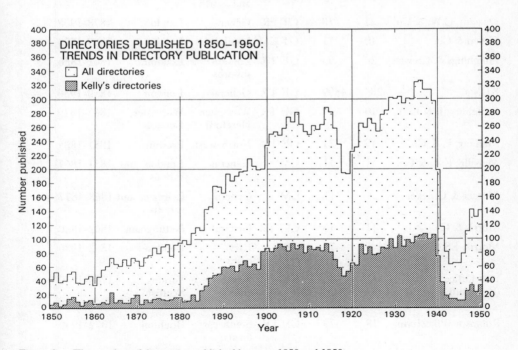

Figure 1   The number of directories published between 1850 and 1950.

Table 1 Characteristics of the main directory publishers

Publisher	Titles	Volumes	Main type	Spatial coverage	Places of publication	Range of dates published (first & last)
Aubrey & Co.	26	125	TR	General	Walsall	1906-1950
Barrett, P.	5	60	GE TR	Lancashire	Preston	1874-1949
Bennett & Co.	29	68	TR	General	Birmingham	1888-1936
Bulmer, T.	13	16	GE TR	Northern counties	Preston, Manchester	1883-1913
Business Directories	7	32	TR	General	Bloxwich	1933-1941
Cassey, E. & Co.	9	13	CM	General	London, Preston and various	1858-1880
Cook, W.J. & Co.	18	39	GE TR	Mainly East Midlands	Boston, Hull, and various	1891-1921
Cope, E.F. & Co.	16	122	TR	Midlands and North	Walsall	1905-1939
Deacon, C.W. & Co.	21	28	CT PR	General	London	1878-1908
Green & Co.	10	11	CT CM	London	London	1869-1874
Hutchings & Crowsley	26	95	GE TR	London suburbs	London	1861-1886
Kelly's	284	4899	GE TR	General	London	1850-1950
Littlebury, J. & Co.	10	21	GE TR	Worcester/ Hereford	Worcester, London	1867-1939
Mannex, P. & Co.	17	21	GE TR	North-west	Preston	1851-1885
Melville, F.R. & Co.	11	11	CM	General	London, and various	1851-1867
Mercer & Crocker	9	11	CM	General	Leicester and various	1868-1877
Morris & Co.	11	16	CM TR	General	Nottingham	1862-1880
Morris, J.S.C.	5	72	TR	Large cities	London	1862-1930
Post Office (Scotland)	11	446	GE TR	Scottish cities	Various Scottish cities	1783-1950
Robinson/Pike/Irving	18	429	GE TR	South-east towns	Brighton	1872-1940
Robinson, J.D.	10	13	GE TR	Yorkshire	Leeds	1901-1906
Slater, I.	60	197	GE TR	General and North	Manchester	1850-1921

Stevens, G.	18	36	GE TR	General towns	London	1879- 1899
Town & County Directories Ltd	53	291	TR	General	Edinburgh	1898-1950
Trades Directories Ltd	10	69	TR	General regional	Edinburgh	1900-1950
Ward, R. & Sons	11	100	GE	North-east	Newcastle	1850-1940
White, F.	11	17	GE TR	North and Midlands	Sheffield	1850-1875
White, W.	25	88	GE TR	General and North	Sheffield	1850-1919
Worrall, J.	21	242	GE TR	North-west	Oldham	1869-1950
Wright, C.N.	10	51	GE TR	East Midlands	Leicester, Nottingham	1854-1920

CM   Commercial
CT   Court
GE   General
TR   Classified Trades

The intensification of competition amongst directory publishers after 1850 was partly responsible for fluctuations in the numbers of directories. Previous research has highlighted these trends for the early part of the nineteenth century and discussed the influence of urban growth and industrialization on stimulating the demand for town directories.[35] Such factors continued to be of importance in the second half of the nineteenth century, a period which witnessed the increasing growth of directories. Figure 1 illustrates the number of surviving directories published between 1850 and 1950. Obviously, these data relate only to the directories discovered in the library searches undertaken for the present volume and as such do not present a complete picture. Even with such limitations, however, this information is the most comprehensive available and gives the best indication of variations over time.

A number of trends are highlighted in figure 1. First, it can be seen that there was only a relatively small increase in publications up to 1870. From then onwards far more directories started to be published, with a period of rapid growth occurring after 1880. The end of the First World War brought a temporary halt to many publications but the 1920s witnessed a recovery, with numbers of directories reaching a peak in 1936. These patterns of growth were conditioned by the commercial revolution that took place in the late nineteenth century, which resulted in the increased importance of retailing and service activities in the British economy.[36] In addition, continued urban growth was another contributing factor in the demand for directories, as were suburbanization processes that intensified after 1920, the latter being especially important in the development of suburban London directories.

A second influence on directory publication was the growth of large-scale publishers, and in particular the work of Kelly. As figure 1 shows, the number of directories published by Kelly's formed a significant proportion of all issues. They were responsible for some of the overall increase in the numbers of directories since, their scale of operations grew most rapidly from the mid-1880s onwards. During this period they not only produced more county and general directories, but also embarked upon the publication of a number of specialized trade directories. In fact between 1850 and 1950 our survey has revealed the existence of almost 3,500 specialist trade directories, the bulk of which were published after 1880.

The publication of directories declined considerably during the Second World War, with the low point being reached in 1944-5 (figure 1). After the war there was a slight recovery in the numbers of volumes published, but the scale of production was never again to approach pre-war levels. There were two main reasons for this. The first was that many directory publishers went out of business during the war years due to both lack of demand and a shortage of paper; for example, during the Second World War only three directories were published annually by Kelly's, these being for the cities of London, Glasgow and Birmingham (see Chapter 4). The second was the increased competition during the immediate post-war years from telephone directories, particularly for business and commercial use. By 1950, therefore, there were only some 140 directories published, and these represented just 44 per cent of the inter-war levels of publication. In many ways this period up to 1950 marked the end of large-scale directory production.

2.3 A classification of British directories

Any attempt to classify directories is a difficult task because of the limited information we have about their development. However, certain generalities about their evolution are known, while others can be inferred from the variety of surviving directories. Figure 2 represents an attempt to develop a typology of

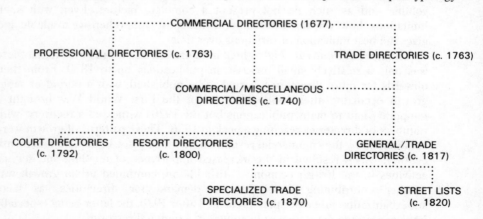

Figure 2   A typology of British directories.

directories in terms of their broad scope and content, as well as placing such publications in a general evolutionary framework. It should be stressed that many of the linkages between different directories are only tentative and for these no hard evidence exists to suggest that one type of development automatically led to another. However, the surviving directories, together with the changing needs of the population, would certainly seem to add strong support to this kind of historical development.

The most important and productive evolutionary line was from the trade directories through to the general directories that included both a classified trades section, and a list of private inhabitants arranged alphabetically. The earliest of these appears to have been the *Universal Director* published, for London, by Mortimer in 1763.[37] This contained a wide range of information, from the usual lists of merchants and bankers through to the introduction of a classified list of tradesmen and shopkeepers. It also represented a move away from directories produced just for merchants, towards publications for more general use by different sectors of society. These later publications took many different forms, as table 2 demonstrates. As can be seen, during the nineteenth century there is an increasing diversity of directories that are based around some variation of the original commercial directories. In this survey, however, such publications comprised only a small proportion of the total number of directories. By comparison, the general trade directories accounted for 35 per cent of all titles and 45 per cent of all volumes. These types of directories began in the early nineteenth century and came to dominate the market. A probable offshoot of the general directories was the production of street lists, usually published by small-scale, local firms. These usually took the form of a list of streets arranged alphabetically, and very often contained little or no other information. They only accounted for a very small proportion of the directories found in this survey (table 2).

A second major line of directory evolution was via the eighteenth century professional directories (figure 2). These publications tended to list only the wealthy and the professional people within the community. In their most specialized form they developed into court lists that covered only the names of important private residents.[38] As table 2 shows, there are a considerable range of combinations of directories based around the court directory. Taken together, however, these publications form only a very small proportion of the directories issued during the period 1850 to 1950. Associated with such information, provided as it was for society's elite, was the growth of 'resort town' directories. The earliest of these were published for established watering places and spa towns; Bath, for instance, had a directory in the late eighteenth century.[39] However, earlier town guides, dating from 1773, contained lists of lodging houses and medical practitioners. Such information was initially found as appendices to guide books before taking the form of a recognizable directory. The trend towards seaside holidays increased the demand for such directories during the early part of the nineteenth century, as more people discovered coastal resorts. Many of these directories contain only selective pieces of information concerning the better-class retailers and fashionable shops, whilst some listed the addresses of villas and houses for holiday lets. By the second half of the

Table 2 Types of directories issued between 1850 and 1950

Directory type[1]	Number of titles	Number of volumes issued
Commercial	184	612
Commercial and professional	1	1
Commercial and classified trade	153	400
Court	69	700
Court and commercial	39	103
Court and professional	19	22
Court and trade	22	119
General[2]	242	1684
General and trade	786	8120
Professional	5	18
Street list	27	69
Street list and trade	4	4
Specialized trade	250	3467
Street directory	69	407
Street and trade	44	171
Trade	308	2046
Total	2222	17943

[1]See chapter 3 for a full discussion of the definitions used in the survey.

[2]This definition differs from that used by Norton. It is used here to describe a directory that contains court and street *or* commercial and street sections; see Chapter 3.

nineteenth century most of the functions of the resort type of directories were covered by the more general trade directories, a factor which goes some way towards explaining the demise of the former publications.

By the second half of the nineteenth century specialized trade directories had made their appearance on a significant scale. For example, in this survey some 250 different titles were identified, which represented just over 11 per cent of all the titles (table 2). A number of the earlier ones concentrated on the activities associated with merchants and wholesalers, and in this sense they were directly associated with the commercial directories (figure 2). Others took on much more specialized forms, some of which were related to the great changes that were occurring in agriculture and more particularly in industry. In effect the ones associated with agriculture made little progress and appeared not to be commercial successes, as is well illustrated in the case of William Kent's publication, *The Agricultural Implement Manufacturers Directory of England*, issued in 1867. This gave an alphabetical list of manufacturers in each county, but in the preface Kent complains about the poor response to his survey which limited the scope of the directory and probably ensured that no other editions were produced. In contrast a few other publications were more successful, as in the case of *The Horticultural Directory*, which was issued regularly between 1867 and 1934.

The greatest proportion of these specialized directories was, however, associated with industrial activity and public utilities. In the case of the former group, some of the earliest were concerned with the worsted and woollen industries of West Yorkshire such as *Collinson, Burton & Co's West Riding Worsted Directory* published in 1851. One of the most famous within this category on textiles was that published by J. Worrall on *The Cotton Spinners and Manufacturers Directory*, issued between 1882 and 1950, which is arranged by place and type of activity, providing the number of spindles and looms for major firms.

By the 1870s specialist directories of all types had become generally accepted and after this period they were being produced in reasonably large numbers. This acceptance is also indicated by the fact that some directories were published over many years, and large firms, like Kelly's, started to issue such volumes. For example, *Kelly's Directory of the Leather Trades* was first published in 1871 and ran through to 1940. Between 1850 and 1950, Kelly's published some 184 specialist directories, which represented some 3.9 per cent of their total number of volumes. In general, the production of these specialist directories continued to increase during the late nineteenth century and peaked in the early years of the twentieth century.

2.4   Changes in content and format

The overall content of directories was related, as we have seen, to their specific role. However, over a period of time all the main types of directory changed their levels of information and general layout. The most significant changes in content and format were associated with the development of the general trade directories (figure 2). The earliest directories were simply alphabetically arranged names of inhabitants together with their addresses. However, throughout the eighteenth century the information and layout of trade directories changed markedly, as is shown in table 3. A second major step was taken with the introduction of separate street sections that gave the names and occupations of residents. Such a change was followed by directories that also contained a classified trades section, giving the names and addresses of each trader. This stage of development had been reached in London by 1763 with the publication of Mortimer's *Universal Director*.

However, in provincial towns such changes tended to come more slowly. In Liverpool, for example, the first directory published in 1766 by John Gore was merely an alphabetical list of names, occupations and addresses.[40] This type of format continued largely unchanged into the 1790s, although by 1790 the Gore directory had increased its level of information to cover a variety of themes (figure

3), and a list of streets had been included.[41] However, it was not until the publication in 1814 of Pigot's *Commercial Directory* that Liverpool was provided with a classified trades directory. Generally, the switch from commercial directories (see Chapter 3) to classified trade directories was slow outside London. Indeed, despite strong attempts by Holden to produce a national directory on a classified trades basis in the early years of the nineteenth century, this was only finally achieved by Pigot from 1814 onwards.

Table 3 Early changes in the general content of directories

Approximate dates	*Basic contents*
1720-1750	Names, alphabetically arranged with addresses, and later occupations were added.
1750-1790	Alphabetical list of names and addresses, together with alphabetical street sections with residents' names.
1790-1800	Names, addresses and occupations, together with alphabetical trades section.
1800-1820	Names, addresses and occupations. Street section. Classified trades section.

The changing format of Scottish directories presents a rather similar picture to that found in provincial England and Wales. However, some notable advances did occur, in particular the publication of *Williamson's Directory for the City of Edinburgh*. The first edition of this series, published in 1774, provided an early example of an alphabetical arrangement of occupations. This style was unfortunately abandoned by Williamson, whose later directories consisted of lists of inhabitants arranged alphabetically by name. It was not until the 1830s that Edinburgh had a comprehensive trades directory, containing a classified list of traders.[42]

The final and major transformation in the evolution of the general trade directories was again to take place in London. In 1817 Andrew Johnstone published a four-part directory that contained the following information:

1. An alphabetical arrangement of London streets that also listed the names and occupations of each householder.

2. An alphabetical list of people together with their occupations.

3. Trades, arranged alphabetically and with the names of persons engaged in each trade.

4. A miscellaneous section containing details on mail, coach and waggon conveyance.

As Goss points out, this was the most comprehensive directory of its time, listing as it did some 27,000 names and a total of nearly 81,000 entries, since each name was repeated in the Street and Trades Sections.[43] Due to a lack of financial

CONTENTS.

Figure 3   The list of contents in *Gore's Liverpool Directory* of 1790. (Not original size.)

support the directory was discontinued after the second edition in 1818, although it had by then paved the way for other compilers to publish similar volumes. In particular, the directories produced by W. Robson and James Pigot during the 1830s widely promoted the general trade directory as originally introduced by Johnstone.

In terms of the changing scope and content of directories two main periods can be identified. The first extended from 1734 to 1816, during which time the style of directories changed only slowly and in a limited fashion, as indicated in table 3. The second period, from 1817 onwards, was marked by a dramatic increase in the size and content of directories, as typified by Johnstone's London directory of 1817. However, it must be stressed that such dates refer mainly to the situation in London, since change in provincial directories, as we have seen, tended to be somewhat later. The increasing size of directories was brought about not merely by changes in classificatory styles, but also through the inclusion of additional types of information. Apart from the names and addresses of residents and traders, directories also contain sections on transport, local histories, maps and town plans, and a wide variety of advertisements.

A major boost to the growing comprehensiveness of general directories in the mid and late nineteenth century came from the activities of the larger firms such as Kelly's. In 1841, Kelly's *Post Office Directory of London* adopted the format introduced by Johnstone, and then produced similar directories for provincial areas after 1845. The success of Kelly's was not only based on the increasing number of their publications, but also on innovations in contents and format. By the late nineteenth century their general directories, especially those covering London, had expanded considerably, often containing well over 3,000 pages and, as table 4 shows, a wide variety of information.

Table 4 The format of Kelly's London directories by the late nineteenth century

Major sections	*Arrangement and content*
1. Official section	Alphabetical list of names of appointments in government offices, and alphabetical list of offices.
2. Street section	List of principal streets, house numbers and names of head of household. Some occupations given.
3. Commercial section	Alphabetical list of tradespeople.
4. Trades and professional section	Classified list of trades and professions.
5. Law section	Lists of judges, recorders, counsels, notaries and solicitors.
6. Court section	Alphabetical list of householders not in commercial section.
7. Parliamentary section	List of all peers of the U.K. and members of the House of Commons.
8. Postal section	Variety of information on postal rates and services.
9. City, clerical and parochial section	Lists of mayors, aldermen and councillors, lists of ministers.
10. Conveyance section	Lists of wharves, names of wharfingers, booking offices and railway carriers.
11. Banking section	List of London banks, foreign banks and country bankers.

DEEPING ST. NICHOLAS (or Deeping Fen) is an extensive village and parish, originally formed in 1846, and is now divided into the middle and north townships: the village is in the Fen, on the high road from Market Deeping to Spalding, with a station called Littleworth, on the East Lincolnshire branch of the London and North Eastern railway, 5 miles south-west from Spalding, about 7 north-east from Market Deeping, 14 north-east from Peterborough, 15 north-east from Stamford, and 87 from London by rail; the Counter Drain station on the Bourne and Spalding branch of the London, Midland and Scottish and London and North Eastern joint line is 3½ miles north-west from the village, and near Tongue End. The parish is in the parts of Holland, Ness and Elloe wapentake, Elloe petty sessional division, Spalding rural district and county court district, rural deanery of West Elloe, and archdeaconry and diocese of Lincoln. The church of St. Nicholas, erected in 1845, from designs by the late Mr. Kirk, of Sleaford, and endowed with funds bequeathed by William and Nicholas Clarke Stevenson, is a building of stone in a modern style of Florid Gothic, and consists of chancel, nave, north aisle and a northern tower, with an octagonal spire relieved by bold dormers and crocketed pinnacles and containing 6 bells, hung in 1904, and a clock provided in 1909: the base of the tower forms a north porch: in 1908 a new reredos was provided: alterations were made in 1891, when a new organ was erected: there are 300 sittings: a lych gate was erected in 1936 by Mrs. Samuel Campain, jun. in memory of her husband. The register dates from the year 1846. The living is a vicarage, net yearly value £375, with residence,

in the gift of the Earl of Lindsey and Dr. Allford, and held since 1925 by the Rev. Herbert Henry Stainsby M.A. of Selwyn College, Cambridge. During the year 1899 a new church Sunday school was built at a cost of £130. Mission services are held at Tongue End in the Public Elementary school. Here is a Methodist chapel, erected in 1867, the site for which was given by the late Mr. James Haynes, of West Deeping Fen; there is also a General chapel at Tongue End. The principal landowners are Thomas Henry Richardson esq. Herbert Parkinson Carter esq. O.B.E., J.P. Sidney Worth esq. William Dennis and Sons Limited and Thomas Arthur Pick esq. The soil is loamy; subsoil, clay and silt. The chief crops are potatoes, rape seed, wheat, barley, oats, peas and beans. The population in 1931 was 1,766; the area is 16,511 acres of land and inland water, parts being nearly the whole of Deeping Fen, which is drained by two powerful engines of 80 and 60 horse power, and is now in a high state of cultivation.

By the Parts of Holland (Alteration of Districts and Parishes) Order, 1932, part of the parish of Spalding was transferred to this parish.

Post, M. O., T. & T. E. D. Office, Deeping St. Nicholas. Letters through Spalding. There is a T. office at Littleworth railway station (L, & N. E. R.) for dispatch, but no delivery; closed on sundays

Post & Tel. Call Office, Tongue End. Letters through Spalding

Railway Stations.—Littleworth (L. & N. E.); Counter Drain (L. M. & S. & L. & N. E. joint)

DEEPING ST. NICHOLAS.

PRIVATE RESIDENTS.

(For T N see general list of Private Residents at end of book.)

Barnett A. R., Tolethorpe house
Stainsby Rev. Herbert Henry M.A. (vicar), Vicarage

COMMERCIAL.

Marked thus ° farm 150 acres or over.

Adcock Leonard & Leslie, farmers, Owens farm
Atkin Harry Russell, smallholder
Atkinson Lucas, farmer Deeping High bank. T N 31
°Atkinson Thos. Hardy, farmer, Deeping High bank. T N 17
Birch G. F. & Son Ltd. farmers. T N 14
Bishop Wm. H. wheelwright. T N 19
Blue Bell P.H. (Albt. Maplethorpe). T N 26
Branton Wltr. Geo. smallholder
Brewster Saml. smallholder
Brittain Geo. T. farmer, Lonsdale ho. T N 4
Burrows Charles A. E. farm bailiff to William Dennis & Sons Ltd. The Beeches. T N 2
°Carter Albt. H. farmer, Bar & Park farms. T N's 9 & 10
°Chappell Albt. Edwd. farmer
Chappell Regnld. W. wheelwright
Clayton Walter, farmer. T N 16

Coleman Arth. smallholder
Cook Sheddle, smallholder
°Cooke Edwd. D. farmer. Market Deeping 223 (postal address, Market Deeping, Peterborough)
Cornwall Fred, smallholder, North Drove bank (letters direct from Spalding)
Cornwall Jn. smallholder
°Dennis William & Sons Ltd. farmers & landowners. T N 2
Ellis & Everard Ltd. coal &c. mers Railway station; & at Stamford
France Chas. butcher. T N 30
°Gandy Jarvis Kilham, farmer (postal address, Langtoft, Peterborough). Market Deeping 227
°Grooby Rt. & Wltr. H. farmers, Little Duke farm. Market Deeping 358
Halfway inn (Jn. W. Kettle)
Harrow inn (Alfd. T. Browning)
Ivatt Geo. E. smallholder
Ives George, smallholder
Jackson George, smallholder
Jackson Herbt. smallholder
Jackson Wm. smallholder
Mann Thos. smallholder
Maplethorpe & Brakes, smallholders
Miller Wm. Seth, smallholder, North Drove bank (letters direct from Spalding)
Munton F.S. farmer, Hop Pole farm. T N 29
Neal Sydney, farmer, The Poplars. T N 20

Noble Thomas, smallholder
Oatsheaf P.H. (Albt. Hare)
Perkins Fred & Sons, saddlers
Perkins Fred, smallholder
°Pick Thos. Arth. farmer. T N 6
Pick Thos. Raymond, farmer, The Chestnuts. T N 24
Plough P.H. (Edwd. Barnatt)
°Pocklington Albt. Ernest, farmer. T N 21
Posey John William, smallholder
°Preston Arth. Cecil, farmer, Oak Tree farm. Market Deeping 229
Reynolds Wm. Hy. smallholder, Willow Tree
°Richardson Thos. Fredk. farmer, The Hollies. T N 5
°Richardson Thos. Hy. farmer & landowner,Church & Hedge farms. T N 18
Steele Jsph. (Mrs.), smallholder
Stennett Wm. smallholder, Willow tree
Taylor Edwd. smallholder, Willow tree
°Tinsley Hy. Cole Cyril, farmer
Vanplew Frank A. shopkpr
°Watts Rt. Knowles, farmer
Webster Jsph. Ernest, smallholder
Wensor James Arthur, smallholder
Wigginton Hy. smallholder
Woodhead Bros. farmers, Halfway farm. T N 11
°Worth Sidney, farmer. T N 3

Figure 4   The format of a typical Kelly's county directory as illustrated by the *Lincolnshire Directory* of 1937. Note how in this agricultural area the large farms, over 150 acres, are identified. (Not original size.)

[21]

In the county directories, Kelly's adopted a very different format. This gave an alphabetical listing of settlements and within each place an alphabetical arrangement of inhabitants. In smaller settlements there were no street sections and the classified trade section was usually arranged for the whole county. Figure 4 shows the typical format, and also illustrates that in agricultural regions, information was often given on the size of farms.

The production of these general directories was not without its difficulties and the complexity of the task required a well-organized company. Such problems were intensified in London because of its sheer size. In an attempt to overcome the increasing size of their volumes for London, which were becoming too cumbersome to use, Kelly's introduced in 1885, their London suburban directories, or 'Buff Books'. Such a move enabled Kelly's to restrict the size of their London directories without any major loss of detail. Other difficulties concerned the volume of names and addresses within the street section of the directories, and the continual growth of new types of economic activities. In the case of the former problem this was solved by the omission of some inhabitants; but on what basis this selection was made Kelly's never specified, only remarking that 'the names are selected with great care, by experienced agents.' [44] It would appear, however, that only the heads of households were selected and that most agents, no matter how experienced, were extremely reluctant to canvass for names in the slums of Victorian cities. Significant problems were encountered with multi-occupied houses, and directories rarely listed all the families in such dwellings. For example, in mid-nineteenth-century Liverpool Gore's directory for 1851 listed only 65 per cent of those households recorded by the 1851 census in those parts of the city dominated by court dwellings and multi-occupied houses.[45] Even in smaller centres, directories tend to emphasize the craftsmen, traders and professional inhabitants at the expense of other occupations. Page's study of Ashby-de-la-Zouch in mid-nineteenth-century Leicestershire gives some measured idea of the extent of such occupational bias.[46] In this study a comparison between White's directory of 1862 and the census enumeration books for 1861 showed that tradesmen accounted for 33 per cent of the names listed in the directory, but that no labourers or domestic servants were listed. In contrast, the census data reveals that tradesmen only accounted for 18 per cent of households in the town, and labourers and domestic servants around 7 per cent. Fortunately, directories tended to be far more complete in their coverage of business and commercial activities, and are often the only reliable source available.

The methods of obtaining information varied according to the resources available and usually involved either visiting houses, or sending or leaving circulars to be filled in by the householders. This system persisted well into the twentieth century and in the 1940s directory compilers were facing the same difficulties. Thus, in the preface of the *Tiverton Directory* of 1947 the author states that 'a canvasser has called on every house, and in the event of a householder being away a slip was deposited. If the slip was not returned the householder was at fault.' This attitude probably accounts for the numbers of empty houses listed in the street section of the directory. The visiting method tended to be more reliable, and by the mid-nineteenth century the larger firms employed teams of agents throughout the country. Results depended very much on the response and cooperation of the public and their willingness to provide information. Initially, many of the uneducated people were suspicious of directory agents, often believing them to be employed by the government. During the latter half of the nineteenth century and the early twentieth century, as more directories were produced, people often became annoyed at being continually pestered for information – a problem that the Eyre brothers encountered in Plymouth, where in 1880 the inhabitants were 'short in their replies to our agents' inquiries, having been pestered beyond enduring in the matter of directories'.[47]

The problem of new commercial activities and the classification of trades was a permanent one for the directory compiler. The development of new trades merely necessitated the addition of new headings, although this could be costly. Kelly's were continually having to introduce new listings in their trades section: for example, in the 1897 edition of the London directory, they added 113 new trade categories, including such activities as 'camomile flower importers', and 'wire key makers'.[48] Much more irksome, however, were the difficulties associated with traders carrying out more than one business at the same site. The grocery trade was particularly prone to this and a tradesman may be listed as grocer, tea dealer, provision dealer and shopkeeper; and such listings changed from one directory to another. Pigot, in an early attempt to overcome this problem, grouped food trades, where specialization was not very developed, into the category 'Shopkeepers and Dealers in Groceries and Sundries'. Unfortunately, this business diversity was not always limited to the same area of trade; hence we find categories such as 'Drapers and Tea Dealers' listed in *Slater's Lancashire Directory* of 1851. In the best of the directories such problems were largely solved by using multiple categories. However, as the total number of trade entries increased in the late nineteenth century most directories abandoned this system in favour of more specific headings. Kelly's, amongst others, sought to make some commercial advantage out of the situation by offering to list the names of traders under more than one heading on payment of a fee.

The aims of the directory compiler obviously depended on the type of book being produced. For example, court directories would collect only a small fraction of a town's population as compared with a general directory. Similarly, specialized trade directories focused mainly on traders or specialized activities, and in some instances depended purely on subscriptions to meet the costs of publication.[49] An example of the latter approach is provided by *Perry's Business Directory* of 1902, the bulk of which consisted of a series of advertisements, classified by types of manufacturing and commercial activity. A similar arrangement is to be found in *London. A Complete Guide to Leading Hotels, Places of Amusement*, published between 1872 and 1902. Each entry consists of an advertisement in a gilt frame illustrating hotels and guesthouses.

Given the increasing number of specialized directories being produced after 1880, it is extremely difficult to encompass their changing contents and format. The majority of these publications were organized around two main sections; one with information arranged geographically by place, and the other by type of activity. Many of Kelly's specialized directories took this format, as illustrated by the *Textile Fabric Directory* of 1880 which listed spinners and manufacturers, together with 25,000 drapers and 18,000 tailors by trade type, and then by place.[50] Another common format was to devote a separate section to London and then arrange the traders in the remainder of the country alphabetically. That many of these publications were able to produce information on a national basis was a testament to the development of directory firms, as well as the growing importance of specialized directories. The latter may be illustrated by the fact that in 1880 only about a quarter of directories issued could be considered specialist ones, whereas in 1950 this proportion had risen to just over 40 per cent.[51]

The growth of specialized directories reflected the increasing diversification of the British economy and also the changing nature of society. Such trends are clearly reflected in the titles of directories. On the industrial front, the development of electricity as a major source of power was mirrored by such publications as *The Electrical Engineers' Central-Station Directory*, first issued in 1896. This was a gazetteer of places which had electricity generating stations, and the directory also gave details of electrical engineers. Similarly, the growth of new industrial locations acted as a spur to specialized directories, as reflected by the *Directory of Firms Located on the Industrial Estate of Trafford Park*, published in 1948.

Changes in tastes and the growth of specialist markets presented some of the more speculative publishers with the opportunity to produce directories of a rather novel nature. For example, *The Vegetarian Directory and Food Reformers Guide*, of 1913, contained a list of vegetarian stores, sanatoria, boarding houses and restaurants. Sadly, these types of publications were of a very ephemeral nature and most never progressed past one issue.

2.5   Maps and town plans

A great number of the directories contained maps or town plans, which, in themselves, are often valuable historical sources. Indeed, it was in recognition of this fact that the present survey not only set out to record which directories possessed maps, but also to give their scale. Like the directories themselves, the growing interest in maps during the nineteenth century reflected the increased demand for information from a society that was becoming fully aware of the importance of having accurate statistics. The development of cartography and the popularization of maps in commercial publications such as directories, was made possible by improvements in surveying with the advent of the Ordnance Survey,[52] together with developments in lithographic techniques.[53] Both trends led to more, and cheaper, maps being available.

The maps and plans within directories served a variety of purposes, ranging from the identification and location of settlements or streets listed in a directory, through to the presentation of specialized economic information. Very often the larger publishing firms had sufficient capital to commission the engraving of their own maps and town plans. Indeed, some of the early directory compilers were also engravers. The best example of this business linkage is that of James Pigot, who was by trade an engraver and copper-plate printer in Manchester.[54] Many of his directories contain maps engraved by his firm, and during the 1830s he published two folios of county maps of England.[55] Some of these were later updated and used to illustrate directories published during the 1840s. Many of the county maps have details on aspects such as turnpike roads, mail routes, the number of Members of Parliament returned by each borough and the location of polling stations (figure 5).

The largest investment in map production was by Kelly's, who produced their own county maps and town plans, and published *The Post Office Directory Atlas of England and Wales* in 1861. This contained 40 county maps at an average scale of 1 inch to 5 miles, and these also appeared in the firm's directories. The maps gave information on the location of polling stations, 'Post Office money-order towns', and details of railways, with the early maps of around 1850 indicating proposed railways. From about 1874 to 1884 a second series of maps were published and these were often at a larger size than the first series, since they were based on the Ordnance Survey's Old Series at 1 inch to 1 mile. In terms of content, they included similar information to the first map series, although details concerning post offices had been removed. Within these two main series many additions and modifications were made to the county maps to keep them up to date and, by the 1930s, with the growing importance of road transport, the main emphasis on Kelly's maps had switched to illustrating road conditions (figure 6). Many of these maps were produced in colour to indicate the different parliamentary divisions of a county.

Obviously, it was only the larger companies like Kelly's that could produce their own county maps. In the majority of cases directory publishers relied very heavily on existing material, and fortunately there was no shortage of this during the nineteenth century. For example, the directories produced by William Robson relied on the reissued county maps of John Murray, whilst Butcher's directories used maps from the work of George Philip.[56] From the 1870s onwards a number of Philip's county maps were used in Butcher's directories; some were overprinted with colours which marked parliamentary divisions and all of them gave information on canals, railways and roads. The scale of these county maps varied between 1 inch to 7 miles and 1 inch to 8 miles, depending on the area covered. Later issues of Philip's county atlas maps of 1881, were issued by Stevens' directories during the 1880s and 1890s. Many of the maps were altered or adapted by the removal of Philip's imprint, which was substituted either by the title 'Stevens' Series of Directory Maps', or a surround of advertisements.[57] Many other directory publishers utilized the smaller-scale maps that were being produced by commercial firms using information gained from the Ordnance Survey. For example, the maps of the Edinburgh-based engravers of Gall & Inglis are to be found in numerous local directories, since they were published at a scale convenient for many directories.

Directories also abound with town plans, although, as with county maps, these are of varying quality. The value of such plans is that they often provide a detailed record of the form and growth of urban areas. Smith, in an assessment of the types of nineteenth-century town plans, has drawn attention to the increasing importance of 'cheap maps to satisfy the growing demands of the ever-more literate and mobile working and middle classes'.[58] It was just such conditions that

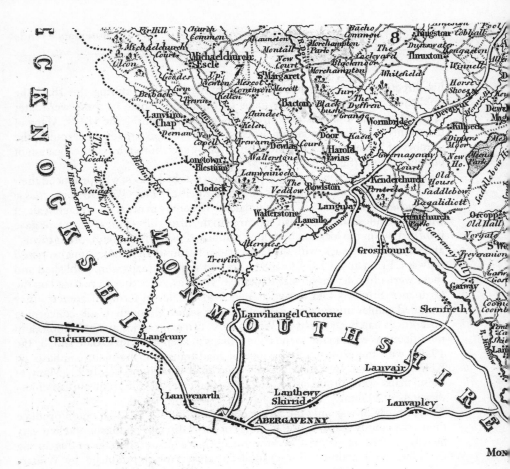

HEREFORD CATHEDRAL.

Figure 5   (overleaf) Part of a map of Herefordshire from Pigot's directory of the county for 1844. (Not original size.)

KELLY'S
MAP OF
LINCOLNSHIRE

1st Class Roads are shewn thus :—
2nd Class Roads „ „ „

Scale of Miles

0   5   10

Figure 6   Part of a typical county map from a Kelly's county directory during the 1930s. The map was drawn and engraved by staff at Kelly's but printed by Suttley and Silverlock of Andover. These maps were generally overprinted with colour to delimit the parliamentary boundaries. (Not original size.)

Table 5 Major types of nineteenth-century town plans for Leeds and Norwich

Category of plan	Leeds	Norwich
Plans in directories	17	5
Street plans in topographical works	21	18
Ordnance Survey plans	13	3
Transport plans	14	3
Insurance plans	1	1
Sanitary district plans	8	5

(Modified from: David Smith, *Victorian Plans of the British Isles*, Batsford, 1985, p.73)

favoured the inclusion of town plans in directories and has left a sizeable collection of such material (table 5). Thus, in an industrial city such as Leeds, plans in directories account for almost 23 per cent of all town plans, and rank second in numerical importance to street plans in topographical works.

Some of the earlier maps are amongst the best town plans and were issued by Edward Baines for use with his directories of Lancashire and Yorkshire.[59] For example, his Lancashire directory contains a series of engraved plans for all the principal settlements, and their quality is illustrated by figure 7 which shows the detail provided for Preston in 1824. By the latter part of the nineteenth century the emphasis of many town plans contained within directories was more functional than decorative, and most were simple street plans. To a great extent these more basic plans were a product of the rapidly changing urban scene and the continual growth of new streets, which necessitated constant updating. In the case of companies such as Kelly's, the town plan had become totally integrated within the directory, with all the streets listed in the directory having map references. The scale of these town plans varied not only depending on the publisher, but also in relation to settlement size. In London, for example, Kelly's produced plans at the scale of 1 inch to 4 miles, although in smaller, provincial cities the scale was more usually 1 inch to 6 miles. Finally, it should be pointed out that not all directories contained high-quality town plans, for in some of the smaller, locally produced publications cartographic skills were often rather basic (figure 8).

A good number of specialized directories also contained maps and plans, usually reflecting their particular specialisms. For example, the *Sheffield Exchange Directory* of 1933 contains a map of the Yorkshire coalfield, whilst the *Timber and Wood Consuming Trades Directory* for Great Britain, published regularly between 1891 and 1950, contains numerous detailed plans of dock areas, at an average scale of just over 1 inch to 1 mile. Some of these plans may well have utilized earlier publications of ports and harbours published during the 1860s.[60]

Figure 7   Baines's map of Preston, issued in *Baines' Directory of Lancashire*, 1824. (Not original size.)

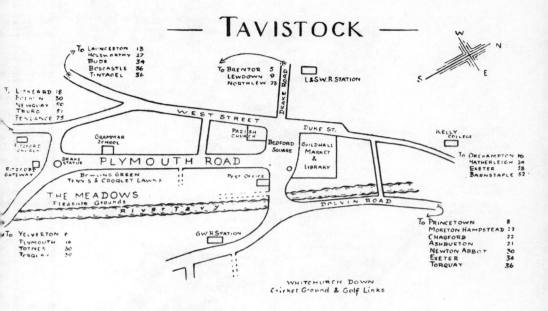

Figure 8   An example of one of the poorer-quality maps issued in some of the more locally produced directories. This is taken from *The Tavistock Directory* of 1918, published by Jolliffe & Son of Tavistock. (Not original size.)

Occasionally, directory publishers used more novel forms of map, as in the case of W.H. Allen's *Commercial London Directory* of 1890. This was mainly a directory of merchants and manufacturers, and was illustrated with 20 bird's-eye views of the main London streets (figure 9). This type of plan followed the re-introduction by Sulman of the Tudor bird's-eye view in order to show buildings in perspective, and was used in Herbert Fry's frequently republished work on London.[61] Unfortunately, this type of map never really caught on in directories, largely because of their cost, and few examples exist.

2.6   Topography and local history

During the early nineteenth century it had become common practice for many directories to contain sections on topography and local history. This material usually introduced the directory and attempted to provide the reader with a background knowledge of a town or county. It appears that such information was regarded as being of considerable importance, particularly in those directories published during the second part of the nineteenth century. The evidence for this stems from two facts. First, the volume and scope of topographical and historical information expanded in many directories; secondly, many of the larger directory-publishing firms engaged well-known authors to write such works. William White engaged both local and national experts of some note, for his *Devonshire Directory* of 1890: thus, Charles Worthy, author of a number of local

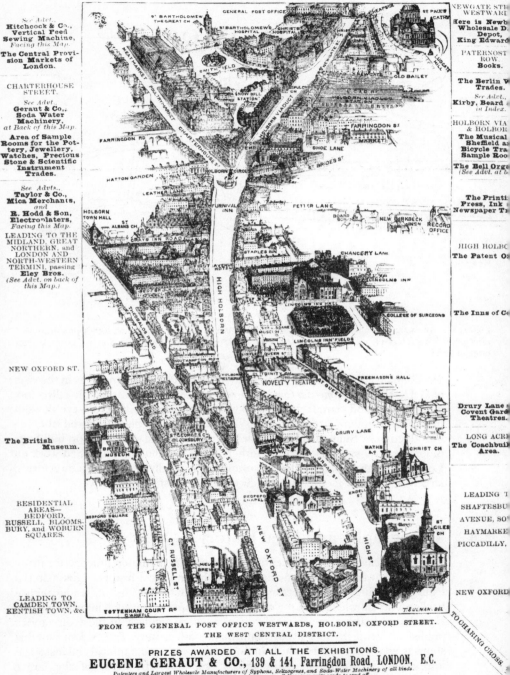

FROM THE GENERAL POST OFFICE WESTWARDS, HOLBORN, OXFORD STREET. THE WEST CENTRAL DISTRICT.

Left margin:

See Advt.
Hitchcock & Co., Vertical Feed Sewing Machine, *Facing this Map.*

The Central Provision Markets of London.

CHARTERHOUSE STREET.
See Advt.
Geraut & Co., Soda Water Machinery, *at Back of this Map.*

Area of Sample Rooms for the Pottery, Jewellery, Watches, Precious Stone & Scientific Instrument Trades.

See Advts.
Taylor & Co., Mica Merchants, *and* R. Hodd & Son, Electroplaters, *Facing this Map.*

LEADING TO THE MIDLAND, GREAT NORTHERN, and LONDON AND NORTH-WESTERN TERMINI, passing Eley Bros. *(See Advt. on back of this Map.)*

NEW OXFORD ST.

The British Museum.

RESIDENTIAL AREAS—BEDFORD, RUSSELL, BLOOMSBURY, and WOBURN SQUARES.

LEADING TO CAMDEN TOWN, KENTISH TOWN, &c.

Right margin:

NEWGATE STH WESTWARD

Here is Newb Wholesale D. Depot, King Edward

PATERNOST ROW. Books.

The Berlin W Trades.
See Advt.
Kirby, Beard *in Index.*

HOLBORN VIA & HOLBORN

The Musical Sheffield a Bicycle Tra Sample Roo

The Bell Orga *(See Advt. at b*

The Printi Press, Ink Newspaper Tr

HIGH HOLBC
The Patent O

The Inns of C

Drury Lane Covent Gard Theatres.

LONG ACR
The Coachbuil Area.

LEADING T SHAFTESBU AVENUE, SO HAYMARKE PICCADILLY,

NEW OXFORD

histories on Devon, was contracted to write the general history and description of the county, whilst a James Britten, of the British Museum, revised the paper on botany in the county.[62] Not all directory publishers were as rigorous as White, however, and many firms probably just copied out any existing topographical material that came to hand. In many other cases it was most probably local clergymen or J.P.s who contributed the section on topography and local history.

It is hardly surprising that such local and regional descriptions became an integral part of most provincial directories, given the increase in personal mobility that was occurring at this time. Some directories took this topographical material to an extreme and appeared almost as regional guidebooks, such as the *Devon and Cornwall Court Guide and County Blue Book of 1896*, which presents a comprehensive series of topographical and historical sketches of the two counties, together with maps of climatological and geological conditions. Other directories emphasized particular local features and institutions. For example, *Venning's Directory of East Cornwall* of 1901 was primarily concerned with describing the history of churches and chapels within the area, so much so that the publishers persuaded a local clergyman to edit the book. Part One of this directory contains a section on local history, whilst Part Two is an account of the local topography, well illustrated by numerous sketches and photographs (figure 10).

The inclusion of topographical and historical material in directories did not diminish, and Kelly's provincial directories published in the twentieth century continued to include a great deal of this information. Indeed, during the 1930s there was, if anything, a renewed interest in topographical material, especially amongst local publishers of directories. This often took the form of views and sketches of the town as it appeared in the nineteenth century or prior to industrialization (figure 11).

2.7   Miscellaneous material

In addition to the previously discussed topics, most directories also included a variety of miscellaneous material. This information can be divided into three main types: that associated with transport, material relating to local public institutions, and commercial advertisements.

Since a great majority of directories were published for reasons of trade it is hardly remarkable that they should contain information on transport. Indeed, such data became a regular feature of many London directories from the mid-eighteenth century onwards. These publications included lists of coaches and their places of departure and destination. In addition, the rates for hackney coaches and watermen were given, together with postal charges. Provincial directories of the eighteenth century provided similar information, but tended to concentrate on commercial carriers.[63] The increasing improvement in the levels

GUNNISLAKE.

CALSTOCK TOWN.

Figure 10   Examples of landscapes and views often accompanied the topographical sections in many directories. These particular ones come from *Venning's Directory of East Cornwall*, 1901. (Not original size.)

Tiverton's Toll Gates

PARK ROAD
leading to Chevithorne.

LOUGHBOROUGH
leading to Cruwys Morchard and Southmolton, and also
to Rackenford.

BOLHAM ROAD
leading to Bampton, Dulverton and Minehead.

Near OLD BLUNDELL'S
leading to Butterleigh and Cullompton.

On the day that the Tolls were abolished, an enterprising citizen drove round them in a dog cart accompanied by a Photographer. These pictures show four of the seven Toll Houses which surrounded Tiverton

(90)

Figure 11   The interest in local history by directory publishers took many forms and continued well into the twentieth century, as illustrated by this collection of photographs from *Musgrove's Tiverton Directory* of 1947. (Not original size.)

of transport during the nineteenth century, especially the coming of the railways, added extra weight to the inclusion of this information within directories. All Kelly's directories contain information on transport, ranging from data on postal charges through to lists of railways carriers and stations (see for example, table 4 above). In Kelly's provincial directories it became usual to insert in the introduction a detailed list of local carriers, along with their times and places of departure. This was often preceded by sections on rail and, where appropriate, water transport, once again giving the frequency of such services. Transportation and related topics also became a theme for specialized directories in the late nineteenth and early twentieth centuries; for instance, between 1916 and 1941 *The Motor Transport Year Book and Directory* was published, containing an index of all garages, together with sections on the different transport companies.

Information on public establishments and institutions increased in those directories published during the nineteenth century as local authorities became more involved in the provision of services and local government spread its influence. In many directories it is normal to find a section listing town or county councillors, city or county officials and magistrates. Lists of educational and religious establishments, hospitals and public buildings were also published. In Kelly's directories such information often appears under a section entitled 'the

Figure 12   A typical trader's card as used in some of the early directory advertisements. (Not original size.)

SAMS' HOTEL

AND

COFFEE HOUSE, 302, STRAND,

LONDON,

(CORNER OF NEWCASTLE STREET.)

SAMS' HOTEL AND COFFEE HOUSE,

302, STRAND, LONDON,

WILL BE FOUND A

CONVENIENT, COMFORTABLE, CENTRAL, & ECONOMICAL RESIDENCE

For Strangers, Country Tradesmen, and Visitors from all parts of England, Ireland, and Scotland;

Being near most of the large Wholesale Warehouses, Banks, Inns of Court, Government and Law Offices, Theatres, Exhibitions, Places of Amusement, &c.

THE CHARGES ARE IN ACCORDANCE WITH THE LIBERAL SPIRIT OF THE TIMES.

Excellent Bed-rooms, 1s. and 1s. 6d. per night.　　Bed and Breakfast, with Egg or Bacon, 2s.
Mutton Chop, 6d.　　Rump Steak, 9d.

PARTIES REMAINING IN TOWN SEVERAL WEEKS, WILL BE ACCOMMODATED UPON LIBERAL TERMS PER AGREEMENT, CHEAPER THAN ANY PRIVATE HOUSE IN LONDON.

Commodious Coffee-rooms, Cigar-room, and cheerful Private Sitting-rooms, 2s. per Day.

A PORTER UP ALL NIGHT.

Omnibuses pass to all parts of London, Fare 4d.　Cab Fare from Great Western Railway Station to SAMS' HOTEL, 1s. 6d.; North Western ditto, 1s.

SAMS' HOTEL IS NEARLY OPPOSITE SOMERSET HOUSE.

HOT, COLD, AND SHOWER BATHS, 1s., ALWAYS READY.

SAMS' HOTEL, 302, STRAND.

Figure 13 Many provincial directories contained advertisements from London, as illustrated by this example from *Kelly's Post Office Directory of Cornwall*, 1856. (Not original size.)

<table>
<tr><td>

Directly
Facing the
Atlantic Ocean

ALFRED BUTLER
Manager

Tel. 8

</td><td>

Officially appointed R.A.C. and A.A. Hotel

HOT AND COLD WATER
in every Bedroom.

**Only Hotel in England with Passenger
Lift from Every Floor to Bathing
Beaches**

</td><td>

Special

Arrangements

for the Comfort

of

Winter Visitors

</td></tr>
</table>

CRANLEIGH PRIVATE HOTEL
Island Estate, NEWQUAY
TELEPHONE: 279.

Cranleigh is situated in a unique position on edge of cliff,
immediately overlooking G.W. Beach, with glorious views
of coast and country (as far as Trevose Head). Central for
Shops, Post Office, Church, Golf Links and Station.

ELECTRIC LIGHT.   SEPARATE TABLES.

PERSONAL SUPERVISION.   GARAGE 1 MINUTE.   WELL RECOMMENDED.

MODERATE TERMS.   MISS L. JONES, *Proprietress.*

Figure 14   Advertisements in directories closely mirrored social and economic trends. By the turn of the century seaside holidays had become important, and directories carried many advertisements from hotels. (Not original size.)

official directory'. Such information, together with the trades sections of the directories, helps to construct a picture of general social and economic conditions prevailing within different communities.

Advertisements also became important during the nineteenth century and were an obvious source of income to the publishers. For example, the Sun Insurance Company paid Kelly's £1,000 a year for the advertising space on the back cover of their London directory between 1898 and 1900. Similarly, the Scottish Widows Insurance Office paid Kelly's £150 for their advertisements to appear before the three main sections of the 1898 London directory.[64]

The advertisements contained within directories are potentially important for two reasons. First, they give some insight into the tradesmen who subscribed to directories, since it seems likely that advertisers would also be subscribers. If this is so, then a review of the main advertisers could give some information on who used directories. Secondly, and of greater importance, advertisements can be used as a data source, albeit a rather fragmented one, for historical research.[65]

Initially, the advertisements placed within directories were nothing more than copies of traders' calling-cards, expressing, as figure 12 shows, the basic facts regarding a particular business. However, by the mid-nineteenth century the power of advertising was fairly well established. A significant boost came from the abolition of the tax on advertisements in 1853. This, together with improvements in transportation, set the scene for the development of modern advertising. Within most directories, advertisements became the norm rather than the exception, and varied considerably in their style (figures 13 and 14).

Notes

1. B. Walker, 'Birmingham directories', *Trans. and Proc. Birmingham Archaeological Soc.*, 58 (1934), 1-36.
2. C.W.F. Goss, *The London Directories, 1677-1855* (1932).
3. W.A. Abram, *Memorials of the Preston Guilds* (1882).
4. S. Lee, *Collection of Names of the Merchants Living in and about the City of London* (1677).
5. Goss, *op. cit.*
6. Goss, *op. cit.*
7. W.H. Beveridge, 'A seventeenth-century labour exchange: a correction', *Economic J.*, 24 (1914), 635-6.
8. J.E. Norton, *Guide to the National and Provincial Directories of England and Wales, excluding London, published before 1856* (1950).
9. M.D. George, 'The early history of registry offices', *Economic History, 1* (1926), 570-90.
10. *Ibid.*; W.H. Beveridge, 'A seventeenth-century labour exchange', *Economic J.*, 24

(1914), 371-6.
11. George, *op. cit.*
12. Walker, *op. cit.*
13. *Ibid.*
14. *Ibid.*
15. J. Harland, 'The oldest Manchester directories, collectanea relating to Manchester', *Chetham Soc. Publication* (1866), 119-66.
16. Anon, 'Mrs Elizabeth Raffald', *The Palatine Note-Book* (1881), 141-2.
17. O. Ashmore, 'Introduction', in *Baines's Directory of Lancashire*, 1823 (repr. 1968).
18. Walker, *op. cit.*
19. *Bailey's Northern Directory* (1781), preface.
20. Walker, *op. cit.*
21. C.W. Chilton, 'The *Universal British Directory* – a warning', *Local Historian, 15* (1982), 144-6.
22. *Holden's Triennial Directory for 1805*, 2 vols.
23. *Holden's Annual London and County Directory, 1811*, 3 vols.

24. J. Pigot, *The Commercial Directory* (1814-15).
25. Norton, *op. cit.*
26. International Publishing Corporation Ltd, 'A brief history of Kelly's directories' (n.d.).
27. *Ibid.*, and Norton, *op. cit.*
28. *Parliamentary Debates*, 85 (1846), 808.
29. *Ibid.*, 809.
30. *Ibid.*, 811.
31. Norton, *op. cit.*
32. *Parliamentary Debates*, 85 (1846), 813.
33. *Ibid.*
34. *Parliamentary Debates*, 91 (1847), 265-9; 94, 593-7.
35. G. Shaw, *British Directories as Sources in Historical Geography* (1982).
36. G. Shaw, 'Retail patterns', and C. Lee, 'Services', in J. Langton and R.J. Morris (eds), *Atlas of Industrializing Britain, 1780-1814* (1986).
37. M. Mortimer, *Universal Director* (1763); Goss, *op. cit.*
38. See, for example, P. Boyle, *Fashionable Court Guide* (1792); a slightly earlier court directory was that by J. Wilkes, *Directory of the Nobility, Gentry and Families of Distinction* (1790).
39. *The New Bath Directory* (1792); printed lists of lodging houses can be found as early as 1772. For a discussion about the spread of eighteenth-century directories, see Shaw, *British Directories as Sources*, and P.J. Corfield and S. Kelly, 'Giving directions to the town: the early town directories', *Urban History Yearbook* (1984), 22-35.
40. J. Gore, *The Liverpool Directory for the Year 1766*. For a detailed discussion of these early Liverpool directories, see G.T. and I. Shaw, *Liverpool's First Directory* (1907); and of Gore's work, see A.C. Wardle, 'John Gore', *Trans. Hist. Soc. Lancashire and Cheshire*, 97 (1946), 223-4.
41. J. Gore, *Gore's Liverpool Directory* (1790).
42. *Gray's Annual Directory for Edinburgh, Leith and Suburbs* (1833).
43. Goss, *op. cit.*; A. Johnstone, *Johnstone's London Commercial Guide and Street Directory* (1817).
44. 'Introduction' in Kelly's *Post Office London Directory* (1897).
45. C. Pooley, 'Migration, mobility and residential areas in nineteenth-century Liverpool' (Ph.D. thesis, University of Liverpool, 1978); see also Shaw, *British Directories as Sources*.
46. D. Page, 'Commercial directories and market towns', *Local Historian, 11.2* (1974), 85-8.
47. Eyre Bros., *Post Office Plymouth Directory* (1880).
48. 'Introduction' to *Kelly's Post Office Directory* (1897).
49. For a detailed discussion of this topic and directory coverage in general, see Shaw, *British Directories as Sources*.
50. For an application of these specialized textile directories, see S. Kenny, 'Sub-regional specialization in the Lancashire cotton industry, 1884-1914', *J. Historical Geography, 8.1* (1982), 41-63.
51. These figures refer only to the directories included in this survey.
52. W.A. Seymour (ed.), *A History of the Ordnance Survey* (1981).
53. G. Wakeman, 'Lithography, photography and map printing', in *Aspects of Victorian Lithography* (1970).
54. Norton, *op. cit.*
55. J. Pigot, *A Pocket Topography and Gazetteer of England* (1841).
56. For details of this link, see D. Smith, *Victorian Plans of the British Isles* (1985), which gives an account of George Philip and his work.
57. *Ibid.*
58. *Ibid.*
59. Shaw, *British Directories as Sources*, and Smith, *op. cit.*
60. Some of these plans may have been based on such publications as A. Fullarton, 'Ports and harbours on the north coast of England', in *The Royal Illustrated Atlas* (1865).
61. H. Fry, *London: Illustrated by Twenty Bird's-Eye Views of the Principal Streets* (1892); T. Sulman, *From Charing Cross Through Whitehall to Westminster* (c.1892).
62. Preface to *White's Devonshire Directory* (1890).
63. For a discussion of this see Shaw, *British Directories as Sources*; for the use of such material see P.R. Odell, 'Urban spheres of influence in Leicestershire in the mid-nineteenth-century', *Geographical*

Studies, 4 (1957), 30-45.

64. Account books of Kelly's Ltd, 1898, from the International Publishing Corporation archives.

65. H. Sampson, *History of Advertising* (1874); for the use of this material see P. Perry, 'Newspaper advertisements', *Local Historian, 9* (1971), 334-7; H. Carter and S. Wheatley, 'Fixation lines and fringe belts, land uses and social areas: nineteenth-century change in the small town', *Trans. Inst. British Geographers*, n.s. *4.2* (1979), 214-38.

Part Two

Bibliography

Chapter 3
THE ORGANIZATION OF THE BIBLIOGRAPHY

3.1 Compilation and arrangement

One of the greatest challenges in compiling and presenting this bibliography of directories was to arrange the information and titles in an order which was both logical and practical to use. This guide refers to approximately 20 times the number of directories covered by Norton in 1950 and consequently it was never feasible to research to the level of detail which she attained, nor to describe the bibliographic particulars of each individual volume in a run of directories, since this would have resulted in nearly 18,000 entries as opposed to the 2,200 titles described here. In this work, the directory *title* is the key identifier, and directories with the same or similar titles published by one or several publishers over a period of time, in a recognizable series or chronological sequence, are generally described by a single entry or reference. When one directory is a continuation of a different and previous one, it is clearly cross-referenced; cross-references are likewise made to titles which are continuations in later years.

The order in which the directories are listed was also the subject of considerable thought. Since directories tend to cover well-defined geographical areas ranging from regions of several counties down to small areas of the London suburbs there was clearly a need to introduce a spatial element into the order along similar lines to Norton. Since this bibliography covers the period before 1950, the spatial unit considered most appropriate for dividing each of the chapters was that of the pre-1974 county (England, Wales and Scotland). However, even this primary classification criterion presented some difficulties in the form of those directories which cover more than one county, or which cover major towns in two or more counties. Furthermore, there are even those which defy the division between England and Wales by including substantial portions of each. Because the number of these 'regional' and 'inter-urban' directories is quite substantial, it was decided to place them in the special sections 4.1 to 4.4 at the beginning of the chapter on England, rather than assign them to the county section which follows; the content of these sections is clearly explained in the introduction to each. The remaining items for England are then arranged alphabetically by county with a separate section for London. The Welsh and Scottish entries are divided into two, with a list of country directories preceding those arranged alphabetically by county.

Having established a spatial basis of classification, the directories required further ordering into a logical sequence within this framework. In each county section, therefore, there are two broad categories relating firstly to directories covering all or a substantial part of that particular county, and secondly to those of the cities, towns and villages in that county. Also included in this latter section are those titles which relate to settlements *mostly* in one county but which may also include a minority of places in a neighbouring county. Within these two broad subdivisions, the titles are arranged chronologically, which in this bibliography relates to the *earliest* date for which that title is known to survive. Should there be two or more titles published on the same date, then the title is taken as the secondary sort criterion and they are placed in alphabetical order. The ordering by date and by title is operative throughout all the subsections of the bibliography, including the specialist Chapter 7, as it is almost impossible to define a well-ordered subject list of these directories without avoiding incongruous overlaps and the need for repeated references.

The bibliography therefore refers to each directory title in one reference. There are no repeated titles and all the bibliographic details and library holdings are outlined under that single reference with the minor exception of the Kelly's regional directories, the arrangements of which are explained in Chapter 4.1.

Finally, it should be noted that where no entry appears under a particular county heading, this is because our survey has been unable to trace any directories specifically relating to that county which were published under separate cover. In all cases the Place Index should be consulted.

3.2 Use of the bibliography

In order to use the bibliography to its full extent, it is essential to consult the place and subject indexes at the back of the book, as each place-name or subject appearing in a directory title also appears in the appropriate index with all the relevant references. Should a place not appear in the place index, it does not necessarily mean that there are no directories for it, as there will almost certainly be entries in the relevant county directory (e.g. Kelly's).

The notes below outline briefly how the bibliography was compiled and presented. Bibliographic information relating to such aspects as pagination, size, edition numbering etc., was not included as it would have necessitated a considerable amount of more detailed research on individual volumes which was beyond the scope of this survey. The bibliography seeks to provide a comprehensive and succinct work of reference containing a balance of information suiting the needs of a wide range of potential users.

REF Each directory is clearly identified by a unique reference which runs in numerical order from 1 to 2222, mainly to facilitate cross-referencing. These reference numbers are used in the place, publisher and subject indexes.

Title Where possible the title of the directory was taken from the title page of the volume, as opposed to the cover, which was only checked if the title page was missing or obscure. If the title was taken from elsewhere in the volume, or if it changed in different editions, such information is recorded in the notes.

Dates The run of dates for each volume is *not exhaustive* and should not be regarded as such: it merely represents those dates for which directories of that title are known to survive and are held in the library collections covered by the survey. To ensure consistency and accuracy, a directory bearing a date of 1923-4, for example, is always assigned to the earlier year (1923) as this was normally the year of publication.

Publisher In most cases the directory publisher is stated on the title page or in the preface to the volume and its transcription was straightforward. In those cases where it is not at all clear who published the directory due to incompleteness of the volume in question, a '?' is entered. Similarly, where the publisher is not stated anywhere through all the directory, a dash (–) is present.

Printer The printer was not always stated in directories, and this is indicated in an identical manner to that described above under 'Publisher'. In many cases the printer and publisher were one and the same.

Place Refers to the place of publication of the directory which is nearly always stated on the title page. This should not be confused with the places to which the directory relates.

Type Describes in code form the contents of the directory as reflected in its various directory sections. The abbreviations used are based on those devised by Norton with two additions and one important modification:

CM Commercial: alphabetical list of names with occupations.

CT Court: alphabetical list of names (occupations not given).

GE General: Norton used the GE abbreviation to describe a directory which contained both CT and CM sections; it is used here, however, to describe one which contains CT and ST *or* CM and ST sections.

PR Professional: a directory related exclusively to a profession – normally consisting of an alphabetical list of persons engaged in that profession; or a general list of professional people. The bibliography generally includes few professional directories as it tends to focus on specialist directories of economic and service activities.

SL Street list (not used by Norton): an alphabetical list of the streets and roads in a particular settlement with no further information about residents or trades etc.

SP Specialized directory: (not used by Norton) used here to describe a directory which is devoted to a particular trade, industry or service. More detailed information on its format is contained in the notes to individual publications.

ST Street directory: alphabetical list of streets with house numbers/names and names of occupiers sometimes with occupations stated, but more usually just names arranged in house order.

TR Classified trades directory: arranged alphabetically by trade with alphabetical list of participants entered under each.

Any two of these types may be combined, such as GE TR and CM PR, describing a general trades and a court and professional directory.

Map scale Where a directory contains a map which has a clearly stated scale, it is entered as a ratio measurement e.g. 1:63360, as opposed to 1 inch = 1 mile. (A conversion list is given at the end of this chapter). Where a map is present but its scale is not stated, it is identified by the abbreviation NS: 'not stated'. If a directory does not contain a map, a dash (–) is entered. It is important to note that even if a scale or 'NS' is present in a reference, not *all* directories in *all* libraries will necessarily contain a map as described, as they tend to be most susceptible to vandalism and some libraries have purposely removed the maps to house them under separate cover or among their map collections. It is therefore advisable to make further enquiries if the map is required for consultation, especially if it is at a large scale which is invaluable for detailed research.

Notes Many of the references or entries contain brief notes describing changes in title, publisher etc., internal cross-references and references to those volumes already described in Norton's guide. Several abbreviations are commonly used besides those relating to Library codes (see below) and shortened forms of counties:

Alph	alphabetical	Xcopy	photocopy
Cont'd	continued	T/P	title page

Library holdings Following the bibliographic information, there is a guide to the library holdings of each directory. Libraries are simply identified by codes of up to three letters (see Chapter 8) and are arranged alphabetically. Holdings are described through the use of the following examples:

(i) 'has': e.g. in the case of a directory whose 'dates' are *1850, 1859-1862, 1865, 1868, 1870, 1872,* 'BL has 1850, 1859-1862, 1865-1870' means that the British Library holds the 1850 volume, and all those published and *known to exist* between 1859 and 1862, and between 1865 and 1870. The latter part does not mean that the BL holds volumes for *every* intervening year (1865, 66, 67, 68, 69, 70), but only for the years specified in the 'dates'; which are 1865, 1868, 1870. It is essential therefore to refer back to the 'dates' above in cases such as this to avoid misinterpretation.

(ii) 'has': e.g. 'RCL has BERK section'. The holdings sometimes describe the county sections of a directory held by different libraries, particularly in the case of regional directories. In this instance Reading Library has the Berkshire extract. In another example 'CLS has HANT section 1859' means that Southampton Library holds the Hampshire section of the 1859 volume. The four-letter abbreviations used here are straightforward and in case of difficulty, reference should be made to the counties in the title or notes for clarification.

(iii)   'not': e.g. 'GL not 1901' means that the Guildhall Library does not hold the 1901 edition in a run of directories whose dates might be 1890-1940, but it does hold all the other volumes.

(iv)   'all' or a blank entry: means that the library holds all of the volumes of a particular run. Blank entries are most commonly used where a directory was only ever produced on a single date.

Map scales and equivalents

Representative fraction	Inches to the mile/ Miles to the inch	Centimetres to metres/ Centimetres to kilometres
1:2500	25in. to 1m	1cm: 25m
1:10000	$6^{1}/_{4}$in. to 1m	1cm: 100m
1:10560	6in. to 1m	1cm: 105.6m
1:25000	$2^{1}/_{2}$in. to 1m	1cm: 250m
1:50000	$1^{1}/_{4}$in. to 1m	1cm: 500m
1:63360	1in. to 1m	1cm: 633.6m
1:100000	$1^{1}/_{2}$m to 1in.	1cm: 1km
1:126720	2m to 1in.	1cm: 1.26km
1:150000	$2^{1}/_{4}$m to 1in.	1cm: 1.5km
1:175000	$2^{3}/_{4}$m to 1in.	1cm: 1.75km
1:200000	$3^{1}/_{4}$m to 1in.	1cm: 2km
1:250000	4m to 1in.	1cm: 2.5km
1:253440	4m to 1in.	1cm: 2.53km
1:500000	8m to 1in.	1cm: 5km
1:633600	10m to 1in.	1cm: 6.33km
1:750000	$11^{3}/_{4}$m to 1in.	1cm: 7.5km
1:1000000	$15^{3}/_{4}$m to 1in.	1cm: 10km

Chapter 4
ENGLISH DIRECTORIES

4.1 The English regions I: directories published by Kelly's

The directory firm of Kelly and Co. (later known as Kelly's Directories Ltd) commenced publication of a series of county directories in 1845, and during the 1850s and 1860s extended their coverage to include all the English counties. The reason it is necessary to devote a special section to these directories is the desirability of providing an uncomplicated guide to a somewhat complex situation. Such complexity may be explained in two ways.

Firstly, Kelly's tended to publish their county directories in regional groups until the late 1920s, when they were published largely in the form of individual county editions. In the 1850s and 1860s such grouping might consist of up to six counties (e.g. *The Post Office Home Counties Directory 1851-1866*), but usually covered two to four counties. As population and urbanization increased, so inevitably did the physical size of the volumes, with the consequence that some of the larger regional directories became too bulky and impractical, thereby inducing the publishers to make minor reorganization and subdivisions. The Home Counties directory, for instance, was divided into two parts from 1870 onwards. By the late 1920s and early 1930s it was more common to find nearly every county published under its own title, although some libraries hold the single-volume regional directories for the late 1930s. The last county directories were published in 1940 and 1941 and never made a reappearance after the war.

The list of titles below therefore provides bibliographic details, but not the library holdings, for regional publications of Kelly's and includes all counties except Cheshire, Lancashire, Lincolnshire, London and Yorkshire, which were only ever published as single-county directories. The full bibliographic details for these five counties may be found in the individual county sections.

The second and more important reason for listing the library holdings of each of the Kelly's county directories under separate entries in the appropriate county section (with the exception of those for Leicestershire and Rutland, and Cumberland and Westmorland which were rarely, if ever, published individually) is largely due to the fact that many libraries have split and rebound the original regional volumes, often only retaining one relevant county directory for their collections. The task of compiling and presenting a potentially complicated mass of information about the various holdings was therefore simplified considerably by treating each county directory as a separate entity, and for the sake of bibliographic completeness, identifying the full titles in this section.

All these directories contain a mixture of court and commercial sections and trade sections. Street sections are uncommon except for the larger towns. Maps were generally published with the directories, but unfortunately many have since been removed or vandalized and the presence of the map can never be assured.

REF	**1**
Title	**Post Office Directory of Birmingham with Staffordshire and Worcestershire**
Dates	1850
Publisher	Kelly & Co
Printer	Kelly & Co
Place	London
Type	GE TR
Map scale	1:253440
Notes	NORTON 116. Cont'd as 6.
Library	BOD
holdings	HBR
	ULC
	WLV
	WSL

REF	**2**
Title	**Post Office Directory of Essex, Hertfordshire, Cambridge, Norfolk and Suffolk**
Dates	1850
Publisher	Kelly & Co
Printer	Kelly & Co
Place	London
Type	CM TR
Map scale	–
Notes	Only COL has this edition, with some pages missing
Library	CHE has ESSX section only
holdings	COL

REF	**3**
Title	**Post Office Directory of the Six Home Counties: Essex, Herts, Middlesex, Kent, Surrey & Sussex**
Dates	1851,1855,1859,1862,1866
Publisher	Kelly & Co
Printer	Kelly & Co
Place	London
Type	GE TR
Map scale	1:348480
Notes	NORTON 117(1851), 123(1855). See 16,17,18,19. For library holdings see under the respective counties (422,576, 997,603,1278,1351).

REF	**4**
Title	**Post Office Directory of Jersey, Guernsey, Alderney, Sark, Herm and Jethon with Hampshire**
Dates	1852
Publisher	Kelly & Co
Printer	Kelly & Co
Place	London
Type	GE TR
Map scale	1:12672
Notes	NORTON 118
Library	BL
holdings	GL
	BOD
	NLS
	ULC

REF	**5**
Title	**Kelly's Directory of Cambridge, Norfolk and Suffolk**
Dates	1853,1858,1865,1869,1875,1879, 1883,1888,1892,1896,1900,1904, 1908,1912,1916,1922,1925,1929, 1933,1937
Publisher	Kelly & Co
Printer	Kelly & Co
Place	London
Type	GE TR
Map scale	1:253440
Notes	NORTON 120 (1853). 1853-1879 editions entitled 'Post Office Directory of Cambridge, Norfolk and Suffolk'. For library holdings see under the respective counties (237, 1042,1260).

REF	**6**
Title	**Kelly's Directory of Birmingham, Staffordshire, Warwickshire and Worcestershire**
Dates	1854,1860,1864,1868,1872,1876, 1880,1884,1888,1892,1896,1900, 1904,1908,1912,1916,1921,1924, 1928,1932,1936,1940
Publisher	Kelly & Co
Printer	Kelly & Co
Place	London
Type	GE TR
Map scale	1:15840
Notes	Cont'd from 1. NORTON 121 (1854). For library holdings see under the respective counties (1222,1422,1508).

REF	**7**
Title	**Post Office Directory of Berkshire, Northamptonshire and Oxfordshire with Hertfordshire, Buckinghamshire and Huntingdonshire**
Dates	1854,1864,1869,1877
Publisher	Kelly & Co
Printer	Kelly & Co
Place	London
Type	GE TR
Map scale	1:285120
Notes	Cont'd by 20. See also 14. NORTON 122 (1854). For library holdings see under the respective counties (195, 1075,1150,576,217,598).

REF	**8**
Title	**Kelly's Directory of Hampshire, Wiltshire and Dorsetshire, including the Isle of Wight**
Dates	1855,1859,1867,1875,1880,1885, 1890,1895,1899,1903,1907,1911, 1915,1920,1923,1927,1931,1935, 1939
Publisher	Kelly & Co
Printer	Kelly & Co
Place	London
Type	GE TR
Map scale	1:253440
Notes	NORTON 124 (1855). 1855-1880 entitled 'Post Office Directory of Hampshire, including the Isle of Wight, Wiltshire & Dorsetshire'. For library holdings see under the respective counties (505, 385,1482).

REF	**9**
Title	**Kelly's Directory of Derbyshire, Leicestershire, Nottinghamshire and Rutlandshire**
Dates	1855,1864,1866,1870,1876,1881, 1888,1891,1895,1899,1904,1908, 1912,1916,1922,1925, 1928 (1932,1936,1941)
Publisher	Kelly & Co
Printer	Kelly & Co
Place	London
Type	GE TR
Map scale	1:253440
Notes	NORTON 126(1855). BL & GL 1864 editions include Cambs. For library holdings see under the respective counties (312,24,1124).

REF	**10**
Title	**Post Office Directory of Gloucestershire, Herefordshire, Shropshire and the City of Bristol**
Dates	1856,1863,1870,1879,1885
Publisher	Kelly & Co
Printer	Kelly & Co
Place	London
Type	GE TR
Map scale	1:304128
Notes	1885 edition entitled 'Kelly's Directory of Gloucestershire ...etc'. Title varies in order of counties listed, but coverage remains identical. Cont'd as 21 & 22. For library holdings see under the respective counties (454,559,1176).

REF	**11**
Title	**Kelly's Directory of Devonshire and Cornwall**
Dates	1856,1873,1883,1889,1893,1897, 1902,1906,1910,1914,1919,1923, 1926,1930,1935,1939
Publisher	Kelly & Co
Printer	Kelly & Co
Place	London
Type	GE TR
Map scale	1:12672
Notes	1856 & 1873 editions entitled 'Post Office Directory of Devonshire and Cornwall'. For library holdings see 287 & 342.

REF	**12**
Title	**Kelly's Directory of Durham, Northumberland, Cumberland and Westmorland**
Dates	1858,1873,1879,1890,1894,1897, 1902,1906
Publisher	Kelly & Co
Printer	Kelly & Co
Place	London
Type	GE TR
Map scale	1:221760
Notes	Cont'd by 23. See also 13 & notes to 23. In 1873 a separate edition was published entitled 'The Post Office Directory of the County of Durham and the principal towns and adjacent places in Northumberland', held at GL,NLS,DAR,DUR. For library holdings see 13,401,1102.

REF   **13**
Title   **Kelly's Directory of Cumberland and Westmorland**
Dates   1858,1873,1879,1890,1894,1897, 1902,1906,1910,1914,1921,1925, 1929,1934,1938
Publisher   Kelly & Co
Printer   Kelly & Co
Place   London
Type   GE TR
Map scale   1:190080
Notes   See 12. Kelly's never published a Westmorland directory under separate cover.
Library holdings   BCL has 1894,1897,1906-1938
BIS has 1938
BL not 1906
BOD all
BPH has 1873,1879,1894,1906, 1929,1938
CAR has 1858,1873,1897(CUMB); 1894,1910,1914, 1925-1938(both counties)
CL has 1938
CLB has 1938
CLN has 1873
DAR has 1894,1897,1906-1938
DUR has 1858,1897
GL not 1873
IHR has 1938
LCL has 1934,1938
MLG has 1894-1906,1914-1938
MOR has 1897,1938
NLS not 1879
NLW has 1914,1929,1938
SOG has 1858,1873,1906-1921, 1928
ULC not 1894
YCL has 1934

REF   **14**
Title   **Kelly's Directory of Bedfordshire, Huntingdonshire & Northamptonshire**
Dates   1864,1869,1885,1890,1894,1898, 1903,1906,1910,1914,1920,1924, 1928,1931,1936,1940
Publisher   Kelly & Co
Printer   Kelly & Co
Place   London
Type   GE TR
Map scale   1:253440

Notes   See 7. For library holdings see under the respective counties (178,598,1075).

REF   **15**
Title   **Post Office Directory of Somerset & Devon with Bristol**
Dates   1866
Publisher   Kelly & Co
Printer   Kelly & Co
Place   London
Type   GE TR
Map scale   NS
Notes   See 342 & 1195 for library holdings

REF   **16**
Title   **Post Office Directory of the Six Home Counties Part I: Essex, Herts, Middlesex, Kent**
Dates   1870,1874,1878
Publisher   Kelly & Co
Printer   Kelly & Co
Place   London
Type   GE TR
Map scale   1:285120
Notes   See 3,17,18,19. See notes to 3.

REF   **17**
Title   **Post Office Directory of the Six Home Counties Part II: Surrey & Sussex**
Dates   1870,1874,1878
Publisher   Kelly & Co
Printer   Kelly & Co
Place   London
Type   GE TR
Map scale   1:285120
Notes   See 3,16,18,19. See notes to 3.

REF   **18**
Title   **Kelly's Directory of the Six Home Counties Part I: Essex, Herts & Middlesex**
Dates   1882,1886,1890,1895,1899,1902, 1906,1908,1910,1912,1914,1917, 1922,1926,1929,1933,1937
Publisher   Kelly & Co
Printer   Kelly & Co
Place   London
Type   GE TR
Map scale   1:105600
Notes   See 422,576,997 for library holdings. Cont'd from 16.

REF	**19**
Title	**Kelly's Directory of the Six Home Counties Part II: Kent, Surrey & Sussex**
Dates	1882,1887,1891,1895,1899,1901, 1903,1905,1907,1909,1911,1913, 1915,1918,1922,1924,1927,1930, 1934,1938
Publisher	Kelly & Co
Printer	Kelly & Co
Place	London
Type	GE TR
Map scale	1:10560
Notes	Part I see 18. See 3,16,17. See notes to 3.

REF	**20**
Title	**Kelly's Directory of Berkshire, Buckinghamshire and Oxfordshire**
Dates	1883,1887,1891,1895,1899,1903, 1907,1911,1915,1920,1924,1928, 1931,1935,1939
Publisher	Kelly & Co
Printer	Kelly & Co
Place	London
Type	GE TR
Map scale	1:380160
Notes	See 195,217,1150 for library holdings. Cont'd from 7.

REF	**21**
Title	**Kelly's Directory of Somersetshire & Gloucestershire with the City of Bristol**
Dates	1889,1894,1897,1902,1906,1910, 1914,1919,1923,1927,1931,1935, 1939
Publisher	Kelly & Co
Printer	Kelly & Co
Place	London
Type	GE TR
Map scale	1:18013
Notes	Cont'd from 10. See notes to 10.

REF	**22**
Title	**Kelly's Directory of Herefordshire and Shropshire**
Dates	1891,1895,1900,1905,1909,1913, 1917,1922,1926,1929,1934,1937, 1941
Publisher	Kelly & Co
Printer	Kelly & Co
Place	London
Type	GE TR
Map scale	1:21120
Notes	Cont'd from 10. 1934,1937 includes Monmouthshire. For library holdings see under the rescpective counties (559, 1176,1757).

REF	**23**
Title	**Kelly's Directory of Durham and Northumberland**
Dates	1910,1914,1921,1925,1929,1934, 1938
Publisher	Kelly's Directories Ltd
Printer	Kelly's Directories Ltd
Place	London
Type	GE TR
Map scale	1:122760
Notes	Cont'd from 12. See 401 & 1102 for library holdings.

REF	**24**
Title	**Kelly's Directory of Leicestershire and Rutland**
Dates	1932,1936,1941
Publisher	Kelly's Directories Ltd
Printer	Kelly's Directories Ltd
Place	London
Type	GE TR
Map scale	1:253440
Notes	See 9. A Rutland directory was never published by Kelly's under a separate cover.
Library holdings	BCL all BL all CLE has 1941 CLL all GL all IHR has 1932 LCL has 1941 NLS has 1932,1936 SCL all SOG has 1932,1941 ULC all YCL has 1941

4.2 The English regions II: other directories covering three or more counties

The titles below, arranged chronologically, comprise the remaining (non-Kelly's) directories covering large regions. They have been distinguished from those covering just two counties which are found in Chapter 4.3. Full bibliographic details and library holdings are stated for each title. Included in this section are directories covering both English and Welsh counties in the same volume, while those covering solely Welsh county groupings are to be found in Chapter 5.1.

REF	**25**
Title	**Slater's National and Commercial Directory of Bedfordshire, Cambridgeshire, Huntingdonshire, Lincolnshire, Norfolk, Northamptonshire, Suffolk**
Dates	**1850**
Publisher	**Slater, I.**
Printer	**Slater, I.**
Place	**Manchester**
Type	**GE TR**
Map scale	**NS**
Notes	**Possibly NORTON 85**
Library	**CAM**
holdings	**GL**
	NOR has NORF section only
	NTH has NHTS section only
	ULC

REF	**26**
Title	**Slater's Royal National and Commercial Directory and Topography for Derbyshire, Herefordshire, Leicestershire, Lincolnshire, Monmouthshire, Northamptonshire, Nottinghamshire, Rutland, Shropshire, Staffordshire, Warwickshire, Worcestershire**
Dates	**1850**
Publisher	**Slater, I.**
Printer	**Slater, I.**
Place	**Manchester**
Type	**GE TR**
Map scale	**1:950400**
Notes	**NORTON 86**
Library	**BCL Volume split & bound**
holdings	**separately**
	BL
	BPH
	CLL
	NCL has NOTT only
	NLW
	WCL

REF	**27**
Title	**Slater's Royal National and Commercial Directory and Topography of ... Derbyshire, Gloucestershire, Herefordshire, Monmouthshire, Shropshire, Staffordshire, Warwickshire, Worcestershire, North & South Wales**
Dates	1850
Publisher	Slater, I.
Printer	Slater, I.
Place	Manchester
Type	GE TR
Map scale	1:396000
Notes	NORTON 87
Library	CLC
holdings	GL
	SHR has SALP section only

REF	**28**
Title	**Slater's Royal National and Commercial Directory and Topography of Bedfordshire, Buckinghamshire, Cambridgeshire, Huntingdonshire, Leicestershire, Lincolnshire, Norfolk, Northamptonshire, Nottinghamshire, Oxfordshire, Rutland, & Suffolk**
Dates	1850,1851
Publisher	Slater, I.
Printer	Slater, I.
Place	Manchester
Type	GE TR
Map scale	1:190080
Notes	NORTON 85 (1851)
Library	AYL has 1850 BUCK
holdings	BED has 1850
	BL has 1851
	IHR has 1851
	NOR has 1850

REF	**29**
Title	**Slater's Royal National Commercial Directory and Topography of ... Gloucestershire, Herefordshire, Monmouthshire, Shropshire, and North and South Wales**
Dates	1850,1859,1868
Publisher	Slater, I.
Printer	Slater, I.
Place	Manchester
Type	GE TR
Map scale	1:253440
Notes	NORTON 89 (1850)
Library	BL not 1850
holdings	GL has 1868
	NLW not 1859
	CLC not 1859
	HPL has 1859
	NPT has 1868 MONM
	SHR has 1859 SALP

REF	**30**
Title	**Slater's Royal National and Commercial Directory and Topography of ... Berkshire, Buckinghamshire, Gloucestershire, Hampshire, Herefordshire, Monmouthshire, Oxfordshire, Warwickshire, Wiltshire, Worcestershire and South Wales**
Dates	1851
Publisher	Slater, I.
Printer	Slater, I.
Place	Manchester
Type	GE TR
Map scale	1:380160
Notes	NORTON 91
Library	CLO has BERK section only
holdings	GL

REF	**31**
Title	**Collinson and Co's West Riding of Yorkshire, Leicestershire & Norwich Woollen and Worsted Directory**
Dates	1852
Publisher	Collinson, J. & Co
Printer	Denton, J. & Co
Place	Bradford
Type	SP
Map scale	–
Notes	CM TR for Bradford, TR for all other places. See 1532.
Library	BRD

REF | **32**
Title | **Scammell & Co's City of Bristol and South Wales Directory**
Dates | 1852
Publisher | Scammell, W. & Co
Printer | Jeffries, C.T.
Place | Bristol
Type | TR
Map scale | –
Notes | NORTON 317. Also CT section for Bristol.
Library | CLC
holdings | NLW
 | NPT
 | SWA

REF | **33**
Title | **Slater's Royal National & Commercial Directory and Topography of the Counties of Cornwall, Devonshire, Dorsetshire, Somersetshire**
Dates | 1852
Publisher | Slater, I.
Printer | Slater, I.
Place | Manchester
Type | CM TR
Map scale | 1:253440
Notes | This edition has similar coverage to 34, but the title page is complete and the volume in DCL has not been rebound or abridged in any way.
Library | DCL

REF | **34**
Title | **Slater's Royal National and Commercial Directory and Topography of ... Berkshire, Cornwall, Devonshire, Dorsetshire, Gloucestershire, Hampshire, Somersetshire, Wiltshire and South Wales**
Dates | 1852
Publisher | Slater, I.
Printer | Slater, I.
Place | Manchester
Type | CM TR
Map scale | 1:380160
Notes | See also 33. NORTON 97.
Library | BCL has BERK section only
holdings | CLM
 | NPT has S. WALES section only
 | PLY has CORN section only
 | SOG
 | SWI has WILT section only (dated 1850)
 | TLH has SMST section only
 | WCS has DEVN section only
 | WIN has HANT section only

REF | **35**
Title | **Slater's Royal National Commercial Directory of the Northern Counties Vol I: Durham, Northumberland & Yorkshire**
Dates | 1854,1864
Publisher | Slater, I.
Printer | Slater, I.
Place | Manchester
Type | TR
Map scale | 1:285120
Notes | NORTON 98 (1854). Vol II see 36.
Library | BRD has 1854
holdings | CLM has 1864
 | CLN has 1854
 | DAR all
 | DUR has 1854;1864 DURH & NHLD only
 | GL has 1854
 | IHR has 1854
 | LAN has 1854
 | MOR has 1854 NHLD
 | SCL has 1854
 | SOG has 1854

REF	**36**
Title	**Slater's Royal National Commercial Directory of the Northern Counties Vol II: Cheshire, Cumberland, Lancashire and Westmorland**
Dates	1855
Publisher	Slater, I.
Printer	Slater, I.
Place	Manchester
Type	TR
Map scale	1:443520
Notes	NORTON 99. Vol I see 35.
Library	BLA
holdings	BPH
	CAR has CUMB 1855
	GL
	LAN
	PHL
	SOG
	WAR

REF	**37**
Title	**Slater's Royal National Commercial Directory and Topography of the Counties of Cheshire, Lancashire, Shropshire and North Wales**
Dates	1856
Publisher	Slater, I.
Printer	Slater, I.
Place	Manchester
Type	GE TR
Map scale	1:396000
Library	CCL
holdings	GL

REF	**38**
Title	**Slater's Royal National Commercial Directory and Topography of the Counties of Lincolnshire, Nottinghamshire, Rutlandshire and Yorkshire**
Dates	1857
Publisher	Slater, I.
Printer	Slater, I.
Place	Manchester
Type	GE TR
Map scale	1:506880
Library	CLL has RUTL only
holdings	GL
	LIN has LINC only
	NCL has NOTT only

REF	**39**
Title	**Slater's Royal National and Commercial Directory and Topography of the Counties of Gloucestershire, Monmouthshire and North and South Wales**
Dates	1858
Publisher	Slater, I.
Printer	Slater, I.
Place	Manchester
Type	TR
Map scale	1:443520
Library	CLB
holdings	CLC
	GL
	GLO has GLOS only
	NLW
	NPT

REF	**40**
Title	**Dutton, Allen & Co's Directory & Gazetteer of the Counties of Oxon, Berks and Bucks**
Dates	1863
Publisher	Dutton, Allen & Co
Printer	–
Place	Manchester
Type	CM
Map scale	1:190080
Library	AYL
holdings	CLO
	GL
	RCL
	SOG

REF	**41**
Title	**Edward Cassey & Co's History, Gazetteer and Directory of Bedfordshire, Hertfordshire and Huntingdonshire**
Dates	1863
Publisher	Cassey, E. & Co
Printer	Danks, T.
Place	London
Type	CM
Map scale	–
Library	HNT
holdings	SOG

REF 42
Title **Slater's Royal National Commercial Directory and Topography of Derbyshire, Leicestershire, Northamptonshire, Nottinghamshire, Staffordshire, Warwickshire and Worcestershire**
Dates 1863
Publisher Slater, I.
Printer Slater, I.
Place Manchester
Type GE TR
Map scale 1:316800
Library GL
holdings NTH has NHTS section only

REF 43
Title **History, Topography and Directory of Buckinghamshire, Cambridgeshire and Hertfordshire**
Dates 1863,1864
Publisher Cassey, E. & Co
Printer Danks, T.
Place London
Type CM
Map scale 1:211200
Library AYL has 1863
holdings GL has 1863,1864
SOG has 1863

REF 44
Title **Webster & Co's Postal and Commercial Directory of the City of Bristol and the Counties of Glamorgan and Monmouth**
Dates 1865
Publisher Webster & Co
Printer Mackintosh. H.F.
Place London
Type CM TR
Map scale –
Notes T/P & front cover missing from volume (NLW)
Library CLC
holdings NLW
NPT

REF 45
Title **J.G. Harrod & Co's Post-Office Directory of Bristol, Glamorganshire and Monmouthshire**
Dates 1866
Publisher Harrod, J.G. & Co
Printer Danks, T.
Place London
Type CM TR
Map scale –
Library CLC

REF 46
Title **Melville & Co's Directory of Berkshire, Oxfordshire, Cambridgeshire, Bedfordshire and Northamptonshire**
Dates 1867
Publisher Melville & Co
Printer Rider, J. & W.
Place London
Type CM
Map scale 1:253440
Library CLO
holdings RCL

REF 47
Title **Mercer and Crocker's General, Topographical and Historical Directory and Gazetteer for Northumberland, Durham and Newcastle**
Dates 1868
Publisher Mercer & Crocker
Printer Mercer & Crocker
Place Newcastle-on-Tyne
Type CM TR
Map scale 1:253440
Library CLN
holdings DAR
MID
SOG

REF	**48**
Title	**Slater's Royal National Commercial Directory and Topography of Shropshire, North and South Wales and the City of Chester**
Dates	1868
Publisher	Slater, I.
Printer	Slater, I.
Place	Manchester
Type	CM TR
Map scale	–
Library	SHR

REF	**49**
Title	**Mercer and Crocker's General Topographical and Historical Directory and Gazetteer for ... Cumberland, Westmorland, North Riding of York, the County of Durham and Newcastle, Sunderland [etc]**
Dates	1869
Publisher	Mercer & Crocker
Printer	Mercer & Crocker
Place	Newcastle-on-Tyne
Type	CM TR
Map scale	1:253440
Library	CAR

REF	**50**
Title	**Slater's Royal National Commercial Directory of Cheshire with North Wales**
Dates	1869
Publisher	Slater, I.
Printer	Slater, I.
Place	Manchester
Type	CM TR
Map scale	–
Library	CCL

REF	**51**
Title	**Slater's Royal National Commercial Directory of Cheshire, Cumberland and Westmorland**
Dates	1869
Publisher	Slater, I.
Printer	Slater, I.
Place	Manchester
Type	TR
Map scale	1:316800
Library	GL

REF	**52**
Title	**Mercer & Crocker's General, Topographical and Historical Directory and Gazetteer for Northamptonshire, Lincolnshire, Huntingdonshire and Rutlandshire**
Dates	1870
Publisher	Mercer & Crocker
Printer	Mercer & Crocker
Place	Hull
Type	CM
Map scale	–
Library	CLL has RUTL only
holdings	NTH has X copy with incorrect T/P

REF	**53**
Title	**Mercer and Crocker's General, Topographical and Historical Directory for Dorsetshire, Bedfordshire, Buckinghamshire and Cambridgeshire**
Dates	1871
Publisher	Mercer & Crocker
Printer	Mercer & Crocker
Place	Leicester
Type	CM
Map scale	1:95040
Library	BED
holdings	LUT has BEDS section only

REF	**54**
Title	**Mercer & Crocker's General, Topographical and Historical Directory for the Counties of Monmouthshire, Herefordshire, Gloucestershire (and the principal towns & places in Glamorganshire & Radnorshire)**
Dates	1871,1875,1876
Publisher	Mercer & Crocker
Printer	Mercer & Crocker
Place	Leicester
Type	CM
Map scale	1:316800
Notes	1876 title includes the last part in brackets
Library	CLC all
holdings	NPT has 1871,1875

REF	55
Title	**J.G. Harrod & Co's Royal County Directory of Bedfordshire, Buckinghamshire, Berkshire, Oxfordshire, Huntingdonshire and Northamptonshire**
Dates	1876
Publisher	Harrod, J.G. & Co
Printer	Harrod, J.G. & Co
Place	Norwich
Type	CM
Map scale	–
Notes	It appears that several editions were published covering different county groupings. The above title relates to the edition covering six counties which is held at NTH & HNT.
Library holdings	AYL has BUCK section BED has BEDS,BUCK,BERK,OXON CLO has BEDS,BUCK,BERK,OXON GL has BEDS & BUCK HNT has all 6 counties NTH has all 6 counties

REF	56
Title	**Slater's Royal National Commercial Directory of the Counties of Cumberland, Westmorland and Lancashire**
Dates	1876
Publisher	Slater, I.
Printer	Slater, I.
Place	Manchester
Type	TR
Map scale	1:380160
Library	GL

REF	57
Title	**Slater's Royal National Commercial Directory of the Counties of Durham, Northumberland & Cleveland**
Dates	1876
Publisher	Slater, I.
Printer	Slater, I.
Place	Manchester
Type	GE TR
Map scale	1:380160
Library holdings	GL BOD NLS ULC

REF	58
Title	**Slater's Royal National Commercial Directory of Cumberland, Durham, Northumberland, Westmorland, Cleveland Districts**
Dates	1876,1877,1879,1884
Publisher	Slater, I.
Printer	Slater, I.
Place	Manchester
Type	GE TR
Map scale	1:15840
Library holdings	BL not 1877,1879 BOD has 1876 CAR has CUMB,WMLD & Cleveland 1876 CLN has 1877-1884 GL not 1876,1884 MID has 1876 NLS has 1876,1877

REF	59
Title	**Mercer & Crocker's General, Typographical and Historical Directory for Shropshire, Herefordshire, Radnorshire etc**
Dates	1877
Publisher	Mercer & Crocker
Printer	Mercer & Crocker
Place	Leicester
Type	CM
Map scale	1:253440
Notes	See 131
Library holdings	GL SHR

REF	60
Title	**The Trades Guide for Midland Counties and Universal Buyers' Guide**
Dates	1879
Publisher	Robinson & Co
Printer	–
Place	Birmingham
Type	CM TR
Map scale	–
Notes	Includes Birmingham, Sheffield, Derbys, Leics, Northants, Notts, Staffs, Warwks, Worcs
Library holdings	BOD NCL

REF **61**
Title **W.E. Owen & Co's General, Typographical and Historical Directory for Gloucestershire, Wiltshire, Somersetshire, Monmouthshire, Radnorshire with the cities of Bristol and Bath**
Dates 1879
Publisher Owen, W.E. & Co
Printer –
Place Leicester
Type CM
Map scale –
Notes See 134
Library GLO
holdings TRW has WILT section only

REF **62**
Title **Slater's Royal National Commercial Directory of North Wales, Cheshire & Shropshire with a Classified Trades Directory of Liverpool**
Dates 1883
Publisher Slater, I.
Printer Slater, I.
Place Manchester
Type GE TR
Map scale 1:316800
Library BL
holdings CCL has CHES & L'pool only
GL
SOG
WAR has CHES & L'pool only

REF **63**
Title **Bennett's Business Directory Norfolk, Cambridge, Suffolk**
Dates 1888
Publisher Bennett & Co
Printer Bennett & Co
Place Birmingham
Type TR
Map scale –
Library NOR

REF **64**
Title **Bennett's Business Directory: Berkshire, Oxfordshire, Bedfordshire, Somerset, Devon, Cornwall, Dorset, Leicestershire, Northants, Yorkshire, Herefordshire, Worcestershire**
Dates 1888
Publisher Bennett & Co
Printer Bennett & Co
Place Birmingham
Type TR
Map scale –
Library CLO

REF **65**
Title **The Steam Users' Directory for the Textile Districts of Lancashire and Yorkshire**
Dates 1888
Publisher Worrall, J.
Printer Worrall, J,
Place Oldham
Type SP
Map scale NS
Notes Classified steam user list (all trades) for each county
Library BL
holdings BOD
NLS
ULC

REF **66**
Title **Bennett's Business Directory: Worcestershire, Gloucestershire, Herefordshire, Shropshire**
Dates 1890
Publisher Bennett & Co
Printer Bennett & Co
Place Birmingham
Type TR
Map scale –
Library WCL

REF	**67**
Title	**Deacon's Berkshire, Buckinghamshire and Oxfordshire Court Guide and County Blue Book**
Dates	1890
Publisher	Deacon, C.W. & Co
Printer	–
Place	London
Type	CT PR
Map scale	1:167904
Library	AYL
holdings	BOD
	NLS
	ULC

REF	**68**
Title	**Deacon's Leicestershire, Rutland and Northamptonshire Court Guide and County Blue Book**
Dates	1890
Publisher	Deacon, C.W. & Co
Printer	–
Place	London
Type	CT PR
Map scale	–
Library	CLL
holdings	NTH

REF	**69**
Title	**Deacon's Cambridgeshire, Norfolk & Suffolk Court Guide and County Blue Book**
Dates	1893
Publisher	Deacon, C.W. & Co
Printer	–
Place	London
Type	CT PR
Map scale	–
Notes	Map missing from BOD edition
Library	BOD
holdings	CAM
	KLL
	NLS
	NOR
	SOG
	ULC

REF	**70**
Title	**Bennett's Business Directory: Herefordshire, Worcestershire and South Wales**
Dates	1895
Publisher	Bennett & Co
Printer	Bennett & Co
Place	Birmingham
Type	TR
Map scale	–
Library	HPL

REF	**71**
Title	**Bennett's Business Directory for Hertfordshire, Essex, Bedfordshire, Buckinghamshire and Oxfordshire**
Dates	1896
Publisher	Bennett & Co
Printer	Bennett & Co
Place	Birmingham
Type	TR
Map scale	–
Notes	See also 78
Library	WAT

REF	**72**
Title	**Bennett's Business Directory for Oxon, Bucks and Hants**
Dates	1898
Publisher	Bennett & Co
Printer	Bennett & Co
Place	Birmingham
Type	CM
Map scale	–
Library	BL
holdings	BOD
	CLO has OXON section only
	ULC

REF	**73**
Title	**Bennett's Business Directory: Section B**
Dates	1898
Publisher	Bennett & Co
Printer	Bennett & Co
Place	Birmingham
Type	CM
Map scale	–
Notes	Covers Bucks, Dorset, Hants, Oxon, Surrey, Sussex & Wilts
Library	BL
holdings	BOD
	ULC

REF **74**
Title **Bennett's Business Directory: South Wales, Devon, Gloucs & Monmouth**
Dates 1898
Publisher Bennett & Co
Printer Bennett & Co
Place Birmingham
Type CM
Map scale –
Notes Also includes counties of Brecknock, Cardigan, Carmarthen, Glamorgan, Pembroke & Radnor
Library BOD
holdings ULC

REF **75**
Title **Bale's Trades Directory comprising the counties of Gloucester, Somerset, Wilts & Dorset**
Dates 1900
Publisher The County Directory Publishing Company
Printer Creber, T.
Place Bath
Type TR
Map scale –
Library CPL

REF **76**
Title **Bennett's Business Directory for Northamptonshire, Leicestershire & Warwickshire**
Dates 1901,1906,1910
Publisher Bennett & Co
Printer Bennett & Co
Place Birmingham
Type TR
Map scale –
Library NTH

REF **77**
Title **The Court Guide and County Blue Book of Warwickshire, Worcestershire and Staffordshire**
Dates 1902
Publisher Deacon, C.W. & Co
Printer –
Place London
Type CT PR
Map scale –
Notes See 1424
Library BCL
holdings BOD
COV
HBR
ULC
WCL
WLV

REF **78**
Title **Bennett's Business Directory for Hertfordshire, Bucks, Cambridge and Essex**
Dates 1902,1908,1909,1911,1914
Publisher Bennett & Co
Printer Bennett & Co
Place Birmingham
Type TR
Map scale –
Notes 1911 edition includes Oxon; 1914 edition includes Northamptonshire
Library STA has 1902,1914
holdings WAT has 1902-1911

REF **79**
Title **Eastern Counties of England Trades' Directory including Norwich**
Dates 1902,1910,1912,1921,1925,1926, 1937
Publisher Trades' Directories Ltd
Printer Macdonald, W. & Co
Place Edinburgh
Type TR
Map scale –
Notes Includes Cambs, Hunts, Lincs, Norfolk & Suffolk
Library CAM has 1902,1926
holdings KLL has 1937
NOR not 1902,1926,1937

REF	**80**
Title	**Bennett's Business Directory Kent, Surrey & Sussex**
Dates	1903-1905,1907
Publisher	Bennett & Co
Printer	Bennett & Co
Place	Birmingham
Type	TR
Map scale	–
Notes	See 143
Library	BRI not 1905
holdings	CRD has 1905 (includes CHAN)

REF	**81**
Title	**Bennett's Business Directory for Derbyshire, Leics, Notts, Northants**
Dates	1904
Publisher	Bennett & Co
Printer	Bennett & Co
Place	Birmingham
Type	CM
Map scale	–
Library	BOD
holdings	NTH has NHTS section only
	ULC

REF	**82**
Title	**Bennett's Business Directory: Midland Counties**
Dates	1904
Publisher	Bennett & Co
Printer	Bennett & Co
Place	Birmingham
Type	CM
Map scale	–
Notes	Includes Berks, Bucks, Derbs, Glos, Leics, Northants, Notts, Oxon, Staffs, Warwks, Worcs & Birmingham
Library	BL
holdings	BOD
	CLO has BERK & OXON sections only
	ULC

REF	**83**
Title	**Bennett's Business Directory for Northern Counties**
Dates	1904,1906,1909,1912,1914
Publisher	Bennett & Co
Printer	Bennett & Co
Place	Birmingham
Type	CM
Map scale	–
Notes	Covers Cumberland, Durham, Northumberland, Westmorland & N. Lancs. 1904 edition includes Lincs & Yorks. 1906 edition includes Lincs.
Library	BOD has 1904
holdings	DUR not 1904
	NLS has 1904

REF	**84**
Title	**North Wales and Chester Official Year Book. A Directory of County, Municipal, Educational and all other public administrative bodies**
Dates	1905-1914
Publisher	Birchall, C. Ltd
Printer	Birchall, C. Ltd
Place	Liverpool
Type	PR
Map scale	–
Notes	Covers Chester & counties of Anglesey, Caernarvon, Denbigh, Flint, Merioneth & Montgomery
Library	CLC has 1905-1907,1909,
holdings	1911-1914
	NLS has 1905
	NLW all
	SWA has 1914

REF	**85**
Title	**Aubrey & Co's Hereford, Shropshire and Monmouthshire Directory**
Dates	1906
Publisher	Aubrey & Co
Printer	Aubrey & Co
Place	Walsall
Type	TR
Map scale	–
Library	GL

REF **86**
Title **Court Guide and Ecclesiastical and Professional Directory for Northumberland, Cumberland and Durham**
Dates 1906
Publisher Ramsay, J.A.
Printer '?'
Place '?'
Type CT PR
Map scale –
Notes No T/P or cover, details of publisher from CLN catalogue
Library CLN

REF **87**
Title **South Eastern Counties of England Trades Directory**
Dates 1906
Publisher Trades Directories Ltd
Printer Macdonald, W. & Co
Place Edinburgh
Type TR
Map scale 1:126720
Notes Covers London, Beds, Berks, Essex, Herts, Kent, Oxon, Surrey, Sussex. Each county divided by place. Also gazetteer section.
Library NLS

REF **88**
Title **Bennett's Business Directory Gloucestershire, Worcestershire, Herefordshire, Wiltshire**
Dates 1908
Publisher Bennett & Co
Printer Bennett & Co
Place Birmingham
Type TR
Map scale –
Library GLO

REF **89**
Title **The Court Guide and County Blue Book of Derbyshire, Nottinghamshire, Leicestershire, Rutland and Northamptonshire**
Dates 1908
Publisher Deacon, C.W. & Co
Printer Deacon, C.W. & Co
Place London
Type CT PR
Map scale –
Library BOD
holdings CLL
DCL
NLS
ULC

REF **90**
Title **North of England Trades Directory**
Dates 1908,1909
Publisher The Newcastle Publishing Co
Printer –
Place Newcastle-on-Tyne
Type GE
Map scale –
Notes Limited trades section. Covers Yorks, Durham & Northumberland.
Library BL
holdings BOD
ULC

REF **91**
Title **Somersetshire, Dorsetshire and Wiltshire Directory**
Dates 1909,1920,1925,1929,1934-1939, 1941
Publisher Aubrey & Co
Printer Aubrey & Co
Place Walsall
Type TR
Map scale –
Library BL has 1934-1939,1941
holdings BRL has 1909-1929

REF **92**
Title **Bennett's Business Directory for Leicestershire, Derbyshire and Nottinghamshire**
Dates 1913
Publisher Bennett & Co
Printer Bennett & Co
Place Birmingham
Type TR
Map scale –
Library NCL

REF	**93**
Title	**Bennett's Business Directory for Staffordshire**
Dates	1914
Publisher	Bennett & Co
Printer	Bennett & Co
Place	Birmingham
Type	TR
Map scale	—
Notes	Includes Birmingham, Staffs, Worcs & Warwks
Library	WLV

REF	**94**
Title	**Bennett's Business Directory for Shropshire and North Wales**
Dates	1916
Publisher	Bennett & Co
Printer	Bennett & Co
Place	Birmingham
Type	TR
Map scale	—
Library	SHR

REF	**95**
Title	**Cambridge, Norfolk and Suffolk Directory**
Dates	1916,1928
Publisher	Aubrey & Co
Printer	Aubrey & Co
Place	Walsall
Type	TR
Map scale	—
Notes	See 96
Library	CAM has 1928
holdings	KLL has 1916

REF	**96**
Title	**Cambridge, Essex, Norfolk & Suffolk Directory**
Dates	1925
Publisher	Aubrey & Co
Printer	Aubrey & Co
Place	Walsall
Type	TR
Map scale	—
Notes	See 95, 148.
Library	SRI

REF	**97**
Title	**Midland Counties of England Trades Directory**
Dates	1926,1931,1932,1934-1942,1944, 1948,1949
Publisher	Trades Directories Ltd
Printer	Macdonald, W. & Co
Place	Edinburgh
Type	TR
Map scale	NS
Notes	Covers Birmingham, Derbs, Herefords, Leics, Northants, Notts, Rutland, Salop, Staffs, Warwks & Worcs
Library	BCL not 1926,1948,1949
holdings	CLL has 1932
	DCL has 1926
	HBR has 1938 STFF
	NCL has 1938,1949
	NTH has 1938
	WCL has 1948

REF	**98**
Title	**Northampton, Hunts & Rutland Trades' Directory**
Dates	1927,1931-1933,1935,1936,1938, 1948
Publisher	Town and County Directories Ltd
Printer	Macdonald, W. & Co
Place	Edinburgh
Type	TR
Map scale	—
Notes	Cont'd from 1080
Library	HNT has 1938
holdings	NTH all

REF	**99**
Title	**Somerset, Wilts and Dorset Trades' Directory**
Dates	1931,1933,1935,1936
Publisher	Town and County Directories Ltd
Printer	Macdonald, W. & Co
Place	Edinburgh
Type	TR
Map scale	—
Library	BRL not 1931
holdings	SOG has 1931

REF	**100**
Title	**Bedfordshire, Northamptonshire, Huntingdonshire and Rutland Directory**
Dates	1932,1934,1936,1940,1941
Publisher	Aubrey & Co
Printer	Aubrey & Co
Place	Walsall
Type	TR
Map scale	–
Library	BL has 1940,1941
holdings	NTH all

REF	**101**
Title	**Western Counties Directory**
Dates	1933–1939
Publisher	Business Directories
Printer	Business Directories
Place	Bloxwich
Type	TR
Map scale	–
Notes	Covers Bristol, Cornwall, Devon, Glos, Somerset & Wilts
Library	BL not 1938
holdings	WCS has 1938

REF	**102**
Title	**Midland Counties Directory**
Dates	1934–1939
Publisher	Business Directories
Printer	–
Place	Bloxwich
Type	TR
Map scale	–
Notes	Covers Birmingham, Derbyshire, Leics, Northants, Notts, Oxon, Salop, Staffs, Warwks & Worcs
Library	BCL has 1934,1936
holdings	BL has 1935–1939

REF	**103**
Title	**South-Western Counties of England Trades' Directory**
Dates	1935
Publisher	Trades' Directories Ltd
Printer	Macdonald, W. & Co Ltd
Place	Edinburgh
Type	TR
Map scale	–
Notes	Includes Bristol, Devonport, Plymouth, Portsmouth, Southampton, Cornwall, Devon, Dorset, Gloucs, Hants, Monmouth, Somerset, Wilts & Channel Isles
Library	RED

REF	**104**
Title	**Kent, Surrey and Sussex Directory**
Dates	1935–1938,1941
Publisher	Aubrey & Co
Printer	Aubrey & Co
Place	Walsall
Type	TR
Map scale	–
Notes	Cont'd as 608, 1356, 1284
Library	BL has 1935–1938
holdings	CRD has 1941
	SLS has 1941

REF	**105**
Title	**Eastern Counties Directory**
Dates	1935–1939
Publisher	Business Directories
Printer	–
Place	Bloxwich
Type	TR
Map scale	–
Notes	Covers Beds, Bucks, Essex, Herts, Hunts, Lincs, Norfolk & Suffolk
Library	BL

REF	**106**
Title	**Northern Counties Directory**
Dates	1935–1939
Publisher	Business Directories
Printer	–
Place	Bloxwich
Type	TR
Map scale	–
Notes	Separate volumes: Vol I covers Durham, Northumberland & Yorks; Vol II covers Lancs, Cumberland & Westmorland
Library	BL all but 1939 Vol I
holdings	only.

REF	**107**
Title	**Southern Counties Directory**
Dates	1935–1939,1941
Publisher	Business Directories
Printer	–
Place	Bloxwich
Type	TR
Map scale	–
Notes	Covers Berks, Hants & IoW, Kent, Surrey & Sussex
Library	BL not 1941
holdings	RCL has 1941 BERK only

REF | **108**
Title | **Berkshire, Buckinghamshire and Oxford Directory**
Dates | 1937-1940
Publisher | Aubrey & Co
Printer | Aubrey & Co
Place | Walsall
Type | TR
Map scale | —
Library holdings | AYL has 1940
| BL all
| RCL has 1940

REF | **109**
Title | **North Eastern Counties of England Trades' Directory**
Dates | 1938,1942,1948
Publisher | Trades' Directories Ltd
Printer | Macdonald, W. & Co
Place | Edinburgh
Type | TR
Map scale | —
Notes | Includes Durham, Northumberland, Yorks. TR section for each place.
Library holdings | CLN has 1942
| DAR has 1948
| DUR has 1938
| LCL has 1938

REF | **110**
Title | **Midland and Southern Counties Trades Directory**
Dates | 1950
Publisher | Counties Trades Publishing Co Ltd
Printer | —
Place | Birmingham
Type | TR
Map scale | —
Notes | Includes Cornwall, Devon, Dorset, Gloucs, Hants, Herefords, Kent, Oxon, Salop, Somerset, Sussex, Warwks, Worcs & Channel Islands
Library | CLO

4.3 The English regions III: other directories covering two counties

This section is arranged as Chapter 4.2 above, chronologically and with full bibliographic details and library holdings.

REF | **111**
Title | **Ward's Northumberland & Durham Directory**
Dates | 1850
Publisher | Ward, R.
Printer | Ward, R.
Place | Newcastle-on-Tyne
Type | CM TR
Map scale | —
Notes | NORTON 576
Library holdings | BL
| CLN
| GL

REF | **112**
Title | **Hunt & Co's Directory of Hampshire and Dorsetshire**
Dates | 1852
Publisher | Hunt, E. & Co
Printer | Benson & Barling
Place | Weymouth
Type | CM TR
Map scale | —
Notes | NORTON 356
Library | CLS
holdings | PCL has Portsmouth sections only (X)

REF **113**
Title **Lascelles & Co's Directory and Gazetteer of the Counties of Monmouth and Hereford**
Dates 1852,1862
Publisher Lascelles & Co
Printer Lascelles & Co
Place Birmingham
Type CM
Map scale –
Library GL has 1852
holdings NPT has 1862

REF **114**
Title **Craven & Co's Commercial Directory of Bedfordshire & Hertfordshire**
Dates 1854
Publisher Craven & Co
Printer Craven & Co
Place Nottingham
Type GE TR
Map scale –
Library BED
holdings GL
HLS

REF **115**
Title **M. Billing's Directory and Gazetteer of the Counties of Berks and Oxon**
Dates 1854
Publisher Billing, M.
Printer Billing, M.
Place Birmingham
Type CM TR
Map scale –
Notes NORTON 131
Library CLO
holdings NEW
RCL

REF **116**
Title **Melville & Co's Directory of Derbyshire and Leicestershire**
Dates 1854
Publisher Melville & Co
Printer –
Place Leicester
Type CM
Map scale –
Notes CLD microfilm copy, T/P missing, title may not be correct
Library DLS

REF **117**
Title **Harrison, Harrod & Co's Bristol Post Office Directory and Gazetteer with the Counties of Gloucester & Somersetshire**
Dates 1859
Publisher Harrison & Harrod
Printer Danks, T.
Place London
Type GE TR
Map scale –
Library BL
holdings GLO
TLH

REF **118**
Title **Gazetteer and Directory of the Counties of Leicester and Rutland**
Dates 1861
Publisher Briggs, J.T. & Co
Printer –
Place Sheffield
Type TR
Map scale –
Library GL

REF **119**
Title **The Devon and Cornwall Mining Directory**
Dates 1861,1862,1870
Publisher Williams, J. (compiler)
Printer Banfield Bros.
Place Hayle
Type SP
Map scale –
Notes Classified by districts, name/location of mine, products etc.
Library BL all
holdings NLS has 1861

REF **120**
Title **Harrison, Harrod & Co's Postal Directory and Gazetteer of Devonshire and Cornwall**
Dates 1862
Publisher Harrison, Harrod & Co
Printer Danks, T. & Co
Place London
Type CM
Map scale –
Library GL
holdings PLY
RED

REF	**121**
Title	**History, Topography and Directory of Bedfordshire and Huntingdonshire**
Dates	1862
Publisher	Cassey, E. & Co
Printer	Danks, T.
Place	London
Type	CT CM
Map scale	1:177408
Library	BED
holdings	GL
	LUT has BEDS section only
	PET

REF	**122**
Title	**Morris & Co's Commercial Directory & Gazetteer of the Counties of Hereford and Monmouth**
Dates	1862
Publisher	Morris & Co
Printer	Stafford & Co
Place	Nottingham
Type	CM
Map scale	–
Library	CLC

REF	**123**
Title	**History, Gazetteer and Directory of the Counties of Leicester and Rutland**
Dates	1863, 1877
Publisher	White, W.
Printer	Leader, R. & Son
Place	Sheffield
Type	GE TR
Map scale	1:190080
Library	BCL all
holdings	BL all
	BPH has 1863
	CLL all
	GL all
	IHR has 1863
	NLW has 1863
	SOG has 1863
	ULC has 1863

REF	**124**
Title	**History, Topography and Directory of Cambridgeshire and Hertfordshire**
Dates	1864
Publisher	Cassey, E. & Co
Printer	Danks, T.
Place	London
Type	CM
Map scale	1:18100
Library	CAM

REF	**125**
Title	**J.G. Harrod & Co's Postal and Commercial Directory of Kent and Sussex**
Dates	1867
Publisher	Harrod, J.G. & Co
Printer	–
Place	London
Type	CM
Map scale	–
Library	GL

REF	**126**
Title	**Edward Cassey & Co's History, Gazetteer and Directory of Berkshire and Oxfordshire**
Dates	1868
Publisher	Cassey, E. & Co
Printer	Danks, T.
Place	London
Type	TR
Map scale	1:158400
Library	BL
holdings	CLO
	GL
	RCL
	SOG

REF	**127**
Title	**Slater's Royal National Commercial Directory of Cheshire and Lancashire**
Dates	1869
Publisher	Slater, I.
Printer	Slater, I.
Place	Manchester
Type	GE TR
Map scale	–
Library	CLM
holdings	GL

REF	**128**
Title	**Slater's Royal National Commercial Directory of Cumberland & Westmoreland**
Dates	1869
Publisher	Slater, I.
Printer	Slater, I.
Place	Manchester
Type	CM TR
Map scale	1:253440
Library	CAR

REF	**129**
Title	**J.G. Harrod & Co's Postal and Commercial Directory of Leicestershire and Rutland**
Dates	1870
Publisher	Harrod, J.G.
Printer	Harrod, J.G.
Place	London
Type	GE TR
Map scale	–
Library	BL
holdings	CLL

REF	**130**
Title	**Mercer & Crocker's General Topographical and Historical Directory for Hampshire, Dorsetshire etc.**
Dates	1871
Publisher	Mercer & Crocker
Printer	Mercer & Crocker
Place	Leicester
Type	CM
Map scale	1:887040
Notes	Also includes Northants, Cambs, Bucks & Beds
Library	CLS
holdings	DCL has DORS section only
	GL
	HRO
	LLB

REF	**131**
Title	**Mercer & Crocker's General Topographical and Historical Directory of Herefordshire, Radnorshire &c**
Dates	1874
Publisher	Mercer & Crocker
Printer	Mercer & Crocker
Place	Leicester
Type	CM
Map scale	1:380160
Notes	See 59
Library	NLW

REF	**132**
Title	**S. Barker & Co's General, Topographical and Historical Directory for the Counties of Leicester, Rutland &c**
Dates	1875
Publisher	Barker, S. & Co
Printer	Barker, S. & Co
Place	Leicester
Type	CM TR
Map scale	1:25344
Library	BOD
holdings	CLL
	NLS

REF	**133**
Title	**J.G. Harrod & Co's Royal County Directory of Devonshire and Cornwall**
Dates	1878
Publisher	Harrod, J.G.
Printer	Harrod, J.G.
Place	Norwich
Type	CM TR
Map scale	–
Library	BL
holdings	BOD
	DEI
	NLS
	PLY
	RED
	ULC
	WCS

REF **134**
Title **W.E. Owen & Co's General, Typographical, and Historical Directory for the counties of Wiltshire, Somersetshire with the cities of Bristol and Bath**
Dates 1878
Publisher Owen, W.E. & Co
Printer –
Place Leicester
Type CM TR
Map scale –
Notes See 61
Library TRW

REF **135**
Title **The Devon and Cornwall Court Guide and County Blue Book**
Dates 1882,1896
Publisher Deacon, C.W. & Co
Printer Deacon, C.W. & Co
Place London
Type CT PR
Map scale 1:422400
Notes 1882 Edition refers to the Eastern Division of Devon.
Library BOD has 1896
holdings DEI has 1882
NLS has 1896
PLY has 1896
SOG has 1882
ULC has 1896
WCS all

REF **136**
Title **Bennett's Business Directory Gloucestershire, Herefordshire, Worcestershire, Somerset, Devon**
Dates 1888
Publisher Bennett & Co
Printer Bennett & Co
Place Birmingham
Type TR
Map scale –
Library PLY

REF **137**
Title **Commercial and General Directory of Leicestershire & Rutland**
Dates 1888,1892,1896,1898,1900
Publisher Wright, C.N.
Printer Barker, S. & Co
Place Leicester
Type GE TR
Map scale –
Library BCL has 1896
holdings BL has 1896,1898
BOD has 1900
CLL all
GL has 1892,1898,1900
NLS has 1888,1896-1900
ULC has 1896-1900

REF **138**
Title **Bennett's Business Directory: Leicestershire and Rutland**
Dates 1888,1901
Publisher Bennett & Co
Printer Bennett & Co
Place Birmingham
Type TR
Map scale –
Notes 1888 edition is a rebound extract from a larger volume. 1901 edition covers Leicestershire only.
Library CLL

REF **139**
Title **Reid's Handy Colliery Guide and Directory for the Counties of Northumberland and Durham**
Dates 1891,1906
Publisher Reid, A. & Sons
Printer Reid, A. & Sons
Place London
Type SP
Map scale NS
Notes Arranged alph. by place, by county & alph. by owner
Library BL

REF	140
Title	**The Hants & Dorset Court Guide and County Blue Book**
Dates	1897
Publisher	Deacon, C.W. & Co
Printer	Deacon, C.W. & Co
Place	London
Type	CT PR
Map scale	1:422400
Library	CLS
holdings	DCL
	LLB
	SCC
	WCS

REF	141
Title	**Jenkins' Berks and Oxon Almanack, Local Directory, Diary & Literary Companion**
Dates	1899,1913
Publisher	Jenkins, W.D.
Printer	Jenkins, W.D.
Place	Wallingford
Type	CT
Map scale	–
Library	CLO

REF	142
Title	**Bennett's Business Directory for Birmingham & Smethwick, Warwickshire & Worcestershire**
Dates	1900,1902,1904,1921
Publisher	Bennett & Co
Printer	Bennett & Co
Place	Birmingham
Type	CM
Map scale	–
Library	BCL has 1902 (B'ham only)
holdings	BL has 1904
	BOD has 1904
	COV has 1921
	LEA has 1900
	NLS has 1904
	ULC has 1904

REF	143
Title	**Bennett's Business Directory for Surrey & Sussex**
Dates	1902,1904
Publisher	Bennett & Co
Printer	Bennett & Co
Place	Birmingham
Type	CM TR
Map scale	–
Notes	See 80
Library	CRD

REF	144
Title	**Herts and Essex Trades' Directory**
Dates	1907,1923,1929-1932,1935,1936
Publisher	Town and County Directories Ltd
Printer	Macdonald, W. & Co
Place	Edinburgh
Type	TR
Map scale	–
Library	GLH has 1931
holdings	WAT all

REF	145
Title	**Bedford, Cambridge and District Trades Directory**
Dates	1909,1910,1917,1918,1921-1925, 1928-1932,1935,1938,1939
Publisher	Town and County Directories Ltd
Printer	Macdonald, W. & Co
Place	Edinburgh
Type	TR
Map scale	–
Notes	Bedford, Beds & Cambs sections
Library	BED has 1925,1935
holdings	CAM has 1921,1939
	LUT has 1909,1910,1938
	ULC has 1917-1932

REF	146
Title	**Bennett's Business Directory for Lincolnshire and Yorkshire**
Dates	1912
Publisher	Bennett & Co
Printer	Bennett & Co
Place	Birmingham
Type	TR
Map scale	–
Library	LIN

REF	147
Title	**Buckinghamshire and South Surrey District Trades' Directory**
Dates	1913,1926
Publisher	Town and County Directories Ltd
Printer	Macdonald, W. & Co
Place	Edinburgh
Type	TR
Map scale	–
Library	AYL

REF	148
Title	**Norfolk and Suffolk Directory**
Dates	1916,1922,1925,1932
Publisher	Aubrey & Co
Printer	Aubrey & Co
Place	Walsall
Type	TR
Map scale	–
Notes	See 96
Library	NOR

REF	149
Title	**Reading, Berks and Oxford Trades Directory**
Dates	1922,1924,1925,1931,1939,1948
Publisher	Town and County Directories Ltd
Printer	Macdonald, W. & Co
Place	Edinburgh
Type	TR
Map scale	–
Library	AYL has 1948
holdings	CLO not 1924
	NLS has 1924

REF	150
Title	**Durham and Northumberland Directory**
Dates	1924,1936-1940
Publisher	Aubrey & Co
Printer	Aubrey & Co
Place	Walsall
Type	TR
Map scale	–
Library	BL has 1936-1940
holdings	DAR has 1934

REF	151
Title	**Derbyshire and Nottinghamshire Directory**
Dates	1927,1931,1937-1939,1941
Publisher	Aubrey & Co
Printer	Aubrey & Co
Place	Walsall
Type	TR
Map scale	–
Library	BL has 1937-1939
holdings	DLS has 1927,1931
	NCL has 1931,1941

REF	152
Title	**Hertfordshire Directory**
Dates	1928
Publisher	Aubrey & Co
Printer	Aubrey & Co
Place	Walsall
Type	TR
Map scale	–
Notes	Includes Essex
Library	STA

REF	153
Title	**Warwickshire and Worcestershire Directory**
Dates	1928,1931,1938,1939
Publisher	Aubrey & Co
Printer	Aubrey & Co
Place	Walsall
Type	TR
Map scale	–
Library	BCL has 1928,1931
holdings	BL has 1938,1939

REF	154
Title	**Northamptonshire and Rutland Directory and Buyer's Guide**
Dates	1933
Publisher	Cope, E.F. & Co
Printer	Cope, E.F. & Co
Place	Walsall
Type	TR
Map scale	–
Library	NTH

REF	155
Title	**Devon & Cornwall Trades' Directory**
Dates	1933,1936,1938
Publisher	Town and County Directories Ltd
Printer	Macdonald, W. & Co
Place	Edinburgh
Type	TR
Map scale	–
Library	RED

REF	**156**
Title	**Norfolk & Suffolk Trades' Directory**
Dates	1933,1946
Publisher	Town and County Directories Ltd
Printer	Macdonald, W. & Co
Place	Edinburgh
Type	TR
Map scale	–
Library holdings	NOR has 1933 SRI has 1946

REF	**157**
Title	**Devonshire and Cornwall Directory**
Dates	1933-1940
Publisher	Aubrey & Co
Printer	Aubrey & Co
Place	Walsall
Type	TR
Map scale	–
Library	BL

REF	**158**
Title	**Cumberland and Westmorland Directory**
Dates	1937-1939
Publisher	Aubrey & Co
Printer	Aubrey & Co
Place	Walsall
Type	TR
Map scale	–
Library	BL

4.4   Directories of towns in two or more counties

Included in this section are those directories whose coverage extends to a range of settlements over a region comprising at least two counties. It does not encompass those whose coverage relates to a majority of towns in one county and perhaps only one or two in a neighbouring county, but rather those whose spatial classification is slightly more complicated. The order is chronological.

REF	**159**
Title	**Almanack and General Town and Country Guide**
Dates	1850
Publisher	'?'
Printer	'?'
Place	'?'
Type	ST TR
Map scale	–
Notes	No T/P or cover & first 13pp missing CAR edition. Covers major towns in Durham & Northumberland and Carlisle.
Library	CAR

REF	**160**
Title	**Hunt & Co's Directory and Topography of the Towns of Cardigan, Carmarthen, Fishguard, Haverfordwest ... Swansea, and Tenby**
Dates	1850
Publisher	Hunt, E. & Co
Printer	Gardiner, B.W.
Place	London
Type	TR
Map scale	–
Notes	NORTON 866. Also includes Bristol.
Library	NLW

REF **161**
Title **Slater's Commercial Directory ... of ... Manchester, Birmingham, Carlisle, Hull, Leeds, Liverpool, Newcastle-upon-Tyne & Sheffield**
Dates 1852
Publisher Slater, I.
Printer Slater, I.
Place Manchester
Type TR
Map scale –
Notes Possibly NORTON 95
Library CL
holdings GL

REF **162**
Title **Slater's Royal National Commercial Directory of the important towns of Glasgow, Paisley, Greenock, Johnstone, Port Glasgow, Birmingham, Bristol, Leeds, Liverpool, Manchester, Sheffield ... & Ireland**
Dates 1857
Publisher Slater, I.
Printer Slater, I.
Place Manchester
Type GE TR
Map scale 1:760320
Notes Map of Ireland
Library BL
holdings CLM

REF **163**
Title **The Goldsmiths', Jewellers', Silversmiths', Watchmakers', Opticians', and Cutlers' Directory for London, Birmingham, Liverpool, Manchester and Sheffield**
Dates 1861,1863
Publisher Hogg, W. & Co
Printer Boot, A.
Place London
Type SP
Map scale –
Notes TR section for each city
Library BL has 1863
holdings BOD has 1863
NLS has 1863
SCL has 1861

REF **164**
Title **Williams's Manufacturers Directory for London & Principal Market Towns in England**
Dates 1864
Publisher Williams, J.
Printer Williams, J.
Place London
Type TR
Map scale –
Notes TR by county
Library BL
holdings BOD
NLS

REF **165**
Title **White's Directory of Birmingham, Wolverhampton, Walsall, Dudley, Wednesbury ... and the principal villages in the Hardware District**
Dates 1869,1873
Publisher White, W.
Printer Leader, R. & Son
Place Sheffield
Type GE TR
Map scale –
Library BCL all
holdings BL all
BOD has 1873
CLM has 1869
GL has 1873
NLS has 1873
ULC has 1873
WSL has 1869

REF **166**
Title **The Export Merchant Shippers of London, Manchester, Liverpool, Glasgow, Birmingham, Bristol, Sheffield, Newcastle, Hull etc**
Dates 1873-1916,1918-1925
Publisher Dean & Son
Printer Dean & Son
Place London
Type SP
Map scale –
Notes Includes a manufacturers trades section
Library BCL has 1918,1919
holdings BL not 1916,1918
BOD not 1878,1888,1908, 1910-1913,1920,1923-1925
MLG has 1921
NLS not 1873-1883,1908, 1910-1913,1920
ULC not 1875,1878,1908, 1910-1913

REF	**167**
Title	**Cassey's Directory of Chester and the Chief Towns in North Wales**
Dates	1876,1878,1880
Publisher	Cassey & Co
Printer	–
Place	Chester
Type	TR
Map scale	–
Notes	1876 edition entitled 'Cassey's Directory of Chester and the following towns in North Wales, viz: Abergele, Carnarvon, Bangor... &c &c'
Library holdings	CLC has 1876 NLW not 1880 WAR has 1880

REF	**168**
Title	**Deacon's Court Guide, Gazetteer and Royal Blue Book ... Western Division of ... Surrey, with Staines, Windsor, Eton, Slough, Maidenhead and the surrounding districts**
Dates	1878
Publisher	Deacon, C.W. & Co
Printer	Deacon, C.W. & Co
Place	London
Type	CT PR
Map scale	–
Notes	See 1281 & 1282. Map vandalized AYL edition.
Library	AYL

REF	**169**
Title	**Deacon's Court Guide, Gazetteer and Royal Blue Book ... of ... the Western Division of Gloucestershire, Chippenham, Devizes, Frome, Marlborough, Shepton Mallet, Swindon, Trowbridge, Yeovil and ... Salisbury, Gloucester, Bristol, Bath & Wells**
Dates	1882
Publisher	Deacon, C.W. & Co
Printer	Deacon, C.W. & Co
Place	London
Type	CT PR
Map scale	–
Library	TRW

REF	**170**
Title	**Cosburn's Directory embracing nearly 100 places in Berks, Hants, Oxon and Wilts**
Dates	1883,1887-1891
Publisher	Cosburn, G.J.
Printer	Cosburn, G.J.
Place	Newbury
Type	CT
Map scale	–
Notes	See 171
Library holdings	BL has 1889 RCL all

REF	**171**
Title	**Cosburn's Illustrated Directory for Newbury & 100 places in Berks, Hants, Oxon & Wilts**
Dates	1896,1898,1900-1916,1921
Publisher	Cosburn, G.J.
Printer	Cosburn, G.J.
Place	Newbury
Type	CT
Map scale	–
Notes	See 170
Library holdings	BL has 1898,1907-1915,1921 BOD has 1898,1904 NEW has 1900,1901,1903-1910, 1912-1917 RCL has 1896,1902,1904,1912, 1914,1916 ULC has 1904

REF	**172**
Title	**Mercantile Directory and Guide to Manufacturers, Merchants, Trades and Hotels in the United Kingdom**
Dates	1908,1909
Publisher	North of England Publishing Co
Printer	–
Place	Newcastle-on-Tyne
Type	TR
Map scale	–
Notes	Covers Northern counties of Yorks, Durham & Northumberland only, major towns
Library holdings	BL BOD NLS ULC

REF **173**
Title **Directory of Manufacturers, Wholesale importers, exporters and merchants on the North Eastern Railway System**
Dates 1916
Publisher North Eastern Railway
Printer –
Place York
Type TR
Map scale NS
Notes Covers towns in Yorks, Durham & Northumberland
Library BL
holdings NLS

REF **174**
Title **Nottingham, Leicester and Derby Trades Directory**
Dates 1933,1936,1938,1939
Publisher Town and County Directories Ltd
Printer Macdonald, W. & Co Ltd
Place Edinburgh
Type TR
Map scale –
Library DLS has 1938,1939
holdings NCL has 1933-1938

REF **175**
Title **Newcastle, Sunderland, Durham and Middlesborough Trades' Directory**
Dates 1936,1937,1948
Publisher Town and County Directories Ltd
Printer Macdonald, W. & Co Ltd
Place Edinburgh
Type TR
Map scale –
Notes Includes Cumberland & Westmorland. See 417.
Library CLN has 1948
holdings DUR all
MID has 1936,1948

REF **176**
Title **North Western Counties of England Trades' Directory including Manchester and Salford, Liverpool and Birkenhead**
Dates 1936,1943,1948
Publisher Trades' Directories Ltd
Printer Macdonald, W. & Co
Place Edinburgh
Type TR
Map scale 1:253440
Notes Cheshire, Cumberland, Lancs, Westmorland & Isle of Man included. Plans of Liverpool & Manchester Central.
Library BOD has 1936
holdings BPH has 1943
GL has 1936
PHL has 1948

4.5 English counties

BEDFORDSHIRE

REF	**177**
Title	**Craven and Co's Commercial Directory of the County of Bedford and the Towns of Hertford, Hitchin and Baldock**
Dates	1853
Publisher	Craven & Co
Printer	Craven & Co
Place	Nottingham
Type	CM TR
Map scale	–
Library holdings	BED LUT

REF	**178**
Title	**Kelly's Directory of Bedfordshire**
Dates	1854,1864,1869,1877,1885,1890, 1894,1898,1903,1906,1910,1914, 1920,1924,1928,1931,1936,1940
Publisher	Kelly & Co
Printer	Kelly & Co
Place	London
Type	GE TR
Map scale	1:380160
Notes	See 14. 1864-1877 editions entitled 'Post Office Directory of Bedfordshire'
Library holdings	AYL has 1869
	BCL has 1890-1940
	BED not 1854,1864
	BIS has 1910,1936
	BL all
	BOD has 1885-1940
	BPH has 1869,1894,1903, 1914-1924,1940
	CLB has 1936
	CLE has 1940
	CLM has 1940
	GL all
	HNT has 1864,1869,1885,1920, 1931,1936
	IHR has 1864,1898,1903,1910, 1940

	LUT has 1864,1885,1890, 1898-1920,1928-1940
	MLG has 1910,1920,1924
	NEW has 1869
	NLS not 1869
	NLW has 1928-1940
	PET has 1869,1890,1903,1924, 1940
	SCL has 1928-1940
	SOG has 1854-1877,1894,1924, 1940
	ULC all

REF	**179**
Title	**The Bedford Directory and Almanack**
Dates	1866
Publisher	Burt, H.
Printer	Burt, H.
Place	Bedford
Type	ST
Map scale	–
Library	BED

REF	**180**
Title	**The Bedford Directory and History of the Town**
Dates	1868
Publisher	Carter, J.H.
Printer	Carter, J.H.
Place	Bedford
Type	GE
Map scale	–
Library	BED

REF	**181**
Title	**The Bedford Directory**
Dates	1884,1893,1897-1901,1903
Publisher	Bedford Publishing Company
Printer	–
Place	Bedford
Type	GE
Map scale	–
Notes	Cont'd by 182. BED also has a pre 1884 edition with no T/P or date etc.
Library	BED

REF	**182**		REF	**185**
Title	**The Bedford Directory**		Title	**The Dunstable Year Book and**
Dates	1887,1904-1918,1920-1923,1925,			**Directory**
	1926,1928-1930,1932,1934,1936,		Dates	1908,1911,1913-1916
	1938,1939		Publisher	Taylor, M.
Publisher	Bedfordshire Times		Printer	Gazette (Dunstable)
Printer	Bedfordshire Times		Place	Dunstable
Place	Bedford		Type	GE
Type	GE		Map scale	–
Map scale	1:9600		Library	BED has 1908-1915
Notes	Cont'd from 181. Later editions		holdings	LUT has 1916
	published by F.R. Hockcliffe.			
Library	BED has 1906-1908,1910-1917,		REF	**186**
holdings	1925,1926,1929,1930,1938,1939		Title	**Rush & Warwick's Leighton**
holdings	BL all			**Buzzard Almanac, Advertiser**
	BOD has 1887			**and Postal Directory**
	GL has 1936,1938,1939		Dates	1911,1913,1938
	LUT has 1939		Publisher	Rush & Warwick
	NLS has 1887		Printer	Rush & Warwick
	SOG has 1913		Place	Leighton Buzzard
	ULC has 1887		Type	ST
			Map scale	–
REF	**183**		Library	BED has 1911,1913
Title	**Luton Directory**		holdings	GL has 1938
Dates	1903,1904,1908,1909			
Publisher	Reporter Press Agency		REF	**187**
Printer	Reporter Press Agency		Title	**James Tibbett's Dunstable**
Place	Luton			**Annual Illustrated Almanack and**
Type	CT			**Local Directory**
Map scale	–		Dates	1912,1914,1921,1922
Notes	1908 edition entitled 'The Luton &		Publisher	Tibbett, J.
	District Almanack and Year Book';		Printer	Tibbett, J.
	1909 edition entitled 'The Luton		Place	Dunstable
	Year Book, Map and Directory' (no		Type	GE
	sign of the map), both editions		Map scale	–
	published by Luton Reporter.		Library	BED not 1914
Library	BL has 1903,1904		holdings	LUT has 1914
holdings	LUT has 1903,1908,1909			
			REF	**188**
REF	**184**		Title	**The New Dunstable Handbook**
Title	**The Luton Year Book and**			**and Directory**
	Directory		Dates	1921
Dates	1904-1923		Publisher	Marchant, W.
Publisher	Town & County Press		Printer	–
Printer	Town & County Press		Place	Dunstable
Place	Luton		Type	ST TR
Type	GE TR		Map scale	–
Map scale	1:7920		Library	BED
Notes	Map scale approx.		holdings	LUT
Library	BL not 1923			
holdings	LUT has 1910,1912,1914-1919,			
	1923			

REF **189**
Title **Dunstable Official Guide and Directory**
Dates 1924
Publisher The British Publishing Company Ltd
Printer Crypt House Press
Place Gloucester
Type ST
Map scale –
Library BED

REF **190**
Title **The Luton News Directory of Luton**
Dates 1925,1926,1931,1933,1936,1939, 1950
Publisher Home Counties Newspapers Ltd
Printer Gibbs, Bamforth & Co Ltd
Place Luton
Type GE TR
Map scale –
Library BED has 1939,1950
holdings GL has 1936,1939,1950
LUT all

REF **191**
Title **The Official Guide to Dunstable and District with Street and Trades Directories**
Dates 1933,1937,1940
Publisher Index Publishers (Dunstable) Ltd
Printer Index Publishers (Dunstable) Ltd
Place Dunstable
Type ST TR
Map scale –
Library BED has 1933,1940
holdings LUT has 1937

REF **192**
Title **Kelly's Directory of Bedford & Neighbourhood**
Dates 1947,1949
Publisher Kelly's Directories Ltd
Printer Kelly's Directories Ltd
Place London
Type GE TR
Map scale –
Library BED all
holdings BL all
GL all
LUT has 1947
NLW has 1949

BERKSHIRE

REF **193**
Title **Rusher's Reading Guide and Berkshire Directory**
Dates 1852,1855,1857
Publisher Rusher & Johnson
Printer Rusher & Johnson
Place Reading
Type CM
Map scale –
Notes Very small CM section
Library GL has 1852,1855
holdings RCL not 1852

REF **194**
Title **Macaulay's Berkshire Directory, Almanac and Official Register**
Dates 1853,1856
Publisher Macaulay, J.
Printer Macaulay, J.
Place Reading
Type ST TR
Map scale –
Notes NORTON 130 (1853)
Library RCL
holdings CLO

REF **195**
Title **Kelly's Directory of Berkshire**
Dates 1854,1864,1869,1877,1883,1887,
1891,1895,1899,1903,1907,1911,
1915,1920,1924,1928,1931,1935,
1939
Publisher Kelly & Co
Printer Kelly & Co
Place London
Type GE TR
Map scale 1:380160
Notes See 7(1854-1877) & 20(1883-1939)
Library AYL has 1869-1887,1895,1907,
holdings 1915,1935
BCL has 1877,1883,1891-1939
BIS has 1928,1931,1939
BL all
BOD has 1891-1931,1939
BPH has 1869,1939
CLB has 1939
CLM has 1924,1928,1939
CLO has 1854-1869,1877,1883,
1891-1911,1920
GL all
HNT has 1864
HRO has 1907,1931,1935
IHR has 1883,1911,1928
LCL has 1935
MLG has 1911-1928
NEW has 1869,1895-1903,1915,
1924-1939
NLS has 1854,1864,1877-1924
NLW has 1887,1903,1907,
1920-1939
RCL has 1854,1864,1877,
1887-1920
SCC has 1928,1931
SCL has 1928-1939
SLS has 1939
SOG has 1865,1864,1877-1887,
1895,1899,1911,1920,1928,
1939
ULC has 1855-1935
WRO has 1931,1939

REF **196**
Title **Macaulay's Reading Directory,**
Almanac and Official Register
Dates 1859,1860,1865,1867,1870,1871
Publisher Macaulay, J.
Printer Macaulay, J.
Place Reading
Type ST TR
Map scale –
Notes Title varies
Library RCL

REF **197**
Title **Lock's Reading Directory, Court**
Guide and Almanack
Dates 1869,1870
Publisher Lock, F.J.
Printer –
Place Reading
Type CT CM
Map scale –
Library RCL

REF **198**
Title **Cosburn's Newbury &**
Speenhamland Directory and
General Local Guide
Dates 1873
Publisher Cosburn, G.J.
Printer Cosburn, G.J.
Place Newbury
Type CT TR
Map scale –
Library BOD

REF **199**
Title **Webster's Reading Directory**
including Henley, Pangbourne
and Goring
Dates 1874
Publisher Webster & Co
Printer –
Place London & Reading
Type GE TR
Map scale –
Library RCL

REF	**200**
Title	**The Postal Directory for Reading & Neighbourhood**
Dates	1875-1879,1882,1884-1916, 1920-1924
Publisher	Smith, G.R.
Printer	Smith, G.R.
Place	Reading
Type	GE TR
Map scale	1:10560
Notes	Early editions have several changes in title: 'Smith's Directory for Reading and Neighbourhood', 'The Directory for Reading & Neighbourhood'
Library holdings	BL has 1889,1905-1924 IHR has 1875 RCL not 1917-1919

REF	**201**
Title	**Directory of Reading & Neighbourhood**
Dates	1884,1888
Publisher	Stevens, G.
Printer	Stevens, G.
Place	London
Type	GE TR
Map scale	–
Library holdings	BL has 1884,1888 BOD has 1888 NLS has 1888 RCL all ULC has 1888

REF	**202**
Title	**Kelly's Directory of Reading**
Dates	1889,1890,1899-1915,1917,1919, 1922-1942,1944,1947,1949
Publisher	Kelly & Co
Printer	Kelly & Co
Place	London
Type	GE TR
Map scale	1:10560
Library holdings	BL all BOD has 1899,1901-1912 CLE has 1949 CLM has 1932 GL not 1890,1906,1908,1911 IHR has 1914 MLG has 1949 NLW has 1949 RCL has 1889-1900,1904,1909, 1912-1914,1917-1932, 1934-1949 ULC not 1900,1913-1947

REF	**203**
Title	**Kelly's Directory of Windsor, Eton & Slough**
Dates	1889,1890,1926,1928,1930,1932, 1934,1936,1938,1940,1947,1950
Publisher	Kelly & Co
Printer	Kelly & Co
Place	London
Type	GE TR
Map scale	–
Library holdings	BL not 1890 BOD has 1908 GL not 1889,1940 NLW has 1950 RCL has 1950 ULC has 1889,1890

REF	**204**
Title	**Hall's Newbury and Hungerford Guide**
Dates	1890
Publisher	Hall, W.
Printer	Hall, W.
Place	Newbury
Type	GE
Map scale	–
Library	RCL

REF	**205**
Title	**W.H. Hooke's Abingdon Almanack, Directory and Diary**
Dates	1892,1900,1903-1905,1907, 1913-1916,1928-1932,1938-1941
Publisher	Hooke, W.H.
Printer	Hooke, W.H.
Place	Abingdon
Type	CT
Map scale	–
Library holdings	BOD has 1914,1938-1941 CLO not 1938-1941 GL has 1914,1938-1941

REF	**206**
Title	**Nichols' Wantage Town & District Almanack with Directory of Wantage, Faringdon, Lambourn & 36 villages**
Dates	1898-1900,1906,1910,1911,1914, 1916,1920
Publisher	Nichols, H.N.
Printer	Nichols, H.N.
Place	Wantage
Type	CM
Map scale	–
Library	CLO has 1898-1900
holdings	RCL has 1900-1920

REF	**207**
Title	**Postal Directory of the Mid-Thames Valley, Maidenhead, Henley, Marlow & Districts**
Dates	1903,1912
Publisher	Smith, G.R. & Co
Printer	Smith, G.R. & Co
Place	Reading
Type	GE TR
Map scale	1:10560
Library	BL

REF	**208**
Title	**Marshall's Royal & Official Directory for Windsor and District**
Dates	1904-1907,1909-1914
Publisher	Marshall, E.
Printer	Marshall, E.
Place	Windsor
Type	GE
Map scale	–
Library	BL all
holdings	RCL has 1911,1914

REF	**209**
Title	**Clegg & Son's Wantage and District Alamanack and Diary with Directory of Wantage, Faringdon, Lambourn and nearly 40 villages**
Dates	1912,1924,1925,1932,1940
Publisher	Clegg & Son
Printer	Clegg & Son
Place	Wantage
Type	CM
Map scale	–
Library	CLO has 1940
holdings	RCL not 1940

REF	**210**
Title	**Blacket's Newbury and District Directory**
Dates	1923,1936
Publisher	Blacket Turner and Company Ltd
Printer	Blacket Turner and Company Ltd
Place	Newbury
Type	CT
Map scale	–
Notes	1936 edition entitled 'Blacket's Newbury and District Directory'. Cont'd as 214.
Library	NEW all

REF	**211**
Title	**Kelly's Directory of Newbury & Neighbourhood**
Dates	1927-1937,1939-1942,1947,1950
Publisher	Kelly's Directories Ltd
Printer	Kelly's Directories Ltd
Place	London
Type	GE TR
Map scale	1:15840
Library	BL not 1940,1942,1950
holdings	CLM has 1930,1933
	GL not 1942
	NEW has 1929,1930,1932,1936, 1937,1941-1950
	NLW has 1950
	RCL has 1932,1934-1936,1938, 1940,1942,1950
	SOG has 1950

REF	**212**
Title	**Kelly's Directory of Maidenhead, Cookham & Taplow**
Dates	1929,1931,1933,1936,1938,1940, 1942,1948
Publisher	Kelly's Directories Ltd
Printer	Kelly's Directories Ltd
Place	London
Type	GE TR
Map scale	1:253440
Library	BL all
holdings	GL not 1940,1942
	RCL not 1929

REF **213**
Title **Kelly's Directory of Wokingham, Bracknell & Neighbourhood**
Dates 1930-1932,1934,1936,1938,1940, 1941
Publisher Kelly's Directories Ltd
Printer Kelly's Directories Ltd
Place London
Type GE TR
Map scale 1:84480
Library BL not 1941
holdings GL not 1936,1940
RCL has 1932-1936

REF **214**
Title **Blacket's Newbury & Hungerford Street Key and District Directory**
Dates 1938,1939,1942
Publisher Blacket Turner & Co
Printer Blacket Turner & Co
Place Newbury
Type GE
Map scale –
Notes Cont'd from 210
Library GL has 1939
holdings NEW all

REF **215**
Title **The Wokingham Times Directory of Wokingham, Bracknell, Ascot, Crowthorne and District**
Dates 1950
Publisher The Wokingham and Bracknell Times
Printer The Wokingham and Bracknell Times
Place Wokingham
Type GE TR
Map scale –
Library GL
holdings RCL

BUCKINGHAMSHIRE

REF **216**
Title **Musson and Craven's Commercial Directory of the County of Buckingham and the town of Windsor**
Dates 1853
Publisher Musson & Craven
Printer Stevenson & Co
Place Nottingham
Type CM
Map scale –
Notes NORTON 134
Library AYL
holdings GL
SOG

REF **217**
Title **Kelly's Directory of Buckinghamshire**
Dates 1854,1864,1869,1877,1883,1887, 1891,1895,1899,1903,1907,1911, 1915,1920,1924,1928,1931,1935, 1939
Publisher Kelly & Co
Printer Kelly & Co
Place London
Type GE TR
Map scale 1:380160
Notes See 7(1854-1977) & 20(1883-1939)
Library AYL not 1854
holdings BCL has 1928,1939
BIS has 1899,1928,1931,1939
BL all
BOD has 1891-1931,1939
BPH has 1869,1939
CLB has 1939
CLM has 1928,1939
CLO has 1864-1883,1891-1911, 1920
GL all
HNT has 1864
IHR has 1911,1928
LUT has 1920,1928,1939
MLG has 1911-1924
NEW has 1869,1915,1939
NLS has 1854,1864,1877-1939
NLW has 1939
RCL has 1887-1920
SCL has 1928-1939
SOG has 1854,1864,1877-1887, 1895,1899,1915,1920,1928, 1939
ULC all

REF **218**
Title **History [and Directory] of the Town of Newport Pagnell and its neighbourhood**
Dates 1868
Publisher Simpson & Son
Printer Simpson & Son
Place Newport Pagnell
Type CM TR
Map scale –
Library AYL

REF **219**
Title **The High Wycombe Directory, Handbook and Advertiser**
Dates 1885
Publisher Stenlake & Simpson
Printer Stenlake & Simpson
Place London
Type ST
Map scale –
Library ULC

REF **220**
Title **The Aylesbury Directory and Official Handbook for the County of Bucks**
Dates 1907,1909,1911,1913,1915,1918, 1922,1925,1927,1932
Publisher De Fraine, G.T.
Printer De Fraine, G.T.
Place Aylesbury
Type GE
Map scale NS
Library AYL has 1913,1925,1927,1932
holdings BL all
BOD has 1907,1932
GL has 1911,1913
ULC has 1907,1932

REF **221**
Title **Fenny Stratford, Bletchley, Winslow, Woburn Sands Year Book and Directory**
Dates 1908
Publisher Jackson, H.
Printer Jackson, H.
Place Leighton Buzzard
Type ST
Map scale –
Library BOD

REF **222**
Title **Palmer's Directory and Year Book for Slough and District**
Dates 1908,1909
Publisher Palmer's
Printer Palmer's
Place Slough
Type GE
Map scale –
Notes Cont'd by 223
Library AYL

REF **223**
Title **Day's (late Palmer's) Directory and Year Book for Slough and District**
Dates 1912,1913
Publisher Day, I.
Printer Day, I.
Place Slough
Type GE
Map scale –
Notes Cont'd from 222
Library AYL

REF **224**
Title **Chesham and District Directory, Year Book and Illustrated Almanac**
Dates 1914
Publisher Page & Thomas Ltd
Printer Bucks Examiner
Place Chesham
Type ST
Map scale –
Library GL

REF **225**
Title **Gerrards Cross & Chalfont St Peter Directory**
Dates 1917
Publisher (For) Gerrards Cross & Chalfont St Peter Volunteer Fire Brigade
Printer Clerkenwell Press
Place London
Type GE
Map scale 1:10560
Library BL
holdings NLS

REF	**226**
Title	**Beaconsfield Directory**
Dates	1925
Publisher	'?'
Printer	Excelsior Printing Works
Place	Beaconsfield
Type	GE
Map scale	NS
Notes	T/P missing AYL edition, This may be an earlier edition of 233. Title uncertain.
Library	AYL

REF	**227**
Title	**Hall's Directory for Amersham, Chesham, Great Missenden and District**
Dates	1930
Publisher	Hall, E. & Co
Printer	Hall, E. & Co
Place	Reading
Type	GE
Map scale	–
Library	AYL

REF	**228**
Title	**High Wycombe Furnishing Trades' Official Directory**
Dates	1931
Publisher	High Wycombe Town Council & Chamber of Commerce
Printer	Freer & Hayter
Place	High Wycombe
Type	SP
Map scale	–
Notes	Classified directory
Library	CLM

REF	**229**
Title	**Binder's Directory of Gerrards Cross and Chalfont St. Peter**
Dates	1931,1938,1940
Publisher	Binder, R.
Printer	–
Place	Gerrards Cross
Type	GE
Map scale	–
Library	AYL

REF	**230**
Title	**Kelly's Directory of Chesham and Amersham**
Dates	1932,1933,1935,1937,1939,1941
Publisher	Kelly's Directories Ltd
Printer	Kelly's Directories Ltd
Place	London
Type	GE TR
Map scale	–
Library holdings	AYL has 1941 BL not 1932 CLM has 1941 GL not 1933

REF	**231**
Title	**Kelly's Directory of Slough & Neighbourhood**
Dates	1936,1938,1940
Publisher	Kelly's Directories Ltd
Printer	Kelly's Directories Ltd
Place	London
Type	GE TR
Map scale	1:10560
Library holdings	BL GL

REF	**232**
Title	**Kelly's Directory of Aylesbury & Neighbourhood**
Dates	1936,1938,1940,1943,1948
Publisher	Kelly's Directories Ltd
Printer	Kelly's Directories Ltd
Place	London
Type	GE TR
Map scale	–
Library holdings	AYL all BL all GL not 1936

REF	**233**
Title	**Directory of Beaconsfield, Knotty Green and Forty Green**
Dates	1938,1949
Publisher	Clarendon Printers Ltd
Printer	Clarendon Printers Ltd
Place	Beaconsfield
Type	GE
Map scale	–
Library	GL

REF | **234**
Title | **E.N. Hillier & Sons Ltd Almanack and Directory for Buckingham, Winslow, Brackley & District**
Dates | 1939
Publisher | Hillier, E.N. & Sons
Printer | Hillier, E.N. & Sons
Place | Buckingham
Type | ST
Map scale | –
Library | GL

REF | **235**
Title | **Illustrated Directory of Gerrards Cross with parts of the parishes of Fulmer and Chalfont St. Peter**
Dates | 1950
Publisher | The Under Twenties Club
Printer | –
Place | Gerrards Cross
Type | GE
Map scale | 1:10560
Library | AYL

CAMBRIDGESHIRE

REF | **236**
Title | **History, Gazetteer and Directory of Cambridgeshire including the Isle of Ely**
Dates | 1851
Publisher | Gardner, R.
Printer | Gardner, R.
Place | Peterborough
Type | CM TR
Map scale | –
Notes | NORTON 135
Library | CAM
holdings | GL
 | IHR
 | PET
 | SOG

REF | **237**
Title | **Kelly's Directory of Cambridgeshire**
Dates | 1853,1858,1865,1869,1875,1879, 1883,1888,1892,1896,1900,1904, 1908,1912,1916,1922,1925,1929, 1933,1937
Publisher | Kelly & Co
Printer | Kelly & Co
Place | London
Type | GE TR
Map scale | 1:253440
Notes | See 5
Library | BCL has 1858,1883-1937
holdings | BIS has 1925
 | BL all
 | BOD all
 | BPH has 1858,1916-1929,1937
 | CAM all
 | CLB has 1937
 | CLE has 1916,1937
 | CLM has 1933,1937
 | GL all
 | HNT has 1937
 | IHR has 1883,1900,1908,1933
 | KLL has 1879,1892,1896, 1904-1912,1925-1937
 | LCL has 1937
 | LIN has 1929
 | MLG has 1904-1937
 | NLS all
 | NLW has 1912,1916,1929-1937
 | NOR has 1853,1892,1908,1916, 1922,1925,1937
 | PET has 1888,1892,1904,1908, 1925,1929,1937
 | SCL has 1929-1937
 | SOG has 1858,1869,1875,1888, 1896,1912,1922-1937
 | SRI has 1869-1879,1904, 1912-1925
 | ULC all

REF | **238**
Title | **J. Morgan & Co's Directory of Cambridge, including Newmarket, Ely and surrounding villages**
Dates | 1865
Publisher | Morgan & Co
Printer | –
Place | London
Type | CT CM
Map scale | –
Library | CAM

REF	**239**
Title	**The Cambridge Directory including Ely and Newmarket**
Dates	1866,1867
Publisher	Johnson, H.
Printer	Mathiesons
Place	Cambridge
Type	GE TR
Map scale	–
Notes	1867 edition entitled 'Mathiesons Cambridge Directory'
Library	BL not 1867
holdings	BOD all
	CAM all

REF	**240**
Title	**Spalding's Street and General Directory of Cambridge**
Dates	1875,1878,1881,1884,1887,1891, 1895,1898,1901,1904,1907, 1910-1916,1919-1939
Publisher	Spalding, W.P.
Printer	Spalding, W.P.
Place	Cambridge
Type	GE
Map scale	–
Notes	Spalding also produced a series of Cambridge almanacks 1874-1919,1921 held at CAM
Library	BL not 1881,1891,1923
holdings	CAM all
	BOD has 1875,1878,1887-1915, 1920-1939
	GL has 1881,1911,1927, 1937-1939
	NLS not 1881,1884,1891, 1927-1939
	ULC all

REF	**241**
Title	**Barber's Littleport and District Directory and Alamanack**
Dates	1909,1915,1917,1918,1920-1935, 1937,1939-1942,1947-1949
Publisher	Barber, W.C.
Printer	Barber, W.C.
Place	Littleport
Type	ST
Map scale	–
Library	CAM

REF	**242**
Title	**Cambridge Annual Directory with map of the Borough of Cambridge**
Dates	1910
Publisher	Dixon, A.P.
Printer	Dixon, A.P.
Place	Cambridge
Type	ST TR
Map scale	1:7040
Library	CAM

REF	**243**
Title	**Heffer's Directory, Diary & Reference Book of Cambridge**
Dates	1913
Publisher	Heffer, W. & Sons Ltd
Printer	Heffer, W. & Sons Ltd
Place	Cambridge
Type	CM
Map scale	–
Library	CAM
holdings	NLW

REF	**244**
Title	**Kelly's Directory of Wisbech and neighbourhood**
Dates	1932,1934,1936,1938,1940
Publisher	Kelly's Directories Ltd
Printer	Kelly's Directories Ltd
Place	London
Type	GE TR
Map scale	–
Library	BL all
holdings	CAM has 1934
	CLM has 1940
	GL all

REF	**245**
Title	**The Blue Book - A Directory of Cambridge and District**
Dates	1936-1940
Publisher	St Tibbs Press
Printer	St Tibbs Press
Place	Cambridge
Type	GE TR
Map scale	–
Library	BOD all
holdings	CAM all
	GL has 1937
	NLS all
	ULC all

REF	246
Title	**The City of Ely Red Book**
Dates	1947-1950
Publisher	Jefferson, W. & Son Ltd
Printer	Jefferson, W. & Son Ltd
Place	Ely
Type	GE
Map scale	–
Library	CAM has 1950
holdings	GL all

REF	247
Title	**Kelly's Directory of Cambridge**
Dates	1948
Publisher	Kelly's Directories Ltd
Printer	Kelly's Directories Ltd
Place	London
Type	GE TR
Map scale	–
Library	BOD
holdings	CAM
	GL
	NLS
	NOR
	ULC

THE CHANNEL ISLANDS

REF	248
Title	**The "Jersey Express" Almanac and General Directory**
Dates	1865,1873-1876,1879,1881-1932, 1934-1936,1938
Publisher	Jersey Express
Printer	Jersey Express
Place	Jersey
Type	GE TR
Map scale	–
Library	BL not 1940
holdings	BOD has 1908-1940
	IHR has 1925
	NLS has 1908-1936
	SOG has 1865
	ULC has 1908-1936

REF	249
Title	**J.W. Hill & Co's Historical Directory of the Channel Islands**
Dates	1874
Publisher	Clarke, F.
Printer	Clarke, F.
Place	Guernsey
Type	CM TR
Map scale	–
Library	BL
holdings	GL

REF	250
Title	**Kelly's Directory of the Channel Islands**
Dates	1898,1903,1907,1911,1915,1927, 1931,1935,1939
Publisher	Kelly's Directories Ltd
Printer	Kelly's Directories Ltd
Place	London
Type	GE TR
Map scale	1:63360
Library	BCL all
holdings	BL not 1907,1927,1939
	BOD has 1898,1903,1931-1939
	BPH has 1939
	CLE has 1939
	GL not 1927,1939
	NLS has 1898,1903,1911
	NLW has 1939
	ULC not 1907,1927,1915
	WCS has 1927

CHESHIRE

REF	251
Title	**History, Gazetteer and Directory of the County Palatine of Chester**
Dates	1850
Publisher	Bagshaw, S.
Printer	Ridge, G.
Place	Sheffield
Type	CM TR
Map scale	NS
Notes	NORTON 142
Library	BCL
holdings	BL
	CLM
	CCL
	CL
	GL
	IHR
	MAC
	SOG
	WAR

REF	252
Title	**Kelly's Directory of Cheshire**
Dates	1857,1865,1878,1892,1896,1902, 1906,1910,1914,1923,1928,1934, 1939
Publisher	Kelly & Co
Printer	Kelly & Co
Place	London
Type	GE TR
Map scale	1:380160
Notes	1857-1878 editions entitled 'Post Office Directory of Cheshire'
Library	BCL has 1896-1939
holdings	BL all
	BOD all
	BPH has 1857,1878,1892,1896, 1910,1923,1939
	CCL not 1865
	CL has 1939
	CLB has 1928
	CLC has 1914,1923,1939
	CLE has 1939
	CLM all
	GL not 1857
	IHR has 1906,1939
	MAC has 1878-1914,1934,1939
	MLG has 1910-1939
	NLS all
	NLW has 1914,1928,1934,1939
	SCL has 1928-1939
	SOG has 1857,1878,1896,1914, 1939
	ULC all
	WAR not 1878
	YCL has 1939

REF	253
Title	**History, Gazetteer and Directory of Cheshire**
Dates	1860
Publisher	White, F.
Printer	Pawson & Brailsford
Place	Sheffield
Type	GE TR
Map scale	1:190080
Library	BCL
holdings	BL
	BPH
	CCL
	CL
	CLM
	GL
	IHR
	MAC
	NLW
	SOG
	WAR

REF	254
Title	**Morris & Co's Commercial Directory and Gazetteer of Cheshire**
Dates	1864,1874
Publisher	Morris & Co
Printer	–
Place	Nottingham
Type	CM
Map scale	–
Notes	1874 edition includes Stalybridge
Library	CCL all
holdings	CLM all
	IHR has 1874
	MAC has 1874

REF	255
Title	**Deacon's Cheshire Court Guide and County Blue Book**
Dates	1886
Publisher	Deacon, C.W. & Co
Printer	Deacon, C.W. & Co
Place	London
Type	CT
Map scale	–
Library	CCL
holdings	GL

REF	256
Title	**Slater's Royal National Commercial Directory of Cheshire**
Dates	1888,1890
Publisher	Slater, I.
Printer	Slater, I.
Place	Manchester
Type	GE TR
Map scale	1:158400
Library	BL has 1888
holdings	BCL has 1890
	BPH has 1890
	GL has 1888

REF	257
Title	**Slater's Royal National Commercial Directory of Cheshire with Liverpool**
Dates	1890
Publisher	Slater, I.
Printer	Slater, I.
Place	Manchester
Type	GE TR
Map scale	NS
Library	GL
holdings	NLS

REF **258**
Title **Bennett's Business Directory of Cheshire**
Dates 1903
Publisher Bennett & Co
Printer Bennett & Co
Place Birmingham
Type TR
Map scale –
Library CCL

REF **259**
Title **Cheshire Directory and Buyers' Guide**
Dates 1909,1913,1928-1930,1932,1935
Publisher Cope, E.F. & Co
Printer Cope, E.F. & Co
Place Walsall
Type TR
Map scale –
Library CCL not 1913
holdings CLM has 1913

REF **260**
Title **Cheshire Directory**
Dates 1933-1940
Publisher Aubrey & Co
Printer Aubrey & Co
Place Walsall
Type TR
Map scale –
Library BL

REF **261**
Title **Pinkney's Directory of Birkenhead & its Environs**
Dates 1851
Publisher Pinkney, R.
Printer Pinkney, R.
Place Birkenhead
Type CM
Map scale –
Notes NORTON 145
Library CLM

REF **262**
Title **A New Alphabetical and Classified Directory of Chester, Bolton, Bury, Wigan, Ashton-under-Lyne, Stalybridge, Oldham, Rochdale ...**
Dates 1854
Publisher Whellan, W. & Co
Printer Galt, Kerrush & Gent
Place Manchester
Type CM TR
Map scale –
Notes NORTON 429
Library BPH

REF **263**
Title **Charles Balshaw's Stranger's Guide and Complete Directory to Altrincham, Bowden, Dunham, Timperley, Baguley, Ashley, Hale and Bollington**
Dates 1855,1857,1859
Publisher Balshaw, C.
Printer Balshaw, C.
Place Altrincham
Type CM
Map scale –
Notes NORTON 143 (1855), GL edition reprint (1973) by E.J. Morten, Didsbury. Dates of post 1855 volumes uncertain.
Library CL all
holdings CLM has 1859
GL has ?1859

REF **264**
Title **Mawdsley and Son's Directory for the Hundred of Wirral, including ... Birkenhead**
Dates 1861
Publisher Mawdsley, J. & Son
Printer Mawdsley, J. & Son
Place Liverpool
Type GE
Map scale –
Library BOD
holdings NLS
ULC

REF **265**
Title **Phillipson and Golder's Directory for Chester**
Dates 1870,1876,1893,1897,1899-1915, 1917,1919-1936
Publisher Phillipson & Golder
Printer Phillipson & Golder
Place Chester
Type GE TR
Map scale 1:12000
Library BL not 1876-1899,1903,1904,
holdings 1917
BOD has 1870,1901,1903,1904, 1906-1915,1919,1921-1935
CCL has 1870-1899,1904-1909, 1911-1915,1917,1919,1921, 1922,1924-1935
CLM has 1914,1922-1933,1935
GL has 1928
NLS has 1901,1904,1906-1915, 1919,1921-1928

REF **266**
Title **Worrall's Directory of Stockport and adjoining townships**
Dates 1872
Publisher Worrall, J.
Printer Worrall, J.
Place Oldham
Type GE TR
Map scale –
Library BL

REF **267**
Title **Eardley's Alphabetical and Trade Directory for Crewe and Neighbourhood**
Dates 1873
Publisher Eardley, W.
Printer Eardley, W.
Place Crewe
Type CM TR
Map scale –
Library GL

REF **268**
Title **Morris & Co's Commercial Directory and Gazetteer of the Cheshire Towns with Wrexham**
Dates 1880
Publisher Morris & Co
Printer –
Place Nottingham
Type GE TR
Map scale –
Library BPH
holdings CLC
GL
NLW

REF **269**
Title **Slater's Post Office Directory of the City of Chester**
Dates 1882,1888
Publisher Slater, I.
Printer Slater, I.
Place Manchester
Type GE TR
Map scale –
Library BL all
holdings BOD has 1882
CCL has 1882
GL not 1888
NLS has 1882

REF **270**
Title **Altrincham, Bowden & Sale District Directory**
Dates 1886
Publisher Hadfield, W.H.
Printer Hadfield, W.H.
Place Altrincham
Type GE TR
Map scale –
Library BOD
holdings NLS
ULC

REF **271**
Title **Altrincham, Bowden, Dunham, Massey, Hale, Timperley & Ashley Directory**
Dates 1886
Publisher Thompson, H.
Printer Percy, T. & R.
Place Manchester
Type CT
Map scale –
Library BL

REF **272**
Title **Postal Directory for Crewe, Middlewich, Nantwich, Sandbach & District**
Dates 1887
Publisher Rockliff Bros
Printer Rockliff Bros
Place Liverpool
Type GE TR
Map scale –
Library GL

REF **273**
Title **R.A. Melsom's Cheadle, etc. Directory**
Dates 1887
Publisher Melsom, R.A.
Printer –
Place Northenden
Type ST TR
Map scale –
Notes Also includes Baguley, Gatley & Northenden
Library CLM

REF **274**
Title **Slater's Directory of Macclesfield and District**
Dates 1887,1890
Publisher Slater, I.
Printer Slater, I.
Place Manchester
Type GE TR
Map scale –
Library BL has 1887
holdings GL has 1887
MAC all

REF **275**
Title **Slater's Royal National Commercial Directory of Stockport, Heaton Norris & District**
Dates 1887,1891,1893
Publisher Slater, I.
Printer Slater, I.
Place Manchester
Type GE TR
Map scale –
Library BL has 1887
holdings CLM has 1891,1893
GL has 1887,1893

REF **276**
Title **Slater's Royal National Commercial Directory of Ashton-under-Lyne, Dukinfield, Hyde & Stalybridge**
Dates 1888
Publisher Slater, I.
Printer Slater, I.
Place Manchester
Type GE TR
Map scale –
Library BL

REF **277**
Title **Hoylake and West Kirby Directory**
Dates 1897
Publisher Gill & Co
Printer Gill & Co
Place Hoylake
Type GE
Map scale –
Library BL

REF **278**
Title **Slater's Directory of Altrincham & Neighbourhood**
Dates 1898-1916
Publisher Slater, I.
Printer Slater, I.
Place Manchester
Type GE TR
Map scale 1:63360
Library BL has 1901-1916
holdings BOD has 1901-1912
CL has 1901
CLM has 1898-1900,1908-1912, 1915
GL has 1916
NLS has 1901-1912
ULC has 1901-1912

REF **279**
Title **The Stockport Directory**
Dates 1899,1902,1905,1907,1910
Publisher New Cheshire County News Co
Printer New Cheshire County News Co
Place Stockport
Type CM TR
Map scale 1:7200
Library BL all
holdings CLM has 1910

REF	**280**
Title	**The Wallasey Directory**
Dates	1901
Publisher	Turner & Dunnett
Printer	–
Place	Liverpool
Type	GE
Map scale	1:8000
Library	BOD
holdings	NLS
	ULC

REF	**281**
Title	**Wood's Wallasey Directory & Year Book**
Dates	1903
Publisher	Wood, P. & Co
Printer	Wood, P. & Co
Place	Liverpool
Type	GE TR
Map scale	1:6000
Library	BL

REF	**282**
Title	**Moss's Directory of Hoylake and West Kirby**
Dates	1906
Publisher	Moss, J.
Printer	Moss, J.
Place	West Kirby
Type	GE TR
Map scale	–
Library	BL
holdings	BOD
	ULC

REF	**283**
Title	**Stockport County Borough Directory and District Express Annual, Street List and Guide**
Dates	1909
Publisher	Connell & Bailey
Printer	Connell & Bailey
Place	Stockport
Type	SL
Map scale	NS
Notes	Contains pictorial map with illustrations of important buildings
Library	BOD

REF	**284**
Title	**Seed's Macclesfield and District Directory**
Dates	1910,1924
Publisher	Seed, R. & Sons
Printer	Seed, R. & Sons
Place	Preston
Type	GE TR
Map scale	–
Library	BL has 1910
holdings	MAC all

REF	**285**
Title	**Johnson's Nantwich Almanac and Directory**
Dates	1934,1936
Publisher	Johnson & Son
Printer	Johnson & Son
Place	Nantwich
Type	ST
Map scale	–
Library	CL

REF	**286**
Title	**Kelly's Directory of Chester & Neighbourhood**
Dates	1936,1938-1941
Publisher	Kelly's Directories Ltd
Printer	Kelly's Directories Ltd
Place	London
Type	GE TR
Map scale	1:10560
Library	BL all
holdings	BPH has 1936,1940
	CCL all
	CLM all
	GL all

CORNWALL

REF	**287**
Title	**Kelly's Directory of Cornwall**
Dates	1856,1873,1883,1889,1893,1897, 1902,1906,1910,1914,1919,1923, 1926,1930,1935,1939
Publisher	Kelly & Co
Printer	Kelly & Co
Place	London
Type	GE TR
Map scale	1:506880
Notes	See 11
Library	BCL all
holdings	BL has 1856-1897,1923-1939
	BOD all
	BPH has 1873,1883,1897, 1919-1926,1939
	CLB has 1939
	CLM has 1926,1939
	DEI has 1873-1923,1935,1939
	FAL has 1910-1939
	GL all
	IHR has 1906,1930
	LCL has 1939
	MLG has 1910-1939
	NLS all
	NLW has 1902,1914,1919, 1930-1939
	PLY not 1930
	RED has 1889,1893,1902,1919, 1914,1923,1935,1939
	SCL has 1930-1939
	SOG has 1856-1883,1893-1910, 1919,1930,1939
	ULC all
	WCS not 1930

REF	**288**
Title	**The Cornwall Trades' Directory**
Dates	1906
Publisher	Town and County Directories Ltd
Printer	Macdonald, W. & Co Ltd
Place	Edinburgh
Type	TR
Map scale	–
Library	RED

REF	**289**
Title	**The Cornwall Directory and Blue Book**
Dates	1930
Publisher	Liddicoat, H.
Printer	Plymouth Printers Ltd
Place	Newquay
Type	TR
Map scale	–
Library	PLY

REF	**290**
Title	**Directory and Guide for Falmouth and Penryn and their vicinities**
Dates	1864
Publisher	Warn, W.
Printer	Earle, F.H.
Place	Falmouth
Type	GE TR
Map scale	–
Library	RED

REF	**291**
Title	**Directory of Penzance and its Immediate Neighbourhood**
Dates	1864
Publisher	Cornish, W.
Printer	Cornish, W.
Place	Penzance
Type	GE TR
Map scale	–
Library	GL

REF	**292**
Title	**Venning's Postal Directory of Twenty Parishes in East Cornwall**
Dates	1881,1887,1901
Publisher	Venning, J.
Printer	Venning, J.
Place	Callington
Type	CT CM
Map scale	1:126720
Library	BL has 1887
holdings	RED all
	WCS has 1901

REF **293**
Title **A Trade and General Directory of the City of Truro**
Dates 1883,1895
Publisher Lake & Lake
Printer –
Place Truro
Type ST
Map scale 1:6864
Notes 1895 edition includes plan of proposed public park
Library RED

REF **294**
Title **The Post Office Directory of Falmouth and Neighbourhood**
Dates 1892,1895,1898,1902,1906,1909, 1912,1921,1925,1928,1933
Publisher Waters, H.R. (editor)
Printer Lake & Co
Place Falmouth
Type GE TR
Map scale 1:7200
Library BL not 1892,1902
holdings BOD has 1895
FAL all
RED has 1892-1898,1909-1925
ULC has 1895

REF **295**
Title **Carter's Illustrated Almanack, Diary & Directory for Launceston**
Dates 1938
Publisher The Launceston Printing Company
Printer The Launceston Printing Company
Place Launceston
Type GE
Map scale –
Library GL

REF **296**
Title **A Complete Guide to the English Lakes ... and a complete directory**
Dates 1855
Publisher Martineau, H. [author]
Printer Garnett, J.
Place Windermere
Type CM
Map scale 1:18103
Notes NORTON 160,161. CAR also has 2nd & 3rd editions which are undated.
Library CAR

REF **297**
Title **Morris, Harrison & Co's Commercial Directory and Gazetteer of the County of Cumberland**
Dates 1861
Publisher Morris, Harrison & Co
Printer Stafford & Co
Place Nottingham
Type CM
Map scale –
Library CAR

REF **298**
Title **Postal Directory for 1882 of Cumberland**
Dates 1882
Publisher Porter, F.
Printer –
Place London
Type CM TR
Map scale –
Library CAR

REF **299**
Title **History, Topography and Directory of West Cumberland**
Dates 1883
Publisher Bulmer, T. & Co
Printer Snape, T. & Co
Place Preston
Type TR
Map scale 1:211200
Library BPH
holdings CAR
GL
SOG

REF	**300**		REF	**304**
Title	**History, Topography and Directory of East Cumberland**		Title	**P.T. Jackson & Co's Postal Address Directory of the City of Carlisle, including adjacent villages in Cumberland and Westmorland**
Dates	1884			
Publisher	Bulmer, T. & Co			
Printer	Snape, T.			
Place	Manchester		Dates	1880
Type	CT		Publisher	Jackson, P.T.
Map scale	1:21120		Printer	Jackson, P.T.
Library	BCL		Place	Newcastle-on-Tyne
holdings	BPH		Type	GE TR
	CAR		Map scale	1:633600
	GL		Library	BL
	SOG			

			REF	**305**
REF	**301**		Title	**Arthur's Directory of Carlisle with a Map of the City & suburbs and a Directory of Stanwix**
Title	**History, Topography and Directory of Cumberland**			
Dates	1901		Dates	1880,1884
Publisher	Bulmer, T. & Co		Publisher	Moss, A.B.
Printer	Snape, T. & Co		Printer	Moss, A.B.
Place	Preston		Place	Carlisle
Type	GE TR		Type	GE TR
Map scale	–		Map scale	1:5068
Library	BCL		Library	BL all
holdings	BL		holdings	BOD has 1884
	BOD			CAR has 1880,1884
	CAR			SOG all
	GL			ULC has 1884
	HRO			
	MOR		REF	**306**
	NLS		Title	**Clarke's Business Directory of Carlisle and Wigton**

			Dates	1893
REF	**302**		Publisher	Clarke, C.
Title	**A Directory and Local Guide or Hand Book to Carlisle and Immediate Vicinity**		Printer	Clarke, C.
			Place	Glasgow
			Type	TR
Dates	1858		Map scale	–
Publisher	Scott, H.		Library	BL
Printer	Scott, H.		holdings	BOD
Place	Carlisle			NLS
Type	GE TR			
Map scale	–		REF	**307**
Library	CAR		Title	**Clarke's Business Directory of Workington, Maryport and Whitehaven**

REF	**303**			
Title	**Directory of the City of Carlisle**		Dates	1893
Dates	1870		Publisher	Clarke, C.
Publisher	Thurnam, C.		Printer	Clarke, C.
Printer	Thurnam, C.		Place	Glasgow
Place	Carlisle		Type	TR
Type	GE TR		Map scale	–
Map scale	–		Library	BL
Library	CAR		holdings	BOD
				NLS

REF **308**
Title **Middleton's Commercial Directory for Carlisle**
Dates 1893
Publisher Middleton, A.E.
Printer Middleton, A.E.
Place Workington
Type ST TR
Map scale –
Library CAR

REF **309**
Title **Post Office Carlisle Directory**
Dates 1902,1905,1907,1910,1913
Publisher Beaty, J. & Sons
Printer Beaty, J. & Sons
Place Carlisle
Type GE TR
Map scale –
Notes Continued as 311
Library BL all
holdings CAR all

REF **310**
Title **Middleton's Commercial Directory for Workington**
Dates 1904
Publisher Middleton, A.E. & Co Ltd
Printer Middleton, A.E. & Co Ltd
Place Workington
Type GE
Map scale NS
Library CAR

REF **311**
Title **Carlisle Directory**
Dates 1920,1924,1927,1931,1934,1937,
1940
Publisher Carlisle & District Chamber of Trade and Commerce
Printer Steel Brothers Ltd
Place Carlisle
Type GE TR
Map scale –
Notes Continued from 309
Library BL not 1920,1937
holdings CAR all
GL has 1937
MLG has 1927,1934,1937

DERBYSHIRE

REF **312**
Title **Kelly's Directory of Derbyshire**
Dates 1855,1864,1870,1876,1881,1888,
1891,1895,1899,1904,1908,1912,
1916,1922,1925,1928,1932,1936,
1941
Publisher Kelly & Co
Printer Kelly & Co
Place London
Type CM
Map scale 1:221760
Notes See 9. 1855-1881 entitled 'Post Office Directory of Derbyshire'.
Library BCL has 1855,1881,1891-1941
holdings BIS has 1925,1941
BL has 1855-1936
BOD not 1870,1888,1932,1941
BPH has 1876-1891,1899,1904,
1912-1922,1928,1936,1941
CLB has 1941
CLL has 1912,1916
CLM has 1870,1932-1941
DLS not 1870
GL all
IHR has 1888,1899
LCL has 1936,1941
MLG has 1855-1928
NCL has 1855
NLS not 1941
NLW has 1928,1936
SCL has 1855,1908,1925-1941
SOG has 1855,1881,1891,1916,
1922,1941
ULC has 1876,1888,1932,1936
WLV has 1932
YCL has 1941

REF	313
Title	**History, Gazetteer and Directory of the County of Derby, with the town of Burton-on-Trent**
Dates	1857
Publisher	White, F.
Printer	Ward, J.
Place	Sheffield
Type	GE TR
Map scale	1:158400
Library	BCL
holdings	BL
	CL
	DCL
	GL
	HBR
	IHR
	SCL
	SOG

REF	314
Title	**Harrison, Harrod & Co's Directory and Gazetteer of Derbyshire with Burton-on-Trent**
Dates	1860
Publisher	Harrison & Harrod
Printer	Danks, T.
Place	London
Type	CM TR
Map scale	–
Library	BL
holdings	DCL

REF	315
Title	**J.G. Harrod & Co's Postal and Commercial Directory of Derbyshire**
Dates	1870
Publisher	Harrod, J.G. & Co
Printer	–
Place	London
Type	CM
Map scale	–
Library	GL

REF	316
Title	**C.N. Wright's Directory of South Derbyshire**
Dates	1874
Publisher	Wright, C.N.
Printer	Bemrose & Sons
Place	Derby
Type	GE TR
Map scale	–
Library	DLS
holdings	GL

REF	317
Title	**Slater's Royal National Commercial Directory of Derbyshire and Burton-on-Trent**
Dates	1884
Publisher	Slater, I.
Printer	Slater, I.
Place	Manchester
Type	GE
Map scale	1:285120
Library	BL
holdings	DCL
	GL

REF	318
Title	**Bennett's Business Directory for Derbyshire**
Dates	1892,1899
Publisher	Bennett & Co
Printer	Bennett & Co
Place	Birmingham
Type	TR
Map scale	–
Library	DLS

REF	319
Title	**History, Topography and Directory of Derbyshire**
Dates	1895
Publisher	Bulmer, T.
Printer	Snape, T. & Co
Place	Preston
Type	CM TR
Map scale	1:253440
Library	BL
holdings	BOD
	CLM
	DCL
	NLS
	SCL
	SOG

REF	**320**
Title	**Derbyshire Directory and Buyer's Guide**
Dates	1923,1928,1929,1931,1933,1935, 1936
Publisher	Cope, E.F. & Co
Printer	Cope, E.F. & Co
Place	Walsall
Type	TR
Map scale	–
Library	DLS

REF	**321**
Title	**The History and Directory of the Borough of Derby**
Dates	1850
Publisher	Rowbottom, W.
Printer	Rowbottom, W.
Place	Derby
Type	CM TR
Map scale	–
Notes	NORTON 172. This edition is identical to the 1849 edition with some additions. Compiled by S. Glover.
Library	DLS

REF	**322**
Title	**Freebody's Directory of the Towns of Derby, Chesterfield, Alfreton, Buxton, Bakewell, Matlock, Wirksworth, Ashbourn, Belper, Melbourn, Ripley, Burton-upon-Trent &c &c**
Dates	1852
Publisher	Richardson & Son
Printer	–
Place	Derby
Type	GE TR
Map scale	–
Notes	NORTON 168
Library	DLS
holdings	GL

REF	**323**
Title	**Glover's Directory of the Borough of Derby**
Dates	1858
Publisher	Glover, S.
Printer	Bemrose, W. & Sons
Place	Derby
Type	CM TR
Map scale	1:10560
Notes	Map scale approx.
Library	GL

REF	**324**
Title	**Drake's Commercial Directory of the Borough of Derby with the towns of Alfreton, Belper, Chesterfield & Wirksworth**
Dates	1862
Publisher	Drake, E.S.
Printer	Drake, E.S.
Place	Sheffield
Type	CM TR
Map scale	–
Library	DLS

REF	**325**
Title	**History, Gazetteer and Directory of the Borough of Derby and of the Town and County of the Town of Nottingham**
Dates	1865
Publisher	White, F. & Co
Printer	Corbitt, C.
Place	Sheffield
Type	TR
Map scale	–
Library	NCL

REF	**326**
Title	**Wright's Directory of Derby and surrounding places**
Dates	1871,1874
Publisher	Bemrose & Sons
Printer	Bemrose & Sons
Place	Derby
Type	GE TR
Map scale	–
Notes	BL 1874 edition has several pages missing
Library	BL all
holdings	DCL has 1871

REF	**327**
Title	**Wilkins & Ellis New Borough of Derby Directory**
Dates	1878
Publisher	Wilkins & Ellis
Printer	Wilkins & Ellis
Place	Derby
Type	GE TR
Map scale	–
Library	GL

REF	328
Title	**Directory of Derby, Belper, Burton & Neighbourhood**
Dates	1880
Publisher	Stevens, G.
Printer	Stevens, G.
Place	London
Type	CM TR
Map scale	1:506880
Library	BL
holdings	DLS

REF	329
Title	**Kelly's Directory of Derby and suburbs**
Dates	1886
Publisher	Kelly & Co
Printer	Kelly & Co
Place	London
Type	GE TR
Map scale	–
Library	BL
holdings	BOD
	DLS
	GL
	NLS
	ULC

REF	330
Title	**Directory of Derby and Neighbourhood**
Dates	1893
Publisher	Stevens, G.
Printer	Stevens, G.
Place	London
Type	GE TR
Map scale	1:506880
Library	BL
holdings	BOD
	DLS
	NLS
	ULC

REF	331
Title	**Derby and District Directory**
Dates	1896,1901,1903,1910,1915,1921
Publisher	Cook, W.J.
Printer	Bemrose & Sons Ltd
Place	Derby
Type	GE TR
Map scale	NS
Library	BL all
holdings	BOD has 1901,1903
	DLS has 1901,1903
	GL has 1901,1903
	NLS has 1901,1903
	SOG has 1903
	ULC has 1901,1903

REF	332
Title	**Kelly's Directory of Derby and District**
Dates	1899
Publisher	Kelly's Directories Ltd
Printer	Kelly's Directories Ltd
Place	London
Type	GE TR
Map scale	1:4800
Library	BL

REF	333
Title	**Jackson's Alfreton and District Year Book with complete Directories of Alfreton, Somercotes and South Normanton**
Dates	1902
Publisher	Jackson, J.N.
Printer	Jackson, J.N.
Place	Alfreton
Type	ST
Map scale	–
Library	BOD

REF	334
Title	**Derby and District Trades Directory**
Dates	1903,1912,1930
Publisher	Town and County Directories Ltd
Printer	Macdonald, W.
Place	Edinburgh
Type	TR
Map scale	–
Notes	CLD also has one undated edition (c. 1900?)
Library	DLS

REF	**335**
Title	**The Wirksworth Directory**
Dates	1908
Publisher	Marsden, G. & Son
Printer	–
Place	Wirksworth
Type	CT
Map scale	–
Library	DLS

REF	**336**
Title	**General and Commercial Directory of Derby and District**
Dates	1910,1915,1921
Publisher	Hobson & Son
Printer	Hobson & Son
Place	Derby
Type	GE TR
Map scale	–
Library	DLS

REF	**337**
Title	**Chesterfield Year Book and Business Directory**
Dates	1913-1922
Publisher	Lee, G.
Printer	Broad Oaks Press
Place	Chesterfield
Type	ST TR
Map scale	–
Library	DLS

REF	**338**
Title	**Norman's Buxton & District Directory**
Dates	1932
Publisher	Norman's Directories
Printer	Norman's Directories
Place	Manchester
Type	GE TR
Map scale	–
Library	DLS

REF	**339**
Title	**The Derby County Borough Directory**
Dates	1935
Publisher	Whipple, R.D. Son & Martin Ltd
Printer	Whipple, R.D. Son & Martin Ltd
Place	Derby
Type	GE TR
Map scale	–
Library	BOD
holdings	CLM
	DCL
	GL

REF	**340**
Title	**Kelly's Directory of Buxton, Chapel-en-le-Frith & Neighbourhood**
Dates	1937,1939,1942
Publisher	Kelly's Directories Ltd
Printer	Kelly's Directories Ltd
Place	London
Type	GE TR
Map scale	1:10560
Notes	Map scale approx.
Library	BL all
holdings	CLM all
	DCL has 1937,1942
	GL all

DEVON

REF **341**
Title **History, Gazetteer and Directory of the County of Devon**
Dates 1850,1878,1890
Publisher White, W.
Printer Spottiswoode
Place Sheffield
Type GE TR
Map scale —
Notes NORTON 174. David & Charles have reprinted the 1850 edition.
Library BCL has 1850 (D & C reprint)
holdings BL all
BIS has 1850
BOD not 1880
BPH has 1850
DEI has 1878
GL not 1890
IHR has 1850
NLS has 1878
PLY all
SOG has 1850,1878
ULC all
WCS all

REF **342**
Title **Kelly's Directory of Devonshire**
Dates 1856,1866,1873,1879,1883,1889, 1893,1897,1902,1906,1910,1914, 1919,1923,1926,1930,1935,1939
Publisher Kelly & Co
Printer Kelly & Co
Place London
Type GE TR
Map scale 1:12672
Notes 1856-1873 entitled 'Post Office Directory of Devonshire'. See 11.
Library BCL has 1893-1939
holdings BIS has 1919,1926,1930-1939
BL has 1856-1897,1923-1939
BOD all
BPH has 1866-1883,1897,1906, 1919-1930
CLB has 1939
CLM has 1939
DEI has 1873-1939
FAL has 1926,1939
GL all
IHR has 1856,1883,1906,1926
LCL has 1935,1939
MLG has 1910-1939
NLS all
NLW has 1902,1914,1919, 1930-1939
PLY not 1866,1930
RED has 1873-1883,1897,1906, 1930
SCL has 1930-1939
SOG has 1856-1883,1893,1897, 1906,1919,1930-1939
TLH has 1866
ULC all
WCS not 1879

REF **343**
Title **M. Billing's Directory and Gazetteer of the County of Devon**
Dates 1857
Publisher Billing, M.
Printer Billing, M.
Place Birmingham
Type GE TR
Map scale —
Library BL
holdings GL
DEI
PLY
SOG
WCS

REF **344**
Title **Smith & Co's Exeter, Plymouth and Devon Directory**
Dates 1866
Publisher Smith & Co
Printer Welch, J.
Place London
Type CT CM
Map scale –
Library PLY

REF **345**
Title **Morris and Co's Directory and Gazetteer of Devon**
Dates 1870
Publisher Morris & Co
Printer –
Place Nottingham
Type GE TR
Map scale –
Library GL
holdings PLY
WCS

REF **346**
Title **Plymouth and District Trades' Directory**
Dates 1900,1903,1906,1912,1915,1926
Publisher Town and County Directories Ltd
Printer Macdonald, W. & Co Ltd
Place Edinburgh
Type TR
Map scale –
Notes 1906 onwards entitled 'The Devonshire Trades' Directory'. 1903 volume covers Devon and Plymouth.
Library PLY has 1900,1903
holdings WCS not 1900

REF **347**
Title **The Exeter Journal & Almanack**
Dates 1850,1851
Publisher Trewman, R.J. & Co
Printer Trewman, R.J. & Co
Place Exeter
Type CM
Map scale –
Notes See 349. NORTON 200,201.
Library WCS

REF **348**
Title **A Directory of Plymouth, Devonport, Stonehouse, Stoke and Moricetown**
Dates 1852
Publisher Brendon, F.
Printer Brendon, F.
Place Plymouth
Type GE TR
Map scale –
Notes NORTON 224. Cont'd as 351.
Library GL
holdings PLY
WCS

REF **349**
Title **West of England and Trewman's Exeter Pocket Journal**
Dates 1853,1856-1861,1864-1884
Publisher Besley, H.
Printer Besley, H.
Place Exeter
Type CM
Map scale –
Notes NORTON 211 (1853). CM section for Exeter. Later editions also contain PR lists for Cornwall, Devon & sometimes Dorset & Somerset. Cont'd as 357.
Library DEI not 1853
holdings WCS has 1853,1860,1861,1863, 1865-1875,1877

REF **350**
Title **M. Billing's Directory and Gazetteer of Plymouth, Stonehouse and Devonport**
Dates 1857
Publisher Billing, M.
Printer Billing, M.
Place Birmingham
Type CM TR
Map scale –
Library PLY

REF **351**
Title **Directory of Plymouth, Stonehouse, Devonport, Stoke and Morice Town**
Dates 1862,1864,1867
Publisher Elvins, J.W.
Printer Brendon, W.
Place Plymouth
Type GE TR
Map scale −
Notes 1867 edition entitled 'Post Office Directory of Plymouth, Stonehouse, Devonport, Stoke and Morice Town'. Cont'd from 348.
Library GL has 1862
holdings IHR has 1862
PLY all
WCS all

REF **352**
Title **J.W. Hill & Co's Historical and Business Directory of Torquay**
Dates 1869
Publisher Hill, J.W. & Co
Printer Hill, J.W. & Co
Place Torquay
Type CT CM
Map scale −
Library GL
holdings WCS

REF **353**
Title **The Three Towns' Directory for Plymouth, Devonport and Stonehouse**
Dates 1873,1875,1877
Publisher Thorne, E.
Printer Thorne, E.
Place Plymouth
Type GE TR
Map scale −
Notes 1877 published & printed by W.J. Trythall
Library PLY has 1873,1877
holdings WCS has 1875,1877

REF **354**
Title **Handbook and Directory for Exeter and its Neighbourhood**
Dates 1874
Publisher Mortimer, H.
Printer Mortimer, H.
Place Exeter
Type GE TR
Map scale −
Library BOD
holdings NLS
WCS

REF **355**
Title **A Directory of the Parish of Plympton St Mary**
Dates 1875
Publisher Birmingham, W.
Printer −
Place Plymouth
Type ST
Map scale −
Library WCS

REF **356**
Title **Eyre Brothers' Post Office Plymouth and Devonport and District Directory**
Dates 1880,1882,1885,1888,1890,1893, 1895-1904
Publisher Eyre Bros.
Printer Eyre Bros.
Place London
Type GE TR
Map scale 1:10560
Notes Cont'd as 363.
Library BL not 1880,1882,1888,
holdings 1890-1897,1899,1901,1903
holdings BOD has 1880-1885,1890,1893, 1901
NLS has 1880,1882,1885,1890, 1896,1898
PLY all
ULC has 1880,1882,1885,1890, 1896,1898,1901
WCS not 1880,1899

REF	**357**
Title	**The Post Office Directory of Exeter and suburbs**
Dates	1881-1884,1894,1896-1950
Publisher	Besley, H. & Son
Printer	Besley, H. & Son
Place	Exeter
Type	GE
Map scale	1:380160
Notes	Continued from 349
Library	BL not 1878,1887-1894,1897,
holdings	1899,1900,1947
	BOD has 1881,1883,1896,1897,
	1899-1950
	DEI has 1878,1881,1883,
	1887-1893,1896,1897,
	1901-1905,1907-1939,
	1941-1944,1946-1950
	GL has 1883,1936-1938,
	1945-1950
	MLG has 1936,1941,1944,1946,
	1948,1950
	NLS has 1896-1899,1901,
	1903-1905,1907-1916,
	1918-1928,1930-1950
	ULC has 1881,1883,1896
	WCS has 1881,1884,1885,1894,
	1906,1909-1950

REF	**358**
Title	**The Tiverton and District Directory**
Dates	1885,1894,1900,1909,1912,1920, 1934,1937
Publisher	Tiverton Gazette
Printer	Gregory, Son & Tozer
Place	Tiverton
Type	CM TR
Map scale	1:158400
Library	BL has 1885
holdings	GL has 1885
	WCS not 1885

REF	**359**
Title	**Torquay, Newton Abbot and District Directory**
Dates	1887
Publisher	Wells & Manton
Printer	–
Place	Shrewsbury
Type	CM TR
Map scale	1:332640
Library	BL
holdings	NLS
	ULC

REF	**360**
Title	**Weeks' Three Towns ABC Directory (Plymouth, Devonport, Saltash)**
Dates	1899
Publisher	Weeks, S.J.
Printer	Weeks, S.J.
Place	Plymouth
Type	GE TR
Map scale	NS
Library	BL
holdings	PLY

REF	**361**
Title	**Totnes District Directory and Almanack**
Dates	1900,1949
Publisher	Mortimer Bros
Printer	–
Place	Totnes
Type	ST TR
Map scale	–
Library	WCS

REF	**362**
Title	**Wheaton's Alphabetical Directory of Exeter, St Thomas and Heavitree**
Dates	1905
Publisher	Wheaton, A. & Co
Printer	Wheaton, A. & Co
Place	Exeter
Type	ST
Map scale	–
Library	WCS

REF	**363**
Title	**The Post Office Directory of Plymouth, Devonport and Stonehouse**
Dates	1905-1915,1920,1923,1928,1932
Publisher	Swiss & Co
Printer	Swiss & Co
Place	Devonport
Type	GE TR
Map scale	1:10560
Notes	Cont'd from 356. 1915 onwards as 'The Post Office Directory of Plymouth & District'. Cont'd as 373.
Library	BL has 1905,1906,1932
holdings	BOD has 1905
	GL has 1932
	NLS has 1905
	PLY all
	SOG has 1909
	ULC has 1905

[109]

REF	364
Title	**Dartmouth and Kingswear Directory**
Dates	1908
Publisher	Evening Post
Printer	Evening Post
Place	Exeter
Type	GE TR
Map scale	–
Library	BOD
holdings	GL

REF	365
Title	**Torbay Household & Business Directory**
Dates	1910
Publisher	McKenzie, W.J.
Printer	McKenzie, W.J.
Place	Torquay
Type	GE
Map scale	–
Notes	Covers Torquay, Paignton & Brixham
Library	WCS

REF	366
Title	**Marshman's Directory of Salcombe**
Dates	1912-1917
Publisher	Marshman, E.P.
Printer	Marshman, E.P.
Place	Salcombe
Type	GE
Map scale	–
Library	BL all
holdings	BOD has 1912-1914

REF	367
Title	**Marshman's Directory of Kingsbridge**
Dates	1914-1917
Publisher	Marshman, E.P.
Printer	Marshman, E.P.
Place	Kingsbridge
Type	GE
Map scale	–
Library	BL

REF	368
Title	**Tavistock Almanack and Directory**
Dates	1916-1919
Publisher	Jolliffe & Son
Printer	Jolliffe & Son
Place	Tavistock
Type	CM
Map scale	–
Library	BL all
holdings	GL has 1918
	WCS has 1918

REF	369
Title	**Kelly's Directory of Torquay & Paignton**
Dates	1928,1929,1931,1933,1935,1937, 1939,1941,1946,1948
Publisher	Kelly's Directories Ltd
Printer	Kelly's Directories Ltd
Place	London
Type	GE TR
Map scale	–
Library	BL all
holdings	GL all
	NLW has 1948
	SOG has 1939
	WCS has 1935

REF	370
Title	**The Plymouth and District Directory**
Dates	1931
Publisher	Liddicott, E.
Printer	Plymouth Printers Ltd
Place	Plymouth
Type	TR
Map scale	–
Library	WCS

REF	371
Title	**Kelly's Directory of Barnstaple & Neighbourhood**
Dates	1931,1933,1935,1937,1939,1941
Publisher	Kelly's Directories Ltd
Printer	Kelly's Directories Ltd
Place	London
Type	GE TR
Map scale	1:253440
Library	BL all
holdings	GL all
	WCS has 1935

REF	**372**
Title	**Kelly's Directory of Newton Abbot**
Dates	1935,1937,1939,1941
Publisher	Kelly's Directories Ltd
Printer	Kelly's Directories Ltd
Place	London
Type	GE TR
Map scale	1:10560
Library	BL all
holdings	GL all
	WCS has 1939

REF	**373**
Title	**Kelly's Post Office Directory of Plymouth and District**
Dates	1935,1937-1940
Publisher	Kelly's Directories Ltd
Printer	Kelly's Directories Ltd
Place	London
Type	GE TR
Map scale	–
Notes	Cont'd from 363
Library	BL all
holdings	GL all
	PLY all
	WCS has 1939

REF	**374**
Title	**Exmouth Chronicle Directory and Gazetteer for Exmouth**
Dates	1936,1938,1940,1947,1948,1950
Publisher	Delderfield, W.J. & Sons
Printer	Delderfield, W.J. & Sons
Place	Exmouth
Type	GE TR
Map scale	1:10560
Library	BL all
holdings	GL not 1938,1940
	NLS has 1947-1950
	NLW has 1948,1950
	ULC has 1947,1948
	WCS has 1947,1948,1950

REF	**375**
Title	**Dawlish Directory**
Dates	1937
Publisher	Cornelius & Morey
Printer	Cornelius & Morey
Place	Dawlish
Type	ST
Map scale	–
Library	GL

REF	**376**
Title	**Gazette North Devon Directory and Year Book**
Dates	1937
Publisher	Bideford Gazette Ltd
Printer	Bideford Gazette Ltd
Place	Bideford
Type	CT
Map scale	–
Library	DEI
holdings	WCS

REF	**377**
Title	**Honiton, Ottery St Mary and District Directory**
Dates	1937
Publisher	East Devon County Press
Printer	East Devon County Press
Place	Honiton
Type	CM
Map scale	–
Library	GL
holdings	WCS

REF	**378**
Title	**Seaton & District Directory**
Dates	1938
Publisher	Three Counties Directories Ltd
Printer	'?'
Place	'?'
Type	CT
Map scale	–
Notes	See notes to 379.
Library	GL

REF	**379**
Title	**Sidmouth & District Directory**
Dates	1938
Publisher	Three Counties Directories Ltd
Printer	'?'
Place	'?'
Type	GE
Map scale	–
Notes	Printer & place of publication not stated. The directory was published in conjunction with The East Devon County Press.
Library	GL

REF **380**
Title **The Ilfracombe, Berry Narbor, Combe Martin, Mortehoe, Woolacombe, West Down and Lee Directory and Year Book**
Dates 1938,1948,1949
Publisher The Chronicle Press (Ilfracombe) Ltd
Printer The Chronicle Press (Ilfracombe) Ltd
Place Ilfracombe
Type GE
Map scale –
Library GL

REF **381**
Title **Street Directory and Gazetteer for Tiverton**
Dates 1947
Publisher Delderfield, W.J. & Sons Ltd
Printer Delderfield, W.J. & Sons Ltd
Place Exmouth
Type GE
Map scale –
Library CLM
holdings GL
NLS
ULC
WCS

REF **382**
Title **Street Directory and Gazetteer for Sidmouth, Sidbury, Sidford and District**
Dates 1947,1949
Publisher Delderfield, W.J. & Sons Ltd
Printer Delderfield, W.J. & Sons Ltd
Place Exmouth
Type GE
Map scale –
Library CLM has 1947
holdings GL all
NLS all
NLW all
ULC has 1949
WCS HAS 1949

REF **383**
Title **The Budleigh Salterton Street Directory and Gazetteer**
Dates 1947,1949,1950
Publisher The Raleigh Press
Printer The Raleigh Press
Place Exmouth
Type GE TR
Map scale 1:10560
Library BL all
holdings BOD not 1947
GL all
NLS not 1947
NLW has 1949,1950
ULC has 1949
WCS all

DORSET

REF **384**
Title **Hunt & Co's Directory of Dorsetshire with part of Hants & Wilts**
Dates 1851
Publisher Hunt, E. & Co
Printer Gardiner, B.W.
Place London
Type GE TR
Map scale –
Notes NORTON 229
Library BL
holdings DCL
GL
IHR
LLB
SOG

REF	**385**
Title	**Kelly's Directory of Dorsetshire**
Dates	1855,1859,1867,1875,1880,1885, 1890,1895,1899,1903,1907,1911, 1915,1920,1923,1927,1931,1935, 1939
Publisher	Kelly & Co
Printer	Kelly & Co
Place	London
Type	GE TR
Map scale	1:253440
Notes	See 8
Library holdings	BCL has 1875,1890-1939
	BIS has 1899,1915,1920,1927, 1931,1939
	BL has 1855-1899,1931-1939
	BOD not 1859,1875
	BPH has 1927,1939
	CHI has 1875
	CLE has 1880
	CLM has 1923,1939
	CLS has 1923
	DCL all
	DEI has 1931,1939
	GL not 1939
	HRO has 1859,1875,1880,1890, 1895,1903,1907,1915,1920, 1931-1939
	IHR has 1880,1903,1923,1939
	LLB has 1880-1903,1911,1915, 1923-1939
	MLG has 1907-1927
	NEW has 1939
	NLS all
	NLW has 1920,1928-1939
	PCL 1895,1911,1931
	SAL has 1875-1899,1911,1915, 1927-1939
	SCC 1885,1911-1923,1939
	SCL has 1927-1939
	SOG has 1859,1867,1895,1899, 1907,1915,1923,1931,1939
	SWI has 1890,1895,1903,1915, 1923,1927,1939
	TRW has 1867,1927
	ULC all
	WCS has 1880,1895,1899, 1915-1939
	WIN has 1880-1890
	WRO has 1859,1867,1885,1899, 1911,1915,1923,1931,1939

REF	**386**
Title	**J.G. Harrod and Co's Postal and Commercial Directory of Dorsetshire**
Dates	1865
Publisher	Harrod, J.G. & Co
Printer	Danks, T.
Place	London
Type	CM
Map scale	–
Notes	X copy in DCL
Library holdings	DCL
	SAL Includes WILT

REF	**387**
Title	**The Weymouth Directory, Visitor's Arrival List and General Advertiser**
Dates	1870
Publisher	Sherren, J. (?)
Printer	–
Place	Weymouth
Type	ST TR
Map scale	–
Notes	X copy in Dorset Record Office
Library	DOR

REF	**388**
Title	**Butcher, Cole & Co's South Dorsetshire Towns Directory**
Dates	1874
Publisher	Butcher, Cole & Co
Printer	–
Place	London
Type	GE
Map scale	1:443520
Library holdings	DCL
	GL

REF	**389**
Title	**The Blandford Directory and Local Handbook**
Dates	1882
Publisher	'?'
Printer	'?'
Place	Blandford (?)
Type	ST
Map scale	–
Notes	X copy. Only part of T/P survives, no details of publisher etc.
Library	DCL

REF	390
Title	**Henry Ling's Dorchester and District Directory and Almanack**
Dates	1893,1934-1937
Publisher	Ling, H.
Printer	Ling, H.
Place	Dorchester
Type	GE
Map scale	NS
Notes	1893 edition entitled 'Henry Ling's Dorchester Illustrated Almanack'
Library	DCL

REF	391
Title	**Derham's Blandford Directory and Almanack**
Dates	1906
Publisher	Derham, E.
Printer	–
Place	Blandford
Type	GE
Map scale	–
Notes	X copy in DCL
Library	DCL

REF	392
Title	**The Blandford Directory**
Dates	1906
Publisher	-
Printer	–
Place	Blandford (?)
Type	GE
Map scale	–
Notes	Although this is a complete edition, there are no details of publisher or place of publication. It may even be a later edition of 389 (?).
Library	WCS

REF	393
Title	**Wheelers' Weymouth Directory**
Dates	1906
Publisher	Wheelers
Printer	Wheelers
Place	Weymouth
Type	GE
Map scale	–
Notes	Date is uncertain
Library	SOG

REF	394
Title	**The Swanage Directory and Almanack**
Dates	1911
Publisher	Mate, S.J.
Printer	Mate, S.J.
Place	Bournemouth
Type	GE TR
Map scale	–
Library	DCL

REF	395
Title	**Sherrens' Directory of Weymouth**
Dates	1923
Publisher	Sherren & Son
Printer	Sherren & Son
Place	Weymouth
Type	GE
Map scale	–
Library	DCL

REF	396
Title	**Weymouth Handbook and Directory**
Dates	1926-1929
Publisher	The Dorset Publishing Co
Printer	The Dorset Publishing Co
Place	Weymouth
Type	GE
Map scale	–
Library	BL all
holdings	DCL has 1929

REF	397
Title	**Kelly's Directory of Weymouth & Portland**
Dates	1929,1930,1932,1934,1936,1938, 1940,1948,1950
Publisher	Kelly's Directories Ltd
Printer	Kelly's Directories Ltd
Place	London
Type	GE TR
Map scale	1:253440
Library	BL all
holdings	DCL not 1938,1950
	GL not 1950
	WCS has 1948

REF **398**
Title **Swanage Official Directory**
Dates 1934
Publisher The Home Publishing Company
Printer –
Place London
Type GE TR
Map scale –
Library DCL
holdings GL

COUNTY DURHAM

REF **399**
Title **Hagar and Co's Directory of the County of Durham**
Dates 1851
Publisher Hagar & Co
Printer Stevenson & Co
Place Nottingham
Type TR
Map scale –
Notes NORTON 235
Library DAR
holdings DUR
GL

REF **400**
Title **History, Topography and Directory of the County Palatine of Durham**
Dates 1856,1894
Publisher Whellan, W.
Printer Galt, Kerrush & Gent
Place London
Type CM
Map scale 1:190080
Library BL all
holdings CLN all
DAR all
DUR all
GL all
MID all
MOR has 1894
SOG has 1856

REF **401**
Title **Kelly's Directory of Durham**
Dates 1858,1873,1879,1890,1894,1897,
1902,1906,1910,1914,1921,1925,
1929,1934,1938
Publisher Kelly & Co
Printer Kelly & Co
Place London
Type GE TR
Map scale 1:221760
Notes See 12 (1858-1906) & 23 (1910-
1938)
Library BCL has 1890-1938
holdings BL not 1906
BOD all
BPH has 1873,1879,1904,1906,
1914-1929,1938
CAR has 1894,1906
CLB has 1938
CLE has 1938
CLM has 1910,1921,1925
CLN not 1897
DAR has 1858,1879-1938
DUR not 1873,1894,1906
GL not 1873
IHR has 1910,1925
MID has 1902,1914,1938
MLG has 1894-1925,1934
MOR has 1873,1879,1897,1910,
1914,1921,1929,1938
NLS not 1879
NLW has 1914,1929-1938
SCL has 1929-1938
SOG has 1873,1879,1890,1910,
1921,1938
ULC not 1894
YCL has 1934

REF **402**
Title **Morris, Harrison and Co's Commercial Directory and Gazetteer of the County of Durham including Newcastle-upon-Tyne**
Dates 1861
Publisher Morris, Harrison & Co
Printer Stafford & Co
Place Nottingham
Type CM
Map scale –
Library DAR

REF	**403**
Title	**Directory and Topography of the County of Durham with Newcastle-upon-Tyne**
Dates	1865
Publisher	Whellan, T. & Co
Printer	Harkness, J.
Place	Preston
Type	CM TR
Map scale	–
Library holdings	DAR DUR GL MID MOR

REF	**404**
Title	**The Durham Directory and Almanack**
Dates	1850-1867,1869,1873-1880, 1882-1884,1887,1888,1891-1939
Publisher	Walker, G.
Printer	Walker, G.
Place	Durham
Type	GE TR
Map scale	–
Notes	NORTON 241-246 (1850-1855). 1892-1896 published by G.M. Watt, 1899 & after published by T. Caldcleugh.
Library holdings	BL has 1851,1853,1857-1864, 1866,1874,1887,1898,1901,1902, 1904-1939 BOD has 1861,1887 CLN has 1850,1852-1854,1857, 1858,1860,1863-1865,1869, 1883,1887,1893-1897, 1899-1916 DUR has 1850,1852-1856,1860, 1861,1867,1873-1880, 1882-1884,1887,1892-1894, 1896,1899,1915 GL has 1851,1853,1857-1864, 1866-1874 SOG has 1865 ULC has 1861,1888,1891

REF	**405**
Title	**Ward's North of England Directory**
Dates	1851,1853-1855,1857,1859,1861
Publisher	Ward, R. & Sons
Printer	Ward, R. & Sons
Place	Newcastle-on-Tyne
Type	CM TR
Map scale	–
Notes	NORTON 577 (1851), 579-581 (1853-1855). Covers major towns in Northumberland & Durham.
Library holdings	CAR has 1851 CLN all DAR has 1851,1859 GL not 1854 MID has 1861

REF	**406**
Title	**Barnes's Alphabetical Directory of Sunderland and Neighbourhood**
Dates	1865
Publisher	Barnes, J.
Printer	Barnes, J.
Place	London
Type	CM
Map scale	–
Library	IHR

REF	**407**
Title	**Directory of Stockton, Middlesborough and Hartlepool**
Dates	1880
Publisher	Porter, F.
Printer	–
Place	London
Type	CM TR
Map scale	1:380160
Library	MCL

REF	**408**
Title	**Directory of Bishop Auckland, Redcar, Darlington, Stockton, Middlesborough, Hartlepool and surrounding villages**
Dates	1881
Publisher	Porter, F.
Printer	–
Place	London
Type	CM
Map scale	1:380160
Notes	DAR edition entitled 'Directory of Stockton, Middlesborough, Hartlepool, Darlington and surrounding villages'
Library holdings	DAR GL

REF	**409**
Title	**Kelly's Directory of South Shields and Jarrow-on-Tyne**
Dates	1885
Publisher	Kelly & Co
Printer	Kelly & Co
Place	London
Type	GE TR
Map scale	–
Library holdings	BL BOD NLS ULC

REF	**410**
Title	**Kelly's Directory of Hartlepool and West Hartlepool**
Dates	1885,1887
Publisher	Kelly & Co
Printer	Kelly & Co
Place	London
Type	GE TR
Map scale	–
Library holdings	BL not 1887 BOD all CLN all DAR has 1885 NLS all ULC all

REF	**411**
Title	**Kelly's Directory of Stockton-on-Tees, Darlington and suburbs**
Dates	1885,1887
Publisher	Kelly & Co
Printer	Kelly & Co
Place	London
Type	GE TR
Map scale	–
Library holdings	BL has 1885 BOD all CLN all DAR all GL has 1887 NLS all ULC all

REF	**412**
Title	**Kelly's Directory of Gateshead and suburbs**
Dates	1886
Publisher	Kelly & Co
Printer	Kelly & Co
Place	London
Type	GE TR
Map scale	–
Library holdings	BL BOD NLS ULC

REF	**413**
Title	**Kelly's Directory of Sunderland and suburbs**
Dates	1886,1887
Publisher	Kelly & Co
Printer	Kelly & co
Place	London
Type	GE TR
Map scale	–
Library holdings	BL has 1886 BOD has 1886 CLN all DAR has 1886 NLS has 1886 ULC has 1886

REF   **414**
Title   **Ward's Directory of Darlington, Hartlepool, West Hartlepool, Middlesborough, Stockton and Thornaby**
Dates   1896,1898,1900,1902,1904,1906, 1908,1910,1912,1914,1917,1921, 1924,1927,1929,1931,1933,1935
Publisher   Ward, R.
Printer   Ward, R.
Place   Newcastle-on-Tyne
Type   GE TR
Map scale   —
Library   BL all
holdings   CLN all
            DAR all
            DUR has 1935
            GL has 1902,1912,1914,1935
            MID has 1896-1924,1929-1933

REF   **415**
Title   **Stockton and District Directory**
Dates   1899
Publisher   Cook, W.J. & Co
Printer   —
Place   Derby
Type   GE TR
Map scale   —
Library   GL

REF   **416**
Title   **Darlington and District Directory**
Dates   1899,1901
Publisher   Cook, W.J. & Co
Printer   Bailey & Co
Place   Hull
Type   GE TR
Map scale   —
Library   BL has 1901
holdings   BOD has 1901
            DAR all
            NLS has 1901
            ULC has 1901

REF   **417**
Title   **Sunderland, Durham and Middlesborough District Trades' Directory**
Dates   1901
Publisher   Town and County Directories Ltd
Printer   Macdonald, W.
Place   Edinburgh
Type   TR
Map scale   —
Notes   See 175
Library   DAR

REF   **418**
Title   **Ward's Directory of Sunderland, Wallsend, Gosforth, Newcastle-on-Tyne, Gateshead**
Dates   1918,1921,1923,1925,1927,1929, 1931,1933,1935,1937,1939
Publisher   Ward, R. & Sons Ltd
Printer   Ward, R. & Sons Ltd
Place   Newcastle-on-Tyne
Type   GE TR
Map scale   NS
Library   BL has 1921-1939
holdings   BPH has 1923-1939
            CLM has 1939
            CLN all
            DAR has 1931-1935,1939
            DUR has 1937,1939
            GL has 1937,1939
            MLG has 1921-1939
            MOR has 1925,1927

REF   **419**
Title   **Darlington Year Book and Business Directory**
Dates   1921-1931,1933-1938,1947-1950
Publisher   North of England Newspaper Co
Printer   North of England Newspaper Co
Place   Darlington
Type   ST TR
Map scale   —
Library   CLN has 1950
holdings   DAR not 1937,1939
            GL has 1936,1937,1949

REF **420**
Title **Durham City Year Book,**
Business Directory and Diary
Dates 1922,1925-1939
Publisher The Durham County Advertiser
& General Printing Co
Printer The Durham County Advertiser
& General Printing Co
Place Durham
Type GE TR
Map scale –
Library CLN not 1922
holdings DUR not 1925-1930
GL has 1936-1938

REF **421**
Title **Sunderland & District including**
Alphabetical Trade Guide for
Ryhope, Silksworth, East Boldon,
Cleadon and Whitburn
Dates 1949
Publisher Local Trades Directories
Printer The Coronation Press
Place Durham
Type TR
Map scale –
Library DUR

ESSEX

REF **422**
Title **Kelly's Directory of Essex**
Dates 1851,1855,1859,1862,1866,1870,
1874,1878,1882,1886,1890,1895,
1899,1902,1906,1908,1910,1912,
1914,1917,1922,1926,1929,1933,
1937
Publisher Kelly & Co
Printer Kelly & Co
Place London
Type GE TR
Map scale 1:105600
Notes See 3 (1851-1866); 16 (1870-1878);
18 (1882-1937). The 1866 edition
contained errors and another version
was published in 1867, some
libraries hold this edition.
Library BCL has 1878,1890-1937
holdings BED has 1851
BIS has 1922,1937
BL not 1851,1926
BOD not 1855,1874,1917
BPH has 1866,1874,1886,1895,
1906,1917-1926,1929,1937
CHE not 1882; has 1888
edition of SUFF & ESSX
CLM has 1859,1937
COL not 1851,1874. Also has
1888,1892,1903,1925
editions published with
other counties.
GL not 1910
GLH not 1851,1929
HLS has 1878,1886,1895,1926,
1929
IHR has 1890,1906,1937
KCL has 1859,1866
LCL has 1937
MLG not 1851-1866,1878-1895
NLS all
NLW has 1912,1914,1929,1937
NOR has 1926
SCL has 1926,1933,1937
SOG has 1851-1862,1874,1882,
1890,1899,1908,1926
SRI has 1862,1912,1929,1937.
Also 1900,1904 editions
NORF,SUFF,ESSX
ULC all
YCL has 1937

REF	**423**		REF	**426**
Title	**History, Gazetteer and Directory of the County of Essex**		Title	**Benham's Colchester & County Almanac: Complete Street and ABC Directory for Colchester**
Dates	1863		Dates	1882,1883,1885-1900,1904-1911, 1913-1950
Publisher	White, W.		Publisher	Benham & Company
Printer	Leader, R. & Sons		Printer	Benham & Company
Place	Sheffield		Place	Colchester
Type	GE TR		Type	GE
Map scale	1:158400		Map scale	NS
Library	BL		Notes	Earlier editions entitled 'Benham's Almanack and Directory'
holdings	CHE		Library	BOD has 1938,1939
	COL		holdings	COL all
	GL			GL has 1938,1945-1950
	GLH			NLS has 1937,1938
	IHR			NLW has 1938,1947
	ULC			

REF	**424**		REF	**427**
Title	**The History of Walthamstow: Its Past, Present and Future with a Directory, Map of the Parish etc**		Title	**Directory for West Ham**
			Dates	1883
Dates	1861		Publisher	Line Bros.
Publisher	Tweedie, W.		Printer	Line Bros.
Printer	Davis & Allen		Place	London
Place	Walthamstow		Type	GE TR
Type	ST TR		Map scale	1:15480
Map scale	1:95040		Library	BL
Library	GLH			

REF	**425**		REF	**428**
Title	**Stevens' Directory for Chelmsford and Neighbourhood**		Title	**The Harwich and Dovercourt Business and Family Almanac, Diary and Directory**
Dates	1881,1894			
Publisher	Stevens, G.		Dates	1885
Printer	Stevens, G.		Publisher	Jackson, G.L.
Place	London		Printer	Jackson, G.L.
Type	GE TR		Place	Harwich
Map scale	1:506880		Type	CT
Library	BL all		Map scale	–
holdings	BOD has 1894		Library	COL
	CHE all			
	GL has 1894			
	NLS has 1894			
	ULC has 1894			

REF	**429**
Title	**Kelly's Stratford, West Ham, Leyton, Leytonstone, Forest Gate, Walthamstow & Plaistow Directory**
Dates	1887,1888,1890-1904
Publisher	Kelly & Co
Printer	Kelly & Co
Place	London
Type	GE TR
Map scale	1:15840
Notes	Walthamstow dropped from title 1891 & after. Leyton & Leytonstone included 1887, 1888.
Library	BL not 1887
holdings	BOD all
	GL not 1887-1891,1897,1904
	ULC has 1887-1904

REF	**430**
Title	**Line Brothers' Directory for Clacton-on-Sea, Essex**
Dates	1888
Publisher	Line Bros.
Printer	Line Bros.
Place	London
Type	CM
Map scale	1:255440
Notes	Date uncertain
Library	BL

REF	**431**
Title	**Kelly's Walthamstow, Leyton & Leytonstone with Snaresbrook Directory**
Dates	1889-1924,1927,1929,1931,1933, 1935,1937,1939
Publisher	Kelly & Co
Printer	Kelly & Co
Place	London
Type	GE TR
Map scale	1:15840
Notes	See as 439. Snaresbrook dropped from title after 1898. Wanstead included from 1893.
Library	BL all
holdings	BOD has 1889-1903,1905
	CRD has 1939
	GL not 1890,1891,1902,1904, 1908
	GLH has 1899,1900,1905,1907
	ULC has 1889-1908

REF	**432**
Title	**Kelly's Ilford, Manor Park, Little Ilford and East Ham Directory**
Dates	1899-1904,1906-1908
Publisher	Kelly's Directories Ltd
Printer	Kelly's Directories Ltd
Place	London
Type	GE TR
Map scale	1:15840
Notes	Cont'd as 438. Little Ilford included 1899,1900.
Library	BL all
holdings	BOD all
	GL all
	GLH has 1905,1907
	ULC all

REF	**433**
Title	**Kelly's Directory of Southend-on-Sea, Leigh-on-Sea and Neighbourhood**
Dates	1899-1916,1920,1922-1940,1948, 1950
Publisher	Kelly's Directories Ltd
Printer	Kelly's Directories Ltd
Place	London
Type	GE TR
Map scale	1:126720
Library	BL all
holdings	BOD has 1899-1908,1910-1912
	CHE has 1937,1950
	COL has 1925,1926,1931,1936, 1940,1950
	GL not 1902,1903,1907,1909, 1912
	NLW has 1950
	ULC has 1899-1912

REF	**434**
Title	**Cullingford's Annual containing Street, Alphabetical and Military Directories of Colchester**
Dates	1900,1903,1905-1907,1909-1915
Publisher	Cullingford, R.W.
Printer	Cullingford, R.W.
Place	Colchester
Type	GE
Map scale	—
Library	COL

REF	**435**	REF	**438**
Title	**Kelly's Woodford with Snaresbrook & Wanstead Directory**	Title	**Kelly's Ilford, Seven Kings and Goodmayes Directory**
Dates	1900-1908	Dates	1909-1918,1921-1927,1929,1931, 1933,1935,1937,1939
Publisher	Kelly's Directories Ltd	Publisher	Kelly's Directories Ltd
Printer	Kelly's Directories Ltd	Printer	Kelly's Directories Ltd
Place	London	Place	London
Type	GE TR	Type	GE TR
Map scale	1:15840	Map scale	1:15840
Notes	Cont'd as 437 and 439	Notes	Cont'd from 432
Library	BL all	Library	BL all
holdings	BOD has 1900-1908	holdings	BOD has 1909-1912
	GL all		CLM has 1929-1939
	GLH has 1905,1907		CRD has 1935
	ULC has 1900-1908		GL all

REF **436**
Title **The Saffron Walden Almanack, Year Book and Directory**
Dates 1905,1933-1939
Publisher Hart & Son
Printer Hart & Son
Place Saffron Walden
Type GE
Map scale –
Library BOD all
holdings COL has 1937
NLS has 1936-1939

REF **438** (continued)
holdings GLH has 1910,1915-1917,1929, 1933,1935
SOG has 1937
ULC has 1909-1912

REF **439**
Title **Kelly's Leytonstone, Wanstead & Snaresbrook Directory**
Dates 1909-1924,1927,1929,1931,1933, 1935,1937,1939
Publisher Kelly's Directories Ltd
Printer Kelly's Directories Ltd
Place London
Type GE TR
Map scale 1:15840
Notes See 431 and 435
Library BL all
holdings CLM has 1939
CRD has 1939
GL not 1916,1939
GLH has 1910,1912-1915, 1923-1935
SOG has 1926,1935
ULC has 1909-1912

REF **437**
Title **Kelly's Woodford, Buckhurst Hill, Loughton & Chingford Directory**
Dates 1909-1915,1927,1929,1931,1933, 1935,1937,1939
Publisher Kelly's Directories Ltd
Printer Kelly's Directories Ltd
Place London
Type GE TR
Map scale 1:15840
Notes Cont'd from 435
Library BL all
holdings BOD has 1909-1912
CHE has 1929
GL all
GLH has 1910-1915,1924, 1927-1933
SOG has 1935
ULC has 1909-1912

REF **440**
Title **Chelmsford Directory and Almanack**
Dates 1910-1913
Publisher Benham & Co Ltd
Printer Benham & Co Ltd
Place Chelmsford
Type GE
Map scale 1:31680
Library CHE

REF **441**
Title **Colchester Almanac, Directory of the Town with much local and general information**
Dates 1912,1913,1916,1923,1927,1928, 1930-1940
Publisher Essex County Telegraph
Printer Essex County Telegraph
Place Colchester
Type GE
Map scale –
Notes Later editions have ST section. After 1927 entitled: 'The County Telegraph Handbook and Directory for Colchester and District', title varies.
Library COL all
holdings GL has 1940

REF **442**
Title **The East Essex Year Book and Directories for Clacton and District**
Dates 1914-1917,1920-1929,1932-1938
Publisher East Essex Advertiser & Clacton News
Printer East Essex Printing Works
Place Clacton-on-Sea
Type GE
Map scale 1:15840
Notes After 1921 entitled 'The Clacton Year Book & Directory'
Library BL

REF **443**
Title **C. Joscelyne's Braintree, Bocking & District Almanack & Directory**
Dates 1920-1922,1926
Publisher Joscelyne, C.
Printer Joscelyne, C.
Place Braintree
Type GE
Map scale –
Library BL

REF **444**
Title **Jewell's Chelmsford Directory**
Dates 1921,1922
Publisher Jewell, G.W.
Printer Jewell, G.W.
Place Chelmsford
Type CM TR
Map scale –
Library BL has 1922
holdings CHE has 1921

REF **445**
Title **Brentwood and District Directory and Year Book**
Dates 1922-1925,1927-1935,1937,1939
Publisher Burgess & Co
Printer Burgess & Co
Place Brentwood
Type GE
Map scale 1:12672
Library BL

REF **446**
Title **Directory of Residents and Guide to Benfleet, N. Benfleet, Canvey Island, Hadleigh, Hockney ... Vange & Wickford**
Dates 1923
Publisher The Benfleet, Canvey & District News
Printer The Benfleet, Canvey & District News
Place Benfleet
Type CT
Map scale –
Library BL

REF **447**
Title **Robus Bros' Almanack with Dunmow Directory**
Dates 1923
Publisher Robus Bros
Printer Robus Bros
Place Dunmow
Type CT CM
Map scale –
Library COL

REF **448**
Title **The Billericay & Wickford Directory and Yearbook**
Dates 1923-1926
Publisher The Brentwood Gazette and Printing Co
Printer The Brentwood Gazette and Printing Co
Place Brentwood
Type CT
Map scale –
Library BL

REF **449**
Title **Romford Official Guide and Directory**
Dates 1924
Publisher The British Publishing Company Ltd
Printer Crypt House Press
Place Gloucester
Type ST
Map scale –
Library COL

REF **450**
Title **Kelly's Directory of Chelmsford & Neighbourhood**
Dates 1927,1929,1931,1933,1935,1938, 1940,1943,1947,1949
Publisher Kelly's Directories Ltd
Printer Kelly's Directories Ltd
Place London
Type GE TR
Map scale 1:95040
Library BL not 1947
holdings CHE not 1931-1935
COL has 1933,1938,1949
GL all
NLW has 1949

REF **451**
Title **The Clacton Directory and Handbook**
Dates 1934,1936,1937,1947
Publisher Quick, A. & Co Ltd
Printer Quick, A. & Co Ltd
Place Clacton-on-Sea
Type GE
Map scale –
Library COL has 1947
holdings GL all

REF **452**
Title **Thurrock ... The Official Guide and Directory**
Dates 1940
Publisher Burrow, E.J. & Co Ltd
Printer –
Place Cheltenham
Type GE TR
Map scale 1:84480
Notes Date approx.
Library COL

REF **453**
Title **The Times Blue Book of Brightlingsea & Wivenhoe and Directory**
Dates 1948
Publisher The Brightlingsea & Wivenhoe Times
Printer The Brightlingsea & Wivenhoe Times
Place Clacton-on-Sea
Type GE
Map scale –
Library COL

GLOUCESTERSHIRE

REF **454**
Title **Kelly's Directory of the County of Gloucester**
Dates 1856,1863,1870,1879,1885,1889, 1894,1897,1902,1906,1910,1914, 1919,1923,1927,1931,1935,1939
Publisher Kelly & Co
Printer Kelly & Co
Place London
Type GE TR
Map scale 1:253440
Notes See 10 & 21
Library BCL has 1870,1885,1894-1939
holdings BIS has 1902,1906,1914,1931, 1939
BL not 1927,1931
BOD all
BPH has 1906,1910,1927,1935, 1939
BRL has 1906-1931,1939
CLB has 1863,1870,1897-1906, 1914,1919,1939
CLE has 1939
CLM has 1927,1939
CPL has 1856-1894,1902-1914, 1923-1939
GL not 1931
GLO not 1863,1870
HPL all
IHR has 1897,1906,1931
LCL has 1939
MLG has 1927
NLS has 1856-1885,1894,1906, 1910
NLW has 1914,1919,1923-1939
SOG has 1856,1863,1885,1894, 1902,1901,1914,1919,1939
TLH has 1889-1923
ULC not 1927
WCS has 1870,1902
WRO has 1902,1935
YCL has 1935

REF **455**
Title **Morris & Co's Directory and Gazetteer of Gloucestershire with Bristol**
Dates 1865,1867,1876
Publisher Morris & Co
Printer –
Place Nottingham
Type GE TR
Map scale 1:190080
Notes See 1198. 1876 edition includes Momnouthshire.
Library CPL has 1867
holdings GL not 1865
GLO all
SOG has 1876

REF **456**
Title **Deacon's Court Guide, Gazetteer and Royal Blue Book ... of the County of Gloucester**
Dates 1880,1899
Publisher Deacon, C.W. & Co
Printer Deacon, C.W. & Co
Place London
Type CT PR
Map scale 1:422400
Notes 1899 edition entitled 'The Gloucester Court Guide and County Blue Book'
Library BOD has 1899
holdings BRL has 1899
GL has 1899
GLO all
NLS has 1899
ULC has 1899

REF **457**
Title **Gloucestershire Directory and Buyers' Guide**
Dates 1910,1933,1935,1936
Publisher Cope, E.F. & Co
Printer Cope, E.F. & Co
Place Walsall
Type TR
Map scale –
Notes Cont'd as 458
Library CPL has 1910,1933
holdings GLO has 1935,1936

REF	**458**		REF	**461**
Title	**Gloucestershire and Bristol Directory**		Title	**Mathews' Annual Bristol and Clifton Directory and Almanack**
Dates	1937,1939,1940		Dates	1850-1857
Publisher	Aubrey & Co		Publisher	Mathews, M.
Printer	Aubrey & Co		Printer	Mathews, M.
Place	Walsall		Place	London
Type	TR		Type	GE TR
Map scale	–		Map scale	NS
Notes	Cont'd from 457		Notes	NORTON 317-312 (1850-1855).
Library	BL			Cont'd as 466. Map only in 1852 edition.

REF **459**

Title **Hunt & Co's Directory and Topography for the City of Bristol, Bedminster, Clifton, Hotwells ... also the towns of Axbridge, Burnham, Clevedon and Weston-super-Mare**

Dates 1850
Publisher Hunt, E. & Co
Printer Gardiner, B.W.
Place London
Type CM TR
Map scale –
Notes NORTON 867
Library TLH

REF **460**

Title **Edwards's New Cheltenham Directory**

Dates 1850-1852,1862
Publisher Edwards, R.
Printer Edwards, R.
Place Cheltenham
Type GE TR
Map scale –
Notes NORTON 346-348 (1850-1852)
Library BOD not 1850,1851
holdings CPL all
GL has 1850
GLO has 1862
IHR has 1850

Library BL all
holdings CLB all
GL all
IHR has 1850,1852,1854,1856
SOG has 1852,1854

REF **462**

Title **The Cheltenham Annuaire with a Directory**

Dates 1850-1912
Publisher Davies, H.
Printer Davies, H.
Place Cheltenham
Type GE TR
Map scale NS
Notes NORTON 334-339 (1850-1855). Map included from 1857 onwards. Cont'd as 499 Although still known as 'The Annuaire' the title changed to 'The Cheltenham and Gloucestershire Directory' in 1900, the directory only relating to Cheltenham.

Library BL not 1850,1851,1853-1855,
holdings 1866,1867
BOD has 1850,1851,1854,
1856-1880
CPL not 1879
GL has 1852,1878,1907,1911
GLO has 1858,1874,1876,1882,
1886,1887,1889,1891-1896,
1900,1903-1912
NLS has 1862
SOG has 1854,1868,1875,1909

REF	**463**
Title	**Scammell & Co's Bristol General Directory**
Dates	1853
Publisher	Scammell, W. & Co
Printer	Jeffries, C.T.
Place	Bristol
Type	GE TR
Map scale	–
Notes	NORTON 318
Library	GL

REF	**464**
Title	**Harper's Cheltenham Directory**
Dates	1853,1857
Publisher	Harper, A.
Printer	Harper, A.
Place	Cheltenham
Type	CM
Map scale	–
Notes	NORTON 349 (1853)
Library	CPL has 1857
holdings	GL has 1857
	GLO all

REF	**465**
Title	**A Directory containing the Names and Residences of Professional Gentlemen, Merchants, Manufacturers and Tradesmen in Cirencester, Swindon [etc]**
Dates	1855,1856,1858,1860,1861, 1863-1865,1868
Publisher	'?'
Printer	Taylor, R. & Francis, W.
Place	London
Type	CM
Map scale	–
Notes	This directory was published as an Appendix to Moores Almanack. Includes Swindon only from 1863.
Library	SWI

REF	**466**
Title	**Mathews' Annual Directory for the city and county of Bristol, including Clifton, Bedminster & surrounding villages**
Dates	1858-1869
Publisher	Mathews, M.
Printer	Mathews, M.
Place	London
Type	GE TR
Map scale	–
Notes	Cont'd from 461, cont'd as 474
Library	BCL has 1858,1860,1866
holdings	BL all
	BOD has 1863,1864
	CLB all
	GL all
	IHR has 1861,1865
	NLS has 1863,1864
	NLW has 1866,1868

REF	**467**
Title	**Cheltenham Free Press Fashionable Directory of Residents and Visitors of Cheltenham**
Dates	1859
Publisher	Harper, A.
Printer	Harper, A.
Place	Cheltenham
Type	ST
Map scale	–
Library	CPL

REF	**468**
Title	**Bretherton's Almanack and Gloucester Directory**
Dates	1862-1873,1875-1877,1879,1880, 1882
Publisher	Bretherton, D.
Printer	–
Place	Gloucester
Type	TR
Map scale	–
Library	BOD has 1871-1873
holdings	GL has 1862
	GLO has 1869,1870,1873, 1875-1882
	ULC has 1863-1873

REF **469**
Title **The Bishopston and Horfield Directory**
Dates 1867
Publisher Jones, W.
Printer Jones, W.
Place Bristol
Type GE TR
Map scale –
Library BL
holdings BOD

REF **470**
Title **Harmer's Cotswold Almanack and Trade Directory**
Dates 1868,1869
Publisher Harmer, H.
Printer Harmer's Steam Press Office
Place Cirencester
Type CT
Map scale –
Notes GCL edition cover missing, bibliographic details from catalogue. Includes Cirencester, Fairford, Cricklade, Lechlade, Tetbury, Malmesbury etc.
Library GLO

REF **471**
Title **Bristol and Clifton Postal Directory**
Dates 1869
Publisher Bristol Printing Co
Printer Bristol Printing Co
Place Bristol
Type ST
Map scale NS
Library BL

REF **472**
Title **Bristol and Clifton Street Directory**
Dates 1870
Publisher Arrowsmith, I.
Printer Arrowsmith, I.
Place Bristol
Type SL
Map scale –
Library BL
holdings BOD

REF **473**
Title **The Royal Cheltenham Directory**
Dates 1870-1872,1874,1876-1878
Publisher Edwards, R.
Printer Edwards, R.
Place Cheltenham
Type GE TR
Map scale –
Notes 1872-1874 entitled 'The Royal Cheltenham & County Directory'. 1876-1878: 'The Royal Cheltenham & District Directory'.
Library BOD has 1871
holdings CPL all
GL has 1870
GLO all

REF **474**
Title **Mathews' Bristol Directory with adjacent villages, remodelled by J. Wright**
Dates 1870-1879
Publisher Wright, J.
Printer Wright, J.
Place Bristol
Type GE TR
Map scale NS
Notes Cont'd from 466, cont'd by 478
Library BL not 1872,1874,1876-1878
holdings BOD has 1870
CLB all
GL has 1871,1877,1878
IHR has 1870
NLS has 1870

REF **475**
Title **The City of Gloucester Directory and Postal Guide**
Dates 1879
Publisher Crocker, W.C.
Printer –
Place Gloucester
Type GE TR
Map scale 1:101370
Library GLO

REF **476**
Title **Arthur's Gloucester Annual Almanack and Diary**
Dates 1880
Publisher Arthur, J.
Printer Arthur, J.
Place Gloucester
Type ST
Map scale –
Library GLO

REF	**477**
Title	**The Cheltenham Post Office Directory**
Dates	1880,1883,1891
Publisher	Edwards, H.
Printer	Edwards, H.
Place	Cheltenham
Type	GE TR
Map scale	1:253440
Library	BL all
holdings	BOD has 1880
	CPL all
	GLO all
	NLS has 1880

REF	**478**
Title	**J. Wright & Co's Bristol & Clifton Directory with nearly 100 adjacent villages**
Dates	1880-1917,1919,192˙,1923
Publisher	Wright, J.
Printer	Wright, J.
Place	Bristol
Type	GE TR
Map scale	1:12672
Notes	Cont'd from 474, published by Kelly's Directories Ltd 1904 onwards. See 482.
Library	BCL has 1901
holdings	BL not 1919,1923
	BOD has 1902-1914,1917,1919
	BRL has 1912,1915,1916,1917, 1919,1923
	CLB has 1880-1917,1923
	CLM has 1916
	GL has 1881,1884,1886-1888, 1901,1903-1908,1910-1917, 1921,1923
	GLO has 1913,1914,1919
	MLG has 1902,1904,1913,1915, 1917,1921,1923
	NLS has 1902-1912,1914,1917, 1919
	NLW has 1884,1898
	SOG has 1913
	ULC has 1880,1902-1912,1914, 1917,1919

REF	**479**
Title	**The East Gloucestershire, Borough of Cricklade and District Directory**
Dates	1882
Publisher	'?'
Printer	'?'
Place	'?'
Type	CM
Map scale	1:443520
Notes	Gloucs & Wilts towns. No T/P or cover GCL edition.
Library	GLO

REF	**480**
Title	**Cheltenham Directory**
Dates	1882,1885
Publisher	Roberts, W.L.
Printer	–
Place	Cheltenham
Type	CT TR
Map scale	–
Notes	T/P & cover missing, title uncertain (both editions)
Library	CPL

REF	**481**
Title	**Smart's City of Gloucester and District Directory**
Dates	1883-1887,1889,1891,1893,1897, 1900,1902,1906,1910,1918,1920, 1927,1930,1936
Publisher	Smart, L.A.
Printer	Smart, L.A.
Place	Gloucester
Type	GE TR
Map scale	–
Notes	1883-7 editions entitled 'The City of Gloucester Diary, Directory & Almanack'
Library	BL not 1920,1930,1936
holdings	CLE has 1910
	GL has 1936
	GLO not 1885,1886,1897-1902, 1936

REF **482**
Title **Kelly's Directory of the City of Bristol and suburbs**
Dates 1889,1891,1892,1894,1897,1902, 1924-1940,1944,1947,1950
Publisher Kelly & Co
Printer Kelly & Co
Place London
Type GE TR
Map scale 1:10560
Library BL not 1889,1891,1902
holdings BOD has 1892,1924-1950
BPH has 1897,1924-1926, 1928-1930,1932-1934,1936, 1939,1940,1944,1950
BRL has 1894,1897,1925,1927, 1928,1931,1933-1950 & extracts from 1906,1910, 1914 (Ref 7)
CLB has 1924-1940,1947,1950
CLM has 1931-1933
GL not 1892,1926
HRO has 1936
MLG has 1924-1950
NLS has 1891,1924-1950
NLW has 1928,1931,1933,1935, 1937,1939,1950
SOG has 1936
ULC has 1891,1924-1950
WCS has 1939,1947,1950

REF **483**
Title **Elliott's Stroud Directory and Household Almanack**
Dates 1891,1895
Publisher Elliott, J.
Printer Elliott, J.
Place Stroud
Type CM
Map scale –
Library GLO

REF **484**
Title **G.J. Harris's Forest of Dean Directory**
Dates 1892,1895,1903,1905-1914
Publisher Harris, G.J.
Printer Harris, G.J.
Place Lydney
Type GE
Map scale –
Library BL has 1905-1914
holdings GLO not 1906,1907,1910

REF **485**
Title **Presley's Illustrated Household Almanack with Directory of Wotton-under-Edge**
Dates 1894,1912,1920
Publisher Presley, G.
Printer Presley, G.
Place Wotton-under-Edge
Type ST
Map scale –
Library GLO

REF **486**
Title **Whitmore's Illustrated Family Almanac and Diary with Local Directory for Dursley, Cam, Coaley, North Nibley, Slimbridge, Cambridge, Stinchcomb and Uley**
Dates 1895,1898,1901,1904,1909-1914
Publisher Whitmore & Son
Printer Whitmore & Son
Place Dursley
Type CT CM
Map scale –
Library GLO

REF **487**
Title **Built-Leonard's Directory for Cheltenham**
Dates 1896,1897,1902-1904,1911,1916, 1921-1937
Publisher Built-Leonard, E.G.
Printer Built-Leonard, E.G.
Place Cheltenham
Type GE TR
Map scale –
Library BL has 1896,1897,1921-1937
holdings CPL has 1902-1916,1922-1925, 1927,1929

REF **488**
Title **The Cheltenham Annual Business Directory**
Dates 1900
Publisher '?'
Printer Hailing, T. (?)
Place Cheltenham
Type TR
Map scale –
Notes Very small TR section. No details of publisher etc. although the volume appears to be complete.
Library CPL

REF	**489**
Title	**The New Bristol Directory**
Dates	1903-1905
Publisher	Sharp & Co
Printer	–
Place	Bristol
Typé	GE TR
Map scale	1:15840
Notes	Map scale approx.
Library	BL

REF	**490**
Title	**Bailey & Woods' Directory and Advertiser ... for the Towns of Cirencester, Fairford, Lechlade, Northleach, Malmesbury & Cricklade**
Dates	1906,1912,1916,1918
Publisher	Bailey & Woods
Printer	Bailey & Woods
Place	Cirencester
Type	CM TR
Map scale	–
Library	GLO

REF	**491**
Title	**Smart's Gloucester Street List**
Dates	1907-1914
Publisher	Gloucester Directory
Printer	Gloucester Directory
Place	Gloucester
Type	ST
Map scale	–
Library	BL all
holdings	GLO has 1908,1912,1914

REF	**492**
Title	**The New Directory of Stroud and District**
Dates	1908,1909
Publisher	Harmer, H.
Printer	Stroud News
Place	Stroud
Type	CT CM
Map scale	1:126720
Notes	Cont'd as 498
Library	GL has 1908
holdings	GLO all

REF	**493**
Title	**The County Almanac and Directory [Cirencester, Tetbury, Fairford, Lechlade]**
Dates	1909,1910,1912-1917,1920,1921
Publisher	Smith, W.H. & Son
Printer	Smith, W.H. & Son
Place	Cirencester
Type	GE TR
Map scale	–
Library	BL has 1915-1921
holdings	GLO has 1909-1914,1917

REF	**494**
Title	**Cheltenham, Gloucester and District Trades' Directory**
Dates	1910,1915,1920
Publisher	Town and County Directories Ltd
Printer	Macdonald, W. & Co Ltd
Place	Edinburgh
Type	TR
Map scale	–
Notes	Cont'd as 501
Library	CPL

REF	**495**
Title	**The Bushley, Longdon, Queenhill and Holdfast Almanack and Year-Book ... Directory of Tewkesbury**
Dates	1911
Publisher	North, W.
Printer	North, W.
Place	Tewkesbury
Type	ST
Map scale	–
Library	GLO

REF	**496**
Title	**Owen's Stroud Directory and Year Book**
Dates	1911,1912-1914
Publisher	Owen, H.M.
Printer	Owen, H.M.
Place	Stroud
Type	CM
Map scale	NS
Library	GLO

REF **497**
Title **Gloucester Year Book**
Dates 1912
Publisher Gloucestershire Chronicle
Printer Gloucestershire Chronicle
Place Gloucester
Type GE
Map scale –
Library GLO

REF **498**
Title **The Stroud and District Residential Guide and Directory**
Dates 1913
Publisher Stroud News Publishing Co Ltd
Printer Stroud News Publishing Co Ltd
Place Stroud
Type CM
Map scale –
Notes Cont'd from 492, cont'd as 500
Library GLO

REF **499**
Title **Looker-On Directory for Cheltenham and Gloucestershire**
Dates 1913-1916
Publisher Looker-On Printing Company Ltd
Printer Looker-On Printing Company Ltd
Place Cheltenham
Type GE
Map scale –
Notes Cont'd from 462. Directory relates to Cheltenham only.
Library BL has 1913,1915
holdings CPL has 1913-1915
GLO has 1913,1914,1916

REF **500**
Title **The Stroud and Mid-Gloucester Directory**
Dates 1914,1916-1918,1920,1922,1923, 1929,1932,1937
Publisher Stroud News Publishing Co
Printer Stroud News Publishing Co
Place Stroud
Type GE
Map scale 1:126720
Notes Cont'd from 498
Library GL has 1932,1937
holdings GLO all

REF **501**
Title **Bristol, Cheltenham and Gloucester Trades' Directory**
Dates 1921-1924,1927-1929,1931, 1933-1936,1938
Publisher Town and County Directories Ltd
Printer Macdonald, W. & Co Ltd
Place Edinburgh
Type TR
Map scale –
Library BRL has 1935,1936,1938
holdings CPL not 1934
GLO has 1936
TLH has 1934

REF **502**
Title **Kelly's Directory of Cheltenham with Charlton Kings, Leckhampton & Prestbury**
Dates 1926-1943,1945,1948,1950
Publisher Kelly's Directories Ltd
Printer Kelly's Directories Ltd
Place London
Type GE TR
Map scale 1:15840
Library BL all
holdings BOD all?
CLE has 1948
CPL not 1929
GL not 1933,1934,1938,1940, 1942,1948
GLO has 1928,1930,1934, 1936-1940,1943-1950
NLW has 1950
SOG has 1948

REF **503**
Title **Directory of Bristol Industries**
Dates 1937-1940,1947,1948,1950
Publisher Bristol City Corporation
Printer St Stephens Bristol Press Ltd
Place Bristol
Type TR
Map scale –
Library BL not 1937-1940
holdings BOD all
NLS has 1937
ULC has 1937,1948,1950

REF	**504**
Title	**Kelly's Directory of the City of Gloucester & District**
Dates	1939,1941,1945,1949
Publisher	Kelly's Directories Ltd
Printer	Kelly's Directories Ltd
Place	London
Type	GE TR
Map scale	–
Library holdings	BL all
	GL not 1941
	GLO all
	NLW has 1949

HAMPSHIRE

REF	**505**
Title	**Kelly's Directory of Hampshire including the Isle of Wight**
Dates	1852,1855,1859,1867,1875,1880, 1885,1890,1895,1899,1903,1907, 1911,1915,1920,1923,1927,1931, 1935,1939
Publisher	Kelly & Co
Printer	Kelly & Co
Place	London
Type	GE TR
Map scale	1:380160
Notes	See 8
Library holdings	BCL has 1931-1939
	BL not 1903-1927
	BIS has 1899,1931,1939
	BOD not 1859,1875
	BPH has 1927,1939
	CHI has 1875,1915
	CLB has 1939
	CLE has 1880,1939
	CLM has 1923,1939
	CLS has 1859-1875,1890-1899, 1907-1915,1923-1939
	DCL has 1885,1895,1903,1923
	GL all
	HRO not 1852,1855,1885,1899, 1923
	IHR has 1923,1935,1939
	LCL has 1939
	LLB has 1859,1867,1885,1890, 1899,1911,1923-1939
	MLG has 1907-1927
	NEW has 1907,1931,1939
	NLS all
	NLW has 1920,1927-1939
	PCL has 1859,1875,1895-1915, 1923-1939

SAL has 1875-1899,1911,1915, 1927-1939
SCC has 1855,1885,1903, 1911-1931,1939
SCL has 1927-1939
SLS has 1939
SOG has 1859,1867,1880,1895, 1899,1907.1915,1931,1939
SWI has 1890,1895,1903,1915, 1923,1927,1939
ULC all
WCS has 1880
WIN not 1852,1927
WRO has 1859,1867,1885,1899, 1911,1915,1939

REF	**506**
Title	**Craven & Co's Commercial Directory of Hampshire**
Dates	1857
Publisher	Craven & Co
Printer	Craven & Co
Place	Nottingham
Type	CM
Map scale	–
Library holdings	GL
	HRO
	IHR
	LLB
	SCC

REF	**507**
Title	**History, Gazetteer and Directory of Hampshire and the Isle of Wight**
Dates	1859,1878
Publisher	White, W.
Printer	Leader, R
Place	Sheffield
Type	GE TR
Map scale	–
Library holdings	BL all
	CLS all
	GL all
	HRO all
	IHR all
	LLB all
	NLS has 1878
	PCL all
	SCC has 1878
	ULC all
	WIN all

REF **508**
Title **J.G. Harrod & Co's Postal and Commercial Directory of Hampshire with the Isle of Wight**
Dates 1865
Publisher Harrod, J.G. & Co
Printer Danks, T.
Place London
Type CM
Map scale –
Library GL
holdings SCC

REF **509**
Title **Smith & Co's Hampshire Directory including the Isle of Wight**
Dates 1866,1867
Publisher Smith & Co
Printer Welch, J.
Place London
Type GE TR
Map scale –
Library GL has 1866
holdings LLB has 1867

REF **510**
Title **Deacon's South Hants Court Guide Gazetteer and Royal Blue Blue Book**
Dates 1879
Publisher Deacon, C.W. & Co
Printer Deacon, C.W. & Co
Place London
Type CT
Map scale –
Notes Covers principal towns in S. Hants
Library PCL

REF **511**
Title **Historical and Commercial Directory of the Isle of Wight**
Dates 1879
Publisher Hill, J.W.
Printer Danks, T.
Place London
Type CT CM
Map scale –
Library CLS
holdings SCC

REF **512**
Title **Kelly's Directory of the Isle of Wight**
Dates 1888,1891,1892,1894,1897,1898, 1900,1902-1906,1910,1912,1914, 1921,1924
Publisher Kelly & Co
Printer Kelly & Co
Place London
Type GE TR
Map scale 1:95040
Library BL not 1904,1908,1914
holdings BOD not 1904,1908,1914,1921, 1924
CLS has 1924
NLS not 1892,1894,1904,1908, 1914,1921,1924
PCL has 1914,1924
SCC has 1914
ULC not 1892,1894,1898,1903, 1905,1914,1921,1924

REF **513**
Title **Hampshire Year Book with Official Directory for Hampshire and the Isle of Wight**
Dates 1912
Publisher Holbrook & Son Ltd
Printer Holbrook & Son Ltd
Place Portsmouth
Type PR
Map scale –
Notes Directory of MPs, Parish Councils, Gentry etc.
Library SCC

REF **514**
Title **Hampshire Directory**
Dates 1920,1935-1940
Publisher Aubrey & Co
Printer Aubrey & Co
Place Walsall
Type TR
Map scale –
Library BL not 1920
holdings PCL has 1920

REF	**515**
Title	**Hampshire and Isle of Wight Trades Directory**
Dates	1924,1928,1931
Publisher	Town and County Directories Ltd
Printer	Macdonald, W. & Co Ltd
Place	Edinburgh
Type	TR
Map scale	–
Library	PCL

REF	**516**
Title	**The Post Office Directory of the Borough of Southampton and neighbourhood**
Dates	1851,1853,1855,1857,1859,1861, 1863,1865
Publisher	Forbes & Knibb
Printer	Forbes & Knibb
Place	Southampton
Type	GE TR
Map scale	–
Notes	NORTON 365-367 (1851,1853, 1855). Published by Forbes & Marshall 1853 & 1855; by A. Forbes 1857; by Forbes & Bennett 1859 & 1861; by J.J. Bennett 1865. Cont'd as 519.
Library	BL has 1853,1855,1859
holdings	CLS all
	GL has 1859,1863,1865
	HRO has 1859
	SCC not 1863

REF	**517**
Title	**Gilmour's Winchester Almanac and Post-Office Directory**
Dates	1854
Publisher	Gilmour, G. & H.
Printer	Gilmour, G. & H.
Place	Winchester
Type	CT TR
Map scale	–
Notes	NORTON 369
Library	HRO
holdings	WIN

REF	**518**
Title	**Simpson's Portsmouth Directory and Court Guide including Southsea, Landport and Kingston, Portsea and Gosport**
Dates	1863
Publisher	Tomkies and Son
Printer	–
Place	London
Type	CM
Map scale	–
Library	PCL

REF	**519**
Title	**The Southampton Directory**
Dates	1867
Publisher	Gutch, T.G. & Co
Printer	–
Place	Southampton
Type	GE
Map scale	–
Notes	Cont'd from 516
Library	CLS
holdings	SCC

REF	**520**
Title	**The Southampton Directory**
Dates	1869,1871,1876,1878
Publisher	Hants Independent
Printer	Hants Independent
Place	Southampton
Type	GE TR
Map scale	–
Notes	1869 & 1871 editions compiled by W. Cox. Cont'd as 525.
Library	CLS all
holdings	GL has 1876,1878
	HRO has 1871
	SCC not 1869

REF	**521**
Title	**Butcher & Co's Borough of Portsmouth Directory**
Dates	1874
Publisher	Butcher & Co
Printer	Butcher & Co
Place	London
Type	CM
Map scale	1:506880
Library	BL

REF	522
Title	**Tucker's Southampton Directory**
Dates	1874
Publisher	Tucker & Son
Printer	Tucker & Son
Place	Southampton
Type	GE
Map scale	–
Library	CLS
holdings	SCC

REF	523
Title	**Warren's Winchester and District Directory**
Dates	1877,1884-1895,1903-1918, 1920-1942
Publisher	Warren & Son
Printer	Warren & Son
Place	Winchester
Type	GE TR
Map scale	1:633600
Library	BL not 1877,1884-1890,1892
holdings	BOD has 1891,1893,1905
	CLS has 1937,1938,1940,1942
	GL has 1914
	HRO has 1906,1915,1924,
	1926-1930,1932-1942
	ULC has 1891-1893,1905
	WIN not 1892,1894,1903,1907,
	1910,1911,1922,1923,1928,
	1929

REF	524
Title	**Chamberlain's Portsmouth including Portsea, Southsea, Landport and District ... List of Streets, Private Residents, Commercial and Trade Directory**
Dates	1879,1881,1887
Publisher	Chamberlain, G.
Printer	Chamberlain, G.
Place	Portsmouth
Type	GE TR
Map scale	–
Library	PCL

REF	525
Title	**Cox's Southampton Directory**
Dates	1880
Publisher	Cox, W. [compiler]
Printer	Randle's General Printing Works
Place	Southampton
Type	CT CM
Map scale	–
Notes	Cont'd from 520, cont'd as 528
Library	MLG
holdings	SCC

REF	526
Title	**Master's City of Winchester Directory**
Dates	1880,1881
Publisher	Masters, F.W.
Printer	–
Place	Winchester
Type	ST TR
Map scale	–
Library	HRO has 1880
holdings	WIN all

REF	527
Title	**The Basingstoke Directory**
Dates	1881
Publisher	Jacob, C.J.
Printer	Jacob, C.J.
Place	Basingstoke
Type	ST TR
Map scale	–
Library	CLS

REF	528
Title	**Foster & Roud's Southampton Directory**
Dates	1883
Publisher	Foster & Roud
Printer	Foster & Roud
Place	Southampton
Type	GE
Map scale	–
Notes	Cont'd from 525
Library	CLS
holdings	SCC

REF	529
Title	**Directory of Portsmouth, Southsea, Landport & Gosport**
Dates	1883,1887,1890
Publisher	Stevens, G.
Printer	Stevens, G.
Place	London
Type	GE TR
Map scale	1:506880
Library	BL all
holdings	BOD not 1883
	NLS not 1883
	PCL has 1887
	ULC not 1883

REF	530
Title	**The Annual Directory of Bournemouth**
Dates	1884
Publisher	Wilson & Prady
Printer	Wilson & Prady
Place	Bournemouth
Type	GE TR
Map scale	–
Library	BL
holdings	BOD
	ULC

REF	531
Title	**Directory of Southampton and Neighbourhood (with 7 miles radius)**
Dates	1884,1887,1891,1895
Publisher	Stevens, G.
Printer	Stevens, G.
Place	London
Type	GE TR
Map scale	1:633600
Library	BL all
holdings	BOD all
	CLS all
	GL has 1884
	NLS all
	SCC not 1884
	ULC all

REF	532
Title	**Kelly's Directory of Portsmouth, Portsea, Landport, Southsea and Gosport**
Dates	1886,1888-1892,1894,1896-1919, 1921-1940,1946,1948
Publisher	Kelly & Co
Printer	Kelly & Co
Place	London
Type	GE TR
Map scale	1:15840
Library	BL not 1886
holdings	BOD has 1888,1890-1911
	BPH has 1932
	CLS has 1934-1939,1946,1948
	GL not 1886,1890-1896,1911, 1915,1919
	MLG has 1946,1948
	NLS has 1897,1902
	NLW has 1917,1948
	PCL not 1889,1891,1900,1902, 1903,1906,1915,1916,1919
	SCC has 1921,1939,1948
	SOG has 1909,1936
	ULC has 1888-1912
	WIN has 1923

REF	533
Title	**Kelly's Directory of Southampton and Neighbourhood**
Dates	1886-1888,1890,1892,1894, 1897-1940,1946,1948
Publisher	Kelly & Co
Printer	Kelly & Co
Place	London
Type	GE TR
Map scale	1:7920
Library	BL not 1886
holdings	BOD has 1887-1890,1892-1912
	CLS not 1901,1906,1917,1919
	GL not 1886,1890,1894,1897, 1913,1917,1919
	HRO has 1922,1931
	NLS has 1887,1897-1907, 1909-1912
	NLW has 1912,1916,1948
	PCL has 1914,1918,1922,1925, 1928,1932-1935,1937-1940, 1946,1048
	SCC has 1886,1890-1898,1900, 1901,1905,1906,1913,1921, 1925,1929,1932-1948
	ULC has 1887-1894,1897-1913
	WIN has 1887

REF **534**
Title **Wallis and Ades' Annual Directory for Southsea**
Dates 1887,1888
Publisher Wallis & Ades
Printer Wallis & Ades
Place Southsea
Type GE
Map scale NS
Library BL all
holdings BOD all
ULC has 1887

REF **535**
Title **W. Mate and Sons' Business, Professional and Private Residents' Directory for Bournemouth, Boscombe and Westbourne**
Dates 1887,1891,1903-1905
Publisher Mate, W. & Sons
Printer Mate, W. & Sons
Place Bournemouth
Type CT TR
Map scale –
Notes 1903 onwards entitled 'W. Mate & Sons' Bournemouth, Boscombe & Westbourne Business Directory'. Cont'd as 545.
Library BL has 1891,1904,1905
holdings LLB has 1887,1903

REF **536**
Title **Directory of Bournemouth (East and West) and Neighbourhood**
Dates 1888,1894
Publisher Stevens, G.
Printer Stevens, G.
Place London
Type GE TR
Map scale NS
Library BL all
holdings BOD all
LLB has 1894
NLS all
ULC all

REF **537**
Title **Directory of Lymington, Ringwood & Christchurch & villages in the New Forest**
Dates 1891
Publisher Stevens, G.
Printer Stevens, G.
Place London
Type GE TR
Map scale 1:506880
Library BL
holdings ULC

REF **538**
Title **Drew's Aldershot and Farnborough Directory and Almanack**
Dates 1893,1904,1907-1915,1920-1928
Publisher Drew, J.
Printer Drew, J.
Place Aldershot
Type GE
Map scale –
Library BL all
holdings BOD has 1893

REF **539**
Title **Directory of Fleet, Hartley Row, Winchfield & North Hants**
Dates 1896,1905-1914
Publisher May, W. & Co
Printer May, W. & Co
Place Aldershot
Type GE TR
Map scale –
Library BL

REF	**540**
Title	**Kelly's Directory of Bournemouth, Christchurch & Poole with Longfleet and Parkstone**
Dates	1897-1899,1901,1903,1905, 1907-1909,1911,1913,1915,1918, 1920-1923,1925-1940,1942,1944, 1947,1950
Publisher	Kelly's Directories Ltd
Printer	Kelly's Directories Ltd
Place	London
Type	GE TR
Map scale	–
Library holdings	BL not 1899,1903 BOD has 1897,1899-1911 CLS has 1935,1937,1938, 1940-1950 DCL has 1931,1944-1950 GL all LLB has 1899-1907,1911-1950 MLG has 1936,1940,1944-1950 NLS has 1897-1911 NLW has 1920,1950 PCL has 1920,1922,1930, 1937-1950 SCC has 1915,1926 ULC has 1897,1899,1901,1903, 1905,1907,1909,1911 WCS has 1947

REF	**541**
Title	**Directory of Lymington, Ringwood, Christchurh, Fordingbridge, Brockenhurst, Lyndhurst**
Dates	1899
Publisher	Stevens, G. & Co
Printer	Stevens, G. & Co
Place	London
Type	CM TR
Map scale	–
Library holdings	BOD NLS

REF	**542**
Title	**Portsmouth, Southampton and District Trades' Directory**
Dates	1902
Publisher	Town and County Directories Ltd
Printer	Macdonald, W. & Co Ltd
Place	Edinburgh
Type	TR
Map scale	–
Library	PCL

REF	**543**
Title	**The Fleet Directory, Timetable and General Business Guide**
Dates	1904
Publisher	The Farnborough Printing Works
Printer	The Farnborough Printing Works
Place	Farnborough
Type	GE
Map scale	–
Library	BOD

REF	**544**
Title	**Hampshire Herald Directory for Alton, Alresford**
Dates	1905,1906,1908
Publisher	Hampshire Herald
Printer	Hampshire Herald
Place	Alton
Type	GE TR
Map scale	–
Library holdings	BL has 1906,1908 HRO has 1905

REF	**545**
Title	**Sidney J. Mate's Bournemouth Business Directory and Year Book**
Dates	1911,1913-1917,1919,1921, 1923-1940
Publisher	Mate, S.J.
Printer	Mate, S.J.
Place	Bournemouth
Type	GE TR
Map scale	–
Notes	Cont'd from 535
Library holdings	BL has 1916,1924,1925, 1927-1940 DCL has 1936,1938,1939 LLB all SOG has 1938

REF **546**
Title **Kelly's Directory of Gosport, Alverstoke, Fareham & District**
Dates 1913-1940
Publisher Kelly's Directories Ltd
Printer Kelly's Directories Ltd
Place London
Type GE TR
Map scale –
Library BL all
holdings CLM has 1940
CLS has 1934-1936,1938,1939
GL not 1915,1919
HRO has 1927,1930
PCL has 1918,1920,1921, 1923-1940
SOG has 1939

REF **547**
Title **Emsworth, Havant, Hayling Island, Southbourne, Westbourne and District Directory**
Dates 1926,1928
Publisher Rogers, D.S. & Co
Printer Rogers, D.S. & Co
Place Emsworth & Havant
Type GE
Map scale –
Library CHI has 1926
holdings PCL has 1928

REF **548**
Title **Portsmouth Commercial Directory including Gosport**
Dates 1927
Publisher South-Western Publishing Co
Printer –
Place Bristol
Type TR
Map scale –
Library PCL

REF **549**
Title **Kelly's Directory of Winchester**
Dates 1927-1933
Publisher Kelly's Directories Ltd
Printer Kelly's Directories Ltd
Place London
Type GE TR
Map scale 1:15840
Library BL all
holdings CLM has 1932
GL not 1927
WIN al`

REF **550**
Title **Kelly's Directory of Basingstoke & Neighbourhood**
Dates 1929-1931,1933,1935,1937,1939, 1941,1948
Publisher Kelly's Directories Ltd
Printer Kelly's Directories Ltd
Place London
Type GE TR
Map scale 1:253440
Library BL not 1931,1935,1937,1941
holdings CLS has 1935-1939,1948
GL not 1930
PCL has 1949,1948

REF **551**
Title **Kelly's Directory of Newport, Cowes & Neighbourhood**
Dates 1931,1933,1935,1937
Publisher Kelly's Directories Ltd
Printer Kelly's Directories Ltd
Place London
Type GE TR
Map scale 1:95040
Library BL all
holdings CLS not 1931
GL all
PCL not 1931

REF **552**
Title **Kelly's Directory of Ryde & Neighbourhood**
Dates 1931,1933,1935,1937
Publisher Kelly's Directories Ltd
Printer Kelly's Directories Ltd
Place London
Type GE TR
Map scale 1:95040
Library BL
holdings GL
PCL

REF **553**
Title **Kelly's Directory of Shanklin, Sandown, Ventnor & Neighbourhood**
Dates 1931,1933,1935,1937
Publisher Kelly's Directories Ltd
Printer Kelly's Directories Ltd
Place London
Type GE TR
Map scale 1:95040
Library BL
holdings GL
PCL

REF **554**
Title **Directory of Romsey**
Dates 1933
Publisher Smith, W.H. & Son
Printer Smith, W.H. & Son
Place Romsey
Type ST
Map scale –
Library GL

REF **555**
Title **Street Directory of the Extended Borough of Christchurch**
Dates 1933
Publisher Christchurch Information Bureau
Printer –
Place Christchurch
Type ST
Map scale –
Library LLB

REF **556**
Title **Kelly's Directory of Andover & Neighbourhood**
Dates 1934,1936,1938,1940,1947,1949, 1950
Publisher Kelly's Directories Ltd
Printer Kelly's Directories Ltd
Place London
Type GE TR
Map scale –
Library BL not 1950
holdings CLS not 1949
GL not 1949
PCL has 1940,1947
SCC has 1950

REF **557**
Title **The Fordingbridge Directory and Almanack**
Dates 1940
Publisher King, A.H.
Printer King, A.H.
Place Fordingbridge
Type ST
Map scale –
Library HRO

HEREFORDSHIRE

REF **558**
Title **Lascelles & Co's Directory and Gazetteer of Herefordshire**
Dates 1851
Publisher Lascelles & Co
Printer Swan Bros.
Place Birmingham
Type CM
Map scale –
Notes NORTON 371
Library BCL
holdings CLC
GL
HPL

REF **559**
Title **Kelly's Directory of Herefordshire**
Dates 1856,1863,1870,1879,1885,1891, 1895,1900,1905,1909,1913,1917, 1922,1926,1929,1934,1937,1941
Publisher Kelly & Co
Printer Kelly & Co
Place London
Type GE TR
Map scale 1:21120
Notes See 10 (1856-1885) & 22 (1891-1941)
Library BCL has 1870,1885-1941
holdings BIS has 199,1934,1941
BL not 1941
BOD not 1891-1937
BPH has 1917,1941
CLB has 1870,1941
CLC has 1895,1913-1941
CLM has 1926,1937,1941
GL all
HPL all
IHR has 1926
MLG has 1870,1905-1913, 1922-1941
NLS all
NLW has 1909,1913,1929,1934, 1941
NPT has 1934,1937
SCL has 1929-1937
SHR has 1956-1885,1900-1917
SOG has 1856,1863,1885,1891, 1900,1909,1929,1937
ULC all
WAR has 1929
WCL has 1891,1922-1934
YCL has 1934

REF **560**
Title **History, Topography and Directory of Herefordshire**
Dates 1858
Publisher Cassey & Co
Printer Bailey, W.
Place Preston
Type GE TR
Map scale NS
Library CLC
holdings GL
HPL

REF **561**
Title **Littlebury's Postal and Commercial Directory and Gazetteer of the County of Hereford**
Dates 1867
Publisher Littlebury, J.
Printer Collingridge, W.H.
Place London
Type GE TR
Map scale —
Library GL
holdings HPL

REF **562**
Title **Postal and Commercial Directory and Gazetteer of the County of Hereford**
Dates 1867
Publisher Littlebury, J.
Printer Collingridge, W.H.
Place London
Type GE TR
Map scale —
Library BL
holdings GL

REF **563**
Title **Littlebury's Directory and Gazetteer of Herefordshire**
Dates 1876
Publisher Littlebury, J.
Printer Ballantyne, Hanson & Co
Place Worcester
Type CM
Map scale —
Library GL
holdings HPL
SOG

REF **564**
Title **Jakeman and Carver's Directory and Gazetteer of Herefordshire**
Dates 1890,1902,1914
Publisher Jakeman & Carver
Printer Jakeman & Carver
Place Hereford
Type GE TR
Map scale 1:126720
Library BL not 1902
holdings BOD has 1890
GL all
HPL all
NLS has 1890
NLW has 1890,1902
ULC has 1890
WCL has 1902,1914

REF **565**
Title **The Post Office Hereford and District Directory**
Dates 1882
Publisher Crocker, W.C.
Printer Jakeman & Carver
Place Hereford
Type GE TR
Map scale —
Library HPL

REF **566**
Title **Directory of the City of Hereford with Ross & District**
Dates 1886,1888
Publisher Wells & Manton
Printer Wells & Manton
Place Shrewsbury
Type GE TR
Map scale 1:190080
Library BL has 1886
holdings BOD has 1886
HPL has 1886
NLS has 1886
ULC all

REF **567**
Title **Hereford and District Directory**
Dates 1888
Publisher Wells & Manton
Printer —
Place Hereford
Type GE TR
Map scale 1:174240
Library BOD
holdings HPL
NLS

REF	**568**
Title	**Jakeman & Carver's City of Hereford & District Directory**
Dates	1895
Publisher	Jakeman & Carver
Printer	Jakeman & Carver
Place	Hereford
Type	GE TR
Map scale	1:10560
Library	HPL

REF	**569**
Title	**Tilley's Ledbury Almanack**
Dates	1903-1950
Publisher	Tilley, L.
Printer	Tilley, L.
Place	Ledbury
Type	ST
Map scale	–
Library	LED

REF	**570**
Title	**The Leominster News Directory**
Dates	1907,1939
Publisher	Leominster Printing Co Ltd
Printer	Leominster Printing Co Ltd
Place	Leominster
Type	ST
Map scale	–
Library	GL has 1939
holdings	NLW has 1907

REF	**571**
Title	**The Hereford Journal Directory**
Dates	1912,1914
Publisher	The Herefordshire Press & Printing Co
Printer	The Herefordshire Press & Printing Co
Place	Hereford
Type	GE TR
Map scale	1:7920
Library	BL
holdings	BOD
	HPL
	NLS
	ULC

REF	**572**
Title	**Hereford City Year Book and Business Directory**
Dates	1922-1924
Publisher	The Herefordshire Press & Printing Co
Printer	The Herefordshire Press & Printing Co
Place	Hereford
Type	ST TR
Map scale	1:7920
Library	BL has 1922
holdings	BOD all
	HPL has 1922,1923
	NLS has 1922

REF	**573**
Title	**Kelly's Directory of Hereford & Neighbourhood**
Dates	1928,1930,1932,1934,1937,1939
Publisher	Kelly's Directories Ltd
Printer	Kelly's Directories Ltd
Place	London
Type	GE TR
Map scale	1:253440
Library	BCL has 1937,1939
holdings	BL all
	GL all
	HPL all
	WCL has 1937

REF	**574**
Title	**Ross Year Book. Directory of Ross and surrounding villages**
Dates	1935
Publisher	Ross Gazette Ltd
Printer	Ross Gazette Ltd
Place	Ross-on-Wye
Type	CM
Map scale	–
Library	GL

REF	**575**
Title	**Hereford and District Directory**
Dates	1950
Publisher	Kent Service Ltd
Printer	The Birmingham Printers Ltd
Place	London
Type	GE
Map scale	–
Library	GL
holdings	HPL
	NLW

HERTFORDSHIRE

REF	**576**
Title	**Kelly's Directory of Hertfordshire**
Dates	1851,1855,1859,1862,1866,1870, 1874,1878,1882,1886,1890,1895, 1899,1902,1906,1908,1910,1912, 1914,1917,1922,1926,1929,1933, 1937
Publisher	Kelly & Co
Printer	Kelly & Co
Place	London
Type	GE TR
Map scale	1:84480
Library	AYL has 1902
holdings	BCL has 1890-1929,1937
	BED has 1851
	BL not 1851,1926
	BIS has 1902,1937
	BOD not 1855,1874,1917,1926
	BPH has 1866,1874,1886,1895, 1906,1926,1929
	CLB has 1937
	CLE has 1937
	CLM has 1859,1937
	COL has 1855,1859,1878
	GL not 1910
	GLH not 1851,1929,1937
	HLS not 1851,1859,1866,1874, 1908,1912
	IHR has 1890,1906,1910
	KCL has 1859,1866
	LUT has 1910,1912,1926,1929, 1933,1937
	MLG has 1870,1874,1899-1937
	NLS not 1926
	NLW has 1912,1914,1929,1937
	SCL has 1926,1933,1937
	SOG has 1851-1862,1874,1882, 1890,1899,1902,1914,1926, 1929
	STA has 1862,1870-1890, 1899-1912,1917-1937
	ULC all
	WAT has 1859,1874-1899,1910, 1926,1937
	YCL has 1937

REF	**577**
Title	**Williams' Directory of the Principal Market Towns in Hertfordshire etc**
Dates	1850
Publisher	Williams, J.
Printer	–
Place	London
Type	GE TR
Map scale	–
Notes	NORTON 372
Library	GL

REF	**578**
Title	**Langley's Almanack & Directory [St Albans]**
Dates	1881,1882
Publisher	Langley, W.
Printer	Langley, W.
Place	St Albans
Type	ST
Map scale	–
Notes	Cont'd by 579
Library	STA

REF	**579**
Title	**Stevens' Almanack & Directory [St Albans]**
Dates	1883,1884
Publisher	Stevens, G.
Printer	Stevens, G.
Place	St Albans
Type	ST
Map scale	–
Notes	Cont'd from 578; cont'd by 581.
Library	STA

REF	**580**
Title	**History of Watford and Trade Directory**
Dates	1884
Publisher	Williams, H.
Printer	Pardon & Sons
Place	London
Type	TR
Map scale	–
Notes	This directory has been reprinted by Chapel Rivers Press, with an introduction by Peter Taylor. WAT holds both the original and the reprinted edition.
Library	WAT

REF **581**
Title **The St Albans Almanack and General Advertiser**
Dates 1886-1889,1891,1893
Publisher Gibbs & Bamforth
Printer Gibbs & Bamforth
Place St Albans
Type ST
Map scale –
Notes Cont'd from 579
Library STA

REF **582**
Title **Brackett's Almanack [Hemel Hempstead]**
Dates 1889-1891,1895,1897,1899, 1901-1903
Publisher Brackett (?)
Printer –
Place Hemel Hempstead
Type CM
Map scale –
Library HLS

REF **583**
Title **Peacock's Watford Directory and Almanack**
Dates 1890-1933
Publisher Peacock, C.H.
Printer Peacock, C.H.
Place Watford
Type ST
Map scale 1:9050
Notes See 585
Library BL not 1891,1894,1896-1899,
holdings 1901
holdings BOD has 1892,1893
HLS has 1929
NLS has 1892,1893
ULC has 1892,1893
WAT all

REF **584**
Title **Kelly's Directory of St Albans, Harpenden & Hatfield**
Dates 1900-1915,1922-1941,1946,1949
Publisher Kelly's Directories Ltd
Printer Kelly's Directories Ltd
Place London
Type GE
Map scale NS
Library BL all
holdings BOD has 1900-1912
GL not 1941
HLS has 1927,1928,1936-1938, 1941,1949
STA not 1902,1904,1905,1908, 1915
ULC has 1900-1912

REF **585**
Title **Kelly's Directory of Watford, Bushey, Harrow, Rickmansworth and district**
Dates 1900-1938,1940-1942,1944,1947, 1949
Publisher Kelly's Directories Ltd
Printer Kelly's Directories Ltd
Place London
Type GE
Map scale 1:63360
Notes See 583. Incorporates Peacock's Watford Directory in 1934.
Library BL all
holdings BOD has 1900-1911
CLM has 1932,1947
GL all
HLS has 1929,1937,1938,1947, 1949
NLW has 1949
ULC has 1900-1912
WAT not 1902,1903,1916-1919

REF **586**
Title **Hertford Directory, Guide and Reference Book**
Dates 1903,1905
Publisher Summers-Gill, J.H.
Printer Henderson & Spalding
Place Hertford
Type ST TR
Map scale –
Notes See 592
Library BL has 1905
holdings BOD has 1903
NLS has 1903

REF	**587**		REF	**591**
Title	**Letchworth Garden City Directory**		Title	**The Letchworth Directory**
Dates	1907		Dates	1920,1923,1930,1933,1935,1937, 1939,1947
Publisher	Wheeler, Odell & Co		Publisher	The Letchworth Printers Ltd
Printer	Wheeler, Odell & Co		Printer	The Letchworth Printers Ltd
Place	Letchworth		Place	Letchworth
Type	CM TR		Type	GE TR
Map scale	–		Map scale	1:10560
Library	GL		Notes	Map scale approx.
			Library	BL all
REF	**588**		holdings	GL has 1939,1947
Title	**Mardon Bros.' Year Book, Directory and Almanack ... Directories for Bishops Stortford, and fifty of the surrounding towns and villages**		REF	**592**
			Title	**Simson's Directory, Guide and Reference Book [Hertford & Ware]**
Dates	1910		Dates	1920,1924,1927,1930
Publisher	Mardon Bros		Publisher	Simson & Co Ltd
Printer	–		Printer	Simson & Co Ltd
Place	Bishops Stortford		Place	Hertford
Type	GE		Type	GE
Map scale	–		Map scale	–
Library	HLS		Notes	See 586
			Library	HLS
REF	**589**			
Title	**Price's Annual Year Book and Almanack containing complete alphabetical Directory... of Ware and District**		REF	**593**
			Title	**The Herts Advertiser Year Book and Directory of St Albans**
Dates	1912		Dates	1922,1932
Publisher	Price, G. & Son		Publisher	Herts Advertiser
Printer	Price, G. & Son		Printer	Herts Advertiser
Place	Ware		Place	St Albans
Type	CT		Type	GE
Map scale	–		Map scale	NS
Library	GL		Library	HLS all
			holdings	STA has 1922
REF	**590**			
Title	**Jennings' & Bewley's Ware and District Almanack**		REF	**594**
			Title	**Welwyn Garden City Directory**
Dates	1916		Dates	1928-1941
Publisher	Jennings & Bewley		Publisher	The Welwyn Garden City & Hertfordshire Pilot
Printer	Jennings & Bewley		Printer	The Welwyn Garden City & Hertfordshire Pilot
Place	Ware		Place	Welwyn Garden City
Type	CT		Type	GE
Map scale	–		Map scale	1:8000
Notes	T/P missing HLS edition.		Notes	1929 onwards published by Welwyn Publications Ltd
Library	HLS		Library	BL not 1920,1929-1931
			holdings	BOD not 1920
				GL has 1937
				HLS not 1928,1938
				NLS not 1928,1929,1931,1933, 1937
				ULC has 1935-1941

REF **595**
Title **Kelly's Directory of Hertford, Hoddesdon, Ware & Neighbourhood**
Dates 1936,1938,1940,1943,1945
Publisher Kelly's Directories Ltd
Printer Kelly's Directories Ltd
Place London
Type GE TR
Map scale –
Library BL all
holdings CLM has 1945
GL not 1936,1943
HLS all

REF **596**
Title **Hitchin Directory**
Dates 1948
Publisher Letchworth Printers Ltd
Printer Letchworth Printers Ltd
Place Letchworth
Type GE TR
Map scale NS
Library BL
holdings GL
HLS

HUNTINGDONSHIRE

REF **597**
Title **History, Gazetteer and Directory of the County of Huntingdon**
Dates 1854
Publisher Hatfield, J.
Printer Hatfield, J.
Place Huntingdon
Type CM
Map scale –
Notes NORTON 373
Library BCL
holdings BL
CAM
GL
HNT
PET
SOG

REF **598**
Title **Kelly's Directory of Huntingdonshire**
Dates 1854,1864,1869,1877,1885,1890,
1894,1898,1903,1906,1910,1914,
1920,1924,1928,1931,1936,1940
Publisher Kelly & Co
Printer Kelly & Co
Place London
Type GE TR
Map scale 1:253440
Notes See 7(1854-1877) & 14(1885-1940)
Library AYL has 1869
holdings BCL has 1890-1936
BED not 1854,1864,1877,1906,
1924
BIS has 1936
BL all
BOD has 1885-1940
BPH has 1869,1894,1903,
1914-1924,1940
CLB has 1936
CLE has 1940
CLM has 1940
CLO has 1869,1877
GL has 1854-1928
HNT not 1854,1877
IHR has 1898,1903,1914
LUT has 1885,1890,1914,1920,
1936,1940
MLG has 1910,1920,1924
NEW has 1869
NLS not 1869
NLW has 1928-1936
PET has 1869,1877,1890,1894,
1903,1906,1924,1940
SCL has 1928-1940
SOG has 1854,1864,1877,1894,
1906,1910,1924,1940
ULC all

REF **599**
Title **Craven & Co's Commercial Directory of the County of Huntingdon and the Town of Cambridge**
Dates 1855
Publisher Craven & Co
Printer Craven & Co
Place Nottingham
Type GE TR
Map scale –
Notes NORTON 374. HNT & PET have editions entitled 'Craven & Co's Commercial Directory of the Counties of Huntingdon and Cambridge'
Library CAM
holdings GL
HNT
PET
SOG

ISLE OF MAN

REF **600**
Title **Residential and Trade Directory to Douglas and Trade Directory to Ramsey**
Dates 1892,1895
Publisher Broadbent, S.K.
Printer Broadbent, S.K.
Place Douglas
Type GE TR
Map scale –
Library BL

REF **601**
Title **The N.M.P. Manx Year Book (Who's Who) and Business Directory**
Dates 1920-1933,1935-1950
Publisher Norris Modern Press
Printer Norris Modern Press
Place Douglas
Type SP
Map scale –
Notes (Who's Who) dropped from title 1940 onwards. No directory sections at all. General information on public bodies, statistics relating to Isle of Man etc.
Library CLM has 1920-1924,1926,1929,
holdings 1932,1933,1935,1938,1940,1942, 1946
holdings NLS not 1920-1924
NLW has 1947,1949

REF **602**
Title **Isle of Man Directory**
Dates 1939
Publisher Business Directories
Printer –
Place Bloxwich
Type TR
Map scale –
Library BL

KENT

REF **603**
Title **Kelly's Directory of Kent**
Dates 1851,1855,1859,1862,1866,1870,
1874,1878,1882,1887,1891,1895,
1899,1901,1903,1905,1907,1909,
1911,1913,1915,1918,1922,1924,
1927,1930,1934,1938
Publisher Kelly & Co
Printer Kelly & Co
Place London
Type GE TR
Map scale 1:380160
Notes See 3, 16 & 19
Library BCL has 1870,1891-1899,
holdings 1903-1938
holdings BED has 1851
BIS has 1938
BL not 1851
BOD not 1855,1874,1901,1918
BPH has 1866,1874,1887,1905,
1905,1918-1930
CHI has 1905,1930,1938
CLB has 1938
CLE has 1895,1938
CLM has 1859,1927,1938
COL has 1855,1859
GL not 1901
GLH not 1851,1901,1913-1918,
1924,1927,1924,1938
HLS has 1878
IHR has 1887,1891,1905
KCL has 1855,1859,1866,
1882-1899,1905-1938
MAI has 1895,1907,1909,
1913-1938
MLG has 1870,1874
NLS all
NLW has 1913,1915,1924,
1930-1938
SCL has 1930-1938
SLS has 1882,1911,1918,1938
SOG has 1851-1866,1874,1882,
1890,1909,1927
ULC all
WOR has 1891,1903
YCL has 1938

REF **604**
Title **Melville & Co's Directory &
Gazetteer of Kent**
Dates 1858
Publisher Melville & Co
Printer Collingridge, W.H.
Place London
Type CM
Map scale –
Library GL
holdings KCL

REF **605**
Title **Green's Mid Kent Court Guide
and County Blue Book**
Dates 1874
Publisher Green & Co
Printer –
Place London
Type CT
Map scale –
Library GL
holdings KCL
MAI

REF **606**
Title **W.E. Owen & Co's General,
Typographical and Historical
Directory for the County of Kent**
Dates 1883
Publisher Owen, W.E. & Co
Printer Owen, W.E. & Co
Place Leicester
Type CM
Map scale 1:570240
Library GL

REF **607**
Title **Kent Trades' Directory,
including Margate, Ramsgate,
Maidstone and Tunbridge Wells**
Dates 1939
Publisher Town and County Directories
Ltd
Printer Macdonald, W.
Place Edinburgh
Type TR
Map scale –
Library KCL

REF	**608**
Title	**Kent Directory**
Dates	1948-1950
Publisher	Aubrey & Co
Printer	Aubrey & Co
Place	Walsall
Type	TR
Map scale	–
Notes	Cont'd from 104
Library	BL

REF	**609**
Title	**Dartford &c Directory**
Dates	1850
Publisher	Williams, J.
Printer	–
Place	London
Type	CM TR
Map scale	–
Notes	T/P missing KCL edition
Library	KCL

REF	**610**
Title	**New and Enlarged Directory for Maidstone and its Environs**
Dates	1850
Publisher	West, W.
Printer	West, W.
Place	Maidstone
Type	CM TR
Map scale	NS
Notes	NORTON 412
Library	GL
holdings	KCL
	MAI
	SOG

REF	**611**
Title	**Monckton's Directory for Maidstone & Neighbouring Villages**
Dates	1854
Publisher	Monckton, W.
Printer	Monckton, W.
Place	Maidstone
Type	CT CM
Map scale	NS
Notes	NORTON 413
Library	BL
holdings	NLS
	ULC

REF	**612**
Title	**A Directory for Rochester, Chatham, Strood**
Dates	1858
Publisher	Phippen, J. & J.
Printer	Ostell, W.
Place	Rochester
Type	CM
Map scale	NS
Library	GL

REF	**613**
Title	**The Sheppey Almanack and Directory**
Dates	1862,1863
Publisher	Rigg, T.M.
Printer	Rigg, T.M.
Place	Blue Town
Type	TR
Map scale	–
Library	BL has 1863
holdings	BOD has 1862

REF	**614**
Title	**Hall's Gravesend, Milton & Northfleet Directory**
Dates	1862-1889
Publisher	Hall, T.
Printer	Hall, T.
Place	London
Type	ST TR
Map scale	–
Library	BL all
holdings	BOD all
	NLS has 1863,1865,1866
	ULC not 1868,1869,1871,1876, 1878

REF	**615**
Title	**The Bromley Directory, includes Bromley, Beckenham, Chislehurst & all Parishes in the Bromley District**
Dates	1866,1883,1885-1887
Publisher	Strong, E. & Sons
Printer	Strong, E. & Sons
Place	Bromley
Type	GE
Map scale	1:42240
Notes	Cont'd as 631
Library	BL not 1866
holdings	BOD has 1885,1886
	GL has 1866
	NLS has 1886
	ULC has 1886

REF	**616**		REF	**620**
Title	**Mathiesons' Tunbridge Wells and Tonbridge Directory**		Title	**Directory of Maidstone & Neighbourhood with East & West Malling**
Dates	1867			
Publisher	Pelton, R.		Dates	1882,1885,1889,1893,1895
Printer	Mathiesons		Publisher	Stevens, G.
Place	Tunbridge Wells		Printer	Stevens, G.
Type	GE TR		Place	London
Map scale	–		Type	GE TR
Library	BL		Map scale	1:63360
holdings	BOD		Library	BL all
	NLS		holdings	MAI has 1892
	ULC			NLS has 1885-1893
				ULC has 1885,1893

REF	**617**		REF	**621**
Title	**The Chatham and Rochester Directory, Family Almanack and Year Book of Useful Information**		Title	**The Chislehurst, Bickley, Sidcup, Cray Valley Directory**
Dates	1867		Dates	1882,1887
Publisher	Taylor, R.		Publisher	Wing, L.
Printer	Taylor, R.		Printer	Wing, L.
Place	Chatham		Place	Chislehurst
Type	CM		Type	CT CM
Map scale	–		Map scale	–
Library	GL		Library	BL has 1887
			holdings	GL has 1882

REF	**618**		REF	**622**
Title	**The Handy Directory and Guide for Maidstone and surrounding villages**		Title	**Directory of Canterbury and Neighbourhood**
Dates	1872		Dates	1882,1889
Publisher	Vivish, W.S.		Publisher	Stevens, G.
Printer	Vivish, W.S.		Printer	Stevens, G.
Place	Maidstone		Place	London
Type	CT TR		Type	GE TR
Map scale	–		Map scale	1:633600
Library	MAI		Library	BL all
holdings	NLS		holdings	BOD has 1889
				NLS has 1889
				ULC has 1889

REF	**619**		REF	**623**
Title	**Rixon, Hill & Co's Canterbury with Faversham, Whitstable and Herne Bay Directory**		Title	**Directory and Guide to the Isle of Thanet**
Dates	1875		Dates	1883
Publisher	Rixon, Hill & Co		Publisher	Hutchings & Crowsley
Printer	–		Printer	Hutchings & Crowsley
Place	London		Place	London
Type	GE TR		Type	GE
Map scale	1:506880		Map scale	NS
Library	GL		Library	GL

REF	**624**
Title	**The Isle of Thanet Directory**
Dates	1883,1886
Publisher	Hutchings & Crowsley
Printer	Hutchings & Crowsley
Place	London
Type	GE TR
Map scale	1:126720
Library	BL
holdings	BOD

REF	**625**
Title	**Kelly's Directory of the Isle of Thanet**
Dates	1883,1886-1916,1920,1922-1939, 1948
Publisher	Kelly & Co
Printer	Kelly & Co
Place	London
Type	GE TR
Map scale	1:126720
Library	BL all
holdings	BOD has 1887-1912
	GL not 1883-1887,1889-1895, 1897,1902,1927
	MLG has 1948
	ULC has 1886-1912

REF	**626**
Title	**W.T. Pike's District Blue Book, Weald of Kent and Romney Marsh Directory**
Dates	1884
Publisher	Pike, W.T.
Printer	Osborne, H.
Place	Hastings
Type	GE
Map scale	–
Library	GL
holdings	KCL

REF	**627**
Title	**Ridout & Flowers' Herne Bay Directory and Year Book**
Dates	1885,1890,1892,1894,1895,1897
Publisher	Ridout & Flowers
Printer	Ridout & Flowers
Place	Herne Bay
Type	GE
Map scale	–
Library	BL all
holdings	BOD not 1897
	GL has 1897
	ULC not 1894,1897

REF	**628**
Title	**Directory of Tunbridge Wells, Tonbridge & Neighbourhood, including all villages within 6 miles**
Dates	1886
Publisher	Stevens, G.
Printer	Stevens, G.
Place	London
Type	GE TR
Map scale	1:633600
Library	BL
holdings	BOD
	NLS
	ULC

REF	**629**
Title	**Wilson's Ramsgate and St Lawrence Directory**
Dates	1886
Publisher	Wilson S.R.
Printer	Wilson, S.R.
Place	Ramsgate
Type	GE TR
Map scale	1:10560
Library	BL

REF	**630**
Title	**Pike's Dover Blue Book and Local Directory**
Dates	1887,1890-1940
Publisher	Robinson & Pike
Printer	Robinson, A.M.
Place	Brighton
Type	GE TR
Map scale	–
Library	BL all
holdings	BOD has 1890-1900,1902-1939
	GL not 1890-1935,1937,1940
	NLS not 1887,1900,1901,1919, 1920,1940
	ULC not 1887,1901,1919,1920, 1925

REF **631**
Title **Strong's Bromley Directory**
Dates 1888,1890-1905
Publisher Strong, E.
Printer Strong, E.
Place Bromley
Type GE TR
Map scale 1:42240
Notes Cont'd from 615, cont'd as 632.
Published by Kelly's Directories Ltd
from 1899.
Library BL all
holdings BOD has 1898-1905
GL has 1898-1905
NLS has 1898-1905
ULC has 1898-1905

REF **632**
Title **Kelly's Bromley, Chislehurst &
Bickley Directory**
Dates 1888-1897,1906-1918,1920-1940,
1950
Publisher Kelly & Co
Printer Kelly & Co
Place London
Type GE TR
Map scale 1:15480
Notes Cont'd from 631. Chislehurst &
Bickley included 1888-1897, 1922-
1940. Orpington included 1922-
1940. 1950 covers Bromley, Hayes
& Keston.
Library BL all
holdings BOD has 1888-1912
CRD has 1930
GL not 1888-1897,1917
GLH has 1907,1911,1915,1916,
1920,1923,1927-1931,1933,
1934,1936
KCL has 1925,1927,1930
MLG has 1950
NLS has 1907
NLW has 1950
SOG has 1930
ULC has 1888-1912

REF **633**
Title **Kelly's Penge, Anerley &
Beckenham Directory**
Dates 1888-1908,1909-1917,1922-1929,
1931,1933-1939
Publisher Kelly & Co
Printer Kelly & Co
Place London
Type GE TR
Map scale 1:15840
Notes Title changes in order of places
listed. Anerley dropped from title
after 1933.
Library BL all
holdings BOD has 1888-1912
CLM has 1939
CRD has 1937,1938
GL not 1889-1891,1900,1928,
GLH has 1904,1906,1907,1910,
1911,1913,1915-1917,
1923-1925,1927,1929-1938
KCL has 1927,1933,1937,1938
SOG has 1938
ULC has 1888-1912

REF **634**
Title **Kelly's Directory of Maidstone &
Neighbourhood**
Dates 1889,1892,1900-1919,1947,1949
Publisher Kelly & Co
Printer Kelly & Co
Place London
Type GE TR
Map scale –
Notes See 649
Library BL all
holdings BOD has 1889-1912
GL not 1892,1915-1919
MAI has 1947,1949
MLG has 1899,1903,1905,1907,
1909,1911,1913,1915,1918,
1922,1924,1927,1930,1934,
1938
SOG has 1914
ULC has 1889-1912

REF **635**
Title **Ward's Beckenham and Penge Advertiser, Almanack and Directory**
Dates 1889-1897
Publisher Ward, J.
Printer Ward, J.
Place London
Type CT
Map scale –
Library BL all
holdings CRD has 1890

REF **636**
Title **Pike's Folkestone, Hythe and Sandgate Directory**
Dates 1889-1910
Publisher Robinson & Pike
Printer Robinson, A.M.
Place Brighton
Type GE TR
Map scale –
Library BL not 1889
holdings BOD has 1889-1900,1902-1910
NLS not 1889,1901
ULC all

REF **637**
Title **Kelly's Directory of Tunbridge Wells, Southborough, Tonbridge and villages in the neighbourhood**
Dates 1889-1917,1919-1940,1948,1950
Publisher Kelly & Co
Printer Kelly & Co
Place London
Type GE TR
Map scale 1:7920
Library BL all
holdings BOD has 1889-1899,1901-1912
GL not 1890-1894,1896,1897,
1899,1903,1906,1908,1910,
1936
KCL has 1914,1940
NLW has 1950
ULC has 1889-1912
WOR has 1948

REF **638**
Title **Kelly's Directory of Canterbury, Whitstable & Herne Bay**
Dates 1890,1891,1899-1906,1925-1940,
1949
Publisher Kelly & Co
Printer Kelly & Co
Place London
Type GE TR
Map scale –
Library BL not 1949
holdings BOD has 1890-1906
GL not 1890-1900,1905,1938,
1949
KCL has 1924
NLW has 1949
ULC has 1890-1906

REF **639**
Title **Webster's Year Book and Directory of Gravesend, Milton, Northfleet and 25 neighbouring Parishes**
Dates 1890-1892
Publisher Webster, E.P.
Printer Webster, E.P
Place Gravesend
Type CM
Map scale 1:7920
Library BL all
holdings BOD all
ULC not 1890

REF **640**
Title **Kelly's Directory of Rochester, Strood & Chatham**
Dates 1890-1892,1894-1916,1919-1939,
1948
Publisher Kelly & Co
Printer Kelly & Co
Place London
Type GE TR
Map scale 1:10560
Library BL all
holdings CLM has 1931
GL not 1891-1897,1902,1903,
1907,1911,1915,1921
ULC has 1890-1911

REF **641**
Title **Maidstone in 1892 Illustrated. Its History, Manufacturers, Trade.**
Dates 1892
Publisher Robinson, Son & Pike
Printer Robinson, Son & Pike
Place London
Type TR
Map scale –
Notes Very detailed descriptive entries for all major manufacturing firms, and well illustrated with engravings & photographs
Library MAI

REF **642**
Title **Walsham Bros' Sidcup, Foot's Cray, Lamorbey and New Eltham Directory**
Dates 1892
Publisher Walsham Bros.
Printer Walsham Bros.
Place Sidcup
Type GE
Map scale –
Library BL

REF **643**
Title **Bush's Bromley Budget with a Directory of Bromley**
Dates 1892-1914
Publisher Bush, S.
Printer Bush, S.
Place London
Type GE
Map scale 1:12672
Notes 1910 & after entitled 'Bush's Directory of Bromley'
Library BL all
holdings BOD all
GL has 1911
KCL has 1908
NLS all
ULC not 1892

REF **644**
Title **Pike's Tunbridge Wells, Tonbridge & Southborough Directory**
Dates 1893-1895
Publisher Robinson & Pike
Printer Robinson, A.M.
Place Brighton
Type GE
Map scale –
Library BL not 1893
holdings BOD all
ULC all

REF **645**
Title **Pike's Canterbury & District, Herne Bay & Whitstable Directory**
Dates 1893-1939
Publisher Robinson & Pike
Printer Robinson, A.M.
Place Brighton
Type GE TR
Map scale –
Library BL all
holdings BOD has 1893-1918,1921-1932, 1934-1939
KCL has 1921,1932,1934,1939
NLS not 1900,1915-1939
ULC not 1920

REF **646**
Title **Herne Bay Press Directory**
Dates 1894
Publisher Herne Bay Press
Printer Herns Bay Press
Place Herne Bay
Type ST
Map scale NS
Library BL

REF **647**
Title **Kelly's Directory of Folkestone, Sandgate, Hythe, Cheriton & villages in the neighbourhood**
Dates 1896-1909,1927-1940,1947,1949
Publisher Kelly's Directories Ltd
Printer Kelly's Directories Ltd
Place London
Type GE TR
Map scale 1:126720
Library BL all
holdings BOD has 1896-1908
BPH has 1947
GL has 1906-1908
KCL has 1940
ULC has 1896-1909

REF **648**
Title **T.F. Pain's Deal, Walmer and Sandwich Directory**
Dates 1897-1899,1903,1904,1906, 1908-1918,1920-1940,1948
Publisher Pain, T.F.
Printer Mercury Printers
Place Deal
Type GE
Map scale –
Library BL all
holdings GL has 1936,1948

REF **649**
Title **Kent Messenger Directory of Maidstone & surrounding villages**
Dates 1898,1903,1907-1911,1913-1915, 1917,1920,1921,1923,1925,1927, 1930,1933,1937
Publisher Kent Messenger
Printer Kent Messenger
Place Maidstone
Type GE TR
Map scale 1:6000
Notes See 634
Library BL not 1898,1903,1914
holdings GL has 1937
KCL has 1898,1903,1910,1921, 1927-1937
SOG has 1914,1933

REF **650**
Title **Kelly's Directory of Gravesend, Milton, Northfleet & District**
Dates 1899-1914,1922,1924
Publisher Kelly's Directories Ltd
Printer Kelly's Directories Ltd
Place London
Type GE TR
Map scale 1:126720
Library BL all
holdings GL not 1902,1903
ULC has 1899-1912

REF **651**
Title **Pike's Blue Book and Local Directory for Deal, Walmer & Sandwich**
Dates 1899-1915
Publisher Robinson & Pike
Printer Robinson, A.M.
Place Brighton
Type GE TR
Map scale –
Library BL all
holdings BOD all
NLS not 1899,1900
ULC has 1899-1912,1914,1915

REF **652**
Title **Milton Union &c Directory and Guide**
Dates 1903
Publisher Parsons, F.J. Ltd
Printer Parsons, F.J. Ltd
Place Hastings
Type GE
Map scale –
Library GL

REF **653**
Title **Salmon's Directory and Handbook of Sevenoaks & Neighbourhood**
Dates 1903
Publisher Salmon, J.
Printer Salmon, J.
Place Sevenoaks
Type GE
Map scale 1:6336
Library BL

REF	**654**
Title	**Jenkins' Local Directory and Advertiser for Abbey Wood, Bexley Heath, Bexley ... Slade's Green, Upton, Welling**
Dates	1903,1907,1912,1920
Publisher	Jenkins, T.
Printer	Jenkins, T.
Place	Bexley Heath
Type	GE
Map scale	–
Library	BL

REF	**655**
Title	**Caddel's Year Book and Directory of Gravesend, Milton, Northfleet & Neighbouring Parishes**
Dates	1903-1913,1915
Publisher	Caddel's
Printer	Caddel's
Place	Gravesend
Type	GE TR
Map scale	1:5280
Library	BL

REF	**656**
Title	**Isle of Sheppey Directory and Guide**
Dates	1904
Publisher	Kent Messenger
Printer	Kent Messenger
Place	Maidstone
Type	GE TR
Map scale	–
Library	GL

REF	**657**
Title	**Perry's Dartford Almanac and Directory**
Dates	1904,1906,1907,1909-1915
Publisher	Perry
Printer	Perry
Place	Dartford
Type	ST
Map scale	–
Library	BL

REF	**658**
Title	**The Beckenham Directory**
Dates	1904-1916
Publisher	Thornton, T.W.
Printer	Thornton, T.W.
Place	Beckenham
Type	GE
Map scale	1:15480
Library	BL

REF	**659**
Title	**The Kent County Examiner Directory of Ashford**
Dates	1904-1918,1920,1922,1924,1926, 1929
Publisher	Boorman, P.B.
Printer	Kent County Examiner
Place	Ashford
Type	GE
Map scale	NS
Library	BL

REF	**660**
Title	**Sidcup Directory including Foot's Cray and Lamorbey**
Dates	1905,1906
Publisher	Forwood, C.
Printer	Sidcup Times
Place	Sidcup
Type	GE
Map scale	–
Library	BL all
holdings	BOD has 1905
	ULC has 1905

REF	**661**
Title	**Turner and Robinson's Directory and Almanack: Eltham, New Eltham and Mottingham**
Dates	1905,1906
Publisher	Turner & Robinson
Printer	Turner & Robinson
Place	Eltham
Type	GE
Map scale	–
Notes	Cont'd as 662
Library	BL

REF	**662**
Title	**Eltham Directory...Eltham, New Eltham, Well Hall and Mottingham**
Dates	1907-1915
Publisher	Digby, H.C.
Printer	–
Place	Eltham
Type	GE
Map scale	–
Notes	Cont'd from 661
Library	BL

REF	663
Title	**The Sittingbourne, Milton and District Directory**
Dates	1908
Publisher	Parrett, W.J.
Printer	–
Place	Sittingbourne
Type	GE
Map scale	–
Library	KCL

REF	664
Title	**The Isle of Sheppey Directory**
Dates	1909
Publisher	Cole, W.J.
Printer	Cole, W.J.
Place	Sheerness
Type	GE
Map scale	1:7920
Library	BL
holdings	BOD

REF	665
Title	**Parsons' Directory and Year Book of Folkestone & District**
Dates	1909,1910,1913-1916,1918-1926
Publisher	Parsons, F.J.
Printer	Parsons, F.J.
Place	Folkestone
Type	GE TR
Map scale	1:10560
Library	BL not 1910
holdings	SOG has 1910

REF	666
Title	**Kentish Express Guide and Directory to Ashford, Romney Marsh, Tenterden & District**
Dates	1911-1918,1920,1926,1930,1935
Publisher	Kentish Express
Printer	Kentish Express
Place	Ashford
Type	GE
Map scale	–
Library	BL all
holdings	BOD has 1912,1930
	NLS has 1930
	NLW has 1930

REF	667
Title	**T.F. Pain & Sons' Sandwich District Directory**
Dates	1914,1915
Publisher	Pain, T.F. & Sons
Printer	Pain, T.F. & Sons
Place	Sandwich
Type	GE
Map scale	–
Library	BL

REF	668
Title	**Hooker's Household Almanack, Diary & Directory [Westerham]**
Dates	1916,1921-1937
Publisher	Hooker Bros.
Printer	Hooker Bros.
Place	Westerham
Type	CT CM
Map scale	–
Library	BL all
holdings	KCL has 1937

REF	669
Title	**Maidstone, Tunbridge Wells, Dover and South Kent District Trades' Directory**
Dates	1916,1925,1930,1932
Publisher	Town and County Directories Ltd
Printer	Macdonald, W. & Co
Place	Edinburgh
Type	TR
Map scale	–
Notes	1916 edition entitled 'Maidstone, Royal Tunbridge Wells, Dover and South Kent District Trades' Directory'
Library	KCL not 1916
holdings	MAI has 1916

REF	670
Title	**Faversham and District Illustrated Directory**
Dates	1921
Publisher	Vickery, Kyrle & Co
Printer	Vickery, Kyrle & Co
Place	London
Type	GE TR
Map scale	1:7920
Library	BL

REF	**671**
Title	**Jenkins' Local Directory and Advertiser for Erith, Belvedere & Abbeywood ... and Northend**
Dates	1921
Publisher	Jenkins, T.W.
Printer	Jenkins, T.W.
Place	Erith
Type	GE
Map scale	–
Library	BL

REF	**672**
Title	**Local Directory for Old Bexley, Bexley Heath, East Wickham, Welling, Barnehurst**
Dates	1929
Publisher	Bexley and District Publications Ltd
Printer	–
Place	Bexley Heath
Type	CT
Map scale	–
Library	KCL

REF	**673**
Title	**Reporter Gravesend Directory**
Dates	1929
Publisher	Reporter
Printer	Reporter
Place	Gravesend
Type	GE
Map scale	–
Library	GL

REF	**674**
Title	**Snowden's Dartford Directory and Almanack**
Dates	1930
Publisher	Snowden Brothers
Printer	Snowden Brothers
Place	Dartford
Type	CT CM
Map scale	–
Library	KCL

REF	**675**
Title	**Headley's Directory of Ashford and District**
Dates	1933,1938
Publisher	Headley Bros.
Printer	Headley Bros.
Place	Ashford
Type	GE TR
Map scale	–
Library holdings	BL has 1933 GL has 1938 KCL all

REF	**676**
Title	**Thomson's Almanac and Directory. Tenterden**
Dates	1934,1939
Publisher	Thomson, W.
Printer	Thomson, W.
Place	Tenterden
Type	CT TR
Map scale	–
Library	GL

REF	**677**
Title	**The Directory and Handbook of Sevenoaks and Neighbourhood**
Dates	1935-1937,1939,1941,1949
Publisher	The Caxton and Holmesdale Press
Printer	The Caxton and Holmesdale Press
Place	Sevenoaks
Type	GE
Map scale	–
Library holdings	GL not 1941 KCL has 1941

REF	**678**
Title	**Faversham and District Directory**
Dates	1939
Publisher	Voile & Roberson
Printer	Voile & Roberson
Place	Faversham
Type	GE
Map scale	–
Library	KCL

REF **679**
Title **Dover and District Local Directory**
Dates 1948
Publisher The Channel Publishing Co
Printer The Channel Publishing Co
Place Hove
Type GE TR
Map scale 1:10560
Notes Map scale approx.
Library GL

REF **680**
Title **Kelly's Directory of Dover and Neighbourhood**
Dates 1950
Publisher Kelly's Directories Ltd
Printer Kelly's Directories Ltd
Place London
Type GE TR
Map scale NS
Library GL

LANCASHIRE

REF **681**
Title **Slater's Royal National Classified Commercial Directory and Topography of the County of Lancashire**
Dates 1851
Publisher Slater, I.
Printer Slater, I.
Place Manchester
Type TR
Map scale 1:15840
Notes NORTON 93
Library BL
holdings CLM
GL
LRO
PHL

REF **682**
Title **History, Topography and Directory of Mid-Lancashire**
Dates 1854
Publisher Mannex & Co
Printer Bailey, W. & Thomson, H.
Place Preston
Type TR
Map scale —
Notes NORTON 430
Library BLA
holdings BPH
BUR
CLM
GL
LAN
LHQ
LRO
PHL

REF **683**
Title **Kelly's Directory of Lancashire with Liverpool and Manchester**
Dates 1858,1864,1873,1881,1887,1892, 1898
Publisher Kelly & Co
Printer Kelly & Co
Place London
Type GE TR
Map scale 1:10560
Notes See 692. 1858-1873 entitled 'Post Office Directory of Lancashire with Liverpool and Manchester'.

Library holdings BCL has 1892 (LIV & MCR),1895 (LIV),1898 (LANC)
BL all
BOD all
BPH has 1873 (L'pool only), 1881,1892,1898
CLM all
GL not 1898
LAN has 1898
LHQ has 1858,1873
NLS all
SOG has 1887
ULC all
WAR has 1864,1881,1892

REF 684
Title **Slater's Royal National Commercial Directory of Lancashire**
Dates 1865,1869,1876,1879,1882,1885, 1887,1890,1892,1895
Publisher Slater, I.
Printer Slater, I.
Place Manchester
Type GE TR
Map scale 1:253440
Library holdings BCL has 1892
BL not 1865-1871,1879,1890, 1892
BLA has 1869
BOD has 1876,1882,1892,1895
CLM has 1876,1890-1895
GL not 1869,1871,1879
LAN has 1879
LHQ all
LRO has 1895
NLS has 1876,1882,1892,1895
NLW has 1882
WAR has 1869,1895
ULC has 1876

REF 685
Title **Directory of North and East Lancashire &c**
Dates 1868
Publisher Mannex, P. & Co
Printer Toulmin, G.
Place Preston
Type GE TR
Map scale –
Notes ST section for Preston only
Library holdings BLA
BUR
GL
LRO

REF 686
Title **Worrall's Commercial Directory of Lancashire and adjoining districts**
Dates 1879
Publisher Worrall, J.
Printer Worrall, J.
Place Oldham
Type TR
Map scale –
Library holdings BL
BOD
NLS
ULC

REF 687
Title **Worrall's Commercial Directory of South-West Lancashire**
Dates 1879
Publisher Worrall, J.
Printer Worrall, J.
Place Oldham
Type TR
Map scale –
Library BPH

REF 688
Title **The Cotton Spinners and Manufacturers Directory**
Dates 1882,1884-1942,1944-1950
Publisher Worrall, J.
Printer Worrall, J.
Place Oldham
Type SP
Map scale –
Notes Arranged by place & type of activity giving approx number of spindles & looms & pay days of major firms. 1920 onwards entitled 'The Lancashire Textile Industry'.
Library holdings BL not 1889
BOD all
BPH has 1940-1942,1944,1945, 1949
BRD has 1916,1925,1928,1931, 1935,1938,1941,1945,1946, 1949,1950
CLM has 1884,1887,1889,1891, 1892,1897-1900,1903, 1908-1946,1948-1950
MLG has 1908,1911,1912,1915, 1920-1922,1924
NLS not 1882-1886,1889,1908, 1920
NLW has 1950
ULC all

REF	689
Title	**Deacon's Lancashire Court Guide and County Blue Book**
Dates	1884,1903
Publisher	Deacon, C.W. & Co
Printer	Deacon, C.W. & Co
Place	London
Type	PR
Map scale	1:253440
Library holdings	BOD has 1903
	BPH has 1903
	CL has 1903
	GL has 1884
	LAN has 1903
	NLS has 1903
	ULC all
	WAR has 1903

REF	690
Title	**Hutton's Agricultural Directory for South West Lancashire**
Dates	1892
Publisher	Hutton, T.
Printer	Ormskirk Advertiser
Place	Ormskirk
Type	SP
Map scale	–
Notes	Farmer's name, farm name, location & distance from nearest town
Library holdings	BL
	BOD
	ULC

REF	691
Title	**Wrench's Merchants', Manufacturers', and Export Shippers' Directory of Lancashire**
Dates	1898
Publisher	Wrench, W.H.
Printer	Taylor & Co
Place	Manchester
Type	SP
Map scale	–
Notes	Sections for export shippers, & TR for merchants & manufacturers
Library	NLS

REF	692
Title	**Kelly's Directory of Lancashire**
Dates	1901,1905,1909,1913,1918,1924
Publisher	Kelly's Directories Ltd
Printer	Kelly's Directories Ltd
Place	London
Type	GE TR
Map scale	1:190080
Notes	Cont'd from 683
Library holdings	BCL all
	BL all
	BLA has 1924
	BOD not 1918
	BPH all
	CL has 1913-1924
	CLB has 1924
	CLM all
	GL all
	LAN has 1901,1905,1913
	LHQ all
	LRO has 1909,1913,1924
	MLG all
	NLW has 1913,1924
	PHL has 1924
	SCL has 1924
	SOG has 1924
	ULC all
	WAR has 1913,1924
	YCL has 1924

REF	693
Title	**Lancashire Directory**
Dates	1932,1936-1940
Publisher	Aubrey & Co
Printer	Aubrey & Co
Place	Walsall
Type	TR
Map scale	–
Library holdings	BL has 1936-1940
	LAN has 1932

REF **694**
Title **The Bury Directory (including all towns in the Bury Union)**
Dates 1850
Publisher Heap, J.
Printer Heap, J.
Place Bury
Type TR
Map scale –
Notes NORTON 434
Library CLM
holdings GL

REF **695**
Title **Slater's General and Classified Directory and Street Register of Manchester and Salford**
Dates 1850-1852,1855-1858,1861,1863, 1865,1869,1871,1874,1876,1877, 1879,1881-1889,1891-1921
Publisher Slater, I.
Printer Slater, I.
Place Manchester
Type GE TR
Map scale 1:10560
Notes NORTON 524,525 (1850, 1851);527 (1852);528 (1855). Cont'd as 801.
Library BCL has 1895
holdings BL has 1850,1851,1863,1869, 1876,1881,1883-1889, 1892-1894,1896-1921
BOD has 1876,1883,1889, 1892-1913,1917,1919
CL not 1891,1899
CLM all
GL has 1850,1855,1869, 1877-1881,1883,1884, 1886-1921
IHR has 1850
LHQ has 1852
LRO has 1852
MLG has 1898,1900,1902,1904, 1906,1908,1910,1912, 1914-1921
NLW has 1912,1915,1920
PHL has 1899,1905,1909,1919
SOG has 1861,1894
ULC has 1876,1893,1894, 1896-1913,1917,1919

REF **696**
Title **Slater's Classified Commercial Directory of the towns and villages in the Manufacturing District round Manchester**
Dates 1851
Publisher Slater, I.
Printer Slater, I.
Place Manchester
Type GE TR
Map scale 1:15840
Notes NORTON 526
Library BL
holdings CL

REF **697**
Title **The History, Topography and Directory of the Borough of Preston and 7 miles round**
Dates 1851
Publisher Mannex, P. & Co
Printer Johnson, W.B.
Place Beverley
Type CM
Map scale –
Notes NORTON 532. Trades section for Central Preston.
Library BLA
holdings BUR
CLM
GL
IHR
LAN
LHQ
LRO
PHL

REF **698**
Title **Oakey's Commercial Directory of Preston**
Dates 1851,1853
Publisher Oakey, H.
Printer Oakey, H.
Place Preston
Type GE
Map scale 1:7826
Notes 1853 edition entitled 'Oakey's Commercial and Trade Directory of Preston'
Library LRO all
holdings PHL has 1853

REF	**699**
Title	**Gore's Directory for Liverpool and its Environs**
Dates	1851,1853,1855,1857,1859,1860, 1862,1864,1865,1867,1868, 1870-1897
Publisher	Mawdsley, J. & Son
Printer	Mawdsley, J. & Son
Place	Liverpool
Type	GE TR
Map scale	–
Notes	NORTON 478-480 (1851,1853, 1855). Cont'd as 771.
Library holdings	BCL has 1873
	BL not 1851-1855,1865
	BOD has 1870-1897
	BPH all
	CL has 1855
	CLM not 1860,1862,1871,1873, 1875,1877,1878,1882,1887, 1888
	GL not 1870-1873,1875, 1887-1891,1894
	IHR has 1851,1857
	LHQ has 1865
	LRO has 1853
	MLG has 1872,1880,1882
	NLS has 1853,1859-1897
	NLW has 1864
	SOG has 1859,1865
	ULC has 1859-1897
	WAR has 1862

REF	**700**
Title	**A New Alphabetical and Classified Directory of Manchester and Salford & vicinity**
Dates	1852,1853
Publisher	Whellan, W.
Printer	Booth & Milthorp
Place	Manchester
Type	GE TR
Map scale	1:380160
Notes	NORTON 426,427
Library holdings	BL has 1853
	CL all
	CLM all
	GL all

REF	**701**
Title	**The Manchester Mercantile & Manufacturing Annual Directory and Record of Industrial Progress**
Dates	1854
Publisher	Collinson & Co
Printer	Ireland, A. & Co
Place	Manchester
Type	CM TR
Map scale	–
Notes	NORTON 529
Library holdings	BL
	CL
	CLM

REF	**702**
Title	**B.H. Gillbanks and Co's Directory and Gazetteer of Preston, Lancaster and Morecambe Bay**
Dates	1857
Publisher	Gillbanks, B.H. & Co
Printer	Bailey, W.
Place	Preston
Type	CM TR
Map scale	–
Library holdings	LHQ
	PHL

REF	**703**
Title	**B.H. Gillbanks and Co's Directory and Gazetteer of Preston, Fleetwood, Blackpool, Lytham, Poulton-le-Fylde &c**
Dates	1857
Publisher	Gillbanks, B.H. & Co
Printer	Bailey, W.
Place	Preston
Type	CM TR
Map scale	–
Library holdings	LHQ
	LRO
	PHL

REF	**704**
Title	**B.H. Gillbanks & Co's Directory and Gazetteer of Preston, Blackburn, Accrington, Church, Enfield etc ...**
Dates	1858
Publisher	Gillbanks, B.H. & Co
Printer	Bailey, W.
Place	Preston
Type	CM TR
Map scale	–
Library	LHQ

REF **705**
Title **Slater's Royal National Commercial Directory of Manchester and Liverpool and the principal manufacturing towns in Lancashire**
Dates 1858, 1861
Publisher Slater, I.
Printer Slater, I.
Place Manchester
Type GE TR
Map scale 1:7920
Library BL has 1858
holdings BLA has 1858
CL all
CLM has 1861
GL has 1861
LHQ all

REF **706**
Title **Commercial Directory of Preston, Fleetwood, Blackpool, Lytham, Poulton-le-Fylde & Kirkham**
Dates 1860
Publisher Brown, J.W.
Printer –
Place Preston
Type GE TR
Map scale –
Library LRO
holdings PHL

REF **707**
Title **Drake's Commercial Directory of Bolton, Bury, Wigan, Chorley, Darwen, Leigh, Radcliffe, Ramsbottom**
Dates 1861
Publisher Drake, E.S. & Co
Printer –
Place Sheffield
Type GE TR
Map scale –
Library CL

REF **708**
Title **The Post Office Directory of Lancaster and Its Vicinity**
Dates 1864
Publisher Kelly & Co
Printer Kelly & Co
Place London
Type CM TR
Map scale –
Notes LAN edition comprises rebound extracts from 683 (Kelly's Lancashire 1864) although the T/P and first part relate specifically to Lancaster
Library LAN

REF **709**
Title **The Post Office Directory of Liverpool**
Dates 1864
Publisher Kelly & Co
Printer Kelly & Co
Place London
Type GE TR
Map scale NS
Library GL

REF **710**
Title **Preston and District: being the First Volume of the Directory and Topography of North Lancashire**
Dates 1865
Publisher Mannex, P.
Printer Harkness, J.
Place Preston
Type GE TR
Map scale –
Library LRO
holdings PHL

REF **711**
Title **Topography and Directory of North and South Lonsdale, Amounderness, Leyland and Southport**
Dates 1866
Publisher Mannex, P. & Co
Printer Harkness, J.
Place Preston
Type GE TR
Map scale –
Library BL
holdings BLA
GL
IHR
LHQ

[165]

REF **712**
Title **Directory and Topography of Southport and North Lancashire District**
Dates 1866,1868
Publisher Mannex, P. & Co
Printer Harkness, J.
Place Preston
Type CM
Map scale –
Notes Limited trades section for Southport
Library BLA has 1866
holdings BPH has 1866
GL has 1868

REF **713**
Title **Directory of Blackburn and East Lancashire**
Dates 1868
Publisher Mannex, P. & Co
Printer Toulmin, G.
Place Preston
Type GE TR
Map scale –
Library BLA

REF **714**
Title **The Business Directory of Manchester**
Dates 1868
Publisher Morris, J.S.C.
Printer Morris, J.S.C.
Place London
Type TR
Map scale –
Library BL
holdings BOD
CL
CLM
NLS
ULC

REF **715**
Title **The Official Directory of Southport and Birkdale**
Dates 1868,1869,1876
Publisher Green, B.L.
Printer Johnson & Green
Place Southport
Type GE TR
Map scale 1:3600
Library BL has 1868
holdings BOD has 1868
GL has 1876
LRO has 1868,1869
[166] NLS has 1868

REF **716**
Title **Commercial and General Directory of Preston including the townships of Ashton, Fulwood, Penwortham & Walton-le-Dale**
Dates 1869
Publisher Gillett, G.A.
Printer Greenall, C.
Place Preston
Type GE TR
Map scale –
Library IHR
holdings LRO
PHL

REF **717**
Title **The Wigan Directory with all the parishes, townships & villages in the Wigan Union and the village of Golborne**
Dates 1869
Publisher Worrall, J.
Printer Worrall, J.
Place Blackburn
Type GE TR
Map scale –
Library BL
holdings CLM
GL
SOG

REF **718**
Title **The Commercial Directory of Liverpool and Shipping Guide**
Dates 1869-1887,1889
Publisher Pascoe & Co
Printer Pascoe & co
Place Liverpool
Type TR
Map scale –
Library BL not 1881,1884,1886
holdings BOD all
NLS has 1869

REF **719**
Title **A. Green & Co's Directory for Liverpool and Birkenhead**
Dates 1870
Publisher Green, A. & Co
Printer –
Place London
Type CM TR
Map scale –
Library BPH

REF	**720**		REF	**725**
Title	**The Blackburn and Darwen Directory**		Title	**Worrall's Directory of Oldham and District**
Dates	1870		Dates	1871,1875,1880,1884,1888,1891
Publisher	Worrall, J.		Publisher	Worrall, J.
Printer	Worrall, J.		Printer	Worrall, J.
Place	Blackburn		Place	Oldham
Type	GE TR		Type	GE TR
Map scale	–		Map scale	NS
Library	BL		Library	BL all
			holdings	BOD not 1871
REF	**721**			NLS not 1871
Title	**The Bolton and District Directory**			ULC not 1871
Dates	1870		REF	**726**
Publisher	Worrall, J.		Title	**Worrall's Directory of Warrington, Wigan, St Helens & adjoining districts**
Printer	Worrall, J.		Dates	1871,1876
Place	Bolton		Publisher	Worrall, J.
Type	GE TR		Printer	Worrall, J.
Map scale	–		Place	Oldham
Library	BL		Type	GE TR
			Map scale	–
REF	**722**		Library	BL all
Title	**Directory and Historical Sketches of St Helens & District**		holdings	BOD has 1876
Dates	1871			CL has 1871
Publisher	Mannex & Co			NLS has 1876
Printer	Toulmin, G.			ULC has 1876
Place	Preston			WAR all
Type	CM TR			
Map scale	–		REF	**727**
Library	BPH		Title	**Worrall's Directory of Burnley, Accrington, Church ... & adjoining townships**
holdings	WAR		Dates	1872
			Publisher	Worrall, J.
REF	**723**		Printer	Worrall, J.
Title	**Porter's Guide to Blackpool, Fleetwood, Lytham &c with a Directory of Blackpool**		Place	Oldham
Dates	1871		Type	CM TR
Publisher	Porter, W.		Map scale	NS
Printer	Porter, W.		Library	BL
Place	Blackpool & Fleetwood		holdings	BUR
Type	CT TR			
Map scale	–			
Library	LHQ			
holdings	PHL			
REF	**724**			
Title	**Worrall's Directory of Bury and Bolton & Neighbourhoods**			
Dates	1871			
Publisher	Worrall, J.			
Printer	Worrall, J.			
Place	Oldham			
Type	GE TR			
Map scale	–			
Library	BL			

REF | 728
Title | **Worrall's Wigan & District Directory with Chorley & Ormskirk**
Dates | 1872
Publisher | Worrall, J.
Printer | Worrall, J.
Place | Oldham
Type | GE TR
Map scale | –
Library | BL
holdings | BPH
 | CLM

REF | 729
Title | **Directory of Preston and District**
Dates | 1873,1877,1885
Publisher | Mannex, P. & Co
Printer | Snape, T. & Co
Place | Preston
Type | GE TR
Map scale | –
Notes | 1873 edition entitled 'Directory of Preston and Six Miles Round'
Library | GL has 1877,1885
holdings | LRO has 1873
 | PHL has 1873,1877

REF | 730
Title | **Worrall's Directory of Rochdale and adjoining townships**
Dates | 1873,1885
Publisher | Worrall, J.
Printer | Worrall, J.
Place | Oldham
Type | GE TR
Map scale | –
Library | BL all
holdings | BOD has 1885
 | NLS has 1885
 | ULC has 1885

REF | 731
Title | **Directory of Preston, Blackburn, Accrington, Darwen, Chorley and Adjacent Villages and Townships**
Dates | 1874
Publisher | Mannex, P. & Co
Printer | Snape, T. & Co
Place | Preston
Type | GE TR
Map scale | –
Library | PHL

REF | 732
Title | **Directory of the Boroughs of Blackburn, Accrington & Darwen**
Dates | 1874,1878,1881,1885,1888,1891, 1894,1897,1900,1903,1906,1909, 1912,1915,1925,1930,1935,1939, 1942,1947
Publisher | Barrett, P.
Printer | Snape, T.
Place | Preston
Type | CM TR
Map scale | –
Notes | Later editions entitled 'Commercial and General Directory of Blackburn, Accrington & Darwen'
Library | BL not 1874
holdings | BLA has 1874,1878,1885-1939, 1947
 | BOD has 1878,1900,1909, 1925-1942
 | BPH has 1942
 | BUR has 1909,1935,1939,1947
 | CLM has 1925,1935-1947
 | GL not 1874
 | NLS has 1900,1909,1925-1947
 | LHQ has 1878,1930
 | LRO has 1878-1894,1900,1906, 1912-1939,1947
 | ULC has 1900,1909,1925-1942

REF | 733
Title | **The Barrow-in-Furness Directory**
Dates | 1875
Publisher | Mather, M.
Printer | Mather, M.
Place | Barrow-in-Furness
Type | GE
Map scale | NS
Library | BL
holdings | BOD
 | NLS

REF | 734
Title | **Directory and Topography of North East Lancashire with Bury and District**
Dates | 1876
Publisher | Mannex, P. & Co
Printer | Snape, T. & Co
Place | Preston
Type | CM TR
Map scale | –
Library | LRO

REF **735**
Title **History and Directory of Barrow-in-Furness and the whole of North Lonsdale**
Dates 1876
Publisher Mannex, P. & Co
Printer Snape, T. & Co
Place Preston
Type CM TR
Map scale –
Library LHQ

REF **736**
Title **P.O. Bolton Directory**
Dates 1876,1877,1887,1894,1896,1898, 1902-1904,1907,1911,1916,1922, 1927,1932
Publisher Tillotson & Son
Printer Tillotson & Son
Place Bolton
Type GE TR
Map scale 1:31680
Library BL not 1876,1877,1887
holdings BOD has 1876
CLM has 1911
GL has 1876,1887
LRO has 1876,1877
MLG has 1876,1932
NLS not 1877
ULC has 1876

REF **737**
Title **Hosking's Mercantile and Professional Directory for Manchester and Salford**
Dates 1877
Publisher Hosking, A.W.
Printer –
Place Manchester
Type CM PR
Map scale –
Library BOD
holdings NLS

REF **738**
Title **Worrall's Commercial Annual and Street Directory of Oldham and Chadderton**
Dates 1878,1880,1882
Publisher Worrall, J.
Printer Worrall, J.
Place Oldham
Type ST
Map scale –
Notes With pay days of major firms
Library BOD has 1882
holdings ULC all

REF **739**
Title **Slater's Royal National Commercial Directory of Southport and Birkdale**
Dates 1878,1882,1883,1886,1887,1890, 1892,1893,1895,1896,1901
Publisher Slater, I.
Printer Slater, I.
Place Manchester
Type GE TR
Map scale 1:12000
Library BL not 1878,1890,1892,1896
holdings BOD not 1878,1882,1892,1896
BPH has 1883-1890,1893
CLM has 1882,1883,1892-1895, 1901
GL all
NLS has 1883,1895,1901
SOG has 1901
ULC has 1893,1901

REF **740**
Title **General and Commercial Directory of Burnley & adjacent villages and townships**
Dates 1879,1883,1887,1890,1893,1896, 1899,1902,1905,1908,1911,1914, 1923,1927,1933,1937,1941,1945, 1949
Publisher Barrett, P.
Printer Barrett, P.
Place Preston
Type GE TR
Map scale –
Notes 1879 edition entitled 'Directory & Topography of Burnley, Nelson, Colne, Padiham'
Library BL not 1933
holdings BOD has 1899,1911-1949
BPH has 1945
BUR all
CLM has 1933,1941-1949
GL has 1887,1896,1902,1908, 1927,1945,1949
LAN has 1949
LHQ has 1923,1927,1949
LRO has 1883,1902,1914-1939
NLS has 1899-1949
NLW has 1949
ULC has 1899-1937,1941-1949

REF	**741**
Title	**The Directory of Preston and Fylde Districts**
Dates	1880
Publisher	Mannex, P. & Co
Printer	Parkinson, R. & Co
Place	Preston
Type	CM TR
Map scale	–
Library	LHQ
holdings	LRO
	PHL

REF	**742**
Title	**Axon's Commercial & General Directory of Bolton, Farnworth, Kearsley, Halliwell, Astley Bridge, Turton, Ainsworth, Walkden, Westhoughton and the townships comprised in the Bolton Union**
Dates	1881
Publisher	Axon, H.
Printer	–
Place	Bolton
Type	GE TR
Map scale	–
Library	LRO

REF	**743**
Title	**Topography and Directory of Lancaster and Sixteen Miles Round**
Dates	1881
Publisher	Mannex, P. & Co
Printer	Parkinson, R. & Co
Place	Preston
Type	CM TR
Map scale	–
Library	BCL
holdings	LAN
	LHQ
	LRO

REF	**744**
Title	**Topography and Directory of Preston, (the Fylde), Lancaster and Districts**
Dates	1881,1886
Publisher	Mannex, P. & Co
Printer	Parkinson, R & Co
Place	Preston
Type	GE TR
Map scale	–
Notes	Title includes the Fylde in 1886
Library	GL has 1881
holdings	LAN has 1886
	LHQ has 1881
	LRO has 1881

REF	**745**
Title	**Axon's Commercial Annual Street and Special Trades Directory for Blackburn, Darwen, Accrington, Oswaldtwistle, Clitheroe and adjoining districts**
Dates	1882
Publisher	Axon, H.
Printer	–
Place	Bolton
Type	SL TR
Map scale	–
Library	BLA

REF	**746**
Title	**History and Directory of Furness and Cartmel**
Dates	1882
Publisher	Mannex, P. & Co
Printer	Snape, T. & Co
Place	Preston
Type	CM TR
Map scale	–
Library	CLM
holdings	GL
	LAN
	LHQ
	LRO
	PHL

REF **747**
Title **General and Commercial Directory of Preston and adjacent villages**
Dates 1882,1885,1889,1892,1895,1898, 1901,1904,1907,1910,1913,1917, 1922,1926,1932,1936,1940,1944, 1948
Publisher Barrett, P.
Printer Snape, T.
Place Preston
Type GE TR
Map scale –
Notes 1882 edition entitled 'General and Commercial Directory of Preston, Chorley, Kirkham, Garstang and adjacent villages'
Library BL not 1917
holdings BLA has 1948
BOD has 1901,1910-1940
BPH has 1898,1936,1944,1948
BUR has 1940,1948
CLM has 1936-1948
GL has 1895,1898,1917, 1932-1948
LHQ has 1892,1904-1913,1922, 1940,1948
LRO not 1944
NLS has 1901,1910-1940
PHL not 1901
ULC has 1901,1910-1917, 1932-1940
WAR has 1948

REF **748**
Title **Axon's Annual Directory and Buyers' Guide for Blackburn and adjoining districts**
Dates 1883
Publisher Axon, H.
Printer –
Place Bolton
Type TR
Map scale –
Library BLA

REF **749**
Title **General and Commercial Directory of Bury, Heywood, Radcliffe, Pilkington, Prestwich, Ramsbottom etc**
Dates 1883
Publisher Barrett, P. & Co
Printer Snape, T. & Co
Place Preston
Type GE TR
Map scale –
Notes Street section for Bury only
Library GL

REF **750**
Title **Slater's Directory of Warrington, Widnes, St Helens, Earlestown**
Dates 1883,1891,1895
Publisher Slater, I.
Printer Slater, I.
Place Manchester
Type GE TR
Map scale –
Library BL has 1883
holdings CLM has 1883,1895
GL has 1891
WAR all

REF **751**
Title **Directory of Barrow-in-Furness and the Furness District**
Dates 1886
Publisher Roberts, C.J. [compiler]
Printer Lord, S.S.
Place Barrow-in-Furness
Type GE TR
Map scale –
Library CAR

REF **752**
Title **Topography and Directory of Lancaster, Morecambe, Carnforth, Milnthorpe**
Dates 1886
Publisher Barrett, P. & Co
Printer Snape, T. & Co
Place Preston
Type CM TR
Map scale –
Library BPH
holdings GL
LAN

REF	**753**
Title	**Burnage, Chorlton, Didsbury, Fallowfield & Withington Directory**
Dates	1887
Publisher	Thompson, H.
Printer	Percy Bros.
Place	Manchester
Type	CT
Map scale	–
Library	BL

REF	**754**
Title	**Eccles, Patricroft, Winton, Monton and Barton Directory**
Dates	1887
Publisher	Hargreaves Thompson
Printer	Percy Bros.
Place	Manchester
Type	CM
Map scale	–
Library	BL

REF	**755**
Title	**Blackburn and District Incorporated Chamber of Commerce Annual Report [and List of Members]**
Dates	1887-1936
Publisher	Blackburn and District Incorporated Chamber of Commerce
Printer	Toulmin, G.
Place	Blackburn
Type	SP
Map scale	–
Notes	19th century editions only contain sketchy information on membership. Later 20th century editions contain lists of members & lists of spindles & looms for Blackburn textile mills.
Library	BLA

REF	**756**
Title	**Slater's Royal National Commercial Directory of Bury, Heywood, Radcliffe and Ramsbottom**
Dates	1888
Publisher	Slater, I.
Printer	Slater, I.
Place	Manchester
Type	GE TR
Map scale	–
Library	BL
holdings	CLM
	GL

REF	**757**
Title	**Directory for the Township of Garston, with ... Wavertree, Woolton, Allerton, Dutton, Hale, Hale Bank, Halewood & Speke**
Dates	1889
Publisher	Rockliff Bros
Printer	Rockliff Bros
Place	Liverpool
Type	GE TR
Map scale	–
Library	BPH

REF	**758**
Title	**Wells' Lancaster & District Directory**
Dates	1889
Publisher	Wells & Co
Printer	–
Place	Shrewsbury
Type	GE TR
Map scale	–
Library	LAN

REF	**759**
Title	**The Blackburn and Districts Directory**
Dates	1891
Publisher	Duncan & Mills
Printer	–
Place	Bolton
Type	GE TR
Map scale	–
Notes	T/P missing from BLA copy
Library	BLA

REF	**760**
Title	**Directory and Guide to the Manchester Royal Exchange Ltd**
Dates	1891,1893,1895,1897,1899, 1901-1950
Publisher	Collinson, R. Ltd
Printer	–
Place	Manchester
Type	SP
Map scale	–
Notes	Sections for firms, towns & trades - all members of the Exchange
Library holdings	BOD all
	CLM not 1897,1918,1931,1941, 1947
	LHQ has 1938
	NLS all
	NLW has 1932,1946-1950

REF	**761**
Title	**Manchester Corn, Grocery & Produce Exchange Directory**
Dates	1893
Publisher	Eckersley & Co [compilers]
Printer	–
Place	Manchester
Type	SP
Map scale	–
Notes	Alph. & TR sections
Library	BL

REF	**762**
Title	**Kelly's Directory of Liverpool and Suburbs with ... Birkenhead**
Dates	1893-1897
Publisher	Kelly & Co
Printer	Kelly & Co
Place	London
Type	GE TR
Map scale	1:10560
Library holdings	BOD all
	BPH has 1894
	NLS all
	ULC all

REF	**763**
Title	**Duncan's Rochdale & District Commercial and Postal Directory**
Dates	1894
Publisher	Duncan, J.G.
Printer	Duncan, J.G.
Place	Bolton
Type	GE TR
Map scale	–
Library holdings	BL
	BOD
	GL
	NLS
	ULC

REF	**764**
Title	**Slater's Directory of Oldham with Chadderton, Glodwick & neighbourhood**
Dates	1895
Publisher	Slater, I.
Printer	Slater, I.
Place	Manchester
Type	GE TR
Map scale	–
Library	CLM

REF	**765**
Title	**Ainsworth's North Manchester Directory comprising Cheetham Hill, Crumpsall, part of Higher Broughton, Kersall & part of Prestwich**
Dates	1896
Publisher	Ainsworth, J.
Printer	Mackie & Co Ltd
Place	Warrington
Type	GE
Map scale	–
Library	CLM

REF **766**
Title **Lancaster, Morecambe & District Directory**
Dates 1896,1899,1901
Publisher Cook, W.J. & Co
Printer Cook, W.J. & Co
Place Hull
Type GE TR
Map scale –
Library BL has 1901
holdings BOD has 1901
CLM has 1901
GL has 1896,1901
LAN all
LRO has 1899
NLS has 1901
SOG has 1901
ULC has 1901

REF **767**
Title **Slater's Directory of Prestwich, Whitefield, Crumpsall**
Dates 1897
Publisher Slater, I.
Printer Slater, I.
Place Manchester
Type GE TR
Map scale 1:63360
Library BL

REF **768**
Title **Slater's Directory of Levenshulme, Heaton Chapel, Heaton Mersey, Heaton Moor, Reddish, Burnage, Withington, Fallowfield & Didsbury**
Dates 1897,1904
Publisher Slater, I.
Printer Slater, I.
Place Manchester
Type GE TR
Map scale 1:63360
Library BL has 1897,1901,1904
holdings BOD has 1901-1904
CL has 1904
CLM has 1898-1900,1903
GL has 1898
LRO has 1904
ULC has 1901-1904

REF **769**
Title **Blackpool and District Directory**
Dates 1898,1900
Publisher Cook, W.J. & Co
Printer Coop, C.J.E.
Place Blackpool
Type GE TR
Map scale –
Library BL all
holdings CLM has 1900

REF **770**
Title **Slater's Directory of Prestwich, Eccles, Patricroft, Barton & District, Stretford and Chorlton-cum-Hardy**
Dates 1898-1904
Publisher Slater, I.
Printer Slater, I.
Place Manchester
Type GE TR
Map scale 1:63360
Library BL has 1901-1904
holdings BOD has 1901-1904
CL has 1900,1902
CLM has 1898-1900
NLS has 1901-1904
ULC has 1901-1904

REF **771**
Title **Kelly's (Gore's) Directory of Liverpool and its suburbs**
Dates 1898-1941,1943,1946,1949
Publisher Kelly's Directories Ltd
Printer Kelly's Directories Ltd
Place London
Type GE TR
Map scale NS
Notes Cont'd from 699
Library BL all
holdings BOD has 1899-1913,1917,1919, 1922-1949
BPH all
CL has 1913,1938
CLE has 1949
CLM not 1939
GL all
LHQ has 1898
LRO has 1899,1905,1909,1914, 1918,1919,1926,1933,1935, 1939,1946
MLG has 1919-1949
NLS not 1898,1914-1916,1921, 1922,1946
NLW has 1907,1911,1913,1915, 1917,1920,1924,1928-1933, 1935-1939,1949
SOG has 1924
ULC not 1914-1916,1919
WAR has 1946,1949

REF **772**
Title **History, Topography, General and Commercial Directory of Burnley, Nelson, Colne, Padiham**
Dates 1899
Publisher Watson, W. & Co
Printer –
Place Preston
Type GE
Map scale –
Library GL

REF **773**
Title **History, Topography, General and Commercial Directory of Lancaster, Morecambe, Skerton, Carnforth, Heysham ... and adjacent villages and townships**
Dates 1899
Publisher Watson, W. & Co
Printer –
Place Preston
Type GE TR
Map scale –
Library LAN

REF **774**
Title **Street Guide and Business Directory for Bury**
Dates 1899
Publisher Bury Times
Printer Bury Times
Place Bury
Type ST TR
Map scale NS
Library BL

REF **775**
Title **The Annual Directory for the Southport Postal District**
Dates 1899,1900,1902
Publisher Weaver, T.
Printer Snape, T. & Co
Place Southport
Type GE TR
Map scale –
Library BL all
holdings BOD all
CLM has 1899
NLS all
ULC all

REF **776**
Title **Morecambe and District Directory**
Dates 1899,1901
Publisher Cook, W.J.
Printer Kitching, T.
Place Derby
Type GE TR
Map scale –
Library BL all
holdings BOD has 1901
GL all
NLS has 1901
ULC has 1901

REF **777**
Title **Blackburn, Burnley & Districts Trades' Directory**
Dates 1900
Publisher Town and County Directories Ltd
Printer Macdonald, W. & Co Ltd
Place Edinburgh
Type TR
Map scale –
Library LRO

REF	**778**		REF	**782**
Title	**Annual Furness Year Book**		Title	**The Twentieth Century Directory for the Wigan Union & Postal Areas**
Dates	1901			
Publisher	Mackereth, H.W.			
Printer	–		Dates	1903
Place	Ulverston		Publisher	Weaver, T. & Co
Type	ST		Printer	Platt, R. & Co
Map scale	–		Place	Wigan
Library	LAN		Type	GE TR
			Map scale	–
REF	**779**		Library	BL
Title	**The Twentieth Century Directory for the Postal Areas of Waterloo, Seaforth, Blundellsands and Hightown**		holdings	BOD
				NLS
				ULC
Dates	1901		REF	**783**
Publisher	Weaver, T. & Co		Title	**Seed's Preston Directory**
Printer	Weaver, T. & Co		Dates	1904
Place	Southport		Publisher	Seed, R.
Type	GE TR		Printer	Seed, R.
Map scale	–		Place	Preston
Library	BL		Type	GE TR
holdings	BOD		Map scale	–
	NLS		Library	BL
	ULC		holdings	GL
				LHQ
REF	**780**			PHL
Title	**The Imperial Directory of Blackpool, Fleetwood, Lytham, St Annes-on-the-Sea and the Fylde**			
			REF	**784**
			Title	**Seed's Southport and District Directory**
Dates	1902		Dates	1904,1906,1908,1910,1912,1914,
Publisher	Designs Ltd			1924,1927,1930,1933,1936,1939
Printer	Designs Ltd		Publisher	Seed, R.
Place	Manchester		Printer	Seed, R.
Type	GE		Place	Preston
Map scale	–		Type	GE TR
Library	LRO		Map scale	1:18103
			Library	BL all
REF	**781**		holdings	BOD not 1904
Title	**McNicol's Liverpool, Bootle and Birkenhead Street Directory, Shipping, Hotel and Business Guide**			CLM has 1904,1908-1936
				GL has 1936,1939
				LHQ has 1924,1930,1939
				LRO has 1908,1914,1924-1933,
Dates	1903			1939
Publisher	McNicol's Publishing Co			NLS not 1904
Printer	–			ULC not 1904
Place	Liverpool			
Type	SL TR			
Map scale	–			
Library	BOD			

REF **785**
Title **Blackburn Tradesmen's Association Annual Report [and List of Members]**
Dates 1904-1917,1922-1950
Publisher Blackburn Tradesmen's Association
Printer Toulmin, G.
Place Blackburn
Type SP
Map scale –
Notes TR section of members
Library BLA

REF **786**
Title **Directory of Waterloo, Blundellsands, Gt Crosby and Seaforth**
Dates 1906,1909,1913,1915,1921,1925, 1929
Publisher Wentworth Publishing Co
Printer Wentworth Publishing Co
Place Liverpool
Type GE
Map scale 1:10560
Library BL all
holdings GL has 1915,1929
LHQ has 1929

REF **787**
Title **Edwards' Manchester and Salford Professional & Trades Directory**
Dates 1906-1910
Publisher Edwards, C.P.
Printer Edwards, C.P.
Place Manchester
Type TR
Map scale –
Library BL all
holdings BOD not 1909
CLM not 1907,1909
NLS not 1909
ULC not 1909

REF **788**
Title **Liverpool and District Trades Directory**
Dates 1908
Publisher Town and County Directories Ltd
Printer Macdonald, W. & Co
Place Edinburgh
Type TR
Map scale NS
Library CLM

REF **789**
Title **Warrington Guardian Directory and History of Warrington and environs**
Dates 1908
Publisher Mackie & Co Ltd
Printer Mackie & Co Ltd
Place Warrington
Type GE TR
Map scale –
Notes See 806
Library CLM
holdings WAR

REF **790**
Title **Seed's Wigan and District Directory**
Dates 1909,1925
Publisher Seed, R. & Sons
Printer Seed, R. & Sons
Place Preston
Type GE TR
Map scale –
Library BL all
holdings BOD has 1909
CLM all
GL has 1925
NLS has 1909
ULC has 1909

REF **791**
Title **The Manchester Coal Exchange Directory**
Dates 1910,1914,1919,1922,1924,1927, 1929,1930,1932,1934-1938,1949, 1950
Publisher Manchester Coal Exchange Committee
Printer
Place Manchester
Type SP
Map scale –
Notes Alph. lists of colliery reps, coal merchants & sundry trades
Library BL has 1910
holdings CLM not 1910
NLS has 1910

REF **792**
Title **Liverpool Shipping: Who's Who? A Complete Directory ... to the Shipping and Allied Trades in the Ports of Liverpool and Manchester**
Dates 1911
Publisher Birchall, C. Ltd
Printer Birchall, C. Ltd
Place Liverpool
Type SP
Map scale 1:16000
Notes Large scale plans of dock areas. Alph. lists of shipping lines, shipowners etc., with details of directors etc.
Library NLS

REF **793**
Title **T. Bulmer & Co's History, Topography and Directory of Furness & Cartmel**
Dates 1911,1912
Publisher Bulmer, T. & Co
Printer Snape, T. & Co
Place Preston
Type GE TR
Map scale –
Library BL has 1911
holdings BOD has 1911
CAR has 1911
GL all
LHQ all
NLS has 1911
ULC has 1911

REF **794**
Title **Directory of the Streets, Roads, Names of Houses etc in Greater Bolton**
Dates 1912,1935
Publisher –
Printer Ikin, G.S.
Place Bolton
Type SL
Map scale –
Notes See 805
Library BL

REF **795**
Title **T. Bulmer & Co's History, Topography and Directory of Lancaster and District**
Dates 1913
Publisher Bulmer, T. & Co
Printer Snape, T. & Co
Place Preston
Type GE TR
Map scale 1:190080
Library BL
holdings BPH
CL
GL
LAN
LHQ
LRO

REF **796**
Title **Preston, Barrow and District Trades' Directory**
Dates 1913,1930,1931
Publisher Town and County Directories Ltd
Printer Macdonald, W. & Co
Place Edinburgh
Type TR
Map scale –
Notes See 777, 815
Library GL has 1913
holdings LAN has 1930,1931

REF **797**
Title **Clegg's Commercial Directory of Rochdale**
Dates 1916
Publisher Clegg, J.
Printer Clegg, J.
Place Rochdale
Type GE TR
Map scale –
Library CLM

REF **798**
Title **Blackburn (Lancashire) & Its Manufactures**
Dates 1919,1923
Publisher Burrow, E.J.
Printer –
Place Cheltenham
Type TR
Map scale 1:42240
Notes Detailed entries for all major manufacturers & TR section
Library BLA

REF	**799**
Title	**The Preston and District Incorporated Chamber of Commerce Statement of Accounts and List of Members**
Dates	1919-1929,1931,1934,1936,1937
Publisher	Preston and District Incorporated Chamber of Commerce
Printer	Toulmin, G. & Sons Ltd
Place	Preston
Type	SP
Map scale	–
Notes	Annual Report & alph. & TR lists
Library	PHL

REF	**800**
Title	**Southport "Visiter" Directory**
Dates	1920
Publisher	Southport Visiter
Printer	Southport Visiter
Place	Southport
Type	GE TR
Map scale	1:18103
Library	BL
holdings	LRO

REF	**801**
Title	**Kelly's (Slater's) Directory of Manchester, Salford and suburbs**
Dates	1922-1940,1942,1945,1948
Publisher	Kelly's Directories Ltd
Printer	Kelly's Directories Ltd
Place	London
Type	GE TR
Map scale	1:10560
Notes	Cont'd from 695
Library	BL not 1948
holdings	BOD all
	BPH has 1940-1945
	CL all
	CLE has 1948
	CLM all
	GL all
	LHQ has 1948
	LRO has 1926,1932,1936,1937, 1939,1942,1945,1948
	MLG not 1934
	NLS all
	NLW has 1924,1929-1933,1935, 1937,1939
	WAR has 1948
	ULC all

REF	**802**
Title	**Blackburn, Burnley & District Directory and Buyers' Guide**
Dates	1923,1930
Publisher	Cope, E.F. & Co
Printer	Cope, E.F. & Co
Place	Walsall
Type	TR
Map scale	–
Library	CLM has 1930
holdings	GL has 1923

REF	**803**
Title	**Barrett's General and Commercial Directory of Blackpool and the Fylde**
Dates	1924,1929,1934,1935,1937-1939, 1941
Publisher	Mather Bros.
Printer	Mather Bros.
Place	Preston
Type	GE TR
Map scale	–
Library	BL has 1924,1929,1934,1938
holdings	BOD has 1924,1929,1934,1938
	BPH has 1938
	BUR has 1934
	CLM has 1934
	GL has 1934,1938
	LHQ has 1929
	LRO has 1929,1934,1938
	NLS has 1924,1929,1934,1938
	SCL has 1934,1935,1937,1939, 1941
	ULC has 1934,1938

REF	**804**
Title	**The Up To Date Directory of Streets, Roads etc Bolton**
Dates	1925
Publisher	Hopkins & Sons
Printer	Hopkins & Sons
Place	Bolton
Type	SL
Map scale	–
Library	BL

REF **805**
Title **Allison's Directory of Streets etc ... in Bolton**
Dates 1926
Publisher Henry, G. & Co
Printer Henry, G. & Co
Place Bolton
Type SL
Map scale –
Notes See 794
Library BL

REF **806**
Title **Warrington Guardian Year Book, Business Directory and Guide**
Dates 1926-1939
Publisher Warrington Guardian
Printer Warrington Guardian
Place Warrington
Type CM
Map scale –
Notes The Business Directory was published as a supplement to the Warrington Guardian Yearbook during the years 1926-1939. WAR has all editions of the Yearbook. 1892-1950.
Library GL has 1938
holdings WAR all

REF **807**
Title **Manchester Chamber of Commerce Handbook ... with a list of members, trade index etc**
Dates 1928,1931
Publisher Manchester Chamber of Commrce
Printer Falkner, G. & Sons Ltd
Place Manchester
Type SP
Map scale –
Notes Alph. list of members (firms) & TR section
Library CLM has 1928
holdings LHQ all

REF **808**
Title **Preston, Blackpool and District Directory and Buyers' Guide**
Dates 1929,1931,1932,1935
Publisher Cope, E.F. & Co
Printer Cope, E.F. & Co
Place Walsall
Type TR
Map scale –
Library LAN has 1929,1931,1935
holdings LRO has 1932
PHL has 1929
12

REF **809**
Title **Cox's Liverpool Commercial Agents' Directory**
Dates 1930,1931
Publisher Cox, F.J.
Printer Daily Post Printers
Place Liverpool
Type SP
Map scale –
Notes Agents listed under societies/ associations etc.
Library BL
holdings BOD
BPH
NLW
ULC

REF **810**
Title **Directory of Merseyside Manufacturers**
Dates 1931
Publisher The Liverpool Organisation Ltd
Printer Duncan, A.W. & Co Ltd
Place Liverpool
Type SP
Map scale –
Notes Alph. list of firms with details of founding, capital, directors, products etc.
Library BL
holdings BOD
BPH
NLS
NLW
ULC
WAR

REF **811**
Title **Dickinson's Popular Directory of Streets, Roads, Lanes, Courts, Villas, Public Offices and Institutions [Blackburn]**
Dates 1932
Publisher Dickinson, J.
Printer Dickinson, J.
Place Blackburn
Type SL
Map scale –
Notes Title taken from cover of directory
Library BLA

REF **812**
Title **Tillotson's Bolton Directory**
Dates 1932
Publisher Tillotsons Newspapers Ltd
Printer Tillotsons Newspapers Ltd
Place Bolton
Type GE TR
Map scale 1:10560
Library BOD
holdings CLM
ULC

REF **813**
Title **Liverpool & District Directory and Buyers' Guide**
Dates 1932,1935
Publisher Cope, E.F. & Co
Printer Cope, E.F. & Co
Place Walsall
Type TR
Map scale –
Library WAR

REF **814**
Title **Liverpool List of Streets**
Dates 1932,1950
Publisher General Post Office
Printer –
Place Liverpool
Type SL
Map scale NS
Library BPH

REF **815**
Title **Blackburn, Burnley, Preston, Barrow & District Trades' Directory**
Dates 1933,1937
Publisher Town and County Directories Ltd
Printer Macdonald, W. & Co Ltd
Place Edinburgh
Type TR
Map scale –
Notes See 796,777
Library BUR has 1933
holdings LAN has 1937
LRO has 1933
12

REF **816**
Title **Lancaster, Morecambe and Suburban Directory**
Dates 1934
Publisher Shires, F.N.
Printer Shires, F.N.
Place Lancaster
Type GE TR
Map scale –
Library LAN

REF **817**
Title **The Warrington County Borough and District Directory**
Dates 1935
Publisher Whipple, R.D. Son & Martin Ltd
Printer Whipple, R.D. Son & Martin Ltd
Place Leeds
Type GE TR
Map scale –
Library GL
holdings WAR

REF	**818**
Title	**The Rochdale County Borough Directory**
Dates	1935,1938
Publisher	Whipple, R.D. Son & Martin Ltd
Printer	Whipple, R.D. Son & Martin Ltd
Place	Leeds
Type	GE TR
Map scale	–
Notes	1938 edition published by Douglas, Osborne & Co Ltd
Library holdings	CLM has 1938
	GL has 1935
	LRO has 1935

REF	**819**
Title	**The Bury County Borough Directory**
Dates	1936
Publisher	Edwards & Bryning Ltd
Printer	Edwards & Bryning Ltd
Place	Rochdale
Type	GE TR
Map scale	–
Library holdings	CLM
	GL
	LRO

REF	**820**
Title	**Laslett's Stretford Street Guide**
Dates	1938
Publisher	Osborne, Rice & Co
Printer	Osborne, Rice & Co
Place	Manchester
Type	SL
Map scale	NS
Library	NLS

REF	**821**
Title	**Bury & District Chamber of Commerce ... Annual Report Also a List of the Members with their Business Classifications**
Dates	1947
Publisher	Bury & District Chamber of Commerce
Printer	–
Place	Bury
Type	SP
Map scale	–
Notes	Alph. & TR lists
Library	BUR

REF	**822**
Title	**Directory of Firms Located on the Industrial Estate of Trafford Park**
Dates	1948
Publisher	The Trafford Park Information Bureau Ltd
Printer	–
Place	Manchester
Type	SP
Map scale	–
Notes	Alph. list of firms located on the estate with description of business, officials, location
Library	CLM

REF	**823**
Title	**Ashton-under-Lyne and District Trades and Industrial Directory**
Dates	1950
Publisher	Grove Publishing Co Ltd
Printer	Edwards & Bryning Ltd
Place	Manchester
Type	TR
Map scale	–
Library	CLM

LEICESTERSHIRE

REF	**824**
Title	**Melville & Co's Directory and Gazetteer of Leicestershire including all the Market Towns**
Dates	1854
Publisher	Melville & Co
Printer	Stanley, J.
Place	Worcester
Type	CM TR
Map scale	1:253440
Notes	NORTON 543
Library	CLL

REF	**825**
Title	**Commercial Directory of Leicestershire**
Dates	1861
Publisher	Drake, E.S. & Co
Printer	Kershaw, K.
Place	Sheffield
Type	CM TR
Map scale	–
Library holdings	CLL
	IHR

REF **826**
Title **Mercer & Crocker's General, Topographical and Historical Directory and Gazetteer for Leicestershire**
Dates 1877
Publisher Mercer & Crocker
Printer Mercer & Crocker
Place Hull
Type CM
Map scale –
Notes CLL edition, T/P missing, title may be incorrect
Library CLL

REF **827**
Title **Leicestershire Directory**
Dates 1934-1937,1939,1940
Publisher Aubrey & Co
Printer Aubrey & Co
Place Walsall
Type TR
Map scale –
Notes Also includes Derbyshire
Library BL

REF **828**
Title **Wright's Midland Directory - Leicester & Loughborough with Burton-on-Trent**
Dates 1864
Publisher Wright, C.N.
Printer Wright, C.N.
Place Nottingham
Type CM TR
Map scale –
Library BL
holdings CLL

REF **829**
Title **Street, Alphabetical and Trade Directory of Leicester**
Dates 1870,1875
Publisher Leicestershire Trade Protection Society
Printer Hunter, J.W. & Co
Place Leicester
Type GE TR
Map scale –
Notes 1875 edition entitled 'Commercial and General Directory & Red Book of Leicester & suburbs'
Library BL has 1870
holdings CLL all

REF **830**
Title **Commercial and General Directory and Blue Book of Leicester and six miles round**
Dates 1878,1880,1882,1894
Publisher Wright, C.N.
Printer Tompkin & Shardlow
Place Leicester
Type GE TR
Map scale –
Notes Cont'd as 831
Library BL not 1878
holdings BOD has 1894
CLL all
GL has 1880
NLS has 1894
ULC has 1894

REF **831**
Title **Commercial and General Directory of Leicester and 15 miles round**
Dates 1884,1886,1890,1892,1900,1902, 1904,1906,1909,1911,1914,1920
Publisher Wright, C.N.
Printer Tompkin & Shardlow
Place Leicester
Type GE TR
Map scale 1:15840
Notes Cont'd from 830. 1886: 10 miles round. 1890: 12 miles round. 1892: 'Greater Leicester'. 1903: 'Wright's Directory of the County Borough of Leicester'. 1909 onwards published by Kelly's Directories Ltd.
Library BL all
holdings BOD not 1914,1920
CLL all
CLM has 1911,1920
GL has 1886,1903,1906,1911, 1914,1923
MLG has 1909-1923
NLS has 1884-1892,1906,1911
ULC has 1884-1892,1903-1911

REF **832**
Title **Leicester and District Trades Directory**
Dates 1911
Publisher Town and County Directories Ltd
Printer Macdonald, W. & Co Ltd
Place Edinburgh
Type TR
Map scale –
Library CLL

REF **833**
Title **Ashby-de-la-Zouch ... Local Directory and Work of Reference**
Dates 1921
Publisher Brown, G.
Printer Brown, G.
Place Ashby-de-la-Zouch
Type CT
Map scale –
Library GL

REF **834**
Title **Directory of Market Harborough**
Dates 1926,1938
Publisher Green & Co
Printer Green & Co
Place Market Harborough
Type ST
Map scale NS
Library CLL has 1926
holdings GL has 1938

REF **835**
Title **The Hinckley Directory**
Dates 1930
Publisher Chronicle Press Ltd
Printer Chronicle Press Ltd
Place Nuneaton
Type GE
Map scale 1:12672
Library GL

REF **836**
Title **Kelly's Directory of Melton Mowbray & neighbourhood**
Dates 1936,1938,1940
Publisher Kelly's Directories Ltd
Printer Kelly's Directories Ltd
Place London
Type GE TR
Map scale –
Library BL all
holdings CLL not 1938
CLM has 1940
GL all

REF **837**
Title **Kelly's Directory of the City of Leicester**
Dates 1938,1947
Publisher Kelly's Directories Ltd
Printer Kelly's Directories Ltd
Place London
Type GE TR
Map scale 1:10560
Library BL all
holdings BOD all
BPH all
CLL all
GL all
MLG all
SCL has 1938
SOG has 1938
ULC all

REF **838**
Title **Loughborough Almamac, Trade and Street Directory**
Dates 1939
Publisher Wills & Hepworth Ltd
Printer Wills & Hepworth Ltd
Place Loughborough
Type ST TR
Map scale –
Library GL

LINCOLNSHIRE

REF **839**
Title **Kelly's Directory of Lincolnshire**
Dates 1855,1861,1868,1876,1885,1889, 1930,1933,1937
Publisher Kelly & Co
Printer Kelly & Co
Place London
Type GE TR
Map scale 1:253440
Notes NORTON 125 (1855). 1855-1876 entitled 'Post Office Directory of Lincolnshire'. See 842.
Library BCL has 1930-1937
holdings BIS has 1937
BL not 1861,1930-1937
BOD all
BPH has 1930,1937
CLB has 1937
CLE has 1937
CLH has 1868,1889-1937
CLM has 1937
GL all
IHR has 1855,1861
LCL has 1937
LIN all
NLS not 1861
NLW has 1930,1937
NOR has 1937
PET has 1889
SCL has 1930-1937
SOG has 1861,1876,1885,1889, 1937
ULC all

REF **840**
Title **History, Gazetteer and Directory of Lincolnshire**
Dates 1856,1863,1872,1882,1892
Publisher White, W.
Printer Spottiswoode
Place Sheffield
Type GE TR
Map scale 1:253440
Notes David & Charles have reprinted the 1856 edition
Library BCL has 1856 (Reprint)
holdings BL not 1856,1863,1892
BIS has 1856,1892
BPH has 1856
DON has 1856,1892
GL all
LIN has 1856,1872-1892
PET has 1856
SCL has 1856
SOG has 1856,1872,1882,1892
ULC has 1882

REF **841**
Title **Morris & Co's Commercial Directory and Gazetteer of Lincolnshire**
Dates 1863,1866,1868
Publisher Morris & Co
Printer –
Place Nottingham
Type CM TR
Map scale –
Notes The date of the '1866' edition is uncertain
Library LIN

REF **842**
Title **Kelly's Directory of Lincolnshire, with the town of Hull and neighbourhood**
Dates 1892,1896,1900,1905,1909,1913, 1919,1922,1926
Publisher Kelly & Co
Printer Kelly & Co
Place London
Type GE TR
Map scale 1:7920
Notes See 839
Library BCL has 1892-1926
holdings BL has 1892-1905,1913,1922
BOD not 1905
CLH all
GL all
IHR has 1905
LIN all
NLS has 1892,1896
NLW has 1913,1919
PET has 1896
SOG has 1909,1926
ULC all

REF **843**
Title **A Guide and Directory to Cleethorpes**
Dates 1850
Publisher Dobson, E, [Author]
Printer –
Place Cleethorpes
Type SP
Map scale –
Notes Alphabetical section listing lodging houses only
Library LIN

REF **844**
Title **Tesseyman's Directory and Guide Book to the Port of Grimsby**
Dates 1852
Publisher Tesseyman, W.
Printer Tesseyman, W.
Place Grimsby
Type GE TR
Map scale –
Notes NORTON 552
Library BL
holdings LIN

REF **845**
Title **The City of Lincoln Directory**
Dates 1857,1867,1877,1881,1885,1894
Publisher Akrill, C.
Printer Akrill, C.
Place Lincoln
Type GE TR
Map scale –
Library LIN

REF **846**
Title **A New & Complete Directory of Great Grimsby and Cleethorpes**
Dates 1860
Publisher Shepherd, J.
Printer Shepherd, J.
Place Grimsby
Type GE TR
Map scale –
Library BL
holdings IHR

REF **847**
Title **General, Commercial and Advertising Directory of Gainsburgh and adjacent villages**
Dates 1882
Publisher Hardy-Ouzman, W. & Taylor, C.
Printer Caldicott, C.
Place Gainsborough
Type GE
Map scale –
Notes See 862
Library BOD
holdings NLS
ULC

REF **848**
Title **Grantham and District Directory**
Dates 1887,1895,1901
Publisher Wells & Manton
Printer Wells & Manton
Place Grantham
Type GE TR
Map scale –
Library BL has 1887
holdings BOD has 1887
NLS all
ULC all

REF	849
Title	**Boston and District Directory**
Dates	1888
Publisher	Wells & Co
Printer	–
Place	Shrewsbury
Type	GE TR
Map scale	–
Library	BOD
holdings	NLS
	ULC

REF	850
Title	**Cook's Boston and District Directory**
Dates	1891
Publisher	Cook, W.J. & Co
Printer	Wing & Broughton
Place	Boston
Type	GE TR
Map scale	–
Library	BOD
holdings	NLS
	ULC

REF	851
Title	**Cook's Grantham & District Directory**
Dates	1892,1895,1899,1901
Publisher	Cook, W.J. & Co
Printer	Wing & Broughton
Place	Boston
Type	GE TR
Map scale	–
Library	BL not 1899
holdings	BOD not 1899
	GL has 1899
	NLS has 1892
	ULC all

REF	852
Title	**Cook's Gainsborough and Retford Directory**
Dates	1893
Publisher	Cook, W.J. & Co
Printer	Wing & Broughton
Place	Boston
Type	GE TR
Map scale	–
Library	BL
holdings	BOD
	NLS
	ULC

REF	853
Title	**Grimsby and Cleethorpes Directory**
Dates	1893,1896,1902
Publisher	Cook, W.J. & Co
Printer	Kelly & Co
Place	Hull
Type	GE TR
Map scale	–
Library	BL has 1902
holdings	BOD has 1893
	GL has 1902
	LIN has 1896
	NLS has 1902
	ULC not 1896

REF	854
Title	**City of Lincoln and District Directory**
Dates	1895
Publisher	Cook, W.J. & Co
Printer	Thomas, C.
Place	Lincoln
Type	GE TR
Map scale	1:693690
Library	BL
holdings	LIN

REF	855
Title	**White's Directory of Grimsby and neighbourhood**
Dates	1895
Publisher	White, W.
Printer	–
Place	Sheffield
Type	GE TR
Map scale	–
Notes	T/P missing from LIN edition
Library	LIN

REF	856
Title	**Directory of the City of Lincoln**
Dates	1897,1899,1901,1903,1905,1907, 1909,1911,1913,1919,1922,1928, 1932
Publisher	Ruddock, J.W. & Sons
Printer	Ruddock, J.W. & Sons
Place	Lincoln
Type	GE TR
Map scale	1:6336
Library	BL all
holdings	BOD has 1901,1905,1907
	GL has 1907
	LIN all
	NLS has 1901,1905
	ULC has 1901,1905

REF	**857**		REF	**861**
Title	**Lincoln, Grimsby and District Trades' Directory**		Title	**Kelly's Directory of Lincoln & Neighbourhood**
Dates	1915,1928		Dates	1937,1939,1941,1946,1949
Publisher	Town and County Directories Ltd		Publisher	Kelly's Directories Ltd
Printer	Macdonald, W.		Printer	Kelly's Directories Ltd
Place	Edinburgh		Place	London
Type	TR		Type	GE TR
Map scale	–		Map scale	1:10560
Library	LIN		Library	BL all
			holdings	BPH has 1937,1946
				GL all
REF	**858**			LIN not 1941
Title	**Lincoln City Year Book and Business Directory**			NLW has 1949
Dates	1922		REF	**862**
Publisher	The Lincolnshire Chronicle Ltd		Title	**Caldicott's Almanac Directory and Year Book [Gainsborough]**
Printer	The Lincolnshire Chronicle Ltd		Dates	1939
Place	Lincoln		Publisher	Caldicott, C.
Type	ST TR		Printer	Caldicott, C.
Map scale	–		Place	Gainsborough
Library	BL		Type	GE
holdings	LIN		Map scale	1:15840
			Notes	See 847. Map scale approx.
			Library	GL
REF	**859**		REF	**863**
Title	**The Grimsby, Cleethorpes and District Directory**		Title	**Harrison's Almanac Directory for Grantham**
Dates	1935		Dates	1939,1946,1947,1950
Publisher	Whipple, R.D. Son & Martin Ltd		Publisher	Harrison, W.G.
Printer	Whipple, R.D. Son & Martin Ltd		Printer	Harrison, W.G.
Place	Leeds		Place	Grantham
Type	GE		Type	ST
Map scale	–		Map scale	1:15840
Library	CLH		Notes	Map scale approx.
holdings	CLM		Library	GL
	GL			
REF	**860**			
Title	**Kelly's Directory of Boston & Neighbourhood**			
Dates	1935,1937,1939			
Publisher	Kelly's Directories Ltd			
Printer	Kelly's Directories Ltd			
Place	London			
Type	GE TR			
Map scale	1:253440			
Library	BL all			
holdings	CLM has 1939			
	GL all			

LONDON

REF	**864**
Title	**Boyle's Fashionable Court & Country Guide & Town Visiting Directory**
Dates	1850-1925
Publisher	Boyle, M.
Printer	Hall, Virtue & Co
Place	London
Type	CT
Map scale	–
Library	BL all
holdings	BOD all
	CLM has 1850-1856
	GLH has 1860,1861,1865,1873, 1875,1879,1898,1900-1908, 1910-1925
	NLS all
	SOG has 1884
	ULC not 1852,1853,1860

REF	**865**
Title	**Royal Blue Book, Fashionable Directory and Parliamentary Guide**
Dates	1850-1940
Publisher	Gardiner, B.W.
Printer	Gardiner, B.W.
Place	London
Type	CT
Map scale	–
Library	BL all
holdings	BOD not 1857
	CLC has 1919,1922,1933,1938, 1939
	CLM has 1924,1925,1927,1929, 1930,1936,1938-1946
	GLH has 1850,1853,1854,1856, 1859,1861,1862,1866, 1876-1878,1880,19071909, 1911-1915,1938
	SOG has 1872,1885,1918,1934
	ULC all
	12

REF	**866**
Title	**Post Office London Directory**
Dates	1850-1950
Publisher	Kelly & Co
Printer	Kelly & Co
Place	London
Type	GE TR
Map scale	NS
Notes	See 867
Library	BL all
holdings	GL all
	BOD not 1927
	ULC not 1862,1873,1874
	MLG has 1889-1950
	CLM not 1856,1909
	CL has 1907
	NLW has 1908,1894,1899,1904, 1910-1940,1942,1944,1945, 1947-1950
	DEI has 1925,1934
	BCL has 1876,1881-1883, 1885-1939
	CLE has 1910,1930,1934,1939, 1942,1944,1946,1948,1950
	BPH has 1869,1892,1895,1900, 1902,1904,1906,1908,1910, 1912,1914,1916,1918,1920, 1922-1931,1933,1935,1937
	CLB has 1899
	GLH has 1850,1851,1853, 1856-1896,1898-1950
	SOG has 1852,1853,1865,1868, 1875,1879,1886-1888,1895, 1905,1908,1912,1914,1917, 1920,1922,1930,1939,1944, 1947,1948

REF	**867**
Title	**The Small Edition of the Post Office London Directory**
Dates	1851,1853-1855,1857,1861,1862
Publisher	Kelly & Co
Printer	Kelly & Co
Place	London
Type	CT CM
Map scale	1:21120
Notes	See 866
Library	GL

REF **868**
Title **Watkins's Commercial and General London Directory and Court Guide**
Dates 1851-1855
Publisher Watkins, F.W. & Longmans
Printer Spottiswoode & Sons
Place London
Type GE TR
Map scale NS
Library BL all
holdings BOD not 1851
GL not 1851
GLH has 1852
NLS not 1851
ULC not 1851

REF **869**
Title **The Municipal Directory**
Dates 1856
Publisher Kelly & Co
Printer Kelly & Co
Place London
Type SP
Map scale –
Notes Lists local government officers & vestrymen
Library BL
holdings ULC

REF **870**
Title **The Post Office London and Suburban Court Guide**
Dates 1861,1866-1868
Publisher Kelly & Co
Printer Kelly & Co
Place London
Type CT
Map scale –
Notes List of persons in Bank of England, govt. offices, MPs etc.
Library BL all
holdings CRD has 1861
GL has 1861
GLH has 1861
NLS all
ULC all

REF **871**
Title **The Business Directory of London**
Dates 1862,1864-1930
Publisher Morris, J.S.C.
Printer Spottiswoode & Co
Place London
Type CM TR
Map scale –
Library BL not 1862,1866
holdings BOD not 1862
GL has 1866
GLH has 1787,1914
NLS all
NLW has 1884,1887,1892, 1895-1904,1928-1930
ULC not 1865,1866
12

REF **872**
Title **Whibley's Shilling Court Directory and London Fashionable Guide**
Dates 1863-1865
Publisher Whibley, T.E.
Printer Whibley, T.E.
Place London
Type CT
Map scale –
Library BL has 1864
holdings ULC all

REF **873**
Title **The Imperial Directory of London**
Dates 1866
Publisher Morris, J.S.C.
Printer Spottiswoode & Co
Place London
Type GE TR
Map scale 1:21120
Library NLS
holdings ULC

REF **874**
Title **Allen's West London Street, Court and Trades Directory**
Dates 1868,1869
Publisher Allen, S.
Printer Allen, S.
Place London
Type GE TR
Map scale 1:10560
Notes Map scale approx.
Library BL has 1869
holdings BOD has 1869
GL has 1868
NLS has 1869
ULC has 1869

REF **875**
Title **The A.B.C. Court Directory & Fashionable Guide, London and 12 miles radius**
Dates 1871
Publisher Elkingham Wilson
Printer Elkingham Wilson
Place London
Type CT
Map scale –
Library BL
holdings BOD
GLH
NLS
SOG
ULC

REF **876**
Title **Kelly's London Medical Directory**
Dates 1872,1889-1897
Publisher Kelly & Co
Printer Kelly & Co
Place London
Type PR
Map scale –
Notes Alph. lists of doctors & ST directory
Library BL all
holdings BOD all
GL has 1894
NLS not 1872
ULC not 1872

REF **877**
Title **London. A Complete Guide to the Leading Hotels, Places of Amusement ... &c; also a Directory ... of First Class Reliable Houses in the Various Branches of Trade**
Dates 1872-1883,1885-1902
Publisher Herbert, H.
Printer –
Place London
Type SP
Map scale –
Notes Each entry consists of an advertisement in a gilt/coloured frame. No particular order. Also several engravings.
Library NLS not 1897
holdings ULC has 1874-1883,1896-1902

REF **878**
Title **A London Street Directory on a New Plan**
Dates 1881
Publisher Morgan, H.
Printer Morgan, H.
Place London
Type ST
Map scale –
Library BL
holdings BOD
GLH
NLS

REF **879**
Title **Walter's Theatrical and Sporting Directory**
Dates 1884-1887,1889,1893
Publisher Seale, E.
Printer –
Place London
Type SP
Map scale –
Notes Classified & alph. directory with sporting/theatrical events in London
Library BOD
holdings NLS
ULC has 1884-1887

REF	**880**
Title	**Kelly's Post Office London and Suburban Local Directories Sections 1,2,3,4,6,9**
Dates	1885
Publisher	Kelly & Co
Printer	Kelly & Co
Place	London
Type	GE TR
Map scale	1:15840
Notes	See 882
Library holdings	BL has sections 1,2
	BOD has all sections
	ULC all

REF	**881**
Title	**The Streets of London**
Dates	1885
Publisher	Kenning, G.
Printer	The Freemason Printing Works
Place	London
Type	SL
Map scale	–
Library holdings	BOD
	NLS

REF	**882**
Title	**Kelly's Post Office London and Suburban Local Directories Sections 1,2,3,4, 5,6,7,8,9,10,11,12,13,15**
Dates	1886
Publisher	Kelly & Co
Printer	Kelly & Co
Place	London
Type	GE TR
Map scale	1:15840
Notes	See 880
Library holdings	BL not sections 5,6,15
	BOD not sections 8,9
	ULC all

REF	**883**
Title	**The London Building Trades Directory and Register**
Dates	1886
Publisher	Hutchings & Crowsley
Printer	Hutchings & Crowsley
Place	London
Type	SP
Map scale	–
Library holdings	BL
	ULC

REF	**884**
Title	**Commercial London**
Dates	1890
Publisher	Allen, W.H. & Co
Printer	Allen, W.H. & Co
Place	London
Type	SP
Map scale	NS
Notes	Directory of merchants & manufacturers. Contains 20 bird's eye views & 2 maps.
Library holdings	BL
	BOD

REF	**885**
Title	**The Mercantile Directory of London**
Dates	1891,1893
Publisher	Heywood Bros & Co
Printer	–
Place	London
Type	TR
Map scale	–
Notes	Also contains a provincial section
Library holdings	BL all
	BOD has 1893
	NLS has 1893
	ULC has 1893

REF	**886**
Title	**The English and Italian Commercial Directory**
Dates	1894
Publisher	Martinenghi, R. & Co
Printer	Martinenghi, R. & Co
Place	London
Type	SP
Map scale	–
Notes	TR sections for London & Italy (Italian traders in London)
Library holdings	BL
	NLS
	ULC

REF **887**
Title **London Directory**
Dates 1894-1896,1898-1939,
1948-1950
Publisher The London Directory Company
Ltd
Printer –
Place London
Type TR
Map scale –
Notes Divided into London, suburban,
and, from 1896, provincial TR
sections
Library BL all
holdings BOD has 1895,1896,1903-1905,
1908,1926-1939,1949,1950
MLG IMP 1894-1950
ULC all

REF **888**
Title **Aves' London Street Directory**
Dates 1897
Publisher Aves & Co
Printer Aves & Co
Place London
Type ST
Map scale –
Library BL

REF **889**
Title **Local London: A Municipal
Directory for the Metropolis and
its Suburbs**
Dates 1901
Publisher King, P.S. & Co
Printer –
Place Westminster
Type SP
Map scale 1:12672
Notes Directory of corporations, councils
& boards
Library BOD
holdings NLS

REF **890**
Title **List of the Streets and Places
within the Administrative County
of London**
Dates 1901,1912,1929
Publisher London County Council
Printer Tarrant, F. & Co Ltd
Place London
Type SL
Map scale –
Library IHR all
holdings SOG has 1912

REF **891**
Title **Post Office London Directory
(County Suburbs)**
Dates 1904-1933
Publisher Kelly's Directories Ltd
Printer Kelly's Directories Ltd
Place London
Type GE TR
Map scale –
Notes Cont'd from 905
Library BL all
holdings BOD all
BPH has 1907,1911,1914,1915
CRD has 1932,1933
GL all
GLH all
MLG not 1906,1907,1909
NLS not 1905-1916
NLW has 1910-1913
ULC has 1904-1912,1914-1916

REF **892**
Title **The London County Courts'
Directory**
Dates 1907,1928
Publisher Wyman & Sons Ltd
Printer Wyman & Sons Ltd
Place London
Type SL
Map scale –
Notes 'Containing the streets & places in
the city & county of London with
their county court districts'
Library BL all
holdings BOD has 1907
NLS has 1907
ULC has 1907

REF **893**
Title **The London Mercantile
Directory**
Dates 1935
Publisher The Newmark Publishing Co
Printer –
Place London
Type TR
Map scale –
Notes London TR section followed by
large provincial TR section
Library NLS
holdings ULC

REF	**894**		REF	**898**
Title	**London and Suburbs Trades'**		Title	**Deptford Directory including**
	Directory			**Blackheath, Lee, Lewisham &**
Dates	1947,1948			**Sydenham**
Publisher	Town and County Directories		Dates	1853
	Ltd		Publisher	Bass, T.
Printer	Macdonald, W. & Co Ltd		Printer	Bass, T.
Place	Edinburgh		Place	London
Type	TR		Type	GE
Map scale	–		Map scale	–
Notes	Includes Middx. Arranged Central		Library	BL
	London, Suburbs, Gazetteer.		holdings	BOD
Library	BL			ULC

REF	**895**
Title	**Directory ... Containing an**
	Alphabetical List of the
	Inhabitants of Hackney, Clapton,
	Homerton, Dalston, Kingsland,
	De Beauvoir Town, Shacklewell
	and Stoke Newington
Dates	1851
Publisher	Turner, C.
Printer	Turner, C.
Place	Hackney
Type	GE
Map scale	–
Library	GL

REF	**899**
Title	**Westminster Local Directory**
Dates	1853
Publisher	Wyld, J.
Printer	–
Place	London
Type	SL
Map scale	–
Library	GL

REF	**896**
Title	**Mason's Greenwich and**
	Blackheath Shilling Directory
Dates	1852
Publisher	Mason, R.H.
Printer	Mason, R.H.
Place	Greenwich
Type	GE
Map scale	–
Library	BL
holdings	BOD

REF	**900**
Title	**The Islington Directory**
Dates	1853,1854,1855,1859-1905
Publisher	Trounce, W.
Printer	Trounce, W.
Place	London
Type	GE TR
Map scale	1:15840
Library	BL not 1852
holdings	BOD has 1864-1905
	GL has 1853-1875,1877,1878,
	1884-1888,1896
	GLH has 1859,1864,1869,1870,
	1872,1875,1878,1882,1884,
	1890,1894,1894,1898-1900,
	1902-1905
	NLS has 1861,1862,1864,1903,
	1905
	ULC has 1864-1905

REF	**897**
Title	**W. Archdeacons's Greenwich and**
	Woolwich Directory
Dates	1852
Publisher	Archdeacon, W. & Wright, C.
Printer	Archdeacon, W. & Wright, C.
Place	London
Type	CT CM
Map scale	–
Library	BL
holdings	BOD
	NLS
	ULC

REF	**901**
Title	**The Hampstead Directory and**
	Guide
Dates	1854
Publisher	Shaw, J.J.
Printer	Hughes, J.
Place	London
Type	GE
Map scale	–
Library	BL

REF **902**
Title **Clapham, with its Common and Environs containing ... a list of Inhabitants**
Dates 1859
Publisher Batten, D.
Printer Batten, D.
Place Clapham
Type GE
Map scale –
Library IHR

REF **903**
Title **Clark's Sydenham and Forest Hill Directory**
Dates 1859
Publisher Clark, W.T.
Printer –
Place Upper Sydenham
Type CM TR
Map scale –
Library GLH

REF **904**
Title **The Hampstead Directory and Almanack**
Dates 1859,1862,1867
Publisher Barrett, R.
Printer Barrett, R.
Place London
Type ST
Map scale –
Library BL

REF **905**
Title **Kelly's London Suburban Directory**
Dates 1860,1863,1865,1868,1871,1872, 1876,1880,1884,1888,1892,1894, 1896,1898,1900-1903
Publisher Kelly & Co
Printer Kelly & Co
Place London
Type GE TR
Map scale –
Notes From 1860-1876 entitled 'Post Office London Suburban Directory'. Cont'd as 891.
Library BL not 1871
holdings BOD all
BPH has 1884,1892,1896,1902, 1903
GLH has 1860-1903
NLS not 1865,1871
SOG has 1894
ULC has 1900-1903

REF **906**
Title **The St John's Wood Directory**
Dates 1861-1864
Publisher Hutchings & Crowsley
Printer Hutchings & Crowsley
Place London
Type GE
Map scale –
Library BL all
holdings BOD has 1862,1863
ULC has 1863

REF **907**
Title **Burt's Sydenham and Forest Hill Guide and Directory**
Dates 1862
Publisher Burt, R.K.
Printer Burt, R.K.
Place Sydenham
Type GE TR
Map scale –
Library BOD
holdings NLS
ULC

REF **908**
Title **Simpson's Street Directory of St Pancras**
Dates 1862
Publisher Tomkies & Son
Printer Tomkies & Son
Place London
Type GE
Map scale –
Library BL
holdings BOD
GL
NLS
ULC

REF **909**
Title **The St Pancras Directory**
Dates 1862
Publisher Giddings, J.
Printer Giddings, J.
Place London
Type CT
Map scale –
Library BL
holdings BOD
GLH
ULC

REF	910
Title	**Dolling's Paddington Directory**
Dates	1862-1864
Publisher	Dolling, J.
Printer	Dolling, J.
Place	London
Type	GE TR
Map scale	NS
Notes	1864 edition entitled 'Paddington, Bayswater & Kensington Directory'
Library	BL has 1862
holdings	BOD has 1862
	GL has 1864
	GLH has 1863
	NLS has 1862
	ULC has 1862

REF	911
Title	**Simpson's Kensington and Hammersmith Directory and Court Guide**
Dates	1863
Publisher	'?'
Printer	'?'
Place	London
Type	GE
Map scale	–
Library	BL

REF	912
Title	**The Marylebone Directory**
Dates	1863,1864
Publisher	Hutchings & Crowsley
Printer	Hutchings & Crowsley
Place	London
Type	GE TR
Map scale	–
Library	BL all
holdings	BOD has 1863
	ULC has 1863

REF	913
Title	**The St Pancras Directory including Hampstead and Highgate**
Dates	1864
Publisher	Hogg, W. & Co
Printer	Boot, A.
Place	London
Type	ST TR
Map scale	–
Library	BOD
holdings	NLS

REF	914
Title	**The Marylebone and St John's Wood Directory**
Dates	1865-1867,1872,1874-1879,1881, 1882,1885,1886
Publisher	Hutchings & Crowsley
Printer	Hutchings & Crowsley
Place	London
Type	GE TR
Map scale	1:15840
Notes	Cont'd as 971
Library	BL all
holdings	BOD has 1886
	GL has 1885,1886
	ULC has 1865

REF	915
Title	**Green's Stoke Newington and Clapton Directory**
Dates	1866
Publisher	Green
Printer	–
Place	London
Type	CM TR
Map scale	–
Library	GL

REF	916
Title	**Allen & Morton's West London Directory**
Dates	1867
Publisher	Allen & Morton
Printer	Allen & Morton
Place	London
Type	GE TR
Map scale	–
Library	GL
holdings	GLH

REF	917
Title	**Green & Co's Forest Hill, Sydenham and Upper Norwood Directory and Court Guide**
Dates	1867
Publisher	Green & Co
Printer	–
Place	London
Type	GE
Map scale	–
Library	GL

REF **918**
Title **Simpson & Green's Hackney and Bow Directory**
Dates 1867
Publisher Green & Simpson
Printer –
Place Stoke Newington
Type CM
Map scale –
Library BL
holdings GL

REF **919**
Title **The Metallurgicon Local Directory of Wandsworth, Putney, Wimbledon, Roehampton, ... Barnes &c &c**
Dates 1867
Publisher Gray, J.W.
Printer Gray, J.W.
Place London
Type GE TR
Map scale –
Library BL
holdings BOD
GL
NLS

REF **920**
Title **The Camden and Kentish Town Directory**
Dates 1867,1871,1873,1876,1877, 1885-1888
Publisher Hutchings & Crowsley
Printer Hutchings & Crowsley
Place London
Type GE TR
Map scale 1:7040
Notes Cont'd as 977
Library BL all
holdings BOD has 1886-1888
ULC has 1887,1888

REF **921**
Title **Jackson's Useful Directory for Woolwich, Plumstead and Charlton**
Dates 1868
Publisher Jackson & Son
Printer Jackson & Son
Place Woolwich
Type GE
Map scale 1:10560
Library GL

REF **922**
Title **Farmery's Sydenham, Forest Hill, Upper Norwood, Anerley, Penge and Beckenham Directory**
Dates 1869
Publisher Farmery, T. & E.
Printer Farmery, T. & E.
Place Sydenham
Type GE TR
Map scale –
Library GL

REF **923**
Title **R. Green & Co's Hackney and North East London Directory**
Dates 1869
Publisher Green, R. & Co
Printer Welch, J.
Place London
Type GE TR
Map scale –
Library GL
holdings GLH

REF **924**
Title **R. Green & Co's Hammersmith, Ealing & South West London Directory**
Dates 1869
Publisher Green, R. & Co
Printer –
Place New Wandsworth
Type CM TR
Map scale –
Library GL

REF **925**
Title **R. Green & Co's South London Blue Book and Royal Court Guide**
Dates 1869
Publisher Green, R. & Co
Printer –
Place New Wandsworth
Type CT
Map scale –
Library GL

REF **926**
Title **The Hampstead and Highgate Almanack, Diary & Directory**
Dates 1869,1870,1873
Publisher Jealous, G.S.
Printer Jealous, G.S.
Place Hampstead
Type GE
Map scale —
Library BL has 1870
holdings GL has 1869,1873

REF **927**
Title **The City of London Directory**
Dates 1871-1915
Publisher Collingridge, W.H. Ltd
Printer Collingridge, W.H. Ltd
Place London
Type GE TR
Map scale 1:3600
Notes After 1909 entitled 'The City of London Year Book and Civic Directory'
Library BCL has 1872,1875,1878
holdings BL all
BOD not 1892
CLM has 1878,1894,1897,1898, 1902
GLH has 1873,1905,1908,1909
NLS has 1871-1877,1879-1891, 1893-1915
SOG has 1878,1879,1902
ULC all

REF **928**
Title **The Borough of Hackney Directory**
Dates 1872
Publisher Brabner, C.W.
Printer Brabner, C.W.
Place London
Type GE TR
Map scale 1:21120
Library BL

REF **929**
Title **The Court Guide and Commercial Directory and Gazetteer for Wandsworth, Wimbledon, Roehampton ... & Brentford**
Dates 1872
Publisher Green & Co
Printer Green & Co
Place London
Type CT CM
Map scale —
Library GL

REF **930**
Title **The South London Suburban Directory**
Dates 1872
Publisher Wilson, E.
Printer Clayton & Co
Place London
Type GE
Map scale —
Library GL

REF **931**
Title **The Kilburn Directory, including Willesden, Cricklewood, West End & Hampstead**
Dates 1872,1874,1876,1882,1885,1886
Publisher Hutchings & Crowsley
Printer Hutchings & Crowsley
Place London
Type GE TR
Map scale 1:15840
Library BL not 1874
holdings BOD has 1886
GLH has 1874

REF **932**
Title **The Paddington and Bayswater Directory**
Dates 1872,1875-1878,1882,1884-1886
Publisher Hutchings & Crowsley
Printer Hutchings & Crowsley
Place London
Type GE TR
Map scale 1:15840
Notes Cont'd as 972
Library BL all
holdings BOD has 1886

REF **933**
Title **Court Guide and Directory for Notting Hill, Acton, Shepherds Bush & Ealing**
Dates 1873
Publisher Green & Co
Printer Green & Co
Place London
Type CM
Map scale –
Library BL

REF **934**
Title **The Court Guide and Commercial Directory and Gazetteer for Chelsea, Kensington, Brompton, Notting Hill, Shepherd's Bush, Acton and Ealing**
Dates 1873
Publisher Green & Co
Printer –
Place London
Type CT CM
Map scale –
Library GL

REF **935**
Title **Green's Court Guide and Commercial Directory and Gazetteer: Greenwich, Deptford, New Cross, Blackheath, Lewisham, Lee**
Dates 1874
Publisher Green & Co
Printer –
Place London
Type CT CM
Map scale –
Library BIS

REF **936**
Title **The Hampstead and Highgate Directory**
Dates 1874,1876,1878,1885,1886
Publisher Hutchings & Crowsley
Printer Hutchings & Crowsley
Place London
Type GE TR
Map scale 1:15840
Notes Cont'd as 964
Library BL all
holdings BOD has 1886
GL has 1876

REF **937**
Title **The Crystal Palace District Handbook and Directory for Sydenham, Forest Hill, Penge, Upper Norwood, Dulwich and Beckenham**
Dates 1875
Publisher Clark & Son
Printer Clark & Son
Place Upper Sydenham
Type CT CM
Map scale 1:10560
Library BL
holdings GL

REF **938**
Title **The Kensington, Notting Hill, Brompton & Knightsbridge Directory**
Dates 1876,1878,1882-1886
Publisher Hutchings & Crowsley
Printer Hutchings & Crowsley
Place London
Type GE TR
Map scale 1:15840
Notes Cont'd as 973
Library BL not 1883
holdings BOD has 1886
GL has 1885,1886
GLH has 1883
ULC has 1886

REF **939**
Title **Directory for Battersea Rise and the Neighbourhoods of Clapham & Wandsworth Common &c**
Dates 1878
Publisher Strong, J.
Printer White, G.
Place Battersea Rise
Type GE TR
Map scale –
Library GL

REF **940**
Title **Morgan & Co's Suburban Street Directory and Court Guide for Sydenham, East & West Dulwich, Forest Hill, Brockley, New Cross and St Johns, Lewisham**
Dates 1878
Publisher Morgan & Co
Printer Morgan & Co
Place London
Type GE
Map scale –
Library GL

REF	**941**
Title	**The Chelsea, Pimlico & Belgravia Directory**
Dates	1878,1881,1885,1886
Publisher	Hutchings & Crowsley
Printer	Hutchings & Crowsley
Place	London
Type	GE TR
Map scale	1:15840
Notes	Cont'd as 970
Library	BL not 1878
holdings	BOD has 1886
	GLH has 1878

REF	**942**
Title	**Directory for Hornsey and Neighbourhood**
Dates	1879
Publisher	Roberts, F.J.
Printer	Roberts, F.J.
Place	London
Type	CT
Map scale	–
Library	BL

REF	**943**
Title	**The Blackheath, Lee and Lewisham Directory**
Dates	1879
Publisher	Wilmhurst, E.
Printer	Wilmhurst, E.
Place	London
Type	CT CM
Map scale	–
Library	BL
holdings	BOD
	NLS

REF	**944**
Title	**The Dulwich, Denmark & Champion Hills Directory, including Tulse Hill & Herne Hill**
Dates	1881,1884-1886
Publisher	Hutchings & Crowsley
Printer	Hutchings & Crowsley
Place	London
Type	GE TR
Map scale	1:15840
Notes	Cont'd as 960
Library	BL all
holdings	BOD has 1886
	GL has 1884,1885

REF	**945**
Title	**The Sydenham and Norwood Directory**
Dates	1881,1884-1886
Publisher	Hutchings & Crowsley
Printer	Hutchings & Crowsley
Place	London
Type	GE TR
Map scale	1:15840
Notes	Cont'd as 969
Library	BL all
holdings	BOD has 1886
	GL has 1885

REF	**946**
Title	**The West Kensington & Hammersmith Directory**
Dates	1881,1885,1886
Publisher	Hutchings & Crowsley
Printer	Hutchings & Crowsley
Place	London
Type	GE TR
Map scale	1:15840
Notes	Cont'd as 966
Library	BL all
holdings	BOD has 1886
	GL has 1885

REF	**947**
Title	**Classified List of the Wholesale Trades including Bankers, Merchants, Warehousemen &c in the City of London**
Dates	1882
Publisher	Seyd & Co
Printer	–
Place	London
Type	TR
Map scale	–
Notes	Classified sections, with merchants/ agents classified under countries
Library	NLS

REF	**948**
Title	**Norris's Stoke Newington Postal Directory**
Dates	1882,1883
Publisher	Norris, W.
Printer	Norris, W.
Place	London
Type	ST
Map scale	–
Library	BL

REF	**949**
Title	**Platt & Burdett's Sydenham & Forest Hill Directory**
Dates	1882,1884
Publisher	Platt & Burdett
Printer	Platt & Burdett
Place	Norwood
Type	GE
Map scale	–
Library	GL has 1884
holdings	GLH has 1882

REF	**950**
Title	**The Brixton, Clapham & South Lambeth Directory**
Dates	1882,1884-1886
Publisher	Hutchings & Crowsley
Printer	Hutchings & Crowsley
Place	London
Type	GE TR
Map scale	1:15840
Notes	Cont'd as 967
Library	BL all
holdings	BOD has 1886
	GL has 1884,1885

REF	**951**
Title	**Chapman's Copyright Index of Woolwich, Charlton and Plumstead**
Dates	1884
Publisher	Chapman & Co
Printer	Chapman & Co
Place	London
Type	CT
Map scale	1:15840
Notes	Arranged as an index book
Library	BL
holdings	BOD

REF	**952**
Title	**The Blackheath, Lee, Lewisham & Greenwich Directory**
Dates	1885,1886
Publisher	Hutchings & Crowsley
Printer	Hutchings & Crowsley
Place	London
Type	GE TR
Map scale	1:15840
Notes	Cont'd as 968
Library	BL all
holdings	BOD has 1886
	GL all

REF	**953**
Title	**The Highbury, Stoke Newington, Stamford Hill & Clapton Directory**
Dates	1885,1886
Publisher	Hutchings & Crowsley
Printer	Hutchings & Crowsley
Place	London
Type	GE TR
Map scale	1:15840
Notes	Cont'd as 961
Library	BL all
holdings	BOD has 1886

REF	**954**
Title	**The Wandsworth, Putney, Wimbledon, Tooting Directory**
Dates	1885,1886
Publisher	Hutchings & Crowsley
Printer	Hutchings & Crowsley
Place	London
Type	GE TR
Map scale	1:15840
Notes	Cont'd as 965
Library	BL all
holdings	BOD has 1886

REF	**955**
Title	**The Bloomsbury and St Pancras Directory**
Dates	1886
Publisher	Hutchings & Crowsley
Printer	Hutchings & Crowsley
Place	London
Type	GE TR
Map scale	1:15840
Notes	Cont'd as 958
Library	BL
holdings	BOD

REF	**956**
Title	**The Mayfair, St James's, Soho & Westminster Directory**
Dates	1886
Publisher	Hutchings & Crowsley
Printer	Hutchings & Crowsley
Place	London
Type	GE TR
Map scale	1:15840
Library	BL
holdings	BOD
	ULC

REF	**957**
Title	**Kelly's Mayfair, St James's, Soho & Westminster Directory**
Dates	1887,1888
Publisher	Kelly & Co
Printer	Kelly & Co
Place	London
Type	GE TR
Map scale	1:15840
Notes	Cont'd from 956
Library	BL has 1887
holdings	BOD has 1887
	GL has 1887
	ULC all

REF	**958**
Title	**Kelly's Bloomsbury and St Pancras Directory**
Dates	1887
Publisher	Kelly & Co
Printer	Kelly & Co
Place	London
Type	GE TR
Map scale	–
Notes	Cont'd from 955
Library	BL
holdings	BOD
	GL
	ULC

REF	**959**
Title	**Kelly's Islington, Canonbury, Barnsbury & Clerkenwell Directory**
Dates	1887,1888
Publisher	Kelly & Co
Printer	Kelly & Co
Place	London
Type	GE TR
Map scale	1:15840
Notes	Clerkenwell included in 1887 only
Library	BL all
holdings	BOD all
	GL has 1888
	ULC all

REF	**960**
Title	**Kelly's Dulwich, Tulse Hill, Herne Hill Directory**
Dates	1887,1890-1914,1916-1920,1922, 1924,1926,1928
Publisher	Kelly & Co
Printer	Kelly & Co
Place	London
Type	GE TR
Map scale	1:15840
Notes	Cont'd from 944. Dulwich also appears in 962.
Library	BL not 1895
holdings	BOD has 1890-1912
	CLM has 1928
	CRD has 1928
	GL not 1887-1891,1894,1928
	GLH has 1906,1907,1909,1911, 1912,1914,1917,1919-1926
	ULC has 1887,1890-1911

REF	**961**
Title	**Kelly's Highbury, Stoke Newington, Stamford Hill & Clapton Directory**
Dates	1887-1889
Publisher	Kelly & Co
Printer	Kelly & Co
Place	London
Type	GE TR
Map scale	1:15840
Notes	Cont'd from 953, cont'd as 980 & 976
Library	BL all
holdings	BOD has 1888,1889
	GL has 1887
	ULC has 1887-1889

REF	**962**
Title	**Kelly's Camberwell, Peckham, Nunhead, Dulwich and Denmark Hill Directory**
Dates	1887-1889,1892-1908
Publisher	Kelly & Co
Printer	Kelly & Co
Place	London
Type	GE TR
Map scale	1:15840
Notes	Dulwich also included in 960
Library	BL not 1887,1890
holdings	BOD has 1892-1908
	GL not 1887,1888,1890
	GLH has 1901,1906,1907
	ULC all

REF	**963**
Title	**Kelly's Hackney, Homerton, Dalston, Old Ford & Bow Directory**
Dates	1887-1890,1892-1915
Publisher	Kelly & Co
Printer	Kelly & Co
Place	London
Type	GE TR
Map scale	1:15840
Notes	Homerton included from 1888. From 1892 only covers Hackney & Homerton.
Library	BL all
holdings	BOD has 1887-1890,1892-1912
	GL not 1887,1888,1890,1905
	GLH has 1898,1901,1903, 1906-1914
	ULC has 1887-1912

REF	**964**
Title	**Kelly's Hampstead & Highgate Directory**
Dates	1887-1896,1898
Publisher	Kelly & Co
Printer	Kelly & Co
Place	London
Type	GE TR
Map scale	1:15840
Notes	Cont'd from 936, cont'd as 988
Library	BL not 1894
holdings	BOD has 1887-1898
	GL has 1889,1892-1898
	GLH has 1895
	ULC has 1887-1898

REF	**965**
Title	**Kelly's Wandsworth, Putney, Wimbledon, Tooting & Merton Directory**
Dates	1887-1901,1903-1936
Publisher	Kelly & Co
Printer	Kelly & Co
Place	London
Type	GE TR
Map scale	1:15840
Notes	Cont'd from 954. Includes Barnes from 1890-1928. Includes Mortlake & Sheen from 1903-1928. Wimbledon & Merton included 1887-1890. Barnes, Mortlake & Sheen cont'd as 1343.
Library	BL not 1901
holdings	BOD has 1887-1912
	CLM has 1930,1936
	GL not 1890,1891,1893,1911, 1917
	GLH has 1891,1927-1931,1933, 1935,1936
	ULC has 1887-1913

REF	**966**
Title	**Kelly's Directory of West Kensington, Shepherds Bush, Fulham & Hammersmith**
Dates	1887-1908,1910-1925,1927,1929, 1931,1933,1935,1937,1939
Publisher	Kelly & Co
Printer	Kelly & Co
Place	London
Type	GE TR
Map scale	1:15840
Notes	Cont'd from 946. Hammersmith dropped after 1898. Walham Green & Fulham included after 1899.
Library	BL all
holdings	BOD has 1887-1912
	CLM has 1939
	GL not 1887,1888,1890,1891, 1900
	GLH has 1897,1900,1901, 1905-1917,1921,1924-1933, 1937
	SOG has 1925,1931
	ULC has 1887-1912

REF	**967**
Title	**Kelly's Brixton, Clapham and South Lambeth Directory**
Dates	1887-1914,1916-1918,1920, 1922-1926,1928
Publisher	Kelly & Co
Printer	Kelly & Co
Place	London
Type	GE TR
Map scale	1:15840
Notes	Cont'd from 950. 1888 & 1889 editions include Tulse Hill & Herne Hill, but exclude South Lambeth.
Library	BL not 1893
holdings	BOD has 1887-1911
	CLM has 1928
	GL not 1889-1891,1894
	GLH has 1897,1898,1903, 1906-1909,1912,1917,1920, 1922-1926
	ULC has 1887-1912

REF	**968**
Title	**Kelly's Blackheath, Lee, Lewisham & Greenwich Directory**
Dates	1887-1917,1919-1925,1927,1929, 1931,1933,1935,1937
Publisher	Kelly & Co
Printer	Kelly & Co
Place	London
Type	GE TR
Map scale	1:15840
Notes	Cont'd from 952. After 1898 includes Eltham & Mottingham, Lewisham dropped from title.
Library	BL all
holdings	BOD has 1887-1912
	CLM has 1937
	GL not 1887,1888,1890,1891, 1935
	GLH has 1900,1907,1909-1917, 1919,1922,1923,1925-1937
	SOG has 1937
	ULC has 1887-1912

REF	**969**
Title	**Kelly's Sydenham, Norwood & Streatham Directory**
Dates	1887-1917,1919-1939
Publisher	Kelly & Co
Printer	Kelly & Co
Place	London
Type	GE TR
Map scale	1:15840
Notes	Cont'd from 945. Forest Hill is included from 1888-1898, 1909-1939. Norwood & Streatham dropped from 1909, after which it is entitled 'Kelly's Sydenham and Forest Hill Directory'.
Library	BL all
holdings	BOD has 1887-1912
	CLM has 1939
	CRD has 1887,1888,1902
	GL not 1887,1888,1890,1891, 1899
	GLH has 1903,1907,1909-1911, 1913-1917,1919,1920,1922, 1923,1929,1931,1933,1935, 1937,1939
	SOG has 1937
	ULC has 1887-1912

REF	**970**
Title	**Kelly's Chelsea, Pimlico and Belgravia Directory**
Dates	1887-1939
Publisher	Kelly & Co
Printer	Kelly & Co
Place	London
Type	GE TR
Map scale	1:15840
Notes	Cont'd from 941
Library	BL all
holdings	BOD has 1887-1912
	CLM has 1939
	GL has 1889,1894-1939
	GLH has 1887,1891,1894,1906, 1907,1909-1917,1919,1921, 1923,1926-1939
	SOG has 1936
	ULC has 1887-1912

REF	**971**		REF	**973**
Title	**Kelly's Marylebone & St John's Wood Directory**		Title	**Kelly's Kensington, Notting Hill, Brompton & Knightsbridge Directory**
Dates	1887-1939			
Publisher	Kelly & Co		Dates	1887-1939,1950
Printer	Kelly & Co		Publisher	Kelly & Co
Place	London		Printer	Kelly & Co
Type	GE TR		Place	London
Map scale	1:15840		Type	GE TR
Notes	Cont'd from 914		Map scale	1:15840
Library	BL all		Notes	Cont'd from 938
holdings	BOD has 1887-1912		Library	BL all
	BPH has 1939		holdings	BOD has 1887-1912
	CLM has 1939			BPH has 1938
	GL not 1887,1888,1890,1891			GL has 1889,1892-1939,1950
	GLH has 1898,1903,1904,1906,			GLH has 1893,1905,1907,
	1907,1909,1911-1917,1921,			1909-1916,1919,1920,1923,
	1923,1926-1931,1933-1939			1924,1936-1950
	ULC has 1887,1912			NLW has 1950
				ULC has 1887-1912
				WAR has 1950

REF **972**
Title **Kelly's Paddington and Bayswater Directory**
Dates 1887-1939
Publisher Kelly & Co
Printer Kelly & Co
Place London
Type GE TR
Map scale 1:15840
Notes Cont'd from 932. From 1889 includes Kensal Green.
Library BL all
holdings BOD has 1887-1912
CLM has 1939
GL not 1887,1888,1903
GLH has 1893,1895,1897, 1903-1916,1919-1921,1923, 1926-1929
ULC has 1887-1912

REF **974**
Title **Kelly's Kilburn & Willesden Directory**
Dates 1887-1940
Publisher Kelly & Co
Printer Kelly & Co
Place London
Type GE TR
Map scale 1:15840
Notes From 1890 includes Harlesden; from 1899 includes Cricklewood; from 1901 includes Brondesbury & West Hampstead.
Library BL all
holdings BOD has 1887-1912
CLM has 1940
GL has 1892-1918,1920-1940
GLH has 1899,1908-1910,1912, 1914,1917,1920-1929, 1931-1933,1935,1937,1938
NLW has 1912
SOG has 1900,1906
ULC has 1887,1913

REF **975**
Title **Kelly's Kennington, Battersea & South Lambeth Directory**
Dates 1888,1889
Publisher Kelly & Co
Printer Kelly & Co
Place London
Type GE TR
Map scale 1:15840
Library BL all
holdings BOD all
GL has 1889
ULC all

REF **976**
Title **Kelly's Highbury, Holloway & Tufnell Park Directory**
Dates 1888-1916
Publisher Kelly & Co
Printer Kelly & Co
Place London
Type GE TR
Map scale 1:15840
Library BL not 1888-1890
holdings BOD has 1888-1912
GL not 1888-1891,1900,1911,
1916
GLH has 1892,1897,1902,
1904-1913
ULC has 1890-1913

REF **977**
Title **Kelly's Camden and Kentish Town Directory**
Dates 1889-1916,1922,1923,1926
Publisher Kelly & Co
Printer Kelly & Co
Place London
Type GE TR
Map scale 1:15840
Notes Cont'd from 920
Library BL all
holdings BOD has 1889-1911
CLM has 1922
GL not 1890,1891
GLH has 1894,1906-1909,
1911-1916,1923
NLW has 1912
ULC has 1889-1912

REF **978**
Title **Blackie's Court Guide with Alphabetical List of the Royal Tradesmen & leading West End Firms**
Dates 1890-1900
Publisher Blackie, J. & Co
Printer Blackie, J. & Co
Place London
Type CT
Map scale –
Library BL all
holdings BOD has 1890

REF **979**
Title **Kelly's Balham, Tooting & Merton Directory**
Dates 1890-1915,1921,1923-1926,1928
Publisher Kelly & Co
Printer Kelly & Co
Place London
Type GE TR
Map scale 1:15840
Library BL all
holdings BOD has 1890-1912
CLM has 1928
GL not 1890,1891,1904,1911
GLH has 1904,1906,1908-1910,
1912-1915,1921,1923-1926
ULC has 1890-1913

REF **980**
Title **Kelly's Stoke Newington, Stamford Hill & Upper & Lower Clapton Directory**
Dates 1890-1929
Publisher Kelly & Co
Printer Kelly & Co
Place London
Type GE TR
Map scale 1:15840
Notes Cont'd from 961. Stamford Hill included 1890,1891, 1909-1929. From 1892-1901 includes South Hornsey.
Library BL all
holdings BOD has 1890-1912
CLM has 1929
GL not 1890,1891,1897,1911,
1917,1920,1928
GLH has 1894,1895,1901,
1903-1906,1908-1915,1919,
1921-1927,1929
ULC has 1890-1912

REF **981**
Title **Kelly's Battersea and South Lambeth Directory**
Dates 1892-1904
Publisher Kelly & Co
Printer Kelly & Co
Place London
Type GE TR
Map scale 1:15840
Library BL not 1901,1904
holdings BOD has 1892-1904
GL not 1900
GLH has 1904
ULC all

REF **982**
Title **Kelly's Dalston, Kingsland, De Beauvoir Town & Canonbury Directory**
Dates 1892-1908
Publisher Kelly & Co
Printer Kelly & Co
Place London
Type GE TR
Map scale 1:15840
Library BL all
holdings BOD all
GL all
GLH has 1892,1898,1903-1908
ULC all

REF **983**
Title **Kelly's Woolwich, Plumstead, Shooter's Hill & Charlton Directory**
Dates 1893-1923
Publisher Kelly & Co
Printer Kelly & Co
Place London
Type GE TR
Map scale 1:15840
Library BL all
holdings BOD has 1893-1912
CLM has 1923
GL not 1917-1919
GLH has 1897,1901,1910-1915, 1920
ULC has 1893-1912

REF **984**
Title **Kelly's Forest Hill, Lower Sydenham and part of Brockley Directory**
Dates 1899-1908
Publisher Kelly's Directories Ltd
Printer Kelly's Directories Ltd
Place London
Type GE TR
Map scale 1:15840
Library BL all
holdings BOD all
GL not 1903
GLH has 1907
ULC all

REF **985**
Title **Kelly's Stamford Hill and Tottenham Directory**
Dates 1899-1908
Publisher Kelly's Directories Ltd
Printer Kelly's Directories Ltd
Place London
Type GE TR
Map scale 1:15840
Notes Cont'd from 1011. Cont'd as 1016.
Library BL all
holdings BOD all
GL not 1900,1907
GLH has 1904-1908
ULC has 1899-1902

REF **986**
Title **Kelly's Hammersmith & Shepherds Bush Directory**
Dates 1899-1908,1910-1925,1927,1929, 1931,1933,1935,1937,1939
Publisher Kelly's Directories Ltd
Printer Kelly's Directories Ltd
Place London
Type GE TR
Map scale 1:15840
Library BL all
holdings BOD has 1899-1912
BPH has 1935
CLM has 1939
GL not 1900,1931
GLH has 1903,1906-1911, 1913-1917,1919-1921, 1925-1937
SOG has 1935
ULC has 1899-1912

REF	987
Title	**Kelly's Lewisham, Brockley & Catford Directory**
Dates	1899-1917,1919-1925,1927
Publisher	Kelly's Directories Ltd
Printer	Kelly's Directories Ltd
Place	London
Type	GE TR
Map scale	1:15840
Library	BL all
holdings	BOD has 1899-1912
	CLM has 1927
	GL all
	GLH has 1907,1912-1916,1919, 1920,1922,1923,1925
	ULC has 1899-1912

REF	988
Title	**Kelly's Hampstead & Child's Hill Directory**
Dates	1899-1918,1920-1940
Publisher	Kelly's Directories Ltd
Printer	Kelly's Directories Ltd
Place	London
Type	GE TR
Map scale	1:15840
Notes	Cont'd from 964
Library	BL all
holdings	BOD has 1899-1912,1936
	CLM has 1940
	GL not 1911,1916
	GLH has 1899,1901-1916, 1920-1932,1934-1937
	NLW has 1912
	SOG has 1939
	ULC has 1899-1913

REF	989
Title	**Suburban Directory**
Dates	1905-1913
Publisher	The London Directory Company Ltd
Printer	–
Place	London
Type	TR
Map scale	–
Notes	For each London suburb - separate TR Directory. Towns in Kent, Surrey & Middx.
Library	BL all
holdings	BOD has 1905-1907,1913
	NLS has 1908-1912

REF	990
Title	**Kelly's Directory of Streatham, Norbury & Norwood**
Dates	1907-1926,1930,1932,1934,1936, 1938
Publisher	Kelly's Directories Ltd
Printer	Kelly's Directories Ltd
Place	London
Type	GE TR
Map scale	1:15840
Library	BL all
holdings	BOD has 1909-1912
	CLM has 1938
	CRD has 1926,1928,1930,1938
	GL not 1907,1908,1918
	GLH has 1909,1911-1914,1916, 1919,1920,1922,1923, 1926-1936
	SOG has 1938
	ULC has 1909-1912

REF	991
Title	**Hampstead Year Book and Directory**
Dates	1928-1939
Publisher	Baines and Scarsbrook Ltd
Printer	Baines and Scarsbrook Ltd
Place	Hampstead
Type	GE TR
Map scale	1:19495
Library	BL all
holdings	BOD all
	GL has 1928,1930,1938
	GLH has 1937
	NLS all
	NLW all

REF	992
Title	**Cope's London Motor & Allied Trades Directory**
Dates	1929
Publisher	Emporium Publications
Printer	Emporium Publications
Place	London
Type	SP
Map scale	–
Notes	TR sections
Library	BL

REF	**993**
Title	**The Larkhall Estate Directory & Handbook**
Dates	1929,1930
Publisher	Larkhall Estate Ltd
Printer	Baltley Bros.
Place	London
Type	GE
Map scale	–
Library	BL all
holdings	NLW has 1929

REF	**994**
Title	**Kelly's Directory of Putney and Roehampton**
Dates	1929-1939
Publisher	Kelly's Directories Ltd
Printer	Kelly's Directories Ltd
Place	London
Type	GE TR
Map scale	1:15840
Library	BL all
holdings	CLM has 1939
	CRD has 1938,1939
	GL all
	GLH all
	SOG has 1937

REF	**995**
Title	**The City Directory and Diary**
Dates	1934-1939,1948
Publisher	Collingridge, W.H. Ltd
Printer	Collingridge, W.H. Ltd
Place	London
Type	CM
Map scale	1:3960
Library	BL not 1948
holdings	NLW has 1948
	SOG has 1935,1939

REF	**996**
Title	**Industrial Islington**
Dates	1937
Publisher	Islington Chamber of Commerce
Printer	–
Place	Islington
Type	SP
Map scale	–
Notes	Alphabetical & classified sections & general industrial/commercial information
Library	GLH

MIDDLESEX

REF	**997**
Title	**Kelly's Directory of Middlesex**
Dates	1851,1855,1859,1862,1866,1870, 1874,1878,1882,1886,1890,1895, 1899,1902,1906,1908,1910,1912, 1914,1917,1922,1926,1929,1933, 1937
Publisher	Kelly & Co
Printer	Kelly & Co
Place	London
Type	GE TR
Map scale	1:63360
Library	BCL has 1890-1937
holdings	BED has 1851
	BIS has 1926,1937
	BL not 1851,1926
	BOD not 1855,1874,1917,1926
	BPH has 1866,1874,1886,1895, 1906,1917-1926
	CLB has 1937
	CLE has 1937
	CLM has 1959,1926,1937
	COL has 1855,1859,1878
	GL not 1910
	GLH not 1851
	HLS has 1878,1886,1895,1926
	IHR has 1890,1906,1926
	KCL has 1859,1866
	MLG has 1870,1874,1899-1926
	NLS not 1926
	NLW has 1912,1914,1937
	SCL has 1926,1933,1937
	SOG has 1851-1862,1874,1882, 1899,1902,1937
	ULC not 1926
	YCL has 1937

REF	**998**
Title	**The West Middlesex Directory**
Dates	1863
Publisher	'?'
Printer	'?'
Place	'?'
Type	GE
Map scale	–
Notes	Bibliographic details missing due to lack of T/P, GL
Library	GL

REF	999
Title	Hand-Book for the Use of Visitors to Harrow-on-the-hill ... with a Directory comprising the residences of the neighbouring gentry, tradesmen, etc.
Dates	1850
Publisher	Wright,W.N.
Printer	Nicol, W.
Place	London
Type	TR
Map scale	–
Notes	NORTON 555. TR section has no addresses. Also very small CT section with few proper addresses.
Library	GLH
holdings	IHR

REF	1000
Title	Mason's Court Guide and General Directory for Brentford, Kew, Ealing, Isleworth, Twickenham, Teddington ... etc etc
Dates	1853
Publisher	Mason, R.H.
Printer	Mason, R.H.
Place	Greenwich
Type	CM TR
Map scale	–
Notes	NORTON 554
Library	BL
holdings	GLH
	NLS
	SOG
	ULC

REF	1001
Title	The Teddington Almanack and Directory
Dates	1884
Publisher	Le Mon, E.S. & M.
Printer	Le Mon, E.S. & M.
Place	Teddington
Type	GE
Map scale	–
Library	BL

REF	1002
Title	Hendon, Finchley and Barnet Directory
Dates	1885
Publisher	Smart, E.A.
Printer	–
Place	Hendon
Type	GE
Map scale	1:15840
Library	BOD

REF	1003
Title	The Hornsey, Upper Holloway & Finsbury Park Directory
Dates	1885,1886
Publisher	Hutchings & Crowsley
Printer	Hutchings & Crowsley
Place	London
Type	GE TR
Map scale	1:15840
Library	BL all
holdings	BOD has 1886
	GL has 1886

REF	1004
Title	The Barnet, Finchley, Hendon, Edgware & District Directory
Dates	1886
Publisher	Hutchings & Crowsley
Printer	Hutchings & Crowsley
Place	London
Type	GE
Map scale	–
Library	BL
holdings	ULC

REF	1005
Title	The Ealing, Acton, Hanwell, Gunnersbury & Chiswick Directory
Dates	1886
Publisher	Hutchings & Crowsley
Printer	Hutchings & Crowsley
Place	London
Type	GE TR
Map scale	1:15840
Notes	Cont'd as 1007
Library	BL all
holdings	BOD has 1886

REF 1006
Title Kelly's Barnet, Finchley, Hendon, Edgware & District Directory
Dates 1887-1911
Publisher Kelly & Co
Printer Kelly & Co
Place London
Type GE TR
Map scale 1:15840
Notes Cont'd as 1018. 1892 Edgware dropped from title, Southgate included; 1900 Friern Barnet included; 1910 Golder's Green included.
Library BL all
holdings BOD all
GL not 1887,1888,1890,1891, 1902,1903,1907,1911
GLH has 1905,1907,1908
ULC all

REF 1007
Title Kelly's Ealing, Acton, Hanwell, Gunnersbury & Chiswick Directory
Dates 1887-1913
Publisher Kelly & Co
Printer Kelly & Co
Place London
Type GE TR
Map scale 1:15840
Notes Cont'd from 1005. Cont'd as 1020 & 1021. From 1896 includes Brentford.
Library BL all
holdings BOD has 1887-1905,1907-1912
GL not 1887,1888,1890,1891, 1898,1900,1906
GLH has 1896,1897,1899,1902, 1904,1905,1907,1908, 1910-1913
ULC has 1887-1912

REF 1008
Title Kelly's Hornsey, Upper Holloway & Finsbury Park Directory
Dates 1887-1918,1920-1923
Publisher Kelly & Co
Printer Kelly & Co
Place London
Type GE TR
Map scale 1:15840
Notes Cont'd as 1024. From 1888-1898 entitled 'Kelly's Hornsey, Wood Green, Crouch End & Finsbury Park with part of Upper Holloway Directory'. After 1898 Wood Green dropped & Highgate included.
Library BL all
holdings BOD has 1887-1912
GL has 1889,1892-1939
GLH has 1892,1904,1906,1909, 1910,1912,1920-1922
SOG has 1915
ULC all

REF 1009
Title Kelly's Directory of Uxbridge, West Drayton, Southall etc
Dates 1890
Publisher Kelly & Co
Printer Kelly & Co
Place London
Type GE TR
Map scale —
Library BL
holdings BOD
GL
ULC

REF 1010
Title Lemon's Teddington Directory
Dates 1890,1891
Publisher Lemon, E.S.
Printer Lemon, E.S.
Place Teddington
Type GE TR
Map scale —
Library BOD
holdings ULC

REF	**1011**		REF	**1014**
Title	**Kelly's Tottenham, Enfield, Edmonton & Winchmore Hill Directory**		Title	**Marshman's Northwood Directory**
			Dates	1905,1906
Dates	1893-1898		Publisher	Marshman, E.P.
Publisher	Kelly & Co		Printer	Marshman, E.P.
Printer	Kelly & Co		Place	Northwood
Place	London		Type	GE
Type	GE TR		Map scale	–
Map scale	1:63360		Library	BL
Notes	Cont'd as 985 & 1016		holdings	BOD
Library	BL			NLS
holdings	BOD			
	GL		REF	**1015**
	ULC		Title	**Kelly's Enfield & Winchmore Hill Directory including Bush Hill Park, Ponder's End, Cockfosters and Hadley Wood**
REF	**1012**			
Title	**Kelly's Enfield, Edmonton & Winchmore Hill Directory**		Dates	1909-1914,1916,1917,1921-1939
			Publisher	Kelly's Directories Ltd
Dates	1899-1908		Printer	Kelly's Directories Ltd
Publisher	Kelly's Directories Ltd		Place	London
Printer	Kelly's Directories Ltd		Type	GE TR
Place	London		Map scale	1:15840
Type	GE TR		Notes	Cont'd from 1012
Map scale	1:15840		Library	BL all
Notes	Cont'd from 1011. Cont'd as 1015.		holdings	BOD has 1909-1911
Library	BL all			CLM has 1939
holdings	BOD all			GL not 1921
	GL not 1900			GLH has 1909-1914,1917,1923,
	GLH has 1902-1906			1924,1926-1937,1939
	ULC all			SOG has 1939
				ULC has 1909-1912
REF	**1013**			
Title	**Kelly's Wood Green, Muswell Hill, Bounds Green, Fortis Green, East Finchley & Palmer's Green Directory**		REF	**1016**
			Title	**Kelly's Tottenham and Edmonton Directory**
			Dates	1909-1915,1922,1923
Dates	1899-1917,1924,1927,1929,1931, 1932,1934,1936,1938		Publisher	Kelly's Directories Ltd
			Printer	Kelly's Directories Ltd
Publisher	Kelly's Directories Ltd		Place	London
Printer	Kelly's Directories Ltd		Type	GE TR
Place	London		Map scale	1:15840
Type	GE TR		Notes	Cont'd from 985
Map scale	1:15840		Library	BL has 1909,1910,1912-1914,
Notes	Palmer's Green included 1900-1914		holdings	1922,1923
Library	BL not 1924,1927			BOD has 1909-1912
holdings	BOD has 1899-1912			CLM has 1922
	CLM has 1938			GL has 1909,1910,1912-1914,
	GL not 1915-1927			1922,1923
	GLH has 1924,1927,1929,1931			GLH all
	SOG has 1938			ULC has 1909,1910,1912
	ULC has 1899-1913			

REF **1017**
Title **Kelly's Directory of Harrow, Wealdstone, Wembley and Sudbury**
Dates 1909-1916,1918-1920,1922-1937
Publisher Kelly's Directories Ltd
Printer Kelly's Directories Ltd
Place London
Type GE TR
Map scale 1:15849
Notes Includes Northwood & Pinner from 1912
Library BL not 1909
holdings BOD has 1909-1911
BPH has 1936
CLM has 1937
GL all
GLH has 1923-1925,1927, 1929-1934,1937
SOG has 1936
ULC has 1909-1912

REF **1018**
Title **Kelly's Barnet, New Barnet, East Barnet, Hadley, Whetstone, Totteridge, Mill Hill, Friern Barnet, Southgate, New Southgate & Palmer's Green Directory**
Dates 1912-1914,1916-1920,1922-1939
Publisher Kelly's Directories Ltd
Printer Kelly's Directories Ltd
Place London
Type GE TR
Map scale 1:15840
Notes Cont'd from 1006. From 1923 includes Potter's Bar; from 1927 includes South Mimms. Friern Barnet dropped after 1922. Mill Hill dropped after 1926.
Library BL all
holdings CLM has 1931,1939
GL all
GLH has 1912-1914,1924,1927, 1929-1933,1935-1937,1939
HLS has 1935,1939
SOG has 1937
ULC has 1912

REF **1019**
Title **Kelly's Finchley, Child's Hill, Hendon & Golders Green Directory**
Dates 1912-1915,1917-1925
Publisher Kelly's Directories Ltd
Printer Kelly's Directories Ltd
Place London
Type GE TR
Map scale 1:15840
Notes Cont'd as 1025. 1923 Child's Hill dropped from title; 1924 includes Friern Barnet.
Library BL all
holdings GL all
GLH has 1920,1923-1925
SOG has 1914

REF **1020**
Title **Kelly's Chiswick, Acton & Gunnersbury Directory**
Dates 1914,1915
Publisher Kelly's Directories Ltd
Printer Kelly's Directories Ltd
Place London
Type GE TR
Map scale 1:15840
Notes Cont'd from 1007
Library BL all
holdings GL all
GLH has 1914

REF **1021**
Title **Kelly's Ealing, Hanwell, Brentford & Southall Directory**
Dates 1914-1920,1922-1940
Publisher Kelly's Directories Ltd
Printer Kelly's Directories Ltd
Place London
Type GE TR
Map scale 1:15840
Notes Cont'd from 1007. Brentford dropped from title after 1927.
Library BL all
holdings CLM has 1940
GL all
GLH has 1914-1917,1919,1920, 1923,1924,1927-1935,1940
SOG has 1937,1939

REF **1022**
Title **Thomason's Directory of Hounslow, Heston, Spring Grove and Osterly**
Dates 1923,1927
Publisher Thomason's Ltd
Printer Thomason's Ltd
Place Hounslow
Type GE
Map scale –
Library BL

REF **1023**
Title **King's "Gazette" Directory of Uxbridge etc**
Dates 1923-1933
Publisher King & Hutchings Ltd
Printer King & Hutchings Ltd
Place Uxbridge
Type CM
Map scale –
Library BL

REF **1024**
Title **Kelly's Directory of Hornsey, Muswell Hill, Crouch End, Highgate etc.**
Dates 1924-1939
Publisher Kelly's Directories Ltd
Printer Kelly's Directories Ltd
Place London
Type GE TR
Map scale 1:15840
Notes Cont'd from 1008
Library BL all
holdings BPH has 1939
CLM has 1939
GLH has 1924,1925,1927-1929, 1931,1932,1935
SOG has 1938
ULC all

REF **1025**
Title **Kelly's Directory of Finchley and Friern Barnet**
Dates 1926-1939
Publisher Kelly's Directories Ltd
Printer Kelly's Directories Ltd
Place London
Type GE TR
Map scale 1:15840
Notes Cont'd from 1019
Library BL all
holdings BPH has 1938
GL all
GLH has 1926-1932,1934,1937
SOG has 1938

REF **1026**
Title **Kelly's Directory of Hendon, Golders Green, Mill Hill, Kingsbury etc**
Dates 1926-1939
Publisher Kelly's Directories Ltd
Printer Kelly's Directories Ltd
Place London
Type GE TR
Map scale 1:15840
Notes Kingsbury dropped from title after 1934
Library BL all
holdings BPH has 1938
CLM has 1939
GL all
GLH has 1927-1933
SOG has 1931,1937

REF **1027**
Title **Kelly's Directory of the Borough of Acton**
Dates 1928-1940
Publisher Kelly's Directories Ltd
Printer Kelly's Directories Ltd
Place London
Type GE TR
Map scale 1:15840
Library BL all
holdings GL all
GLH has 1929,1931,1932,1935, 1939
SOG has 1937

REF	**1028**
Title	**Kelly's Directory of Wembley, Alperton & Sudbury**
Dates	1929-1937,1948
Publisher	Kelly's Directories Ltd
Printer	Kelly's Directories Ltd
Place	London
Type	GE TR
Map scale	1:15840
Library	BL not 1948
holdings	BPH has 1936
	CLM has 1937
	GL all
	GLH has 1929-1937
	SOG has 1935

REF	**1029**
Title	**Kelly's Directory of Edgware & Neighbourhood**
Dates	1929-1939
Publisher	Kelly's Directories Ltd
Printer	Kelly's Directories Ltd
Place	London
Type	GE TR
Map scale	1:255440
Library	BL not 1939
holdings	CLM has 1939
	GL not 1938
	GLH has 1929-1933,1936
	SOG has 1933,1934,1938

REF	**1030**
Title	**Kelly's Directory of Pinner, Hatch End & Northwood**
Dates	1929-1939
Publisher	Kelly's Directories Ltd
Printer	Kelly's Directories Ltd
Place	London
Type	GE TR
Map scale	1:15840
Library	BL all
holdings	BPH has 1939
	CLM has 1939
	GL not 1937
	GLH has 1930,1931-1934,1939
	SOG has 1937

REF	**1031**
Title	**Kelly's Directory of Twickenham, Teddington & Neighbourhood**
Dates	1929-1940
Publisher	Kelly's Directories Ltd
Printer	Kelly's Directories Ltd
Place	London
Type	GE TR
Map scale	1:15840
Notes	Cont'd from 1313
Library	BL all
holdings	CLM has 1931,1940
	GL all
	GLH has 1929-1933,1936
	SOG has 1908

REF	**1032**
Title	**Beddoe's Directory Staines and District**
Dates	1947
Publisher	Beddoe, B. Ltd
Printer	Beddoe, B. Ltd
Place	Staines
Type	ST
Map scale	1:84480
Library	GL

REF	**1033**
Title	**Wembley Directory**
Dates	1948
Publisher	The London & Provincial Publications Ltd
Printer	Knight, T. & Co
Place	Wembley
Type	CT TR
Map scale	1:15840
Library	BOD
holdings	CLM
	NLS
	ULC

REF	**1034**
Title	**Ealing Blue Book**
Dates	1949
Publisher	Commercial Guides Ltd
Printer	Harrow Observer
Place	Harrow
Type	ST TR
Map scale	1:10560
Notes	Map scale approx.
Library	GL

REF **1035**
Title **Finchley Directory**
Dates 1949
Publisher The London & Provincial Publications Ltd
Printer Rawlinson's Printing Works
Place Wembley
Type CT TR
Map scale –
Library BOD
holdings GL
ULC

REF **1036**
Title **Harrow Directory**
Dates 1949,1950
Publisher Commercial Guides Ltd
Printer Harrow Observer Ltd
Place Harrow
Type ST TR
Map scale 1:15840
Notes 1950 edtion entitled 'Kemp's Harrow and District Local Directory'. Map scale approx.
Library BL all
holdings GL all
NLS has 1950

REF **1037**
Title **Uxbridge & District Local Directory**
Dates 1949,1950
Publisher Kemp's Commercial Guides Ltd
Printer Kemp's Commercial Guides Ltd
Place London
Type ST TR
Map scale 1:253440
Library GL all
holdings NLS has 1950
ULC has 1950

REF **1038**
Title **Hendon Directory including Cricklewood, Edgware and Golders Green**
Dates 1950
Publisher The London & Provincial Publications Ltd
Printer The London & Provincial Publications Ltd
Place Wembley
Type ST TR
Map scale –
Library GL
holdings NLW

REF **1039**
Title **Kemp's Directory of Ealing and Hanwell (Incorporating Perivale)**
Dates 1950
Publisher '?'
Printer '?'
Place '?'
Type ST TR
Map scale 1:10560
Notes GL title page and first 30pp missing when re-bound. Map scale approx.
Library GL
holdings GLH

REF **1040**
Title **Southgate Directory**
Dates 1950
Publisher The London & Provincial Publications Ltd
Printer –
Place London
Type ST TR
Map scale –
Library GL

NORFOLK

REF **1041**
Title **Hunt & Co's Directory of East Norfolk with part of Suffolk**
Dates 1850
Publisher Hunt, E. & Co
Printer Gardiner, B.W.
Place London
Type TR
Map scale –
Notes NORTON 561
Library GL
holdings KLL
NOR
SOG

REF	**1042**
Title	**Kelly's Directory of Norfolk**
Dates	1853,1858,1865,1869,1875,1879, 1883,1888,1892,1896,1900,1904, 1908,1912,1916,1922,1925,1929, 1933,1937
Publisher	Kelly & Co
Printer	Kelly & Co
Place	London
Type	GE TR
Map scale	1:253440
Notes	See 5
Library	BCL has 1933,1937
holdings	BIS has 1879,1904,1912,1933, 1937
	BL all
	BOD all
	BPH has 1858,1900,1916-1929, 1937
	CAM not 1896,1908
	CLB has 1937
	CLE has 1916,1937
	CLM has 1937
	COL has 1892. Also 1903 edition ESSX,NORF,SUFF
	GL all
	HRO has 1912
	IHR has 1892,1908,1937
	KLL not 1853,1875,1883,1888
	LCL has 1933
	MLG has 1904-1939
	NLS not 1933
	NLW has 1912,1916,1929-1937
	NOR all
	PET has 1888,1892,1908, 1925-1933
	SOG has 1858,1869,1875,1888, 1896,1900,1922-1937
	SRI has 1869-1879,,1900,1904, 1912-1929,1937
	ULC all

REF	**1043**
Title	**History, Gazetteer and Directory of Norfolk**
Dates	1854
Publisher	White, F.
Printer	Burton, E.
Place	Sheffield
Type	GE TR
Map scale	1:316800
Notes	NORTON 562. See 1046.
Library	BCL
holdings	BL
	BOD
	GL
	IHR
	KLL
	NOR
	SOG

REF	**1044**
Title	**Craven and Co's Commercial Directory of the County of Norfolk**
Dates	1856
Publisher	Craven & Co
Printer	Craven & Co
Place	Nottingham
Type	CM TR
Map scale	–
Library	NOR

REF	**1045**
Title	**J.G. Harrod & Co's Postal and Commercial Directory of Norfolk with Lowestoft in the County of Suffolk**
Dates	1863,1868,1872,1877
Publisher	Harrod, J.G. & Co
Printer	–
Place	Norwich
Type	CM TR
Map scale	–
Notes	1877 edition entitled 'J.G. Harrod & Co's Royal County Directory of Norfolk including Lowestoft in the County of Suffolk'
Library	GL has 1877
holdings	KLL all
	NOR all
	SOG has 1863

REF **1046**
Title **History, Gazetteer and Directory of Norfolk**
Dates 1864,1883,1890
Publisher White, W.
Printer Leader, R. & Sons
Place Sheffield
Type GE TR
Map scale 1:253440
Notes See 1043
Library BCL has 1864
holdings BL all
BOD not 1864
BPH has 1864
GL all
IHR has 1864,1883
KLL all
NOR all
SOG has 1864
SRI has 1864,1883
ULC not 1864

REF **1047**
Title **Deacon's Norfolk Court Guide and County Blue Book**
Dates 1885
Publisher Deacon, C.W. & Co
Printer Deacon, C.W. & Co
Place London
Type CT PR
Map scale –
Library NOR

REF **1048**
Title **Mason's Norwich General and Commercial Directory and Handbook**
Dates 1852
Publisher Mason
Printer Adlard & Palmer
Place London
Type CT CM
Map scale –
Notes NORTON 570
Library BOD
holdings IHR
NOR
ULC

REF **1049**
Title **Melville and Co's Directory and Gazetteer of Norwich, Yarmouth, Dereham, Swaffham ... Ipswich, Bury St. Edmunds, Woodbridge [etc]**
Dates 1856
Publisher Melville, F.R. & Co
Printer Jarrold & Sons
Place Norwich
Type CM
Map scale –
Library NOR

REF **1050**
Title **Rogers' Directory of Norwich and Neighbourhood**
Dates 1859
Publisher Rogers
Printer Jarrold & Sons
Place Norwich
Type CM TR
Map scale –
Library GL
holdings NOR

REF **1051**
Title **Cobb's Directory of the Borough of Gt. Yarmouth in the County of Norfolk with Southtown and Gorleston in Suffolk**
Dates 1863
Publisher Cobb, W. & Co
Printer Cobb, W. & Co
Place Great Yarmouth
Type GE TR
Map scale –
Library NOR

REF **1052**
Title **Simpson's Norwich Directory and Court Guide including Aylsham and Wymondham**
Dates 1864
Publisher Simpson & Co
Printer –
Place London
Type GE
Map scale –
Library GL
holdings IHR
NOR

REF	**1053**
Title	**Mathieson's Norwich Directory**
Dates	1867
Publisher	Mathieson
Printer	Fletcher & Son
Place	Norwich
Type	GE TR
Map scale	–
Library holdings	BL
	BOD
	GL
	NLS
	ULC

REF	**1054**
Title	**Mathiesons' Yarmouth and Lowestoft Directory**
Dates	1867
Publisher	Nall, G.
Printer	–
Place	Yarmouth
Type	GE TR
Map scale	–
Library holdings	BL
	BOD
	NOR
	ULC

REF	**1055**
Title	**The Thetford Household Almanack and Directory**
Dates	1869-1874
Publisher	Lucy, F.
Printer	Lucy, F.
Place	Thetford
Type	CM
Map scale	–
Notes	1870 published by M. Breeds; 1871-1874 published by F.T. Groom
Library	NOR

REF	**1056**
Title	**Godfrey's Directory of the Borough of Great Yarmouth ... with Southtown and Gorleston**
Dates	1874
Publisher	Godfrey, C.W.
Printer	Godfrey, C.W.
Place	Great Yarmouth
Type	GE
Map scale	–
Notes	Cont'd by 1058
Library	NOR

REF	**1057**
Title	**Colman's Directory of Norwich**
Dates	1877
Publisher	Colman, J.A. & Fuller, T.B.
Printer	–
Place	Norwich
Type	GE TR
Map scale	–
Library	NOR

REF	**1058**
Title	**Commercial and General Directory of the Town and Borough of Great Yarmouth ... Gorleston and Southtown**
Dates	1878
Publisher	Steer, C.
Printer	Steer, C.
Place	Great Yarmouth
Type	ST
Map scale	–
Notes	Cont'd from 1056
Library	NOR

REF	**1059**
Title	**The Imperial Postal Directory of the City and County of Norwich**
Dates	1879
Publisher	Hamilton, J.J. & Co
Printer	Allen, W.
Place	Norwich
Type	GE TR
Map scale	–
Library	NOR

REF	**1060**
Title	**Post Office Norwich District Directory**
Dates	1883
Publisher	Eyre Brothers
Printer	–
Place	London
Type	GE TR
Map scale	–
Library	NOR

REF **1061**
Title **Directory of the City of Norwich and its Hamlets**
Dates 1887,1889,1894,1896,1900,1905, 1908,1911,1913,1914,1922
Publisher Jarrold & Sons
Printer —
Place Norwich
Type GE
Map scale 1:10560
Notes Title varies
Library BL has 1887,1905-1911,1914
holdings BOD has 1889
NLS has 1889
NOR all
ULC has 1889

REF **1062**
Title **Jarrold's Directory of Cromer and Neighbourhood**
Dates 1889
Publisher Jarrold & Sons
Printer Jarrold & Sons
Place London
Type GE TR
Map scale —
Library BL
holdings BOD
NLS
NOR

REF **1063**
Title **Kelly's Directory of Great Yarmouth with Gorleston & Southtown**
Dates 1900,1903-1907,1909,1911,1913, 1915,1921-1924,1927,1930,1934, 1936,1938,1948
Publisher Kelly's Directories Ltd
Printer Kelly's Directories Ltd
Place London
Type GE
Map scale 1:126720
Library BL not 1906
holdings BOD has 1903-1911
GL not 1900
NLW has 1948
NOR has 1911,1915,1921,1922, 1927,1930,1936,1948
SOG has 1948
ULC has 1903-1911

REF **1064**
Title **Great Yarmouth, Gorleston and Southtown Directory**
Dates 1901
Publisher Jarrold & Sons
Printer Jarrold & Sons
Place Great Yarmouth
Type GE TR
Map scale —
Library BL
holdings BOD
GL
NLS
ULC

REF **1065**
Title **Norwich and District Trades' Directory**
Dates 1901,1902,1907,1911,1922-1930, 1932
Publisher Town and County Directories Ltd
Printer Macdonald, W. & Co
Place Edinburgh
Type TR
Map scale —
Notes 1932 edition entitled 'Norwich and Norfolk Trades' Directory'
Library KLL has 1932
holdings NOR all

REF **1066**
Title **East Dereham & District Almanack and Directory**
Dates 1901,1903,1904,1910,1913,1920
Publisher Coleby, G.
Printer Coleby, G.
Place East Dereham
Type GE
Map scale —
Library NOR

REF **1067**
Title **City of Norwich Business Directory**
Dates 1902
Publisher Pioneer Printing and Publishing Co
Printer Pioneer Printing and Publishing Co
Place Norwich
Type CM TR
Map scale —
Library NOR

REF **1068**
Title **F.W. Count's Illustrated Dereham Almanack ... Private and Commercial Directory**
Dates 1904
Publisher Count, F.W.
Printer Count, F.W.
Place East Dereham
Type CT CM
Map scale –
Library NOR

REF **1069**
Title **The New Directory of Norwich**
Dates 1914
Publisher Goose & Son Ltd
Printer Goose & Son Ltd
Place Norwich
Type GE
Map scale 1:12000
Library BL
holdings BOD
NLS
NOR
ULC

REF **1070**
Title **Kelly's Directory of the City of Norwich**
Dates 1924-1927,1929,1931,1933,1935, 1937,1939,1941,1947,1950
Publisher Kelly's Directories Ltd
Printer Kelly's Directories Ltd
Place London
Type GE TR
Map scale 1:10560
Library BL all
holdings GL all
MLG has 1947,1950
NLW has 1950
NOR all

REF **1071**
Title **Kelly's Directory of King's Lynn & Neighbourhood**
Dates 1928,1930,1932,1934,1936,1938
Publisher Kelly's Directories Ltd
Printer Kelly's Directories Ltd
Place London
Type GE TR
Map scale –
Library BL all
holdings CLM has 1930
GL all
KLL all
NOR has 1930,1936

REF **1072**
Title **The Cromer Almanack & Directory**
Dates 1929,1930
Publisher Rounce & Wortley
Printer Rounce & Wortley
Place Holt
Type ST
Map scale –
Library NOR

REF **1073**
Title **Thetford and District Almanac**
Dates 1929,1930,1937
Publisher Green, H.
Printer Green, H.
Place Thetford
Type ST
Map scale –
Library NOR

REF **1074**
Title **Rounce & Wortley's Sheringham Almanack including alphabetical directory of householders**
Dates 1933
Publisher Rounce & Wortley
Printer Rounce & Wortley
Place Holt
Type CT
Map scale –
Library NOR

NORTHAMPTONSHIRE

REF	**1075**
Title	**Kelly's Directory of Northamptonshire**
Dates	1854,1864,1869,1877,1885,1890, 1894,1898,1903,1906,1910,1914, 1920,1924,1928,1931,1936,1940
Publisher	Kelly & Co
Printer	Kelly & Co
Place	London
Type	GE TR
Map scale	1:285120
Notes	See 7(1854-1877) & 14(1885-1940)
Library holdings	AYL has 1869
	BCL has 1890-1936
	BED not 1854,1864,1877,1906, 1924
	BIS has 1936
	BL all
	BOD has 1885-1940
	BPH has 1869,1894,1903, 1914-1924,1940
	CLB has 1936
	CLE has 1940
	CLM has 1931-1940
	GL all
	HNT has 1864,1895,1931
	IHR has 1898,1903,1931,1936
	LUT has 1885,1890,1914,1920, 1936,1940
	MLG has 1910,1920,1924
	NEW has 1869
	NLS has 1885-1940
	NLW has 1928-1936
	NTH all
	PET has 1854,1869,1877,1890, 1894,1903,1906,1914,1924, 1931-1940
	SCL has 1928-1940
	SOG has 1894,1906,1910, 1920-1928,1940
	ULC has 1885-1940

REF	**1076**
Title	**Melville & Co's Directory of Northamptonshire**
Dates	1861
Publisher	Melville, F.R. & Co
Printer	Rider, J. & W.
Place	London
Type	CM
Map scale	–
Library	GL
holdings	NTH

REF	**1077**
Title	**Commercial Directory and Gazetteer for Northamptonshire**
Dates	1866
Publisher	The Royal Directory Printing and Publishing Company
Printer	Wilkes & Pollard
Place	London
Type	CM
Map scale	–
Library	NTH

REF	**1078**
Title	**History, Topography and Directory of Northamptonshire**
Dates	1874
Publisher	Whellan, F. & Co
Printer	Whittaker & Co
Place	London
Type	CM
Map scale	–
Library holdings	BCL
	GL
	IHR
	NTH
	PET
	SOG

REF	**1079**
Title	**Commercial and General Directory and Blue Book of Northamptonshire**
Dates	1884
Publisher	Wright, C.N.
Printer	Tompkin & Shardlow
Place	Leicester
Type	GE TR
Map scale	1:253440
Library	NTH
holdings	PET

REF	**1080**
Title	**Northampton & District Trades' Directory**
Dates	1905,1911,1918,1922,1923
Publisher	Town and County Directories Ltd
Printer	Macdonald, W. & Co
Place	Edinburgh
Type	TR
Map scale	–
Notes	Cont'd by 98. Relates to the county of Northants.
Library holdings	HNT has 1905 NTH all

REF	**1081**
Title	**The Northamptonshire County Trades' Journal and Directory**
Dates	1924
Publisher	The County Publicity Co
Printer	The County Publicity Co
Place	London
Type	TR
Map scale	–
Library	NTH

REF	**1082**
Title	**Directory of the Town of Northampton**
Dates	1853
Publisher	-
Printer	Phillips, T.
Place	Northampton
Type	TR
Map scale	–
Notes	NORTON 572
Library	NTH

REF	**1083**
Title	**J. Taylor & Son's Northampton Directory**
Dates	1858,1864
Publisher	Taylor, J. & Son
Printer	Taylor, J. & Son
Place	Northampton
Type	GE TR
Map scale	–
Notes	1858 edition entitled 'A General Directory of Northampton'
Library holdings	NTH all ULC has 1864

REF	**1084**
Title	**Clarke's Shilling Directory of Peterborough & Neighbourhood**
Dates	1871
Publisher	Clarke, J.S. & Son
Printer	Clarke, J.S. & Son
Place	Peterborough
Type	CM TR
Map scale	–
Notes	Cont'd as 1086
Library holdings	BL BOD PET

REF	**1085**
Title	**The Northampton Alphabetical Postal and Street Guide**
Dates	1876
Publisher	Clarke, F.W.S.
Printer	Clarke, F.W.S.
Place	Leicester
Type	SL
Map scale	–
Notes	Publisher & printer not stated, but Clarke advertises throughout the directory
Library	NTH

REF	**1086**
Title	**The Peterborough Directory**
Dates	1876
Publisher	Clarke, J.S.
Printer	Clarke, J.S.
Place	Peterborough
Type	CM TR
Map scale	1:19200
Notes	Cont'd from 1084. Cont'd as 1089. PET also holds a series of 'Companions to the Almanacks' from 1850 intermittently through to 1867 which contain ST and TR sections for Peterborough.
Library holdings	GL NTH PET

REF **1087**
Title **Directory of Northampton & Neighbourhood**
Dates 1878
Publisher Provincial & Metropolitan Directories Publishing Company
Printer –
Place London
Type CM TR
Map scale NS
Library BL
holdings BOD
NTH

REF **1088**
Title **Roberts' Northampton Directory**
Dates 1884
Publisher Roberts, W.L.
Printer –
Place Northampton
Type GE TR
Map scale –
Library GL
holdings NTH

REF **1089**
Title **The Peterborough Directory**
Dates 1884,1888,1892,1896,1901,1907, 1912
Publisher Caster, G.C,
Printer Caster, G.C,
Place Peterborough
Type CM TR
Map scale –
Notes Cont'd from 1086
Library NTH has 1888
holdings PET not 1888

REF **1090**
Title **Stevens' Directory of Northampton & Neighbourhood**
Dates 1889,1893
Publisher Stevens, G. & Co
Printer Stevens, G. & Co
Place London
Type GE TR
Map scale 1:506880
Library BL
holdings BOD
NLS
NTH all
ULC

REF **1091**
Title **Cook's Peterborough and District Directory**
Dates 1892,1894
Publisher Cook, W.J.
Printer Wing & Broughton
Place Boston
Type GE TR
Map scale –
Library BL all
holdings BOD all
NLS all
PET has 1894
ULC has 1892

REF **1092**
Title **Directory of Wellingborough, Kettering, Market Harborough & District**
Dates 1893
Publisher Stevens, G. & Co
Printer Stevens, G. & Co
Place London
Type GE TR
Map scale –
Library BL
holdings BOD
NLS
NTH
ULC

REF **1093**
Title **Lea's Northampton Directory**
Dates 1893,1900,1906,1907,1912,1914, 1915
Publisher Lea & Company Ltd
Printer Lea & Company Ltd
Place Northampton
Type GE TR
Map scale 1:9051
Library BL has 1915
holdings NTH not 1915

REF	**1094**
Title	**White's Directory of Northampton & Neighbourhood**
Dates	1896
Publisher	White, W.
Printer	Leader, R.
Place	Sheffield
Type	GE TR
Map scale	1:506880
Notes	Cont'd from 1090
Library	BL
holdings	BOD
	GL
	NLS
	NTH
	ULC

REF	**1095**
Title	**White's Directory of Wellingborough, Kettering & Neighbourhood**
Dates	1896
Publisher	White, W.
Printer	Leader, R. & Son
Place	Sheffield
Type	GE TR
Map scale	NS
Notes	Cont'd from 1092
Library	BL
holdings	BOD
	GL
	NLS
	NTH
	ULC

REF	**1096**
Title	**The Peterborough and District Directory and Year Book**
Dates	1922,1925,1928
Publisher	The Peterborough Advertiser
Printer	Advertiser Press
Place	Peterborough
Type	GE TR
Map scale	1:6336
Library	BL all
holdings	PET not 1922

REF	**1097**
Title	**Mark's Northampton Directory and Guide Book**
Dates	1928,1929
Publisher	Mark, W. & Co
Printer	Mark, W. & Co
Place	Northampton
Type	GE TR
Map scale	1:10560
Library	BL
holdings	BOD
	NLW
	NTH
	ULC

REF	**1098**
Title	**Leayton's Oundle Almanack and Directory**
Dates	1928,1931,1934,1937,1939
Publisher	Leayton, V.E.
Printer	Leayton, V.E.
Place	Oundle
Type	GE
Map scale	–
Library	GL has 1939
holdings	PET not 1939

REF	**1099**
Title	**The Northampton County Borough Directory**
Dates	1936
Publisher	Whipple, R.D. Son & Martin Ltd
Printer	Whipple, R.D. Son & Martin Ltd
Place	Leeds
Type	GE TR
Map scale	–
Library	GL
holdings	NTH

REF	**1100**
Title	**Peterborough Standard Directory of the City of Peterborough and Fletton Urban District**
Dates	1940
Publisher	Peterborough Standard
Printer	Peterborough Standard
Place	Peterborough
Type	GE
Map scale	–
Library	PET

NORTHUMBERLAND

REF	**1101**
Title	**History, Topography and Directory of Northumberland**
Dates	1855
Publisher	Whellan, W.
Printer	Galt & Co
Place	London
Type	GE TR
Map scale	1:190080
Notes	NORTON 582
Library	BL
holdings	DUR
	DAR
	CLN
	GL
	IHR
	MOR
	SOG

REF	**1102**
Title	**Kelly's Directory of Northumberland**
Dates	1858,1873,1879,1890,1894,1897, 1902,1906,1910,1914,1921,1925, 1929,1934,1938
Publisher	Kelly & Co
Printer	Kelly & Co
Place	London
Type	GE TR
Map scale	1:253440
Library	BCL has 1890-1938
holdings	BIS has 1914
	BL not 1906
	BOD all
	BPH has 1873,1879,1894,1906, 1914-1929
	CAR has 1894,1906
	CLB has 1938
	CLE has 1938
	CLM has 1910,1921,1925
	CLN not 1894,1897
	DAR not 1873
	DUR not 1873,1894,1906
	GL not 1873
	IHR has 1934
	LCL has 1934
	MID has 1902,1938
	MLG has 1894-1925,1934,1938
	MOR has 1873,1879,1897,1910, 1914,1921,1929,1938
	NLS not 1879
	NLW has 1914,1929-1938
	SCL has 1929,1938
	SOG has 1873,1879,1890,1910, 1921,1938
	ULC not 1894
	YCL has 1934

REF	**1103**
Title	**History, Topography and Directory of Northumberland (Hexham Division)**
Dates	1886
Publisher	Bulmer, T. & Co
Printer	Snape, T. & Co
Place	Manchester
Type	TR
Map scale	—
Library	CLN
holdings	GL
	MOR

REF **1104**
Title **History, Topography and Directory of Northumberland (Tyneside, Wansbeck and Berwick Divisions)**
Dates 1887
Publisher Bulmer, T. & Co
Printer Snape, T. & Co
Place Preston
Type GE TR
Map scale –
Library CLN
holdings GL
MOR
NLS

REF **1105**
Title **Ward's Directory of Newcastle and Gateshead with their Localities**
Dates 1863
Publisher Ward, R. & Sons
Printer Ward, R. & Sons
Place Newcastle-on-Tyne
Type GE TR
Map scale –
Library CLN

REF **1106**
Title **Ward's Directory of North and South Shields**
Dates 1865
Publisher Ward, R.
Printer Ward, R.
Place Newcastle-on-Tyne
Type CM TR
Map scale –
Library CLN

REF **1107**
Title **Ward's Directory (comprehending the towns) of Newcastle, Gateshead & South Shields**
Dates 1865,1867,1869,1871,1873,1875, 1877,1879,1881,1883,1885,1887, 1889,1891,1893,1895,1897,1899, 1901,1903,1905,1907,1909,1911, 1913,1915
Publisher Ward, R.
Printer Ward, R.
Place Newcastle-on-Tyne
Type GE TR
Map scale –
Notes Coverage increases in 1890s. Cont'd as 1119 & 418.
Library BL all
holdings BOD has 1887,1893,1895
BPH has 1885,1895,1905,1915
CLN all
DAR has 1871
GL has 1873,1879
MOR has 1915
NLS has 1887,1893,1895
ULC has 1887,1893,1895

REF **1108**
Title **The Newcastle and Gateshead Annual Directory**
Dates 1870,1873,1874
Publisher Christie, J.
Printer Christie, J.
Place Newcastle-on-Tyne
Type GE TR
Map scale –
Notes 1873 edition entitled 'Christie's Annual Directory for Newcastle, Gateshead, Jarrow'. 1874 edition entitled 'Christie's Combined Annual Directory for Newcastle, Gateshead, North and South Shields, Jarrow etc'.
Library CLN

REF **1109**
Title **The Blyth Pictorial Almanack, Diary, Tide Tables, Directory**
Dates 1879,1898
Publisher Alder and Company
Printer Alder and Company
Place Blyth
Type TR
Map scale 1:190080
Notes 1879 edition, T/P missing, but has identical format to 1898 edition
Library CLN

REF **1110**
Title **P.J. Jackson's Postal Address Directory of Newcastle-on-Tyne and Tyneside**
Dates 1880
Publisher Jackson, P.J. & Co
Printer Lambert, M. & M.W.
Place Newcastle-on-Tyne
Type GE TR
Map scale 1:10560
Library CLN

REF **1111**
Title **Robinson's Penny Illustrated Household Almanac, Blyth, Amble and Warkworth Directory**
Dates 1880
Publisher Robinson, J. (Junior) and Son
Printer Robinson, J. (Junior) and Son
Place Blyth
Type TR
Map scale –
Library CLN

REF **1112**
Title **Kelly's Directory of Newcastle, Gateshead, Sunderland, North & South Shields & suburbs**
Dates 1883,1886,1887
Publisher Kelly & Co
Printer Kelly & Co
Place London
Type GE TR
Map scale 1:10560
Library BL not 1887
holdings BOD not 1886
CLN not 1887
GL not 1887
NLS not 1886
SOG has 1887

REF **1113**
Title **Kelly's Directory of North Shields & Tynemouth**
Dates 1886
Publisher Kelly & Co
Printer Kelly & Co
Place London
Type GE TR
Map scale –
Library BL
holdings BOD
GL
NLS
ULC

REF **1114**
Title **Kelly's Directory of Newcastle and suburbs**
Dates 1886,1887
Publisher Kelly & Co
Printer Kelly & Co
Place London
Type GE TR
Map scale 1:10560
Library BL has 1887
holdings BOD has 1886
GL has 1887
NLS has 1886
ULC all

REF **1115**
Title **History and Directory of Newcastle-upon-Tyne**
Dates 1887
Publisher Bulmer, T. & Co
Printer Snape, T. & Co
Place Preston
Type CM TR
Map scale –
Library CLN

REF **1116**
Title **History, Directory and Topography of Newcastle-upon-Tyne**
Dates 1887
Publisher Bulmer, T. & Co
Printer Snape, T. & Co
Place Preston
Type CM TR
Map scale –
Library GL
holdings MOR

REF **1117**
Title **Ward's Directory of Newcastle-upon-Tyne (and the adjacent villages)**
Dates 1888,1890,1892,1894,1896,1898, 1900,1902,1904,1906,1908,1910, 1912,1914,1916,1919
Publisher Ward, R. & Sons
Printer Ward, R. & Sons
Place Sunderland
Type GE TR
Map scale NS
Notes Title includes 'adjacent villages' 1888-1896
Library BL not 1888,1890
holdings CLN all
GL has 1888,1916
MOR has 1888,1890,1902,1904

REF **1118**
Title **McInnes' Illustrated Amble Almanack**
Dates 1895
Publisher McInnes, R.G.
Printer –
Place Amble
Type CT TR
Map scale –
Library CLN

REF **1119**
Title **Ward's Directory of Newcastle-on-Tyne, North & South Shields, Jarrow, Wallsend**
Dates 1917,1920,1922,1924
Publisher Ward, R. & Sons
Printer Ward, R. & Sons
Place Newcastle-on-Tyne
Type GE TR
Map scale 1:380160
Notes Cont'd as 1120. Map scale approx.
Library BL all
holdings BPH has 1922,1924
CLN all
GL has 1920-1924
MLG has 1924

REF **1120**
Title **Ward's Directory of Whitley Bay, Tynemouth, North & South Shields, Jarrow, Wallsend, Gosforth, Newcastle-on-Tyne**
Dates 1926,1928,1930,1932,1934,1936, 1938,1940
Publisher Ward, R. & Sons Ltd
Printer Ward, R. & Sons Ltd
Place Newcastle-on-Tyne
Type GE
Map scale –
Notes Cont'd from 1119
Library BL all
holdings BPH not 1940
CLM has 1940
CLN all
DAR has 1930
DUR has 1930
GL has 1928,1936-1940
MLG not 1936
MOR has 1926,1932,1936-1940

REF **1121**
Title **The Advertiser Directory of Berwick and N. Northumberland**
Dates 1936-1938
Publisher Berwick Advertiser
Printer Berwick Advertiser
Place Berwick-upon-Tweed
Type GE
Map scale –
Library CLN

REF **1122**
Title **Kelly's Directory of the City of Newcastle-upon-Tyne**
Dates 1947,1950
Publisher Kelly's Directories Ltd
Printer Kelly's Directories Ltd
Place London
Type GE TR
Map scale –
Library BL all
holdings BOD all
BPH has 1950
CLE has 1950
CLN all
DUR has 1950
GL all
MOR all
NLS all
NLW has 1950
SCL all
SOG all
ULC all

[229]

NOTTINGHAMSHIRE

REF	**1123**
Title	**History, Directory and Gazetteer of the County, and of the Town and County of the Town of Nottingham**
Dates	1853,1864
Publisher	White, F. & Co
Printer	Harrison, S.
Place	Sheffield
Type	GE TR
Map scale	–
Notes	1864 edition entitled 'History, Gazetteer & Directory of the County of Nottingham'
Library holdings	BL all
	DON has 1864
	GL all
	NCL all
	SCL all

REF	**1124**
Title	**Kelly's Directory of Nottinghamshire**
Dates	1855,1864,1870,1876,1881,1888, 1891,1895,1899,1904,1908,1912, 1916,1922,1925,1928,1932,1936, 1941
Publisher	Kelly & Co
Printer	Kelly & Co
Place	London
Type	GE TR
Map scale	1:190080
Notes	See 9
Library holdings	BCL has 1855,1881,1891–1941
	BIS has 1925
	BL all
	BOD not 1870,1888
	BPH has 1876–1891,1899,1904, 1912–1922,1928,1936,1941
	CL has 1855
	CLB has 1941
	CLE has 1936
	CLL has 1855,1876–1895,1912, 1916
	CLM has 1870,1932–1941
	DLS has 1855,1864,1876
	GL all
	IHR has 1899
	MLG all
	NLS all
	NLW has 1928,1936
	SCL has 1855,1908,1925–1941
	SOG has 1855,1881,1891,1916, 1925,1936,1941
	ULC has 1876,1888
	YCL has 1941

REF	**1125**
Title	**Morris & Co's Commercial Directory and Gazetteer of Nottinghamshire with Grantham, Chesterfield and Gainsborough**
Dates	1869
Publisher	Morris & Co
Printer	–
Place	Nottingham
Type	CM TR
Map scale	–
Library holdings	GL
	NCL

REF **1126**
Title **History, Gazetteer and Directory of Nottinghamshire**
Dates 1885,1894
Publisher White, W.
Printer Spottiswoode
Place Sheffield
Type GE TR
Map scale 1:190080
Library BL not 1864
holdings BOD has 1894
GL not 1864
NCL has 1885
NLS has 1894
NLW has 1885
SOG has 1864
ULC has 1894

REF **1127**
Title **Nottinghamshire Directory and Buyer's Guide**
Dates 1930,1934,1935
Publisher Cope, E.F. & Co
Printer Cope, E.F. & Co
Place Walsall
Type TR
Map scale –
Library NCL

REF **1128**
Title **Wright's Nottingham Directory and Borough Register**
Dates 1854
Publisher Wright, C.N.
Printer Wright, C.N.
Place Nottingham
Type GE TR
Map scale –
Notes NORTON 609
Library GL
holdings NCL

REF **1129**
Title **Wright's Nottingham & Suburban Directory (and Red Book)**
Dates 1858,1862,1866
Publisher Wright, C.N.
Printer Wright, C.N.
Place Nottingham
Type GE TR
Map scale –
Notes Cont'd as 1133
Library BIS has 1858
holdings BL has 1862
GL has 1866
IHR has 1862
NCL all

REF **1130**
Title **Directory of the Town and County of the Town of Nottingham**
Dates 1860
Publisher Drake, E.S. & Co
Printer Kershaw, J. & Son
Place Leeds
Type GE TR
Map scale –
Library GL
holdings NCL

REF **1131**
Title **History and Directory of Nottingham**
Dates 1864
Publisher White, F. & Co
Printer Harrison, S.
Place Sheffield
Type CM TR
Map scale –
Library GL

REF **1132**
Title **Wright's Midland Directory (Nottingham, Radford, Sneinton & Hyson Green)**
Dates 1864
Publisher Wright, C.N.
Printer Wright, C.N.
Place Nottingham
Type GE TR
Map scale –
Library GL
holdings NCL

REF	**1133**
Title	**Wright's Directory of Nottingham and 12 miles round**
Dates	1868,1871,1874,1879,1881,1883, 1885,1887,1889,1891,1893,1895, 1897,1899,1900,1902,1905,1907, 1910,1913,1915,1920
Publisher	Wright, C.N.
Printer	Tompkin & Shardlow
Place	Nottingham
Type	CM TR
Map scale	–
Notes	Title varies. 1907 & after published by Kelly's Directories Ltd and entitled 'Wright's Directory of the City of Nottingham'.
Library holdings	BL not 1892,1897,1899, 1902-1920 BOD has 1874-1910 CLM has 1892,1897,1902-1920 GL has 1881,1883,1892,1897, 1902-1920 MLG has 1905,1910,1915,1920 NCL not 1893,1895 NLS has 1874-1910 NLW has 1879,1897 SOG has 1885 ULC has 1887,1891,1893,1895, 1897,1899-1910

REF	**1134**
Title	**Morris & Co's Commercial Directory and Gazetteer of Nottingham and District**
Dates	1877
Publisher	Morris & Co
Printer	–
Place	Nottingham
Type	CM TR
Map scale	–
Library holdings	GL NCL

REF	**1135**
Title	**White's General and Commercial Directory of the Borough of Nottingham**
Dates	1885
Publisher	White, W.
Printer	Spottiswoode & Co
Place	Sheffield
Type	GE
Map scale	–
Library	GL

REF	**1136**
Title	**Bedells' Pocket Street Directory of the Borough of Nottingham**
Dates	1887,1889,1892,1894,1901,1905, 1910,1916,1921,1926,1931,1937, 1946
Publisher	Bedells, E.J.
Printer	Bedells, E.J.
Place	Nottingham
Type	SL
Map scale	–
Library holdings	BL not 1892 NCL not 1916,1926 NLS not 1910

REF	**1137**
Title	**Sissons & Son's Illustrated Almanack and Local Directory [Worksop]**
Dates	1888
Publisher	Sissons, H.P. & Son
Printer	Sissons, H.P. & Son
Place	Worksop
Type	CM
Map scale	–
Library	NCL

REF	**1138**
Title	**Newark and District Directory**
Dates	1892,1897
Publisher	Cook, W.J. & Co
Printer	Wing & Broughton
Place	Boston
Type	GE TR
Map scale	1:506880
Library holdings	BL has 1892 BOD has 1892 GL has 1897 NCL has 1892 NLS has 1892 ULC has 1892

REF	**1139**
Title	**The Nottingham Lace and Hosiery Trades Directory**
Dates	1897
Publisher	Fisher & Co
Printer	Fisher & Co
Place	London
Type	SP
Map scale	–
Library holdings	BL NLS

REF **1140**
Title **Nottingham and District Trades Directory**
Dates 1904,1906,1915,1921,1924,1930
Publisher Town and County Directories Ltd
Printer Macdonald, W. & Co Ltd
Place Edinburgh
Type TR
Map scale –
Library NCL

REF **1141**
Title **Allen's Commercial Directory for Nottingham**
Dates 1907
Publisher Johnson, A.
Printer Johnson, A.
Place Nottingham
Type TR
Map scale –
Library NCL

REF **1142**
Title **Wharton's Directory of Retford and District**
Dates 1926
Publisher Wharton
Printer –
Place Retford
Type GE TR
Map scale –
Library GL

REF **1143**
Title **Allen's Street Directory of Nottingham & West Bridgford**
Dates 1929,1933,1935,1937,1939
Publisher Johnson, A.
Printer Johnson, A.
Place Nottingham
Type SL
Map scale NS
Library NCL

REF **1144**
Title **Street Directory and Map of Hucknall**
Dates 1933
Publisher Haywood & Davenport
Printer Haywood & Davenport
Place Hucknall
Type ST
Map scale NS
Library NCL

REF **1145**
Title **Kelly's Directory of Newark & Neighbourhood**
Dates 1938,1940,1942,1950
Publisher Kelly's Directories Ltd
Printer Kelly's Directories Ltd
Place London
Type GE TR
Map scale –
Library BL all
holdings BOD has 1950
CLM has 1950
GL all
NCL has 1950
NLS has 1950
NLW has 1950

REF **1146**
Title **Linney's Illustrated Mansfield and North Notts Almanack, Directory, Street Plan, Guide and Diary**
Dates 1939,1947-1950
Publisher Linney, W. & J.
Printer –
Place Mansfield
Type ST
Map scale 1:47520
Library GL

REF **1147**
Title **Kelly's Directory of the City of Nottingham and the Urban District of West Bridgford**
Dates 1950
Publisher Kelly's Directories Ltd
Printer Kelly's Directories Ltd
Place London
Type GE TR
Map scale –
Library BL
holdings BOD
BPH
CLE
DLS
GL
MLG
NCL
NLS
NLW
SCL
SOG
ULC

OXFORDSHIRE

REF	**1148**
Title	**History, Gazetteer and Directory of the County of Oxford**
Dates	1852
Publisher	Gardner, R.
Printer	Gardner, R.
Place	Peterborough
Type	CM TR
Map scale	–
Notes	NORTON 611
Library	CLO
holdings	GL
	IHR
	SOG

REF	**1149**
Title	**Lascelles and Co's Directory and Gazetteer of the County of Oxford**
Dates	1853
Publisher	Lascelles & Co
Printer	Lascelles & Co
Place	Birmingham
Type	CM TR
Map scale	–
Library	CLO

REF	**1150**
Title	**Kelly's Directory of Oxfordshire**
Dates	1854,1864,1869,1877,1883,1887, 1892,1895,1899,1903,1907,1911, 1915,1920,1924,1928,1931,1935, 1939
Publisher	Kelly & Co
Printer	Kelly & Co
Place	London
Type	GE TR
Map scale	1:253440
Notes	See 7(1854-1877) & 20(1883-1939)
Library	AYL has 1869-1887,1895,1907,
holdings	1915,1935
holdings	BCL has 1883,1891-1939
	BIS has 1924,1931,1939
	BL not 1935
	BOD has 1891-1931,1939
	BPH has 1869,1939
	CLB has 1939
	CLM has 1939
	CLO has 1854-1883,1891-1939
	GL all
	HNT has 1864
	IHR has 1899,1928
	LUT has 1939
	MLG has 1911-1924
	NEW has 1869,1915,1939
	NLS has 1854,1864,1877-1939
	NLW has 1887,1903,1907, 1920-1939
	RCL has 1887-1920
	SOG has 1854,1877-1887,1895, 1899,1915,1920,1928,1935, 1939
	ULC all

REF	**1151**
Title	**Oxfordshire Directory and Buyers' Guide**
Dates	1910
Publisher	Cope, E.F. & Co
Printer	Cope, E.F. & Co
Place	Walsall
Type	TR
Map scale	–
Notes	CLO volume also includes Gloucs & Warwks
Library	CLO

REF	**1152**
Title	**Rusher Banbury List and Directory**
Dates	1850-1896
Publisher	Rusher
Printer	Rusher
Place	London
Type	TR
Map scale	–
Notes	NORTON 612
Library holdings	BL not 1850,1875-1896
	BOD has 1850-1866,1868-1896
	CLO has 1850-1874,1877-1895
	GL not 1872-1874
	IHR all

REF	**1153**
Title	**Almanack with Bicester Directory**
Dates	1854,1856,1865
Publisher	Smith, E. & Son
Printer	Smith, E. & Son
Place	Bicester
Type	PR
Map scale	–
Library	CLO

REF	**1154**
Title	**The Banbury Almanack and Local Directory**
Dates	1856
Publisher	Potts, W. & Son
Printer	–
Place	Banbury
Type	CT TR
Map scale	–
Notes	The directory section is Rusher's (see 1152)
Library	CLO

REF	**1155**
Title	**The Oxford Directory**
Dates	1861
Publisher	Mansell, W.
Printer	Mansell, W.
Place	Oxford
Type	ST TR
Map scale	–
Library	CLO

REF	**1156**
Title	**Hewiett's Almanack and Bicester Directory**
Dates	1862,1863,1865,1867,1871,1873, 1883,1885,1886,1888,1890-1892
Publisher	Hewiett, G.
Printer	Hewiett, G.
Place	Bicester
Type	CM TR
Map scale	–
Notes	Earlier editions contain CT section only
Library	CLO

REF	**1157**
Title	**The Directory of Banbury and its neighbourhood**
Dates	1865
Publisher	Walford, G.
Printer	Advertiser
Place	Banbury
Type	CM TR
Map scale	–
Notes	Date uncertain
Library	CLO

REF	**1158**
Title	**The Oxford Directory**
Dates	1866,1867
Publisher	Wheeler & Day
Printer	Mathieson, J. & F.C.
Place	London
Type	GE TR
Map scale	–
Notes	1867 edition entitled 'Mathieson's Oxford Directory (including Abingdon)'
Library holdings	BL all
	CLO all
	NLS has 1866
	ULC all

REF	**1159**
Title	**Webster's Oxford, Wallingford, Abingdon and Banbury Directory**
Dates	1869
Publisher	Webster, W.M.
Printer	–
Place	Oxford
Type	GE TR
Map scale	–
Library	CLO

REF **1160**
Title **The Post Office Directory of the City of Oxford**
Dates 1871
Publisher The Oxford Times
Printer The Oxford Times
Place Oxford
Type ST TR
Map scale —
Library CLO

REF **1161**
Title **Webster's Oxford Directory**
Dates 1872
Publisher Webster, W.M.
Printer Webster, W.M.
Place Oxford
Type GE TR
Map scale —
Library CLO

REF **1162**
Title **G. Shrimpton's Oxford Directory**
Dates 1875
Publisher Shrimpton, G.
Printer —
Place Oxford
Type GE TR
Map scale —
Library CLO

REF **1163**
Title **Oxford City and Suburban Directory**
Dates 1876
Publisher The Oxford Times
Printer The Oxford Times
Place Oxford
Type GE
Map scale —
Library CLO

REF **1164**
Title **The Vale of the White Horse Directory, Diary and Almanack**
Dates 1878,1911,1912,1915
Publisher Luker, C.
Printer Luker, C.
Place Faringdon
Type CM
Map scale —
Library CLO

REF **1165**
Title **Valters' Oxford and District Post Office Directory**
Dates 1880,1882,1884,1889-1891, 1893-1896,1898,1899
Publisher Valters, J.C.
Printer Bowden, W.R.
Place Oxford
Type GE TR
Map scale —
Notes 1880 & 1882 editions entitled 'The Oxford Post Office Directory'
Library BIS has 1889
holdings BL has 1889,1893,1894
CLO not 1893
NLS has 1889,1895
ULC has 1889-1891,1893-1895

REF **1166**
Title **Kelly's Directory of Oxford and Neighbourhood**
Dates 1889,1890,1893-1896,1898-1941, 1943,1945,1947,1949
Publisher Kelly & Co
Printer Kelly & Co
Place London
Type GE TR
Map scale 1:5280
Notes After 1895 entitled 'Kelly's Directory of Oxford, Abingdon & Neighbourhood'
Library BL all
holdings BOD has 1889,1890
CLO has 1889-1896,1898-1901, 1903,1905,1907-1915,1919, 1921-1923,1925,1928-1949
GL not 1890-1899,1901,1902, 1917,1920,1924,1943
NLW has 1918,1919,1923,1925, 1929,1931,1949
SOG has 1943
ULC has 1889,1890

REF **1167**
Title **The Telegraph Combined Oxford Directory**
Dates 1902
Publisher The Oxfordshire Telegraph Newspaper Co Ltd
Printer The Oxfordshire Telegraph Newspaper Co Ltd
Place Oxford
Type GE TR
Map scale —
Library CLO

REF **1168**
Title **Oxford and District Trades' Directory**
Dates 1908
Publisher Town and County Directories Ltd
Printer Macdonald, W. & Co Ltd
Place Edinburgh
Type TR
Map scale –
Library CLO

REF **1169**
Title **Directory of Witney**
Dates 1915,1916
Publisher Knight, J.E.
Printer –
Place Witney
Type ST
Map scale –
Library CLO

REF **1170**
Title **Bicester Notes on the Town and a Directory of Traders**
Dates 193-?
Publisher Bicester and District Chamber of Commerce
Printer –
Place Bicester
Type TR
Map scale –
Notes No date on this volume. CLO catalogue assigns date to 1930s, but may be more recent.
Library CLO

REF **1171**
Title **Kelly's Directory of Henley-on-Thames & Neighbourhood**
Dates 1932,1934,1936,1938,1940,1942
Publisher Kelly's Directories Ltd
Printer Kelly's Directories Ltd
Place London
Type GE TR
Map scale 1:126720
Library BL all
holdings CLM has 1942
CLO has 1936-1942
GL all

REF **1172**
Title **Kelly's Directory of Banbury and neighbourhood**
Dates 1932,1934,1936,1938,1940,1950
Publisher Kelly's Directories Ltd
Printer Kelly's Directories Ltd
Place London
Type GE TR
Map scale 1:126720
Library BL all
holdings CLM has 1950
CLO has 1936-1950
GL not 1936
NLW has 1950

RUTLAND

REF **1173**
Title **Dolby's Almanack & Directory of Stamford, Uppingham, Oakham, Bourne, the Deepings and 123 villages**
Dates 1927,1932,1934,1939,1949,1950
Publisher Dolby Brothers Ltd
Printer Dolby Brothers Ltd
Place Stamford
Type ST
Map scale NS
Notes 1939 onwards entitled 'Dolby's Stamford and Rutland Almanack and Directory'
Library GL has 1939-1950
holdings PET has 1927-1934

REF **1174**
Title **Matkin's Oakham Almanack and County Directory**
Dates 1939-1941
Publisher Matkin
Printer Matkin
Place Oakham
Type GE
Map scale –
Library GL

SHROPSHIRE

REF	**1175**
Title	**History, Gazetteer and Directory of Shropshire**
Dates	1851
Publisher	Bagshaw, S.
Printer	Bagshaw, S.
Place	Sheffield
Type	CM
Map scale	–
Notes	NORTON 615
Library	CLC
holdings	CLM
	GL
	SHR
	SOG
	WSL

REF	**1176**
Title	**Kelly's Directory of Shropshire**
Dates	1856,1863,1870,1879,1885,1891, 1895,1900,1905,1909,1913,1917, 1922,1926,1929,1934,1937,1941
Publisher	Kelly & Co
Printer	Kelly & Co
Place	London
Type	GE TR
Map scale	1:15840
Notes	See 10(1856-1885) & 22(1891-1941)
Library	BCL has 1870,1885-1941
holdings	BIS has 1909,1941
	BL all
	BOD not 1891-1941
	BPH has 1917,1937,1941
	CLB has 1870,1941
	CLC has 1895,1913-1941
	CLM has 1926,1937
	GL not 1941
	HPL has 1856-1909,1934-1937
	IHR has 1900,1926
	LCL has 1937
	MLG has 1905-1913,1922-1937
	NLS all
	NLW has 1909,1913,1929,1934, 1941
	NPT has 1934,1937
	SCL has 1929-1941
	SHR all
	SOG has 1856,1863,1885,1891, 1900,1937
	ULC not 1941
	WAR has 1929
	WCL has 1891
	WCS has 1870
	YCL has 1934

[238]

REF	**1177**
Title	**Edward Cassey and Co's History, Gazetteer and Directory of Shropshire**
Dates	1871,1875
Publisher	Cassey, E. & Co
Printer	–
Place	Shrewsbury
Type	CM
Map scale	–
Library	CLC has 1871
holdings	GL all
	SHR all

REF	**1178**
Title	**Directory for the County of Salop**
Dates	1888
Publisher	Rockliff Bros Ltd
Printer	Rockliff Bros Ltd
Place	Liverpool
Type	CM
Map scale	–
Notes	Compiled by F. Porter
Library	SHR

REF	**1179**
Title	**Randall's Tom Moody Almanack, "All Round the Wrekin Advertiser", and Directory**
Dates	1879
Publisher	Randall, J.
Printer	Randall, J.
Place	Madeley
Type	ST
Map scale	–
Notes	Very small directory section. Other editions were published [SHR] but do not contain directories.
Library	SHR

REF	**1180**
Title	**The Wellington Directory, Almanack and Diary**
Dates	1879,1880,1898,1907-1913
Publisher	Hobson & Co
Printer	Hobson & Co
Place	Wellington (Salop)
Type	TR
Map scale	–
Library	BL has 1879,1880
holdings	SHR has 1898,1907-1013

REF **1181**
Title **Crocker's Shrewsbury Directory and Postal Guide**
Dates 1880,1882
Publisher Crocker, W.C.
Printer Crocker, W.C.
Place Shrewsbury
Type GE TR
Map scale 1:443520
Notes 1882 edition entitled 'The Post Office Shrewbury Directory'
Library SHR

REF **1182**
Title **Directory of Shrewsbury and its Environs**
Dates 1886,1888
Publisher Wells & Manton
Printer Wells & Manton
Place Shrewsbury
Type GE TR
Map scale 1:253440
Notes Cont'd as 1183
Library BL has 1888
holdings BOD has 1888
NLS has 1888
SHR all
ULC has 1888

REF **1183**
Title **Wells's Directory of Shrewsbury, Ludlow, Oswestry, Wellington & District**
Dates 1890
Publisher Wells & Co
Printer –
Place Shrewsbury
Type CM
Map scale –
Notes See 1182
Library SHR

REF **1184**
Title **Wilding's Directory of Shrewsbury and District**
Dates 1893,1896,1899,1903,1906,1910, 1916,1922,1925,1928,1931
Publisher Wilding, L.
Printer Wilding, L.
Place Shrewsbury
Type GE TR
Map scale –
Notes Cont'd by 1193
Library BL all
holdings BOD not 1906-1910
CLM has 1928
CLC has 1903,1906
GL has 1925
NLS not 1931
NLW has 1916,1922,1931
SHR not 1893
ULC has 1893-1903,1916-1931

REF **1185**
Title **The Advertiser Almanack, Diary and Directory, Newport and Gnosall Edition**
Dates 1898
Publisher Bennion, Horne, Smallman & Co Ltd
Printer –
Place Newport (Salop)
Type GE
Map scale –
Notes See 1186,1188
Library GL

REF **1186**
Title **The Advertiser Almanack and Directory Albrighton and Brewood Edition**
Dates 1901
Publisher Bennion, Horne, Smallman & Co Ltd
Printer –
Place Newport & Market Drayton
Type CM
Map scale –
Notes See 1185,1188
Library WSL

REF	**1187**
Title	**Shrewsbury and District Trades Directory**
Dates	1903
Publisher	Town and County Directories Ltd
Printer	Macdonald, W.
Place	Edinburgh
Type	TR
Map scale	–
Library	GL

REF	**1188**
Title	**The Advertiser Almanack and Directory Shifnal and Oakengates Edition**
Dates	1904
Publisher	Bennion, Horne, Smallman & Co
Printer	–
Place	Newport & Market Drayton
Type	CM
Map scale	–
Notes	See 1185,1186
Library	SHR

REF	**1189**
Title	**B's Directory of Church Stretton and District**
Dates	1906
Publisher	Norgate, C.E.
Printer	Norgate, C.E.
Place	Church Stretton
Type	CM
Map scale	–
Library	BOD

REF	**1190**
Title	**The Newport and Market Drayton Advertiser, Almanack and Directory**
Dates	1928-1941
Publisher	Newport & Market Drayton Advertiser
Printer	Newport & Market Drayton Advertiser
Place	Newport (Salop)
Type	CT
Map scale	–
Library	BL all
holdings	GL has 1939

REF	**1191**
Title	**Shrewsbury, Hereford and District Trades' Directory**
Dates	1932
Publisher	Town and County Directories Ltd
Printer	Macdonald, W. & Co Ltd
Place	Edinburgh
Type	TR
Map scale	–
Library	HPL

REF	**1192**
Title	**Wellington and District Directory**
Dates	1934,1937
Publisher	Jones, J. & Son
Printer	Jones, J. & Son
Place	Wellington (Salop)
Type	ST TR
Map scale	–
Library	BL has 1934
holdings	BOD has 1937
	SHR all
	ULC all

REF	**1193**
Title	**Kelly's Directory of Shrewsbury & Neighbourhood**
Dates	1936,1938,1940
Publisher	Kelly's Directories Ltd
Printer	Kelly's Directories Ltd
Place	London
Type	GE TR
Map scale	–
Notes	Continuation of 1184
Library	BL all
holdings	BOD all
	CLM has 1940
	GL all
	NLS all
	SHR all
	ULC all

REF	**1194**
Title	**The Ludlow Standard Directory**
Dates	1938
Publisher	The Ludlow Standard
Printer	The Ludlow Standard
Place	Ludlow
Type	CT
Map scale	–
Library	GL

SOMERSET

REF	**1195**
Title	**Kelly's Directory of Somersetshire**
Dates	1861,1866,1875,1883,1889,1894, 1897,1902,1906,1910,1914,1919, 1923,1927,1931,1935,1939
Publisher	Kelly & Co
Printer	Kelly & Co
Place	London
Type	GE TR
Map scale	1:253440
Library holdings	BCL has 1894,1927-1939
	BIS has 1910,1914,1927-1939
	BL all
	BOD all
	BPH has 1906,1910,1927,1935, 1939
	BRL has 1875-1914,1923-1931, 1939
	CLB not 1861,1866,1894,1910
	CLM has 1927,1939
	CPL has 1927,1939
	DCL has 1889,1897,1939
	DEI has 1897,1919,1935,1939
	GL all
	GLO has 1897,1906
	HRO has 1939
	IHR has 1897,1906,1927
	LCL has 1935
	MLG has 1894,1906,1910
	NLS all
	NLW has 1914,1919-1939
	SCL has 1931-1939
	SOG not 1875,1889,1897,1906, 1919,1927-1935
	TLH all
	ULC not 1927,1935
	WCS has 1897-1939
	WCL has 1914,1919,1931
	WRO has 1902,1907,1914,1935

REF	**1196**
Title	**Post Office Directory of Somerset and Bristol**
Dates	1861,1875,1883
Publisher	Kelly & Co
Printer	Kelly & Co
Place	London
Type	GE TR
Map scale	1:10560
Notes	See 1195 for library holdings

REF	**1197**
Title	**Smith & Co's Bath & Somerset Directory**
Dates	1865
Publisher	Smith & Co
Printer	Welsh, J.
Place	London
Type	GE
Map scale	–
Library	BRL

REF	**1198**
Title	**Morris & Co's Commercial Directory and Gazetteer of Somersetshire with Bristol**
Dates	1872
Publisher	Morris & Co
Printer	–
Place	Nottingham
Type	CM
Map scale	–
Notes	See 455
Library holdings	BRL
	GL
	TLH
	WCS

REF	**1199**
Title	**Bath Annual Directory**
Dates	1850
Publisher	Clark, C.
Printer	Clark, C.
Place	Bath
Type	GE TR
Map scale	–
Library holdings	BRL
	GL

REF	**1200**
Title	**Hunt & Co's Directory and Topography of the Towns of Axbridge, Burnham, Bruton, Castle Cary, ... Weston-super-Mare, Wincanton and Yeovil (including Bristol)**
Dates	1850
Publisher	Hunt, E. & Co
Printer	Gardiner, B.W.
Place	London
Type	CM
Map scale	–
Notes	NORTON 622
Library holdings	GL
	TLH

REF	**1201**
Title	**A Directory for the City & Borough of Bath and the City of Wells**
Dates	1852,1854
Publisher	Vivian, S.
Printer	Simpkin & Marshall
Place	Bath
Type	GE TR
Map scale	–
Notes	NORTON 623 (1854), 649? (1852)
Library	BL has 1854
holdings	BOD has 1854
	BRL all
	GL has 1852
	NLS has 1854
	TLH has 1854
	ULC has 1854

REF	**1202**
Title	**The Bath Directory**
Dates	1856
Publisher	Peach, R.E.
Printer	–
Place	Bath
Type	GE TR
Map scale	–
Library	BRL
holdings	GL
	IHR

REF	**1203**
Title	**Post Office Bath Directory**
Dates	1858,1860,1862,1864,1866,1868, 1870,1872,1874,1876,1878,1880, 1882,1884,1886,1888,1890,1892, 1894-1927,1930-1940
Publisher	Lewis, W.
Printer	Lewis, W.
Place	Bath
Type	GE TR
Map scale	1:10560
Library	BL has 1858,1860,1864,
holdings	1882-1896,1898-1940
	BRL not 1931,1934-1937
	GL has 1858,1864,1880-1931, 1933,1936-1938
	IHR has 1870
	NLS has 1860
	NLW has 1880
	SOG has 1870
	TLH has 1874,1876,1886,1888, 1897,1902,1903,1906-1908, 1910-1916,1919,1921, 1923-1927,1930-1934,1936, 1938-1940

REF	**1204**
Title	**Goodman's Directory of Taunton and its neighbourhood**
Dates	1864
Publisher	Goodman, E.
Printer	Goodman, E.
Place	Taunton
Type	CT TR
Map scale	–
Notes	See 1207
Library	TLH

REF	**1205**
Title	**J. Wright & Co's Weston-super-Mare & Clevedon Directory**
Dates	1880,1883,1887,1891
Publisher	Wright, J.
Printer	Houlston & Sons
Place	Bristol
Type	GE TR
Map scale	NS
Library	BL all
holdings	BOD has 1880
	NLS has 1880
	ULC has 1880

REF	**1206**
Title	**John Whitby & Son's Handy Directory of Bridgwater and Neighbourhood**
Dates	1883,1897
Publisher	Whitby, J. & Son
Printer	Whitby, J. & Son
Place	Bridgwater
Type	CT CM
Map scale	1:15840
Library	BOD has 1883
holdings	NLS has 1883
	TLH all
	ULC has 1883

REF	**1207**
Title	**Goodman and Son's Illustrated Guide and Directory of Taunton**
Dates	1887,1888,1900,1902,1906
Publisher	Goodman & Son
Printer	Goodman & Son
Place	Taunton
Type	GE TR
Map scale	1:10560
Notes	See 1204
Library	BL has 1887,1888
holdings	TLH not 1888
	ULC has 1887

REF	1208
Title	E.T. Page's Directory of Bridgwater and neighbourhood
Dates	1890
Publisher	Page, E.T.
Printer	Page, E.T.
Place	Bridgwater
Type	CT CM
Map scale	–
Library	BL
holdings	BOD
	ULC

REF	1209
Title	Kelly's Directory of Bath & Neighbourhood
Dates	1904-1908,1929-1937,1947,1950
Publisher	Kelly's Directories Ltd
Printer	Kelly's Directories Ltd
Place	London
Type	GE TR
Map scale	1:15840
Library	BL all
holdings	BRL has 1929-1931,1934-1937, 1947,1950
	DEI has 1935
	GL not 1906,1908
	MLG has 1936,1947,1950
	NLW has 1950
	ULC has 1904-1908
	WCS has 1947,1950

REF	1210
Title	Collins' History of Yeovil and Directory
Dates	1905,1907
Publisher	Beale Collins, W.
Printer	Beale Collins, W.
Place	Yeovil
Type	ST TR
Map scale	–
Library	BL all
holdings	BOD has 1905
	NLS has 1905

REF	1211
Title	Bridgwater Directory and Guide, including fifty villages
Dates	1908
Publisher	Whitby, J. & Sons Ltd
Printer	Whitby, J. & Sons Ltd
Place	Bridgwater
Type	CM
Map scale	–
Library	GL

REF	1212
Title	The Wellington and Wiveliscombe Directory
Dates	1912-1923,1925-1933
Publisher	Tozer, I.
Printer	Wellington Weekly News
Place	Wellington (Somerset)
Type	CT
Map scale	–
Library	BL all
holdings	TLH has 1923

REF	1213
Title	Frome Almanack and Directory and Chamber of Commerce Guide
Dates	1916,1927-1931
Publisher	Harvey & Woodland
Printer	Harvey & Woodland
Place	Frome
Type	GE TR
Map scale	–
Notes	1927-1931 editions entitled 'Harvey & Woodland's Frome Directory and Chamber of Commerce Guide'
Library	TLH

REF	1214
Title	Yeovil, Sherborne & District Directory
Dates	1927,1930,1932,1934,1936,1938, 1949
Publisher	Snell, E.
Printer	Snell, E.
Place	Yeovil
Type	GE TR
Map scale	1:50688
Notes	1934 edition entitled 'Yeovil and District Directory'
Library	BL not 1949
holdings	DCL has 1934
	GL has 1936,1949
	TLH has 1936
	WCS has 1949

REF	1215
Title	Kelly's Directory of Taunton
Dates	1928,1929,1931,1933,1935,1937, 1939,1941,1944,1948
Publisher	Kelly's Directories Ltd
Printer	Kelly's Directories Ltd
Place	London
Type	GE TR
Map scale	1:253440
Library	BL not 1941,1948
holdings	GL all
	TLH all
	WCS has 1948

[243]

REF **1216**
Title **The Frome Almanack, Directory and Guide**
Dates 1936,1937,1948,1949
Publisher Frome Newspaper Co Ltd
Printer Frome Newspaper Co Ltd
Place Frome
Type GE TR
Map scale –
Library BL not 1936,1937
holdings GL all

REF **1217**
Title **Bridgwater, Burnham-on-Sea and District Directory**
Dates 1937,1938
Publisher Whitby, Light & Lane Ltd
Printer Whitby, Light & Lane Ltd
Place Bridgwater
Type GE
Map scale –
Notes 1938 edition entitled 'Bridgwater Directory, Almanack & Tide Table' (GE TR)
Library GL has 1937
holdings TLH all

REF **1218**
Title **Wells Directory and Almanack**
Dates 1938
Publisher Clare, Son & Co Ltd
Printer Clare, Son & Co Ltd
Place Wells
Type CT
Map scale –
Library GL

REF **1219**
Title **The Weston-super-Mare Directory**
Dates 1938-1940,1946
Publisher Lawrence Bros.
Printer Lawrence Bros.
Place Weston-super-Mare
Type GE TR
Map scale –
Library GL has 1938-1940
holdings TLH has 1946

REF **1220**
Title **The Wellington (Somerset) Street Directory and Gazetteer including Tonedale, Rockwell Green, Westford etc.**
Dates 1948,1949
Publisher Delderfield, W.J. & Sons Ltd
Printer Delderfield, W.J. & Sons Ltd
Place Exmouth
Type ST
Map scale –
Library BOD has 1948
holdings GL all
NLS all
TLH has 1948
ULC all

REF **1221**
Title **Kelly's Directory of Weston-super-Mare**
Dates 1949
Publisher Kelly's Directories Ltd
Printer Kelly's Directories Ltd
Place London
Type GE TR
Map scale –
Library BL
holdings GL
NLW
WCS

STAFFORDSHIRE

REF	**1222**
Title	**Kelly's Directory of Staffordshire**
Dates	1850,1854,1860,1864,1868,1872, 1876,1880,1884,1888,1892,1896, 1900,1904,1908,1912,1916,1921, 1924,1928,1932,1936,1940
Publisher	Kelly & Co
Printer	Kelly & Co
Place	London
Type	GE TR
Map scale	1:253440
Notes	See 6
Library	BCL not 1850
holdings	BIS has 1940
	BL has 1868-1921,1928-1940
	BOD has 1850-1864,1872-1940
	BPH has 1868,1888,1916,1924, 1940
	CLB has 1940
	CLE has 1940
	CLM has 1924,1928,1940
	COV has 1884,1888,1932,1936
	GL has 1868,1876-1928
	HBR has 1850-1860,1872,1876, 1892-1904,1912,1916,1924, 1932-1940
	IHR has 1908,1940
	LEA has 1872-1884,1892,1900, 1908-1921,1928,1932,1940
	LCL has 1936,1940
	MLG has 1880,1921-1928
	NLS has 1854,1860,1868,1876, 1921-1940
	NLW has 1916,1924,1928,1936
	SCL has 1928-1940
	SOG has 1860,1880,1884,1896, 1912-1921
	ULC all
	WCL has 1854,1868,1872, 1932-1940
	WLV has 1850,1860,1876, 1888-1900,1932-1940
	WRK has 1928,1940
	WSL has 1850-1916,1924-1940
	YCL has 1940

REF	**1223**
Title	**History, Gazetteer and Directory of Staffordshire**
Dates	1851
Publisher	White, W.
Printer	Leader, R.
Place	Sheffield
Type	GE TR
Map scale	1:190080
Notes	NORTON 650
Library	BCL
holdings	BL
	BPH
	CLM
	CL
	GL
	HBR
	IHR
	SOG
	WLV
	WCL
	WSL

REF	**1224**
Title	**Harrison, Harrod & Co's Directory and Gazetteer of Staffordshire and Shropshire with Dudley in Worcestershire**
Dates	1861
Publisher	Harrison, Harrod & Co
Printer	Danks, T.
Place	London
Type	CM
Map scale	1:253440
Library	BCL
holdings	GL
	SHR
	WLV
	WSL

REF	**1225**
Title	**Jones's Mercantile Directory of the Pottery District of Staffordshire**
Dates	1864
Publisher	Jones & Proud
Printer	Jones & Proud
Place	London
Type	CM TR
Map scale	—
Library	HBR
holdings	IHR

REF | 1226
Title | **J.G. Harrod & Co's Postal and Commercial Directory of Staffordshire**
Dates | 1870
Publisher | Harrod, J.G. & Co
Printer | –
Place | Norwich
Type | CM
Map scale | –
Library | HBR

REF | 1227
Title | **Staffordshire Directory and Buyers' Guide**
Dates | 1905,1908,1910-1914,1916, 1921-1925,1927-1936,1938
Publisher | Cope, E.F. & Co
Printer | Cope, E.F. & Co
Place | Walsall
Type | TR
Map scale | –
Library | BL all
holdings | HBR has 1938
WLV has 1929,1930
WSL has 1921

REF | 1228
Title | **Staffordshire Directory**
Dates | 1933-1940
Publisher | Aubrey & Co
Printer | Aubrey & Co
Place | Walsall
Type | TR
Map scale | –
Library | BL all
holdings | WSL has 1934

REF | 1229
Title | **Melville & Co's Directory of Wolverhampton**
Dates | 1851
Publisher | Melville, F.R. & Co
Printer | Stanley, J.
Place | Worcester
Type | CM TR
Map scale | –
Notes | NORTON 660
Library | GL
holdings | HBR
WLV

REF | 1230
Title | **Trades Directory of Wolverhampton, Wednesfield, Bilston, Willenhall, Sedgley, Tipton, Wednesbury, Darlaston & Moxley**
Dates | 1862
Publisher | Jones & Co
Printer | Jones & Co
Place | London
Type | TR
Map scale | –
Library | WLV

REF | 1231
Title | **Jones's Mercantile Directory of the Iron District of South Staffordshire and East Worcestershire**
Dates | 1865
Publisher | Jones & Proud
Printer | Jones & Proud
Place | London
Type | CM TR
Map scale | –
Notes | Includes large & small towns in the district
Library | WLV
holdings | WSL

REF | 1232
Title | **Keates & Ford's Annual Potteries and Newcastle Street and Trade Directory**
Dates | 1865,1867
Publisher | Keates & Ford
Printer | Keates & Ford
Place | Hanley
Type | ST TR
Map scale | –
Notes | 1867 edition entitled 'Keates & Ford's Annual Directory of the Potteries and Newcastle with Almanack'. Cont'd as 1233.
Library | GL
holdings | HBR

REF **1233**
Title **Keates's Gazetteer and Directory of the Staffordshire Potteries, Newcastle and District**
Dates 1869,1873,1875,1879,1882,1889, 1892
Publisher Keates, J.
Printer Keates, J.
Place Hanley
Type GE TR
Map scale –
Notes Cont'd from 1232. Slight variations in title & publishers. See EMERY & BEARD pp7-8.
Library BL has 1875
holdings GL has 1869
HBR all
WSL has 1875-1882,1892

REF **1234**
Title **Directory of Newcastle-under-Lyme with Historical Records**
Dates 1871,1881
Publisher Dilworth, D.
Printer Dilworth, D.
Place Newcastle-under-Lyme
Type CM
Map scale –
Library BCL all
holdings CLM has 1871
GL has 1881
HBR all

REF **1235**
Title **Hulley's Directory of the Parliamentary Borough of Wolverhampton which includes ... Bilston, Sedgley, Wednesfield and Willenhall**
Dates 1874
Publisher Hulley, J.
Printer Barford & Newitt
Place Birmingham
Type GE TR
Map scale –
Library WLV
holdings WSL

REF **1236**
Title **The Wolverhampton District Year Book, Commercial and Trades Directory with Almanack, Diary and General Guide**
Dates 1877
Publisher Edward Brothers
Printer Rowland, E.J.
Place Wolverhampton
Type TR
Map scale –
Library WLV

REF **1237**
Title **Directory of Wolverhampton and Six Miles Round**
Dates 1879
Publisher Stevens, G.
Printer Stevens, G.
Place London
Type CM TR
Map scale –
Library WLV

REF **1238**
Title **The Walsall Annual Red Book and Directory**
Dates 1880,1911-1917,1932,1933, 1935-1938
Publisher Kirby, T. & Sons Ltd
Printer –
Place Walsall
Type GE TR
Map scale 1:8448
Notes Published by H. Robinson (1894-1911) with CT & ST sections
Library BCL not 1912-1917
holdings BOD has 1912-1917

REF **1239**
Title **Crocker's Post Offfice Wolverhampton and District Directory**
Dates 1884
Publisher The Birmingham Publishing Company
Printer The Birmingham Publishing Company
Place Birmingham
Type GE TR
Map scale –
Library WLV

REF	**1240**		REF	**1243**
Title	**Halden and Sons' Almanack and**		Title	**The Wolverhampton Red Book**
	Directory of Stafford and District			**and Directory**
Dates	1885,1891-1900,1903-1911,		Dates	1892,1894,1896,1897,1899-1918,
	1913-1916,1920,1922,1924-1939,			1920-1942
	1946,1947		Publisher	Hinde, A.
Publisher	Halden, J. & Sons		Printer	Hinde, A.
Printer	–		Place	Wolverhampton
Place	Stafford		Type	CT TR
Type	CT TR		Map scale	1:5280
Map scale	–		Notes	Later editions contain map
Notes	1885 edition entitled 'The Stafford		Library	BCL has 1894,1934,1936-1942
	and District Directory and		holdings	WLV all
	Almanack'. Title & publishers vary.			WSL has 1899
	For full details see EMERY &			
	BEARD p.11.		REF	**1244**
Library	BL has 1895		Title	**Lomax's Red Book and**
holdings	WSL all			**Almanack for the City and**
				County of Lichfield
REF	**1241**		Dates	1898,1901,1903-1915,1934-1940
Title	**Barker's Wolverhampton Trade**		Publisher	Lomax, A.C.
	Directory and Guide		Printer	Lomax, A.C.
Dates	1887		Place	Lichfield
Publisher	Barker, J.W.		Type	TR
Printer	–		Map scale	–
Place	Wolverhampton		Library	BL all
Type	TR		holdings	BOD has 1934-1940
Map scale	–			GL has 1938
Library	WLV			ULC has 1934-1940
REF	**1242**		REF	**1245**
Title	**Postal Directory for the Potteries**		Title	**Burton-on-Trent and District**
	with Newcastle and District			**Directory**
Dates	1887		Dates	1902
Publisher	Rockliff Bros		Publisher	Cook, W.J. & Co
Printer	Rockliff Bros		Printer	Perfect, J.C. & Co
Place	Liverpool		Place	Hull
Type	CM TR		Type	GE TR
Map scale	–		Map scale	–
Notes	Compiled by F. Porter. T/P missing		Library	BL
	HBR edition.		holdings	BOD
Library	HBR			NLS
				ULC

REF **1246**
Title **Hanley and Potteries District Trades' Directory**
Dates 1902,1913,1917
Publisher Town and County Directories Ltd
Printer Macdonald, W. & Co
Place Edinburgh
Type TR
Map scale –
Notes 1913 & after entitled 'Potteries and District Trades' Directory'
Library HBR

REF	**1247**
Title	**Adie's Annual consistng of Almanac, Diary & Directory of Stone, Eccleshall & surrounding places**
Dates	1902,1930
Publisher	Adie, T.G. & Co
Printer	Adie, T.G. & Co
Place	Stone
Type	GE
Map scale	–
Library	WSL

REF	**1248**
Title	**Hughes & Harber's Almanack, Local Information, Trade Directory and Year Book [Longton]**
Dates	1902-1907
Publisher	Hughes & Harber Ltd
Printer	Hughes & Harber Ltd
Place	Longton
Type	TR
Map scale	–
Notes	1906 onwards entitled 'Hughes & Harber's Almanack, Local Information, Year Book and Business Directory'
Library	HBR

REF	**1249**
Title	**Pascoe's Almanack, Directory and Year Book ... Rugeley**
Dates	1904,1906,1907,1909,1911-1915, 1920,1921
Publisher	Pascoe & Sons
Printer	–
Place	Rugeley
Type	GE
Map scale	–
Library holdings	BL all WSL has 1904

REF	**1250**
Title	**The Potteries Newcastle & District Directory**
Dates	1907,1912
Publisher	Staffordshire Sentinel Ltd
Printer	Staffordshire Sentinel Ltd
Place	Hanley
Type	GE TR
Map scale	–
Library holdings	BL BOD HBR NLS ULC

REF	**1251**
Title	**The Walsall Trades Directory and Year Book**
Dates	1910
Publisher	Griffin, J.W. Ltd
Printer	Griffin, J.W. Ltd
Place	Walsall
Type	CM TR
Map scale	–
Library	BL

REF	**1252**
Title	**Burton-on-Trent and District Directory**
Dates	1911,1925,1932
Publisher	Tresises
Printer	Tresises
Place	Burton-on-Trent
Type	ST TR
Map scale	NS
Notes	CLM edition (1911) is a 1977 reprint of principal parts of the directory
Library holdings	CLM has 1911 DLS has 1932 WSL has 1925

REF	**1253**
Title	**Walsall Blue Book and Directory**
Dates	1912-1916,1920-1939
Publisher	Cope, E.F. & Co
Printer	Cope, E.F. & Co
Place	Walsall
Type	GE TR
Map scale	–
Library holdings	BL not 1939 BOD has 1920 GL has 1938,1939

REF	**1254**
Title	**Cannock Chase Blue Book & Directory**
Dates	1920,1922-1927
Publisher	Cope, E.F. & Co
Printer	Cope, E.F. & Co
Place	Walsall
Type	GE TR
Map scale	–
Library	BL

REF **1255**
Title **Spennell's Wolverhampton Directory**
Dates 1921
Publisher Jones, P. Ltd
Printer Jones, P. Ltd
Place Birmingham
Type GE TR
Map scale –
Library BCL
holdings WLV

REF **1256**
Title **Cope's Wednesbury & Darlaston Blue Book and Directory**
Dates 1921,1922,1924,1927
Publisher Cope, E.F. & Co
Printer Cope, E.F. & Co
Place Walsall
Type GE TR
Map scale –
Library BL

REF **1257**
Title **The Willenhall Red Book**
Dates 1933,1935
Publisher Cartwright, A. & Sons
Printer Cartwright, A. & Sons
Place Willenhall
Type TR
Map scale –
Library WSL

REF **1258**
Title **Trades Directory of Smethwick**
Dates 1938,1939
Publisher Littlebury & Co
Printer –
Place Worcester
Type TR
Map scale –
Notes Alphabetical list of industrial firms
Library BCL

REF **1259**
Title **Wolverhampton Production Exchange List of Members Rules & Byelaws**
Dates 1943,1944
Publisher Ministry of Production
Printer –
Place Wolverhampton
Type SP
Map scale –
Notes Alph. & TR sections
Library BCL

SUFFOLK

REF **1260**
Title **Kelly's Directory of Suffolk**
Dates 1853,1858,1865,1869,1875,1879,
1883,1888,1892,1896,1900,1904,
1908,1912,1916,1922,1925,1929,
1933,1937
Publisher Kelly & Co
Printer Kelly & Co
Place London
Type GE TR
Map scale 1:253440
Notes See 5
Library BCL has 1858,1883-1937
holdings BIS has 1879,1900,1904,
1922-1933
BL all
BOD all
BPH has 1858,1916-1929,1937
CAM not 1896,1908
CLB has 1937
CLE has 1916,1937
CLM has 1937
COL has 1888,1892,1925,1937.
Also 1903 edition ESSX,
NORF,SUFF
GL has 1853-1929
HRO has 1912
IHR has 1900,1908,1937
KLL has 1879,1892,1896,
1904-1912,1925-1937
MLG has 1904-1929
NLS all
NLW has 1912,1916,1929-1937
NOR has 1853,1858,1879,1885,
1892,1904,1908,1912,1922,
1929-1937
PET has 1888,1892,1925
SCL has 1929-1937
SOG has 1858,1869,1875,1888,
1896,1900,1912,1922-1937
SRI not 1853,1865
ULC all

REF **1261**
Title **History, Gazetteer and Directory
of Suffolk**
Dates 1855,1874,1885,1892
Publisher White, W.
Printer Leader, R.
Place Sheffield
Type GE TR
Map scale –
Notes NORTON 662
Library BCL has 1885,1874
holdings BL all
BOD all
GL not 1892
IHR has 1855,1874
NLS has 1892
NOR has 1855,1874,1885
SCL has 1874
SOG has 1855,1885
SRI all
ULC all

REF **1262**
Title **J.G. Harrod and Co's Postal and
Commercial Directory of Suffolk**
Dates 1864,1873,1877
Publisher Harrod, J.G. & Co
Printer Danks, T.
Place London
Type CM
Map scale –
Notes 1873 CAM edition & 1877 NOR
edition include Cambridgeshire
Library CAM has 1873
holdings GL has 1864,1873
NOR has 1877
SRI has 1864,1873

REF **1263**
Title **Morris & Co's Commercial
Directory and Gazetteer of
Suffolk with Great Yarmouth and
Newmarket**
Dates 1868
Publisher Morris & Co
Printer –
Place Nottingham
Type CM
Map scale –
Library NOR
holdings SRI

REF **1264**
Title **Directory of Ipswich and Neighbourhood**
Dates 1881,1885,1889,1894
Publisher Stevens, G.
Printer Stevens, G.
Place London
Type GE TR
Map scale 1:633600
Library BL all
holdings BOD not 1881
NLS not 1881
SRI not 1889
ULC has 1885,1889

REF **1265**
Title **Arthur Stebbings' Directory to Beccles**
Dates 1887
Publisher Stebbings, A.
Printer Lowestoft Journal Press
Place Lowestoft
Type CT CM
Map scale –
Library BL
holdings BOD

REF **1266**
Title **Arthur Stebbings' Directory to Halesworth**
Dates 1887
Publisher Stebbings, A.
Printer Stebbings, A.
Place Lowestoft
Type CM
Map scale –
Library BL
holdings BOD

REF **1267**
Title **Read's Illustrated Family Almanack and Woodbridge Directory**
Dates 1888
Publisher Read, M.
Printer Read, M.
Place Woodbridge
Type CM
Map scale –
Library SRI

REF **1268**
Title **Directory of Ipswich ... with Felixstowe, Walton, Harwich, Dovercourt**
Dates 1890
Publisher Jarrold & Sons
Printer –
Place London
Type GE TR
Map scale 1:12000
Library SRI

REF **1269**
Title **Jewell's Ipswich Directory ... with Felixstowe, Hadleigh, Stowmarket, Walton, Woodbridge**
Dates 1898
Publisher Jewell, G.W.
Printer –
Place Ipswich
Type GE
Map scale –
Library SRI

REF **1270**
Title **Kelly's Directory of Ipswich**
Dates 1899-1915,1918-1941,1943,1947, 1949
Publisher Kelly's Directories Ltd
Printer Kelly's Directories Ltd
Place London
Type GE TR
Map scale 1:253440
Library BL not 1899
holdings BOD has 1899,1900,1902-1912
GL not 1901,1940,1943
NLW has 1949
NOR has 1941
SRI has 1906,1909,1910, 1912-1915,1918,1920-1949
ULC has 1899-1912

REF	**1271**
Title	**Kelly's Directory of Lowestoft**
Dates	1899-1916,1922,1924,1925,1927, 1930,1932,1934,1936,1938,1948, 1949
Publisher	Kelly's Directories Ltd
Printer	Kelly's Directories Ltd
Place	London
Type	GE TR
Map scale	1:253440
Library	BL all
holdings	BOD has 1899,1900,1902-1912 GL not 1901,1916,1949 NLW has 1948 NOR has 1930,1948 SRI has 1925,1930,1934,1948 ULC has 1899-1912

REF	**1272**
Title	**Ipswich and District Trades' Directory**
Dates	1906,1919,1925,1927,1928,1932
Publisher	Town and County Directories Ltd
Printer	Macdonald, W. & Co
Place	Edinburgh
Type	TR
Map scale	–
Library	SRI

REF	**1273**
Title	**Directory of Felixstowe, Walton and Trimley**
Dates	1924,1927,1934
Publisher	Cowell, W.S. Ltd
Printer	Cowell, W.S. Ltd
Place	Felixtowe
Type	GE
Map scale	1:7920
Library	BL has 1934
holdings	SRI has 1924,1927

REF	**1274**
Title	**Kelly's Directory of Bury St Edmunds & Neighbourhood**
Dates	1930,1931,1933,1935,1937,1939, 1940
Publisher	Kelly's Directories Ltd
Printer	Kelly's Directories Ltd
Place	London
Type	GE TR
Map scale	1:253440
Library	BL all
holdings	GL all SRI has 1930,1933

REF	**1275**
Title	**The New Directory of Felixstowe and District**
Dates	1932
Publisher	Henderson & Spalding
Printer	Henderson & Spalding
Place	London
Type	GE
Map scale	–
Library	SRI

REF	**1276**
Title	**The E.C. Supplies Co Newmarket & District Annual and Directory**
Dates	1932-1936
Publisher	Eastern Counties Supplies Co
Printer	Eastern Counties Supplies Co
Place	Newmarket
Type	GE
Map scale	–
Library	BL

REF	**1277**
Title	**Kelly's Directory of Felixstowe**
Dates	1936,1938,1950
Publisher	Kelly's Directories Ltd
Printer	Kelly's Directories Ltd
Place	London
Type	GE TR
Map scale	1:6336
Library	BL all
holdings	GL all NLW has 1950 SRI has 1950

SURREY

REF **1278**
Title **Kelly's Directory of Surrey**
Dates 1851,1855,1859,1862,1866,1870,
1874,1878,1882,1887,1891,1895,
1899,1901,1903,1905,1907,1909,
1911,1913,1915,1918,1922,1924,
1927,1930,1934,1938
Publisher Kelly & Co
Printer Kelly & Co
Place London
Type GE TR
Map scale 1:76032
Library BCL has 1882,1891-1899,
holdings 1903-1938
BED has 1851
BIS has 1934,1938
BL not 1851
BOD not 1855,1901
BPH has 1866,1887,1895,1905,
1918-1930,1938
CHI has 1905,1930,1938
CLB has 1938
CLM has 1859,1927,1938
CRD has 1855,1874-1882,
1891-1899,1903-1938
COL has 1855,1859
GL not 1901
GLH has 1855-1878,1899,
1903-1911,1922-1930,1938
HLS has 1878
HRO has 1938
IHR has 1862,1887,1891,1905,
1909,1913,1930
KCL has 1859,1866,1878,1895
LCL has 1934
NLS all
NLW has 1913,1915,1924,
1930-1938
SCL has 1930-1938
SLS has 1855,1874,1882-1891,
1899,1905-1938
SOG has 1851-1862,1874,1882,
1899,1915,1938
ULC all
WOR has 1891,1903
YCL has 1938

REF **1279**
Title **Larkin's Directory for West
Surrey and the Neighbourhood**
Dates 1872
Publisher Larkin, R.H.B.
Printer Larkin, R.H.B.
Place Chertsey
Type CM
Map scale –
Library BOD
holdings ULC

REF **1280**
Title **Arnold's West Surrey Court
Guide, Gazetteer and Royal Blue
Book**
Dates 1876
Publisher Arnold, A. & Co
Printer Arnold, A. & Co
Place London
Type CT
Map scale NS
Library GL

REF **1281**
Title **Deacon's Mid-Surrey Court
Guide, Gazetteer and Royal Blue
Book**
Dates 1878
Publisher Deacon, C.W. & Co
Printer Deacon, C.W. & Co
Place London
Type CT PR
Map scale 1:126720
Notes See 168 & 1282
Library CRD

REF **1282**
Title **Deacon's Surrey Court Guide,
Gazetteer and Royal Blue Book**
Dates 1879
Publisher Deacon, C.W. & Co
Printer Deacon, C.W. & Co
Place London
Type CT PR
Map scale –
Notes Map vandalized CRD edition. See
168 & 1281.
Library CRD

REF	**1283**
Title	**North West Surrey Directory and Trade Guide**
Dates	1929-1939
Publisher	Rawlings & Walsh Ltd
Printer	–
Place	Chertsey
Type	GE
Map scale	–
Library	BL all
holdings	GL has 1938

REF	**1284**
Title	**Surrey Directory**
Dates	1947-1950
Publisher	Aubrey & Co
Printer	Aubrey & Co
Place	Walsall
Type	TR
Map scale	–
Notes	Cont'd from 104
Library	BL

REF	**1285**
Title	**W. Archdeacon's Directory for Richmond, Kew, Twickenham, Kingston, Hampton, Staines, Windsor ... Slough &c &c**
Dates	1851
Publisher	Archdeacon, W.
Printer	Wright, C. & Co
Place	London
Type	CM
Map scale	1:10560
Notes	NORTON 663
Library	GL

REF	**1286**
Title	**A New Commercial and General Directory of the Town of Croydon**
Dates	1851,1853,1855,1859,1861
Publisher	Gray, J.
Printer	Gray, J.
Place	Croydon
Type	GE TR
Map scale	–
Notes	NORTON 664-666 (1851,1853, 1855). 1855 edition entitled 'The Commercial and General Directory of the Town of Croydon' & published by Gray & Warren. Cont'd by 1290.
Library	BL has 1851,1855
holdings	CRD all
	GL not 1859

REF	**1287**
Title	**Russell's Almanac for Guildford and West Surrey**
Dates	1853,1859
Publisher	Russell, G., W. & J.
Printer	Russell, G., W. & J.
Place	Guildford
Type	CT
Map scale	–
Library	SLS

REF	**1288**
Title	**Andrew's Guildford Almanac and Directory**
Dates	1854,1855,1857,1859,1863-1869, 1871-1874,1876,1878,1879
Publisher	Andrews and Son
Printer	–
Place	Guildford
Type	GE
Map scale	–
Notes	Cont'd as 1307
Library	SLS

REF	**1289**
Title	**A Handbook of Dorking**
Dates	1855
Publisher	Rowe, J.
Printer	Rowe, J.
Place	Dorking
Type	CT CM
Map scale	1:63360
Notes	NORTON 667
Library	IHR

REF	**1290**
Title	**The Commercial and General Directory of the Town and Parish of Croydon**
Dates	1864,1869
Publisher	Warren, F.
Printer	Warren, F.
Place	Croydon
Type	GE TR
Map scale	–
Library	CRD all
holdings	GL all
	GLH has 1864

REF	**1291**
Title	**R. Simpson & Co's Reigate, Redhill and Guildford Directory and Court Guide**
Dates	1865
Publisher	Simpson, R. & Co
Printer	–
Place	London
Type	CM
Map scale	–
Library	GL

REF	**1292**
Title	**The Godalming Almanac and Directory**
Dates	1868,1875,1876
Publisher	Chennell, T.
Printer	Chennell, T.
Place	Godalming
Type	CM
Map scale	–
Notes	1876 edition published & printed by H.T. Craddock
Library	SLS

REF	**1293**
Title	**A History and Description of Sutton, Surrey with a Directory of the Inhabitants**
Dates	1869
Publisher	Morgan, J.
Printer	–
Place	Sutton
Type	GE
Map scale	1:7200
Library	GL

REF	**1294**
Title	**The Court Guide and Commercial Directory and Gazetteer for Richmond, Twickenham, Hampton Court, Mortlake etc ...**
Dates	1872
Publisher	Green & Co
Printer	–
Place	London
Type	CT CM
Map scale	–
Library	GL

REF	**1295**
Title	**Wilkins' Street Directory and Court Guide of Croydon**
Dates	1872
Publisher	Tomkies, W.
Printer	–
Place	London & Croydon
Type	ST TR
Map scale	–
Notes	See 1299 & 1303
Library	CRD

REF	**1296**
Title	**The Reigate & Redhill Almanac and Directory**
Dates	1873
Publisher	Allingham, W.
Printer	Allingham, W.
Place	Reigate
Type	TR
Map scale	–
Library	GL

REF	**1297**
Title	**Sutton's Redhill Annual with Directory and Diary**
Dates	1874
Publisher	Sutton, H.
Printer	Sutton, H.
Place	London
Type	ST
Map scale	–
Library	BL

REF	**1298**
Title	**Ward's Commercial and General Croydon Directory**
Dates	1874,1876,1878,1880,1882,1884, 1885,1887-1930,1932,1934,1937, 1939
Publisher	Ward, J.W.
Printer	Ward, J.W.
Place	London
Type	GE TR
Map scale	–
Library	BL not 1874-1887
holdings	CRD all
	GL has 1887,1932,1934,1937, 1939
	GLH has 1900-1904,1906,1913, 1917
	SLS has 1899 & extracts from most other years 1878, 1884-1930
	SOG has 1889,1891,1898,1929

REF	1299
Title	**The Croydon Court Guide and Directory**
Dates	1876
Publisher	Wilkins & Co
Printer	Wilkins & Co
Place	London
Type	GE
Map scale	–
Notes	See 1295 & 1303
Library	GL

REF	1300
Title	**Atwood's Standard Directory of Croydon and Norwood**
Dates	1878
Publisher	Atwood, T.
Printer	Marshall, F.B.
Place	Croydon
Type	GE
Map scale	–
Library	CRD
holdings	GL

REF	1301
Title	**Worth's Croydon, Norwood & Penge Directory**
Dates	1878
Publisher	Worth & Co
Printer	Gooch, E.F. & Son
Place	Croydon
Type	GE
Map scale	–
Library	CRD

REF	1302
Title	**Ward's Norwood & Penge Directory with Map of Norwood and District**
Dates	1878,1880
Publisher	Ward, J.W.
Printer	Ward, J.W.
Place	Croydon
Type	GE TR
Map scale	–
Notes	Map missing CRD edition
Library	CRD

REF	1303
Title	**The Croydon Court Guide and Street Directory**
Dates	1879
Publisher	Tomkies, W.
Printer	Tomkies, W.
Place	London
Type	GE
Map scale	–
Library	CRD
holdings	GL

REF	1304
Title	**Church's Illustrated Sutton with a Street Directory**
Dates	1880
Publisher	Church, W.R.
Printer	–
Place	Sutton
Type	GE TR
Map scale	–
Notes	Reprint by Derek W. James (1978)
Library	GL
holdings	GLH
	SLS

REF	1305
Title	**Richmond and Twickenham Times Almanack and Directory**
Dates	1880,1881,1887,1888,1890
Publisher	Times Steam Printing Co
Printer	Times Steam Printing Co
Place	Richmond (Surrey)
Type	GE TR
Map scale	–
Library	BL has 1880
holdings	GL not 1880

REF	1306
Title	**Craddock's Godalming Almanac and Directory**
Dates	1880,1883,1885,1886,1888,1889, 1891-1896,1898-1908,1910,1911, 1913
Publisher	Craddock, H.T.
Printer	Craddock, H.T.
Place	Godalming
Type	CM
Map scale	–
Notes	Cont'd from 1292. From 1888 has street sections.
Library	BOD has 1899
holdings	SLS all
	SLS all

REF **1307**
Title **Lasham's Guildford Almanac and Directory**
Dates 1880-1895,1897-1919,1921-1935
Publisher Lasham, F.
Printer Lasham, F.
Place Guildford
Type GE
Map scale –
Notes 1880-1883 editions entitled 'The Guildford Almanac and Directory'. Cont'd from 1288
Library BL has 1904,1907-1912, 1919-1935
holdings CRD has 1922,1925,1929,1931, 1934
SLS not 1921

REF **1308**
Title **Purnell's Directory of Croydon**
Dates 1882
Publisher Purnell, G.T.
Printer Purnell, G.T.
Place Croydon
Type GE TR
Map scale –
Library CRD

REF **1309**
Title **Pile's Beddington, Carshalton, Wallington and District Directory**
Dates 1884,1888,1890
Publisher Pile, W. Ltd
Printer Pile, W. Ltd
Place Sutton
Type GE
Map scale –
Notes Cont'd as 1324
Library BL not 1884,1888,1890
holdings CRD has 1884
GL not 1884

REF **1310**
Title **Watford Hooke's Almanack and Directory for Guildford & surrounding villages**
Dates 1885
Publisher Hooke, W.
Printer Hooke, W.
Place Guildford
Type GE
Map scale –
Library BOD
holdings ULC

REF **1311**
Title **Burdett & Co's Upper Norwood, Penge & Anerley Directory**
Dates 1886
Publisher Burdett & Co
Printer Burdett & Co
Place Norwood
Type GE
Map scale –
Library CRD

REF **1312**
Title **The Richmond, Kew, Twickenham, St Margarets, Petersham, Barnes, Mortlake, Sheen & Teddington Directory**
Dates 1886
Publisher Hutchings & Crowsley
Printer Hutchings & Crowsley
Place London
Type GE TR
Map scale 1:15840
Notes Cont'd as 1313
Library BL
holdings BOD

REF **1313**
Title **Kelly's Richmond, Kew, Twickenham, St Margarets, Petersham, Barnes, Mortlake, Sheen & Teddington Directory**
Dates 1887-1905,1907-1916,1919-1928
Publisher Kelly & Co
Printer Kelly & Co
Place London
Type GE TR
Map scale 1:15840
Notes Cont'd from 1312, cont'd as 1344, 1031 & 1343. Barnes included 1887,1888 only.
Library BL all
holdings BOD has 1887-1912
CRD has 1888,1928
GL not 1887,1890,1891,1894, 1918,1922
GLH has 1904,1907,1910,1911, 1914,1919,1920,1923,1927
ULC has 1887-1912

REF	**1314**
Title	**Kelly's Directory of Croydon & South Norwood**
Dates	1888-1917,1919,1920,1922-1928
Publisher	Kelly & Co
Printer	Kelly & Co
Place	London
Type	GE TR
Map scale	1:15840
Notes	See also 1298. After 1922 includes Coulsdon, Kenley, Purley etc.
Library holdings	BL all
	BOD has 1888-1912
	CRD not 1894,1896,1897,1900, 1901-1903,1905,1909,1910, 1920
	GL not 1888,1890,1891
	GLH has 1905,1907,1910,1912, 1914-1919,1923,1926-1928
	SOG has 1926
	ULC has 1888-1912

REF	**1315**
Title	**Ward's Commercial and General Norwood Directory**
Dates	1889
Publisher	Ward, J.W.
Printer	Ward, J.W.
Place	Croydon
Type	GE TR
Map scale	–
Library	CRD

REF	**1316**
Title	**Christopher Holt's Almanack & Directory of Sutton**
Dates	1890
Publisher	Holt, C.
Printer	Holt, C.
Place	Sutton
Type	CT
Map scale	–
Library	GL

REF	**1317**
Title	**Kelly's Directory of Redhill, Reigate & Neighbourhood**
Dates	1890-1916,1922-1942,1944,1948
Publisher	Kelly & Co
Printer	Kelly & Co
Place	London
Type	GE TR
Map scale	–
Library holdings	BL all
	BOD has 1890-1910,1912
	CLM has 1933
	CRD has 1891,1892,1894-1896, 1902,1933-1940
	GL not 1891-1897,1903,1907, 1910,1912,1927,1942
	GLH has 1931-1933
	SOG has 1948
	SLS has 1890,1900,1902, 1904-1910,1912,1913,1915, 1923-1926,1930-1932,1934, 1936-1950
	ULC has 1890-1912

REF	**1318**
Title	**Kelly's Wimbledon, Merton, Mitcham, Sutton & District Directory**
Dates	1891-1940
Publisher	Kelly & Co
Printer	Kelly & Co
Place	London
Type	GE
Map scale	1:15840
Notes	Sutton dropped from title 1908; Wallington included 1907,1908; Morden included after 1908.
Library holdings	BL all
	BOD has 1891-1912
	CLM has 1931
	CRD has 1927,1938
	GL not 1891,1894,1901,1917, 1938
	GLH has 1904,1910,1911-1913, 1915,1919,1921,1922,1924, 1927-1931,1934-1939
	SLS has 1936
	SOG has 1930
	ULC has 1891-1913

REF **1319**
Title **Kelly's Kingston, Norbiton, Surbiton & District Directory**
Dates 1891-1940,1948
Publisher Kelly & Co
Printer Kelly & Co
Place London
Type GE
Map scale 1:15840
Notes Surbiton dropped from title after 1937 (cont'd as 1349), Malden & Coombe included from 1938
Library BL all
holdings BOD has 1891-1900,1902-1912
BPH has 1936
CRD has 1927,1930,1935,1938
GL not 1891,1904,1919,1948
GLH has 1898,1923,1924,1927, 1929-1931,1933,1935,1937
SLS has 1948
ULC has 1892-1903,1905-1912

REF **1320**
Title **The Richmond District Directory and Almanack**
Dates 1895,1896,1905,1907,1909-1913
Publisher Dimbleby, E.W.
Printer Dimbleby. E.W.
Place Richmond (Surrey)
Type GE
Map scale –
Notes 1905 edition entitled 'Richmond District Directory'
Library BL

REF **1321**
Title **Edward Cock's Local Directory of Addlestone, Chertsey, Weybridge and Walton-on-Thames**
Dates 1897
Publisher Cock, E.
Printer Cock, E.
Place Weybridge
Type TR
Map scale –
Library BL

REF **1322**
Title **Kelly's Directory of Dorking and District**
Dates 1899-1915,1950
Publisher Kelly's Directories Ltd
Printer Kelly's Directories Ltd
Place London
Type GE
Map scale 1:15840
Library BL not 1914,1915,1950
holdings BOD has 1899-1908,1910-1912
CLM has 1950
GL not 1906,1907
NLW has 1912,1950
SOG has 1950
SLS has 1950
ULC has 1899-1912

REF **1323**
Title **Kelly's Directory of Epsom and Leatherhead**
Dates 1899-1916,1922-1924,1926,1928, 1930,1932,1934,1936,1938,1940
Publisher Kelly's Directories Ltd
Printer Kelly's Directories Ltd
Place London
Type GE
Map scale 1:63360
Library BL all
holdings BOD has 1899-1905,1907-1912
CRD has 1924,1940
GL not 1902,1906,1907,1922
GLH has 1907,1932,1934
NLW has 1912
SLS has 1934
ULC has 1899-1912

REF	**1324**
Title	**Pile's Commercial and General Sutton & District Directory**
Dates	1900-1902,1904,1907,1908, 1910-1916,1919,1921,1923,1924, 1926-1929,1931,1932,1935,1938
Publisher	Pile, W. Ltd
Printer	Pile, W. Ltd
Place	Sutton
Type	GE
Map scale	1:15840
Notes	Cont'd from 1309. After 1903 entitled 'William Pile's Sutton, Carshalton, Wallington & District Directory'.
Library	BL all
holdings	CRD has 1935,1937
	GL has 1926,1935,1937
	GLH has 1923,1935,1937
	SLS has 1937 (volume is undated)
	SOG has 1902,1929,1935,1937

REF	**1325**
Title	**Kelly's Directory of Guildford, Godalming, Woking & villages in neighbourhood of Guildford**
Dates	1900-1915,1922,1924-1941,1943, 1944,1948,1950
Publisher	Kelly's Directories Ltd
Printer	Kelly's Directories Ltd
Place	London
Type	GE
Map scale	1:63360
Library	BL all
holdings	BOD has 1900-1912
	CLM has 1944
	CRD has 1933-1939,1944-1950
	GL not 1901,1906,1943
	SLS has 1924-1950
	ULC has 1900-1912

REF	**1326**
Title	**Caterham District Directory**
Dates	1901,1902
Publisher	Caterham Free Press
Printer	Caterham Free Press
Place	Caterham Valley
Type	CT CM
Map scale	–
Library	SLS

REF	**1327**
Title	**Barnes & Mortlake Directory**
Dates	1904
Publisher	Simpson, R.W. & Co
Printer	Simpson, R.W. & Co
Place	Barnes
Type	GE
Map scale	–
Library	BL

REF	**1328**
Title	**Andrews' Epsom and Leatherhead District Directory**
Dates	1904,1906,1909
Publisher	Andrews, L.W. & Son
Printer	Andrews, L.W. & Son
Place	Epsom
Type	GE
Map scale	–
Library	BL

REF	**1329**
Title	**Drew's York Town, Camberley & District Directory**
Dates	1904,1907-1920
Publisher	Drew, J.
Printer	Drew, J.
Place	Camberley
Type	GE
Map scale	–
Library	BL

REF	**1330**
Title	**The Woking Year Book and Directory**
Dates	1904-1907,1913,1915-1939, 1948-1950
Publisher	Woking News & Mail
Printer	Woking News & Mail
Place	Woking
Type	GE
Map scale	–
Library	BL all
holdings	CRD has 1949
	GL has 1937,1939,1949
	SLS has 1921-1928,1930-1932, 1935-1938,1948,1949

REF **1331**
Title **Phillipson's Almanack and Directory for Kingston & Neighbourhood**
Dates 1904-1908
Publisher Phillipson, G. & Sons
Printer Phillipson, G. & Sons
Place Kingston-on-Thames
Type GE TR
Map scale 1:15840
Library BL

REF **1332**
Title **F.M. Smith & Co's Directory of South Croydon, Purley, Sanderstead, Beddington, Kenley, Smitham and Coulsdon, Wallington**
Dates 1906
Publisher Smith, F.M. & Co
Printer The Edridge Press
Place Croydon
Type GE TR
Map scale –
Library CRD

REF **1333**
Title **Trim's Wimbledon Directory**
Dates 1906-1908
Publisher Trim, E.
Printer Trim, E.
Place Wimbledon
Type GE
Map scale 1:15840
Library BL

REF **1334**
Title **The Holmesdale Directory to the Borough of Reigate & District**
Dates 1907-1914,1917,1920-1940
Publisher The Holmesdale Press Ltd
Printer The Holmesdale Press Ltd
Place Redhill
Type GE
Map scale NS
Library BL not 1940
holdings CRD has 1924,1925,1927, 1929-1931,1934-1938,1940
GL has 1911,1939
SLS has 1908,1914,1917,1921, 1927,1929,1931-1940

REF **1335**
Title **Kelly's Sutton, Carshalton, Beddington, S. Beddington, Wallington, Cheam, Cuddington, Hackbridge & Worcester Park Directory**
Dates 1909-1940
Publisher Kelly's Directories Ltd
Printer Kelly's Directories Ltd
Place London
Type GE TR
Map scale –
Notes See 1318
Library BL all
holdings BOD has 1909-1912
CLM has 1924
CRD has 1925
GL not 1911,1916-1923, 1928-1940
GLH has 1926,1927
SOG has 1938
ULC has 1909-1913

REF **1336**
Title **Elliott's Cranleigh Directory & Almanac**
Dates 1910
Publisher Elliott, F.P.
Printer Elliott, F.P.
Place Cranleigh
Type CT
Map scale –
Library BL

REF **1337**
Title **Weekly Record Directory of Beddington, Carshalton & Wallington**
Dates 1910,1911
Publisher Weekly Record
Printer Weekly Record
Place Wallington
Type GE TR
Map scale –
Library BL all
holdings GL has 1911

REF	1338
Title	**The Holmesdale Directory to Dorking and Leatherhead**
Dates	1911-1916,1918,1920,1921,1923, 1926,1928-1936,1938,1940
Publisher	The Holmesdale Press Ltd
Printer	The Holmesdale Press Ltd
Place	Redhill
Type	GE
Map scale	NS
Notes	Later (1930s) editions published by the Dorking & Leatherhead Advertiser
Library	BL all
holdings	GL has 1935-1938
	SLS has 1932

REF	1339
Title	**Caterham District Directory**
Dates	1912-1916,1920,1922,1924,1926, 1928,1930,1932,1934,1937,1939
Publisher	The Holmesdale Press Ltd
Printer	The Holmesdale Press Ltd
Place	Redhill
Type	GE
Map scale	–
Library	BL not 1934,1939
holdings	CRD has 1924-1928,1927,1939
	GL has 1934
	SLS has 1912,1922,1926, 1934-1939

REF	1340
Title	**Ward's Commercial and General Coulsdon, Purley, Kenley, Sanderstead and Selsdon Directory**
Dates	1913-1915,1918,1930,1932,1934, 1937,1939
Publisher	Ward, J.W.
Printer	Ward, J.W.
Place	Croydon
Type	GE
Map scale	–
Notes	Title variable. Later editions published & printed by The Croydon Advertiser.
Library	CRD all
holdings	GL has 1932-1939
	SLS has 1939

REF	1341
Title	**The Woldingham Directory and Guide**
Dates	1924
Publisher	(In aid of) Caterham Cottage Hospital
Printer	Holdbrook
Place	Caterham Valley
Type	CT
Map scale	–
Library	SLS

REF	1342
Title	**Directory for Farnham and District**
Dates	1924,1928,1930-1932,1934-1939, 1947
Publisher	Langham, E.W.
Printer	Langham, E.W.
Place	Farnham
Type	GE
Map scale	NS
Library	BL not 1924,1928,1947
holdings	BOD has 1932-1935,1938,1939
	CRD has 1924-1930,1934,1935
	NLS has 1937
	SLS has 1947
	ULC has 1931-1935,1937-1939

REF	1343
Title	**Kelly's Directory of Barnes, Mortlake and Sheen**
Dates	1929-1939
Publisher	Kelly's Directories Ltd
Printer	Kelly's Directories Ltd
Place	London
Type	GE TR
Map scale	1:15840
Notes	Cont'd from 1313
Library	BL all
holdings	CRD has 1937
	GL all
	GLH has 1929,1931,1933,1934
	SOG has 1933,1937

REF **1344**
Title **Kelly's Directory of Richmond, Kew, Petersham & Ham**
Dates 1929-1940,1948
Publisher Kelly's Directories Ltd
Printer Kelly's Directories Ltd
Place London
Type GE TR
Map scale 1:15840
Notes Cont'd from 1313 & 965
Library BL all
holdings BPH has 1936,1939
CRD has 1930-1933,1937,1940, 1948
GL all
GLH has 1929-1931,1933

REF **1345**
Title **Lucas's Cranleigh and Ewhurst Directory**
Dates 1930,1935
Publisher Lucas, R.
Printer The Cranleigh Press
Place Cranleigh
Type CM
Map scale —
Notes GL title page missing when re-bound, date uncertain. SLS edition also undated although complete, probably c.1935.
Library GL has 1930
holdings SLS has 1935

REF **1346**
Title **Kelly's Directory of Esher, Claygate, The Dittons, Cobham, East & West Molesey &c**
Dates 1932-1939,1948
Publisher Kelly's Directories Ltd
Printer Kelly's Directories Ltd
Place London
Type GE TR
Map scale 1:76032
Notes 1932 edition only covers Esher & Neighbourhood
Library BL all
holdings CRD has 1937,1938,1948
GL all
GLH has 1933,1938
SLS has 1934,1948

REF **1347**
Title **Esher Directory and Trade Guide**
Dates 1933
Publisher Thompson, E.V. & Co Ltd
Printer Thompson, E.V. & Co Ltd
Place Esher
Type GE
Map scale —
Library SLS

REF **1348**
Title **May's Directory of Camberley and Frimley**
Dates 1938
Publisher May, W. & Co Ltd
Printer May, W. & Co Ltd
Place Aldershot
Type GE
Map scale —
Library GL

REF **1349**
Title **Kelly's Directory of Surbiton**
Dates 1938-1940
Publisher Kelly's Directories Ltd
Printer Kelly's Directories Ltd
Place London
Type GE TR
Map scale 1:15840
Notes Cont'd from 1319
Library BL
holdings GL

REF **1350**
Title **The Croydon Directory and Handbook**
Dates 1949,1950
Publisher The Heath Press
Printer The Heath Press
Place Thornton Heath
Type TR
Map scale —
Library BL
holdings GL

SUSSEX

REF **1351**
Title **Kelly's Directory of Sussex**
Dates 1851,1855,1859,1862,1866,1870,
1874,1878,1882,1887,1891,1895,
1899,1901,1903,1905,1907,1909,
1911,1913,1915,1918,1922,1924,
1927,1930,1934,1938
Publisher Kelly & Co
Printer Kelly & Co
Place London
Type GE TR
Map scale 1:126720
Notes See 3,17 & 19
Library BCL has 1891-1899,1903-1938
holdings BED has 1851
BIS has 1927,1934,1938
BL not 1851
BOD not 1855,1901,1918
BPH has 1866,1887,1895,1905,
1918-1930,1938
BRI not 1851,1901,1934
CHI has 1851,1862,1866,1874,
1878,1887,1891,1899,
1903-1909,1913,1918-1938
CLB has 1938
CLE has 1938
CLM has 1859,1927,1938
COL has 1855,1859
GL not 1901,1930,1934
GLH has 1855-1899,1903-1911,
1922,1930
HLS has 1878
HRO has 1938
IHR has 1866,1887,1891,1905,
1930-1938
KCL has 1859,1866,1878,1895
NLS all
NLW has 1913,1915,1924,
1930-1938
SLS has 1882,1911,1918,1938
SCL has 1930-1938
SOG has 1851-1862,1874,1882,
1899,1913,1922,1938
ULC all
WOR has 1855,1866,1874,1878,
1891-1899,1903-1915,1922,
1927-1938
YCL has 1938

REF **1352**
Title **Melville & Co's Directory and
Gazetteer of Sussex**
Dates 1858
Publisher Melville & Co
Printer Collingridge, W.H.
Place London
Type GE
Map scale 1:253440
Library BRI
holdings CHI
GL
WOR

REF **1353**
Title **J.G. Harrod & Co's Postal and
Commercial Directory of Sussex**
Dates 1867
Publisher Harrod, J.G. & Co
Printer Harrod, J.G. & Co
Place London
Type CM
Map scale –
Library BRI
holdings GL

REF **1354**
Title **Deacon's Court Guide, Gazetteer
and County Blue Book [Sussex]**
Dates 1881,1894
Publisher Deacon, C.W. & Co
Printer Deacon, C.W. & Co
Place London
Type CT
Map scale 1:253440
Library BOD has 1894
holdings BRI has 1894
GL has 1881
NLS has 1894
SOG all
WOR all

REF **1355**
Title **The Sussex Blue Book and Court
Directory**
Dates 1905
Publisher The Robinson Printing Co
Printer The Robinson Printing Co
Place Brighton
Type CT
Map scale –
Library CHI
holdings WOR

REF	1356
Title	**Sussex Directory**
Dates	1947-1950
Publisher	Aubrey & Co
Printer	Aubrey & Co
Place	Walsall
Type	TR
Map scale	–
Notes	Cont'd from 104
Library	BL

REF	1357
Title	**Folthorpe's General Directory for Brighton, Hove and Cliftonville**
Dates	1850,1852,1854,1856,1859-1862, 1864-1866
Publisher	Folthorpe, R.
Printer	Spottiswoode & Co
Place	Brighton
Type	GE TR
Map scale	–
Notes	NORTON 683-685 (1850,1852, 1854). See 1363.
Library	BL not 1850-1856
holdings	BOD has 1859,1861,1862,1864, 1866
	BRI has 1850-1859,1861,1862, 1864
	GL has 1850,1852
	IHR has 1856
	NLS has 1852,1859,1861,1862, 1864
	ULC has 1852,1859,1861,1862, 1864-1866
	WOR has 1850,1856

REF	1358
Title	**Osborne's Stranger's Guide and Directory to Hastings & St Leonards**
Dates	1852,1854
Publisher	Osborne, H.
Printer	Osborne, H.
Place	Hastings
Type	CM
Map scale	1:31680
Notes	NORTON 689
Library	BL has 1852
holdings	GL has 1854

REF	1359
Title	**The Original Brighton & Hove Directory, including Cliftonville**
Dates	1854
Publisher	Taylor, W.J.
Printer	Taylor, W.J.
Place	Brighton
Type	GE TR
Map scale	1:23760
Notes	NORTON 686
Library	BL
holdings	BRI
	GL
	WOR

REF	1360
Title	**French and Watkis's Hand Book and Directory for Worthing**
Dates	1857
Publisher	Phillipps, J.
Printer	French & Watkis
Place	Worthing
Type	CT
Map scale	–
Notes	See 1361
Library	GL
holdings	WOR

REF	1361
Title	**French & Son's Handbook and Directory for Worthing**
Dates	1859
Publisher	French and Son
Printer	French and Son
Place	Worthing
Type	CM
Map scale	–
Notes	See 1360
Library	IHR
holdings	WOR

REF	1362
Title	**Simpson's Brighton and Cliftonville Directory and Court Guide**
Dates	1864
Publisher	Simpson & Co
Printer	–
Place	London
Type	GE TR
Map scale	–
Library	BRI
holdings	GL

REF **1363**
Title **Page's Court Guide & General Directory of Brighton, Hove, Cliftonville and Preston (late Folthorpe's)**
Dates 1864-1868,1870-1873,1877-1898
Publisher Page, T.
Printer Page, T.
Place Brighton
Type GE TR
Map scale –
Notes Cont'd from 1357, cont'd as 1393
Library BL not 1869,1874-1876
holdings BOD has 1867,1868,1870-1873, 1880-1895
BRI has 1865-1895
GL has 1867,1870,1878,1886, 1887
IHR has 1865
NLS has 1865-1868,1870-1873, 1880-1895
ULC has 1864-1867,1870-1873, 1880-1885,1887-1895
WOR has 1871,1877,1880,1882, 1884

REF **1364**
Title **Mathiesons' Hastings & St Leonards Directory**
Dates 1867
Publisher Burg & Daniel
Printer Mathiesons
Place St Leonards
Type GE TR
Map scale –
Library BL
holdings BOD
ULC

REF **1365**
Title **Mathiesons' Brighton & Suburban Directory**
Dates 1868-1870
Publisher Beal, J.
Printer Beal, J.
Place Brighton
Type GE TR
Map scale –
Library BL has 1868
holdings BOD has 1868
BRI all
GL has 1869,1870
NLS has 1868
ULC has 1868
WOR has 1869

REF **1366**
Title **The Worthing Directory and Almanack**
Dates 1870-1903
Publisher Lucy, F.
Printer –
Place Worthing
Type GE
Map scale 1:1200
Notes 1874-1903 published by G.D.S. Kirshaw. Map included in 1896 & later editions.
Library BL has 1896
holdings BRI has 1887,1900
WOR all

REF **1367**
Title **The Brighton, Kemp-Town, Hove and Cliftonville Court Guide**
Dates 1871
Publisher Wilkins & Co
Printer –
Place London
Type CT
Map scale –
Library BRI

REF **1368**
Title **The Brighton Quarterly Directory and Sussex Court Guide**
Dates 1872-1875
Publisher Pike, W.T.
Printer Hilton, G.
Place Brighton
Type GE TR
Map scale –
Library BL not 1875
holdings GL not 1872

REF **1369**
Title **Butcher, Cole and Co's Hastings, St Leonards and Eastbourne Directory**
Dates 1874
Publisher Butcher, Cole & Co
Printer –
Place London
Type CT CM
Map scale 1:633600
Library BRI

REF 1370
Title Pike & Ivimy's Annual Hastings and St Leonards Directory and Sussex Court Guide
Dates 1876
Publisher Pike & Ivimy
Printer –
Place Brighton
Type GE
Map scale –
Library BRI

REF 1371
Title The Half Crown Brighton Directory with Map
Dates 1876
Publisher Pike & Ivimy
Printer –
Place Brighton
Type GE TR
Map scale –
Notes Map missing from SOG volume
Library SOG

REF 1372
Title The Shilling Brighton Directory and Court Guide
Dates 1876
Publisher Steven & Co
Printer Robinson, A.M.
Place Brighton
Type GE TR
Map scale –
Library BRI

REF 1373
Title Clarke's Local Directory and Year Book for Cuckfield, Haywards Heath, Lindfield & Burgess Hill
Dates 1879,1883-1885,1887-1889
Publisher Clarke, C.
Printer Clarke, C.
Place Haywards Heath
Type GE
Map scale –
Notes 1889,1890 editions entitled 'Clarke's Local Directory and Year Book for Hurstpierpoint, Hassocks, Burgess Hill, Lindfield, Haywards Heath, Cuckfield'
Library BOD has 1888,1889
holdings BRI has 1883,1887,1888
GL has 1879
ULC has 1879,1888,1889
WOR has 1884,1885

REF 1374
Title The Chichester Directory Handbook and Almanack
Dates 1880,1883,1887,1889-1891,1900
Publisher Moore, J.W.
Printer Moore, J.W.
Place Chichester
Type GE
Map scale –
Library BRI has 1900
holdings CHI not 1900
WOR has 1891

REF 1375
Title The Lewes, Newhaven etc etc Directory
Dates 1881
Publisher Tomkies, W.
Printer –
Place Brighton
Type GE
Map scale –
Library WOR

REF 1376
Title Hastings and St Leonards Directory and Guide
Dates 1882,1883,1885
Publisher Hutchings & Crowsley
Printer Hutchings & Crowsley
Place London
Type GE TR
Map scale 1:63360
Library BL has 1885
holdings BRI has 1882,1883

REF	**1377**
Title	**Holman's Lewes Directory**
Dates	1883,1887
Publisher	Holman, G.
Printer	Holman, G.
Place	Lewes
Type	GE TR
Map scale	–
Library	BL all
holdings	SOG has 1887
	ULC has 1887

REF	**1378**
Title	**Robinson's Popular Brighton Directory and Street Guide**
Dates	1884-1886
Publisher	Robinson, A.M.
Printer	Robinson, A.M.
Place	Brighton
Type	GE TR
Map scale	–
Library	BL has 1885
holdings	BRI has 1884,1886

REF	**1379**
Title	**W.T. Pike's Local Blue Book and Directory of the Eastern or Rye Parliamentary Division of Sussex**
Dates	1885,1886
Publisher	Pike, W.T.
Printer	Osborne, H.
Place	Hastings
Type	GE
Map scale	–
Library	BRI has 1886
holdings	GL has 1885

REF	**1380**
Title	**W.T.Pike's Local Blue Book and Directory of the Chichester Parliamentary Division of Sussex**
Dates	1886
Publisher	Pike, W.T.
Printer	Pike, W.T.
Place	Brighton
Type	GE
Map scale	–
Notes	Rebound with no T/P & entitled 'Sussex Directory', further clues about title taken from W.T. Pike's advertisement inside the directory and the title of 1379, title is therefore uncertain
Library	CHI

REF	**1381**
Title	**Long's Worthing Directory and Postal Guide**
Dates	1886,1892,1893
Publisher	Long, W.J.C.
Printer	Long, W.J.C.
Place	Worthing
Type	ST
Map scale	–
Library	BL has 1886
holdings	BOD has 1886
	BRI has 1892
	WOR all

REF	**1382**
Title	**W.T. Pike's Hastings and St Leonards Directory**
Dates	1886-1888,1890-1900,1902-1939
Publisher	Pike, W.T.
Printer	Robinson, A.M.
Place	Hastings
Type	GE TR
Map scale	–
Notes	1910 onwards published by Garnett, Mepham & Fisher
Library	BL not 1892
holdings	BOD not 1886,1887,1892
	BRI has 1891,1892,1894, 1902-1905,1907
	GL has 1886,1888
	ULC not 1892,1920,1921
	WOR has 1910-1912

REF	**1383**
Title	**Kelly's Hastings and St Leonards Directory**
Dates	1887-1914,1919,1921-1940,1948, 1950
Publisher	Kelly & Co
Printer	Kelly & Co
Place	London
Type	GE TR
Map scale	1:9052
Library	BL all
holdings	BOD has 1888-1912
	BPH has 1948,1950
	BRI has 1900,1901,1919,1921, 1924,1925,1927,1928, 1930-1934,1936-1950
	GL not 1890-1896
	SOG has 1950
	ULC has 1888-1913
	WOR has 1925,1938-1940,1950

REF **1384**
Title **Pike's Brighton & Hove Blue Book and Local Directory**
Dates 1887-1939
Publisher Robinson & Pike
Printer Robinson, A.M.
Place Brighton
Type GE TR
Map scale –
Library BL not 1887,1889
holdings BOD not 1887,1889,1901,1919, 1920
BRI all
GL has 1888
ULC not 1887,1889,1901,1919, 1920
WOR has 1911,1917

REF **1385**
Title **Brooker's Guide and Directory for Uckfield and District**
Dates 1888
Publisher Brooker, J.
Printer Brooker, J.
Place Uckfield
Type CM
Map scale –
Library NLS

REF **1386**
Title **Downsborough's Guide and Directory of Bexhill-on-Sea**
Dates 1888
Publisher Downsborough, J.
Printer Osborne, H.
Place Bexhill-on-Sea
Type GE
Map scale 1:4800
Library BL
holdings ULC

REF **1387**
Title **Clarke's Illustrated Mid-Sussex Directory and Year Book**
Dates 1888,1890-1896,1898,1900-1905, 1912-1917,1922,1924-1940
Publisher Clarke, C.
Printer Clarke, C.
Place Haywards Heath
Type CT
Map scale –
Notes Later editions entitled 'The Mid-Sussex Directory and Visitors' Guide'
Library BL not 1888,1891,1900-1905
holdings BOD has 1890-1893,1896,1898, 1900,1902-1911,1926-1940
BRI has 1895,1900-1917, 1924-1940
CHI has 1938
GL has 1912,1938-1940
NLS has 1888,1890-1893,1896, 1898-1913,1915-1917,1922, 1924-1926,1928,1931,1932, 1938-1940
ULC has 1890-1893,1896,1900, 1903-1905,1935-1940
WOR has 1914

REF **1388**
Title **Pike's Eastbourne Blue Book and Local Directory**
Dates 1888,1890-1939
Publisher Robinson & Pike
Printer Robinson & Pike
Place Brighton
Type GE TR
Map scale –
Notes 1910 onwards published by Garnett, Mepham & Fisher. Title then changes to 'Eastbourne, Hailsham & District Local Directory'.
Library BL not 1888,1935
holdings BOD not 1888,1919,1935
BRI has 1890-1894,1901-1904, 1906,1914-1916,1920,1921, 1923-1929,1932,1934,1936
GL has 1888,1910,1939
ULC has 1890-1939
WOR has 1910,1911,1923,1933

REF **1389**
Title **Kelly's Directory of Brighton, Hove and Preston**
Dates 1889-1940,1947,1949
Publisher Kelly & Co
Printer Kelly & Co
Place London
Type GE TR
Map scale 1:10560
Library BL all
holdings BOD has 1889-1912
BRI not 1907-1910,1921,1925
CLE has 1947
GL not 1890,1891,1893-1896,
1908,1921
MLG has 1947,1949
NLS has 1897,1899
NLW has 1949
ULC has 1889-1912
WOR has 1907,1920,1921,1923,
1925,1932-1935,1937-1949

REF **1390**
Title **The Chronicle Bexhill-on-Sea Directory, Almanack & Guide**
Dates 1891,1892,1902-1919,1922-1930
Publisher Bexhill Chronicle
Printer Bexhill Chronicle
Place Bexhill-on-Sea
Type GE TR
Map scale –
Library BL

REF **1391**
Title **Parsons' Hastings, St Leonards and District Directory and Local Red Book**
Dates 1894,1895,1910-1917,1920
Publisher Parsons, F.J.
Printer Parsons, F.J.
Place Hastings
Type GE TR
Map scale 1:10560
Library BL

REF **1392**
Title **John Davis & Co's Lewes Directory**
Dates 1896,1898
Publisher Davis, J. & Co
Printer Davis, J. & Co
Place Brighton
Type GE
Map scale –
Library BRI

REF **1393**
Title **Towner's Brighton, Hove and Suburban Directory**
Dates 1896-1908
Publisher Towner, W.J.
Printer Towner, W.J.
Place Brighton
Type GE TR
Map scale –
Notes Cont'd from 1363
Library BL all
holdings BOD not 1896-1898,1906,1907
BRI all
NLS not 1896-1898,1906
ULC not 1906,1907

REF **1394**
Title **Pike's Horsham, Crawley & District Blue Book & Local Directory**
Dates 1898-1917,1920,1921,1923,1925,
1927,1929,1931,1933,1935,1937,
1939
Publisher Robinson & Pike
Printer Robinson, A. M.
Place Brighton
Type GE TR
Map scale –
Notes 1910 onwards published by Garnett, Mepham & Fisher
Library BL all
holdings BOD not 1920
BRI has 1899,1900,1902,1904,
1905,1910,1914-1916,1920,
1923-1939
CHI has 1900,1925,1929-1937
CRD has 1937
GL has 1920,1927
NLS has 1901-1939
ULC has 1898-1917,1921-1939
WOR has 1910,1911,1925,1933,
1935

REF **1395**
Title **The Bognor, Aldwick, Felpham and South Bersted Directory and Almanack**
Dates 1900,1905,1906,1913
Publisher Webster & Webb
Printer Webster & Webb
Place Bognor
Type GE
Map scale 1:10560
Notes Cont'd as 1409
Library BRI not 1913
holdings CHI has 1913

[271]

REF	**1396**
Title	**The Bexhill Directory, Year Book and Illustrated Almanack**
Dates	1900,1925
Publisher	The Bexhill Publishing and Printing Company
Printer	The Bexhill Publishing and Printing Company
Place	Bexhill-on-Sea
Type	GE TR
Map scale	1:6336
Notes	1925 edition entitled 'The Bexhill & District Directory', published by The Bexhill Printing Company
Library	BRI has 1900
holdings	WOR has 1925

REF	**1397**
Title	**Kelly's Directory of Chichester, Bognor and Littlehampton**
Dates	1900-1908,1930-1940,1950
Publisher	Kelly's Directories Ltd
Printer	Kelly's Directories Ltd
Place	London
Type	GE TR
Map scale	NS
Notes	Title varies, later editions cover Chichester, Selsey & neighbourhood
Library	BL all
holdings	BOD has 1900-1906,1908
	BRI has 1900,1901,1930,1933, 1936,1937,1939,1950
	CHI has 1929,1931,1934-1950
	GL all
	PCL has 1936-1950
	NLW has 1950
	ULC has 1900-1908
	WOR has 1934,1936,1937,1939, 1950

REF	**1398**
Title	**Kelly's Directory of Worthing and Neighbourhood**
Dates	1900-1915,1921-1940,1946,1949
Publisher	Kelly's Directories Ltd
Printer	Kelly's Directories Ltd
Place	London
Type	GE TR
Map scale	1:126720
Library	BL not 1922
holdings	BOD has 1900-1912
	BPH has 1946,1949
	BRI has 1900,1901,1914,1915, 1924-1927,1930,1932,1933, 1935-1937,1939,1946,1949
	GL all
	NLW has 1949
	ULC has 1900-1913
	WOR not 1901,1905,1907-1909, 1915,1922,1925,1933

REF	**1399**
Title	**Pike's Lewes, Newhaven & Seaford Directory**
Dates	1900-1920,1922,1924,1927,1929, 1931,1932,1934,1936,1938,1940
Publisher	Robinson & Pike
Printer	Robinson, A.M.
Place	Brighton
Type	GE TR
Map scale	–
Notes	1910 onwards published by Garnett, Mepham & Fisher
Library	BL not 1940
holdings	BOD not 1901,1918,1919,1940
	BRI has 1900,1903,1905-1907, 1910,1914,1916,1920-1940
	GL has 1912,1931,1934-1938
	NLS not 1900,1901,1918-1920, 1926,1940
	SOG has 1931
	ULC not 1901,1918,1919,1940
	WOR has 1911,1924,1932,1938

REF	**1400**
Title	**Dixon's East Grinstead, Ashurst Wood and Forest Row Family Almanack and Directory**
Dates	1901
Publisher	Dixon, W.H.
Printer	–
Place	East Grinstead
Type	GE
Map scale	–
Library	WOR

REF **1401**
Title **Gowland's Eastbourne Postal & Borough Directory**
Dates 1904,1906-1917,1920-1925
Publisher Gowland Bros.
Printer Gowland Bros.
Place Eastbourne
Type GE TR
Map scale 1:10560
Notes Cont'd by 1314
Library BL all
holdings GL has 1912,1913,1917,1920, 1922,1924,1925

REF **1402**
Title **Brighton and District Trades' Directory**
Dates 1904,1909,1910,1918,1921-1924, 1927,1936
Publisher Town and County Directories Ltd
Printer Macdonald, W. & Co Ltd
Place Edinburgh
Type TR
Map scale –
Library BRI has 1904
holdings CHI has 1936
WOR has 1909-1927

REF **1403**
Title **Worthing Mercury Directory, Almanack and Year Book**
Dates 1904-1906
Publisher South Coast Mercury Company Ltd
Printer South Coast Mercury Company Ltd
Place Worthing
Type GE
Map scale 1:10560
Notes Map scale approx. Cont'd as 1405.
Library BL all
holdings WOR has 1905

REF **1404**
Title **Pike's Hailsham, Pevensey and Local District Blue Book and Directory**
Dates 1906-1908
Publisher Robinson Printing Company
Printer Robinson Printing Company
Place Brighton
Type GE TR
Map scale –
Notes Cont'd as 1388
Library BL all
holdings BOD all
BRI has 1906,1907
GL has 1907
NLS all
ULC all

REF **1405**
Title **Worthing Mercury Red Book, Directory & Household Guide for Worthing**
Dates 1907,1909,1910
Publisher Worthing Mercury
Printer Worthing Mercury
Place Worthing
Type ST
Map scale –
Notes Cont'd from 1403
Library BL has 1907,1910
holdings WOR all

REF **1406**
Title **Pike's Bognor, Littlehampton, Arundel District Blue Book and Local Directory**
Dates 1910,1912
Publisher Garnett, Mepham & Fisher
Printer –
Place Brighton
Type GE
Map scale –
Library BL all
holdings BOD all
BRI has 1910
CHI has 1912
NLS all
ULC all
WOR has 1910

REF **1407**
Title **Worthing and District Blue Book and Local Directory**
Dates 1911-1939
Publisher Garnett, Mepham & Fisher Ltd
Printer –
Place Brighton
Type GE TR
Map scale –
Library BL all
holdings BOD all
BRI has 1911,1915,1926,1929, 1932,1936
NLS has 1911-1913
SOG has 1939
ULC all
WOR has 1912,1914-1922, 1924-1939

REF **1408**
Title **The Shoreham, Southwick and District Local Directory**
Dates 1914
Publisher Garnett, Mepham & Fisher Ltd
Printer Garnett, Mepham & Fisher Ltd
Place Brighton
Type ST
Map scale –
Library BOD

REF **1409**
Title **The Bognor Observer Directory ... including Aldwick, Felpham, New City, South Bersted, North Bersted**
Dates 1922,1925,1927,1929
Publisher Acford, R.J. Ltd
Printer Acford, R.J. Ltd
Place Bognor
Type GE
Map scale –
Notes Cont'd from 1395, cont'd as 1417
Library CHI

REF **1410**
Title **Pike's Blue Book Bexhill Directory with South Coast Map, Guide and Register**
Dates 1923
Publisher Garnett, Mepham & Fisher Ltd
Printer Garnett, Mepham & Fisher Ltd
Place Brighton
Type GE TR
Map scale NS
Library BRI

REF **1411**
Title **The Chichester Observer Directory with... Selsey, Fishbourne and District**
Dates 1923
Publisher Acford, R.J. Ltd
Printer Acford, R.J. Ltd
Place Chichester
Type ST
Map scale –
Library CHI

REF **1412**
Title **The Peacehaven Handbook and Illustrated Guide with Directory**
Dates 1923,1924,1930,1933
Publisher The Central Agency
Printer –
Place Peacehaven
Type GE TR
Map scale NS
Notes 1930,1933 editions entitled: 'The South Downs Directory'
Library BL all
holdings BOD not 1923
NLS has 1933
ULC not 1923

REF **1413**
Title **Kelly's Directory of Eastbourne, Hailsham & Neighbourhood**
Dates 1926-1940,1946,1948
Publisher Kelly's Directories Ltd
Printer Kelly's Directories Ltd
Place London
Type GE TR
Map scale 1:10560
Notes Cont'd from 1401
Library BL all
holdings BRI has 1926,1928,1929,1946, 1948
GL not 1936
WOR has 1937,1938

REF **1414**
Title **Littlehampton and District Directory**
Dates 1928,1938,1947,1950
Publisher Littlehampton Chamber of Commerce
Printer Mitchell & Co
Place Arundel
Type GE
Map scale 1:10560
Notes Map scale approx. Details of 1928 edition uncertain GL.
Library CHI has 1938,1947,1950
holdings GL has 1928,1950
WOR has 1947

REF **1415**
Title **Kelly's Directory of Bognor Regis & Neighbourhood**
Dates 1929-1940,1950
Publisher Kelly's Directories Ltd
Printer Kelly's Directories Ltd
Place London
Type GE TR
Map scale 1:15840
Library BL all
holdings BRI has 1929,1933,1936,1937, 1939,1950
CHI has 1931-1935,1937, 1939-1950
GL all
NLW has 1950
SOG has 1940,1950
WOR has 1934,1938-1950

REF **1416**
Title **Willis' Directory & Handbook of Chichester City**
Dates 1934
Publisher Willis, W.G. & T.R.
Printer Willis, W.G. & T.R.
Place Chichester
Type GE
Map scale –
Library CHI

REF **1417**
Title **Street and Alphabetical Directory of Bognor Regis and District**
Dates 1935,1936
Publisher Acford, R.J. Ltd
Printer Acford, R.J. Ltd
Place Chichester
Type GE
Map scale –
Notes Cont'd from 1409
Library CHI

REF **1418**
Title **The Official Mayfield Directory and Guide**
Dates 1935,1939,1949
Publisher Thomas, H.
Printer Thomas, H.
Place Mayfield
Type CT
Map scale –
Library BL all
holdings WOR has 1935

REF **1419**
Title **Who's Who in Worthing and District**
Dates 1938
Publisher Ludovic Grant & Co Ltd
Printer Love & Malcolmson
Place Worthing
Type CT PR
Map scale –
Notes Alphabetical list of local notables, professions etc.
Library WOR

REF **1420**
Title **Kelly's Directory of Bexhill**
Dates 1948,1950
Publisher Kelly's Directories Ltd
Printer Kelly's Directories Ltd
Place London
Type GE TR
Map scale –
Library BL all
holdings BPH has 1950
BRI all
GL all
NLW has 1950
SOG has 1950

WARWICKSHIRE

REF **1421**
Title **History, Gazetteer and Directory of Warwickshire**
Dates 1850,1874
Publisher White, F.
Printer Blurton, J.
Place Sheffield
Type GE
Map scale 1:126720
Notes NORTON 694 (1850)
Library BCL has 1874
holdings BL all
CL has 1850
COV all
GL all
IHR has 1850
LEA all
RUG all
SOG all
ULC has 1874
WCL all
WRK all

REF **1422**
Title **Kelly's Directory of Warwickshire**
Dates 1854,1860,1864,1868,1872,1876, 1880,1884,1888,1892,1896,1900, 1904,1908,1912,1916,1921,1924, 1928,1932,1936,1940
Publisher Kelly & Co
Printer Kelly & Co
Place London
Type GE TR
Map scale 1:253440
Notes See 6
Library BCL all
holdings BIS has 1940
BL has 1868-1921,1928,1940
BPH has 1868,1888,1916,1924, 1940
BOD has 1854-1864,1872-1940
CLB has 1940
CLE has 1940
CLM has 1924,1928,1940
COV has 1864,1876-1892, 1900-1912,1921-1940
GL has 1868,1876-1928
HBR has 1854
IHR has 1908,1936
LEA has 1864,1872-1884,1892, 1900-1921,1928,1932,1940
MLG has 1880,1921-1928,1940
NLS has 1854,1860,1868,1876, 1940
NLW has 1916,1924,1928,1936
RUG has 1896,1940
SCL has 1928-1940
SOG has 1860,1880,1884,1896, 1900,1916,1921,1936
ULC all
WCL has 1854,1868,1872, 1932-1940
WLV has 1860,1876,1932-1940
WRK has 1864,1896-1908,1916, 1928-1940
WSL has 1854,1860,1908,1936
YCL has 1940

REF	**1423**
Title	**Morris & Co's Commercial Directory and Gazetteer of Warwickshire with Birmingham**
Dates	1866
Publisher	Morris & Co
Printer	–
Place	Nottingham
Type	CM
Map scale	–
Library	BCL
holdings	COV
	GL
	LEA
	WRK

REF	**1424**
Title	**Deacon's Warwickshire Court Guide and County Blue Book**
Dates	1888
Publisher	Deacon, C.W. & Co
Printer	Deacon, C.W. & Co
Place	London
Type	CT PR
Map scale	1:158400
Notes	See 77
Library	COV

REF	**1425**
Title	**Warwickshire Directory and Buyers' Guide**
Dates	1911,1925,1926
Publisher	Cope, E.F. & Co
Printer	Cope, E.F. & Co
Place	Walsall
Type	TR
Map scale	–
Library	BCL

REF	**1426**
Title	**Lascelles & Co's Directory and Gazetteer of the City of Coventry and Neighbourhood**
Dates	1850
Publisher	Lascelles & Co
Printer	Lewin, D.
Place	Coventry
Type	CM TR
Map scale	–
Notes	NORTON 745
Library	BCL
holdings	BL
	COV
	GL

REF	**1427**
Title	**Slater's Classified Directory of the Manufacturing District 15 miles round Birmingham including Worcester and the Potteries**
Dates	1852
Publisher	Slater, I.
Printer	Slater, I.
Place	Manchester
Type	TR
Map scale	–
Notes	NORTON 695. BL volume dated 1858 in pencil.
Library	BL
holdings	HBR Xcopy of part of directory, local area only.
	WLV

REF	**1428**
Title	**Slater's General and Classified Directory of Birmingham and its vicinities**
Dates	1852
Publisher	Slater, I.
Printer	Slater, I.
Place	Manchester
Type	CM TR
Map scale	–
Notes	NORTON 742
Library	BCL
holdings	GL

REF	**1429**
Title	**The Edgbaston Directory and Guide**
Dates	1853
Publisher	Josebury, W. & Howe, W.H.
Printer	–
Place	Birmingham
Type	GE
Map scale	NS
Notes	NORTON 743
Library	BCL

REF	**1430**
Title	**Shalder's Birmingham Directory**
Dates	1854
Publisher	Wrightson & Bell
Printer	–
Place	Birmingham
Type	TR
Map scale	–
Notes	NORTON 744
Library	BCL
holdings	GL

REF	**1431**		REF	**1434**
Title	**General and Commercial Directory & Topography of the Borough of Birmingham**		Title	**Corporation, General and Trades Directory of Birmingham ... and Wolverhampton**
Dates	1855,1856		Dates	1861,1863,1864
Publisher	White, F.		Publisher	Cornish, W.
Printer	Harrison, S.		Printer	–
Place	Sheffield		Place	Birmingham
Type	GE TR		Type	CM TR
Map scale	–		Map scale	–
Notes	NORTON 696 (1855)		Library	BCL all
Library	BCL has 1855		holdings	BL has 1861
holdings	BL has 1855			BOD has 1861
	GL has 1856			NLS has 1861
	IHR has 1855			ULC has 1861
	WSL has 1855			WSL has 1861

REF	**1432**		REF	**1435**
Title	**The Post Office Directory of Birmingham with its suburbs and the principal towns of the Hardware District**		Title	**Rogers's Rugby Family Almanack and Year Book of Useful Information**
Dates	1856,1860,1863,1865,1867,1869		Dates	1861-1864
Publisher	Kelly & Co		Publisher	Rogers, T.
Printer	Kelly & Co		Printer	Rogers, T.
Place	London		Place	Rugby
Type	GE TR		Type	TR
Map scale	NS		Map scale	–
Notes	Cont'd as 1441		Notes	Cont'd as 1443
Library	BCL has 1856,1860,1865,1867		Library	GL has 1861
holdings	BL has 1856,1865,1867,1869		holdings	RUG all
	BPH has 1863,1867			
	CLM has 1856,1865,1867,1869		REF	**1436**
	GL has 1869		Title	**The Business Directory of Birmingham**
	NLS has 1867		Dates	1862
	SOG has 1865		Publisher	Morris, J.S.C.
	ULC has 1856		Printer	Morris, J.S.C.
			Place	London
REF	**1433**		Type	TR
Title	**General and Commercial Directory of the Borough of Birmingham**		Map scale	–
Dates	1858		Library	BCL
Publisher	Dix, W.H. and Co		holdings	BL
Printer	Upton, J.			BOD
Place	Birmingham			CLM
Type	GE TR			NLS
Map scale	–			SOG
Library	BCL			
holdings	GL			
	IHR			
	SOG			
	WLV			
	WSL			

REF **1437**
Title **Tait's Household Rugby Almanack**
Dates 1862-1884,1886-1888,1890-1894
Publisher Tait & Sons
Printer Tait & Sons
Place Rugby
Type CM
Map scale –
Notes Cont'd as 1460. 1879-1884 editions entitled 'Tait & Hopewell's Rugby Almanack'. 1885-1894: 'J. Hopewell's Rugby Almanack'.
Library BL has 1893
holdings GL has 1864,1869,1876,1879, 1881,1884,1885,1887,1893
RUG all

REF **1438**
Title **Jones's Mercantile Directory of Birmingham**
Dates 1865
Publisher Jones & Proud
Printer Jones & Proud
Place London
Type CM TR
Map scale –
Library BCL

REF **1439**
Title **C. Buchanan & Co's Postal and Commercial Directory of Coventry, Leamington, Warwick, Kenilworth, Nuneaton and District**
Dates 1868
Publisher Buchanan, C. & Co
Printer Corns & Bartleet
Place Portsmouth
Type CM TR
Map scale –
Library COV

REF **1440**
Title **Hulley's Birmingham Directory**
Dates 1870,1872,1876,1881,1886
Publisher Hulley, J.
Printer Hulley, J.
Place Birmingham
Type GE TR
Map scale –
Library BCL all
holdings BL has 1886
BOD has 1876-1886
CLM has 1870
GL not 1876,1886
NLS has 1876-1886
ULC has 1876-1886
WSL has 1870

REF **1441**
Title **Kelly's Directory of Birmingham**
Dates 1870-1872,1874,1875,1876, 1878-1880,1882-1884,1886,1888, 1890,1892,1894-1950
Publisher Kelly & Co
Printer Kelly & Co
Place London
Type GE TR
Map scale 1:10560
Library BCL has 1871,1872,1875,1876,
holdings 1878,1879,1882-1913,1915-1950
BIS has 1926,1929
BL has 1871,1874-1883,1886, 1890,1891,1893-1895, 1897-1907,1909-1915, 1917-1950
BOD has 1871,1874,1878,1879, 1883,1886,1890,1894,1895, 1897-1907,1909-1921,1923, 1924
BPH has 1875,1883,1895,1898, 1902,1905,1906,1908,1910, 1913-1916,1918-1921,1923, 1925,1927,1929-1931,1933, 1934,1938,1939,1941-1950
CLE has 1947
CLM has 1870,1882-1886,1890, 1894,1895,1897,1898, 1907-1915,1917-1932,1934, 1936-1950
COV has 1934,1940,1946,1950
GL has 1874-1950
IHR has 1931
MLG has 1880-1898,1902,1906, 1914,1915,1917-1950
NLS has 1871-1879,1882-1950
NLW has 1911,1915,1920, 1928-1930,1932,1935,1936, 1939,1949,1950
SOG has 1904,1934,1944
ULC has 1874-1879,1882-1886, 1890,1891,1893-1895, 1899-1907,1909-1911,1920, 1922,1925-1950
12

REF **1442**
Title **Beck's Directory for Leamington**
Dates 1870-1887,1890-1897
Publisher Beck, J.
Printer –
Place Leamington
Type GE TR
Map scale –
Notes Title varies.
Library COV has 1882
holdings GL has 1894
LEA not 1894
WRK not 1894

REF **1443**
Title **Kenning's Illustrated Rugby Family Almanack**
Dates 1871-1900
Publisher Kenning, J.W.
Printer Kenning, J.W.
Place Rugby
Type ST
Map scale –
Notes Cont'd from 1435
Library GL has 1874-1900
holdings RUG has 1871-1890

REF **1444**
Title **Percy, Butcher & Co's Stratford-upon-Avon, Leamington and Warwick Directory**
Dates 1873
Publisher Percy, Butcher & Co
Printer Percy, Butcher & Co
Place London
Type CT CM
Map scale –
Library BL
holdings LEA
WRK

REF **1445**
Title **Curtis & Beamish's Directory of Coventry**
Dates 1874,1881
Publisher Curtis & Beamish
Printer Curtis & Beamish
Place Coventry
Type GE TR
Map scale –
Notes See 1455
Library BCL has 1874
holdings COV all

REF **1446**
Title **Francis White & Co's Commercial and Trades Directory of Birmingham**
Dates 1875
Publisher White, F.
Printer White, F.
Place Sheffield
Type GE TR
Map scale –
Library BCL
holdings BL
COV

REF **1447**
Title **Palmer's Stratford-on-Avon Almanack and Directory**
Dates 1875
Publisher Palmer, A.
Printer Palmer, A.
Place Stratford-on-Avon
Type CM
Map scale –
Library BOD

REF **1448**
Title **Sutton & Co's Directory of Birmingham**
Dates 1876
Publisher Sutton & Co
Printer Sutton & Co
Place Birmingham
Type GE TR
Map scale –
Library BCL

REF **1449**
Title **Charles Cooper & Co's Street Directory of Birmingham**
Dates 1877,1878
Publisher Cooper, C. & Co
Printer –
Place Birmingham
Type SL
Map scale NS
Notes With timetable (omnibuses & trams)
Library BCL

REF **1450**
Title **Hulley's Directory of the Hardware District**
Dates 1879,1889
Publisher Hulley, J.
Printer –
Place Birmingham
Type CM TR
Map scale –
Library BCL has 1889
holdings WLV has 1879

REF **1451**
Title **Dirctory of Coventry, Leamington, Kenilworth, Nuneaton and Warwick including the towns and villages within 12 miles of Coventry**
Dates 1880
Publisher Stevens, G. & Co
Printer Stevens, G. & Co
Place London
Type CT CM
Map scale –
Library BL
holdings COV
LEA

REF **1452**
Title **Spennell's Annual Directory Royal Leamington Spa, Warwick and District**
Dates 1880-1917,1919-1927
Publisher Spennell, R.
Printer Spennell, R.
Place Warwick
Type ST TR
Map scale 1:380160
Notes Title varies, but coverage is largely South Warwickshire & includes Stratford in 1880s and 1890s. Early editions only include Warwick; Leamington included from 1886 onwards.
Library BCL has 1881-1885,1887-1915,
holdings 1917,1919
BL has 1881-1885,1887-1891, 1898,1909-1912,1915
BOD has 1884,1885,1917,1919
COV has 1883,1884,1891,1894, 1896,1908,1910,1911,1926
GL has 1883
LEA not 1880-1882
NLS has 1917,1919
WRK all

REF **1453**
Title **The Birmingham Post Office Directory**
Dates 1882
Publisher Houghton & Co
Printer Houghton & Co
Place Birmingham
Type GE TR
Map scale –
Library BCL

REF **1454**
Title **Coventry Year Book and Directory**
Dates 1883
Publisher Hopper, T.
Printer Hopper, T.
Place Coventry
Type CT TR
Map scale –
Notes Map missing from COV volume
Library COV

REF **1455**
Title **A New Directory of the City and suburbs of Coventry**
Dates 1886
Publisher Mills, Curtis & Beamish
Printer Mills, Curtis & Beamish
Place Coventry
Type GE TR
Map scale 1:9600
Notes See 1445
Library BCL
holdings BL
BOD
COV
ULC

REF **1456**
Title **The Midland Times and Rugby Gazette Directory and Official Year Book**
Dates 1886-1900,1902-1908
Publisher Midland Times and Rugby Gazette
Printer Midland Times and Rugby Gazette
Place Rugby
Type ST
Map scale –
Library COV has 1905
holdings GL has 1902-1908
RUG all

REF **1457**
Title **Sutton's Postal Directory of Aston Manor, Erdington, Gravelly Hill & neighbourhood**
Dates 1890
Publisher Sutton, F.
Printer Hunt & Randall
Place Aston Cross
Type CM TR
Map scale –
Library BCL

REF **1458**
Title **The Edgbastonia Directory**
Dates 1893-1896,1898,1900-1922,1925, 1927,1929,1933
Publisher Edgbastonia
Printer Edgbastonia
Place Birmingham
Type GE TR
Map scale –
Library BCL all
holdings BL has 1893-1895,1920-1925, 1929

REF **1459**
Title **Coventry Complete Directory**
Dates 1894,1896,1898,1903,1905,1907, 1909
Publisher Robertson & Gray
Printer Robertson & Gray
Place Coventry
Type GE TR
Map scale –
Library BCL has 1909
holdings COV all

REF **1460**
Title **The Advertiser Rugby Almanack**
Dates 1895-1950
Publisher The Rugby Advertiser Ltd
Printer The Rugby Advertiser Ltd
Place Rugby
Type GE
Map scale 1:10560
Notes Map included from early 1900s. Cont'd from 1437. 1916-1925 editions entitled 'The Advertiser Rugby Directory'. 1926-1950: 'Rugby Directory'.
Library BCL has 1927
holdings BL has 1900,1909-1950
COV has 1927,1947
GL has 1900,1916,1917,1938, 1948,1949
[282] RUG all

REF **1461**
Title **Peck's Circular Trades' Directory to the Manufacturers of Birmingham & District**
Dates 1896,1899,1901,1903,1905-1916, 1918,1920,1922,1923
Publisher Peck, W.E.
Printer Peck, W.E.
Place Birmingham
Type SP
Map scale –
Notes Alph. & TR sections
Library BCL has 1896-1905,1907-1913,
holdings 1916,1923
BL not 1896,1901,1903
WLV has 1896

REF **1462**
Title **Everson's Moseley, King's Heath & Balsall Heath Directory and Year Book**
Dates 1896,1901
Publisher Bill, C.
Printer Hudson & son
Place Birmingham
Type ST
Map scale –
Library BCL

REF **1463**
Title **Lovett's Harborne, Selly Oak and Northfield Local Directory and Timetable**
Dates 1901
Publisher Lovett & Co
Printer Lovett & Co
Place Birmingham
Type GE
Map scale –
Library BCL

REF **1464**
Title **Sutton Coldfield, Erdington & District Directory**
Dates 1901
Publisher Beaumont & Co
Printer –
Place Birmingham
Type GE
Map scale 1:15840
Notes Map scale approx.
Library BCL
holdings BL
BOD
NLS
ULC

REF **1465**
Title **Spennell's (Annual) Directory of the City of Coventry and District**
Dates 1904,1912,1919,1921
Publisher Spennell, R.
Printer Spennell, R.
Place Warwick
Type GE
Map scale –
Notes 1919,1921 published by P. Jones. Cont'd as 1471.
Library BCL has 1912,1921
holdings BL has 1904
COV all
GL has 1912

REF **1466**
Title **Spennell's Coventry Directory**
Dates 1911
Publisher Robert Spennell Press
Printer Robert Spennell Press
Place Warwick
Type GE
Map scale –
Library BL
holdings COV

REF **1467**
Title **Spennell's Annual Directory: Rugby with New Bilton, Nuneaton, Bedworth, Hinckley and District**
Dates 1912
Publisher The Robert Spennell Press
Printer The Robert Spennell Press
Place Warwick
Type GE TR
Map scale 1:126720
Library COV

REF **1468**
Title **Birmingham Trades, Traders and Professional Addresses**
Dates 1914,1921,1922
Publisher Bennett & Co
Printer Bennett & Co
Place Birmingham
Type TR
Map scale –
Notes The 1914 edition is undated but bound with 1914 'Bennett's Business Directory for Staffordshire'
Library BCL has 1921,1922
holdings WLV has 1914

REF **1469**
Title **Birmingham & Hardware District Trades' Directory**
Dates 1915-1935,1937-1942,1944
Publisher Town and County Directories Ltd
Printer Macdonald, W. & Co Ltd
Place Edinburgh
Type TR
Map scale 1:1257200
Library BCL all
holdings HBR has 1937
WCL has 1938

REF **1470**
Title **Moseley & King's Heath Directory**
Dates 1924
Publisher Trout, L.E.
Printer Hudson & Son
Place Birmingham
Type GE
Map scale –
Library BCL

REF **1471**
Title **Directory of the City of Coventry and District**
Dates 1924,1926,1929,1931,1933,1935, 1937,1939
Publisher Jones, P. Ltd
Printer Jones, P. Ltd
Place Birmingham
Type GE TR
Map scale 1:10560
Notes Cont'd from 1465. From 1929 published & printed by The Press at Coombelands Ltd, Addlestone.
Library BCL has 1924,1926,1933-1937
holdings BL not 1924,1926
BOD not 1924-1929
BPH has 1937
COV all
GL has 1937,1939
MLG has 1935,1939
NLS not 1924-1929
NLW has 1931,1933
ULC not 1924-1929
WRK has 1939

REF	**1472**
Title	**The Three Towns Directory Nuneaton, Atherstone, Bedworth**
Dates	1926
Publisher	Chronicle Press Ltd
Printer	Chronicle Press Ltd
Place	Nuneaton
Type	GE TR
Map scale	1:10560
Notes	See 1475
Library	COV

REF	**1473**
Title	**Kelly's Directory of Warwick, Leamington Spa, Stratford-upon-Avon, Kenilworth**
Dates	1927-1942,1945,1948,1950
Publisher	Kelly's Directories Ltd
Printer	Kelly's Directories Ltd
Place	London
Type	GE TR
Map scale	1:10560
Library holdings	BCL has 1928-1930,1933,1934, 1936-1950
	BL all
	COV has 1927,1929-1935,1938, 1941,1948
	GL not 1942
	LEA all
	NLW has 1950
	SOG has 1950
	WRK all

REF	**1474**
Title	**Denham's Timetable & Business Directory [Birmingham]**
Dates	1929,1934
Publisher	Railway & Shipping Publishing Co Ltd
Printer	Buckler & Webb
Place	Birmingham
Type	TR
Map scale	–
Library	BCL

REF	**1475**
Title	**The Nuneaton Directory and Commercial List**
Dates	1932,1938
Publisher	Chronicle Co Ltd
Printer	Chronicle Co Ltd
Place	Nuneaton
Type	ST TR
Map scale	1:12000
Notes	Date of 1932 edition uncertain. BL:1932, GL:1933. See 1472.
Library holdings	BCL has 1932
	BL all
	GL all

REF	**1476**
Title	**Wakelin's Street Guide of the City of Birmingham, Smethwick, Coventry, Wolverhampton**
Dates	1933
Publisher	Wakelin, F.H.
Printer	Wakelin, F.H.
Place	Birmingham
Type	SL
Map scale	–
Library	BL

REF	**1477**
Title	**Directory of Coventry Manufacturers**
Dates	1936,1939,1950
Publisher	The Corporation of Coventry
Printer	–
Place	Coventry
Type	TR
Map scale	1:36206
Library holdings	BCL all
	BL not 1939
	BOD not 1939
	MLG not 1939
	NLS has 1950
	ULC not 1939

REF	**1478**
Title	**Buyers' Guide to Birmingham Industries and Commercial Directory**
Dates	1940
Publisher	Brown, A. & Sons
Printer	–
Place	London
Type	TR
Map scale	–
Library	BCL

REF **1479**
Title **The Birmingham Exchange Directory of Members, Subscribers and Representatives**
Dates 1942-1950
Publisher Birmingham Exchange Committee
Printer –
Place Birmingham
Type SP
Map scale –
Notes Alph. & classified sections
Library NLW

WESTMORLAND

REF **1480**
Title **History, Topography and Directory of Westmorland and the Hundreds of Lonsdale and Amounderness in Lancashire**
Dates 1851
Publisher Mannex, P. & Co
Printer Johnson, W.B.
Place Beverley
Type CM
Map scale NS
Library BCL
holdings BIS
CAR
CLM
GL
IHR
LHQ

REF **1481**
Title **History, Topography and Directory of Westmorland**
Dates 1885,1906
Publisher Bulmer, T. & Co
Printer Snape, T. & Co
Place Manchester
Type CM
Map scale 1:158400
Library BOD has 1906
holdings BPH has 1906
CAR has 1906
GL all
IHR has 1885
NLS has 1906
SOG all

WILTSHIRE

REF **1482**
Title **Kelly's Directory of Wiltshire**
Dates 1855,1859,1867,1875,1880,1885, 1890,1895,1899,1903,1907,1911, 1915,1920,1923,1927,1931,1935, 1939
Publisher Kelly & Co
Printer Kelly & Co
Place London
Type GE TR
Map scale 1:221760
Notes See 8
Library BCL has 1875,1890-1939
holdings BIS has 1907,1915,1927,1931, 1939
BL not 1903-1927
BOD not 1859,1875
BPH has 1927,1939
BRL has 1875,1880,1903-1920, 1927,1931,1939
CHI has 1875
CLB has 1939
CLE has 1939
CLM has 1923,1939
CLS has 1923
DCL has 1885,1895,1903,1923
GL all
HRO has 1859,1875,1880,1890, 1895,1903,1907,1915,1920, 1931-1939
IHR has 1923,1939
LCL has 1935
LLB has 1885,1890,1899, 1923-1939
MLG has 1907-1927
NEW has 1939
NLS all
NLW has 1920,1927-1939
PCL has 1895,1911,1931
SAL has 1855,1875-1903,1911, 1915,1927-1939
SCC has 1885,1911-1923,1939
SCL has 1927-1939
SOG has 1859,1867,1895,1899, 1907,1915,1923,1931,1939
SWI has 1855,1880,1890-1903, 1915,1923,1927,1935,1939
TLH has 1875
TRW has 1859,1867,1880, 1889-1939
ULC all
WCS has 1880
WIN has 1880-1890
WRO all

[285]

REF **1483**
Title **J.G. Harrod & Co's Postal and Commercial Directory of Wiltshire**
Dates 1865
Publisher Harrod, J.G. & Co
Printer Danks, T.
Place London
Type CM
Map scale –
Library GL
holdings IHR
SAL Includes DORS

REF **1484**
Title **Gillman's Devizes Public Register, Business Directory and Family Almanack**
Dates 1858,1859,1861,1863-1933
Publisher Gillman, C.
Printer Gillman, C.
Place Devizes
Type ST
Map scale –
Notes Cont'd as 1505. During the 1920s publication was taken over by the Wiltshire Advertiser (Devizes), CT section also included.
Library GL all
holdings SAL has 1869-1875,1882-1892, 1894-1921
SOG has 1879
TRW has 1880-1889,1891-1899, 1926-1932
WRO has 1858,1859,1864-1910, 1912,1914,1922-1933

REF **1485**
Title **The Bradford-on-Avon Annual, Household Almanack, Directory and Advertiser**
Dates 1869,1886-1888,1890-1892,1895
Publisher Rawling, C.
Printer Rawling, C.
Place Bradford-on-Avon
Type CM
Map scale –
Library WRO

REF **1486**
Title **The Swindon and District Illustrated Almanack and Directory**
Dates 1875,1876,1878
Publisher North Wilts Herald
Printer North Wilts Herald
Place Swindon
Type CM
Map scale 1:443520
Notes Cont'd as 1489
Library GL has 1875
holdings SWI has 1876,1878

REF **1487**
Title **Astill & Co's Original Swindon Almanack and Directory**
Dates 1877,1878
Publisher Astill, R. & Co
Printer Astill, R. & Co
Place Swindon
Type ST
Map scale –
Notes Previous and later editions do not contain directory sections (SWI).
Library SWI

REF **1488**
Title **Lucy's Marlborough and District Directory**
Dates 1879,1883,1897,1901,1903,1904, 1906-1934
Publisher Lucy & Co
Printer Lucy & Co
Place Marlborough
Type CM
Map scale –
Notes Cont'd by 1507
Library BL has 1914-1934
holdings SWI has 1914
TRW has 1910,1915,1920,1925, 1933
WRO has 1879-1915,1919-1926, 1928-1931,1933

REF	**1489**
Title	**The North Wilts, Borough of Cricklade & District Directory**
Dates	1879-1923
Publisher	North Wilts Herald
Printer	North Wilts Herald
Place	Swindon
Type	CT
Map scale	1:506880
Notes	After 1885 entitled 'The North Wilts and District Directory'. 1923 edition published by the Swindon Press. Cont'd from 1486, cont'd as 1502
Library holdings	BL not 1879-1888 GL has 1888 SWI has 1879-1898,1901-1904, 1906-1913,1915-1923

REF	**1490**
Title	**Smith's Highworth Almanac, Diary & Directory**
Dates	1888
Publisher	Smith, J.J.
Printer	Smith, J.J.
Place	Highworth
Type	CM
Map scale	–
Library	WRO

REF	**1491**
Title	**Collins's Directory of Trowbridge and neighbourhood and almanack**
Dates	1888,1893-1900,1902-1907
Publisher	Collins, W.
Printer	Collins, W.
Place	Trowbridge
Type	CT CM
Map scale	–
Notes	Cont'd by 1498
Library holdings	SOG has 1888 WRO not 1888

REF	**1492**
Title	**Heath's Calne Almanack and Directory**
Dates	1888-1891,1894,1896,1898,1901, 1902,1930
Publisher	Heath, A.
Printer	Heath, A.
Place	Calne
Type	ST
Map scale	–
Notes	Title varies
Library holdings	TRW not 1930 WRO has 1930

REF	**1493**
Title	**F. Mundy & Co's Street & Trade Directory of the City of Salisbury and District**
Dates	1891
Publisher	Mundy, F. & Co
Printer	Mundy, F. & Co
Place	Southampton
Type	GE TR
Map scale	–
Library	BL

REF	**1494**
Title	**Dotesio's Illustrated Commercial Diary, Almanack and Directory [Bradford-on-Avon]**
Dates	1894-1902,1908,1910-1912,1914
Publisher	Dotesio, W.
Printer	Dotesio, W.
Place	Bradford-on-Avon
Type	GE
Map scale	–
Notes	Earlier editions exist, but are only almanacks and do not contain directory sections
Library	WRO

REF	**1495**
Title	**Directory of Salisbury and District**
Dates	1897
Publisher	Langmead & Evans
Printer	Western Gazette Co
Place	Salisbury
Type	GE TR
Map scale	–
Library holdings	BL SAL TRW

REF	**1496**
Title	**Brown's Directory of Salisbury**
Dates	1906,1907,1909-1916
Publisher	Brown & Co
Printer	Western Gazette Co
Place	Salisbury
Type	GE TR
Map scale	–
Notes	Cont'd as 1501
Library holdings	BL all SAL has 1912 TRW has 1913

REF	**1497**		REF	**1500**
Title	**Coleman's Trowbridge, Bradford and Westbury Directories**		Title	**Riddick's Directory of Malmesbury and Adjoining Villages**
Dates	1906-1908		Dates	1922,1925,1930,1931,1934,1937, 1938
Publisher	Coleman, G.			
Printer	–		Publisher	Riddick, J.
Place	Trowbridge		Printer	Riddick, J.
Type	TR		Place	Malmesbury
Map scale	–		Type	CT
Library	WRO		Map scale	–
			Notes	Title varies
REF	**1498**		Library	GL has 1938
Title	**West Wilts Directory: Trowbridge, Bradford-on-Avon, Melksham, Mere, Westbury, Warminster**		holdings	TRW all

REF	**1501**
Title	**Directory of Salisbury and the Neighbourhood**
Dates	1908,1909,1911-1916,1921-1936, 1938-1940,1948-1950

REF **1501**
Title **Directory of Salisbury and the Neighbourhood**
Dates 1923,1925
Publisher Salisbury & District Chamber of Commerce
Printer Bennett Bros
Place Salisbury
Type GE
Map scale –
Notes Cont'd from 1496, cont'd as 1503
Library BL has 1923
holdings SAL has 1925

REF **1498**
Title **West Wilts Directory: Trowbridge, Bradford-on-Avon, Melksham, Mere, Westbury, Warminster**
Dates 1908,1909,1911-1916,1921-1936, 1938-1940,1948-1950
Publisher Lansdown, B. & Sons Ltd
Printer Lansdown, B. & Sons Ltd
Place Trowbridge
Type GE
Map scale –
Notes Cont'd from 1491. Early editions were entitled 'Collin's Almanack with West Wilts Directory'. After 1923 published by the Wiltshire Times.
Library GL has 1938,1939,1848,1949
holdings TRW has 1939,1940,1949,1950
WRO has 1908,1909,1911-1916, 1921-1936,1938-1940, 1948-1950

REF **1502**
Title **The Swindon and District Directory and Year Book**
Dates 1924-1940,1947-1949
Publisher Swindon Press Ltd
Printer Swindon Press Ltd
Place Swindon
Type GE
Map scale –
Notes Cont'd from 1489
Library BL all
holdings GL has 1936-1938,1947-1949
SWI all
WRO has 1947

REF **1499**
Title **The Warminster and District Directory**
Dates 1914,1937-1939
Publisher Coates & Parker
Printer Coates & Parker
Place Warminster
Type GE
Map scale –
Notes 1914 edition published by Coates
Library GL has 1938
holdings WRO not 1938

REF	**1503**
Title	**Kelly's Directory of Salisbury and neighbourhood**
Dates	1927,1929,1931,1933,1935,1937, 1939,1941,1944,1947,1950
Publisher	Kelly's Directories Ltd
Printer	Kelly's Directories Ltd
Place	London
Type	GE TR
Map scale	1:15840
Notes	Cont'd from 1501
Library	BCL has 1927
holdings	BL all
	CLM has 1929-1935
	GL all
	NLW has 1950
	SAL has 1927-1931,1935-1950
	SWI has 1941,1950
	TRW has 1927,1931
	WRO has 1935,1950

REF	**1504**
Title	**Taylor's Directory Malmesbury, Cirencester & District, Purton, Cricklade, Wootton Bassett**
Dates	1933
Publisher	Taylor & Sons
Printer	Taylor & Sons
Place	Minety
Type	CM
Map scale	–
Library	TRW

REF	**1505**
Title	**Devizes & District Almanack & Directory**
Dates	1934-1940,1947-1950
Publisher	Wiltshire Gazette Ltd
Printer	The Swindon Press
Place	Devizes
Type	ST
Map scale	–
Notes	Cont'd from 1482
Library	GL not 1940,1947
holdings	SWI has 1939,1949,1950
	TRW all
	WRO has 1934,1936-1939, 1947-1949

REF	**1506**
Title	**Westbury Directory**
Dates	1935,1938-1940
Publisher	Holloway, A.E. & H.
Printer	–
Place	Westbury
Type	GE
Map scale	–
Library	WRO

REF	**1507**
Title	**The Marlborough and District Directory**
Dates	1937-1943,1945,1948-1950
Publisher	Gale, W.
Printer	Gale, W.
Place	Marlborough
Type	GE
Map scale	–
Notes	Cont'd from 1488
Library	GL has 1938,1948-1950
holdings	TRW has 1937,1942,1948,1950
	WRO all

[289]

WORCESTERSHIRE

REF	**1508**
Title	**Kelly's Directory of Worcestershire**
Dates	1850,1854,1860,1868,1872,1876, 1880,1884,1888,1892,1896,1900, 1904,1908,1912,1916,1921,1924, 1928,1932,1936,1940
Publisher	Kelly & Co
Printer	Kelly & Co
Place	London
Type	GE TR
Map scale	1:253440
Notes	See 6
Library holdings	BCL not 1850
	BIS has 1908,1921-1928,1936, 1940
	BL has 1868-1921,1928
	BOD not 1868
	BPH has 1868,1888,1916,1924, 1940
	CLB has 1940
	CLE has 1912
	CLM has 1924,1928,1940
	COV has 1884,1888,1932,1936
	GL has 1868,1876-1928
	HBR has 1850,1854
	HPL has 1896
	IHR has 1908,1912,1940
	LEA has 1872-1884,1892,1900, 1908-1921,1928,1932,1940
	MLG has 1880,1921-1928
	NLS has 1854,1860,1868, 1932-1940
	NLW has 1916,1924,1928,1936
	SCL has 1928-1940
	SOG has 1860,1880,1884,1896, 1916,1921,1932
	ULC all
	WCL has 1865-1876,1884-1940
	WLV has 1850,1860,1876, 1932-1940
	WRK has 1928,1940
	WSL has 1850-1860,1908,1936
	YCL has 1940

REF	**1509**
Title	**M. Billing's Directory & Gazetteer of the County of Worcester**
Dates	1855
Publisher	Billing, M.
Printer	Billing, M.
Place	Birmingham
Type	GE TR
Map scale	–
Notes	NORTON 777
Library holdings	BCL
	BL
	GL
	SOG
	WCL

REF	**1510**
Title	**History, Topography and Directory of Worcestershire**
Dates	1860
Publisher	Cassey, E. & Co
Printer	Bailey, W.
Place	Preston
Type	CM
Map scale	1:190080
Library holdings	BCL
	GL
	WCL

REF	**1511**
Title	**Littlebury's Directory and Gazetteer of the County of Worcester**
Dates	1873,1879
Publisher	Littlebury, J.
Printer	Littlebury, J.
Place	Worcester
Type	CM
Map scale	1:126720
Library holdings	BCL has 1873
	GL all
	IHR has 1873
	SOG all
	WCL all

REF	**1512**
Title	**General and Topographical Directory of Worcester**
Dates	1881
Publisher	Owen, W.E. & Co
Printer	'?'
Place	'?'
Type	CM TR
Map scale	–
Notes	T/P missing when rebound and 'Owen' is stated to be the publisher. It is likely that this directory was published by W.E. Owen & Co at Leicester.
Library	WCL

REF	**1513**
Title	**Worcestershire Directory and Buyers' Guide**
Dates	1905,1907,1910,1911,1913,1915, 1916,1922-1926,1929-1938
Publisher	Cope, E.F. & Co
Printer	Cope, E.F. & Co
Place	Walsall
Type	TR
Map scale	–
Library	BL all
holdings	WCL has 1933,1934

REF	**1514**
Title	**Lascelles & Co's Directory and Gazetteer of the City of Worcester and Neighbourhood**
Dates	1851
Publisher	Lascelles & Co
Printer	Stanley, J.
Place	Worcester
Type	CM TR
Map scale	–
Notes	NORTON 785. GL edition has Kidderminster in title.
Library	GL
holdings	IHR
	WCL

REF	**1515**
Title	**Littlebury's Directory of the City of Worcester**
Dates	1869
Publisher	Littlebury, W.
Printer	Collingridge, W.
Place	London
Type	GE TR
Map scale	–
Library	BL
holdings	GL
	WCL

REF	**1516**
Title	**Percy, Butcher & Co's City of Worcester and Malvern Directory**
Dates	1873
Publisher	Percy, Butcher & Co
Printer	–
Place	London
Type	CM
Map scale	–
Library	WCL

REF	**1517**
Title	**Littlebury's Guide to Worcester and its neighbourhood**
Dates	1882
Publisher	Littlebury & Spencer
Printer	Littlebury & Spencer
Place	Worcester
Type	SL TR
Map scale	1:12870
Library	WCL

REF	**1518**
Title	**Littlebury's Street Directory of the City of Worcester**
Dates	1884
Publisher	Littlebury & Co
Printer	Littlebury & Co
Place	Worcester
Type	ST
Map scale	–
Library	WCL

REF	**1519**
Title	**Littlebury's Directory of Worcester and District**
Dates	1885,1905,1907,1908,1910,1912, 1915,1922
Publisher	Littlebury & Co
Printer	Littlebury & Co
Place	Worcester
Type	GE TR
Map scale	1:10666
Notes	1910 & after entitled 'Littlebury's Directory of the City of Worcester'
Library	BL has 1885,1910-1922
holdings	GL has 1915
	WCL all

REF	**1520**
Title	**Blocksidge's Illustrated Dudley Almanack, Diary and Directory**
Dates	1896
Publisher	Blocksidge, E.
Printer	Blocksidge, E.
Place	Dudley
Type	CM
Map scale	–
Library	ULC

REF	**1521**
Title	**Littlebury's Annual**
Dates	1896-1898
Publisher	Littlebury & Co
Printer	Littlebury & Co
Place	Worcester
Type	ST
Map scale	–
Notes	Contains street directory for Worcester & diary section
Library	WCL

REF	**1522**
Title	**Smith's Droitwich Borough Almanack and Directory**
Dates	1897
Publisher	Smith, M.
Printer	Smith, M.
Place	Droitwich
Type	ST
Map scale	–
Library	WCL

REF	**1523**
Title	**Stevens' Annual of Malvern & District**
Dates	1898-1916,1920-1928,1930,1933
Publisher	Stevens & Co
Printer	Stevens & Co
Place	Malvern
Type	GE TR
Map scale	1:10560
Library holdings	BCL has 1924
	BL all
	GL has 1914
	ULC has 1898
	WCL has 1910

REF	**1524**
Title	**Littlebury's Worcester Directory**
Dates	1900
Publisher	Littlebury & Co
Printer	Littlebury & Co
Place	Worcester
Type	GE TR
Map scale	–
Library	WCL

REF	**1525**
Title	**Redditch and District Directory**
Dates	1900
Publisher	Beaumont & Company
Printer	–
Place	Birmingham
Type	CM
Map scale	–
Library	BOD

REF	**1526**
Title	**Worcester, Hereford and District Trades' Directory**
Dates	1906,1919
Publisher	Town and County Directories Ltd
Printer	Macdonald, W. & Co Ltd
Place	Edinburgh
Type	TR
Map scale	–
Library	WCL

REF	**1527**
Title	**Fearnside & Martin's Pershore Almanac, Diary and Directory**
Dates	1909
Publisher	Fearnside & Martin
Printer	Fearnside & Martin
Place	Pershore
Type	CT
Map scale	–
Library	WCL

REF	**1528**
Title	**W. & H. Smith's Household Almanack and Evesham & District Directory**
Dates	1911,1939,1947
Publisher	Smith, W. & H. Ltd
Printer	Smith, W. & H. Ltd
Place	Evesham
Type	GE
Map scale	–
Library	BOD has 1911
holdings	GL has 1939,1947

REF	1529
Title	**Bromsgrove Almanack and Directory**
Dates	1918,1926,1935-1947,1949
Publisher	Bromsgrove Messenger
Printer	Bromsgrove Messenger
Place	Bromsgrove
Type	CM
Map scale	–
Library	BCL

REF	1530
Title	**Kelly's Directory of Worcester & Neighbourhood**
Dates	1928,1930,1937
Publisher	Kelly's Directories Ltd
Printer	Kelly's Directories Ltd
Place	London
Type	GE TR
Map scale	1:253440
Library	BCL
holdings	BL
	GL
	WCL

REF	1531
Title	**Kelly's Directory of Great Malvern & Neighbourhood**
Dates	1936,1938,1940,1942,1950
Publisher	Kelly's Directories Ltd
Printer	Kelly's Directories Ltd
Place	London
Type	GE TR
Map scale	1:10560
Library	BCL has 1942,1950
holdings	BL all
	CLM has 1950
	GL all
	HPL has 1950
	NLW has 1950
	SOG has 1950
	WCL has 1938,1950

YORKSHIRE

REF	1532
Title	**Collinson, Burton & Co's West Riding Worsted Directory**
Dates	1851
Publisher	Collinson, Burton & Co
Printer	Burton, D.
Place	Bradford
Type	SP
Map scale	–
Notes	Arranged by towns with alph. & classified lists for larger places. See 31.
Library	BRD
holdings	GL
	LCL

REF	1533
Title	**Post Office Directory of Yorkshire**
Dates	1857
Publisher	Kelly & Co
Printer	Kelly & Co
Place	London
Type	GE TR
Map scale	1:6336
Library	BL
holdings	BOD
	BRD
	CLM
	GL
	HUD
	LCL
	SCL
	SOG
	ULC

REF	1534	REF	1535
Title	**Post Office Directory of the West Riding of Yorkshire with the city of York**	Title	**Kelly's Directory of the West Riding of Yorkshire**
Dates	1861,1867	Dates	1871,1877,1881,1889,1893,1897, 1901,1904,1908,1912,1917,1922, 1927,1936
Publisher	Kelly & Co	Publisher	Kelly & Co
Printer	Kelly & Co	Printer	Kelly & Co
Place	London	Place	London
Type	GE TR	Type	GE TR
Map scale	1:6336	Map scale	1:6336
Notes	Cont'd as 1535	Notes	1871 & 1877 editions entitled 'Post Office Directory of the West Riding of Yorkshire'. Cont'd from 1534
Library holdings	BL all BOD all BRD all CLM has 1867 DON has 1867 GL has 1867 HFX has 1861 LCL all NLS all SOG has 1861 ULC all YCL all	Library holdings	BCL has 1893-1936 BIS has 1936 BL all BOD not 1917 BPH has 1881,1893,1901,1912, 1917,1922,1936 BRD has 1871,1877,1893,1897, 1908,1917,1922,1936 CL has 1936 CLB has 1936 CLE has 1936 CLM not 1936 DAR has 1904,1927,1936 DON has 1936, & extracts from 1877,1889,1893,1908,1917, 1927 GL not 1893 HFX has 1871,1877,1889,1893, 1908,1922-1936 HUD has 1901,1904,1912-1936 IHR has 1927 LCL not 1871 MID has 1927,1936 MLG has 1893-1936 NLS all NLW has 1912,1936 SCL has 1871,1881,1922,1927, 1936 SOG has 1892,1936 ULC all WAR has 1936 YCL not 1871

REF	1536
Title	**Kelly's Directory of the North and East Ridings of Yorkshire with the city of York**
Dates	1872,1879,1889,1893,1897,1901, 1905,1909,1913,1921,1925,1929, 1933,1937
Publisher	Kelly & Co
Printer	Kelly & Co
Place	London
Type	GE TR
Map scale	NS
Notes	1872, 1879 editions entitled 'Post Office Directory of the North and East Ridings of Yorkshire with the city of York'. 1937 edition does not include York.
Library holdings	BCL has 1893-1933
	BIS has 1933
	BL all
	BOD all
	BPH has 1929,1937
	BRD has 1937
	CLB has 1937
	CLE has 1937
	CLH all (1889 E.R. only)
	CLM not 1905
	CLN has 1937
	DAR has 1872,1889-1909,1925, 1933,1937
	DUR has 1937
	GL all
	IHR has 1905,1937
	LCL has 1879,1897,1901,1929, 1933,1937
	MID not 1872
	MLG not 1889
	NLS not 1913
	NLW has 1913,1921,1929,1937
	SCL has 1929-1937
	SOG has 1872,1909,1937
	ULC all
	YCL all

REF	1537
Title	**Slater's Royal National Commercial Directory of (the West Riding of) Yorkshire**
Dates	1875,1887,1891
Publisher	Slater, I.
Printer	Slater, I.
Place	Manchester
Type	GE TR
Map scale	1:506880
Notes	1891 title includes West Riding
Library holdings	BL not 1891
	BOD has 1891
	BRD has 1875
	CLM not 1891
	DAR has 1875
	GL has 1891
	HFX has 1875,1887
	LCL has 1887,1891
	MID has 1875 (dated 1873)
	NLS all
	ULC has 1875

REF	1538
Title	**The Yorkshire Textile Directory**
Dates	1883,1885-1950
Publisher	Worrall, J.
Printer	Worrall, J.
Place	Oldham
Type	SP
Map scale	—
Notes	Arranged alph. by place with a classified section for each place
Library holdings	BL all
	BOD not 1883,1943
	BRD has 1916,1925,1932-1950
	CLM has 1911,1912,1914-1916, 1919,1921-1932,1934, 1936-1938,1941,194-
	HUD has 1910-1916,1918-1920, 1923-1928,1930,1931,1934, 1935,1938,1941,1942,1944, 1945,1947-1950
	LCL has 1900,1945-1950
	MLG has 1908,1909,1911, 1915-1921,1930,1938,1941, 1945-1947,1949
	NLS not 1898,1904,1906,1908, 1927
	NLW has 1928-1942,1944-1950
	ULC has 1892-1950

REF **1539**
Title **Deacon's Court Guide, Gazetteer and County Blue Book ... of Yorkshire**
Dates 1883,1900,1901
Publisher Deacon, C.W. & Co
Printer Deacon, C.W. & Co
Place London
Type CT
Map scale –
Notes 1900: West Riding. 1901: North & East Ridings
Library BOD has 1900
holdings DON has 1900
GL all
HFX has 1883
IHR has 1900
LCL has 1883,1901
NLS has 1900
SOG all
ULC has 1900
YCL all

REF **1540**
Title **The Yorkshire Textile Directory (Pocket Edition)**
Dates 1889,1895-1909,1911-1914, 1920-1942
Publisher Worrall, J.
Printer Worrall, J.
Place Oldham
Type SP
Map scale –
Notes Smaller edition of 1538
Library BL all
holdings LCL has 1914

REF **1541**
Title **History, Topography and Directory of North Yorkshire**
Dates 1890
Publisher Bulmer, T. & Co
Printer Snape, T. & Co
Place Preston
Type GE TR
Map scale 1:380160
Library GL
holdings BRD
LCL
MID
SOG
YCL

REF **1542**
Title **History, Topography and Directory of East Yorkshire**
Dates 1890,1892
Publisher Bulmer, T.
Printer Snape, T.
Place Preston
Type GE TR
Map scale –
Library BL not 1890
holdings CL has 1892
GL all
YCL has 1892

REF **1543**
Title **Hanson's Directory of the Musicians, Music Trades, Dancing Masters, Elocutionists and Entertainers in Yorkshire**
Dates 1894
Publisher West Riding Advertising Agency
Printer –
Place Leeds
Type SP
Map scale –
Notes 'List of Music Societies, Bands, Newspapers, Printers etc. in every town'
Library LCL

REF **1544**
Title **Robinson's Business Directory for Yorkshire**
Dates 1904
Publisher Robinson, J. & D. Ltd
Printer Robinson, J. & D. Ltd
Place Leeds
Type GE TR
Map scale –
Library BL
holdings LCL
NLS
YCL

REF **1545**
Title **Mid-Yorkshire Directory of Manufacturers and Merchants and Trade Annual**
Dates 1910
Publisher West Riding ABC Publishing Co
Printer West Riding ABC Publishing Co
Place Leeds
Type TR
Map scale –
Library BL
holdings BOD
HUD
NLS
ULC

REF **1546**
Title **The Yorkshire Federation of Building Trade Employers' Official Directory**
Dates 1913
Publisher Yorkshire Federation of Building Trade Employers (?)
Printer –
Place Leeds
Type SP
Map scale –
Notes Bibliographic details uncertain. Alph. list of places with Building Trades Federations, classified list of members for each.
Library LCL

REF **1547**
Title **Yorkshire Directory**
Dates 1933-1940
Publisher Aubrey & Co
Printer Aubrey & Co
Place Walsall
Type TR
Map scale –
Library BL all
holdings HFX One undated volume
HUD has 1933,1936

REF **1548**
Title **Charlton & Company's Directory of Huddersfield, Leeds, Dewsbury and the adjacent villages**
Dates 1850
Publisher Charlton & Company
Printer Roebuck, D.I.
Place Leeds
Type GE TR
Map scale 1:8712
Notes NORTON 815
Library HUD

REF **1549**
Title **Directory of Halifax, Huddersfield, Holmfirth and adjacent villages**
Dates 1850
Publisher Collinson, Burton & Co
Printer Burton, D.
Place Bradford
Type CM TR
Map scale –
Notes NORTON 813. Publisher uncertain.
Library HFX

REF **1550**
Title **Ibbetson's General and Classified Directory, Street List and History of Bradford**
Dates 1850
Publisher Ibbetson, J.
Printer Ibbetson, J.
Place Bradford
Type CM TR
Map scale 1:19200
Notes NORTON 811
Library BRD
holdings IHR

REF **1551**
Title **Freebody's Directory of Kingston-upon-Hull**
Dates 1851
Publisher Freebody, T.
Printer Pulleyn, J.
Place Hull
Type GE TR
Map scale –
Notes NORTON 831
Library BOD
holdings CLH

REF **1552**
Title **Slade and Roebuck's Directory of Leeds**
Dates 1851
Publisher Slade & Roebuck
Printer Mitchell, C.
Place Leeds
Type GE TR
Map scale –
Notes NORTON 845
Library BL
holdings GL
LCL

REF	**1553**		REF	**1555**

REF **1553**
Title **General Directory and Topography of Kingston-upon-Hull and the City of York**
Dates 1851,1858,1859
Publisher White, F.
Printer Blurton, J.
Place Sheffield
Type GE TR
Map scale –
Notes NORTON 801 (1851). 1859 edition entitled 'General Directory and Topography of Kingston-upon-Hull and the City of York with Beverley, Bridlington, Driffield, ... Great Grimsby, Barton, Brigg, Gainsborough etc'.
Library BL has 1851,1858
holdings CLH all
GL has 1851,1858
IHR has 1851,1858
LCL has 1851
YCL has 1851,1858

REF **1554**
Title **Gazetteer and General Directory of Sheffield**
Dates 1852
Publisher White, W.
Printer Leader, R.
Place Sheffield
Type GE
Map scale –
Notes NORTON 803
Library GL
holdings HFX
IHR
SCL
YCL

REF **1555**
Title **Directory and Topography of the Boroughs of Leeds, Bradford, Halifax, Huddersfield and Wakefield (White's Clothing District Directory)**
Dates 1853,1854,1857,1858,1861,1866, 1870,1875,1881,1887,1894
Publisher White, W.
Printer Leader, R.
Place Sheffield
Type CM TR
Map scale –
Notes NORTON 804 (1853) 806 (1854). 1853 edition reprinted in 1969 by David & Charles. White also published parts of this directory separately e.g. Bradford, Halifax & Huddersfield. See under library holdings for details.
Library BCL has 1853 (reprint)
holdings BPH has 1853 (reprint)
BL has 1866,1870,1875,1881, 1887,1894
BOD has 1853,1870,1881,1887, 1894
BRD has 1853,1854,1866-1881, 1894; 1861 (Part II B'ford, K'ley, Bingley, D'bury); 1887 (B'ford)
CLM has 1894
DAR has 1853 (reprint)
DON has 1853
GL not 1875,1894
HFX has 1853 Part I (Bradford, H'fax, H'dfld), 1894 (H'fax)
HUD has 1853,1857,1861,1866, 1881; 1894 (H'dfld)
IHR has 1853,1875
LCL not 1854,1858
NLS has 1866,1870,1881,1887, 1894
NLW has 1853
SCL has 1853,1861,1866
SOG has 1853,1861
ULC has 1870,1881-1894
YCL has 1853

REF **1556**
Title **Post Office Directory of Sheffield with neighbouring towns and villages**
Dates 1854,1865
Publisher Kelly & Co
Printer Kelly & Co
Place London
Type GE TR
Map scale –
Notes NORTON 860
Library BL
holdings BOD
NLS
SCL
ULC

REF **1557**
Title **B.H. Gillbanks & Co's Visitors and Residents' Directory and Gazetteer of Scarborough, Whitby, Bridlington Quay, Filey, Hunmanby, Flamborough &c**
Dates 1855
Publisher Gillbanks, B.H. & Co
Printer Kirk, W.
Place Hull
Type TR
Map scale –
Notes NORTON 809
Library GL
holdings YCL

REF **1558**
Title **Melville & Co's Directory and Gazetteer of the City of York, Kingston-upon-Hull, Beverley etc.**
Dates 1855
Publisher Melville, F.R. & Co
Printer –
Place York
Type CM
Map scale 1:1013760
Notes NORTON 808. See 1559.
Library YCL

REF **1559**
Title **Melville & Co's Directory and Gazetteer of the Town and Borough of Kingston-upon-Hull, Beverley, Market Weighton, Driffield &c &c**
Dates 1855
Publisher Melville & Co
Printer Kirk, W.
Place Hull
Type CM TR
Map scale –
Notes NORTON 807. See 1558.
Library CLH

REF **1560**
Title **Leeds and Neighbourhood Directory and Gazetteer**
Dates 1856
Publisher Gillbanks, B.H. & Co
Printer –
Place Leeds
Type CM TR
Map scale –
Notes Title taken from spine of rebound Xcopy, no title page (LCL)
Library LCL

REF **1561**
Title **Lunds' Bradford Directory**
Dates 1856
Publisher Lund, J. & C.
Printer Firth & Field
Place Bradford
Type GE TR
Map scale –
Library BRD
holdings HFX
LCL

REF **1562**
Title **General Directory and Topography of the Borough of Sheffield**
Dates 1856,1864
Publisher White, W.
Printer Leader, R. & Sons
Place Sheffield
Type GE TR
Map scale –
Library BCL has 1856
holdings BL all
DON has 1864
GL all
SCL has 1856
SOG has 1856

[299]

REF	1563
Title	**Melville & Co's Commercial Directory of Sheffield, Rotherham and the Neighbourhood**
Dates	1859
Publisher	Melville & Co
Printer	Algar, T.S.
Place	Sheffield
Type	CM TR
Map scale	–
Library	GL
holdings	SCL

REF	1564
Title	**General Directory of the Town, Borough and Parish of Sheffield**
Dates	1860
Publisher	White, W.
Printer	Leader, R.
Place	Sheffield
Type	GE TR
Map scale	–
Library	GL has 1860

REF	1565
Title	**White's General and Commercial Directory of Sheffield & Rotherham and Towns within a distance of 7 miles**
Dates	1860,1862,1864,1872,1876,1879, 1884,1889,1891,1893-1898, 1900-1917,1919
Publisher	White, W.
Printer	White, W.
Place	Sheffield
Type	GE TR
Map scale	–
Notes	Cont'd as Kelly's, see 1606
Library	BCL has 1901
holdings	BL has 1876,1884,1893,1894, 1901,1902,1904,1905,1908, 1910
	BOD not 1860-1876,1891,1897, 1913-1915,1917
	BPH has 1876,1906,1916,1919
	BRD has 1911
	CLM has 1898,1901-1903, 1906-1915,1917,1919
	GL has 1876,1884,1893, 1900-1902,1904,1905,1908, 1910
	MLG has 1898,1903,1906,1910, 1911,1914-1917,1919
	NLS has 1876,1884,1893,1897, 1900-1902,1904,1905,1908, 1910
	NLW has 1919
	SCL has 1860-1893,1895,1896, 1900-1919
	ULC has 1884,1889,1893,1895, 1896,1898,1900-1912,1916, 1919
	YCL has 1901

REF	1566
Title	**General and Commercial Directory of the Borough of Sheffield**
Dates	1861,1862
Publisher	White, F. & Co
Printer	Corbitt, C.
Place	Sheffield
Type	GE TR
Map scale	1:31680
Library	BL has 1862
holdings	DON has 1862
	GL all
	HUD has 1862
	NLS has 1862
	SOG has 1862

REF	**1567**
Title	**White's General and Commercial Directory of Sheffield, Rotherham, Barnsley, Chesterfield & Worksop**
Dates	1861,1868,1871,1879
Publisher	White, W.
Printer	Leader, R. & Son
Place	Sheffield
Type	GE TR
Map scale	–
Notes	See 1565. 1868 & after entitled 'Directory of the Boroughs of Sheffield, Doncaster, Chesterfield, Rotherham & all villages in the cutlery district'
Library holdings	BL has 1868,1871,1879
	BOD has 1871,1879
	GL has 1868,1871,1879
	NLS has 1871,1879
	SCL all
	ULC has 1871,1879

REF	**1568**
Title	**Business Directory of Sheffield, Rotherham, Masboro' & Attercliff**
Dates	1862
Publisher	Morris, J.S.C.
Printer	Spottiswoode & Co
Place	London
Type	TR
Map scale	–
Library holdings	BL
	BOD
	NLS
	SCL
	SOG

REF	**1569**
Title	**Drake's Directory of Rotherham**
Dates	1862
Publisher	Drake, E.S. & Co
Printer	–
Place	Sheffield
Type	CM TR
Map scale	–
Notes	Also includes 24 other townships, parishes & villages
Library	SCL

REF	**1570**
Title	**Drake's Commercial & Trades' Directory of Sheffield**
Dates	1863
Publisher	Drake, E.S. & Co
Printer	–
Place	Sheffield
Type	CM TR
Map scale	–
Library	SCL

REF	**1571**
Title	**Jones's Mercantile Directory of Bradford & District**
Dates	1863
Publisher	Jones & Proud
Printer	Jones & Proud
Place	London
Type	CM TR
Map scale	–
Library holdings	BL
	BRD
	GL
	HFX
	LCL

REF	**1572**
Title	**Jones's Mercantile Directory of Halifax, Huddersfield and Dewsbury**
Dates	1863
Publisher	Jones & Proud
Printer	Jones & Proud
Place	London
Type	CM TR
Map scale	–
Library holdings	CLM
	GL
	HFX
	HUD

REF	**1573**		REF	**1577**
Title	**Jones's Mercantile Directory of Leeds**		Title	**Ackrill's Harrogate Directory**
			Dates	1863,1879
Dates	1863		Publisher	Ackrill, R.
Publisher	Simpkin, Marshall & Co		Printer	Ackrill, R.
Printer	Jones & Proud		Place	Harrogate
Place	London		Type	GE
Type	CM TR		Map scale	–
Map scale	–		Library	GL has 1879
Library	GL		holdings	LCL has 1863

REF	**1574**		REF	**1578**
Title	**Jones's Mercantile Directory of the Shipping Ports of Hull, Great Grimsby & Goole**		Title	**Charlton and Anderson's Directory of the Woollen Districts of Leeds, Huddersfield, Dewsbury and the surrounding villages**
Dates	1863		Dates	1864
Publisher	Jones & Proud		Publisher	Charlton and Anderson
Printer	Jones & Proud		Printer	Moxon, S.
Place	London		Place	Leeds
Type	TR		Type	GE TR
Map scale	–		Map scale	–
Notes	Commercial section for Hull only		Library	HUD
Library	CLH		holdings	LCL
holdings	GL			

REF	**1575**		REF	**1579**
Title	**The Middlesborough Directory and Guide**		Title	**Halifax Municipal Borough Directory**
Dates	1863		Dates	1866
Publisher	Mills, J.H.		Publisher	Stephenson and Holdsworth
Printer	–		Printer	Crabtree and Son
Place	Middlesborough		Place	Halifax
Type	TR		Type	CM TR
Map scale	–		Map scale	–
Library	MCL		Library	HFX

REF	**1576**		REF	**1580**
Title	**Wright's Directory of Kingston-upon-Hull and Suburbs**		Title	**Tindall's Huddersfield Directory & Year Book**
Dates	1863		Dates	1866
Publisher	Plaxton, J.		Publisher	Tindall, G.
Printer	Wright, C.		Printer	Tindall, G.
Place	Hull		Place	Huddersfield
Type	GE TR		Type	GE
Map scale	–		Map scale	–
Library	BL		Notes	Cont'd as 1584
holdings	CLH		Library	BL
			holdings	BOD
				GL
				HUD
				NLS
				ULC

REF	**1581**		REF	**1584**
Title	**Directory of the Boroughs of Hull, Grimsby, Beverley, Doncaster and Hedon (Part I)**		Title	**Huddersfield Directory and Year Book**
Dates	1867		Dates	1867,1868,1870,1873
Publisher	White, W.		Publisher	Harper, G.
Printer	Leader & Sons		Printer	Harper, G.
Place	Sheffield		Place	Huddersfield
Type	GE TR		Type	GE TR
Map scale	–		Map scale	–
Notes	See 1582		Notes	Cont'd as 1599
Library	DON		Library	BL not 1867,1873
holdings	SCL		holdings	BOD has 1867
				GL not 1873
				HUD all
REF	**1582**			NLS has 1867
Title	**Directory of the Boroughs of Hull, York, Grimsby, Scarborough ... Middlesborough, Stockton-upon-Tees ... and the North and East Ridings of Yorkshire (Part II)**			ULC has 1867,1868
			REF	**1585**
			Title	**A Directory of Scarborough and Falsgrave**
Dates	1867		Dates	1868
Publisher	White, W.		Publisher	Theakston, S.W.
Printer	Leader, R. & Sons		Printer	Theakston, S.W.
Place	Sheffield		Place	Scarborough
Type	GE TR		Type	GE TR
Map scale	–		Map scale	–
Notes	See 1581		Library	BL
Library	BL			
holdings	BOD		REF	**1586**
	DAR		Title	**The Hand-Book and Directory of Middlesborough, Guisborough and their localities**
	GL			
	IHR			
	LCL		Dates	1871,1873,1874
	MID		Publisher	Burnett & Hood
	NLS		Printer	–
	ULC		Place	Middlesborough
	YCL		Type	CT TR
			Map scale	–
REF	**1583**		Library	DAR has 1874
Title	**Directory of the City of York ... Scarborough, Whitby ... Stockton-upon-Tees and Middlesborough ... Darlington and ... the North Riding of Yorkshire**		holdings	GL has 1871
				MID all
			REF	**1587**
			Title	**Buchanan & Co's Postal and Commercial Directory of Kingston-upon-Hull**
Dates	1867			
Publisher	White, W.		Dates	1872
Printer	White, W.		Publisher	Buchanan & Co
Place	Sheffield		Printer	Hudson, Scott & Sons
Type	CM TR		Place	Manchester
Map scale	–		Type	GE TR
Library	GL		Map scale	–
holdings	MID		Library	BL
			holdings	CLH

REF	1588
Title	**Porter's Topographical and Commercial Directory of Leeds**
Dates	1872
Publisher	Provincial Directories Company
Printer	McCorquodale & Co
Place	Leeds
Type	GE TR
Map scale	–
Library	BL
holdings	GL
	LCL

REF	1589
Title	**Smith's Directory of Bradford and Neighbourhood**
Dates	1872
Publisher	Smith, F.
Printer	Simpkin, Marshall & Co
Place	London
Type	CM TR
Map scale	1:2400
Library	BL
holdings	BOD
	BRD
	HFX

REF	1590
Title	**Directory of the City of York and Neighbourhood**
Dates	1872,1876
Publisher	Johnson & Tesseyman
Printer	Johnson & Tesseyman
Place	York
Type	GE TR
Map scale	1:15840
Notes	Map scale approx.
Library	BOD has 1872
holdings	CL has 1872
	NLS has 1872
	ULC has 1872
	YCL all

REF	1591
Title	**The Directory of the City of York and Neighbourhood**
Dates	1872,1876
Publisher	Johnson & Tesseyman
Printer	Johnson & Tesseyman
Place	York
Type	GE TR
Map scale	NS
Library	BL has 1872
holdings	GL has 1876

REF	1592
Title	**Johnson's Street Directory of Leeds & Neighbourhood**
Dates	1873,1899,1900
Publisher	Johnson, J.
Printer	Johnson, J.
Place	Leeds
Type	ST
Map scale	–
Library	BL has 1873
holdings	LCL all

REF	1593
Title	**Butcher and Co's Kingston-upon-Hull Directory**
Dates	1874
Publisher	Butcher and Co
Printer	–
Place	London
Type	GE
Map scale	–
Library	CLH

REF	1594
Title	**Smith's Directory of Halifax and Neighbourhood**
Dates	1874
Publisher	Smith, F.
Printer	Oldfield & Horsfall
Place	Bradford
Type	CM TR
Map scale	–
Library	BL
holdings	HFX

REF	1595
Title	**Smith's Directory of Wakefield**
Dates	1875
Publisher	Smith, F.
Printer	McCorquodale & Co
Place	Leeds
Type	CM TR
Map scale	–
Library	GL

REF **1596**
Title **Spencer's Richmond Almanac, Diary, Directory**
Dates 1875,1901,1905,1911
Publisher Spencer, T.
Printer Spencer, T.
Place Richmond (Yorks)
Type CM TR
Map scale –
Notes 1875 edition entitled 'Spencer's Richmond Almanack & Swaledale & Wensleydale Book of Reference'
Library DAR

REF **1597**
Title **Hull Year Book and Directory**
Dates 1876
Publisher Hunt, W.
Printer Hunt, W.
Place Hull
Type GE TR
Map scale –
Library CLH

REF **1598**
Title **McCorquodale & Co's Topographical and Commercial Directory of Leeds and neighbourhood**
Dates 1876,1878
Publisher McCorquodale & Co
Printer McCorquodale & Co
Place Leeds
Type GE TR
Map scale –
Notes See 1608
Library LCL

REF **1599**
Title **Huddersfield and District (Postal) Directory**
Dates 1876,1879,1884,1900
Publisher Daily Chronicle Steam Printing Works
Printer Daily Chronicle Steam Printing Works
Place Huddersfield
Type GE TR
Map scale –
Notes Cont'd from 1584, cont'd as 1659. 'Postal' included in title in 1884.
Library BL all
holdings BOD not 1884
GL all
HUD all
NLS has 1876,1879
ULC has 1879,1900

REF **1600**
Title **Almanac and Directory for Saltburn-by-the-Sea & District**
Dates 1877
Publisher Moss, A.B.
Printer Moss, A.B.
Place Saltburn-by-the-Sea
Type CM TR
Map scale –
Library BL
holdings BOD

REF **1601**
Title **Smith's Directory of Dewsbury and Batley**
Dates 1878
Publisher Smith, F.
Printer Wright, W.
Place Bradford
Type CM
Map scale –
Library HFX

REF **1602**
Title **The Post Office Bradford Directory**
Dates 1879,1883,1887,1891,1893,1894, 1898,1900,1903,1906,1909,1912, 1916,1921,1924,1928
Publisher Byles, W. & Son
Printer Byles, W. & Son
Place Bradford
Type GE TR
Map scale 1:15840
Library BL all
holdings BOD has 1879,1883,1891,1893, 1898,1900
BRD all
CLM has 1898
GL has 1879
NLS has 1879,1883,1891,1893, 1898,1900
ULC has 1879,1883,1891,1893, 1898

REF **1603**
Title **Kelly's Directory of Bradford and Neighbourhood**
Dates 1881
Publisher Kelly & Co
Printer Kelly & Co
Place London
Type GE TR
Map scale –
Notes See 1639. This volume, 1604 & 1605 were published only in 1881, and are slightly different in size/format to all other Kelly's town directories. They might possibly have been reproduced from the West Riding Directory for 1881 (1535) with added ST sections.
Library BRD

REF **1604**
Title **Kelly's Directory of Halifax and Neighbourhood**
Dates 1881
Publisher Kelly & Co
Printer Kelly & Co
Place London
Type GE TR
Map scale –
Notes A handwritten note in HFX copy states that 'Messrs Kelly have now discontinued publishing this Directory. November 1890.' See notes to 1603.
Library HFX

REF **1605**
Title **Kelly's Directory of Huddersfield and Neighbourhood**
Dates 1881
Publisher Kelly & Co
Printer Kelly & Co
Place London
Type GE TR
Map scale –
Notes See notes to 1603.
Library HUD

REF **1606**
Title **Kelly's (White's) Directory of Sheffield & Rotherham**
Dates 1881,1883,1888,1890,1893, 1922-1942,1944,1948
Publisher Kelly & Co
Printer Kelly & Co
Place London
Type GE TR
Map scale 1:10560
Notes Cont'd from White's, see 1565
Library BL not 1893
holdings BPH has 1883,1924-1931, 1940-1942,1944
BOD not 1881,1893
CLM has 1922-1927,1929-1948
GL not 1881,1883,1890,1893, 1940
LCL has 1922,1927,1932,1948
MLG has 1922-1948
NLS has 1922-1944
NLW has 1924,1927-1930,1933, 1935-1938
SCL all
ULC not 1881,1893

REF **1607**
Title **Stevens' Directory of York and Neighbourhood**
Dates 1881,1886
Publisher Stevens, G.
Printer Stevens, G.
Place London
Type GE TR
Map scale 1:760320
Library BL has 1886
holdings GL has 1881
LCL has 1886
YCL all

REF **1608**
Title **The Leeds Post Office Directory**
Dates 1882
Publisher McCorquodale & Co
Printer McCorquodale & Co
Place Leeds
Type GE TR
Map scale 1:5280
Notes See 1598
Library BOD
holdings LCL
NLS

REF **1609**
Title **White's General and Commercial Directory of Hull and District**
Dates 1882,1895
Publisher White, W.
Printer Leader, R. & Son
Place Sheffield
Type GE TR
Map scale –
Library BL all
holdings CLH all
GL has 1895
NLS all
ULC all

REF **1610**
Title **A. Craven's Commercial and General Directory of Keighley, Bingley, Skipton and surrounding districts**
Dates 1884
Publisher Craven, A.
Printer Craven, A.
Place Keighley
Type CM TR
Map scale –
Library BRD

REF **1611**
Title **Hulley's Alphabetical and Classified Directory of Sheffield, Rotherham and Neighbourhood**
Dates 1884
Publisher Hulley, J.
Printer –
Place Birmingham
Type CM TR
Map scale –
Library BOD
holdings NLS
SCL

REF **1612**
Title **Middlesborough Directory and Guide**
Dates 1884
Publisher Jordison & Co
Printer Jordison & Co
Place Middlesborough
Type GE TR
Map scale –
Library MID

REF **1613**
Title **Kelly's Directory of Middlesborough and suburbs**
Dates 1885,1887
Publisher Kelly & Co
Printer Kelly & Co
Place London
Type GE TR
Map scale –
Library BL has 1885
holdings BOD all
GL has 1887
MID all
NLS all
ULC all

REF **1614**
Title **Kelly's Directory of Hull and its neighbourhood**
Dates 1885,1889,1892,1899,1900, 1903-1916,1919,1921,1922,1925, 1926,1929,1930,1933,1936,1937, 1939
Publisher Kelly & Co
Printer Kelly & Co
Place London
Type GE TR
Map scale 1:10560
Notes 1885-1892 editions entitled 'Kelly's Directory of the Port of Hull'
Library BCL has 1892,1900,1922,1926,
holdings 1930,1933,1937
BIS has 1939
BL not 1885-1892,1903,1937
BOD has 1933-1939
BPH has 1939
BRD has 1939
CLE has 1936
CLH all
CLM has 1904,1906-1916,1919, 1926,1930,1937,1939
GL not 1889,1892,1900,1903, 1906,1907,1909,1913, 1917-1919
LCL has 1937,1939
MLG has 1900,1903,1906,1909, 1912,1915,1916,1921,1926, 1930-1939
NLS has 1900,1903-1913, 1925-1939
NLW has 1929,1933,1936,1939
SCL has 1939
SOG has 1939
ULC has 1900,1903-1913,1921, 1925-1933,1936-1939
YCL has 1939   [307]

REF **1615**
Title **Reliance Almanac and Directory for Ripon**
Dates 1886
Publisher Fall & Babington
Printer Reliance Printing Works
Place Ripon
Type CM TR
Map scale –
Library BOD
holdings NLS
ULC

REF **1616**
Title **Kelly's Directory of Leeds**
Dates 1886,1888,1893,1897,1899-1917,
1920-1925,1927,1929,1932,1936,
1938,1940,1947
Publisher Kelly & Co
Printer Kelly & Co
Place London
Type GE TR
Map scale 1:10560
Library BL not 1893,1897,1901-1904,
holdings 1906,1924,1929
BOD not 1893,1897,1901,1904,
1917,1921
BPH has 1886,1893,1905,1916,
1922,1923,1925,1927-1932,
1940,1947
BRD has 1888,1925,1947
CLM has 1899,1905-1907,1913,
1917,1920-1923,1925-1947
GL not 1893,1897,1901,1904,
1906,1924,1929
IHR has 1929
LCL has 1886-1889,1901,1903,
1904,1906-1912,1915-1917,
1920,1921,1923,1925,
1927-1947
MLG has 1899,1903,1906,1909,
1911,1914-1917,1920-1923,
1925,1927,1932-1947
NLS not 1893,1897,1901,1904,
1914,1917,1921
NLW has 1920,1923,1929,1936,
1938,1947
ULC not 1893,1897,1901,1904
YCL has 1947

REF **1617**
Title **Mercantile & General Directory of Middlesborough, North Ormesby, South Bank etc**
Dates 1887
Publisher The Printing & Publishing Co
Printer The Printing & Publishing Co
Place Middlesborough
Type CT TR
Map scale –
Library MID

REF **1618**
Title **Slater's Directory of Sheffield and Rotherham**
Dates 1887
Publisher Slater, I.
Printer Slater, I.
Place Manchester
Type GE TR
Map scale 1:158400
Library BL
holdings GL
SCL

REF **1619**
Title **Taylor's Business Directory of Bridlington & the Bridlington Union**
Dates 1888
Publisher Taylor, W.
Printer Harland, M.
Place Bridlington
Type GE TR
Map scale –
Library BL

REF **1620**
Title **Hull and District Directory and Grimsby Trade Directory**
Dates 1888,1891
Publisher Atkinson, F.
Printer Brown, A.
Place Hull
Type GE TR
Map scale –
Library BL has 1888
holdings BOD has 1888
CLH has 1888
GL has 1888
NLS all
ULC all

REF **1621**
Title **Borough of Halifax List of Streets**
Dates 1889
Publisher Whitley & Booth
Printer Whitley & Booth
Place Halifax
Type SL
Map scale –
Library HFX

REF **1622**
Title **Halifax Street Guide and Select Business Directory**
Dates 1890
Publisher Womersley, W.C.
Printer Womersley, W.C.
Place Halifax
Type SL TR
Map scale –
Library HFX

REF **1623**
Title **Slater's Directory of Halifax and District**
Dates 1890
Publisher Slater, I.
Printer Slater, I.
Place Manchester
Type CM TR
Map scale –
Library GL

REF **1624**
Title **Slater's Directory of Wakefield, Normanton, Ossett and their Vicinities**
Dates 1890
Publisher Slater, I.
Printer Slater, I.
Place Manchester
Type GE TR
Map scale –
Library GL

REF **1625**
Title **Slater's Directory of Leeds and District**
Dates 1890,1892
Publisher Slater, I.
Printer Slater, I.
Place Manchester
Type GE TR
Map scale –
Library LCL all
holdings NLS has 1892

REF **1626**
Title **Slater's Directory of Huddersfield and District**
Dates 1891
Publisher Slater, I.
Printer Slater, I.
Place Manchester
Type GE TR
Map scale –
Library GL
holdings HUD

REF **1627**
Title **Slater's Directory of Rotherham, Masborough and District**
Dates 1891
Publisher Slater, I.
Printer Slater, I.
Place Manchester
Type GE TR
Map scale –
Library GL

REF **1628**
Title **A Directory of Scarborough and Filey**
Dates 1892
Publisher Hagyard, J.
Printer –
Place Scarborough
Type GE TR
Map scale –
Library GL

REF **1629**
Title **The Sheffield Street List**
Dates 1893
Publisher Pawson & Brailsford
Printer Pawson & Brailsford
Place Sheffield
Type SL
Map scale –
Library BL

REF **1630**
Title **York and District Directory**
Dates 1893,1896,1898,1900,1902
Publisher Cook, W. J. & Co
Printer Wing & Broughton
Place Boston
Type GE TR
Map scale 1:760320
Library BL not 1896,1898
holdings BOD not 1896,1898
CLM has 1900
GL has 1902
NLS not 1896,1898
ULC not 1896,1898
YCL all

REF **1631**
Title **The Gazette Commercial and General Doncaster Directory**
Dates 1893-1915,1921,1923
Publisher Doncaster Gazette
Printer Doncaster Gazette
Place Doncaster
Type GE TR
Map scale 1:10560
Notes Cont'd as 1674
Library BL has 1899,1900,1902-1906,
holdings 1908-1923
BOD has 1908
DON not 1910-1913
NLS has 1908

REF **1632**
Title **White's Directory of York and Neighbourhood**
Dates 1895
Publisher White, W.
Printer Morrison & Gibb
Place Sheffield
Type GE TR
Map scale 1:15840
Library BL
holdings BOD
GL
ULC
YCL

REF **1633**
Title **The Sheffield City Directory**
Dates 1895,1896,1900
Publisher Pawson & Brailsford
Printer Pawson & Brailsford
Place Sheffield
Type GE TR
Map scale –
Library BL has 1896
holdings CLM has 1900
GL has 1896,1900
SCL all
SOG has 1895

REF **1634**
Title **Hull and District Directory**
Dates 1895,1897,1899,1901
Publisher Cook, W.J.
Printer –
Place London
Type GE TR
Map scale –
Library BL has 1901
holdings CLH all

REF **1635**
Title **Robinson's Business Directory for the City of Leeds**
Dates 1897-1911
Publisher Robinson, J.
Printer Robinson, J.
Place Leeds
Type GE TR
Map scale NS
Notes 1898 & after entitled 'Robinson's Leeds Directory'
Library BL all
holdings BOD not 1902,1904,1908
LCL not 1908
NLS not 1902,1904,1908
ULC all

REF **1636**
Title **Sheffield and District Trades' Directory**
Dates 1898,1901,1902,1904,1918,1926, 1949
Publisher Town and County Directories Ltd
Printer Macdonald, W.
Place Edinburgh
Type TR
Map scale –
Library LCL has 1918
holdings SCL not 1918

REF **1637**
Title **Whitby and District Directory**
Dates 1899,1901
Publisher Cook, W.J. & Co
Printer Newton & Son
Place Hull
Type GE TR
Map scale –
Library BL all
holdings BOD has 1901
GL all
NLS has 1901
ULC has 1901

REF **1638**
Title **Halifax, Huddersfield and District Trades' Directory**
Dates 1899,1902-1907,1909,1914,1915, 1917-1919,1922-1931
Publisher Town and County Directories Ltd
Printer Macdonald, W. & Co Ltd
Place Edinburgh
Type TR
Map scale –
Library HFX has 1903,1904,1906,1919,
holdings 1922-1926,1929,1931
HUD has 1899,1902-1905,1907, 1909,1914,1915,1917-1919, 1922-1925,1927-1931

REF **1639**
Title **Kelly's Directory of Bradford and suburbs**
Dates 1900-1902,1904,1908,1912,1917, 1922,1927,1936,1938
Publisher Kelly's Directories Ltd
Printer Kelly's Directories Ltd
Place London
Type GE TR
Map scale –
Notes See 1603
Library BCL has 1922
holdings BL not 1901,1902,1904
BOD not 1901-1904,1917,1936, 1938
BPH has 1936
BRD not 1900,1904,1908,1927
CLM not 1901,1902,1938
GL not 1901,1902,1917
LCL has 1912,1936,1938
MLG has 1917-1938
NLS not 1901,1902
NLW has 1936,1938
ULC not 1901,1902,1904

REF **1640**
Title **Leeds and District Trades Directory**
Dates 1900-1903,1906,1909,1917,1919, 1920,1922-1925,1931
Publisher Town and County Directories Ltd
Printer Macdonald, W. & Co Ltd
Place Edinburgh
Type TR
Map scale –
Notes 1919 onwards entitled 'Leeds, Bradford & District Trades' Directory'. See 1678.
Library BRD has 1919
holdings LCL not 1919

REF **1641**
Title **Kelly's Directory of Leeds and Bradford**
Dates 1900-1903,1908
Publisher Kelly's Directories Ltd
Printer Kelly's Directories Ltd
Place London
Type GE TR
Map scale 1:10560
Library BCL has 1901
holdings BL not 1901,1908
BRD has 1908
LCL has 1900,1902
NLS not 1901,1908
YCL has 1901

REF **1642**
Title **Robinson's Harrogate, Knaresboro', Ripon, Pateley Bridge & District Directory**
Dates 1900-1936
Publisher Robinson, J.
Printer –
Place Leeds
Type GE TR
Map scale –
Library BL not 1904
holdings BOD has 1900,1904-1936
CLM has 1932
GL has 1909,1912
LCL has 1901,1910,1913,1936
NLS not 1901-1903
ULC has 1900,1904-1936

REF **1643**
Title **Beverley and District Directory**
Dates 1901
Publisher Cook, W.J. & Co
Printer Green & Son
Place Hull
Type GE TR
Map scale –
Library BL
holdings NLS
ULC

REF **1644**
Title **Bridlington and District Directory**
Dates 1901
Publisher Cook, W.J. & Co
Printer Cook, W.J. & Co
Place Hull
Type GE TR
Map scale –
Library BL
holdings BOD
CLM
GL
NLS
SOG
ULC

REF **1645**
Title **The Wakefield Express Directory for Wakefield & District**
Dates 1901
Publisher Robinson, T.
Printer Robinson, T.
Place Wakefield
Type CM
Map scale –
Library BL

REF **1646**
Title **Robinson's Directory for Ilkley, Burley, Otley & the Mid-Wharfe Valley**
Dates 1901,1904,1909
Publisher Robinson, J. & D. Ltd
Printer Robinson, J. & D. Ltd
Place Leeds
Type GE TR
Map scale –
Library BL all
holdings BOD has 1909
LCL has 1901,1904

REF **1647**
Title **Robinson's Barnsley Directory**
Dates 1902,1905
Publisher Robinson, J. & D. Ltd
Printer Robinson, J. & D. Ltd
Place Leeds
Type GE TR
Map scale –
Library BL
holdings NLS
ULC

REF **1648**
Title **Robinson's Leeds Suburban Directory**
Dates 1903
Publisher Robinson, J. & D. Ltd
Printer Robinson, J. & D. Ltd
Place Leeds
Type GE TR
Map scale NS
Library BL

REF **1649**
Title **Robinson's Directory for the Borough of Morley including Gildersome, Drightlington, Tingley, Ardsley etc**
Dates 1905
Publisher Robinson, J.D.
Printer Robinson, J.D.
Place Leeds
Type GE TR
Map scale –
Library BL
holdings BOD
ULC

REF **1650**
Title **Robinson's Directory for the Borough of Ossett including Horbury & District**
Dates 1905
Publisher Robinson, J.D.
Printer Robinson, J.D.
Place Leeds
Type GE TR
Map scale –
Library BL
holdings BOD
ULC

REF **1651**
Title **Robinson's Directory of the Borough of Pudsey**
Dates 1905
Publisher Robinson, J.D. Ltd
Printer Robinson, J.D. Ltd
Place Leeds
Type GE TR
Map scale –
Library BL
holdings BOD
ULC

REF **1652**
Title **Robinson's Halifax & District Directory**
Dates 1905
Publisher Robinson, J.D.
Printer Robinson, J.D.
Place Leeds
Type GE TR
Map scale –
Library BL
holdings BOD
HFX
NLS
ULC

REF **1653**
Title **The Headingley, Meanwood & Adel Directory and Almanack**
Dates 1905,1906,1910-1914,1920,1921, 1923,1934-1937
Publisher Saville, J.S. & Co
Printer Saville, J.S. & Co
Place Leeds
Type CT
Map scale –
Library LCL

REF **1654**
Title **Robinson's Headingley & Meanwood Directory**
Dates 1906
Publisher Robinson, J.D.
Printer –
Place Leeds
Type GE
Map scale –
Library BL
holdings BOD
NLS

REF **1655**
Title **Robinson's Roundhay and Chapeltown Directory**
Dates 1906
Publisher Robinson, J.D.
Printer –
Place Leeds
Type GE
Map scale 1:10560
Notes Map scale approx.
Library BL
holdings BOD

REF **1656**
Title **Annual Report of the Huddersfield Chamber of Trade**
Dates 1907
Publisher –
Printer Cook, W.H.
Place Huddersfield
Type SP
Map scale –
Notes TR section of subscribers to the Chamber
Library HUD

REF **1657**
Title **Directory of the City of York**
Dates 1909
Publisher Arthur and Company Ltd
Printer Arthur and Company Ltd
Place York
Type GE TR
Map scale 1:10560
Library GL
holdings YCL

REF **1658**
Title **Cookes' Almanack and Directory of Richmond, Swaledale &c**
Dates 1909,1914,1915
Publisher Cookes, C.E. & Son
Printer Cookes, C.E. & Son
Place Richmond (Yorks)
Type GE TR
Map scale –
Library DAR has 1909,1915
holdings GL has 1914
LCL has 1909

REF	1659
Title	**Huddersfield Directory**
Dates	1909,1924
Publisher	Jubb, A. & Son Ltd
Printer	Jubb, A. & Son Ltd
Place	Huddersfield
Type	GE TR
Map scale	–
Notes	See 1681. Cont'd from 1599.
Library	BOD has 1909
holdings	GL has 1909
	HUD all
	NLS has 1909
	ULC has 1909

REF	1660
Title	**The Leeds, Bradford, Harrogate, Wakefield & Districts Trade Directory**
Dates	1912,1914
Publisher	Crewe, J. & Co
Printer	Goddall & Suddick Ltd
Place	Leeds
Type	TR
Map scale	–
Library	BL all
holdings	HUD has 1912
	LCL has 1912

REF	1661
Title	**Robinson's Directory of Ripon, Boroughbridge, Pateley Bridge & Country Districts**
Dates	1912,1915
Publisher	West Riding ABC Publishing Co Ltd
Printer	West Riding ABC Publishing Co Ltd
Place	Leeds
Type	GE TR
Map scale	–
Library	BL
holdings	BOD

REF	1662
Title	**Halifax A Commercial and Industrial Centre**
Dates	1915
Publisher	Sells Ltd
Printer	–
Place	London
Type	SP
Map scale	–
Notes	TR list & articles on advertisers & much local, commercial, historical, general information
Library	HFX

REF	1663
Title	**The Commercial Year Book of the Halifax Chamber of Commerce with Classified Trade Indices ... and Trade Mark Section**
Dates	1918
Publisher	Halifax Chamber of Commerce
Printer	Bemrose & Sons Ltd
Place	Leeds
Type	TR
Map scale	–
Notes	With articles & other information, 4 different languages
Library	HFX

REF	1664
Title	**The Commercial Year Book of the Huddersfield Incorporated Chamber of Commerce with Classified Trades Indices ... and Trade Mark Section**
Dates	1918
Publisher	Mills, C. [compiler]
Printer	Bemrose & Sons
Place	Derby
Type	SP
Map scale	–
Notes	TR section. In 4 languages.
Library	HUD

REF	1665
Title	**Annual Report of ... the Huddersfield Incorporated Chamber of Commerce .. with a list of members**
Dates	1918-1950
Publisher	Huddersfield Incorporated Chamber of Commerce
Printer	Brown, B. & Sons
Place	Huddersfield
Type	SP
Map scale	–
Notes	Alph. list of firms in Chamber of Commerce. 1923 onwards includes TR section.
Library	HUD

REF	1666
Title	**York City Year Book and Business Directory**
Dates	1920-1939,1949,1950
Publisher	Yorkshire Gazette Newspaper
Printer	Yorkshire Gazette Newspaper
Place	York
Type	GE TR
Map scale	1:15840
Library	BL all
holdings	GL has 1937
	YCL not 1934

REF	1667
Title	**Waddington's Scarborough Almanac, Farmers' Guide and Directory**
Dates	1922-1937
Publisher	Waddington, T.A.J.
Printer	Waddington, T.A.J.
Place	York
Type	ST
Map scale	–
Library	BL

REF	1668
Title	**York, Hull and District Trades' Directory**
Dates	1923,1933,1934,1936,1938
Publisher	Town and County Directories Ltd
Printer	Macdonald, W. & Co
Place	Edinburgh
Type	TR
Map scale	–
Library	YCL

REF	1669
Title	**Bradford Exchange Directory**
Dates	1925,1938,1941,1947
Publisher	The Exchange Publishing Co Ltd
Printer	Robertson, R.E.
Place	Bradford
Type	SP
Map scale	–
Notes	Alph. & TR sections
Library	BRD

REF	1670
Title	**Ward's Directory of Redcar and Coatham... with Saltburn, Middlesborough ... Stockton, ... and Thornaby**
Dates	1926,1928,1930,1932,1934,1936, 1938
Publisher	Ward, R. & Sons
Printer	Ward, R. & Sons
Place	Newcastle-on-Tyne
Type	GE
Map scale	–
Library	BPH has 1938
holdings	CLM has 1936
	CLN all
	DAR has 1930-1934,1938
	DUR has 1936
	GL has 1926,1936,1938
	MID all

REF	1671
Title	**Huddersfield, Halifax and District Directory and Buyers' Guide**
Dates	1927-1929,1931-1933,1935,1936
Publisher	Cope, E.F. & Co
Printer	Cope, E.F. & Co
Place	Walsall
Type	TR
Map scale	–
Library	HFX has 1927-1939,1932-1935
holdings	HUD has 1928,1931,1935,1936

REF	1672
Title	**Bradford and District Trades' Directory**
Dates	1927-1931
Publisher	Town and County Directories Ltd
Printer	Macdonald, W. & Co Ltd
Place	Edinburgh
Type	TR
Map scale	–
Notes	Cont'd as 1678
Library	BRD

REF **1673**
Title **Hull and District Trades'**
Directory
Dates 1928,1930
Publisher Town and County Directories
Ltd
Printer Macdonald, W. & Co Ltd
Place Edinburgh
Type TR
Map scale –
Library CLH

REF **1674**
Title **The Chronicle Doncaster Year**
Book and Street Directory
Dates 1928,1932,1934,1936,1938
Publisher The Chronicle Co Ltd
Printer The Chronicle Co Ltd
Place Doncaster
Type GE TR
Map scale –
Notes Cont'd from 1631
Library DON

REF **1675**
Title **Sheffield Street Guide**
Dates 1929-1935
Publisher Sheffield Telegraph
Printer Sheffield Telegraph
Place Sheffield
Type SL
Map scale –
Library BL

REF **1676**
Title **Sheffield Exchange (Coal, Iron,**
Steel & Allied Trades) Directory
and List of Members
Dates 1933
Publisher Bemrose Publicity Co Ltd
Printer –
Place Derby
Type SP
Map scale NS
Notes Alph. & TR sections. Map of Yorks
coalfield.
Library SCL

REF **1677**
Title **Huddersfield Classified Trades**
Directory to Manufacturers,
Wholesalers and Retailers
Dates 1934
Publisher U-Need-A Publicity Service
Printer Wheatley, Dyson & Son
Place Huddersfield
Type TR
Map scale –
Library HUD

REF **1678**
Title **Bradford, Leeds, Halifax,**
Huddersfield & District Trades
Directory
Dates 1934,1935,1937-1940,1948
Publisher Town and County Directories
Ltd
Printer Macdonald, W. & Co Ltd
Place Edinburgh
Type TR
Map scale –
Notes Cont'd from 1640 and 1672
Library BRD has 1938
holdings HFX has 1939
HUD has 1934,1935,1937,1938,
1940
LCL has 1948

REF **1679**
Title **Scarborough, Scalby, Newby and**
District Directory
Dates 1936
Publisher St Nicholas Press
Printer St Nicholas Press
Place Scarborough
Type GE TR
Map scale –
Notes Title page missing from YCL
edition
Library YCL

REF **1680**
Title **The Halifax County Borough**
Directory
Dates 1936
Publisher Whipple, R.D. Son & Martin
Ltd
Printer Whipple, R.D. Son & Martin
Ltd
Place Leeds
Type GE TR
Map scale –
Library CLM
holdings GL
HFX

REF	**1681**
Title	**The Huddersfield County Borough Directory**
Dates	1937
Publisher	Jubb, A. & Son Ltd
Printer	Jubb, A. & Son Ltd
Place	Huddersfield
Type	GE TR
Map scale	–
Library	GL
holdings	HUD
	LCL
	SCL

REF	**1682**
Title	**The Yorkshire Post Year Book and Directory of Barnsley**
Dates	1937
Publisher	The Chronicle Co Ltd
Printer	The Chronicle Co Ltd
Place	Doncaster
Type	GE TR
Map scale	–
Library	GL

REF	**1683**
Title	**Kelly's Directory of Harrogate and neighbourhood**
Dates	1937-1941,1943,1945,1948,1950
Publisher	Kelly's Directories Ltd
Printer	Kelly's Directories Ltd
Place	London
Type	GE TR
Map scale	1:15840
Library	BL all
holdings	DAR has 1948
	GL not 1937
	LCL has 1945
	NLW has 1950
	YCL has 1939

REF	**1684**
Title	**Wrigley's Thorne Almanac and Directory**
Dates	1938
Publisher	Wrigley, W. & Son
Printer	Wrigley, W. & Son
Place	Thorne
Type	CT
Map scale	–
Library	DON

REF	**1685**
Title	**Kelly's Directory of Bridlington & neighbourhood**
Dates	1939
Publisher	Kelly's Directories Ltd
Printer	Kelly's Directories Ltd
Place	London
Type	GE TR
Map scale	–
Library	BL all
holdings	CLM all
	GL all
	YCL has 1939

REF	**1686**
Title	**Kelly's Directory of Scarborough, Filey & District**
Dates	1939
Publisher	Kelly's Directories Ltd
Printer	Kelly's Directories Ltd
Place	London
Type	GE TR
Map scale	1:7594
Library	BL
holdings	GL

REF	**1687**
Title	**Tellway Leeds Directory**
Dates	1949
Publisher	Franks, A.W.
Printer	Partridge Printers Ltd
Place	Leeds
Type	SL
Map scale	1:126720
Library	LCL

REF	**1688**
Title	**The Keighley Year Book and Business Directory**
Dates	1950
Publisher	The Keighley Year Book and Business Directory
Printer	Parker, W. (Keighley) Ltd
Place	Keighley
Type	ST TR
Map scale	–
Library	BCL
holdings	CLM

Chapter 5
WALES AND WELSH COUNTIES

5.1 Welsh directories

REF	**1689**
Title	**Kelly's Directory of Monmouthshire and (the principal towns and places of) South Wales**
Dates	1871,1884,1891,1895,1901,1906, 1910,1914,1920,1923,1926,1934
Publisher	Kelly & Co
Printer	Kelly & Co
Place	London
Type	GE TR
Map scale	1:158400
Notes	Penultimate part of title dropped from 1901. 1871 edition entitled 'Post Office Directory of Monmouthshire etc'.
Library holdings	BCL has 1891-1934
	BIS has 1926
	BL not 1934
	BOD not 1934
	BPH has 1884,1926
	CLC all
	CLM has 1926
	GL all
	IHR has 1926
	LCL has 1934
	MLG has 1906-1920,1926
	NLS all
	NLW not 1906
	NPT all
	SCL has 1926,1934
	SOG has 1871,1895,1914,1923, 1926
	SWA not 1910,1934
	ULC all

REF	**1690**
Title	**Worrall's Directory of North Wales**
Dates	1874
Publisher	Worrall, J.
Printer	Worrall, J.
Place	Oldham
Type	GE TR
Map scale	–
Notes	Covers Anglesey, Caernarvon, Flint, Merioneth & Montgomery (counties); Chester, Shrewsbury, Oswestry & Aberystwyth (towns)
Library holdings	BL
	BPH
	CLC
	GL
	NLS
	NLW
	SHR
	ULC

REF	**1691**
Title	**Worrall's Directory of South Wales**
Dates	1875
Publisher	Worrall, J.
Printer	Worrall, J.
Place	Preston
Type	TR
Map scale	–
Notes	Covers Newport & counties of Glamorgan, Carmarthen, Pembroke, Brecknock & Radnor
Library holdings	BL
	CLC
	GL
	NLS
	NLW
	NPT
	SWA
	ULC

REF	**1692**
Title	**W.E. Owen & Co's General and Commercial Directory for Glamorganshire, Monmouthshire etc**
Dates	1877,1878
Publisher	Owen, W.E. & Co
Printer	–
Place	Leicester
Type	CM
Map scale	–
Notes	1878 edition entitled 'W.E. Owen & Co's General, Topographical and Historical Directory for Glamorganshire, Monmouthshire etc'
Library	CLC

REF	**1693**
Title	**The Wales Register and Guide**
Dates	1878
Publisher	Eyre Bros.
Printer	–
Place	London
Type	CM
Map scale	–
Notes	Mainly a topography, but small CM section for most places
Library	CLC

REF	**1694**
Title	**Slater's Royal National Commercial Directory of North and South Wales, Monmouthshire, Shropshire & the Cities of Bristol and Chester**
Dates	1880
Publisher	Slater, I.
Printer	Slater, I.
Place	Manchester
Type	GE TR
Map scale	1:396000
Library	CCL
holdings	CLC
	GL
	NLW
	SOG

REF	**1695**
Title	**Slater's Directory of North and Mid Wales**
Dates	1885,1895
Publisher	Slater, I.
Printer	Slater, I.
Place	Manchester
Type	GE TR
Map scale	NS
Library	BCL has 1895
holdings	BL all
	CLC has 1895
	GL has 1895
	NLS has 1895
	NLW has 1895
	SOG has 1895
	SWA has 1895
	ULC has 1895

REF	**1696**
Title	**Postal Directory of Caernarvonshire and Anglesey**
Dates	1886
Publisher	Rockliff Bros Ltd
Printer	Rockliff Bros Ltd
Place	Liverpool
Type	CM TR
Map scale	–
Library	CLC
holdings	NLW

REF	**1697**
Title	**Postal Directory of Flintshire & Denbighshire**
Dates	1886
Publisher	Rockliff Bros
Printer	Rockliff Bros
Place	Liverpool
Type	CM TR
Map scale	–
Notes	See 1717
Library	CLC

REF	**1698**
Title	**Postal Directory of Merionethshire and Montgomeryshire**
Dates	1886
Publisher	Rockliff Bros Ltd
Printer	Rockliff Bros Ltd
Place	Liverpool
Type	CM TR
Map scale	–
Library	CLC
holdings	NLW

REF **1699**
Title **Deacon's North and South Wales Court Guide and County Blue Book**
Dates 1887
Publisher Deacon, C.W. & Co
Printer –
Place London
Type CT PR
Map scale 1:316800
Library NLW

REF **1700**
Title **Sutton's Directory of North Wales**
Dates 1889
Publisher Sutton, A.
Printer Looney & Pilling
Place Manchester
Type GE TR
Map scale –
Notes Covers the counties of Anglesey, Caernarvon, Denbigh, Flint, Merioneth & Montgomery, & the city of Chester
Library BCL
holdings BL
CLC
GL
NLW

REF **1701**
Title **Bennett's Business Directory for South Wales**
Dates 1893,1895,1897,1899-1901,1915
Publisher Bennett & Co
Printer Bennett & Co
Place Birmingham
Type CM TR
Map scale –
Notes CLC also has 1914 edition for Monmouthshire & Wales
Library CLC has 1900,1915
holdings NLW not 1893,1899,1915
SWA has 1893,1899,1900

REF **1702**
Title **Trades' Directory of Wales**
Dates 1901,1903,1909,1910,1912-1932, 1934-1937,1948,1950
Publisher Trades' Directories Ltd
Printer Macdonald, W. & Co Ltd
Place Edinburgh
Type TR
Map scale –
Notes 1909 onwards entitled 'Wales Trades' Directory'
Library CLC has 1901,1909,1912-1914,
holdings 1918,1922,1923,1925-1929,1931, 1934,1935,1937-1950
NLW not 1901,1909,1913,1914, 1931,1932,1934,1937-1950
SWA has 1909,1912,1914,1918, 1922,1927-1929,1931,1932

REF **1703**
Title **North Wales Directory and Guide**
Dates 1907,1909-1912,1914,1915,1917, 1919,1923,1925,1926,1928-1938
Publisher Cope, E.F.
Printer Cope, E.F.
Place Walsall
Type TR
Map scale –
Notes Covers counties of Anglesey, Caernarvon, Denbigh, Flint, Merioneth, Montgomery
Library BL not 1923
holdings NLW has 1923

REF **1704**
Title **South Wales and Monmouthshire Directory and Buyers' Guide**
Dates 1907,1918,1923,1931,1933
Publisher Cope, E.F. & Co
Printer Cope, E.F. & Co
Place Walsall
Type TR
Map scale –
Library CLC not 1923
holdings SWA has 1923

REF	1705
Title	**Bennett's Business Directory for North Wales**
Dates	1911,1912,1915-1917,1920,1922, 1923,1927,1929,1933,1936
Publisher	Bennett & Co
Printer	Bennett & Co
Place	Birmingham
Type	GE TR
Map scale	–
Notes	TR & CM sections for each place
Library	CCL has 1916
holdings	CLC has 1923
	GL has 1936
	NLS has 1936
	NLW not 1916
	ULC not 1916

REF	1706
Title	**The Directory of South Wales including Monmouthshire**
Dates	1920-1932
Publisher	The Town & Counties Publishing Co
Printer	Mason, C.J. & Sons
Place	Bristol
Type	TR
Map scale	–
Notes	Major towns with alph. lists of traders in each
Library	BL all
holdings	NPT has 1920

REF	1707
Title	**South Wales Directory**
Dates	1926,1935,1936,1938
Publisher	Aubrey & Co
Printer	Aubrey & Co
Place	Walsall
Type	TR
Map scale	–
Notes	Covers counties of Glamorgan, Brecknock, Carmarthen & Pembroke.
Library	BL not 1926
holdings	CLC has 1926

REF	1708
Title	**Business Directory of Wales**
Dates	1933,1940
Publisher	Business Directories
Printer	–
Place	Bloxwich
Type	TR
Map scale	–
Library	BPH has 1933
holdings	CLC has 1940

REF	1709
Title	**North and Central Wales Directory**
Dates	1935,1936,1938
Publisher	Aubrey & Co
Printer	Aubrey & Co
Place	London
Type	TR
Map scale	–
Notes	Covers counties of Anglesey, Cardigan, Caernarvon, Denbigh, Flint, Radnor, Montgomery & Merioneth
Library	BL

REF	1710
Title	**Industrial Directory of Wales and Monmouthshire**
Dates	1948
Publisher	The Industrial Association of Wales & Monmouthshire
Printer	Western Mail & Echo Ltd
Place	Cardiff
Type	SP
Map scale	–
Notes	Alph. lists of firms & TR section
Library	CLC
holdings	NLS
	ULC

5.2   Welsh counties

CAERNARVONSHIRE

REF	**1711**
Title	**Llandudno, Craig-y-don and Deganwy Complete Directory and Guide**
Dates	1903
Publisher	Jones, R.E. & Bros
Printer	Weekly News
Place	Conway
Type	GE TR
Map scale	–
Library	NLW

REF	**1712**
Title	**The Llandudno, Deganwy, Conway & Llandudno Junction Directory**
Dates	1911,1914,1922,1925,1929
Publisher	The Wentworth Publishing Co
Printer	The Wentworth Publishing Co
Place	Liverpool
Type	GE
Map scale	1:10560
Library	BL all
holdings	GL has 1929

REF	**1713**
Title	**Kelly's Directory of Llandudno & Conway**
Dates	1939
Publisher	Kelly's Directories Ltd
Printer	Kelly's Directories Ltd
Place	London
Type	GE TR
Map scale	–
Library	BL
holdings	BPH
	CLM
	GL

CARMARTHENSHIRE

REF	**1714**
Title	**Chalinder's Llanelly Directory**
Dates	1872
Publisher	Chalinder, J.J.
Printer	Broom & Thomas
Place	Llanelly
Type	CM TR
Map scale	–
Library	NLS

REF	**1715**
Title	**James Davies & Co's Llanelly Directory and Local Guide**
Dates	1897
Publisher	Davies, D.J.
Printer	Davies, D.J.
Place	Llanelly
Type	GE TR
Map scale	–
Library	NLW

DENBIGHSHIRE/ FLINTSHIRE

REF	**1716**
Title	**Crocker's Wrexham Directory and Postal Guide**
Dates	1881
Publisher	Crocker, W.C.
Printer	Crocker, W.C.
Place	Shrewsbury
Type	GE
Map scale	–
Library	WRX

REF	**1717**
Title	**Wrexham Directory**
Dates	1886
Publisher	Clywd Record Office
Printer	Clywd County Council
Place	Deeside
Type	GE TR
Map scale	–
Notes	GL Edition is a facsimile reprint of the Wrexham section of the 'Postal Directory of Flintshire and Denbighshire', see 1697
Library	GL

REF | 1718
Title | **The Red Book and Trades Directory and Diary for Wrexham and District**
Dates | 1892,1893
Publisher | Woodall, Minshall & Thomas
Printer | Woodall, Minshall & Thomas
Place | Wrexham
Type | GE TR
Map scale | 1:190080
Library | BL has 1892
holdings | BOD has 1893
 | WRX has 1892

REF | 1719
Title | **The Wrexham & District Directory**
Dates | 1907,1909
Publisher | Bennett & Co
Printer | Bennett & Co
Place | Birmingham
Type | CT TR
Map scale | –
Library | NLW has 1907
holdings | WRX all

REF | 1720
Title | **Jarman's Wrexham Year Book and Local Directory**
Dates | 1908-1915,1919-1939
Publisher | Jarman & Sons Ltd
Printer | Jarman & Sons Ltd
Place | Wrexham
Type | SP
Map scale | –
Notes | Directory of professional/municipal bodies, some of the later editions contain telephone directories
Library | NLW has 1908-1939
holdings | WRX all

REF | 1721
Title | **Directory of Colwyn Bay, Rhos-on-Sea, Old Colwyn, Upper Colwyn, Upper Colwyn Bay & Mochdre**
Dates | 1911,1914,1922,1925,1929
Publisher | The Wentworth Publishing Co
Printer | The Wentworth Publishing Co
Place | Liverpool
Type | GE TR
Map scale | 1:10560
Library | BL all
holdings | CLM has 1929
 | GL has 1929
 | NLW has 1911

REF | 1722
Title | **The Wrexham Leader Official Commercial Directory for Wrexham**
Dates | 1931,1932,1934,1936-1939,1946, 1947,1950
Publisher | Wrexham Leader
Printer | Wrexham Leader
Place | Wrexham
Type | GE TR
Map scale | 1:253440
Library | BL has 1947,1950
holdings | CCL has 1947
 | GL has 1938,1946-1950
 | WRX all

REF | 1723
Title | **Kelly's Directory of Colwyn Bay**
Dates | 1937,1939,1941
Publisher | Kelly's Directories Ltd
Printer | Kelly's Directories Ltd
Place | London
Type | GE TR
Map scale | –
Library | BL all
holdings | BPH not 1937
 | CLM has 1941
 | GL not 1941
 | NLW has 1939
 | SOG has 1937

REF | 1724
Title | **The Leader Directory of Rhyl**
Dates | 1935,1937
Publisher | Rhyl Leader
Printer | Rhyl Leader
Place | Rhyl
Type | ST
Map scale | –
Library | CLM has 1937
holdings | GL all

GLAMORGANSHIRE

REF | 1725
Title | **Pearse's Swansea Directory including Neath, Llanelly and the neighbourhood**
Dates | 1854,1856
Publisher | Pearse, E.
Printer | Pearse, E.
Place | Swansea
Type | CM TR
Map scale | –
Library | CLC has 1856
holdings | SWA all

[323]

REF **1726**
Title **Ewen's Guide and Directory for the Town of Cardiff and is environs**
Dates 1855
Publisher Ewen, J.
Printer Jones, W.
Place Cardiff
Type GE TR
Map scale –
Notes NORTON 872
Library CLC

REF **1727**
Title **Wakeford's Cardiff Directory**
Dates 1855,1863
Publisher Wakeford, C.
Printer Wakeford, C.
Place Cardiff
Type GE TR
Map scale –
Notes NORTON 873 (1855)
Library BL has 1855
holdings BOD has 1855
CLC all
GL has 1855
NLS has 1855

REF **1728**
Title **The Cardiff Directory and Handbook**
Dates 1858
Publisher Bird, H.
Printer Bird, H.
Place Cardiff
Type ST TR
Map scale –
Library NLW

REF **1729**
Title **Duncan & Ward's Cardiff Directory**
Dates 1863
Publisher Duncan & Ward
Printer Duncan & Ward
Place Cardiff
Type CM TR
Map scale –
Library CLC

REF **1730**
Title **Pearse & Brown's Swansea Directory including Oystermouth, Sketty, Swansea Valley etc**
Dates 1869
Publisher Pearse & Brown
Printer –
Place Swansea
Type CM TR
Map scale –
Library CLC

REF **1731**
Title **Percy, Butcher & Co's Swansea & Neath Directory**
Dates 1873
Publisher Percy, Butcher & Co
Printer Percy, Butcher & Co
Place London
Type GE
Map scale 1:506880
Library BL
holdings CLC

REF **1732**
Title **The Official Directory, Handbook and General Postal Guide for Merthyr Tydfil**
Dates 1873
Publisher Morgan, D.
Printer Eyre & Spottiswoode
Place Merthyr Tydfil
Type TR
Map scale –
Library NLW

REF **1733**
Title **Butcher & Co's Directory of Swansea, Neath, Llanelly, Bridgend etc**
Dates 1873,1875,1881
Publisher Butcher, G.P.
Printer –
Place London
Type GE TR
Map scale –
Notes 1881 edition entitled 'Butcher's Swansea District Directory'
Library BOD has 1881
holdings NLS has 1881
NLW not 1873
SWA not 1875
ULC has 1881

REF	**1734**
Title	**Percy, Butcher & Co's Cardiff & Newport Directory**
Dates	1873,1880
Publisher	Percy, Butcher & Co
Printer	Percy, Butcher & Co
Place	London
Type	CT CM
Map scale	1:506880
Library	BL all
holdings	CLC has 1873
	NLW has 1873
	NPT has 1873

REF	**1735**
Title	**Butcher & Co's Directory of Cardiff, Newport, Pontypool, Pontypridd, Llandaff etc**
Dates	1875,1880,1882
Publisher	Butcher & Co
Printer	–
Place	London
Type	GE
Map scale	1:443520
Notes	1880 & 1882 entitled 'Butcher's Cardiff District Directory including Pontypridd, Llandaff etc'. Cont'd as 1738.
Library	CLC all
holdings	NLW has 1875
	SWA has 1875

REF	**1736**
Title	**Slater's Post Office Directory of Cardiff & its suburbs**
Dates	1882,1883,1885
Publisher	Slater, I.
Printer	Slater, I.
Place	Manchester
Type	GE TR
Map scale	–
Library	BL not 1882
holdings	BOD has 1883
	CLC has 1882,1885
	GL has 1882
	NLS has 1883
	NLW has 1882

REF	**1737**
Title	**The Swansea Directory, Almanack, Diary & Tide Tables**
Dates	1883
Publisher	Williams, D. & Wright, A.C.
Printer	Owen, D. & Co
Place	Swansea
Type	ST TR
Map scale	NS
Library	CLC all
holdings	SWA

REF	**1738**
Title	**J. Wright & Co's Cardiff Directory**
Dates	1883-1886
Publisher	Wright, J. & Co
Printer	Wright, J. & Co
Place	Cardiff
Type	GE TR
Map scale	1:10560
Notes	Cont'd from 1735, cont'd as 1740.
Library	GL has 1885

REF	**1739**
Title	**Swansea and District Directory**
Dates	1887,1894
Publisher	Cambria Daily Leader
Printer	Cambria Daily Leader
Place	Swansea
Type	GE TR
Map scale	–
Library	CLC has 1894
holdings	SWA all

REF	**1740**
Title	**Daniel Owen & Co's Cardiff Directory**
Dates	1887-1897
Publisher	Owen, D. & Co
Printer	Owen, D. & Co
Place	Cardiff
Type	GE
Map scale	1:10560
Notes	Cont'd from 1738, cont'd as 1745
Library	BL has 1895,1897
holdings	CLC not 1895
	NLW has 1890

REF **1741**
Title **Wright's Swansea Directory**
Dates 1889,1899,1904
Publisher Wright, A.C.
Printer Wright, A.C.
Place Swansea
Type GE TR
Map scale –
Library BL has 1904
holdings NLW has 1899
SWA all

REF **1742**
Title **Western Mail Barry & District Directory**
Dates 1897,1907,1909,1911,1914
Publisher Western Mail Ltd
Printer Western Mail Ltd
Place Cardiff
Type GE TR
Map scale 1:10560
Notes Map scale approx.
Library BL not 1897
holdings CLC has 1897,1909
NLW not 1897,1914

REF **1743**
Title **Western Mail Pontypridd and District Directory**
Dates 1897,1908,1910,1913
Publisher Western Mail Ltd
Printer Western Mail Ltd
Place Cardiff
Type GE TR
Map scale 1:12000
Library BL has 1913
holdings CLC has 1897,1913
NLW not 1897

REF **1744**
Title **Cardiff (Swansea, Newport) and District Trades' Directory**
Dates 1899,1901,1907,1909,1910,1912,
1914,1915,1920-1931,1934,1936,
1948,1950
Publisher Town and County Directories
Ltd
Printer Macdonald, W. & Co
Place Edinburgh
Type TR
Map scale –
Notes See 1747. From 1907 title includes
Swansea & Newport.
Library CLC not 1926,1928
holdings NLW has 1899
NPT has 1912,1921,1923,1927,
1928,1936;1931(MONM & Npt
only)
SWA has 1919,1922-1924,
1926-1930

REF **1745**
Title **Cardiff Directory including Penarth and Llandaff**
Dates 1899-1916,1918-1920,1922,1924,
1927,1929,1932,1937
Publisher Western Mail Co
Printer Western Mail Co
Place Cardiff
Type GE TR
Map scale 1:10560
Notes Cont'd from 1740, cont'd as 1754
Library BL all
holdings BOD has 1937
CLC all
GL has 1924,1932
MLG has 1922
NLS has 1937
NLW has 1907,1909,1910,1912,
1913,1915-1929,1937
ULC has 1937

REF **1746**
Title **South Wales Daily Post Swansea & District Directory**
Dates 1900
Publisher South Wales Daily Post
Printer South Wales Daily Post
Place Swansea
Type GE
Map scale –
Library SWA

REF **1747**
Title **Swansea and District Trades' Directory**
Dates 1900,1904-1906
Publisher Town and County Directories Ltd
Printer Macdonald, W. & Co
Place Edinburgh
Type TR
Map scale –
Notes Cont'd by 1744
Library SWA

REF **1748**
Title **Purrier's Swansea Directory**
Dates 1907,1908,1910,1911,1913
Publisher Purrier, A.
Printer –
Place Swansea
Type ST TR
Map scale –
Library BOD has 1907
holdings CLC all
NLS has 1907
SWA all
ULC has 1907

REF **1749**
Title **Pontypridd, Treforest and District Directory**
Dates 1908
Publisher Glossop, S.
Printer –
Place Cardiff
Type GE
Map scale –
Library CLC

REF **1750**
Title **Cowbridge, Llantrisant and Bridgend Directory including Llantwit Major and Vale of Glamorgan**
Dates 1912
Publisher Journal of Commerce Printing Works
Printer Journal of Commerce Printing Works
Place Cardiff
Type GE
Map scale –
Library CLC

REF **1751**
Title **Cardiff Year Book**
Dates 1921-1933
Publisher Williams, A.S. & Kewer-Williams, R.F. [eds]
Printer –
Place Cardiff
Type CM
Map scale 1:316800
Notes Although mainly a year book, there are CM & exports sections
Library CLC

REF **1752**
Title **The Swansea Directory**
Dates 1929
Publisher The Bart Cronin Advertising Agency Ltd
Printer The Bart Cronin Advertising Agency Ltd
Place Swansea
Type GE TR
Map scale –
Notes Cont'd by 1753
Library SWA

REF **1753**
Title **The Swansea County Borough Directory**
Dates 1938
Publisher Western Express Newspaper Ltd
Printer Western Express Newspaper Ltd
Place Swansea
Type GE TR
Map scale –
Notes Cont'd from 1752
Library BCL
holdings CLC
SWA

REF **1754**
Title **Kelly's "Western Mail" Directory of Cardiff**
Dates 1949
Publisher Kelly's Directories Ltd
Printer Kelly's Directories Ltd
Place London
Type GE TR
Map scale –
Notes Cont'd from 1745
Library BL
holdings BOD
CLC
GL
MLG
NLS
SOG
ULC

[327]

REF	**1755**		REF	**1758**
Title	**The Swansea Area Industrial and Trades Directory**		Title	**Johns' Directory of Newport & Neighbourhood**
Dates	1950		Dates	1877,1880-1890,1892-1917,1919, 1920,1922-1942,1946
Publisher	Thomas & Pryer		Publisher	Johns, R.
Printer	Swansea Printers Ltd		Printer	Johns, R.
Place	Swansea		Place	Newport (Mon)
Type	ST TR		Type	GE TR
Map scale	–		Map scale	1:16896
Library	CLC		Notes	1877 edition published by Johns Brothers
holdings	CLM		Library	BL has 1884,1900-1917,1920,
	SWA		holdings	1923-1930,1932-1941,1946

MONMOUTHSHIRE

				BOD has 1900-1902
				GL has 1916,1936,1937,1946
REF	1756			MLG has 1936,1940,1941,1946
Title	**Lascelles & Co's Directory & Gazetteer of the County of Monmouth**			NLW has 1881,1888,1892,1897, 1900,1901,1903,1907-1930, 1933-1941
Dates	1852			NLS has 1900,1901
Publisher	Lascelles & Co			NPT not 1881
Printer	Lascelles & Co			ULC has 1900-1902
Place	Birmingham			
Type	CM TR		REF	**1759**
Map scale	1:190080		Title	**Hillman's Directory of Chepstow and the Parishes comprising the Chepstow Union**
Notes	NORTON 556			
Library	CLC			
holdings	NPT		Dates	1882,1884,1887,1888
			Publisher	Hillman & Co
REF	**1757**		Printer	Hillman & Co
Title	**Kelly's Directory of Monmouthshire**		Place	Chepstow
			Type	CT CM
Dates	1937		Map scale	–
Publisher	Kelly's Directories Ltd		Library	NLW
Printer	Kelly's Directories Ltd			
Place	London		REF	**1760**
Type	GE TR		Title	**W.N. Johns's Newport Directory and Year Book of Useful Information**
Map scale	NS			
Notes	Cont'd from 1689			
Library	BL		Dates	1885
holdings	GL		Publisher	Johns, W.N.
	BOD		Printer	–
	NLS		Place	Newport (Mon)
	ULC		Type	GE
	CLM		Map scale	–
	SCL		Notes	Distinguishes voters & non-voters. Only one edition of this directory ever appears to have been published. It should not be confused with 1758.
	NLW			
	BCL			
	BPH			
	CLB		Library	NPT
	NPT			

REF	**1761**
Title	**Johns' Directory of Pontypool**
Dates	1901,1906
Publisher	Johns, R.H.
Printer	Johns, R.H.
Place	Newport (Mon)
Type	GE TR
Map scale	NS
Library	BL all
Holdings	BOD has 1901
	CLC has 1901
	NLW has 1906
	ULC has 1901

REF	**1762**
Title	**The Abergavenny Mail Directory and Year Book**
Dates	1906
Publisher	Vaughan, T.G.
Printer	Vaughan, T.G.
Place	Ledbury
Type	ST TR
Map scale	1:10560
Library	BL

REF	**1763**
Title	**Kelly's Directory of Newport**
Dates	1950
Publisher	Kelly's Directories Ltd
Printer	Kelly's Directories Ltd
Place	London
Type	GE TR
Map scale	1:14908
Library	BL
Holdings	GL
	MLG
	NLW
	NPT

MONTGOMERYSHIRE

REF	**1764**
Title	**The Montgomeryshire Almanac and Official Directory**
Dates	1908,1909
Publisher	County Times
Printer	County Times
Place	Welshpool
Type	SP
Map scale	–
Notes	Directory relates to public and official bodies only
Library	NLW

PEMBROKESHIRE

REF	**1765**
Title	**The Haverfordwest and Milford Haven Telegraph Almanack and Directory**
Dates	1889,1897,1905,1906,1908-1915
Publisher	Telegraph
Printer	Lewis, W.
Place	Haverfordwest
Type	TR
Map scale	–
Library	NLW

RADNORSHIRE

REF	**1766**
Title	**Radnor Redbook, Directory and Almanack**
Dates	1909-1912
Publisher	Oldbury, E.J.
Printer	–
Place	Llandrindod Wells
Type	GE
Map scale	–
Library	NLW

Chapter 6
SCOTLAND AND SCOTTISH COUNTIES

6.1   Scottish directories

REF	1767
Title	**The Commercial Directory of Ireland, Scotland, and the four most Northern Counties of England for 1820-21 & 22**
Dates	1820
Publisher	Pigot, J. & Co
Printer	Pigot, J. & Co
Place	Manchester
Type	TR
Map scale	–
Notes	See 1768
Library holdings	CLA DDL NLS SLP WLG

REF	1768
Title	**Pigot & Co's National Commercial Directory of the Whole of Scotland and the Isle of Man**
Dates	1825, 1837
Publisher	Pigot, J. & Co
Printer	–
Place	London
Type	CM TR
Map scale	1:871200
Notes	See 1767
Library holdings	ACL has 1825 BOD has 1837 CLM has 1837 ELD all FLK has 1837 (dated 1825) GL has 1837 IHR has 1837 MLG all MTH has 1825 NLS all SLP has 1837

REF	1769
Title	**The Circulation of the Edinburgh, Leith, Glasgow & North British Commercial Advertiser**
Dates	1827
Publisher	Gray, J. & J.
Printer	Peacock & Fairgreave
Place	Edinburgh
Type	SP
Map scale	–
Notes	Alph. list of persons taking the 'North British Advertiser' in major Scottish towns, with ST sections for Edinburgh, Leith & Glasgow
Library	GL

REF	1770
Title	**The Angus and Mearns Commercial and Agricultural Remembrancer**
Dates	1829-1832,1834,1836-1838,1840, 1842,1845,1846,1848,1851
Publisher	Mitchell, J.
Printer	Mitchell, J.
Place	Montrose
Type	CT
Map scale	–
Notes	List of freeholders/electors only
Library holdings	BPL has 1837 DDL has 1845-1851 FPL not 1845,1848,1851

REF	1771
Title	**Directory to Noblemen and Gentlemens' Seats, Villages in Scotland**
Dates	1843,1852,1857
Publisher	Sutherland & Knox
Printer	Ballantyne & Co
Place	Edinburgh
Type	CT
Map scale	1:1267200
Notes	Continued as 1774

Library holdings	ACL has 1852
	BL has 1857
	BOD all
	CLA has 1843,1857
	ELD all
	IHR has 1852
	MLG all
	NLS all
	SOG has 1843
	ULC not 1843

REF	**1772**
Title	**The Angus and Mearns Directory**
Dates	1846,1847
Publisher	Watt, J.
Printer	Montrose Standard
Place	Montrose
Type	CM
Map scale	–
Library holdings	BPL has 1847
	DDL has 1847
	FPL has 1846
	NLS has 1846

REF	**1773**
Title	**Slater's Royal National Commercial Directory and Topography of Scotland**
Dates	1852,1860,1861,1867,1873,1878, 1882,1886,1889,1893,1896,1899, 1900,1903,1905,1907,1911,1915
Publisher	Slater, I.
Printer	Slater, I.
Place	Manchester
Type	GE TR
Map scale	1:1267200
Notes	Also includes large English towns. Cont'd as 1798
Library holdings	BCL has 1852,1882,1889-1915
	BL not 1878,1889,1899
	BOD has 1882,1889-1896,1900, 1903,1907-1915
	CLA has 1867
	CLM has 1860,1867,1873,1886, 1893,1896-1915
	ELD has 1852
	FLK has 1889 STIR only
	GL not 1852,1861,1882,1886, 1900
	MLG not 1899,1905
	NLS all
	NLW has 1915
	SLP has 1860,1893
	SOG has 1867,1878,1896,1911
	ULC has 1893,1896,1915

REF	**1774**
Title	**The County Directory of Scotland**
Dates	1862,1868,1872,1875,1878,1882, 1886,1894,1902,1912
Publisher	Grant, R. & Son
Printer	Ballantyne & Co
Place	Edinburgh
Type	CT
Map scale	1:760320
Notes	Cont'd from 1771. Edited by W.W. Halliburton.
Library holdings	ACL has 1862,1875
	BCL has 1872
	BL not 1872
	BOD has 1862-1882,1894,1902, 1912
	CLA has 1912
	ELD has 1862,1872
	GL not 1862,1875,1878,1894, 1912
	HAM has 1862,1868,1902,1912
	MLG all
	NLS all
	SOG has 1868
	STR has 1886
	ULC has 1862-1882,1886,1894, 1902,1912

REF	**1775**
Title	**The Southern Counties Register and Directory for Roxburgh, Berwick & Selkirk**
Dates	1866
Publisher	Rutherford, J. & J.H.
Printer	Rutherford, J. & J.H.
Place	Kelso
Type	CT
Map scale	–
Library holdings	BL
	GL
	MLG
	NLS
	SOG

REF	**1776**
Title	**The Commercial Directory of Glasgow and the West of Scotland**
Dates	1870,1872,1874
Publisher	Dougall, J.
Printer	Bruce and Martin
Place	Glasgow
Type	CM TR
Map scale	–
Library	MLG

REF 1777
Title **The Poor Law Directory for Scotland**
Dates 1874
Publisher Duncan Grant & Co
Printer Duncan Grant & Co
Place Edinburgh
Type SP
Map scale –
Notes Alph. list of parishes with post town, county, chairman's name, inspector's name & medical officers etc.
Library NLS

REF 1778
Title **Worrall's Directory of the North Eastern Counties of Scotland comprising ... Forfar, Fife, Kinross, Aberdeen, Banff and Kincardine**
Dates 1877
Publisher Worrall, J.
Printer Worrall, J.
Place Oldham
Type GE TR
Map scale –
Notes ACL edition entitled 'Worrall's Directory for the counties of Aberdeen, Banff and Kincardine'
Library ACL
holdings BL
BOD
NLS

REF 1779
Title **Macdonald's Scottish Directory and Gazetteer**
Dates 1884-1886,1889-1891,1893, 1897-1944,1947-1950
Publisher Macdonald, W. & Co
Printer Avery, J. & Co
Place Edinburgh
Type TR
Map scale –
Library BL not 1886,1891,1895
holdings BOD has 1884,1885,1891, 1899-1944,1950
CLM has 1932
GL has 1914
MLG has 1884-1886,1891,1893, 1895,1897-1932,1934,1935, 1947,1948,1950
NLS not 1884-1890,1893-1896, 1922,1923,1947-1950
NLW has 1913-1944

REF 1780
Title **Clark's Trades and Professions Directory for the Counties of Forfar, Perth and Fife**
Dates 1885
Publisher Clark, D.R. & Son
Printer Clark, D.R. & Son
Place Dundee
Type CT TR
Map scale –
Library DDL

REF 1781
Title **The West Coast Almanack and Business Directory**
Dates 1886
Publisher Higgie & Paterson
Printer Higgie & Paterson
Place Rothesay
Type TR
Map scale –
Notes Covers counties of Ayr, Argyll, Bute & Ross
Library NLS

REF 1782
Title **Parochial Directory of Scotland**
Dates 1887-1892,1894
Publisher Adshead, N. & Son
Printer Adshead, N. & Son
Place Glasgow
Type SP
Map scale –
Notes List of county council & burgh officials, parishes with chairmen, officials of local boards, registrars Cont'd as 1787
Library BOD has 1894
holdings MLG has 1892,1894
NLS all

REF 1783
Title **Ayrshire, Dumfriesshire, Wigtownshire and Kirkcudbrightshire Business Directory**
Dates 1893
Publisher Lamburn, C.
Printer –
Place Edinburgh
Type TR
Map scale –
Library NLS

REF	**1784**
Title	**Fifeshire, Clackmannanshire and Kinross-shire Business Directory**
Dates	1893
Publisher	Lamburn, C.
Printer	–
Place	Edinburgh
Type	TR
Map scale	–
Library	MLG

REF	**1785**
Title	**Roxburghshire, Selkirkshire, Peeblesshire and Berwickshire Business Directory**
Dates	1893
Publisher	Lamburn, C.
Printer	–
Place	Edinburgh
Type	TR
Map scale	–
Library	MLG
holdings	NLS

REF	**1786**
Title	**Stirlingshire, Dunbartonshire and Linlithgowshire Business Directory**
Dates	1893
Publisher	Lamburn, C.
Printer	–
Place	Edinburgh
Type	TR
Map scale	–
Library	MLG
holdings	NLS

REF	**1787**
Title	**The Local Government Directory of Scotland**
Dates	1895,1896,1899-1918,1920-1930, 1932,1933
Publisher	Adshead, N. & Son
Printer	Adshead, N. & Son
Place	Glasgow
Type	SP
Map scale	–
Notes	Cont'd from 1782. See notes to 1782.
Library	MLG

REF	**1788**
Title	**Clarke's Business Directory of Scotland**
Dates	1895,1898
Publisher	Clarke, C. & Co
Printer	Clarke, C. & Co
Place	Glasgow
Type	TR
Map scale	–
Library	BL all
holdings	BOD has 1895
	MLG has 1898
	NLS has 1895
	ULC has 1895

REF	**1789**
Title	**The Border Counties ... Business Directory**
Dates	1897
Publisher	Lamburn, C.
Printer	–
Place	Glasgow
Type	TR
Map scale	–
Notes	Covers counties of Berwick, Haddington, Peebles, Roxburgh & Selkirk
Library	MLG
holdings	NLS

REF	**1790**
Title	**Collins' Business Directory of Scotland**
Dates	1899
Publisher	Collins Bros.
Printer	Collins Bros.
Place	Glasgow
Type	TR
Map scale	–
Library	BL

REF	**1791**
Title	**Edinburgh and South of Scotland Trades Directory**
Dates	1900
Publisher	Trades' Directories Ltd
Printer	Macdonald, W. & Co Ltd
Place	Edinburgh
Type	TR
Map scale	–
Notes	Includes Edinburgh & counties of Berwick, Haddington, Linlithgow, Peebles, Roxburgh & Selkirk
Library	NLS

REF **1792**
Title **Glasgow and West of Scotland Carriers Directory**
Dates 1900
Publisher The Leader Publishing Co
Printer The Leader Publishing Co
Place Glasgow
Type SP
Map scale –
Notes Alph. list of destinations, with carriers & departures
Library NLS

REF **1793**
Title **Glasgow and West of Scotland Trades Directory**
Dates 1903-1907
Publisher Trades' Directories Ltd
Printer Macdonald, W. & Co
Place Edinburgh
Type TR
Map scale –
Notes Covers counties of Argyll, Ayr, Bute, Dumbarton, Dumfries, Kirkcudbright, Lanark, Renfrew & Wigtown
Library MLG

REF **1794**
Title **Munro's Scottish Licensed Trade Directory**
Dates 1904,1906,1908,1910-1914, 1921-1949
Publisher Munro, J.M. Ltd
Printer Munro, J.M. Ltd
Place Glasgow
Type SP
Map scale –
Notes Public Houses arranged by county
Library BL

REF **1795**
Title **The Court Guide and Royal Blue Book of Scotland**
Dates 1905,1906
Publisher Deacon, C.W. & Co
Printer Deacon, C.W. & Co
Place London
Type CT PR
Map scale –
Library CLA has 1905
holdings MLG has 1905
NLS all
ULC all

REF **1796**
Title **The Chemists and Druggists Year Book and Directory for Scotland**
Dates 1914,1916-1918,1936-1939
Publisher Munro & Co
Printer –
Place Glasgow
Type SP
Map scale –
Library BL not 1914-1918
holdings MLG all
NLS not 1914,1917,1918

REF **1797**
Title **George Souter's Directory ... for counties of Inverness, Ross, Caithness and Sutherland**
Dates 1920
Publisher Souter, G.
Printer –
Place Dingwall
Type SP
Map scale –
Notes Contains valuation rolls, parish & county information. Arranged by parish, alph. by name.
Library NLS

REF **1798**
Title **Kelly's (Slater's) Directory of Scotland**
Dates 1921,1928
Publisher Kelly's Directories Ltd
Printer Kelly's Directories Ltd
Place London
Type CM TR
Map scale 1:1267200
Notes Cont'd from 1773
Library BCL all
holdings BL all
BOD all
BPH has 1928
CLB has 1928
CLM all
GL all
LCL has 1928
MLG all
NLS all
SCL all
SLP has 1921
SOG has 1928
ULC all

REF	**1799**
Title	**The Mercantile Directory (Jepson's) of Scotland and the North of England**
Dates	1922-1939
Publisher	Jepson's Publishing Co
Printer	–
Place	Birmingham
Type	TR
Map scale	–
Notes	Includes Lancs & Yorks
Library	MLG

REF	**1800**
Title	**Scottish Press Directory and Advertisers Guide**
Dates	1924
Publisher	Cuthbertson, D.C. & Co Ltd
Printer	Walker, A. & Son
Place	Glasgow
Type	SP
Map scale	–
Notes	Directory of newspapers arranged by county, with gazetteer of places (stating population, shops, general & specific industries etc.)
Library holdings	NLS ULC

REF	**1801**
Title	**The British Trades Directory**
Dates	1924
Publisher	The British Publishing Company
Printer	The British Publishing Company
Place	Glasgow
Type	TR
Map scale	–
Notes	Coverage of Scottish counties only
Library	MLG

REF	**1802**
Title	**Stirling, Linlithgow and Clackmannan Trades' Directory**
Dates	1925,1926,1937,1938
Publisher	Town and County Directories Ltd
Printer	Macdonald, W. & Co Ltd
Place	Edinburgh
Type	TR
Map scale	–
Library holdings	SHQ has 1937,1938 STR has 1925,1926

REF	**1803**
Title	**Dumfries, Kirkcudbright and Wigtown Trades' Directory**
Dates	1925,1928
Publisher	Town and County Directories Ltd
Printer	Macdonald, W. & Co Ltd
Place	Edinburgh
Type	TR
Map scale	–
Notes	With lists of farmers and county residents
Library holdings	ELD has 1925 NLS has 1928

REF	**1804**
Title	**Aberdeen, Banff, Kincardine, Moray and Nairn Trades' Directory**
Dates	1928,1939
Publisher	Town and County Directories Ltd
Printer	Macdonald, W. & Co Ltd
Place	Edinburgh
Type	TR
Map scale	–
Library	ACL

REF	**1805**
Title	**Murray's Glasgow and West of Scotland Trades Directory**
Dates	1934,1936
Publisher	The Mercantile and Commercial Directory Ltd
Printer	The Mercantile and Commercial Directory Ltd
Place	Glasgow
Type	TR
Map scale	–
Notes	Covers counties of Argyll, Ayr, Bute, Dumbarton, Dumfries, Kirkcudbright, Lanark, Renfrew & Wigtown. See notes to 1810.
Library holdings	BL all BOD all MLG has 1934 NLS all ULC all

REF	**1806**		REF	**1809**
Title	**ABC General Directory**		Title	**The Trades and Commercial Directory**
Dates	1934-1936		Dates	1935,1936
Publisher	Jack, J.		Publisher	McCall, J. & Co
Printer	Jack, J.		Printer	–
Place	Edinburgh		Place	Edinburgh
Type	TR		Type	TR
Map scale	–		Map scale	–
Library	BL all		Library	BL
holdings	NLS has 1936			

REF	**1807**
Title	**Murray's Dundee, Perth and Central Scotland Directory**
Dates	1935,1936
Publisher	The Mercantile and Commercial Directory Ltd
Printer	The Mercantile and Commercial Directory Ltd
Place	Glasgow
Type	TR
Map scale	–
Notes	Covers counties of Clackmannan, Fife, Forfar, Kinross, Perth & Stirling
Library	BL
holdings	BOD
	NLS
	ULC

REF	**1808**
Title	**Murray's Edinburgh & South East of Scotland Trades Directory**
Dates	1935,1936
Publisher	The Mercantile and Commercial Directory Ltd
Printer	The Mercantile and Commercial Directory Ltd
Place	Glasgow
Type	TR
Map scale	–
Notes	Covers Berwicks, Midlothian, Peebles, Roxburgh, Selkirk, Haddington & Linlithgow
Library	BL all
holdings	BOD all
	NLS all
	ULC has 1935

REF	**1810**
Title	**Murray's Aberdeen, Inverness and North of Scotland Trades Directory**
Dates	1936
Publisher	The Mercantile and Commercial Directory Ltd
Printer	The Mercantile and Commercial Directory ltd
Place	Glasgow
Type	TR
Map scale	–
Notes	Covers counties of Aberdeen, Banff, Caithness, Inverness, Kincardine, Moray, Nairn, Shetland, Ross & Cromarty & Sutherland. Also published under the title 'Brown's Trades Directory of Aberdeen etc'.
Library	BL
holdings	BOD
	NLS
	ULC

REF	**1811**
Title	**Aberdeen, Inverness and Northern Counties Trades' Directory**
Dates	1938,1944,1950
Publisher	McCormick, Son & Co
Printer	McCormick, Son & Co
Place	Glasgow
Type	TR
Map scale	–
Notes	Includes the counties of Aberdeen, Banff, Caithness, Inverness, Kincardine, Moray, Nairn, Shetland, Ross & Cromarty, Sutherland
Library	ACL

REF **1812**
Title **The Scottish National Register of Classified Trades**
Dates 1938-1942,1944,1946,1947,1949, 1950
Publisher Business Directories Ltd
Printer –
Place London
Type TR
Map scale –
Library BOD all
holdings MLG all
NLS all
NLW has 1938-1946,1950

REF **1813**
Title **Dumfries, Kirkcudbright and Ayr Trades' Directory**
Dates 1943,1946
Publisher McCormick, Son & Co'
Printer McCormick, Son & Co
Place Glasgow
Type TR
Map scale –
Notes 1946 edition entitled: 'Dumfries, Kirkcudbright, Wigtown and Ayr Trades' Directory'
Library ELD

REF **1814**
Title **Western Counties Trades' Directory**
Dates 1945,1948
Publisher McCormick, Son & Co
Printer McCormick, Son & Co
Place Glasgow
Type TR
Map scale –
Notes Includes the counties of Ayr, Argyll, Bute, Dumbarton, Dumfries, Kirkcudbright, Renfrew, Stirling & Wigtown. 1948 edition entitled 'McCormick's Scottish Western Counties Trades' Directory'.
Library ELD

REF **1815**
Title **Aberdeen and North of Scotland Trades' Directory**
Dates 1947,1948
Publisher Trades' Directories Ltd
Printer Macdonald, W. & Co Ltd
Place Edinburgh
Type TR
Map scale –
Notes Includes the counties of Aberdeen, Banff, Caithness, Inverness, Kincardine, Moray, Nairn, Shetland, Ross & Cromarty, Sutherland & Skye
Library ACL

REF **1816**
Title **Stirling, West Lothian and Kinross Trades' Directory**
Dates 1948
Publisher McCormick, Son & Co
Printer McCormick, Son & Co
Place Glasgow
Type TR
Map scale –
Library SHQ

REF **1817**
Title **Scotland and Northern Counties Trades Directory**
Dates 1950
Publisher Renfield Publishing Co
Printer –
Place Glasgow
Type TR
Map scale –
Notes Glasgow section & TR section alph. by place
Library MLG

6.2 Scottish counties

ABERDEENSHIRE

REF **1818**
Title **A Directory for the City of Aberdeen and its vicinity**
Dates 1824,1825,1827-1839
Publisher Gordon, Clark, Stevenson, Spark & Wyllie
Printer Chalmers, D. & Co
Place Aberdeen
Type CM
Map scale –
Library ACL not 1828,1830
holdings GL has 1830,1831,1833
NLS has 1828

REF **1819**
Title **The Aberdeen Almanack and Northern Register**
Dates 1839
Publisher Chalmers, C.D.
Printer Chalmers, C.D.
Place Aberdeen
Type CT PR
Map scale –
Library GL

REF **1820**
Title **The Bon Accord Directory [Aberdeen]**
Dates 1840-1845
Publisher Wilson, J.H.
Printer Finlayson, J.
Place Aberdeen
Type CM
Map scale 1:506880
Library ACL all
holdings GL has 1842
NLS has 1842
NLW has 1840

REF **1821**
Title **The Post Office and Bon Accord Directory [Aberdeen]**
Dates 1846,1847
Publisher Post Office
Printer Bennett, W.
Place Aberdeen
Type CM
Map scale –
Library ACL

REF **1822**
Title **Post Office Aberdeen Directory**
Dates 1848-1853,1856-1943,1946-1950
Publisher Post Office
Printer King, A.
Place Aberdeen
Type GE TR
Map scale 1:7554
Library ACL not 1864
holdings BL not 1848-1878,1880,1883, 1890-1892,1943
BIS has 1928
BOD has 1902-1950
CLM has 1927.1930-1932
GL not 1848-1859,1861-1863, 1865-1867,1871-1874, 1876-1878,1880,1881,1883, 1890-1892,1899-1946
MLG has 1882,1899-1916,1919, 1920,1922-1939,1941-1948
NLS not 1850-1867,1870-1878, 1880,1883,1890-1892, 1899-1901
NLW has 1852
SOG has 1903,1926
ULC has 1902-1950

REF **1823**
Title **Cornwall's New Aberdeen Directory**
Dates 1853
Publisher Cornwall, G.
Printer Cornwall, G.
Place Aberdeen
Type GE TR
Map scale –
Library ACL
holdings NLS

REF	**1824**
Title	**Peterhead Almanac and Directory**
Dates	1853
Publisher	Stuart, P.
Printer	Stuart, P.
Place	Peterhead
Type	CM
Map scale	–
Library	ACL
holdings	NLS

REF	**1825**
Title	**Directory of the City of Aberdeen**
Dates	1854,1855
Publisher	Bennett, W.
Printer	Bennett, W.
Place	Aberdeen
Type	GE
Map scale	–
Library	ACL all
holdings	GL has 1855

REF	**1826**
Title	**The Peterhead Almanac and Buchan Directory**
Dates	1864,1865
Publisher	Anderson, W.
Printer	Sentinel
Place	Peterhead
Type	TR
Map scale	–
Library	ACL

ANGUS

REF	**1827**
Title	**Hood's Forfarshire Almanac and Official Directory for the Burghs of Dundee, Arbroath, Montrose, Forfar, Brechin, Kirriemuir**
Dates	1880,1881
Publisher	Hood, J.F.
Printer	Hood, J.F.
Place	Arbroath
Type	PR
Map scale	–
Library	NLS

REF	**1828**
Title	**Forfarshire Directory**
Dates	1887
Publisher	Lamburn, C.
Printer	Avery, J. & Co
Place	Edinburgh
Type	CT TR
Map scale	–
Library	DDL

REF	**1829**
Title	**The Dundee Register and Directory**
Dates	1782,1783,1809,1818,1824
Publisher	Colville, A. & Co
Printer	Colville, A. & Co
Place	Dundee
Type	CM
Map scale	1:9600
Notes	1782 edition entitled 'The Dundee Register of Merchants & Trades' TR
Library	DDL not 1782
holdings	FPL has 1782
	GL has 1818,1824
	NLS has 1818,1824

REF	**1830**
Title	**Dundee Delineated (with a General Directory)**
Dates	1822
Publisher	Colville, A.
Printer	Colville, A. & Sandeman, A.
Place	Dundee
Type	CM
Map scale	–
Library	MLG

REF	**1831**
Title	**The Dundee Directory**
Dates	1829,1837,1840,1842,1850,1853, 1856
Publisher	Chalmers, C.D.
Printer	Chalmers, C.D.
Place	Dundee
Type	CT CM
Map scale	–
Library	DDL all
holdings	GL has 1840,1856
	IHR has 1829
	NLS has 1829

REF	**1832**
Title	**The Dundee Directory and General Register**
Dates	1834
Publisher	Allardice, A.
Printer	Dundee Chronicle
Place	Dundee
Type	CM
Map scale	1:5940
Library	DDL
holdings	GL

REF	**1833**
Title	**The Dundee Post Office Directory**
Dates	1845,1846,1858,1861,1864,1867, 1869,1871
Publisher	Dundee Post Office
Printer	Advertiser
Place	Dundee
Type	CM TR
Map scale	–
Notes	Cont'd as 1835
Library	DDL all
holdings	GL has 1845-1861
	NLS not 1845,1858

REF	**1834**
Title	**The Dundee Directory**
Dates	1853
Publisher	Stephen, A.M.
Printer	Stephen, A.M.
Place	Dundee
Type	CM TR
Map scale	–
Library	GL

REF	**1835**
Title	**The Dundee Directory**
Dates	1874-1915,1918-1927
Publisher	Mathew, J.P. & Co
Printer	Mathew, J.P. & Co
Place	Dundee
Type	GE TR
Map scale	1:10560
Notes	Cont'd from 1833, cont'd by 1841
Library	BL has 1876,1878,1880,1882,
holdings	1884-1914,1918,1920,1922,1927
holdings	BOD has 1874,1885,1888-1897,
	1903-1914,1920,1922,1923,
	1925-1927
	CLM has 1926
	GL has 1876
	MLG has 1874,1882,1895-1904,
	1920-1923,1925-1927
	NLS has 1882,1885-1923,
	1925-1927
	NLW has 1927
	SOG has 1871,1926
	ULC has 1885,1887-1897,
	1903-1915,1920-1927

REF	**1836**
Title	**The Montrose Year Book and Directory**
Dates	1884,1885,1887,1888,1890-1903, 1905-1923,1925-1950
Publisher	Foreman, J.
Printer	Foreman, J.
Place	Montrose
Type	CT
Map scale	–
Notes	Initially published by the Review Press
Library	BPL has 1898
holdings	FPL all
	MLG has 1934,1939,1940, 1942-1946,1948,1950

REF	**1837**
Title	**The Forfar Directory and Year Book**
Dates	1885-1895,1897-1911,1913-1916, 1927-1929,1935-1939
Publisher	Shepherd, W.
Printer	Shepherd, W.
Place	Forfar
Type	CT
Map scale	–
Library	BL has 1885,1888,1889
holdings	FPL all
	NLS has 1888
	ULC has 1888,1892

REF **1838**
Title **The Brechin Almanac and Directory**
Dates 1886-1893
Publisher Black & Johnston
Printer Black & Johnston
Place Brechin
Type TR
Map scale –
Library BPL

REF **1839**
Title **The Arbroath Year Book and Directory**
Dates 1889-1940,1948-1950
Publisher Brodie & Salmond
Printer Brodie & Salmond
Place Arbroath
Type GE TR
Map scale 1:9600
Library BL not 1889-1891,1916-1919,
holdings 1938-1950
DDL has 1891,1895
FPL not 1915
NLS has 1891,1894,1899

REF **1840**
Title **Glimpses of Old and New Dundee**
Dates 1925
Publisher Macleod, M.C.
Printer Jamieson & Munro Ltd
Place Dundee
Type SP
Map scale –
Notes By A.H. Millar. TR section followed by very detailed entries/histories of each firm, together with section on Dundee street names.
Library DDL
holdings FPL

REF **1841**
Title **The Dundee Directory**
Dates 1928-1942,1944,1946-1950
Publisher Burns & Harris Ltd
Printer Burns & Harris Ltd
Place Dundee
Type GE TR
Map scale 1:23760
Notes Cont'd from 1835
Library BL not 1944
holdings BOD not 1946-1950
CLM has 1929,1946,1947
DDL not 1944
GL has 1930,1933,1936-1939,
1941,1947-1950
MLG not 1944
NLS all
ULC all

REF **1842**
Title **The Forfar Annual and Directory**
Dates 1935
Publisher The Forfar Press
Printer The Forfar Press
Place Forfar
Type CM TR
Map scale –
Library FPL

REF **1843**
Title **Dundee, Forfar and Perth Trades' Directory**
Dates 1938
Publisher Town and County Directories Ltd
Printer Macdonald, W. & Co Ltd
Place Edinburgh
Type TR
Map scale –
Library BPL
holdings FPL

REF **1844**
Title **The Dundee Register of Trades and Professions**
Dates 1950
Publisher The Scottish Advertisers
Printer Smith, R.K. & Son
Place Dundee
Type TR
Map scale –
Library DDL

AYRSHIRE

REF	1845
Title	**Ayrshire containing Map of the County ... and Directory for Ayr**
Dates	1830,1832
Publisher	McCarter, W.
Printer	–
Place	Ayr
Type	CM
Map scale	NS
Notes	Contains both town & county maps. Also has list of county freeholders. 1830 edition entitled 'Brief Historical Reminiscences of the County and Town of Ayr ... Directory for Ayr, Newton and Wallacetown', by A. Burgess.
Library	CLA all
holdings	KIL has 1832
	MLG has 1832

REF	1846
Title	**The Ayrshire Directory**
Dates	1851
Publisher	Ayr Advertiser
Printer	Ayr Advertiser
Place	Ayr
Type	CT
Map scale	–
Library	BL
holdings	CLA
	KIL
	MLG
	NLS

REF	1847
Title	**North Ayrshire Directory**
Dates	1935
Publisher	Hunter, J.
Printer	The Herald
Place	Ardrossan
Type	CM
Map scale	–
Library	BOD
holdings	GL
	MLG
	NLS
	ULC

REF	1848
Title	**Kilmarnock Directory**
Dates	1833
Publisher	Brown, W. [compiler]
Printer	Paterson, J.
Place	Kilmarnock
Type	CM
Map scale	–
Library	KIL

REF	1849
Title	**Kilmarnock and Riccarton Directory**
Dates	1840
Publisher	Angus, J. (compiler)
Printer	Crawford, H. & Son
Place	Kilmarnock
Type	TR
Map scale	–
Library	NLS

REF	1850
Title	**Directory for Ayr, Newton, Wallacetown & Troon**
Dates	1841,1845,1858,1861,1864,1867, 1870
Publisher	Lockhart, C. [compiler]
Printer	Ayr Observer
Place	Ayr
Type	CM
Map scale	–
Notes	Cont'd as 1855. 1858-1870 entitled: 'Post Office Directory for Ayr, Newton, Wallacetown & Troon'
Library	CLA all
holdings	CLM has 1841
	KIL has 1841
	MLG not 1845

REF	1851
Title	**The Kilmarnock and Riccarton Post Office Directory**
Dates	1846,1855
Publisher	Post Office
Printer	Muir, W.
Place	Kilmarnock
Type	CM TR
Map scale	–
Library	KIL

REF **1852**
Title **The Post Office Directory for Ayr, Newton and Wallacetown**
Dates 1849
Publisher –
Printer Ayr Advertiser
Place Ayr
Type CM
Map scale –
Library CLA

REF **1853**
Title **The Kilmarnock Directory**
Dates 1851
Publisher Millar & Guthrie
Printer Millar & Guthrie
Place Kilmarnock
Type CM TR
Map scale –
Library KIL
holdings MLG

REF **1854**
Title **Post Office Kilmarnock Directory**
Dates 1868,1872
Publisher Post Office
Printer McKie, J.
Place Kilmarnock
Type CM TR
Map scale 1:10560
Notes Cont'd as 1857
Library BCL has 1868
holdings CLA has 1868
KIL all
MLG has 1868

REF **1855**
Title **Post Office General and Trades Directory for Ayr, Newton and Wallacetown**
Dates 1873,1876,1878,1880,1882,1884, 1886,1888,1890,1892,1894,1896, 1898,1900,1902-1904,1906-1912
Publisher Post Office
Printer Observer Office
Place Ayr
Type CM TR
Map scale –
Notes Cont'd from 1850. From 1894-1912 entitled 'Ayr Post Office General and Trades Directory for Ayr, Newton and Wallacetown', GE TR, printed by The Ayrshire Post Ltd.
Library CLA all
holdings NLS has 1873

REF **1856**
Title **Jonas' Kilmarnock Directory**
Dates 1879
Publisher Jonas, A.C.
Printer Jonas, A.C.
Place Kilmarnock
Type GE TR
Map scale –
Library CLA
holdings KIL

REF **1857**
Title **Kilmarnock Post Office Directory**
Dates 1882,1884,1887,1892,1895,1898, 1901,1904,1907,1910,1913
Publisher Smith. J.M. & Co
Printer –
Place Kilmarnock
Type CM TR
Map scale 1:10666
Notes Cont'd from 1854, cont'd as 1861. 1892 onwards published by Dunlop & Brennan.
Library CLA has 1913
holdings GL has 1901
KIL all
MLG has 1913

REF **1858**
Title **The Carrick Directory**
Dates 1883
Publisher Latta, J.
Printer Latta, J.
Place Maybole
Type CM
Map scale –
Library CLA

REF **1859**
Title **Post Office General and Trades Directory for Irvine**
Dates 1896
Publisher –
Printer Irvine Herald
Place Irvine
Type GE TR
Map scale –
Library NLS

REF	**1860**
Title	**Ayr and District Directory**
Dates	1913-1915,1918,1920,1922,1924, 1926,1928,1930,1934,1936,1938, 1940,1949
Publisher	Ayrshire Post Ltd
Printer	Ayrshire Post Ltd
Place	Ayr
Type	GE TR
Map scale	1:15840
Notes	Published by J. Browning & Co Ltd 1934-1940, and by Dallas Advertising Agency 1949
Library holdings	CLA all CLM has 1940 GL has 1934-1940 MLG has 1918,1926,1928, 1930-1936 NLS not 1913,1918,1949 SOG has 1930 SOG has 1930

REF	**1861**
Title	**Kilmarnock and District Directory**
Dates	1923,1928,1930,1933,1936,1939
Publisher	Standard Printing Works
Printer	Standard Printing Works
Place	Kilmarnock
Type	GE TR
Map scale	1:10667
Notes	Cont'd from 1857
Library holdings	CLA has 1923-1936 KIL has 1923,1928,1933,1939 MLG has 1928-1936

BANFFSHIRE

REF	**1862**
Title	**Banffshire Year Book and County Directory**
Dates	1890,1892-1896,1898-1915,1918, 1919
Publisher	Banffshire Journal Office
Printer	Banffshire Journal Office
Place	Banff
Type	CM
Map scale	–
Notes	Contains lists of voters
Library holdings	ACL all NLS has 1901-1906,1908-1912

BUTE

REF	**1863**
Title	**The West Coast Directory**
Dates	1883-1888
Publisher	Higgie, G.
Printer	Higgie, G.
Place	Rothesay
Type	GE
Map scale	–
Notes	See 1864
Library holdings	BL all BOD has 1883,1885,1888 MLG has 1884 NLS has 1883,1885,1886 ULC has 1883-1886

REF	**1864**
Title	**Bute County Directory**
Dates	1889,1891-1893,1895-1935
Publisher	Higgie & Coy
Printer	Higgie & Coy
Place	Rothesay
Type	GE TR
Map scale	–
Notes	See 1863
Library holdings	BL not 1889,1891,1892,1896, 1897 BOD not 1889,1891,1892,1934, 1935 MLG has 1889,1896,1898-1933 NLS not 1918 NLW has 1912-1931 ULC has 1889,1893,1895, 1900-1906,1909,1912, 1917-1919,1920,1922

CLACKMANNANSHIRE

REF	**1865**
Title	**Lothian's Annual Register for the County of Clackmannan**
Dates	1877,1878,1884,1887
Publisher	Lothian, J.
Printer	Lothian, J.
Place	Alloa
Type	CM
Map scale	–
Notes	Contains plan of public park of Alloa
Library	NLS

REF	**1866**
Title	**The County Register and Business Directory for Clackmannanshire**
Dates	1889-1912
Publisher	Buchan Bros.
Printer	Buchan Bros.
Place	Alloa
Type	CT
Map scale	–
Library holdings	BL all STR has 1892

DUMFRIESSHIRE

REF	**1867**
Title	**The County Directory of Dumfriesshire**
Dates	1910
Publisher	Courier and Herald
Printer	Courier and Herald
Place	Dumfries
Type	CT
Map scale	–
Notes	Small general directory, mostly information on parishes, clubs etc.
Library	NLS

REF	**1868**
Title	**Johnston's Directory of Dumfries, Maxwelltown &c**
Dates	1882
Publisher	Johnston & Sons
Printer	Johnston & Sons
Place	Dumfries
Type	GE TR
Map scale	NS
Notes	Map in very poor condition ELD
Library	ELD

REF	**1869**
Title	**The Visitors' Guide to Sanquhar & Neighbourhood with a list of the People in Business**
Dates	1886
Publisher	Wilson, W.
Printer	Wilson, W.
Place	Sanquhar
Type	TR
Map scale	–
Library	ELD

REF	**1870**
Title	**The Stewartry Illustrated Almanac and Directory**
Dates	1890-1892,1895,1897,1913
Publisher	Macbean, A.
Printer	Macbean, A.
Place	Kirkcudbright
Type	TR
Map scale	–
Notes	Covers towns in Dumfriesshire & Kirkcudbrightshire. In 1913 published by the Standard Branch Office.
Library	ELD

REF	**1871**
Title	**Post Office Dumfries, Maxwelltown and District Directory**
Dates	1893,1895,1897
Publisher	Post Office
Printer	Dumfries and Galloway Standard
Place	Dumfries
Type	GE TR
Map scale	–
Notes	1897 edition entitled 'Post Office Dumfries Directory'
Library	ELD

REF	**1872**
Title	**Dumfries and Maxwell Town Post Office Directory**
Dates	1901,1903
Publisher	Post Office
Printer	Courier and Herald
Place	Dumfries
Type	GE TR
Map scale	–
Library	ELD

REF	**1873**
Title	**Guide to Annan and Neighbourhood ... with ... Business Directory**
Dates	1902
Publisher	Watt, D. & Son
Printer	Watt, D. & Son
Place	Annan
Type	TR
Map scale	–
Library	ELD

REF	**1874**
Title	**Dumfries and District Post Office Directory**
Dates	1911,1913,1920,1923,1927,1930, 1933,1936,1939
Publisher	Post Office
Printer	Standard
Place	Dumfries
Type	GE TR
Map scale	NS
Library	ELD not 1923,1927
holdings	MLG not 1911-1920
	NLS has 1911

REF	**1875**
Title	**Annandale Post Office Directory**
Dates	1922
Publisher	Courier and Herald
Printer	Courier and Herald Press
Place	Dumfries
Type	GE
Map scale	—
Library	ELD

DUNBARTONSHIRE

REF	**1876**
Title	**Macneur and Bryden's Guide and Directory to Helensburgh and neighbourhood**
Dates	1875,1880,1881,1883,1885, 1895-1900,1925,1928,1930,1931, 1933,1935,1937,1939
Publisher	Macneur & Bryden
Printer	—
Place	Helensburgh
Type	GE TR
Map scale	1:14080
Library	MLG not 1875
holdings	NLS has 1875

FIFESHIRE

REF	**1877**
Title	**The Dunfermline Almanack and Register**
Dates	1835
Publisher	Miller, J. & Son
Printer	Miller, J. & Son
Place	Dunfermline
Type	GE
Map scale	—
Library	NLS

REF	**1878**
Title	**Westwood's Parochial Directory of Fife and Kinross**
Dates	1862,1866
Publisher	Westwood, A.
Printer	Westwood, A.
Place	Cupar
Type	TR
Map scale	1:126720
Library	BL has 1866
holdings	BOD all
	MLG has 1866
	NLS all
	SLP has 1866
	ULC all

REF	**1879**
Title	**The Tayside Annual and Directory for Newport, Wormit and Tayport**
Dates	1907,1908
Publisher	McFarlane, A.R. [editor]
Printer	Leng, J. & Co
Place	Dundee
Type	CM
Map scale	NS
Library	DDL

REF	**1880**
Title	**St Andrews Directory**
Dates	1909
Publisher	Wilson, G.
Printer	—
Place	St Andrews
Type	CM TR
Map scale	—
Library	BOD

REF **1881**
Title **Kirkcaldy and Dysart Directory**
Dates 1924
Publisher Strachan & Livingston, Ltd
Printer –
Place Kirkcaldy
Type CM TR
Map scale –
Library MLG

REF **1882**
Title **St Andrews Directory**
Dates 1935
Publisher The Atlas Press Ltd
Printer Paul & Matthew
Place Dundee
Type CT TR
Map scale –
Library NLS

INVERNESS-SHIRE

REF **1883**
Title **Inverness County Directory**
Dates 1887,1889,1899,1901,1902,1920
Publisher Fraser, J.A.
Printer Carruthers, R. & Sons
Place Inverness
Type CM
Map scale –
Notes For each address the yearly rent/
value is stated. Occupations not
always stated.
Library NLS

REF **1884**
Title **The Inverness Directory
containing street and alphabetical
lists, professional lists and other
useful information**
Dates 1873
Publisher -
Printer Advertiser
Place Inverness
Type GE
Map scale –
Library NLS

REF **1885**
Title **Inverness Burgh Directory**
Dates 1899,1901,1902,1904-1946,1949,
1950
Publisher Carruthers, R.
Printer Carruthers, R.
Place Inverness
Type GE TR
Map scale 1:6933
Library BL not 1899-1903,1943-1945
holdings BOD has 1946,1949
GL has 1936-1940,1949,1949
MLG has 1922-1925,1927,1931,
1933,1935,1937,1939,1941,
1946,1949
NLS not 1904,1936,1941
ULC has 1946-1950

KIRKCUDBRIGHTSHIRE

REF **1886**
Title **Stewartry of Kirkcudbright Post
Office Directory**
Dates 1921,1924
Publisher -
Printer Dinwiddie, R.
Place Dumfries
Type GE TR
Map scale –
Library ELD all
holdings MLG has 1924
NLS has 1924

LANARKSHIRE

REF **1887**
Title **The Lanarkshire Business
Directory**
Dates 1895
Publisher Lamburn, C.
Printer –
Place Glasgow
Type TR
Map scale –
Library HAM

REF **1888**
Title **Glasgow and Lanark Trades Directory**
Dates 1901,1902,1905,1906,1909,1916, 1919,1948
Publisher Town and County Directories Ltd
Printer Macdonald, W. & Co
Place Edinburgh
Type TR
Map scale —
Notes Also contains a county supplement (CT section)
Library LAN has 1901
holdings MLG not 1901

REF **1889**
Title **Glasgow Trades Directory, including Lanarkshire**
Dates 1905-1909,1916-1919,1921,1923, 1928
Publisher McCormick, Son & Co
Printer McCormick, Son & Co
Place Glasgow
Type TR
Map scale —
Library MLG

REF **1890**
Title **John Tait's Directory for the City of Glasgow ... also for the towns of Paisley, Greenock, Port-Glasgow and Kilmarnock**
Dates 1783
Publisher Tait, J.
Printer —
Place Glasgow
Type CM
Map scale —
Notes 1871 reprint of the original edition
Library BCL
holdings CLP
GL
IHR
KIL
MLG
NLS
SOG
WLG

REF **1891**
Title **Post Office Glasgow Directory**
Dates 1783-1921
Publisher Post Office
Printer Mackenzie, W.
Place Glasgow
Type GE TR
Map scale 1:1200
Notes Cont'd as 'Kelly's Directory of Glasgow', see 1911
Library BL all
holdings BIS has 1875
BOD has 1828,1862-1870, 1872-1882,1886-1921
GL has 1828,1831,1834, 1838-1847,1852,1854-1856, 1861-1867,1872-1877,1879, 1882,1883,1886-1890,1903, 1907,1908,1910,1913,1914, 1917,1920
IHR has 1843
MLG all
NLS not 1829-1834,1838,1841, 1845,1848-1851,1855,1871, 1874
NLW has 1921-1923,1925-1928, 1930-1950
SOG has 1848,1913
ULC has 1839,1863-1870, 1872-1921

REF **1892**
Title **Jones's Directory or Useful Pocket Companion for ... the City of Glasgow**
Dates 1787,1789,1790
Publisher Jones
Printer Mennons, J.
Place Glasgow
Type CM
Map scale —
Notes 1789 edition is a 1973 reprint by Blackie & Sons, Glasgow (BOD). 1787 edition is 1868 reprint (GL)
Library BIS has 1789
holdings BOD has 1789
CLP has 1787,1789
GL all
IHR has 1787,1789
NLS has 1789
MLG all
SOG has 1787,1789
WLG has 1787

REF	1893
Title	**The Glasgow Directory**
Dates	1804,1817-1827
Publisher	McFeat, W.
Printer	Land, W.
Place	Glasgow
Type	CM
Map scale	–
Library	GL has 1804,1817,1823,1826
holdings	NLS not 1804,1817
	12

REF	1894
Title	**The Hamilton Directory**
Dates	1847
Publisher	Brown and Naismith
Printer	Brown and Naismith
Place	Hamilton
Type	CT CM
Map scale	–
Notes	CT section is a list of electors.
Library	HAM

REF	1895
Title	**Brown's Hamilton Directory**
Dates	1855
Publisher	Brown, J.
Printer	Brown, J.
Place	Hamilton
Type	CM
Map scale	1:6336
Notes	Map scale approx.
Library	HAM
holdings	NLS

REF	1896
Title	**Hamilton Directory**
Dates	1859,1878
Publisher	Naismith, W.
Printer	Naismith, W.
Place	Hamilton
Type	CT CM
Map scale	–
Notes	1878 edition entitled 'Naismith's Hamilton Directory'.
Library	HAM

REF	1897
Title	**Handbook of Hamilton, Bothwell, Blantyre and Uddingston with a Directory**
Dates	1862
Publisher	Naismith, W.
Printer	Naismith, W.
Place	Hamilton
Type	CM
Map scale	NS
Notes	Author: A. MacPherson
Library	HAM
holdings	MTH

REF	1898
Title	**Slater's Royal National Commercial Directory of Glasgow**
Dates	1880
Publisher	Slater, I.
Printer	Slater, I.
Place	Manchester
Type	GE
Map scale	1:792000
Library	GL

REF	1899
Title	**The Hamilton Directory**
Dates	1883,1889
Publisher	Dick, R.W.
Printer	Dick, R.W.
Place	Hamilton
Type	CM
Map scale	–
Notes	1889 edition includes ST section
Library	HAM

REF	1900
Title	**Peat & Forrest's Directory of Hamilton, Blantyre & Larkhall**
Dates	1884
Publisher	Peat & Forrest
Printer	Peat & Forrest
Place	Hamilton
Type	CM TR
Map scale	–
Library	HAM

REF	1901
Title	**Uddingston Directory**
Dates	1887,1889,1891,1893,1895,1899
Publisher	Myles, W.
Printer	Myles, W.
Place	Uddingston
Type	CM
Map scale	–
Notes	1889 onwards entitled 'Uddingston and Bothwell Directory'. 1895 & 1899 editions also contain a reprint of an unidentified 1862 Uddingston Directory (CM).
Library	HAM

REF	1902
Title	**Pomphrey's Directory and Handbook of Wishaw with Shotts Supplement**
Dates	1887,1893
Publisher	Pomphrey, W.
Printer	Pomphrey, W.
Place	Wishaw
Type	TR
Map scale	–
Library	MLG

REF	1903
Title	**Russell's Glasgow and Suburban Street Guide**
Dates	1890
Publisher	Russell & Co
Printer	Russell & Co
Place	Glasgow
Type	SL
Map scale	–
Library	BL

REF	1904
Title	**Adshead's Penny Street Directory of Greater Glasgow**
Dates	1892,1914,1915,1917,1919-1924, 1935,1936
Publisher	Adshead, N. & Son
Printer	Adshead, N. & Son
Place	Glasgow
Type	SL
Map scale	–
Library	BL not 1935,1936
holdings	NLS has 1892,1935,1936

REF	1905
Title	**History and Directory of Motherwell**
Dates	1894,1899
Publisher	Naismith, W.
Printer	Naismith, W.
Place	Hamilton
Type	TR
Map scale	1:10560
Notes	1894 edition entitled 'Handbook & Directory of Motherwell'
Library	MLG has 1894
holdings	MTH all
	NLS has 1899

REF	1906
Title	**Clarke's Airdrie Directory**
Dates	1896
Publisher	Clarke, C.
Printer	Clarke, C.
Place	Glasgow
Type	GE
Map scale	–
Library	BL
holdings	MLG
	NLS
	ULC

REF	1907
Title	**Clarke's Motherwell Directory**
Dates	1896
Publisher	Clarke, C.
Printer	Clarke, C.
Place	Glasgow
Type	GE
Map scale	–
Library	BL
holdings	NLS
	ULC

REF	1908
Title	**Directory for Hamilton and district including Cadzow, Eddlewood, Ferniegair, Larkhall, High Blantyre and Bothwell**
Dates	1909
Publisher	Hamilton Herald
Printer	Hamilton Herald
Place	Hamilton
Type	CM TR
Map scale	–
Notes	T/P missing, details from HAM catalogue
Library	HAM

REF **1909**
Title **Directory for Wishaw and District**
Dates 1909
Publisher Hamilton Herald Printing and Publishing Company Ltd
Printer Hamilton Herald Printing and Publishing Company Ltd
Place Hamilton
Type CM
Map scale –
Notes Incomplete volume, surnames A-M only
Library MTH

REF **1910**
Title **Directory for Motherwell and District**
Dates 1910
Publisher Hamilton Herald Printing and Publishing Company Ltd
Printer Hamilton Herald Printing and Publishing Company Ltd
Place Hamilton
Type CM
Map scale –
Library MTH

REF **1911**
Title **Kelly's Directory of Glasgow**
Dates 1923-1950
Publisher Kelly's Directories Ltd
Printer Kelly's Directories Ltd
Place London
Type GE TR
Map scale 1:63360
Notes Cont'd from 1891
Library BCL has 1927
holdings BL all
BOD all
BPH has 1940,1942-1950
CLM has 1926-1950
CLE has 1941,1947
GL not 1942
MLG all
NLS all
NLW has 1923,1924,1928,
1931-1933,1936,1937,1939,
1949
ULC all

REF **1912**
Title **Glasgow Royal Exchange Directory of Members, Firms and Trades etc.**
Dates 1933,1934
Publisher Glasgow Royal Exchange Ltd
Printer –
Place Glasgow
Type SP
Map scale –
Notes Alph. list of firms followed by TR section
Library MLG

REF **1913**
Title **V.P. Street Directory of Greater Glasgow**
Dates 1948
Publisher Frame, M.M.
Printer –
Place Glasgow
Type SL
Map scale –
Library BL

MIDLOTHIAN

REF **1914**
Title **Williamson's Directory for the City of Edinburgh, Canongate, Leith and Suburbs**
Dates 1773-1776,1778,1780,1782
Publisher Williamson, P.
Printer Wilson, J. & Coke, W.
Place Edinburgh
Type TR
Map scale –
Notes 1773 edition is an 1889 reprint by W. Brown, Edinburgh. Directory is arranged with a TR section for each letter of the alphabet.
Library BOD has 1773
holdings GL has 1773,1778
IHR has 1773,1778
MLG has 1773
NLS all
SOG has 1773

REF	1915
Title	**The Edinburgh Directory**
Dates	1793,1797,1800,1801
Publisher	Aitchison, T. (selected by)
Printer	–
Place	Edinburgh
Type	CM
Map scale	–
Notes	1801 edition entitled 'The Edinburgh and Leith Directory'
Library holdings	CLM has 1793 GL has 1801 NLS not 1793

REF	1916
Title	**Denovan & Co's Edinburgh and Leith Directory**
Dates	1804
Publisher	Denovan & Co
Printer	Denovan & Co
Place	Edinburgh
Type	CM
Map scale	–
Library holdings	GL MLG NLS

REF	1917
Title	**Post Office Edinburgh and Leith Directory**
Dates	1805-1950
Publisher	Post Office
Printer	Ballantyne, J.A.
Place	Edinburgh
Type	GE TR
Map scale	1:10560
Notes	1805-1845 entitled 'The Post Office Annual Directory of Edinburgh and Leith etc.'
Library holdings	BCL has 1839,1855,1925,1935, 1943 BL all? BOD has 1826,1828,1829,1833, 1834,1840,1841,1845,1849, 1852,1854,1860,1863,1867, 1870-1876,1878-1927, 1929-1950 BPH has 1855,1865,1876,1886, 1895,1906,1916,1921, 1923-1935,1940-1950 CLM has 1805-1865,1940-1944, 1947-1950 GL has 1807-1810,1817,1819, 1820,1824-1840,1842,1843, 1845,1849-1851,1853-1855, 1857-1862,1869,1873-1875, 1877-1879,1881,1883,1884, 1886,1891,1923,1927-1945, 1947-1950 IHR has 1807,1822,1825,1828, 1835,1846,1848,1855 MLG has 1805,1808,1810,1816, 1817,1819,1820,1822-1950 NLS has 1805-1814,1816-1890, 1893,1895-1908,1918-1950 SOG has 1840,1864,1918,1923, 1938 ULC has 1833,1834,1845,1847, 1852,1854,1863,1867,1868, 1870-1950

REF	1918
Title	**The New and Improved Directory for Edinburgh, Leith and Suburbs**
Dates	1824
Publisher	Anderson, J.
Printer	Shaw, J. & Co
Place	Edinburgh
Type	CM
Map scale	–
Library holdings	MLG NLS

REF	1919
Title	**Gray's Annual Directory ... of Edinburgh and its vicinity**
Dates	1833,1834,1836,1837
Publisher	Gray, J.
Printer	Shortrede, A.
Place	Edinburgh
Type	GE
Map scale	1:12000
Library	BOD has 1833,1837
holdings	NLS has 1833
	MLG not 1833

REF	1920
Title	**The New Edinburgh, Leith and County Directory**
Dates	1867,1868
Publisher	-
Printer	Ballantyne & Co
Place	Edinburgh
Type	GE TR
Map scale	1:12672
Library	NLS

REF	1921
Title	**The Edinburgh County Directory**
Dates	1870
Publisher	Doig, W.
Printer	–
Place	Portobello
Type	CM
Map scale	1:253440
Library	BOD
holdings	NLS

REF	1922
Title	**Carment's Directory for Dalkeith and District**
Dates	1887-1889,1891,1899,1902-1907, 1909-1917
Publisher	Carment, J.
Printer	Pardon & Sons
Place	Dalkieth
Type	CM
Map scale	–
Library	MLG has 1899-1917
holdings	NLS has 1887-1902

REF	1923
Title	**Parochial Directory for Edinburgh and Leith**
Dates	1888,1893
Publisher	Sinclair, W. (Compiler)
Printer	–
Place	Edinburgh
Type	SL
Map scale	1:10560
Library	BL all
holdings	BOD all
	NLS has 1888
	ULC all

REF	1924
Title	**The Portobello & District Directory**
Dates	1889,1892,1894
Publisher	Douglas & Smart
Printer	Blair, T.C.
Place	Portobello
Type	GE
Map scale	1:21120
Library	NLS

REF	1925
Title	**Dalkeith District Directory and Household Almanac**
Dates	1890,1894
Publisher	Lyle, P. & D.
Printer	Lyle, P. & D.
Place	Dalkieth
Type	CM
Map scale	–
Library	NLS

REF	1926
Title	**McLaren's Edinburgh and Leith Street Directory**
Dates	1902,1921
Publisher	McLaren, J.W. & Co
Printer	McLaren, J.W. & Co
Place	Edinburgh
Type	SL
Map scale	–
Library	BL

REF	1927
Title	**Musselburgh Directory and Yearbook**
Dates	1903
Publisher	Musselburgh Merchants Association
Printer	Sinclair, W.
Place	Haddington
Type	GE TR
Map scale	–
Library	NLS

[353]

REF	**1928**
Title	**Musselburgh Directory**
Dates	1934,1937
Publisher	–
Printer	–
Place	Musselburgh
Type	GE
Map scale	–
Notes	Publisher & printer not stated
Library	NLS

REF	**1929**
Title	**Edinburgh, Peebles and Linlithgow Trades' Directory**
Dates	1940
Publisher	Town and County Directories Ltd
Printer	Macdonald, W. & Co
Place	Edinburgh
Type	TR
Map scale	–
Library	NLS

MORAYSHIRE

REF	**1930**
Title	**Russell's Morayshire Register and Elgin & Forres Directory**
Dates	1844,1847,1850
Publisher	Russell, A.
Printer	Russell, A.
Place	Elgin
Type	CM
Map scale	–
Library	MLG has 1844
holdings	NLS all

REF	**1931**
Title	**Black's Morayshire Directory including the Upper District of Banffshire**
Dates	1863
Publisher	Black, J.
Printer	Black, J.
Place	Elgin
Type	CM
Map scale	–
Library	MLG
holdings	NLS

ORKNEY AND SHETLAND

REF	**1932**
Title	**Zetland Directory and Guide**
Dates	1861
Publisher	Davidson, G.
Printer	Cornwall, G. & Son
Place	Aberdeen
Type	CM
Map scale	1:126720
Library	NLS

REF	**1933**
Title	**Peace's Orkney Almanac and County Directory**
Dates	1873-1875,1878,1886-1893, 1898-1902,1904,1911-1916,1920, 1928,1934-1939
Publisher	Orkney Herald
Printer	Orkney Herald
Place	Kirkwall
Type	TR
Map scale	–
Library	GL has 1938,1939
holdings	MLG has 1887-1890,1891-1893, 1898-1902,1904,1911-1916, 1918,1934-1939 NLS has 1873,1932

REF	**1934**
Title	**The Orkney & Shetland Guide Directory and Almanac**
Dates	1882,1883,1885-1893
Publisher	Anderson, J.
Printer	The Orcadian
Place	Kirkwall
Type	CM
Map scale	–
Library	BL has 1883,1887-1893
holdings	MLG all

REF	**1935**
Title	**Manson's Shetland Almanac and Directory**
Dates	1892-1950
Publisher	Manson, T. & J.
Printer	Manson, T. & J.
Place	Lerwick
Type	TR
Map scale	–
Library	BL all
holdings	GL has 1950 MLG has 1936-1940,1942-1944, 1950

PERTHSHIRE

REF **1936**
Title **Leslie's Directory for Perth and Perthshire**
Dates 1885,1887,1889,1891,1893,1895, 1897,1899,1901,1903,1905,1907, 1909,1911,1913,1915,1919,1921, 1923,1925,1927,1929,1931,1933, 1935,1937,1939
Publisher Leslie, P.
Printer Leslie, P.
Place Perth
Type GE
Map scale 1:7920
Notes 1905 published by Watson & Annandale, 1919 onwards published by K. Annandale
Library BL not 1885-1915
holdings DDL has 1939
MLG has 1891,1899,1907,1911, 1919-1925,1929-1937
NLS has 1891,1889,1907,1911, 1929,1937
SLP all

REF **1937**
Title **Morison's Perthshire Register and City of Perth Directory**
Dates 1886,1887
Publisher Cowan, S. & Co
Printer Cowan, S. & Co
Place Perth
Type CM
Map scale —
Notes Previous & later editions do not contain directory sections
Library SLP

REF **1938**
Title **Perthshire Directory**
Dates 1889
Publisher Lamburn, C.
Printer —
Place Dundee
Type CT TR
Map scale —
Library NLS
holdings SLP

REF **1939**
Title **Perth Town and County Directory**
Dates 1948
Publisher The Scottish Advertisers Ltd
Printer Leslie, D.
Place Dundee
Type ST TR
Map scale —
Library SLP

REF **1940**
Title **Directory for the City of Perth and Vicinity**
Dates 1837,1841
Publisher Mackie, J.
Printer Sidey, C.G.
Place Perth
Type CM
Map scale —
Library SLP

REF **1941**
Title **The Post Office Perth Directory**
Dates 1843,1845,1848,1850,1852,1854, 1856,1858,1860,1862,1865,1866, 1868,1872,1874,1878,1882,1884
Publisher Post Office
Printer Sidey, C.G.
Place Perth
Type CT
Map scale 1:12000
Library BL has 1852-1860,1884
holdings GL has 1860,1872
MLG has 1872,1880,1882
NLS has 1880
SLP all

REF **1942**
Title **Lunan's Alyth Almanack and List of Voters**
Dates 1888
Publisher Lunan, A.
Printer Lunan, A.
Place Alyth
Type CT
Map scale —
Library SLP

REF	**1943**
Title	**The Annual Directory of the City of Perth**
Dates	1890
Publisher	Jackson, J.H.
Printer	Jackson, J.H.
Place	Perth
Type	GE TR
Map scale	–
Library	SLP

REF	**1944**
Title	**Stewart's Coupar Angus and District Directory and Alamanac**
Dates	1905
Publisher	Stewart, D.
Printer	–
Place	Coupar Angus
Type	TR
Map scale	–
Library	SLP

REF	**1945**
Title	**McMurray's Alyth Directory and Almanac**
Dates	1911,1913
Publisher	McMurray, T.
Printer	McMurray, T.
Place	Alyth
Type	GE
Map scale	–
Library	SLP

RENFREWSHIRE

REF	**1946**
Title	**Fowler's Commercial Directory of the Principal Towns and Villages in the Upper Ward of Renfrewshire**
Dates	1829-1832,1834,1836
Publisher	Fowler, G.
Printer	Fowler, G.
Place	Paisley
Type	CM
Map scale	–
Library	CLP all
holdings	MLG not 1830
	NLS has 1831
	WLG has 1831,1832,1836

REF	**1947**
Title	**Fowler's Commercial Directory of the Lower Ward of Renfrewshire**
Dates	1831,1832,1834,1836
Publisher	Fowler, G.
Printer	Fowler, G.
Place	Paisley
Type	CM
Map scale	–
Notes	NLS 1831 edition bound with 1946
Library	MLG not 1836
holdings	NLS has 1831,1836
	WLG all

REF	**1948**
Title	**The Paisley Directory**
Dates	1810,1812,1820,1823
Publisher	Bell, A.
Printer	Neilson, J.
Place	Paisley
Type	CM
Map scale	–
Notes	Cont'd by 1950
Library	CLP

REF	**1949**
Title	**The Greenock Directory**
Dates	1815,1820,1829
Publisher	Hutchison, W. [compiler]
Printer	Scott, W.
Place	Greenock
Type	CM
Map scale	–
Library	WLG

REF	**1950**
Title	**The Paisley Directory**
Dates	1827,1828
Publisher	Fowler, G.
Printer	–
Place	Paisley
Type	CM
Map scale	–
Notes	Cont'd from 1948, cont'd as 1951
Library	CLP

REF	1951
Title	**Fowler's Paisley Commercial Directory**
Dates	1838,1841,1845,1848,1851,1853
Publisher	Fowler, G.
Printer	Neilson, J.
Place	Paisley
Type	CM
Map scale	–
Notes	Cont'd from 1950. From 1841 entitled 'Fowler's Paisley & Johnstone Commercial Directory and General Advertiser'.
Library	CLP all
holdings	MLG all
	NLS has 1838,1851

REF	1952
Title	**The Paisley New Directory**
Dates	1840
Publisher	Murray & Stewart [sold by]
Printer	Neilson, J.
Place	Paisley
Type	TR
Map scale	–
Library	CLP

REF	1953
Title	**Hutcheson's Greenock Register, Directory and General Advertiser**
Dates	1841,1845
Publisher	Hutcheson
Printer	Scott & Mackenzie
Place	Greenock
Type	CM
Map scale	–
Library	GL has 1845
holdings	MLG has 1845
	NLS has 1845
	WLG all

REF	1954
Title	**Paisley Commercial Directory**
Dates	1844
Publisher	Biggar & McFarlane
Printer	Gardner, A.
Place	Paisley
Type	CM
Map scale	–
Library	CLP

REF	1955
Title	**The Post Office Greenock Directory**
Dates	1847,1849,1851,1853,1855,1857, 1858-1915
Publisher	Hutchison, W.
Printer	Hutchison, W.
Place	Greenock
Type	GE
Map scale	1:10560
Notes	1847 edition entitled 'The Post Office Annual Greenock Directory'. Cont'd as 1964.
Library	BL has 1855,1890,1892,
holdings	1895-1898,1904,1906-1915
holdings	CLM has 1858
	GL has 1855,1892,1895-1897, 1915
	MLG has 1849,1862,1875-1880, 1895-1898
	NLS has 1853,1861,1862,1868, 1873,1875
	WLG all

REF	1956
Title	**Sproull's Paisley Commercial Directory**
Dates	1848
Publisher	Sproull, M.
Printer	Neilson, J.
Place	Paisley
Type	CM
Map scale	–
Library	CLP

REF	1957
Title	**Hinshelwood's Directory for Paisley & Neighbourhood**
Dates	1857,1859,1861
Publisher	Hinshelwood, P.
Printer	Paisley Herald
Place	Paisley
Type	CM TR
Map scale	–
Library	CLP
holdings	MLG

REF	**1958**		REF	**1961**
Title	**Watson's Directory for Paisley, Renfrew, Johnstone, Elderslie, Linwood, Quarrelton, Thornhill, Balaclava and Inkerman**		Title	**Clarke's Barrhead & Neilston Directory**
			Dates	1896
			Publisher	Clarke, C.
Dates	1862,1865-1883		Printer	Clarke, C.
Publisher	The Paisley Herald		Place	Glasgow
Printer	The Paisley Herald		Type	GE TR
Place	Paisley		Map scale	–
Type	CM TR		Library	BL
Map scale	–		holdings	MLG
Notes	Cont'd by 1960			NLS
Library	CLP not 1870,1878			
holdings	GL has 1878		REF	**1962**
	MLG not 1862,1866		Title	**Kilmacolm Directory**
			Dates	1906
REF	**1959**		Publisher	Pollock, J.M.
Title	**Winning's Paisley Directory and General Advertiser**		Printer	Pollock, J.M.
			Place	Greenock
Dates	1864,1866		Type	CM
Publisher	Winning, J.		Map scale	–
Printer	Cook, J. & J.		Library	WLG
Place	Paisley			
Type	CM TR		REF	**1963**
Map scale	–		Title	**The Handbook for the Burgh of Greenock**
Library	CLP			
holdings	MLG		Dates	1923,1926
			Publisher	Haughey, N.
REF	**1960**		Printer	Haughey, N.
Title	**The Paisley Directory and General Advertiser**		Place	Greenock
			Type	SL
Dates	1884-1915,1924,1926,1927,1929, 1931,1934,1937		Map scale	–
			Library	WLG
Publisher	Cook, J. & J.			
Printer	Cook, J. & J.		REF	**1964**
Place	Paisley		Title	**The Greenock Directory**
Type	GE TR		Dates	1923-1933,1935,1937,1938,1940
Map scale	1:8013		Publisher	Haughey, N.
Library	BL not 1885-1903,1908,1909,		Printer	Haughey, N.
holdings	1914,1937		Place	Greenock
	CLM has 1934		Type	GE TR
	CLP all		Map scale	–
	GL has 1897,1905,1934,1937		Notes	1925 onwards entitled 'The Greenock and District Directory'. Cont'd from 1955.
	MLG has 1885-1892,1895-1898, 1900,1901,1904-1907, 1910-1915,1924-1934			
			Library	BL not 1923
			holdings	MLG has 1923,1924
				NLS has 1923,1930,1938,1940
				ULC has 1923
				WLG all

REF | **1965**
Title | **The Gourock Directory**
Dates | 1925,1935
Publisher | Simpson, J. & R.
Printer | Simpson, J. & R.
Place | Gourock
Type | CM TR
Map scale | –
Library | WLG

SELKIRKSHIRE

REF | **1966**
Title | **The Galashiels and Selkirk Almanac and Directory**
Dates | 1889,1891-1894,1896-1950
Publisher | McQueen, J.
Printer | McQueen, J.
Place | Galashiels
Type | TR
Map scale | –
Library | BL has 1889,1894,1896-1950
holdings | MLG has 1936,1950
NLS not 1899,1900,1913-1918, 1920,1922,1923,1925,1928, 1931,1932,1935

STIRLINGSHIRE

REF | **1967**
Title | **The Stirlingshire (Burgh and County) Directory**
Dates | 1886
Publisher | Rowe-Gliddon, J.S.
Printer | –
Place | Dundee
Type | CM TR
Map scale | –
Library | SHQ
holdings | STR

REF | **1968**
Title | **Threepenny Guide and Directory for Stirling, Bridge of Allan, Dunblane, Doune, St Ninians & Bannockburn**
Dates | 1866
Publisher | Miller, D. & Son
Printer | –
Place | Stirling
Type | GE TR
Map scale | –
Notes | GE TR Stirling only, CM smaller places
Library | NLS

REF | **1969**
Title | **The Stirling Directory including Bridge of Allan, St Ninians, Cambusbarron, Whins of Milton and Bannockburn**
Dates | 1870
Publisher | Duncan & Jamieson
Printer | Duncan & Jamieson
Place | Stirling
Type | GE TR
Map scale | –
Library | SHQ

REF | **1970**
Title | **The Stirling Directory including Bridge of Allan etc**
Dates | 1872-1888
Publisher | Miller, A.
Printer | –
Place | Stirling
Type | GE TR
Map scale | –
Notes | GE TR for Stirling only, CM for smaller places
Library | MLG all
holdings | NLS has 1882
SHQ has 1881
STR has 1881

REF | **1971**
Title | **Wilson's Business Directory of Stirling, Bridge of Allan, Causewayhead, Bannockburn and Neighbourhood**
Dates | 1887,1888
Publisher | Wilson & Co
Printer | Wilson & Co
Place | Glasgow
Type | GE TR
Map scale | 1:126720
Library | SHQ has 1888
holdings | STR all

REF | **1972**
Title | **Harvey's Stirling Directory and Almanack**
Dates | 1888,1889,1894
Publisher | Harvey, C.
Printer | Harvey, C.
Place | Stirling
Type | CM TR
Map scale | –
Notes | 1888 edition entitled 'Harvey's Alamanck and Business Directory of Stirling'
Library | SHQ has 1888
holdings | STR has 1889,1894

[359]

REF	1973
Title	**Cook & Wylie's Stirling Directory and Almanac**
Dates	1896,1897,1901,1903,1906,1909
Publisher	Cook & Wylie
Printer	Cook & Wylie
Place	Stirling
Type	CM TR
Map scale	NS
Notes	Map only in 1901 edition
Library	SHQ all
holdings	STR all

REF	1974
Title	**Industries of Stirling and District**
Dates	1909
Publisher	Mackay, E. & Jamieson, J.
Printer	Stirling Observer Press
Place	Stirling
Type	SP
Map scale	–
Notes	Contains detailed articles, historical information, illustrations of Stirling firms in 1909
Library	STR

REF	1975
Title	**Falkirk and District Illustrated Almanack, Diary and Directory**
Dates	1913
Publisher	McCulloch & Mackie
Printer	McCulloch & Mackie
Place	Falkirk
Type	TR
Map scale	–
Library	FLK

REF	1976
Title	**Scott, Learmonth & Allan's Directory for Stirling**
Dates	1913
Publisher	Scott, Learmonth & Allan
Printer	Scott, Learmonth & Allan
Place	Stirling
Type	GE TR
Map scale	–
Library	SHQ
holdings	STR

REF	1977
Title	**Stirling District Directory**
Dates	1913,1914,1924,1932
Publisher	McIntyre & Pearson
Printer	McIntyre & Pearson
Place	Stirling
Type	GE TR
Map scale	NS
Notes	1924 edition entitled 'Stirling Directory'
Library	GL has 1932
holdings	SHQ not 1914
	STR all

REF	1978
Title	**Stirling and District Directory (Official)**
Dates	1925
Publisher	The Simmath Press
Printer	The Simmath Press
Place	Dundee
Type	GE TR
Map scale	NS
Library	STR

REF	1979
Title	**Falkirk, Grangemouth and District Directory**
Dates	1934
Publisher	Falkirk, Grangemouth and District Directory
Printer	Paul, T. Ltd
Place	Larbert
Type	CT TR
Map scale	–
Library	SHQ

REF	1980
Title	**The Grangemouth Directory and Guide**
Dates	1949
Publisher	Johnston, F. & Co Ltd
Printer	Johnston, F. & Co Ltd
Place	Grangemouth
Type	GE
Map scale	1:14080
Library	BL
holdings	MLG

Chapter 7
BRITISH DIRECTORIES OF COMMERCE, INDUSTRY AND TRADES

REF	**1981**
Title	**The Building Societies' Directory and Almanack**
Dates	1850
Publisher	Effingham Wilson
Printer	–
Place	London
Type	SP
Map scale	–
Notes	Alph. list of names (managers, agents), building societies, addresses etc
Library	BL
holdings	NLS

REF	**1982**
Title	**A Directory of the Joint Stock & Private Banks in England & Wales**
Dates	1851
Publisher	Groombridge, R. & Sons
Printer	Waterlow & Sons
Place	London
Type	SP
Map scale	–
Notes	List of banks with alph. list of shareholders for each
Library	BL
holdings	NLS
	ULC

REF	**1983**
Title	**The Chemical Directory and Pharmaceutists' Compendium**
Dates	1851
Publisher	Wright, C. & Co
Printer	Wright, C. & Co
Place	London
Type	SP
Map scale	–
Notes	Alph. & place directory & general pharmaceutical information
Library	BL
holdings	NLS

REF	**1984**
Title	**The Newspaper Press Directory**
Dates	1851,1856,1859,1860,1862-1940, 1945,1946,1948,1949
Publisher	Mitchell, C. & Co
Printer	–
Place	London
Type	SP
Map scale	1:1584000
Notes	Alph. list of newspapers, magazines, periodicals; London, provincial & Irish sections
Library	BL all
holdings	BOD not 1851-1860
	CLC has 1865,1920,1938-1949
	CLM has 1851,1859,1860, 1867-1885,1887-1927, 1929-1949
	DEI has 1889
	MLG has 1878,1880-1949
	NLS has 1856-1949
	NLW has 1895,1897,1906,1907, 1910-1912,1914-1949
	ULC not 1851,1859

REF	**1985**
Title	**The London & Provincial Builders & Building Trades Directory**
Dates	1851,1857
Publisher	Piper, W. & T.
Printer	Marchant Singer & Co
Place	London
Type	SP
Map scale	–
Notes	London followed by counties. 1857 edition entitled 'The Metropolitan & Provincial Builders & Building Trades Directory'.
Library	BL

REF	**1986**		REF	**1989**
Title	**Ralph's Stock and Share Brokers Directory**		Title	**Hodson's Booksellers, Publishers and Stationers Directory for London and Country**
Dates	1851-1858			
Publisher	Longman, Brown, Green & Longmans		Dates	1855
			Publisher	Hodson, W.H.
Printer	–		Printer	Hodson, W.H.
Place	London		Place	London
Type	SP		Type	SP
Map scale	–		Map scale	–
Notes	Alph. list of stock brokers on London & provincial exchanges		Library holdings	BL BOD ULC
Library holdings	BL all BOD has 1852-1854 NLS has 1852,1853,1857 ULC all			

REF	**1990**
Title	**The Musical Directory, Annual and Almanack**
Dates	1855,1857,1859,1861-1863,1865, 1867,1870-1872,1875,1876, 1878-1882,1891,1892,1896-1931
Publisher	Rudall, Carte & Co
Printer	–
Place	London
Type	SP
Map scale	–
Notes	Alph. list of professions, music sellers, songs etc.
Library holdings	BL all BOD not 1855-1881 NLS has 1855,1862 ULC all

REF	**1987**
Title	**Webster's Royal Red Book or Court and Fashionable Register**
Dates	1852-1939
Publisher	Webster & Co
Printer	Webster & Co
Place	London
Type	CT
Map scale	–
Library holdings	BL all GLH has 1878,1900,1902,1907, 1913-1915,1926-1933, 1935-1937 NLS all

REF	**1988**
Title	**The Register Insurance Directory and Almanac**
Dates	1854,1856-1858
Publisher	Tweedie, W.
Printer	Tweedie, W.
Place	London
Type	SP
Map scale	–
Notes	Alph. list of insurance firms, directors names etc.
Library holdings	NLS ULC

REF	**1991**
Title	**Owen's New Book of Fairs to be held in England, Wales, Scotland & Ireland**
Dates	1856,1859
Publisher	Donaldson, J.
Printer	Cornish, J.
Place	London
Type	SP
Map scale	–
Notes	List of fairs by place & date. also by type (e.g. livestock, general, county etc.)
Library	BL

REF **1992**
Title **Blower's Architect's, Surveyor's, Engineer's and Builder's Directory**
Dates 1860
Publisher Blower, T.
Printer –
Place London
Type SP
Map scale –
Notes Classified directory
Library BOD
holdings NLS
ULC

REF **1993**
Title **The Auctioneers', Land Agents', Valuers', & Estate Agents' Directory**
Dates 1860,1862
Publisher Estates Gazette
Printer –
Place London
Type SP
Map scale –
Notes Alph. list
Library BL

REF **1994**
Title **The Paper Mills Directory**
Dates 1860,1862,1865-1941
Publisher The Stationer
Printer The Stationer
Place London
Type SP
Map scale –
Notes Alph. list of paper mills in Great Britain
Library BL all
holdings BOD has 1901-1940
CLM has 1938
NLW has 1913-1935
ULC has 1871,1872,1874-1880, 1882-1885,1887-1935,1938, 1940

REF **1995**
Title **Thom's British Directory and Official Handbook of the United Kingdom**
Dates 1862,1863,1873
Publisher Groombridge & Sons
Printer Groombridge & Sons
Place London
Type CT
Map scale –
Library BCL has 1863
holdings BL all
BOD all
CLM all
NLS all
ULC all

REF **1996**
Title **The United Kingdom Bill Posters Association Directory**
Dates 1864-1869,1871,1873,1874, 1878-1888
Publisher Bill Posting Association
Printer Yorkshire Post
Place Leeds
Type SP
Map scale –
Notes Alph. by place
Library BL all
holdings MLG has 1884

REF **1997**
Title **The Joint Stock Directory of Banking, Financial, Insurance & other Public Companies**
Dates 1865-1867
Publisher Sampson, Low, Son & Marston
Printer Regent Press
Place London
Type SP
Map scale –
Notes Bank, finance & miscellaneous sections
Library BL
holdings BOD
NLS
ULC

REF	**1998**
Title	**The Joint Stock Companies Directory**
Dates	1865-1869
Publisher	Barker, C. & Son
Printer	King, J. & Co
Place	London
Type	SP
Map scale	–
Notes	Lists joint stock railway, insurance, banking, credit, shipping, hotel, mining & dock companies
Library	BL all
holdings	BOD all
	CLM has 1865-1867
	NLS all
	ULC all

REF	**1999**
Title	**Post Office European Directory, Containing lists of Bankers, Leading Merchants & Manufacturers of the Principal Ports of the Continent of Europe**
Dates	1866
Publisher	Kelly & Co
Printer	Kelly & Co
Place	London
Type	SP
Map scale	–
Notes	Continental, England, Wales, Ireland & Scotland sections
Library	BL
holdings	BOD
	ULC

REF	**2000**
Title	**The Agricultural Implement Manufactories Directory of England**
Dates	1867
Publisher	Kent & Co
Printer	Kent & Co
Place	London
Type	SP
Map scale	–
Notes	Alph. list of names by county. In preface, Kent notes poor response to survey, hence the limited scope of this directory.
Library	BL
holdings	NLS
	ULC

REF	**2001**
Title	**The Horticultural Directory**
Dates	1867,1868,1871-1920,1923,1934
Publisher	Journal of Horticulture
Printer	Journal of Horticulture
Place	London
Type	SP
Map scale	–
Notes	Alph. list of seedsmen, gardeners & nurserymen by London, counties & rest of G.B.
Library	BL not 1868,1871,1872,
holdings	1874-1876,1878,1880,1882,1884, 1917-1924
	BOD has 1867,1868,1871, 1882-1924
	ULC has 1867,1868,1871-1920, 1923,1934

REF	**2002**
Title	**The Tanneries' Directory of England**
Dates	1867-1869
Publisher	Kent & Co
Printer	Unwin Bros.
Place	London
Type	SP
Map scale	–
Notes	Alph. & county lists
Library	BL all
holdings	NLS has 1867

REF	**2003**
Title	**The Chemical Manufacturers' Directory of England, (Wales & Scotland)**
Dates	1867-1869,1871-1950
Publisher	Simpkin, Kent & Co
Printer	Newnham, Cowell & Gripper
Place	London
Type	SP
Map scale	–
Notes	List of chemicals & producers. Alph. list of manufacturers. Wales & Scotland included from 1913 (possibly earlier).
Library	BL not 1867-1869,1872,1873
holdings	BOD not 1874-1876,1880,1884
	NLS not 1867-1869,1874,1879, 1887
	NLW has 1913-1950
	ULC not 1874,1876,1880,1884

REF	**2004**
Title	**The Architects', Engineers' and Building Trades' Directory**
Dates	1868
Publisher	Wyman & Sons
Printer	Wyman & Sons
Place	London
Type	SP
Map scale	–
Notes	Classified directory
Library	BL
holdings	BOD
	NLS
	ULC

REF	**2005**
Title	**Trades Directory of Great Britain and Ireland or the Foreign Buyer's Pocket Guide**
Dates	1869
Publisher	Parisot, E.
Printer	Bradbury, Evans & Co
Place	London
Type	SP
Map scale	–
Notes	List of businesses by location, classified by trade. In German, French & Spanish.
Library	BL

REF	**2006**
Title	**The Illustrated Guide and Directory of Manufacturers of Great Britain and Ireland**
Dates	1869,1871,1873,1875,1876
Publisher	Deacon, S.
Printer	Spottiswoode & Co
Place	London
Type	TR
Map scale	–
Notes	Arranged alph. by place with TR sections. General section with many engravings of products etc. 1876 edition in English, French & German. Title varies.
Library	BL all
holdings	BOD has 1876
	NLS has 1869,1876

REF	**2007**
Title	**Kelly's Directory of Chemists and Druggists**
Dates	1869,1872,1876,1880,1885,1889, 1893,1896,1900,1904,1908,1912, 1916
Publisher	Kelly & Co
Printer	Kelly & Co
Place	London
Type	SP
Map scale	–
Notes	Cont'd as 2153. 1869,1872, 1876 editions entitled 'The Post Office Directory of Chemists & Druggists, Manufacturing Chemists & Wholesale Druggists'.
Library	BL all
holdings	BOD not 1869
	MLG has 1889-1916
	NLS all
	NLW has 1912,1916
	ULC all

REF	**2008**
Title	**Kelly's Directory of the Engineers and Iron & Metal Trades**
Dates	1870,1874,1878,1883,1886,1890, 1894,1897,1901,1905,1909,1913, 1917,1920,1922,1924,1926,1928, 1930,1932,1934,1936,1938,1940
Publisher	Kelly & Co
Printer	Kelly & Co
Place	London
Type	SP
Map scale	–
Notes	1870-1878 entitled 'Post Office Directory of the Engineers and Iron & Metal Trades'. 1928 onwards entitled 'Kelly's Directory of the Engineering, Hardware, Metal and Motor Trades'.
Library	BL all
holdings	BOD not 1917,1920
	BPH has 1924-1934,1940
	CLM has 1940
	GL has 1940
	HBR has 1940
	LCL has 1922
	MLG has 1890-1940
	NLS all
	NLW has 1909,1920,1922, 1926-1930,1934-1938
	ULC all

REF 2009
Title **Kelly's Directory of the Building Trades**
Dates 1870,1874,1878,1883,1886,1890, 1894,1898,1902,1906,1910,1914, 1920,1923,1925,1927,1929,1931, 1933,1935,1937,1939
Publisher Kelly & Co
Printer Kelly & Co
Place London
Type SP
Map scale –
Notes 1870,1874 entitled 'Post Office Directory of the Building Trades'
Library BL all
holdings BOD all
BPH has 1933,1939
CLM has 1935,1939
GL has 1939
HBR has 1939
LCL has 1937,1939
MLG has 1890-1939
NLS all
NLW has 1923,1931-1937
ULC all

REF 2010
Title **Kelly's Directory of the Leather Trades**
Dates 1871,1875,1880,1885,1889,1893, 1896,1901,1903,1908,1911,1915, 1918,1920,1922,1925,1929,1933, 1937,1940
Publisher Kelly & Co
Printer Kelly & Co
Place London
Type SP
Map scale –
Library BL not 1896,1903
holdings BOD not 1918,1920
CLL has 1896,1937,1940
CLM has 1940
GL has 1937,1940
LCL has 1937,1940
MLG has 1889-1950
NLS has 1918,1920
NLW has 1915,1920,1933,1937
ULC all

REF 2011
Title **The Artificial Manure Directory of England**
Dates 1872
Publisher Kent, W. & Co
Printer –
Place London
Type SP
Map scale –
Notes Alph. lists for London & rest of England
Library BL

REF 2012
Title **Kelly's Directory of the Watch and Clock Trades**
Dates 1872,1875,1880,1887,1892,1897, 1901,1905,1909,1913,1917,1921, 1924,1927,1932,1937
Publisher Kelly & Co
Printer Kelly & Co
Place London
Type SP
Map scale –
Library BCL has 1887,1901,1905,1913,
holdings 1917,1927
BL all
BOD all
BPH has 1924-1937
CLM has 1937
GL not 1872,1875
LCL has 1932,1937
MLG has 1892-1937
NLS not 1917
NLW has 1937
ULC all

REF	**2013**
Title	**Kelly's Directory of the Grocery, Oil and Colour Trades including Confectionery, Tobacco and Provision Trades of England, Scotland and Wales**
Dates	1872,1875,1884,1895,1904,1922
Publisher	Kelly & Co
Printer	Kelly & Co
Place	London
Type	SP
Map scale	–
Notes	1872,1875 entitled 'Post Office Directory of the Grocery, Oil and Colour Trades including Confectionery, Tobacco and Provision Trades of England, Scotland and Wales'
Library	BL all
holdings	BOD not 1872
	CLM has 1922
	MLG has 1904,1922
	NLS all
	ULC not 1872

REF	**2014**
Title	**Kelly's Directory of Stationers, Printers, Booksellers and Papermakers of England, Scotland, Wales & Ireland**
Dates	1872,1876,1880,1885,1889,1891, 1893,1896,1900,1904,1908,1912, 1916,1919,1921,1924,1927,1931, 1936,1939
Publisher	Kelly & Co
Printer	Kelly & Co
Place	London
Type	SP
Map scale	–
Notes	1872-1880 entitled 'Post Office Directory of Stationers, Printers, Booksellers and Papermakers of England, Scotland, Wales & Ireland'
Library	BL all
holdings	BOD has 1876,1904-1939
	BPH has 1916,1924,1927,1936, 1939
	GL has 1936,1939
	HBR has 1939
	LCL has 1936
	MLG all
	NLS all
	NLW has 1908-1924
	ULC all

REF	**2015**
Title	**Wilson's Mercantile Directory of the World Vol I Great Britain & Ireland**
Dates	1873,1877,1889-1897
Publisher	Wilson, W. & Sons
Printer	–
Place	London
Type	TR
Map scale	–
Library	BL all
holdings	NLS has 1894
	ULC has 1894

REF	**2016**
Title	**The Artists Directory**
Dates	1874
Publisher	Tarrant, A.
Printer	Hackett, R.
Place	London
Type	SP
Map scale	–
Notes	Alph. lists of artists & sculptors
Library	BL
holdings	NLS

REF	**2017**
Title	**The London and Suburban Licensed Victuallers, Hotel and Tavern Keepers Directory**
Dates	1874
Publisher	Miles, H.D.
Printer	–
Place	London
Type	SP
Map scale	1:63360
Notes	Alph. list by name
Library	BOD
holdings	NLS

REF	**2018**
Title	**The Paper Stainers Directory of Great Britain**
Dates	1874
Publisher	Kent & Co
Printer	Kent & Co
Place	London
Type	SP
Map scale	–
Notes	Reprinted from 'The House Furnisher and Decorator'. Small directory section, mainly adverts.
Library	BL
holdings	ULC

REF	**2019**	REF	**2022**
Title	**Lamb's International Guide to British and Foreign Merchants and Manufacturers**	Title	**The Coal Trades Directory comprising all important trades and professions connected with Coal and Iron throughout England, Scotland & Wales with a foreign appendix**
Dates	1874,1875,1878,1881,1890, 1904-1907,1909,1910,1912,1913, 1915-1925,1927,1930-1938		
Publisher	Lamb's Press Ltd	Dates	1877
Printer	Lamb's Press Ltd	Publisher	Eyre Bros.
Place	London	Printer	Eyre Bros.
Type	TR	Place	London
Map scale	–	Type	SP
Library	BL not 1895,1906	Map scale	–
holdings	MLG has 1895,1906,1907,1909, 1910,1920,1931	Notes	TR section arranged by location
		Library	BL

REF	**2020**	REF	**2023**
Title	**The Local Government Directory**	Title	**Wine & Spirit Trade Directory of England and South Wales**
Dates	1874-1950		
Publisher	Knight & Company	Dates	1877
Printer	–	Publisher	Harvey, H. & Sons
Place	London	Printer	Harvey, H. & Sons
Type	SP	Place	London
Map scale	–	Type	SP
Notes	Details of Poor Law Unions, Sanitary Authorities, School Boards etc. 1923 onwards entitled 'The Local Government Manual and Directory'	Map scale	–
		Notes	Mimeographed hand written manuscript. Arranged alph. by place.
Library	BOD all	Library	BL
holdings	CLB has 1909-1918,1920-1922 CLC has 1930,1938,1943 CLM has 1934-1940,1944-1950 LCL has 1931-1950 MLG has 1917-1938,1940-1950 NLS not 1899,1902,1908 ULC all	REF	**2024**
		Title	**The Gas and Water Companies Directory**
		Dates	1877,1880,1883-1891,1893-1902, 1904,1905,1907-1914,1916,1920, 1924,1928,1930
REF	**2021**	Publisher	Hastings, C.W.
Title	**The Country Stockbrokers Directory**	Printer	Ward, M. & Co
		Place	Belfast
Dates	1875	Type	SP
Publisher	Allen, E.W.	Map scale	–
Printer	Straker, S. & Sons	Notes	Arranged alph. by town, with details of company formation, legislation, capital, chairmen etc. 1890-1899 entitled 'The Gas, Water & Electric Companies Directory'. 1900 onwards entitled 'Gasworks Directory & Statistics'.
Place	London		
Type	SP		
Map scale	–		
Notes	Alph. list of 100 towns in UK with stockbrokers & alph. directory of stockbrokers		
Library	BL	Library	BL not 1877,1930
holdings	BOD NLS	holdings	BOD all CLM has 1907-1928 MLG has 1883-1928 NLS has 1880,1884,1886-1896, 1899-1930 ULC has 1877-1880,1895,1896, 1899,1902,1904,1905,1914, 1916,1924,1928

REF	**2025**
Title	**Kelly's Directory of Merchants, Manufacturers and Shippers**
Dates	1877,1882,1884,1887,1888, 1891-1950
Publisher	Kelly & Co
Printer	Kelly & Co
Place	London
Type	TR
Map scale	–
Library holdings	BL not 1888
	BOD not 1887
	BPH has 1924,1927-1936, 1940-1943,1945-1950
	BRD has 1918,1922,1927,1933, 1935,1937,1939,1940-1945, 1948-1950
	CLM has 1921
	LCL has 1940 (inc)
	NLS all
	NLW has 1913,1916,1917, 1919-1922,1924-1933, 1936-1940,1946,1949,1950
	ULC all

REF	**2026**
Title	**Kelly's Directory of the Wine & Spirit Trades, Brewers & Maltsters**
Dates	1877,1884,1887,1892,1895,1898, 1902,1906,1910,1914,1923,1926, 1930,1935,1939
Publisher	Kelly & Co
Printer	Kelly & Co
Place	London
Type	SP
Map scale	–
Library holdings	BL all
	BOD all
	BPH has 1923,1939
	CLM has 1939
	GL has 1939
	LCL has 1935,1939
	MLG has 1898-1939
	NLS all
	ULC all

REF	**2027**
Title	**Kelly's Directory of the Cabinet, Furniture and Upholstery Trades**
Dates	1877,1886,1894,1899,1903,1907, 1911,1915,1921,1925,1931,1936
Publisher	Kelly & Co
Printer	Kelly & Co
Place	London
Type	SP
Map scale	–
Notes	1877 edition entitled 'Post Office Directory of the Cabinet, Furniture and Upholstery Trades'
Library holdings	BL all
	BOD all
	BPH has 1921-1936
	CLM has 1936
	GL has 1936
	LCL has 1931,1936
	MLG all
	NLS all
	NLW has 1915,1931,1936
	ULC all

REF	**2028**
Title	**The Exporters' Directory**
Dates	1878-1881
Publisher	Jones, T. & Co
Printer	Jones, T. & Co
Place	London
Type	SP
Map scale	–
Notes	List of merchants in Manchester, Birmingham & London
Library holdings	BL all
	NLS has 1879
	ULC has 1879

REF	**2029**
Title	**The Fanciers Directory containing the Names & Addresses of all Judges & Exhibitions of Dogs, Poultry, Pigeons, Cage Birds, Rabbits & Cats in the UK**
Dates	1879
Publisher	Cassell, Petter, Gilpin & Co
Printer	–
Place	London
Type	SP
Map scale	–
Notes	Includes details of shows & alph. list of judges etc.
Library holdings	BL
	BOD
	NLS
	ULC

[369]

REF **2030**
Title **Reeves' Musical Directory**
Dates 1879-1902
Publisher Reeves, W.
Printer Reeves, W.
Place London
Type SP
Map scale –
Notes Alph. & classified directory of all persons connected with music, teachers, players etc.
Library BL all
holdings BOD not 1880,1890
MLG has 1900,1902
NLS not 1890
ULC not 1890

REF **2031**
Title **J.G. Harrod's Royal Despatch and Special Directory of England**
Dates 1880
Publisher Harrod, J.G. & Co
Printer –
Place Norwich
Type SP
Map scale –
Notes Alph. place postal/telegraph directory & commercial directory for alph. places
Library BL has 1880
holdings GLH has 1886
NLS has 1880

REF **2032**
Title **The Wine, Spirit and Liquor Trades Directory of the U.K**
Dates 1880
Publisher Molyneux, W. & Co
Printer Molyneux, W. & Co
Place London
Type SP
Map scale –
Notes Alph. list of towns with classified lists
Library BL
holdings BOD
NLS
ULC

REF **2033**
Title **Kelly's Directory of the Manufacturers of Textile Fabrics**
Dates 1880,1885,1889,1893,1897,1906, 1920,1922,1928
Publisher Kelly & Co
Printer Kelly & Co
Place London
Type SP
Map scale –
Notes From 1920 onwards entitled 'Kelly's Directory of the Textile Industries'
Library BL all
holdings BOD not 1920
BRD has 1906,1928
CLM has 1880,1928
MLG has 1889-1928
NLS not 1920
ULC not 1920

REF **2034**
Title **Stubbs' Directory**
Dates 1880-1900,1902,1904-1943,1946, 1948,1950
Publisher Stubbs & Co
Printer –
Place London
Type TR
Map scale –
Notes London & provincial sections
Library BL has 1880-1988,1912-1950
holdings BOD has 1880,1883-1896,1898, 1899,1905-1943
BPH has 1926,1928-1934, 1940-1943,1946-1950
NLS not 1881,1882,1905,1915
NLW has 1898,1900-1904,1906, 1913,1915-1943,1946-1950
ULC not 1881,1882,1900

REF **2035**
Title **The Directory of Directors**
Dates 1880-1950
Publisher Skinner, T. & Co
Printer –
Place London
Type SP
Map scale –
Notes Alph. list of company directors in GB
Library BL all
holdings BOD not 1887
BPH has 1885-1936,1938-1950
CLB has 1944,1945,1947-1950
CLM has 1880-1885,1889,1892, 1893,1895-11921,1922-1950
NLS all
ULC has 1880-1944

REF **2036**
Title **The Registers of Pharmaceutical Chemists and Chemists and Druggists**
Dates 1880-1950
Publisher Pharmaceutical Society of Great Britain
Printer Pharmaceutical Society of Great Britain
Place London
Type SP
Map scale –
Notes Alph. list by name, with residence, qualifications etc.
Library BOD all
holdings CLC has 1936,1939,1949,1950

REF **2037**
Title **The International Mercantile Directory**
Dates 1881,1883-1886,1888,1890-1893, 1895-1911,1913,1915,1916,1918, 1921,1923-1925,1927-1930
Publisher Collingwood Bros.
Printer –
Place London
Type TR
Map scale –
Notes 'A classified list of the manufacturers, merchants, bankers, shipping companies, insurance companies, warehousemen, agents &c &c of GB and the continent'
Library BL all
holdings BOD all
MLG has 1893,1898,1901,1903, 1905,1906,1909,1910,1913
NLS has 1890
ULC not 1907

REF **2038**
Title **Ryland's Iron, Steel and Allied Trades Directory with Brands & Trade Marks**
Dates 1881,1884,1887,1890,1896,1899, 1902,1906,1908,1910,1912,1915, 1918,1920,1922,1924,1926,1928, 1930,1932,1934,1936,1938,1940, 1942,1945,1947,1950
Publisher Ryland's
Printer Ryland's
Place Birmingham
Type SP
Map scale NS
Notes Alph. & TR sections arranged by county. Iron, steel, tinplate & allied trades.
Library BCL has 1881,1890,1896,1902,
holdings 1906,1910,1912,1918-1924, 1928-1932,1936-1942
BL not 1881,1908,1920
BOD not 1881,1906,1908, 1912-1918
BRD has 1932,1940,1942,1950
CLM has 1934-1938,1940,1942, 1950
LCL has 1945-1950
MLG has 1906-1922,1924, 1926-1950
NLS not 1881,1896,1906,1908, 1912,1915,1918
NLW has 1926,1947,1950
ULC not 1881,1906,1908, 1912-1918

REF **2039**
Title **The United Kingdom Stock and Sharebrokers Directory**
Dates 1881,1885,1890,1892,1896-1915, 1917,1919-1940
Publisher Adams & Sons
Printer Adams & Sons
Place London
Type SP
Map scale –
Notes Section for London Stock Exchange followed by provincial membership
Library BL not 1900,1917-1920
holdings BOD all
CLM has 1939
NLS not 1896,1934
NLW has 1913,1917,1919-1938
ULC has 1881,1885,1892-1914, 1917,1919-1940

REF **2040**
Title **Freeman's Mercantile & Maritime Handbook and Export Trades Directory**
Dates 1881,1886
Publisher Freeman, S.
Printer Shaw & Co
Place London
Type SP
Map scale –
Library BL

REF **2041**
Title **Berly's British, American & Continental Electrical Directory**
Dates 1882-1917
Publisher Berly & Dawson
Printer Berly & Dawson
Place London
Type SP
Map scale –
Notes Classified sections. 1885 edition entitled 'Berly's Universal Electrical Directory'. 1886 & after entitled 'The Universal Electrical Directory'.
Library BL all
holdings BOD has 1883,1888,1889, 1895-1916
NLS has 1917
NLW has 1913-1917
ULC has 1883,1888,1895-1905, 1907-1916

REF **2042**
Title **The British Fisheries Directory**
Dates 1883
Publisher Sampson, Low, Marston, Searle & Rivington
Printer –
Place London
Type SP
Map scale –
Notes Arranged by place, with lists of fish merchants, curers, buyers, boat builders etc.
Library BL
holdings NLS
ULC

REF **2043**
Title **The Dramatic and Musical Directory of the United Kingdom**
Dates 1883,1884,1886-1893
Publisher Fox, C.H.
Printer –
Place London
Type SP
Map scale 1:1520640
Notes Alph. & classified sections of all singers, musicians, actors etc.
Library BL all
holdings BOD has 1884,1887-1893
NLS has 1884,1887-1893
ULC has 1884,1887-1893

REF **2044**
Title **Directory of the Tobacco Trade in Great Britain and Ireland**
Dates 1883,1892,1895,1898,1905,1909, 1914,1922
Publisher Tobacco Journal
Printer Tobacco Journal
Place London
Type SP
Map scale –
Library BL

REF **2045**
Title **The Electricians' Directory**
Dates 1883-1885
Publisher The Electrician
Printer –
Place London
Type SP
Map scale –
Notes Alph. & TR sections
Library BL not 1885
holdings BOD all
ULC all

REF **2046**
Title **Electrical Trades' Directory and Handbook**
Dates 1883-1885,1889-1943,1945-1950
Publisher The Electrician
Printer The Electrician
Place London
Type SP
Map scale –
Notes Classified list covering UK, USA & continent. 1927-1943 entitled 'The Blue Book Electrical Trades Directory & Handbook'. 1945-1950 entitled 'The Blue Book'.
Library BL not 1885
holdings BOD has 1894-1896,1898, 1902-1950
NLS has 1894-1896,1898, 1902-1950
NLW has 1915-1950
ULC has 1883-1885,1894-1896, 1898,1902-1950

REF **2047**
Title **London and Provincial Directory and Commercial Guide**
Dates 1883-1886,1889,1895,1896,1908, 1910-1941,1944-1950
Publisher Kay Fisher, A. & Co
Printer –
Place London
Type TR
Map scale –
Library BL all
holdings MLG has 1896-1937 (imperfect run)

REF **2048**
Title **The Cycle Directory**
Dates 1884
Publisher Cassell & Company Ltd
Printer –
Place London
Type SP
Map scale –
Notes Alph. list of all cycling clubs & unions & list of manufacturers, tradesmen etc in the cycle trade
Library BOD
holdings NLS
ULC

REF **2049**
Title **The Directory of Building Societies**
Dates 1884,1885
Publisher Kent, M. & Braund, V.M.
Printer Kent, M. & Braund, V.M.
Place London
Type SP
Map scale –
Notes Alph. lists of building societies with details of location, assets, directors, date of establishment etc.
Library BL
holdings BOD
NLS
ULC

REF **2050**
Title **The Paper Makers' Directory of all Nations**
Dates 1884,1885,1887,1891,1895, 1897-1946,1948,1950
Publisher Phillipps, S.C.
Printer Dean & Son
Place London
Type SP
Map scale –
Notes Claims to contain every paper & pulp mill in the world. Arranged by country, and alphabetically in each section giving location, number of machines & capacity.
Library BL all
holdings BOD not 1891
MLG has 1906,1926,1933
NLS not 1887,1891,1895,1917
NLW has 1915,1923-1928,1930, 1931,1942-1950
ULC all

REF **2051**
Title **Johnson's Handbook of Cattle Fairs, Markets & Auctions**
Dates 1884,1885,1887-1890,1892-1898
Publisher Johnson, C.M.
Printer Johnson, C.M.
Place Leeds
Type SP
Map scale –
Notes List by county of fairs & main auctions & dates (England). List by dates for Scotland & Wales.
Library BL

REF **2052**
Title **Russell's Mercantile Directory and Merchants' Guide**
Dates 1885
Publisher Russell, K.
Printer Russell, K.
Place London
Type TR
Map scale –
Notes See also 2075
Library BL

REF **2053**
Title **Sell's Directory of Registered Telegraphic Addresses**
Dates 1885,1894-1944,1946-1950
Publisher Sell, H.
Printer –
Place London
Type SP
Map scale –
Notes Alph. list of names & addresses followed by telegraphic addresses
Library BL all
holdings BOD has 1895,1896,1898-1944
BRD has 1929
CLM has 1922,1943-1950
NLS has 1895,1896,1898, 1900-1950
NLW has 1914-1950
ULC all

REF **2054**
Title **Perry's Directory of Great Britain and Ireland and Continental & Colonial Mercantile Guide**
Dates 1885,1895,1896,1898-1940
Publisher Perry, W. & Co Ltd
Printer –
Place London
Type TR
Map scale –
Library BL has 1885,1895,1905-1940
holdings BOD has 1885-1899,1914-1940
CLM has 1940
MLG has 1885-1924 (imperfect run)
NLS has 1898-1940
ULC has 1889,1896,1898,1899, 1903,1914-1940

REF **2055**
Title **Smith's Trades' Guide to Manufacturers, Merchants, Shippers, Business & Professions**
Dates 1886
Publisher Smith & Co
Printer Smith & Co
Place London
Type TR
Map scale –
Notes TR by place
Library BOD
holdings NLS
ULC

REF **2056**
Title **The Directory of Second Hand Booksellers**
Dates 1886
Publisher Gyles, A. (editor)
Printer –
Place Nottingham
Type SP
Map scale –
Notes Alph. by place
Library BL

REF **2057**
Title **The Metropolitan Dairymens' Directory and Handbook**
Dates 1886,1887
Publisher Easton, E.G.
Printer Easton, E.G.
Place London
Type SP
Map scale –
Notes Alph. list of cowkeepers & vendors
Library BL

REF **2058**
Title **Directory of Paper Makers of the U.K.**
Dates 1886-1950
Publisher Paper Makers' Journal
Printer Paper Makers' Journal
Place London
Type SP
Map scale –
Notes Alph. lists of mills & occupiers, lists of mills by county, TR section
Library BL all
holdings BOD has 1908,1910-1950
BPH has 1947,1948,1950
MLG has 1931,1936-1940, 1942-1950
NLS has 1908,1910-1938, 1940-1945,1947-1950
NLW has 1916,1918,1919,1921, 1922,1925-1931,1940,1941, 1943,1944,1947-1950
ULC has 1908,1910-1945, 1947-1950

REF **2059**
Title **The Licensed Victuallers Diary and Trades Directory**
Dates 1887
Publisher Francis, J. & Co
Printer –
Place London
Type SP
Map scale –
Notes TR sections arranged alph. by place
Library BL

REF **2060**
Title **The London and County Trades Directory**
Dates 1887-1938
Publisher Moody, T. & Co
Printer –
Place London
Type TR
Map scale –
Library BL all
holdings MLG has 1899-1903,1905,1907, 1910,1912,1914,1915,1918, 1919,1921,1925,1929
NLS has 1887-1891
TRW has 1896

REF **2061**
Title **The Counties Directory and Trades Guide**
Dates 1888
Publisher Blackie, J. & Co
Printer Multing, W.H. & A.
Place London
Type TR
Map scale –
Notes TR by county
Library BL
holdings BOD
NLS
ULC

REF **2062**
Title **The Soap Makers' Directory of Great Britain**
Dates 1888,1890,1892,1894,1898,1900, 1902,1904,1906,1908-1950
Publisher Simpkin, Kent & Co
Printer Simpkin, Kent & Co
Place London
Type SP
Map scale –
Notes Alph. list, arranged by London & rest of country
Library BL not 1909
holdings BOD all
MLG has 1935-1950
NLS has 1890-1950
NLW has 1913-1943,1945,1947, 1949,1950
ULC all

REF **2063**
Title **Clegg's Directory of Booksellers**
Dates 1888,1891,1894,1899,1903,1906, 1910,1914,1927,1930,1936,1940, 1950
Publisher Clegg, J.
Printer Clegg, J.
Place Rochdale
Type SP
Map scale –
Notes International Directory
Library BL all
holdings BOD all
CLM has 1899-1906,1914-1936
MLG all
NLS has 1888-1914
ULC has 1894-1914
CLM has 1899-1906,1914-1936

REF **2064**
Title **The Bill Posters' Directory**
Dates 1888,1893-1896,1898-1915,1920, 1922-1924,1926-1930
Publisher Bill Posters' Association Ltd
Printer McCorquodale & Co Ltd
Place London
Type SP
Map scale –
Notes 1927-1929 entitled 'Directory of the British Poster Advertising Association'. Arranged alph. by place, with population of town, number of bill posters etc. Cont'd from 1996.
Library BL all
holdings ULC has 1888,1895

REF **2065**
Title **Rylands List of Merchant Exporters**
Dates 1888,1895,1898,1901,1904,1906
Publisher Ryland's
Printer Ryland's
Place Birmingham
Type SP
Map scale –
Notes Iron, steel tinplate & metal merchants only
Library BL all
holdings BOD not 1888
NLS all
ULC has 1898-1904

REF **2066**
Title **A Diary and Directory for the use of Surveyors, Auctioneers, Land and Estate Agents**
Dates 1888-1890,1893-1939
Publisher Estates Gazette Ltd
Printer Estates Gazette Ltd
Place London
Type SP
Map scale –
Notes Also contains information & tables. After 1939 merely becomes a diary.
Library BL all
holdings BOD has 1935
CLM has 1928-1939

REF **2067**
Title **Pott's Mining Register and Directory for the Coal and Ironstone Trades of Great Britain and Ireland**
Dates 1888-1890,1895,1900,1903,1905, 1912,1915
Publisher Potts, W.J.
Printer Potts, W.J.
Place North Shields
Type SP
Map scale 1:1267200
Library BL has 1895-1920
holdings MLG has 1890
NLS all
ULC all

REF **2068**
Title **The Mercantile Year Book and Directory of Exporters in London, Manchester, Liverpool, Birmingham, Glasgow & Bristol**
Dates 1888-1893,1896-1939,1941,1945, 1947-1950
Publisher Jones, W.L.
Printer Mercantile Guardian
Place Birmingham
Type SP
Map scale –
Notes For each town, ST section of principal merchant area. TR section for London. CM sections for other towns.
Library BCL has 1890,1918-1922,
holdings 1924-1927,1929,1931
BL not 1888-1892,1948
BOD has 1888,1889,1891-1893, 1901,1902,1904-1950
NLS has 1888,1889,1891-1893, 1901,1903-1950
NLW has 1914-1919,1921-1950
ULC has 1888,1889,1891-1893, 1901-1903,1905-1950

REF **2069**
Title **The Music Trades Pocket Directory**
Dates 1888-1894,1898
Publisher Ernest, G.D. & Co
Printer –
Place London
Type SP
Map scale –
Notes List of musical instrument dealers, music sellers etc by place
Library BL all
holdings BOD not 1889,1893
NLS not 1898
ULC not 1898

REF **2070**
Title **The County Councillors Directory containing a list of the Aldermen & Councillors with addresses for all counties & county boroughs under the Act of 1888**
Dates 1889,1890,1892
Publisher Contract Journal Company Ltd
Printer –
Place London
Type SP
Map scale –
Notes Alph. by place
Library BL all
holdings BOD not 1892
NLS not 1890

REF **2071**
Title **Bourne's Insurance Directory**
Dates 1889,1890,1897-1950
Publisher Effingham Wilson
Printer –
Place London
Type SP
Map scale –
Notes Alph. list of insurance companies, addresses, class of assurance & numerous other details
Library BL not 1889,1890,1931
holdings BOD not 1889,1901,1931
CLM has 1889,1897,1904-1918, 1920-1933,1936-1950
LCL has 1924-1950
MLG has 1890,1904,1925
NLS all
ULC has 1897-1930

REF **2072**
Title **Jepson's Mercantile Directory and Manufacturers Guide**
Dates 1889,1891,1893-1896,1911-1914, 1919-1937
Publisher Jepson
Printer –
Place London
Type TR
Map scale 1:724114
Notes Publisher uncertain
Library BCL has 1920
holdings BL all
HBR has 1937
MLG has 1933-1936
NLS has 1921
ULC has 1894

REF **2073**
Title **The Advertiser's ABC of Official Scales & Charges and Advertisement Press Directory**
Dates 1889,1891-1893,1895-1898,1910, 1915-1917,1921-1927
Publisher Browne, T.R.
Printer –
Place London
Type SP
Map scale –
Notes Contains newspaper index, sections for London, provinces (alph. by place), magazines & reviews, colonial & foreign. Other large libraries may also hold runs of this directory which was only added to the list at a late stage.
Library DEI has 1897
holdings NLW all

REF	**2074**
Title	**Worrall's Textile Directory of the Manufacturing Districts of Ireland, Scotland, Wales and the Counties of Chester, Derby, Leicester and Nottingham**
Dates	1889-1919,1924,1927,1933,1936, 1939,1943-1950
Publisher	Worrall, J.
Printer	Worrall, J.
Place	Oldham
Type	SP
Map scale	–
Notes	Arranged by place & type of activity. In 1930s title changed to 'British & Dominion Textile Industry'.
Library holdings	BL not 1924-1942 BRD has 1912,1913,1916, 1924-1939,1944-1950 MLG has 1909,1911,1913,1915, 1917-1919 NLS not 1901,1919-1942 NLW has 1943-1950 ULC not 1890,1898,1924-1942

REF	**2075**
Title	**Mercantile Directory and Provincial Guide**
Dates	1890,1891
Publisher	Russell, K.
Printer	–
Place	London
Type	TR
Map scale	–
Notes	Mainly London coverage. This may be a subsequent edition of 2052.
Library holdings	NLS all ULC has 1890

REF	**2076**
Title	**Woodhead's Directory of the Credit Drapers of England & Wales**
Dates	1890,1901,1907,1909
Publisher	Woodhead, G. & Co
Printer	Woodhead, G. & Co
Place	Manchester
Type	SP
Map scale	–
Library	BL

REF	**2077**
Title	**The Eastern Importers Directory**
Dates	1891
Publisher	Jones, L. & Co
Printer	–
Place	London
Type	SP
Map scale	NS
Notes	Lists of importers by country of origin of goods. Small scale maps of countries/continents etc.
Library	NLS

REF	**2078**
Title	**Timber and Wood Consuming Trades Directory for Great Britain**
Dates	1891,1892,1896-1901,1906,1910, 1914,1920,1924,1928,1936,1939, 1948,1950
Publisher	Rider, W. & Sons
Printer	Rider, W. & Sons
Place	London
Type	SP
Map scale	1:6000
Notes	TR sections for London & provincial towns. Contains many maps of dock areas.
Library holdings	BL not 1893 BOD has 1893,1906-1950 NLS not 1891,1892 NLW has 1920,1939,1948

REF	**2079**
Title	**Street's Newspaper Directory**
Dates	1891,1899-1917,1920
Publisher	Street Bros.
Printer	Street Bros.
Place	London
Type	SP
Map scale	1:1425600
Notes	List of provincial newspapers, publishers etc, alph. by place
Library holdings	BOD not 1891 NLS not 1891,1911,1917,1919 ULC not 1915,1920

REF	**2080**
Title	**The Directory of Contractors**
Dates	1892-1894,1896-1899,1901,1902, 1906-1913,1925-1950
Publisher	Biggar, W.
Printer	Veale, Chifferiel & Co Ltd
Place	London
Type	SP
Map scale	–
Notes	Includes railway contractors, waterworks, gasworks, dock & harbour engineers, builders etc.
Library holdings	BL all NLS has 1946-1950 ULC has 1946-1950

REF	**2081**
Title	**Directory of the Electrical Industry**
Dates	1893
Publisher	Electrical Plant & Electrical Industry (In conj. with)
Printer	–
Place	London
Type	SP
Map scale	–
Notes	Alph. by name, alph. by place
Library	NLS

REF	**2082**
Title	**The Bookman Directory of Booksellers, Publishers & Authors**
Dates	1893
Publisher	Hodder & Stoughton
Printer	–
Place	London
Type	SP
Map scale	–
Notes	London, country & Scottish sections (alph. by place) & alph. list of publishers
Library holdings	BL BOD MLG NLS

REF	**2083**
Title	**The International Directory of Patent Agents**
Dates	1893
Publisher	Reeves, W.
Printer	Reeves, W.
Place	London
Type	SP
Map scale	–
Notes	Alph. lists of patent agents by country
Library holdings	BL NLS ULC

REF	**2084**
Title	**Traders' Directory to the Warehousemen's, Textile Fabrics and Drapery Trades**
Dates	1893,1894
Publisher	Johnson, W.B.
Printer	Johnson, W.B.
Place	London
Type	SP
Map scale	–
Notes	Classified list of trades, probably a subscription directory
Library holdings	BL all NLS has 1894 ULC has 1894

REF	**2085**
Title	**Slater's Textile Directory of the World - Europe Volume**
Dates	1894
Publisher	Slater, I.
Printer	Slater, I.
Place	Manchester
Type	SP
Map scale	–
Notes	Alph. lists by country & type of activity. Sections on agents, merchants, warehousemen & shipping.
Library holdings	BL BOD CLM NLS ULC

REF **2086**
Title **Traders' Directory to the Brewers, Corn, Seed, Provision & Wine & Spirit Trades**
Dates 1894
Publisher Johnson, W.
Printer Johnson, W.
Place London
Type SP
Map scale –
Notes Classified list of trades
Library BL

REF **2087**
Title **Ryland's Hardware: A complete Directory of Midland & other Manufacturers**
Dates 1894,1902
Publisher Iron Trades Circular (Ryland's)
Printer –
Place Birmingham
Type SP
Map scale 1:21120
Notes Alph. section, alph. by place & TR section
Library BL
holdings BOD
NLS

REF **2088**
Title **The Commercial Directory**
Dates 1894-1896,1911-1913,1916-1918, 1921-1928,1930
Publisher Harrison & Co Ltd
Printer –
Place London
Type TR
Map scale 1:905143
Library BL

REF **2089**
Title **Municipal Directory for the United Kingdom**
Dates 1895
Publisher The Sanitary Publishing Co
Printer –
Place London
Type SP
Map scale –
Notes Alph. list of Urban District Councils & general information on sanitary legislation, societies etc.
Library BL
holdings NLS

REF **2090**
Title **The Engineer Directory**
Dates 1895-1917,1919-1934,1936-1939, 1950
Publisher The Engineer
Printer Reviers, G. Ltd
Place London
Type SP
Map scale –
Library BL all
holdings NLS has 1909-1917,1920, 1926-1928,1931-1932, 1936-1950
ULC has 1936-1950

REF **2091**
Title **The Universal Directory of Railway Officials**
Dates 1895-1950
Publisher The Directory Publishing Company Ltd
Printer –
Place London
Type SP
Map scale –
Notes International directory, arranged by continent
Library BOD all
holdings CLC has 1935,1938-1940,1943, 1944
LCL has 1925-1950
NLW has 1914-1922,1924-1950
ULC all
12

REF	**2092**
Title	**Postal Directory of the Cycle Trades of Great Britain and Ireland**
Dates	1896
Publisher	Rockliff Bros Ltd
Printer	Rockliff Bros Ltd
Place	Liverpool
Type	SP
Map scale	–
Notes	Alph. list of places with cycle agents, dealers, makers & alph. names directory
Library	BL
holdings	NLS

REF	**2093**
Title	**The Electrical Engineers' Central-Station Directory**
Dates	1896-1902,1905-1907
Publisher	Biggs & Son
Printer	–
Place	London
Type	SP
Map scale	–
Notes	Gazetteer of places with electricity generating stations, details of electrical engineers, electricity supply etc.
Library	BL not 1897
holdings	CLM has 1900
	NLS has 1897,1905,1907
	ULC has 1896,1905-1907

REF	**2094**
Title	**Walker's Press Directory**
Dates	1897
Publisher	Walker, H.T. & Co
Printer	–
Place	London
Type	SP
Map scale	–
Notes	Alph. lists of newspapers etc. & place directory
Library	NLS

REF	**2095**
Title	**Chambers' Directory of the United Kingdom**
Dates	1897,1899-1902,1904-1907,1909, 1927-1936
Publisher	Chambers' Publishing Co
Printer	–
Place	London
Type	TR
Map scale	–
Library	BL all
holdings	BOD has 1905-1907,1928-1933, 1935,1936
	NLS has 1905,1907
	ULC has 1905-1907,1928-1936

REF	**2096**
Title	**Directory of Gas Undertakings**
Dates	1898
Publisher	Hammond, J.G. & Co Ltd
Printer	–
Place	Birmingham
Type	SP
Map scale	–
Notes	Alph. list of places with details of engineers, output of gas, population of district, capital etc.
Library	BL
holdings	NLS

REF	**2097**
Title	**Macdonald's English Directory and Gazetteer (2 Vols)**
Dates	1898-1950
Publisher	Macdonald, W. & Co Ltd
Printer	Macdonald, W. & Co Ltd
Place	Edinburgh & London
Type	TR
Map scale	1:10560
Notes	Vol I devoted to large cities. Vol II devoted to counties. It is possible that this directory was the 'Master Directory' for other provincial directories published by Town and County Directories Ltd.
Library	BL all
holdings	BOD all
	GLH has 1925,1938
	MLG has 1898,1900-1907,1913, 1914,1921-1926,1930,1931, 1935,1937,1943
	NLS not 1914,1915 (VOL 1 for 1911,1912)
	NLW has 1900,1914-1944

REF	2098
Title	**The National Trades Directory of Great Britain and Ireland**
Dates	1900
Publisher	The Improved Trades' Directory Publishing Co
Printer	–
Place	London
Type	TR
Map scale	–
Notes	TR by place
Library	NLS
holdings	ULC

REF	2099
Title	**Ice and Cold Storage Trades' Directory**
Dates	1900,1901,1903-1914,1920-1932
Publisher	Ice and Cold Storage Co
Printer	Ice and Cold Storage Co
Place	London
Type	SP
Map scale	–
Notes	Alph. list for GB, USA & continent; TR section
Library	BL all
holdings	BOD has 1910-1914,1920-1932
	NLS not 1901-1909,1915-1919
	NLW has 1914,1925-1932
	MLG has 1903,1904,1928-1931

REF	2100
Title	**Ryland's Directory of Ironmongers**
Dates	1900,1904
Publisher	Iron Trades Circular (Ryland's)
Printer	–
Place	Birmingham
Type	SP
Map scale	–
Library	BL
holdings	BOD
	NLS
	ULC

REF	2101
Title	**Barton's British & Foreign Manufacturers and County Merchants, Shippers and Trades Directory**
Dates	1900,1905,1908,1909,1911,1912, 1914,1916-1918
Publisher	Barton
Printer	–
Place	Edinburgh
Type	TR
Map scale	–
Notes	Publisher uncertain. With special TR section for Scotland.
Library	BL has 1900-1909
holdings	NLS has 1911-1918

REF	2102
Title	**The Directory of Clayworkers**
Dates	1901,1904,1924
Publisher	The British Clayworker
Printer	–
Place	London
Type	SP
Map scale	–
Notes	Alph. by county & alph. list
Library	BL has 1901,1904
holdings	MLG has 1924

REF	2103
Title	**Porter's Motor Trades Directory of Great Britain & Ireland**
Dates	1902
Publisher	The Lancashire Publishing Co
Printer	Rockliff Bros Ltd
Place	Liverpool
Type	SP
Map scale	–
Notes	TR, alph. & place directory
Library	NLS
holdings	ULC

REF	2104
Title	**The Automotor Directory**
Dates	1902
Publisher	King, F. & Co
Printer	King, F. & Co
Place	London
Type	SP
Map scale	–
Library	BL

REF **2105**
Title **Kemp's Trades Directory: Manufacturers, Merchants, Shippers and Professional for the UK**
Dates 1902,1904
Publisher Kemps Publishing Co
Printer –
Place London
Type TR
Map scale –
Library BL
holdings BOD
NLS
ULC

REF **2106**
Title **London and Provincial Directory and Continental Guide ... of the United Kingdom, Europe, Australia and New Zealand**
Dates 1902,1906-1942,1944-1950
Publisher Crane, Crane & Co
Printer Carlton Press
Place London
Type TR
Map scale –
Notes London, provincial, colonial, hotel & continental sections
Library BOD has 1908,1910-1938,
holdings 1940-1950
MLG has 1909,1910,1924,1927,
1929-1931,1934,1936-1938
NLS all
ULC not 1902,1906,1909

REF **2107**
Title **Perry's Business Directory**
Dates 1902,1914-1918,1935-1938
Publisher The Commercial Publishing Co
Printer –
Place Leeds
Type TR
Map scale –
Notes London section; remainder of directory divided into classified advertisements for all types of firm throughout the country.
Manufacturers, merchants, shippers, professional & general traders included.
Library BL has 1935-1938
holdings NLW has 1902,1914-1918

REF **2108**
Title **Directory of Electric Lighting and Electric Traction**
Dates 1902-1905
Publisher Hazell, Watson & Viney Ltd
Printer Hazell, Watson & Viney Ltd
Place London
Type SP
Map scale –
Notes Arranged alph. by place. Also contains statistics etc.
Library BL
holdings BOD

REF **2109**
Title **The London Commercial Trades Directory**
Dates 1903
Publisher Boyce, F. & Co
Printer –
Place London
Type TR
Map scale –
Notes London & provincial sections
Library BOD
holdings NLS

REF **2110**
Title **The Oil Mills Directory**
Dates 1903,1905-1907
Publisher Simpkin, Marshall, Hamilton, Kent & Co Ltd
Printer –
Place London
Type SP
Map scale –
Notes Alph. list of products & alph. directory of oil manufacturers etc.
Library BL has 1903,1905,1907
holdings NLS has 1905,1907
ULC not 1907

REF **2111**
Title **Waterworks Directory and Statistics**
Dates 1903,1907,1909,1911,1912,1915
Publisher Hazell, Watson & Viney
Printer –
Place London
Type SP
Map scale –
Notes Arranged alph. by place, with detailed information relating to water supply & management
Library BL
holdings BOD

REF **2112**
Title **The Paper Trade Diary Directory**
Dates 1903-1920,1922,1924-1949
Publisher Paper Making
Printer Paper Making
Place London
Type SP
Map scale –
Notes Alph. directory
Library BL all
holdings BOD has 1924-1941,1947,1949
NLS not 1904-1924,1930,1931,
1934,1935,1937

REF **2113**
Title **The Directory of Shipowners,
Shipbuilders and Marine
Engineers**
Dates 1903-1950
Publisher The Directory Publishing
Company Ltd
Printer Nosilla Stationary Co
Place London
Type SP
Map scale –
Notes Alph. directory of shipping lines with
TR section
Library BL all
holdings BOD all
BPH has 1919,1921-1936,1938,
1939,1941-1946,1948-1950
CLC has 1925-1940,1943,
1948-1950
CLM has 1923-1932,1935-1950
NLS all
NLW has 1916-1950
ULC all

REF **2114**
Title **Woods' Directory of
Manufacturers, Merchants and
Shippers**
Dates 1904
Publisher Woods, E.B.
Printer –
Place Manchester
Type TR
Map scale –
Library BL
holdings ULC

REF **2115**
Title **The National Directory**
Dates 1904,1905
Publisher The National Publishing Co
Printer –
Place London
Type TR
Map scale –
Notes Cont'd as 'The ABC Commercial
Directory' (2121)
Library BL all
holdings BOD has 1904
NLS has 1904
ULC all

REF **2116**
Title **Phillips' Paper Trade Directory
of the World**
Dates 1904,1906,1908,1910-1931,1933,
1935-1942,1944,1946,1948-1950
Publisher Phillips, S.C. & Co
Printer Phillips, S.C. & Co
Place London
Type SP
Map scale –
Notes Alph. section & alph. by county
Library BL not 1930
holdings BOD has 1914-1918,1920-1926,
1930,1933,1935-1940,
1946-1950
CLE has 1949
CLM has 1918,1920,1923
NLS not 1917,1918,1922,1927,
1929,1944
NLW has 1912,1914,1923,1925,
1926,1929,1944,1946,
1948-1950
ULC has 1913-1921,1923-1940,
1946-1950

REF **2117**
Title **Port-to-Port Directory**
Dates 1905
Publisher Unwin Bros.
Printer –
Place London
Type SP
Map scale –
Notes Directory of international shipping
ports, shipping lines & departure
ports
Library NLS

REF	**2118**
Title	**Pottery Gazette & Glass Trade Review Directory**
Dates	1905,1907,1910-1922,1924-1950
Publisher	The Pottery Gazette and Glass Trade Review
Printer	The Surrey Fine Art Press
Place	London
Type	SP
Map scale	–
Notes	Alph. lists of British pottery & glass manufacturers, buyers' guide, overseas agents etc.
Library	CLM has 1932-1935,1939,1940,
holdings	1942-1950
holdings	HBR has 1905,1907,1910-1922, 1924-1944,1946-1950
	MLG has 1947-1950
	NLS has 1947-1950

REF	**2119**
Title	**The Motor and Cycle Trades Directory of Great Britain and Ireland**
Dates	1905-1908,1912,1915
Publisher	Lancashire Publishing Co Ltd
Printer	Rockliff Bros Ltd
Place	London
Type	SP
Map scale	–
Notes	Alph. by county & alph. section, TR section
Library	BL not 1915
holdings	BOD not 1906
	NLS not 1915
	ULC all

REF	**2120**
Title	**The National Commercial Directory and Business Guide North of England**
Dates	1906
Publisher	The Commercial Publishing Co
Printer	–
Place	Newcastle-on-Tyne
Type	TR
Map scale	–
Library	BL
holdings	NLS

REF	**2121**
Title	**The ABC Commercial Directory (London & Provincial)**
Dates	1906,1907
Publisher	The National Publishing Co
Printer	–
Place	London
Type	TR
Map scale	–
Library	BL all
holdings	BOD has 1907
	NLS has 1907

REF	**2122**
Title	**The National Provincial Trades Directory**
Dates	1907
Publisher	Hick Bros. & Co
Printer	–
Place	Hull
Type	TR
Map scale	–
Notes	TR section & large advertisements section
Library	BL
holdings	NLS

REF	**2123**
Title	**The Chemical Trade Directory**
Dates	1907,1911,1913
Publisher	Davis Bros.
Printer	–
Place	London
Type	SP
Map scale	–
Notes	TR & alph. sections
Library	BL all
holdings	NLS has 1913
	NLW has 1913

REF	**2124**
Title	**The Architects and Surveyors Directory & Referendum & Diary**
Dates	1907-1912
Publisher	Truscott, J. & Son Ltd
Printer	Truscott, J. & Son Ltd
Place	London
Type	SP
Map scale	–
Notes	Arranged by place
Library	BL all?
holdings	BOD all
	NLS has 1908
	ULC all

REF	2125
Title	**The Autocar Directory**
Dates	1908
Publisher	Iliffe & Sons Ltd
Printer	Iliffe & Sons Ltd
Place	London
Type	SP
Map scale	–
Notes	TR directory of the automobile industry & alph. section
Library	BL
holdings	BOD
	NLS

REF	2126
Title	**The Laundry Trade Directory and Launderers Handbook**
Dates	1908
Publisher	The Laundry Record
Printer	The Laundry Record
Place	London
Type	SP
Map scale	–
Notes	Alph. sections for London & rest of country
Library	BL
holdings	BOD
	NLS
	ULC

REF	2127
Title	**Women Workers Directory**
Dates	1909
Publisher	Bale, J. Sons & Danielsson Ltd
Printer	Bale, J. Sons & Danielsson Ltd
Place	London
Type	SP
Map scale	–
Notes	TR & alph directory of specialist women craft etc. workers
Library	BL
holdings	NLS

REF	2128
Title	**Sell's National Directory**
Dates	1909-1912,1918-1935,1944,1946, 1947,1949,1950
Publisher	Sell, H.
Printer	–
Place	London
Type	TR
Map scale	–
Library	BL not 1946
holdings	BOD has 1918-1950
	MLG has 1921-1935 (imperfect run)
	NLS has 1918-1950
	NLW has 1944-1950
	ULC has 1930-1950

REF	2129
Title	**Lloyd's Directory of Manufacturers, Merchants & Shippers**
Dates	1909-1940
Publisher	Lloyd's Publishing Company Ltd
Printer	–
Place	Birmingham
Type	TR
Map scale	–
Notes	Classified sections, then alph. by place
Library	BL all
holdings	BOD has 1909
	BPH has 1939
	CLM has 1940
	MLG has 1920-1937,1939
	NLS has 1909
	ULC has 1909

REF	2130
Title	**Directory of Agricultural Associations in Great Britain**
Dates	1910
Publisher	H.M.S.O.
Printer	Darling & Son
Place	London
Type	SP
Map scale	–
Notes	Arranged by county
Library	BL
holdings	NLS

REF **2131**
Title **The Directory of Commercial Inquiry Agents**
Dates 1911
Publisher Voyce & Co
Printer –
Place Nottingham
Type SP
Map scale –
Notes Arranged by county
Library BL
holdings NLS
ULC

REF **2132**
Title **The Trader Handbook & Diary and Garage Reference Book**
Dates 1911-1940,1946-1950
Publisher The Cycle Trade Publishing Co
Printer Hudson & Co
Place London
Type SP
Map scale –
Notes Alph. & TR sections. Later editions entitled 'The Traders' Handbook'. There is also an undated 'War Time' edition.
Library BL

REF **2133**
Title **Insurance Shareholders Directory**
Dates 1912
Publisher The Policy-Holder Journal Company Ltd
Printer The Policy-Holder Journal Company Ltd
Place Manchester
Type SP
Map scale –
Notes Alph. list of insurance firms with details of capital, shares, interest etc etc.
Library NLW

REF **2134**
Title **The Vegetarian Directory and Food Reformers Guide**
Dates 1913
Publisher Daniel, C.W. Ltd
Printer The Walter Scott Publishing Co Ltd
Place London
Type SP
Map scale –
Notes Directory of vegetarian stores, pensions/sanatoriums, boarding houses, restaurants
Library BL
holdings NLS

REF **2135**
Title **The Trading Directory**
Dates 1913,1914
Publisher The Trading Publishing Co
Printer –
Place London
Type TR
Map scale –
Library BL

REF **2136**
Title **The Trades' Directory of Manufacturers, Merchants and Traders in the United Kingdom**
Dates 1914
Publisher Crewe, J. & Son
Printer Crewe, J. & Son
Place Leeds
Type TR
Map scale –
Library BL

REF **2137**
Title **The Universal Musical & Dramatic Directory: English Section**
Dates 1914
Publisher Risacher, E.
Printer Risacher, E.
Place London & Paris
Type SP
Map scale –
Notes London & provincial classified sections, remainder of directory published in French
Library NLW

REF **2138**
Title **Black's Commercial Directory of British & Russian Manufacturers, Exporters, Importers etc**
Dates 1914,1916
Publisher Black, L. & Co
Printer –
Place London
Type TR
Map scale –
Notes In English & Russian
Library BL

REF **2139**
Title **The Leather Trades Year Book**
Dates 1914-1917,1919,1921-1923, 1925-1938
Publisher Anglo-American Technical Co Ltd
Printer Anglo-American Technical Co Ltd
Place London
Type SP
Map scale –
Notes 1914 published as 'The Tanners Year Book'. International volume containing directory, statistics & articles.
Library BL not 1922
holdings CLM has 1930,1931,1933-1937
LCL has 1922,1927,1928,1931, 1935-1938

REF **2140**
Title **Harpur's Manual: The Standard Work of Reference for the Wine and Spirit Trade**
Dates 1914-1918,1920-1928,1930-1950
Publisher The Wine & Spirit Gazette
Printer Straker, S. & Son
Place London
Type SP
Map scale –
Notes Section on bonded warehouses & alph. sections. 1927-1929 are pocket editions. From 1930-1932 entitled 'Harpur's Manual & Directory'; from 1933 onwards entitled 'Harpur's Directory & Manual'.
Library BL all
holdings BOD has 1924-1943,1945, 1948-1950
NLS not 1924,1944,1945
ULC has 1934-1950

REF **2141**
Title **The All-British Engineering and Building Trades Directory**
Dates 1915
Publisher Angold's Ltd
Printer –
Place London
Type SP
Map scale –
Notes Alph. & classified lists. This directory only contains 16 pages.
Library BL
holdings NLS

REF **2142**
Title **Kemps' Directory**
Dates 1915,1917-1936
Publisher Kemps Publishing Co
Printer Smith, W.A.
Place Leeds
Type TR
Map scale –
Library BL not 1936
holdings BOD has 1918-1936
ULC has 1919-1935

REF **2143**
Title **The Co-Operative Directory**
Dates 1916,1922,1928,1932,1934,1940
Publisher The Co-Operative Union Ltd
Printer C.W.S.
Place Manchester
Type SP
Map scale –
Notes Alph. list of places in UK with CWS/CRS branches, with type of business, number of members etc.
Library BL not 1916
holdings CLM has 1916,1922,1932,1924, 1940
MLG has 1940
NLS has 1928

REF **2144**
Title **Music Trade Directory**
Dates 1916-1918,1920-1939
Publisher Musical Opinion and Musical Trade Review
Printer –
Place London
Type SP
Map scale –
Notes See 2030. Arranged by London & country sections.
Library BL all
holdings BOD not 1917,1924
MLG IMP 1916-1939
ULC not 1917,1924

REF **2145**
Title **The Manual of Electrical Undertakings**
Dates 1916-1924,1926-1950
Publisher Electrical Press Ltd
Printer –
Place London
Type SP
Map scale NS
Notes 1948-1950 entitled 'Garcke's Manual of Electricity Supply'. Alph. list of Electricity Corporations with details of date of establishment, capital, system, directors etc. Maps at various scales.
Library CLB has 1927,1928,1930-1937,
holdings 1946
CLC has 1937-1939,1946,1947
LCL has 1927-1950
NLW has 1916-1924,1926-1928, 1930-1940,1947,1948

REF **2146**
Title **The British Commercial Directory**
Dates 1916-1935
Publisher Davies & Co
Printer Davies & Co
Place Birmingham
Type TR
Map scale –
Notes Classified, Hotels, London, England & Scotland sections
Library BL not 1924
holdings BOD has 1933-1935
MLG has 1923-1925
ULC has 1922,1925,1933-1935

REF **2147**
Title **The Motor Transport Year Book and Directory**
Dates 1916-1941
Publisher Electrical Press Ltd
Printer Electrical Press Ltd
Place London
Type SP
Map scale –
Notes Contains geographical index of garages & sections on motor transport companies, manufacturers & miscellaneous & directory of officials
Library BL all
holdings BOD all
CLC has 1933,1934,1935,1938
CLM has 1919-1941
MLG all
NLS all
NLW not 1940

REF **2148**
Title **The Electrical Review's Electrical and Allied Trades Directory**
Dates 1917
Publisher Alabaster, Gatehouse & Kempe
Printer Clowes, W. & Sons Ltd
Place London
Type SP
Map scale –
Notes Alph. & TR sections; British, colonial & continental
Library MLG
holdings ULC

REF **2149**
Title **Universal Mercantile Directory**
Dates 1917-1934
Publisher Homer, J.A.
Printer –
Place Birmingham
Type GE TR
Map scale –
Library BL all
holdings BOD has 1924-1934
MLG has 1921,1925
NLS has 1924-1934
ULC has 1923-1934

REF	**2150**		REF	**2153**
Title	**Directory of British Manufacturers of Jewellery, Silver, Electroplate**		Title	**Kelly's Directory of the Chemical Industries**
Dates	1918		Dates	1919,1921,1923,1926,1930,1935, 1938
Publisher	Birmingham Jewellers & Silversmiths Association		Publisher	Kelly's Directories Ltd
			Printer	Kelly's Directories Ltd
Printer	Silk & Terry Ltd		Place	London
Place	Birmingham		Type	SP
Type	SP		Map scale	–
Map scale	–		Notes	See 2007
Notes	Classified list of members		Library	BL all
Library	BCL		holdings	BOD all
				BPH has 1938

REF **2151**
Title **Engineering Directory**
Dates 1918-1936,1938
Publisher Engineering Ltd
Printer The Bedford Press
Place London
Type SP
Map scale –
Notes TR section, lists of addresses, trade names etc.
Library MLG not 1938
holdings NLS has 1938

Kelly's Directory of the Chemical Industries holdings continued:
CLM has 1921,1938
GL has 1938
HBR has 1938
LCL has 1935,1938
MLG all
NLS all
NLW has 1923-1938
ULC all

REF **2152**
Title **The Hardware Trades Directory**
Dates 1919,1921,1923,1925,1927, 1929-1940
Publisher Armstrong, Horton & Co Ltd
Printer Brendon, W. & Son
Place London
Type SP
Map scale –
Notes Alph. list of firms; alph. list of branded goods. TR section.
Library BCL has 1919,1932-1938
holdings BL not 1919
CLM has 1939,1940
MLG has 1931,1934-1940

REF **2154**
Title **Directory of Manufacturers & Wholesalers of Sporting Goods**
Dates 1920-1932,1934-1941
Publisher Tattershall, W.B. Ltd
Printer The Sports Trader
Place London
Type SP
Map scale –
Notes Alph. & TR sections
Library BL

REF **2155**
Title **Games and Toys Trade Directory and Diary**
Dates 1920-1942
Publisher Games and Toys [Magazine?]
Printer The International Trades Press Ltd
Place London
Type SP
Map scale –
Notes Alph. list of branded goods, firms, TR section
Library BL all
holdings MLG has 1939-1941

REF **2156**
Title **Directory of Antiquarian Booksellers**
Dates 1921,1927,1932
Publisher International Association of Antiquarian Booksellers
Printer –
Place London
Type SP
Map scale –
Notes Arranged alph. by place
Library BL all
holdings NLS has 1932

REF **2157**
Title **The Insurance Directory, Reference and Year Book (Post Magazine Almanack)**
Dates 1921,1929,1931-1950
Publisher The Post Magazine and Insurance Monitor Ltd
Printer –
Place London
Type SP
Map scale –
Notes Alph. list of insurance companies with branches, details of company, capital, objects etc.
Library BOD not 1921,1929
holdings CLC has 1943,1944,1948,1949
LCL has 1929,1931-1946,1947, 1949
NLW has 1921
ULC not 1921-1931
12

REF **2158**
Title **The Fruit Grower Directory and Handbook**
Dates 1921-1925
Publisher Benn Brothers Ltd
Printer Benn Brothers Ltd
Place London
Type SP
Map scale –
Notes Alph. & classified sections
Library BL
holdings NLS ·

REF **2159**
Title **The Directory of Insurance Brokers**
Dates 1922-1950
Publisher Cawley's Publicity Service
Printer Metchim & Son
Place London
Type SP
Map scale –
Notes Alph. lists by place. Alph. list of claims assessors.
Library BL has 1922,1935-1950
holdings BPH has 1922,1924,1926-1928, 1940,1943,1945,1947,1948, 1950
CLM has 1925,1931,1932
NLS has 1922
NLW not 1924
ULC has 1935-1950
12

REF **2160**
Title **Directory for the British Glass Industry**
Dates 1923,1928,1934,1939
Publisher The Society of Glass Technology
Printer Sir W.C. Leng & Co Ltd
Place Sheffield
Type SP
Map scale –
Notes TR & alph. sections
Library BL all?
holdings MLG not 1923
NLS all
ULC not 1923

REF **2161**
Title **Skinner's Cotton Trade Directory of the World**
Dates 1923-1942,1944-1948,1950
Publisher Skinner, T. & Co
Printer Skinner, T. & Co
Place London
Type SP
Map scale –
Notes TR sections arranged alphabetically, also international section
Library BL all
holdings BOD all
BPH has 1947-1950
BRD has 1928,1931,1932,1938, 1942,1947,1948
CLM all
MLG all
NLS all
NLW not 1950
ULC all

REF **2162**
Title **The Colliery Year Book and Coal Trades Directory**
Dates 1923-1950
Publisher Louis Cassier Co Ltd
Printer Broadway Press
Place London
Type SP
Map scale –
Notes Lists of colliery owners, index to mines, statistics, articles etc.
Library BL all
holdings CLE has 1950
CLM has 1923,1925-1940, 1942-1950
MLG all
NLS all
NLW has 1925-1933,1935-1950
ULC all

REF **2163**
Title **Kelly's Directory of the Electrical Industry, Wireless and Allied Trades**
Dates 1924-1926
Publisher Kelly's Directories Ltd
Printer Kelly's Directories Ltd
Place London
Type SP
Map scale –
Library BL all
holdings BOD all
BPH all
CLM has 1926
HBR has 1926
MLG all
NLS all
NLW has 1924,1925
ULC all

REF **2164**
Title **The Textile Manufacturer Buyers' Directory**
Dates 1924-1934,1936
Publisher Emmott & Co
Printer Emmott & Co
Place Manchester
Type SP
Map scale –
Notes TR, alph, & international sections
Library BL all
holdings CLM has 1936

REF **2165**
Title **The British European Commercial Directory (Chambers')**
Dates 1924-1936
Publisher Chambers' Publishing Co Ltd
Printer New Goswell Printing Co Ltd
Place London
Type TR
Map scale –
Notes Large London section followed by brief provincial section
Library BL all
holdings MLG has 1930-1934

REF **2166**
Title **The Concrete Year Book: A Handbook and Directory for the Concrete Industry**
Dates 1924-1950
Publisher Concrete Publications Ltd
Printer Butler & Tanner Ltd
Place London
Type SP
Map scale –
Notes TR & place sections & lists of consulting engineers etc & other general information
Library CLM has 1924-1926,1928,1931,
holdings 1931,1933,1935,1936,1939-1944, 1946-1950
NLS not 1948

REF **2167**
Title **The Metal Industry Handbook and Directory**
Dates 1925,1931,1939-1945,1947-1950
Publisher The Louis Cassier Co Ltd
Printer Premier Press Ltd
Place London
Type SP
Map scale –
Notes Small directory section (alph. & TR), mainly a handbook with articles & tables etc.
Library CLM

REF **2168**
Title **Music Industries Directory**
Dates 1925-1929
Publisher Federation of British Music Industries
Printer Pollock, W.J. & Co
Place London
Type SP
Map scale –
Library BL

REF	**2169**
Title	**The Silk and Rayon Directory & Buyers Guide of Great Britain**
Dates	1925-1938,1940,1942,1946,1948
Publisher	Heywood, J. Ltd
Printer	Heywood, J. Ltd
Place	Manchester
Type	SP
Map scale	–
Notes	Alph. & TR sections
Library	BL all
holdings	BOD all
	MLG has 1926-1936
	NLS all
	NLW has 1925-1932
	ULC has 1937-1948

REF	**2170**
Title	**The Hatters' Gazette Diary and Trade Directory**
Dates	1925-1948
Publisher	Trade Journals
Printer	Edwards Ltd
Place	London
Type	SP
Map scale	–
Notes	TR & alph. sections
Library	BL all
holdings	BOD has 1928-1940,1942-1944, 1947
	NLS has 1937-1948,1950
	ULC has 1935-1948

REF	**2171**
Title	**Tillotson's Directory of Pedigree Stock Breeders and Year Book of the Breeding Industry**
Dates	1926,1929,1930
Publisher	Tillotsons Publishing Co
Printer	Tillotsons (Bolton) Ltd
Place	Bolton
Type	SP
Map scale	–
Notes	1929 & 1930 editions entitled 'International Directory of Pedigree Stock Breeders and Year Book of the Breeding Industry'. Alph. names by county.
Library	BL not 1929
holdings	BOD not 1928
	NLS has 1928-1930
	ULC not 1928

REF	**2172**
Title	**British Trades Directory and Continental Guide**
Dates	1926-1936
Publisher	Lloyds Advertising Co
Printer	Richardsons, Printers Ltd
Place	London
Type	TR
Map scale	–
Notes	Most of the directory devoted to London
Library	BL all
holdings	MLG has 1927-1936

REF	**2173**
Title	**The Advertising Register: A Directory of Advertisers ... and Advertising Agents**
Dates	1927,1928
Publisher	(at) Rolls House
Printer	The Garden City Press Ltd
Place	London
Type	SP
Map scale	–
Notes	Alph. lists by name & place
Library	BL has 1927
holdings	ULC has 1928

REF	**2174**
Title	**The Knitting Trades Directory**
Dates	1927,1929,1931,1932,1937,1938
Publisher	Heywood, J. Ltd
Printer	Heywood, J. Ltd
Place	Manchester
Type	SP
Map scale	–
Notes	TR & place directory
Library	BL not 1929,1937
holdings	CLM has 1929,1937
	NLS has 1929-1932,1938
	NLW has 1931
	ULC has 1934,1937

REF **2175**
Title **The Directory of Quarries, Clayworks, Sand and Gravel Pits etc**
Dates 1927,1929,1931,1933,1935,1937, 1939,1941,1943,1948
Publisher The Quarry Managers' Journal Ltd
Printer Times Printing Co Ltd
Place Birmingham
Type SP
Map scale –
Notes Directory of quarries by county
Library BCL has 1927-1933
holdings BL all
BPH has 1939-1943
NLW has 1931-1937
NLS has 1933-1948
ULC has 1933-1948
12

REF **2176**
Title **The Incorporated Brewers' Directory**
Dates 1927,1934,1936,1938-1942, 1944-1946,1948-1950
Publisher The Incorporated Brewers' Guild
Printer Warde, T. & Sons Ltd
Place London
Type SP
Map scale –
Notes 1927 edition entitled 'The Operative Brewers Directory'
Library BL

REF **2177**
Title **The World's Wool**
Dates 1927-1930,1932,1946,1947,1949
Publisher Skinner, T. & Co
Printer Skinner, T. & Co
Place Bradford
Type SP
Map scale –
Notes TR sections arranged alphabetically. International directory. 1947 & 1949 editions entitled 'Skinner's Wool Trade Directory of the World'.
Library BL all
holdings BOD all
BPH has 1927-1929,1932-1949
BRD has 1928-1930,1946,1947, 1949
CLM has 1928,1930,1949
MLG has 1947,1949
NLS has 1947,1949
NLW all
ULC all

REF **2178**
Title **The Motor and Allied Trades Directory**
Dates 1927-1939
Publisher The Motor Trades Directory Ltd
Printer –
Place London
Type SP
Map scale –
Library BL all
holdings BOD not 1927
CLM has 1938
NLS not 1927
ULC not 1927

REF **2179**
Title **The Chemical Trade Directory**
Dates 1928
Publisher Brandon & Morris
Printer Messent & Bond
Place London
Type SP
Map scale –
Notes Classified directory
Library BL
holdings NLS

REF	**2180**
Title	**Blair's Commercial Directory and Buyers' Guide**
Dates	1928-1938
Publisher	Blair, T. & Co
Printer	Whitehead, J. & Son
Place	Leeds
Type	CM
Map scale	–
Library	BL not 1931
holdings	BOD has 1929-1932,1934,1936
	ULC has 1929-1932,1934

REF	**2181**
Title	**The Gas Journal Directory**
Dates	1928-1950
Publisher	King, W. Ltd
Printer	–
Place	London
Type	SP
Map scale	–
Notes	Alph. list of places with details of gas works, articles & other information
Library	BOD all
holdings	MLG has 1934-1950
	ULC has 1935-1950

REF	**2182**
Title	**The Market Man's Manual and Directory**
Dates	1929,1930
Publisher	Walter Rose Publishing Co
Printer	Walter Rose Publishing Co
Place	London
Type	SP
Map scale	–
Notes	List of markets, with information for sellers
Library	BOD
holdings	ULC

REF	**2183**
Title	**Cook's Directory: Manufacturers, Merchants, Exporters, Importers**
Dates	1929,1938,1939
Publisher	Cook's Publishing Co
Printer	–
Place	Leeds
Type	TR
Map scale	–
Library	BL

REF	**2184**
Title	**Leather Goods Directory and Year Book**
Dates	1929-1931,1936-1941
Publisher	Tattershall, W.D.
Printer	Tattershall, W.D.
Place	London
Type	SP
Map scale	–
Notes	Alph. & TR sections
Library	BCL has 1926,1937,1939-1941
holdings	BL all

REF	**2185**
Title	**The British Mercantile and Trades Directory**
Dates	1929-1934
Publisher	The Mercantile and Commercial Directory Ltd
Printer	The Mercantile and Commercial Directory Ltd
Place	Glasgow
Type	TR
Map scale	–
Library	BL all
holdings	BOD not 1929
	NLS has 1931-1934
	ULC has 1930-1934

REF	**2186**
Title	**The Mercantile and Commercial Directory (Scrivens')**
Dates	1929-1934
Publisher	The Mercantile and Commercial Directory Co
Printer	Duncan, A. & Son
Place	Glasgow
Type	GE TR
Map scale	–
Library	BL
holdings	BOD
	NLS
	ULC

REF	**2187**
Title	**The Commercial and Mercantile Directory**
Dates	1929-1935
Publisher	The Oxford Publishing Co
Printer	Richardsons Ltd
Place	Leeds
Type	SP
Map scale	–
Notes	Classified section & alph. by place
Library	BL
holdings	BOD
	NLS
	ULC

[395]

REF	2188
Title	**The Commercial and Mercantile Directory**
Dates	1929-1938
Publisher	Law Publishing Co
Printer	Whitehead, J. & Son
Place	Leeds
Type	TR
Map scale	–
Library	BL all
holdings	BOD not 1931,1935-1938
	ULC has 1929-1936

REF	2189
Title	**The Water Engineer's Pocket Book and Directory**
Dates	1929-1939,1945-1950
Publisher	Water and Water Engineering
Printer	Water and Water Engineering
Place	London
Type	SP
Map scale	–
Notes	Directory of water engineers & water undertakings, by place
Library	BOD all
holdings	NLS all
	ULC has 1930-1950

REF	2190
Title	**Iron and Steel Directory and Handbook**
Dates	1930-1932,1934,1939,1950
Publisher	Louis Cassier Co
Printer	Premier Press Ltd
Place	London
Type	SP
Map scale	–
Library	BL
holdings	BOD
	ULC

REF	2191
Title	**British Trades and Commercial Directory**
Dates	1930-1934
Publisher	Morston Publishing Co
Printer	St Albans Press
Place	Leeds
Type	TR
Map scale	–
Notes	London, Suburban & Provincial sections
Library	BL

REF	2192
Title	**The London and Provincial Classified Trades Register**
Dates	1930-1934
Publisher	The Mercantile and Commercial Directory Ltd
Printer	The Mercantile and Commercial Directory Ltd
Place	Glasgow
Type	TR
Map scale	–
Notes	TR directory arranged alph. by place
Library	BOD all
holdings	NLS all
	ULC has 1930

REF	2193
Title	**British Commercial and Mercantile Directory**
Dates	1930-1935
Publisher	Morston Publishing Co
Printer	St Alban Press
Place	Leeds
Type	GE TR
Map scale	–
Library	BL all
holdings	NLS has 1933-1935

REF	2194
Title	**The Commercial Trades Directory**
Dates	1930-1938
Publisher	Blains' Publishing Co
Printer	Whitehead, J. & Son
Place	Leeds
Type	TR
Map scale	–
Library	BL all
holdings	BOD has 1930
	ULC has 1930,1933

REF	2195
Title	**Grocery & the Provision Merchant Directory of Brands, Trade Marks and Trade Names**
Dates	1930-1941
Publisher	Heywood & Company Ltd
Printer	–
Place	London
Type	SP
Map scale	–
Notes	Alph. by trade mark with proprietor & address
Library	BL all
holdings	BOD all
	NLS all
	ULC all

REF	**2196**
Title	**Poster Advertising Year Book and Directory**
Dates	1931-1937,1939,1949
Publisher	British Poster Advertising Association
Printer	Western Times
Place	London
Type	SP
Map scale	–
Notes	Arranged alph. by place
Library	BL all
holdings	NLW has 1931-1935,1949

REF	**2197**
Title	**The British Book Trade Directory**
Dates	1933
Publisher	Whitaker, J. & Sons Ltd
Printer	Whitaker, J. & Sons Ltd
Place	London
Type	SP
Map scale	–
Library	BL
holdings	CLM
	MLG
	NLS
	ULC

REF	**2198**
Title	**The British Counties Trades Directory**
Dates	1933,1935-1938
Publisher	Harmsworth Publishing Co
Printer	Harmsworth Publishing Co
Place	Leeds
Type	GE TR
Map scale	–
Library	BL not 1933
holdings	ULC has 1933

REF	**2199**
Title	**Nuttall's Business Directory, British, Colonial & Foreign**
Dates	1933-1936
Publisher	Nuttall & Co
Printer	Whipple, R.D.
Place	London
Type	TR
Map scale	–
Library	BL all
holdings	MLG has 1934

REF	**2200**
Title	**Kelly's Directory of the Wireless and Allied Trades**
Dates	1934
Publisher	Kelly's Directories Ltd
Printer	Kelly's Directories Ltd
Place	London
Type	SP
Map scale	–
Library	BL
holdings	CLM
	GL
	LCL
	MLG
	NLS
	NLW
	ULC

REF	**2201**
Title	**Kelly's Directory of the Laundry and Allied Trades**
Dates	1934,1938
Publisher	Kelly's Directories Ltd
Printer	Kelly's Directories Ltd
Place	London
Type	SP
Map scale	–
Library	BL all
holdings	BOD all
	BPH has 1938
	CLM has 1938
	GL has 1938
	LCL all
	NLS all
	NLW all
	ULC all

REF	**2202**
Title	**Harmsworth Business Directory**
Dates	1934-1937
Publisher	Harmsworth Publishing Co
Printer	–
Place	Leeds
Type	TR
Map scale	–
Library	BL

REF	**2203**
Title	**Collins Commercial and Mercantile Directory**
Dates	1935,1936
Publisher	Oxford Publishing Co
Printer	Chadwick, W.
Place	Leeds
Type	CM
Map scale	–
Library	BL all
holdings	BOD has 1936

REF	**2204**
Title	**The London Directory & International Register of Manufacturers, Wholesalers and Shippers**
Dates	1935,1936,1948-1950
Publisher	The London Directory Company Ltd
Printer	–
Place	London
Type	TR
Map scale	–
Notes	International coverage, TR arranged by place
Library	NLW

REF	**2205**
Title	**Roads and Road Construction Year Book and Directory**
Dates	1936-1950
Publisher	The Chambers Publishing Company Ltd
Printer	–
Place	London
Type	SP
Map scale	–
Notes	General information & directory of highway officials, road contractors, with TR section
Library	BL all?
holdings	BOD all
	CLM has 1930,1934,1937
	MLG all
	NLS has 1936
	ULC all

REF	**2206**
Title	**Coal and Colliery Directory and Manual**
Dates	1938
Publisher	Harper & Co
Printer	Straker, S. & Sons
Place	London
Type	SP
Map scale	–
Notes	Alph. list of colliery firms & coal merchants
Library	MLG

REF	**2207**
Title	**The British Empire Timber Trades Directory**
Dates	1938
Publisher	The Mercantile & Commercial Printing Co Ltd
Printer	The Mercantile & Commercial Printing Co Ltd
Place	Glasgow
Type	SP
Map scale	–
Notes	TR sections for London, England & Wales, Scotland, Ireland & continents
Library	BL
holdings	CLM
	NLS
	ULC

REF	**2208**
Title	**The Metal Bulletin Directory of Europe**
Dates	1938
Publisher	Metal Information Bureau
Printer	Grubb, H.R. Ltd
Place	London
Type	SP
Map scale	–
Notes	Alph. & classified sections covering all metal trades
Library	BL
holdings	NLS

REF	**2209**
Title	**Department, Chain, Co-operative Store Annual & Directory**
Dates	1939,1940,1946-1950
Publisher	Store Magazine
Printer	–
Place	London
Type	SP
Map scale	–
Notes	Alph. & TR sections & other general information
Library	BL all
holdings	BOD not 1947
	NLS not 1946,1948
	NLW has 1949,1950
	ULC has 1949,1950

REF **2210**
Title **Winckelmann Fur Trade Directory of Great Britain**
Dates 1946-1950
Publisher Winckelmann, R.
Printer –
Place London
Type SP
Map scale –
Notes Alph. & foreign sections
Library BL

REF **2211**
Title **Skinner's Hosiery and Knit Goods Directory**
Dates 1947,1948,1950
Publisher Skinner, T. & Co
Printer Skinner, T. & Co
Place Manchester
Type SP
Map scale –
Notes Arranged alph. by county & TR sections
Library BL all
holdings BOD all
BPH has 1950
MLG not 1947
NLS all
NLW all
ULC all

REF **2212**
Title **British Iron & Steel Directory**
Dates 1947,1949
Publisher The Metal Information Bureau Ltd
Printer Clark, C.W. & Co
Place London
Type SP
Map scale –
Notes Arranged alph. by product
Library BL all
holdings MLG has 1947

REF **2213**
Title **Carter's Flax, Hemp and Jute Year Book and Directory**
Dates 1947,1949
Publisher H.R. Carter Publications Ltd
Printer McCaw, Stevenson & Orr Ltd
Place Belfast
Type SP
Map scale –
Notes Alph. & TR sections & other information
Library BOD
holdings NLW

REF **2214**
Title **The British Non-Ferrous Metals Directory**
Dates 1947,1949
Publisher Metal Information Bureau Ltd
Printer Clark, C.W. & Co
Place London
Type SP
Map scale –
Notes Arranged alph. by metal
Library BL
holdings MLG
NLS
ULC

REF **2215**
Title **Power Laundry Directory and Year Book**
Dates 1948
Publisher The Trades Publishing Co Ltd
Printer –
Place London
Type SP
Map scale –
Notes TR & alph. sections & legal & technical guide
Library BL
holdings MLG
NLS
NLW
ULC

REF **2216**
Title **Directory of the Brush and Allied Trades**
Dates 1948,1949,1950
Publisher Wheatland Journals Ltd
Printer Ling, H. Ltd
Place London
Type SP
Map scale –
Notes British & international suppliers listed
Library BL all
holdings BOD has 1950
NLS has 1950

REF	**2217**
Title	**The Waste Trades Manual and Directory**
Dates	1948-1950
Publisher	British Continental Trade Press Ltd
Printer	British Continental Trade Press Ltd
Place	London
Type	SP
Map scale	–
Notes	Alph. by country (international directory). Rubber & cotton waste only.
Library holdings	BL all NLS has 1950

REF	**2218**
Title	**Town & Country Trades Directory**
Dates	1948-1950
Publisher	United Publicity Services
Printer	Furnack Ltd
Place	London
Type	TR
Map scale	–
Library holdings	BL all BOD has 1948

REF	**2219**
Title	**Charles Skilton's Directory of Printers' and Bookbinders' Suppliers**
Dates	1949
Publisher	Skilton, C. Ltd
Printer	–
Place	London
Type	SP
Map scale	–
Notes	Classified directory
Library holdings	BL MLG NLS NLW ULC

REF	**2220**
Title	**Small Printers' Directory and Year Book**
Dates	1949
Publisher	Aquarius Press
Printer	Aquarius Press
Place	London
Type	SP
Map scale	–
Notes	Alph. list of printers & other information
Library holdings	BL MLG NLS ULC

REF	**2221**
Title	**The British Antique Trades and Collectors' Directory**
Dates	1949
Publisher	Woodhouse & Co
Printer	The Leagrave Press Ltd
Place	London
Type	SP
Map scale	–
Notes	Alph. & place lists
Library holdings	BL MLG NLS

REF	**2222**
Title	**Provincial Business Directories (Romford) Ltd**
Dates	1949,1950
Publisher	Provincial Business Directories (Romford) Ltd
Printer	–
Place	Romford
Type	TR
Map scale	–
Notes	1950 edition 'Covers 37 Counties of England & Special Sections for London, Scotland, Wales & IoW'. This directory was also issued in individual county parts (also held by NLW).
Library	NLW

Part Three

Library Holdings and Index

Chapter 8
LIBRARY HOLDINGS AND THE
LOCATIONS OF DIRECTORIES

This chapter provides a list of the libraries covered in the survey, which were nearly all visited personally as part of the research programme. Each is identified by the code used throughout the bibliography, followed by name, address and the type of library which is identified by the following abbreviations:

CL   Copyright Library
HQL   Headquarters Library
PL   Private Library
PRL   Public Reference Library
RO   Record Office
SC   Special Collection: University Library

Also recorded here is the type of check which was carried out: CAT meaning that the catalogue was examined; STK meaning that the directories themselves were checked manually to ascertain the holdings of a given library. Where CAT/STK is entered, a combination of both methods was used, with greater emphasis on the first mentioned. It should be noted that not all library catalogues are 100 per cent accurate and it is not unusual to find in a catalogue reference to a directory which has since gone missing or has been transferred to another library. Similarly, a check of the book stacks may not always turn up every single directory held by a library.

Finally, conditions of access are stated, 'open' implying that the directories are on open shelves and may be freely browsed, and 'closed' that they are stored in closed access book stacks behind the scenes or in locked glass-fronted cases to which only librarians have access. Many libraries have a collection which may be partly open and partly closed. An increasing number of libraries are trying to preserve irreplaceable stocks either by restricting access or by reproducing the directories for public use and retaining the originals behind closed doors.

8.1   List of libraries visited

ACL
Aberdeen Central Library
Rosemount Viaduct, Aberdeen AB9 1GU
PRL STK
Closed

AYL
Buckinghamshire County Library
Walton Street, Aylesbury HP20 1UU
PRL STK
Mostly open

BCL
Birmingham Central Library
Chamberlain Square, Birmingham B3 3HQ
PRL STK
Local D's closed, Kelly's county D's
    open

BED
Bedford Central Library
Harpur Street, Bedford MK40 1PG
PRL STK/CAT
Mostly open   [403]

BIS
Bishopsgate Institute
230 Bishopsgate, London EC2M 4QH
PRL STK
Open

BL
British Library
Department of Printed Books, Great
    Russell Street, London WC1B 3DG
CL STK/CAT
Closed
Reader's Ticket required, 24 hours
    advance notice needed for
    consultation of directories

BLA
Blackburn Library
Town Hall Street, Blackburn BB2 1AG
PRL STK
Mostly closed, some local D's open

BOD
Bodleian Library
University of Oxford, Broad Street,
    Oxford OX1 3BG
CL STK
Closed
Reader's Ticket required, fee payable

BPH
Brown, Picton & Hornby Libraries
    Liverpool
William Brown Street, Liverpool L3 8EW
PRL CAT
Closed

BPL
Brechin Public Library
St Ninian's Square, Brechin DD9 7AA
PRL STK
Closed

BRD
Bradford Central Library
Prince's Way, Bradford BD1 1NN
PRL STK
Closed

BRI
Brighton Library
Church Street, Brighton BN1 1UE
PRL CAT
Closed

BRL
Bath Reference Library
Queen Square, Bath BA1 2HP
PRL STK
Closed

BUR
Burnley Library
Grimshaw Street, Burnley BB11 2BD
PRL STK/CAT
Closed

CAM
Cambridge Central Library
7 Lion Yard, Cambridge CB2 3QD
PRL CAT
Closed

CAR
Carlisle Library
11 Globe Lane, The Lanes,
    Carlisle CA3 8NX
PRL STK
Closed

CCL
Chester Central Library
Northgate Street, Chester
PRL STK/CAT
Mostly closed

CHE
Chelmsford Library
Duke Street, Chelmsford CM1 1JF
PRL STK
Open, some microfilmed material

CHI
Chichester Library
Tower Street, Chichester PO19 1PD
PRL STK
Mostly open, older D's closed

CL
Chetham's Library
Long Millgate, Manchester M3 1SB
PL STK
Open
Appointment necessary

CLA
Carnegie Library Ayr
12 Main Street, Ayr KA8 8ED
PRL STK
Closed

CLB
Central Library Bristol
College Green, Bristol BS1 5TL
PRL STK/CAT
Local D's open, rest closed

CLC
Central Library Cardiff
The Hayes, Cardiff CF1 2QU
PRL STK
Closed
A new library was due to open in Cardiff
    late in 1986

CLE
Central Library Exeter
Castle Street, Exeter EX4 3PQ
PRL STK
Kelly's county D's open, rest closed

CLH
Central Library Hull
Albion Street, Hull HU1 3TF
PRL STK/CAT
Closed

CLL
Central Leicestershire Library
Belvoir Street, Leicester LE1 6QG
PRL STK
Some open, mostly closed

CLM
Central Library Manchester
St Peter's Square, Manchester M2 5PD
PRL CAT/STK
Closed, Manchester D's microfilmed

CLN
Central Library Newcastle-upon-Tyne
Princess Square, Newcastle-upon-Tyne
    NE99 1DX
PRL STK
Closed

CLO
Central Library Oxford
Westgate Street, Oxford OX1 1DJ
PRL CAT/STK
Mostly open, rarer material closed

CLP
Paisley Central Library
High Street, Paisley PA1 2BB
PRL STK
Closed

CLS
Southampton Central Library
Civic Centre, Southampton SO9 4XP
PRL STK
Open

COL
Colchester Library
Trinity Square, Colchester CO1 1JB
PRL STK
Mostly open

COV
Coventry Library
Smithford Way, Coventry CV1 1FY
PRL STK
Nearly all open

CPL
Cheltenham Public Library
Clarence Street, Cheltenham GL50 3JT
PRL STK
Closed

CRD
Croydon Library
Katherine Street, Croydon CR9 1ET
PRL STK
Some open, mostly closed

DAR
Darlington Library
Crown Street, Darlington DL1 1ND
PRL STK
Closed

DCL
Dorset County Library
Colliton Park, Dorchester DT1 1XJ
PRL STK/CAT
Closed
There is also a good collection of
    Dorset Directories in the Dorset
    Record Office, Colliton Park. With
    one exception they duplicate the
    DCL holding.

DDL
Dundee Central Library
The Wellgate, Dundee DD1 1BB
PRL STK
Closed

DEI
Devon & Exeter Institution Library
7 Cathedral Close, Exeter
PL STK
Open
Members only

DLS
Derby Central Library
Local Studies Library, 25b Irongate,
    Derby DE1 3GL
PRL CAT
All D's on microfiche

DON
Doncaster Central Library
Waterdale, Doncaster DN1 3JE
PRL STK
Closed

DUR
Durham City Library
South Street, Durham DH1 4QS
PRL CAT/STK
Closed

ELD
Ewart Library Dumfries
Catherine Street, Dumfries DG1 1JB
PRL SK
Open

FAL
Falmouth Library
The Moor, Falmouth, Cornwall
PRL STK
Open

FLK
Falkirk Library
Hope Street, Falkirk FK1 5AU
PRL STK
Closed

FPL
Forfar Public Library
West High Street, Forfar DD8 1BB
PRL STK/CAT
Closed

GL
Guildhall Library London
Aldermanbury, London EC2P 2EJ
PRL STK/CAT
Closed; PO London D's open.
Max 6 volumes for consultation.

GLH
Greater London History Library
40 Northampton Road, London EC1R 0HB
RO CAT
Mostly closed
This library forms part of the Greater
    London Record Office

GLO
Gloucester Library
Brunswick Road, Gloucester GL1 1HT
PRL STK/CAT
Mostly open, some closed

HAM
Hamilton Library
98 Cadzow Street, Hamilton ML3 6HQ
PRL STK
Closed

HBR
Horace Barks Reference Library
City Central Library, Bethesda Street,
    Hanley, Stoke-on-Trent ST1 3RS
PRL CAT
Closed

HFX
Halifax Central Library
Northgate House, Northgate, Halifax HX1
    1UN
PRL STK
Closed

HLS
Hertfordshire Local Studies Library
County Hall, Hertford SG13 8EJ
HQL STK
Open
Appointment advisable

HNT
Huntingdon Library
Princes Street, Huntingdon PE18 6PH
PRL STK
Open

HPL
Hereford Public Library
Broad Street, Hereford HR4 9AU
PRL STK
Closed

HRO
Hampshire Record Office
20 Southgate Street, Winchester SO23 9EF
RO STK/CAT
Mostly open

HUD
Huddersfield Central Library
Princess Alexandra Walk, Huddersfield
   HD1 2SU
PRL STK
Open

IHR
Institute of Historical Research
University of London, Senate House,
   London WC1E 7HU
See notes CAT/STK
Open
The IHR is part of London University & a
   Member's Ticket is required for
   access

KCL
Kent County Library
Springfield, Maidstone ME14 2LH
PRL STK/CAT
Open

KIL
Kilmarnock Library
Dick Institute, Elmbank Avenue,
   Kilmarnock KA1 3BU
PRL STK
Closed

KLL
King's Lynn Central Library
London Road, King's Lynn PE30 5EZ
PRL STK
Closed

LAN
Lancaster Library
Market Square, Lancaster LA1 1HY
PRL CAT
Mostly closed

LCL
Leeds Central Library
Calverley Street, Leeds LS1 3AB
PRL STK
Local D's open, rest closed

LEA
Leamington Library
Avenue Road, Leamington CV31 3PP
PRL CAT
Closed

LED
Ledbury Library
Homend, Ledbury HR8 1BT
PRL STK
Closed

LHQ
Lancashire Library HQ
143 Corporation Street, Preston PR1 2TB
HQL STK
Open
Appointment advisable

LIN
Lincoln Library
Free School Lane, Lincoln LN2 1EL
PRL CAT
Closed

LLB
Lansdowne Library
Meyrick Road, Bournemouth BH1 3DJ
PRL STK
Closed

LNK
Lanark Library
Lindsay Institute, Hope Street, Lanark
   ML11 7LZ
PRL STK
Open

LRO
Lancashire Record Office
Bow Lane, Preston PR1 8ND
RO STK
Mostly open, rarer D's closed

LUT
Luton Central Library
St Georges Square, Luton LU1 2NG
PRL STK
Mostly open

MAC
Macclesfield Library
Park Green, Macclesfield, SK11 6TW
PRL CAT
Closed

MAI
Maidstone Reference Library
St Faith's Street, Maidstone, Kent
PRL STK
Closed

MID
Middlesborough Library
Victoria Square, Middlesborough TS1 2AY
PRL STK
Closed

MLG
Mitchell Library Glasgow
North Street, Glasgow G3 7DN
PRL CAT/STK
Closed

MOR
Northumberland County Library
The Willows, Morpeth NE61 1TA
PRL STK
Closed

MTH
Motherwell Library
Hamilton Road, Motherwell ML1 3BZ
PRL CAT
Closed

NCL
Nottingham Central Library
Angel Row, Nottingham NG1 6HP
PRL STK
Closed

NEW
Newbury Library
Carnegie Road, Newbury RG14 5DW
PRL STK
Open

NLS
National Library of Scotland
George IV Bridge, Edinburgh EH1 1EW
CL CAT
Closed
Reader's Ticket required

NLW
National Library of Wales
Aberystwyth, Dyfed SY23 3BU
CL STK
Local D's open, rest closed;
Reader's Ticket required

NOR
Norwich Central Library
Bethel Street, Norwich NR2 1NJ
PRL STK/CAT
Closed

NPT
Newport Library
John Frost Square, Newport, Gwent NP9
    1PA
PRL CAT
Closed

NTH
Northampton Central Library
Abington Street, Northampton NN1 2BA
PRL STK
Mostly open

PCL
Portsmouth Central Library
Guildhall Square, Portsmouth PO1 2DX
PRL STK
Half open, half closed

PET
Peterborough Library
Broadway, Peterborough PE1 1RX
PRL STK
Closed

PHL
Harris Library
Market Square, Preston PR1 2PP
PRL STK
Mostly open

PLY
Plymouth Library
Drake's Circus, Plymouth PL4 8AL
PRL STK
Mostly open, older D's closed

RCL
Reading Central Library
Abbey Square, Reading, RG1 3BQ
PRL STK
Approx. half open, half closed

[408]

RED
Redruth Library
Clinton Road, Redruth TR15 2QE
PRL STK
Open

RUG
Rugby Library
St Matthews Street, Rugby CV21 3BZ
PRL STK
Closed

SAL
Salisbury Library
Market Place, Salisbury SP1 1BL
PRL STK
Closed

SCC
Cope Collection Southampton University
University Library, University,
    Southampton SO9 5NH
SC STK
Closed
Appointment advisable.

SCL
Sheffield Central Library
Surrey Street, Sheffield S1 1XZ
PRL STK
Local D's open, rest closed

SHQ
Stirling District Library HQ
Borrowmeadow Road, Springkerse
    Industrial Estate, Stirling FK7 7TN
HQL STK
Open
Appointment advisable.

SHR
Shropshire County Library
Local Studies Department, Castle Gates,
    Shrewsbury SY1 2AS
PRL STK
Mostly open

SLP
Sandeman Library
Kinnoull Street, Perth PH1 5ET
PRL STK
Open

SLS
Surrey Local Studies Library
North Street, Guildford GU1 4AL
PRL STK
Closed

SOG
Society of Genealogists
14 Charterhouse Buildings, London EC1M
    7BA
PL STK/CAT
Open
Members only (fee payable)

SRI
Suffolk Record Office Ipswich
St Andrew House, County Hall, St Helen
    Street, Ipswich
RO CAT/STK
Mostly open

STA
St Albans Central Library
Victoria Street, St Albans AL1 3JQ
PRL STK
Open

STR
Stirling Central Library
Corn Exchange Road, Stirling FK8 2HX
PRL STK
Closed

SWA
Central Library Swansea
Alexandra Road, Swansea SA1 5DX
PRL CAT
Closed

SWI
Swindon Library
Regent Circus, Swindon SN1 1BL
PRL STK
Closed

TLH
Taunton Local History Library
The Castle, Castle Green, Taunton TA1
    4AD
PRL STK
Open

TRW
Wiltshire Library HQ
Bythesea Road, Trowbridge BA14 8BS
PRL STK
Open

ULC
University Library Cambridge
West Road, Cambridge CB3 9DR
CL CAT
Closed
Reader's Ticket required

WAR
Warrington Library
Museum Street, Warrington WA1 1JB
PRL STK
Closed
Also holds Warrington extracts from
    county D's

WAT
Watford Central Library
Hampstead Road, Watford, Herts
PRL STK
Closed

WCL
Worcester Central Library
Foregate Street, Worcester WR1 1DT
PRL STK
Closed

WCS
Westcountry Studies Library
Castle Street, Exeter EX4 3PQ
PRL STK
Approx. half open, half closed;
West Country D's only

WIN
Winchester Library
Jewry Street, Winchester SO23 8RX
PRL CAT
Some open, mostly closed

WLG
Watt Library Greenock
9 Union Street, Greenock PA16 8JH
PRL STK
Open

WLV
Wolverhampton Central Library
Snow Hill, Wolverhampton WV1 3AX
PRL STK
Closed

WOR
Worthing Library
Richmond Road, Worthing BN11 1HD
PRL STK
Closed

WRK
Warwick Library
Barrack Street, Warwick CV34 4TH
PRL STK
Mostly open, some closed

WRO
Wiltshire Record Office
Bythesea Road, Trowbridge BA14 8BS
RO STK
Mostly closed, county D's open

WRX
Wrexham Area Library
Rhosddu Road, Wrexham LL11 1AU
PRL STK
Closed

WSL
William Salt Library
Eastgate Street, Stafford ST16 2LZ
PL STK
Open
Appointment advisable

YCL
York Central Library
Museum Street, York YO1 2DS
PRL STK
Closed

8.2　Publishers index

Acford, R.J. Ltd 1409,1411,1417
Ackrill, R. 1577
Adams & Sons 2039
Adie, T.G. & Co 1247
Adshead, N. & Son 1782,1787,1904
Ainsworth, J. 765
Aitchison, T. (selected by) 1915
Akrill, C. 845
Alabaster, Gatehouse & Kempe 2148
Alder and Company 1109
Allardice, A. 1832
Allen & Morton 916
Allen, E.W. 2021
Allen, S. 874
Allen, W.H. & Co 884
Allingham, W. 1296
Anderson, J. 1918,1934
Anderson, W. 1826
Andrews and Son 1288
Andrews, L.W. & Son 1328
Anglo-American Technical Co Ltd 2139
Angold's Ltd 2141
Angus, J. (compiler) 1849
Aquarius Press 2220
Archdeacon, W. 1285
Archdeacon, W. & Wright, C. 897
Armstrong, Horton & Co Ltd 2152
Arnold, A. & Co 1280
Arrowsmith, I. 472
Arthur and Company Ltd 1657
Arthur, J. 476
Astill, R. & Co 1487
Atkinson, F. 1620
Atwood, T. 1300
Aubrey & Co 85,91,95,96,100,104,108,
　　148,150,151,152,153,157,158,260,
　　458,514,608,693,827,1228,1284,1356,
　　1547,1707,1709
Aves & Co 888
Axon, H. 742,745,748
Ayr Advertiser 1846
Ayrshire Post Ltd 1860

Bagshaw, S. 251,1175
Bailey & Woods 490
Baines and Scarsbrook Ltd 991
Bale, J. Sons & Danielsson Ltd 2127

Balshaw, C. 263
Banffshire Journal Office 1862
Barber, W.C. 241
Barker, C. & Son 1998
Barker, J.W. 1241
Barker, S. & Co 132
Barnes, J. 406
Barrett, P. 732,740,747
Barrett, P. & Co 749,752
Barrett, R. 904
Barton 2101
Bass, T. 898
Batten, D. 902
Beal, J. 1365
Beale Collins, W. 1210
Beaty, J. & Sons 309
Beaumont & Co 1464
Beaumont & Company 1525
Beck, J. 1442
Beddoe, B. Ltd 1032
Bedells, E.J. 1136
Bedford Publishing Company 181
Bedfordshire Times 182
Bell, A. 1948
Bemrose & Sons 326
Bemrose Publicity Co Ltd 1676
Benham & Co Ltd 440
Benham & Company 426
Benn Brothers Ltd 2158
Bennett & Co 63,64,66,70,71,72,73,74,
　　76,78,80,81,82,83,88,92,93,94,136,
　　138,142,143,146,258,318,1468,1701,
　　1705,1719
Bennett, W. 1825
Bennion, Horne, Smallman & Co 1188
Bennion, Horne, Smallman & Co Ltd 1185,
　　1186
Berly & Dawson 2041
Berwick Advertiser 1121
Besley, H. 349
Besley, H. & Son 357
Bexhill Chronicle 1390
Bexley and District Publications Ltd
　　672
Bicester and District Chamber of
　　Commerce 1170
Bideford Gazette Ltd 376
Biggar & McFarlane 1954
Biggar, W. 2080
Biggs & Son 2093
Bill Posters' Association Ltd 2064
Bill Posting Association 1996
Bill, C. 1462
Billing, M. 115,343,350,1509

8.3 Place index

Note In this index, numbers refer
to the reference system used in the
bibliography.

8.4   Subject index